ETHNIC DYNAMICS

Patterns of intergroup relations in various societies

SECOND EDITION

CHESTER L. HUNT, Ph.D.
Professor of Sociology

and

LEWIS WALKER, Ph.D.
Professor of Sociology

both of Western Michigan University

Chapter 12 was contributed by
GEORGE KLEIN, Ph.D.

and

PATRICIA V. KLEIN, M.A.

also of Western Michigan University

Lp 1979

LEARNING PUBLICATIONS, INC.
P.O. Box 1326
Holmes Beach, Florida 33509

Learning Publications, Inc.
P.O. Box 1326
Holmes Beach, Florida 33509

Hardback: ISBN 0-918452-16-3
Paperback: ISBN 0-918452-17-1
Library of Congress Catalog No. 78-73117
Printing: 1 2 3 4 5 6 7 8   Year: 9 8 0 1 2
Printed in the United States of America

To Victor
whose life and death symbolize
the triumph and tragedy of our era
and to
Joanna and Leigh Rae—
members of a generation who
may move beyond ethnicity
into humanity.

Preface

This book has grown out of our conviction that there is a need to provide more of a balance in our discussions and investigations of so-called race relations. In the last decade or so, the volume of popular literature and serious study on majority-minority relationships in the United States has grown larger and larger. While this is good in itself, a concentration on the United States runs the risk of a parochialism that may blind us not only to the rest of the world but also to important factors on the American scene. Consequently, we felt that a look at social relations among varied peoples at different levels of national and economic development, in different parts of the world, would provide the student of "race relations" a greater depth and a broader perspective.

The task of this book is to examine a number of intergroup situations and to determine whether each case is unique or whether there are certain underlying principles that are found operating in many situations. In so doing, we have focused our attention on patterns of social structure rather than on unique individual relationships or psychological perspectives, and on ethnicity rather than on race per se.

The selection of intergroup arrangements to be studied was based on our desire to examine areas or situations which exemplified four major patterns of ethnic relationships: (1) integration, (2) segregation, (3) cultural pluralism, and (4) temporary accommodation. None of these patterns of ethnic interaction can be divorced from the milieu in which they occur and no two examples are ever completely comparable. Nevertheless, it is our contention that each of these patterns is moulded by certain inherent factors which are present in all societies and can only be ignored at our peril. Despite major social and cultural differences, cultural pluralism in Switzerland does have some features in common with cultural pluralism in the Soviet Union. Segregation in South Africa has some of the same sources of both tension and support as segregation in the pre-World War II American South. Problems of integration of aliens and natives show some similar tendencies in Europe and in the United States. Obviously, social and cultural differences between countries should not be ignored or minimized, but neither should we refuse to recognize common elements of social dynamics that reappear in many situations. From an examination of each situation discussed in this book, we have formulated what we think are important and generalizable principles of social relations which we hope will be helpful to the reader as he considers other countries or situations.

Most of the topics treated will be at least moderately familiar to students of the field, but some may be surprised at the inclusion of a chapter concerning the Peace Corps. The Peace Corps was not included because of a desire to appraise its impact on either international relations or economic development. It has already an ample share of both fulsome praise and bitter denunciation for its alleged effects on these matters. Regardless of the readers' reactions to the Peace Corps image, they may still be interested in its "technique" of temporary accommodation. The relationships between natives and aliens temporarily in the land is an important topic. Permanent migration may be declining but world cooperation will require many functionaries to spend temporary sojourns in foreign lands and to work out some type of adjustment with an unfamiliar people. The Peace Corps method of seeking adjustment by modifying ethnocentrism is not without problems, but it is a challenge to conventional wisdom which is worthy of consideration.

ACKNOWLEDGMENTS

In preparing this volume, we are indebted to our colleagues in the academic profession, both in the United States and abroad, who have contributed greatly to our understanding of the processes involved in ethnic relationships. We owe a continuing debt to the Department of Sociology and the Institute of International and Area Studies of Western Michigan University, partially for facilities and assistance, but more for providing a stimulating atmosphere for scholarly activity. We are especially grateful to Robin Luckham, Patrick Daudu, Leila Bradfield, Edward T. Callan, Ibrahim Tahir, and Consuela Reed for reading parts of the manuscript and making suggestions. Major assistance has come from Robin Williams who has patiently probed our assumptions, checked our syntax and clarified our presentation. Without imposing his own views, he has deftly helped us to make a more rigorous statement of our own ideas.

In addition to benefiting from contacts with professional colleagues, we have profited greatly from contact with students in various courses touching on ethnic relationships. Three of these students are mentioned in footnotes, but many others, too numerous to name, have also contributed by sharing their experiences. We are indebted to our co-authors George Klein and Patricia Klein of Western Michigan University for chapter 12 and for helpful sugges-tions on chapter 4. We wish to acknowledge the special service of Ellyn Robert for her many helpful suggestions and the countless hours spent checking sources and materials. We also owe a debt of gratitude to Susan Warner, Karen Yinger, and Patricia Martin for their valuable clerical and secretarial assistance and to Virginia Reynolds and Karla Zakrzewski. Finally, a special word of appreciation to our wives, Maxine and Georgia, for their patience and encouragement, as well as their editorial and typing assistance.

December 1973

PREFACE TO 2D EDITION

In this second edition, we have updated the text to include current developments. We have added maps to help the student grasp more easily the geographic factors. They are located at either the beginning or the end of the chapters.

We are grateful to Leslie Lance and Professor Thomas Hodler for their cartographic assistance and to our publisher, Edsel Erickson for his advice and encouragement.

September, 1978   Chester L. Hunt
                                                    Lewis Walker

Contents

heterogeneity. Classic cultural pluralism. Other multi-ethnic countries. Temporary ethnic minorities. Crescive influences in intergroup relations. Freedom for the individual and for the group. Social unity and ethnic diversity. Majoritarian and minoritarian perspectives. Outlook for the future.

Chapter 1

Divergent patterns of intergroup living

One of the paradoxical aspects of our times is that, even as improvements in communication and transportation make a world community conceivable and national sovereignty almost an anachronism, we have counter-movements which would divide up existing states and would multiply the number of units trying to perpetuate national sovereignty in an increasingly interdependent world. The argument seems plausible that our existing national units serve to fragment a world in which scientific endeavor is creating the potential basis for a world society. On the other hand, spokesmen for minority groups protest that their identity is threatened by forced incorporation within a larger state.

Complaints of the minorities—i.e., distinguishable groups that receive unequal and differential treatment—may be classified under two headings: (1) discrimination against the individuals of the minority group in favor of members of the majority groups and (2) threats to the validity and viability of the minority culture. Such problems form a basic component of many of the battles recorded in world history for several millennia, but probably have become more salient with the breakup of empires and the rise of nation states. The latter trend culminated in the process described by the late American president, Woodrow Wilson, as "the self-determination of peoples."[1] Presumably the implication of Wilson's statement is that every group which considers itself a "people" should have the right to decide its own form of territorial and governmental organization. When the Ottoman and Hapsburg empires met defeat in World War I, it was taken for granted that their realms should be broken up rather than reconstituted, since they included a number of "nations" which had unwillingly been placed under a single government. Thus the Hapsburg Empire shrank to tiny Austria, and the Ottoman Empire to the nation of Turkey, while the rest of their territories were carved up into separate and independent states.

The process did not stop with the dissolution of the Hapsburg and Ottoman Empires, and the question of whether and how minorities can survive as parts of larger units is a live issue everywhere in the world today. In the United States, some blacks have despaired of the possibility (and perhaps the desirability) of real integration in American society and call for the erection of the "Republic of New Africa" on American soil. In Northern Ireland, the Protestant attempt to retain a portion of the island where they can be free from Catholic rule has led to charges of Protestant oppression of the Catholic minority. In Belgium there is a question whether it is really practical for Walloons and Flemish to try to coexist under the same governmental regime. In Nigeria, as well as in many other countries of Africa, the issue is whether or not several ethnically distinct groupings—tribes, "peoples", incipient nationalities—can be contained within the boundaries of a single state.

In many countries of the world, there are small minorities that have been strikingly successful in commerce and trade but are now threatened with expulsion from the countries which have become their home. In the Soviet Union, Communist theorists tried to construct a system which would combine specific ethnic identity with loyalty to an overall Communist regime. In the Republic of South Africa, few men are optimistic about the chances of constructing any type of arrangement by which blacks and whites can live in peace and harmony. One might find similar problems in nearly every country in the world.

ETHNICITY AND SOCIAL STRUCTURE

The goal of this book is to examine a number of such intergroup situations, and to determine whether each case is unique and specific or whether certain principles operate in many situations. In making this type of a

---

[1] Woodrow Wilson, "Pueblo Speech on the League of Nations," ". . . the sacredness of the right of self-determination, the sacredness of the right of any body of people to say that they would not continue to live under the government they were then living under. . ." cited in the Staff of Social Sciences of the University of Chicago (eds.), *The People Shall Judge* (Chicago, University of Chicago Press, 1949), p. 387.

survey, the focus will be on ethnicity rather than race per se and on patterns of social structure rather than on unique individual relationships or psychological perspectives.

Now a word as to what is meant by these terms. Our definition of ethnicity is taken from Gordon.[2] Gordon's definition is based on the American situation, but appears to have a wider applicability.

When I use the term "ethnic group," I shall mean by it any group which is defined or set off by race, religion, or national origin, or some combination of these categories. I do not mean to imply that these three concepts mean the same thing. They do not. Race, technically, refers to differential concentrations of gene frequencies responsible for traits which, so far as we know, are confined to physical manifestations such as skin color or hair form; it has no intrinsic connection with cultural patterns and institutions. Religion and national origins, while both cultural phenomena, are distinctly different institutions which do not necessarily vary concomitantly. However, all of these categories have a common social-psychological referent, in that all of them serve to create, through historical circumstances, a sense of peoplehood.[3]

This highly inclusive definition simply says that there are a number of factors which lead people to consider themselves (and to be considered by others) as an ethnic group. An ethnic group is a collection of people whose membership is largely determined by ancestry and which regards its place in society as being affected by its ethnicity. Thus the test of differences in physical appearance (frequently referred to as racial), national origin, or religion is not the difference per se, but whether this difference is considered socially significant. Some societies will disregard a rather wide range of differences in physical appearance, while others will relate social privileges to rather minute types of variations. Likewise, some societies will be greatly concerned about the national (or tribal) origins of the people in a given territory, while, to other societies, this will be a matter of indifference. Finally, religious diversity may simply indicate a variation in the interpretation of ultimate reality by various groups within the nation, or it may constitute a rigid dividing line which affects practically every phase of life. Sometimes ethnic differences are based upon a variation in all three of the criteria, physical appearance, national origin and religion; sometimes, upon one or two. In any case, what matters is not the nature of the difference, but the intensity of feeling about the importance of the difference, and the way in which this difference is associated with economic stratification, political power, and other elements of social structure.

Intergroup conflicts along racial lines have been so prominent in recent

---

[2] Milton M. Gordon, *Assimilation in American Life: The Role of Race, Religion and National Origins* (New York, Oxford University Press, 1964).

[3] Ibid., pp. 27–28.

years that sometimes the term *race relations* is viewed as a synonym for *intergroup relations*. Since this is not the viewpoint of this particular book, some elaboration may be in order. If *race relations* were a synonym for *intergroup relations,* one would expect to find harmony in any society which is racially homogenous and conflict in any society which is racially heterogeneous. A brief look at the world indicates that such a proposition will hardly stand close examination. It is true that there are many cases of racial conflict, but it is also true that there are examples of conflict among those who are members of the same race. In Africa, one looking for racial conflict would find it in the fierce warfare between Arabs and black Africans in the Sudan or in the seething discontent which pervades racial relationships in the Republic of South Africa. However, one would also find that one of the bloodiest civil wars of recent decades took place in Nigeria, where the combatants, although separated by ethnic affiliations, were all members of the Negroid race. Again, in Ireland or in Belgium, one would find Caucasians of similar appearance assailing each other with considerable bitterness.

Admittedly, the reverse cases, in which people who are racially different live together in a fair degree of peace and harmony, are more difficult to find. There are, however, some examples which can be cited. One could, for instance, point to the relatively harmonious and cooperative relationships existing between the British and black Africans in Northern Nigeria. Race relationships on the mainland of the United States have often been difficult but, in Hawaii, Caucasians, Polynesians, and Orientals have lived together in relative tranquility. Similarly, the "colored" inhabitants of Martinique and Guadeloupe seem to be happy with incorporation in the predominantly Caucasian French nation. Such examples are rare and may represent changing situations, but they do indicate that major friction between racial groups is not inevitable. Racial differences do frequently form lines along which intergroup conflict occurs. This pattern, however, is not always present, and there are many cases in which equally bitter conflict may occur among members of the same race.

It may be argued that racial differences, since they are rooted in physical heredity, are more durable than differences based on nationality, regional origin, or religious affiliation. This seems to be a self-evident truth, but the evidence in its favor is somewhat less than overwhelming. Those who assume that genetic heredity is a constant, forget that sexual attraction operates across racial lines and may largely replace the original peoples with a new hybrid strain. Mexico, where the majority of the populace are classed as mestizo, is a case in point. On the other hand, groups with a high degree of phenotypical similarity, such as the Flemish and Walloons in Belgium, have preserved a separate identity for centuries. In sum, groups whose identity is based on cultural distinctiveness sometimes survive for long periods, while groups identified by distinctive physical characteristics may diminish or even disappear.

Since there are no specific types of patterns which are associated with differences in race, as contrasted to religious, regional, or nationality differences, it seems best to place all types of fairly durable socially significant classifications under the ethnic rubric. However, not all authorities in the field are happy with this use of the term ethnic, and where the authorities whom we cite speak of *nationality*, or *regional, tribal, religious*, or *racial* differences, we shall follow their usage in our discussion.

Voluminous literature has appeared dealing with the psychodynamics of prejudices which grow out of ethnic conflict. There seems little doubt that our perception of the attitudes and actions of other individuals is shaped to a great degree by our respective ethnic affiliations. This ethnic stereotyping serves to justify the attitudes of our own group and to invalidate the attitudes or demands of other groups. It represents what Gunnar Myrdal referred to as "beliefs with a purpose."[4] There are also psychological problems which hinge on the relation between self-concept and group pride. These important problems having to do with individuals and individual attitudes, however, are not a major topic of concern in this volume, rather we are concerned with systems of group behavior or, in other words, relationships in social structure. It is assumed, for present purposes, that psychological processes may be viewed as constants which operate in all types of human relationships. However, there are some patterns of relations between groups which appear, at least for the time being, to have produced a tolerable situation for all concerned, while there are other patterns in which severe conflict appears to be endemic.

The best description we have seen of social patterns is found in Gordon's discussion of social structure. Like many other terms used by sociologists, social structure has a variety of meanings, but its use in the present context is indicated by the following statement:

> By the social structure of a society we mean the set of crystallized social relationships which its members have with each other which places them in groups, large or small, permanent or temporary, formally organized or unorganized, and which relates them to the major institutional activities of the society, such as economic and occupational life, religion, marriage and the family, education, government, and recreation. . . . It is a large definition but a consistent one in that it focuses on *social relationships*, and social relationships that are *crystallized*—that is, which are not simply occasional and capricious but have a pattern of some repetition and can to some degree be predicted, and are based, at least to some extent, on a set of shared expectations.[5]

Perhaps one concrete example might indicate the significance of social structure. Blacks and whites in the United States frequently react psychologically to each other. This interaction results in stereotypes, prejudices,

---

[4] Gunnar Myrdal, *American Dilemma* (New York, Harper & Bros., 1944), pp. 101–6.

[5] Gordon, *Assimilation in American Life*, pp. 30–31.

racially tinged notions of the self concept, and numerous other behavior patterns and attitudes which have been classified by psychologists and social psychologists. No study of American race relationships, however, can ignore the differences which came with one massive change in social structure—the shift from slavery to emancipation. Undoubtedly, many of the psychological processes operating during slavery have continued afterwards, but certainly the nature of race relations in the United States was drastically changed when blacks moved from the category of slaves to that of citizens.

To take another example, people of French ancestry and people of British ancestry interact in ways which produce various psychological reactions to the French or British labels that are probably somewhat similar in a great many circumstances, but French and British differences are far more salient in Canada, under a social system which maximizes their significance, than in the United States under a system which minimizes the importance of national ancestry. It will be the task of this book to investigate a number of social structural ethnic patterns and to indicate their significance for intergroup relationships.

SOCIAL STRUCTURAL PATTERNS

As with most other types of sociological classification, there is no "right" number of classifications which is inherent in the nature of the phenomena. The number of such classifications inevitably varies with the viewpoint of the writer and with the criteria which he uses. For our purposes, four main headings would seem to be adequate. These are segregation, cultural pluralism, integration, and temporary accommodation. These structural patterns are "ideal types" which are never found in their pure form in the real world. Indeed, Max Weber,[6] who is generally credited with developing the concept of the ideal type, argued that social scientists should even exaggerate significant features of social reality rather than describe them with photographic accuracy. The justification for this procedure is that thereby salient aspects of social life are brought inescapably to our attention for purposes of analysis. Admittedly the patterns of social structure we have mentioned will never be found in a form which is identical with their definitions. In spite of such disparity between these social structural patterns and reality, they are still of value if they direct our attention to significant features of intergroup relations.

Segregation. The segregated society is one in which contacts between various groups are restricted by law, by custom, or by both. It is assumed that the group differences, whether cultural or biological, are permanent

---

[6] H. H. Gerth and C. Wright Mills, *From Max Weber, Essays in Sociology* (New York, Oxford University Press, 1958), pp. 59–60.

in nature and determine one's total social role. The segregated society is organized on terms agreeable to the dominant ethnic group. This pattern is based on the premise that individuals have few rights apart from their ethnic group and that ethnic groups are unequal. Members of subordinate ethnic groups are allowed to engage only in the type of activities which are seen as contributing to the interests of the dominant group.

Cultural pluralism. Cultural pluralism is similar to segregation in that a variety of cultures continue to exist in the society. It differs from segregation in the degree to which the dominance of any one ethnic group is recognized. In a situation of cultural pluralism all groups, theoretically, have equal rights. It is a system which flourishes best when each ethnic group in a society has a specific territory in which it is a numerical majority and when there is at least an approximate equality of economic development between groups. When there is a marked overlapping of territorial ethnicity or when there is a marked divergence of economic development, there are likely to be fears for group survival and charges of discrimination.

Internal peace in a nation which espouses cultural pluralism is facilitated when the various territorial districts of the nation at least approximate ethnic homogeneity. Such a situation makes it possible for the ethnic group to follow its own way of life without being harassed by either cultural competition or charges of discrimination against other ethnic groups. However, even territorial homogeneity may not eliminate conflict about economic discrimination. Territories are likely to be unequal in resources or in economic development, or in both, with the result that per capita incomes in the richer district may be several times those in the poorer. Even socialism is little help in avoiding this kind of disparity, since a poor territory can not bring up low per capita incomes by redistributing nonexistent revenues. Consequently, the poorer territory will demand that the national government bring about economic parity between the regions and that it do this without giving "alien" (nonethnic) experts control over the depressed territories.

Acquiescence to such demands requires not only that the more prosperous regionally based ethnic groups share the wealth with ethnically distinguishable fellow countrymen but that in giving aid they limit the use of the most competent personnel in order to avoid charges of "internal colonialism." In addition to demanding a rare type of magnanimity from the wealthier ethnic groups such a decision also poses a dilemma for the national government—the choice between the most rapid economic development and the amelioration of the needy districts. Revenues are always in short supply and the national authorities usually desire to maximize the growth of the gross national product. Uusually the already prosperous districts are best equipped to make use of additional investment, and it is here that scarce capital will yield the greatest return. A decision on this basis may be criticized as shortsighted, but demands on revenues are always greater than resources, and if the national government accepts a slower rate of overall economic growth it is even less able to help develop the poorer regions. On the other hand, if its developmental efforts are focused on the richer regions, the gap between them and the poorer areas will increase and the discontent of the less prosperous ethnic groups will grow. Problems of this type have emerged in most nations which follow patterns of cultural pluralism and are outlined in some detail in the chapter dealing with Yugoslavia. Experience indicates that, while peaceful reconciliation of the economic demands of regionally based ethnic groups may not be an impossible task, it is certainly a difficult one.

A basic premise of cultural pluralism is that there is no need to sacrifice ethnic identity. Switzerland is frequently offered as a classic example of cultural pluralism. It is a nation characterized by a diversity of religion and national origin and by the complete absence of any one tongue which may be classified as the "Swiss language." Swiss are divided by national origin, religious affiliation, and language of common usage, and yet are united in their devotion to a Swiss nation which transcends these ethnic characteristics. There are few nations in which the path of cultural pluralism has been as tranquil as that of Switzerland or where differing ethnic identities could be combined with a common national loyalty with such apparent success. In fact, as we shall see, even the Swiss have at times had difficulty in maintaining this type of structure.

In spite of its difficulties, cultural pluralism is an attractive pattern, as it offers the hope of combining the preservation of ethnic distinctiveness with the advantages of coordination in a larger state.

Integration. Integration may be defined as a situation in which all citizens of the nation, or possibly even all members of the society regardless of citizenship, participate freely in all forms of social interaction without concern for ethnic affiliation. Integration differs from cultural pluralism in that it is not concerned with group privileges but with the rights of individuals. The integrated society is not directly concerned with ethnic group equality, inequality, survival, or disappearance. Its legal and social structure is not concerned with ethnicity. If ethnic groups survive this is because of the cumulative effect of individual choices rather than because of governmental guarantees to protect ethnically based institutions or privileges.

Integration differs from both cultural pluralism and segregation in that ethnic affiliation loses its salience in the social structure. The integrated nation may allow for some degree of cultural diversity, such as the toleration of religious differences in the United States, but its basic premise is a denial of any social obligation to preserve ethnic distinctions. Efforts to preserve special privileges on the basis of ethnicity are seen as a denial of integration and as an injustice to other ethnic groups. Likewise, efforts to preserve distinctive minority cultures tend to be regarded as separatist and divisive.

Minorities sometimes view this lack of protection for their cultures as tyranny, especially when their children are compelled to attend a school system which functions in terms of the majority culture. Some of the more cohesive and isolated minorities, such as the Amish and the stronger American Indian tribes, may succeed in maintaining a distinctive culture, but the general trend is toward homogenization. In the United States, this has meant the acceptance of a high degree of "Anglo-conformity"[7] which is most vividly seen in the dominance of the English language.

The philosophy of integration implies that individual frustrations will not furnish the basis for the development of ethnic grievances because salient attachment to the ethnic group has disappeared. This, however, is a process which, at best, takes a period of time and in the case of groups with distinctive physical traits or tenaciously held cultural patterns may never occur.

The question as to the extent to which integration is dependent on assimilation is illuminated by the distinction which Gordon makes between cultural and structural assimilation.[8] Cultural assimilation is seen as one of the subprocesses whereby members of the "guest" group become acculturated to the cultural patterns of the "host" society; in religion, for instance. General attitudes also come under the heading of cultural assimilation, and their direction influences the pace of structural assimilation even though not necessarily on a one to one ratio. Structural assimilation involves interaction at the primary group level between members of the "host" society and those of the "guest" group; i.e., widespread patterns of face-to-face relationships in clubs, organizations, and institutions of the "host" society.

Cultural assimilation threatens ethnic identity, but does not necessarily destroy it. Some individuals, for instance, may have largely forgotten their ancestral culture but yet restrict their group participation to those of their own ethnic background—or they may be excluded by those who claim ancestry which is either more prestigious or has been longer in the country. In other circumstances, structural assimilation, even including marriage, may occur before cultural assimilation is far advanced. In sum, assimilation is the basis of an integrated society, but assimilation is often incomplete and may not move at an equal rate at the structural and the cultural level.

In this book, we attempt to focus on patterns and hence on social struc-

---

[7] Stewart G. Cole and Mildred Wiese Cole, *Minorities and the American Promise* (New York, Harper and Brothers, 1954), pp. 135–40.

[8] Gordon, *Assimilation in American Life*, pp. 71–72.

ture rather than on attitudes, but attitudes and actions always interact and this is especially true in an integrated society. This interaction between attitudes and action patterns is the key to the understanding of Kenneth Clark's insistence on the difference between desegregation and integration.[9] Desegregation is the term applied to the removal of legal barriers which enforce ethnic segregation. Integration requires removal not only of legal barriers, but also of the prejudiced attitudes and social pressures which maintain ethnic barriers even after legal restrictions have been eliminated.

Gordon describes integration in terms of a social structural situation which would be impossible to approximate without the attitudinal changes which come from a lessening of prejudice:

in social structural terms, integration presupposes the elimination of hard and fast barriers in the primary group relations and communal life of the various ethnic groups of the nation. It involves easy and fluid mixture of peoples of diverse racial, religious, and nationality backgrounds in social cliques, families (i.e., inter-marriage), private organizations and intimate friendships.[10]

Integration even approximating this description is certainly rare and thus (like the other patterns that we have considered), represents an "ideal type" rather than an actual situation. Nevertheless, the insistence that the individual, rather than the ethnic group, should be the focus of social and legal concern is a pattern with continuing appeal.

Temporary accommodation. The types of social structure considered up to this point represent fairly permanent arrangements. There is another type of situation which we have labeled temporary accommodation. This form of adjustment may be made when foreigners live in a country with the expectation that they will never become a permanent part of the host nation, as when military, commercial, or religious personnel are on specific and temporary assignments in a foreign country. The example used in this book is of a particular group, the Peace Corps, which is organized for the purpose of providing specific services in a foreign country for a limited period of time.

ETHNIC PATTERNS AND THE DRIVE FOR EQUALITY

Since there are no national states without some variety of ethnic identification, the rejection of ethnic group rights in favor of individual rights appears to occur only when men feel either that their ethnic background is no handicap in the competition for success or that they can easily leave their ethnic identity and "pass" into the more favored group. Moreover, if

---

[9] Kenneth B. Clark; "Desegregation: The Role of the Social Sciences," *Teachers College Record,* 62 (October 1960): 16–17.

[10] Gordon, *Assimilation in American Life,* p. 246.

the members of an ethnic group are doing well individually, the group as a whole achieves a higher status; conversely, the group is placed at a lower level if the proportion of individuals who are successful is low. Thus, the concept of "equal rights" merges into the demand for ethnic as well as individual social and economic equality.

While the structures which a segregated society erects to maintain the supremacy of the favored group are easy to recognize, it is much more difficult to delineate those which make for equality. Not only is true equality difficult to obtain, it is even hard to define the conditions under which true equality may be said to exist. Does true equality, for instance, mean equality before the law? Does it mean equality of opportunity? Does it mean equality of achievement? Does true equality assume that the various groups will be equally distributed in all areas of the nation's life, or are the demands for equality satisfied when the domains in which the members of different ethnic categories participate are different but considered approximately equal? In other words, does equality imply proportionate ethnic representation in every occupation? If some groups are underrepresented are others overrepresented?

It is seldom, if ever, true that all groups in a society will agree that true equality exists. For the segregationist this is not much of a problem, since he is ideologically committed to maintaining the superiority of his ethnic group. Even the segregationist, however, will speak of the benefits which his rule brings to the subordinate ethnic groups and will compare their situation with allegedly more unfavorable conditions elsewhere. Cultural pluralists find that absolute ethnic self-determination is frequently compromised by a national drive to eliminate or minimize inequality between regions. Integrationists shift the focus from the group to the individual, but, if many individuals identified with an ethnic group feel that society is unfair, then the whole structure of integration is in danger. Even though equality may be hard either to achieve or to define the drive for it is a constant factor in any pattern of ethnic relationships.

ETHNIC PATTERNS IN OPERATION

We said earlier that our structured patterns of ethnic behavior are "ideal types" never found in their pure form in the real world. Even though there is no perfect replication of the conditions implied in the definition, however, some countries do illustrate to some degree the patterns described. Any example may be faulted on the grounds of imperfect representation of the ideal type, but it is still from an examination of living societies that such concepts emerge as aids to social analysis. For this reason, we have taken a variety of societies which, to some extent, represent the types we have listed. Through an examination of these societies we may expect to gain further insight into the problems which arise under various patterns of intergroup relationships and, conversely, into the factors which contribute to the stability of these patterns.

Integration

Integration assumes that the problem of ethnic group conflict is solved through the adoption of a common identity and the disappearance of separate ethnic interests. To cite an example previously mentioned—if people cease to identify themselves as French and British, as has happened with the longtime descendants of these groups in the United States, then we may expect that there will be no conflict which runs along the lines of separate French and British identification. Integration, in other words, solves group conflict through the merger of separate groups into a common whole. Such a process is not necessarily inconsistent with a lingering consciousness of a distinct ethnic subcultural identity, but it assumes that such identity will be chiefly one of historical identification which does not have any great significance in terms of present interest.

Integration assumes a high amount of cultural assimilation such as the adoption of a common language and a considerable consensus on basic values and standards. Sharp cultural differences obviously tend to provide lines along which conflict can emerge and therefore appear to be inconsistent with effective integration.

A real question is whether the same observation applies to biological differences; that is, whether there can be a national unity along lines of integration in a nation which preserves two or more groups differing rather sharply in physical appearances. Two nations which appear, to a large extent, to have adopted the path of integration have followed different practices in this matter. In the United States, there has been widespread intermarriage between those of European ancestry; this has tended to bring about a biological as well as a cultural unification of the Caucasian population. Such intermarriage has occurred to a lesser degree between blacks and whites. One estimate is that as many as 21 percent of the Caucasian population of the United States may have some black ancestry and that perhaps as many as three fourths of blacks have some degree of white ancestry.[11] Most of this intermixture, however, apparently occurred during the days of slavery and the years immediately following Emancipation. At any rate, at the present time, in spite of a small number of people who may "pass" from one race to another, the majority of people in the United States can be rather easily categorized as white or nonwhite, and this situation does not appear to be changing with any degree of rapidity.

In Mexico, on the other hand, intermarriage has been so widespread that a mestizo population is dominant both numerically and socially. The

---

[11] Robert P. Stuckert, "African Ancestry of the White American Population," *Ohio Journal of Science,* 58 (1958): 155–160, and John H. Burma, "The Measurement of Negro Passing," *American Journal of Sociology,* 52 (1946): 18–22.

black population has practically disappeared and pure Indians and pure whites constitute only a small minority. Thus Mexico represents a pattern of integration which includes both racial amalgamation (biological intermixture) and cultural assimilation, while in the United States amalgamation has not been pervasive enough to eliminate or greatly diminish recognizable racial categories.

Segregation

Segregation, or a separation of racial groups by both law and custom, was for a long time the unchallenged practice in the southern part of the United States. In the 1970s it is more starkly represented in the Union of South Africa and in Rhodesia than in other countries. In the United States, segregation was a part of the tactics used by white supremacists to overturn the reconstruction government after the Civil War. Between 1880 and 1910, laws were passed in many southern states ordering the separation of white and black in schools, libraries, restaurants, public transportation, and, in general, prohibiting the common use of any type of facilities when this use might imply an equality of the races.[12]

These practices of segregation were practically unchallenged until the 1950s, when a series of court decisions pronounced legalized segregation unconstitutional. At the same time, both in many state legislatures and in the national Congress, civil rights laws were passed which sought to outlaw segregation and discrimination in all the areas where, in a previous era, the law had commanded that segregation should be the practice. For some time, these laws and court decisions were largely formal procedures with little effect on day-to-day living and the practices of segregation which had been outlawed by judicial decisions continued to be the normal pattern in many communities. During the late 1950s and early 1960s, however, several forces narrowed the gap between theory and practice in a way that brought about significant change in black and white relationships. More effective enforcement of civil rights laws made it apparent that segregation placed one outside the legal order. Additional lawsuits by the NAACP (National Association for the Advancement of Colored People) produced additional court decisions which made it abundantly clear that no legal technicalities would be allowed to thwart the move toward equal rights. Finally, the demonstrations led by the Reverend Martin Luther King, Jr., dramatized the issue and gave evidence of mass support for the ideal of a desegregated society. By the end of the 1960s, formal public separation of the races in the use of public facilities had ceased to exist.

This does not mean that there is no longer separation between the races in the United States. Mutual suspicion and unfamiliarity of black and white do not vanish overnight. Many people will continue to pursue traditional

---

[12] C. Vann Woodward, *The Strange Career of Jim Crow* (Fair Lawn N.J., Oxford University Press, 1957).

patterns even though the force of both law and custom that support these patterns has been greatly weakened.

Nor have all of the events of social life reinforced the decision of the courts and legislatures in discouraging racial separation. In the cities two types of migratory movements have brought an actual increase in separate racial housing. The first movement is the migration of whites from the central cities to the suburbs, and the other movement is a massive black urban migration. The combined effect of these two population movements has made many central cities largely black in population. This development has been accompanied by a more critical attitude on the part of many blacks toward policies of integration and the adoption by some blacks of a separatist philosophy.

In spite of all the reservations which must be made, it still remains true that the general course of events in the United States since 1950 has been away from segregation. Formal legal rules requiring segregation have been scrapped in all cases, and all types of activities in which joint participation was once taboo are, to some extent, now the scene of integrated activity.

In the Republic of South Africa events have taken an exactly opposite course. When the Nationalist Party acquired control of South Africa in 1948, it adopted a formal stated policy to eliminate every possible vestige of integration and to make segregation the rule and practice as far as possible in South African life. To most observers, South Africa would already have seemed a segregated society before this time, but the aim of the Nationalists was to make segregation complete and total. South Africa has evolved an elaborate system of racial classification whereby people are issued cards indicating the racial category in which they belong. All political rights have been denied the nonwhite population, and hundreds of thousands of black Africans have been forcibly removed from supposedly white areas.

There are two major questions in the South African situation. One is how long a segregationist regime can be maintained by whites who are a minority of around 20 percent inside the Republic of South Africa, are a still smaller minority in the continent of Africa, and, in addition, are condemned by the bulk of world opinion. Another question is the viability of a program of segregation in a country with a rapidly growing economy where the demand for skilled personnel is beyond that which can be supplied by the white population. In any event, the Republic of South Africa and, to a slightly lesser extent, Rhodesia offer a case study of the results of the efforts to maintain segregation in a modernizing society.

Cultural pluralism

Cultural pluralism, according to Hoult, is "the doctrine that society benefits when it is made up of a number of interdependent ethnic groups, each of which maintains a degree of autonomy."[13] As we added earlier, this implies, in contrast to segregation, some degree of equality. Admittedly, though, it is seldom, if ever, true that all the various groups feel that they have equal privileges in the society. Under cultural pluralism, however, group relationships are so ordered that the extremes of inequality found in segregation are avoided and each group feels that it is gaining some benefit from association in the common society.

It should be added that such a feeling is not necessarily unanimous in any group and that it does not preclude the existence of extremists who feel that the sacrifices demanded by membership in a common society are so great that the group itself should secede and form a separate entity. The term cultural pluralism used in this way covers a wide and varied number of social patterns. In addition to Belgium, Switzerland, the Soviet Union, and Yugoslavia in Europe, there are examples in other continents. Canada, Malaya, and possibly Brazil could be so classified. There are also several African countries which have diverse, and apparently persisting, ethnic groups. So far, however, it is unclear whether the African trend is toward cultural pluralism or toward integrated societies based on assimilation to core cultures.

One of the most successful examples of cultural pluralism is the Republic of Switzerland. It is based on an arrangement whereby Swiss of Protestant or Catholic religious beliefs and of German, French, and Italian descent live in districts which are, to a great extent, ethnically homogeneous, but which are united in a federal republic that proclaims a respect for the cultures of all its ethnic groups without insisting on the dominance of any.

Much more difficult and conflictive than the Swiss experience is that of the Kingdom of Belgium and the district of Northern Ireland. Both are examples of a situation in which a partition had been accepted in the efforts to end conflict through arrangement of territories in which, supposedly, ethnic conflict could be escaped. Belgium was a result of the division of an area which, at one time, embraced both the largely Protestant Netherlands and largely Catholic Belgium. Partition did, it is true, create a Belgium which is homogeneous with respect to religion but which included two national groups, the Flemish and the Walloons, who have lived together in a decidedly uneasy relationship since that time. Northern Ireland was created at the time of the formation of the Irish Free State and was divided from the rest of the island in order to form an enclave in which Protestants might be free from Catholic rule. This partition did create an area in which Protestants were the majority, but it included a substantial Roman Catholic minority who came to resent bitterly what

---

[13] Thomas Ford Hoult, *Dictionary of Modern Sociology* (Totowa, N.J., Littlefield, Adams & Co., 1969), p. 239.

they regarded as classification as second-class citizens. Both Belgium and Northern Ireland may be regarded as examples of countries in which democratic cultural pluralism has seemingly failed to develop a society satisfactory to the contending groups.

The largest European country in which cultural pluralism is the official state policy is the Soviet Union. During the time of the Czars, the Russian government regarded the non-Russian minorities in the country as a menace to national unity. The government's answer to this problem was a program of forced assimilation known as "Russification." This program brought resentment and hostility from the minority groups, which constituted about half of the population of the empire, without producing the cultural assimilation sought. When the Communists came to power, in 1917, they denounced the Czarist regime as a "prison of the peoples" and announced a policy of cultural freedom for all the ethnic groups in the area. As a result, varied political units based on ethnic lines were developed which were subordinate to Moscow politically and economically, and which were not only allowed, but encouraged, to develop the language and arts indigenous to the particular culture. The Communists had proclaimed that ethnic conflict is the result of capitalistic oppression and would be absent in a socialist state. Thus an examination of intergroup relations in the Soviet Union may serve as a test case for examination of the hypothesis that ethnic quarrels are simply a manifestation of a capitalist social system.

Yugoslavia, although much smaller than the Soviet Union, also includes a variety of ethnic groups and has endeavored to maintain cultural pluralism through the establishment of "republics" constructed on ethnic lines. In Yugoslavia regional-ethnic autonomy has been carried into the economic field by a policy of decentralization which allowed individual enterprises controlled by workers' councils to make policy on wages and investment. The result has been a spurt of economic growth in the more industrialized regions, along with a growing gap between them and the agricultural areas.

The changing Yugoslav policies on centralism and local autonomy vividly illustrate the difficulty in maintaining a satisfactory pattern of cultural pluralism in a nation which has great differences in regional economic development. Two of the issues which emerge are (1) whether socialist equality implies equality between regions, and (2) whether a nation should submit to top-heavy centralized dictation in order to even out regional disparities. Along with the Soviet Union, the Yugoslav experience offers a case study of the opportunities and problems which arise when a noncapitalist, multi-ethnic state attempts to follow a policy of cultural pluralism.

The relations of the onetime colonial powers and their former subjects had elements of both integration and cultural pluralism. During the course of empire some degree of acculturation occurred, usually it was confined to a minority of the population who had the most intense interaction with the colonial power. There were, however, some cases in which the indigenous culture either was totally destroyed or survived only in small pockets and in which the postcolonial culture was an amalgam of the precolonial and the colonial cultures.

When the indigenous culture was not destroyed, there was usually at least a de facto cultural pluralism in which the colonial power conceded the legitimacy of some parts of the indigenous culture and social structure. After the withdrawal of colonial military suppression, the question still remained whether the inhabitants of the onetime colony should direct their major emphasis toward further assimilation of the culture of the "mother country" or should seek to strengthen what were regarded as indigenous cultural forms. This issue emerges sharply both in the newly independent countries and in those overseas territories which have chosen to retain their links with the imperial country. The assimilation of the colonial culture, incidentally, does not necessarily predispose a country to forgo independence nor does a distinct culture necessarily dictate political separatism. Rather, the question seems to be whether the relationship between the two territories is regarded as inhibiting and stifling or as promoting the welfare of the inhabitants of the former colony. The empires were usually edifices maintained by force which were quickly destroyed as soon as a native elite developed a national consciousness. There are, however, some exceptions to this cycle of colonialism succeeded by nationalism and, consequently, by independence and separation from the imperial country. In the United States this can be seen in the case of Hawaii, in which the predominantly non-Caucasian people of a distant Pacific island have accepted statehood for Hawaii. A somewhat different example is also afforded by the Commonwealth of Puerto Rico, the majority of whose inhabitants prefer a link with the United States although there is a small and fervent independence party.

Hawaii would probably be considered an example of integration, with the various Oriental and Polynesian groups functioning as subcultures in which people acknowledge the neccessity of conforming to an American core culture even as they struggle to maintain some elements of their traditional heritage.

In Puerto Rico, on the other hand, Spanish is still the language of basic education and a Latin culture coexists with Yankee practices and values. It is a somewhat uneasy kind of coexistence with many Puerto Ricans fearful that their political links with the United States may threaten Latin culture—a fear most vividly expressed in the independence party which, as yet, represents only a small minority of the island's people.

One of the most striking examples of a onetime colony which has expressed a preference for an organic relationship with the imperial country rather than independence is found in the case of Martinique and Guadeloupe. Martinique and Guadeloupe contrast rather sharply with the African territory of Senegal. Senegal was also the scene of an assimilative French colonial policy which attempted to bring Africans into a relationship with France in which French culture would be assimilated and French political ties accepted. Senegalese, though, decided that, however strong the French influence might be, their real destiny lay in independence. Martinique and Guadeloupe are in the West Indies, and they also contrast sharply with other West Indian islands of roughly similar economic and ethnic attributes which had been under the British control and which opted for independence at the first opportunity. Consideration of the question why Martinique and Guadeloupe followed a course different from that of either other French colonies or other Carribean islands will illuminate many of the factors involved in the choice of independence or of union with a metropolitan power.

Colonialism was one method of bringing other peoples under the rule of Europeans. Another method which, in a sense, accomplished the same objective was that of the migration from former colonies to European countries. During the colonial periods there was a small trickle of immigration from the colonies to France and Britain, and after the end of World War II this flow of immigrants from the former colonies sharply increased. Whatever their overseas policies, neither France nor Great Britain had a history of racial intolerance at home, and ethnocentric colonial attitudes were assumed to be historical anachronisms with no present viability. France and Britain were both inclined to look with some bewilderment at countries such as the United States in which racial prejudices and discrimination seemed rife. However, a sudden increase in their non-European population brought problems of many types. A study of the relationship of France and Great Britain with their new immigrants provides some indication as to the extent to which racial patterns are determined by present situations as contrasted to the impact of historical precedent.

Turning away from Europe, let us look at Africa, where the boundaries of most national states reflect the strategic or economic concerns of former colonial powers rather than African ethnic distinctions. Indeed, one of the main problems of several African states is the gross lack of correlation between political and ethnic boundary lines. Several ethnic groups commonly live within the same national boundary lines and yet also spread beyond the national limits. To mention only a few cases: Hausa- and Yoruba-speaking peoples are not confined to Nigeria, Swahili-speaking groups are found in several East African nations, and significant numbers of Somali comprise minority populations in Ethiopia and Kenya.

In discussing African populations, "tribalism" is often used as a term indicating any kind of ethnic distinction. The "tribe" may be a diffuse category of several million people with no common government, a cohesive band of a few hundred, or any number in between. Actually, Africa has had as great a variety of governmental entities as Europe. These include empires ruling diverse peoples, as in the case of the Egyptians, Ethiopians, and Songhai; collectivities often referred to as nations, such as the Zulu and the Ashanti; kingdoms comparable to smaller European states, such as Buganda or the six Hausa kingdoms; city states, several of which flourished among the Yoruba; along with thousands of small tribal units found throughout the continent. Colonialism paid little attention to any of these patterns and developed a network of territories with little relation to indigenous African ethnicity.

When independence movements developed in Africa the leaders generally accepted the boundary lines agreed upon by the European colonial powers. The result is that practically every country in Africa includes a number of ethnic groups, practicing different customs, speaking different languages, and following different religions. Often an ethnic group spread beyond the country's borders and its identification with any of the newly independent nations was weak. Similarly, there was frequently little sense of any common bond with other ethnic groups in the same country, a situation similar to that often found in Europe.

The leaders of African governments seek to foster a national consciousness which will supersede ethnic loyalties, but this is a difficult task. Ethnic rivalries were in fact, exacerbated by a differential assimilation of European culture. Some ethnic groups were heavily exposed to Western education and technology, while others followed a traditional pattern of life with little intrusion from the outside world. In Nigeria, competition between the highly westernized Ibo and Yoruba and conflict between both of them and the Hausa-Fulani stimulated dissension which erupted in a bloody civil war. It was a war watched with much anxiety by the rest of Africa. This anxiety was based partly upon sympathy and concern for the contending groups and also upon a fear that similar conflicts might erupt elsewhere from the pluralist ethnic basis on which all African nations were erected.

Africa is also one of the areas which saw the development of cultural pluralism on the basis of religious precepts. The expansion of Islamic territory from a tiny portion of the Middle East to North Africa, Asia, and Europe brought about a type of cultural pluralism which followed the precepts laid down in the Islamic law. This type of society found its most outstanding expression in the Ottoman Empire, which allowed the Turks to rule an area running in a sort of semicircle from Cairo to the Balkans for a period of over 500 years. It was an empire in which, although the political power was exercised by those of Turkish nationality, the basic distinction was between Muslims and those outside of the faith. Ideally the infidels would accept conversion, but, in practice, this did not always follow and some arrangements had to be made for the dissenting minority. In addition to considerations of expediency, tolerance of those who rejected the faith was justified on the ground that Christians and Jews were also "People of the Book" and therefore shared some elements of Islam.

The resulting accommodation was known as the *millet* system, in which each religious group was allowed to have autonomy in its own territory although required to pay tribute to the Muslim ruler. This system had nearly constant discontent, saw occasional massacres, and yet retained a degree of peace in an area of the world which, since the end of the Ottoman Empire, has often been involved in conflict.

Still another type of cultural pluralism is that in which ethnicity is rather sharply correlated with economic function. In societies of this type, it is common for a minority ethnic group to be successful in commercial undertakings which appear risky to the majority group. The social contribution of this minority group does not, however, serve to facilitate their acceptance by the majority. Usually they thrive best in a colonial regime in which the government is more concerned with economic development than with the ethnic identity of those engaged in economic activities. When independence occurs, the ethnic majority then sees the minority persons who constitute the commercial middle class as a group occupying economically profitable positions which should be held by members of the majority group.

Frequently there are legal provisions, such as ratification of the United Nations' Human Rights covenants or the extension of citizenship to non-indigenous inhabitants, which would seem to guarantee certain rights to the despised minority. These legal restrictions are usually broken or ignored while various governmental measures are taken to drive the "aliens" out of the economy and to replace them with indigenous inhabitants. Two situations which contrast sharply with respect to history and ethnic composition but which represent a somewhat similar experience in this regard are offered as test cases. These are the Indian minority in Kenya and the overseas Chinese minority in the Philippine Islands.

One might question placing these, and similar situations, under the rubric of cultural pluralism, since both the Indians in Kenya and the Chinese in the Philippines have suffered discrimination. Such discrimination conflicts with the previous statement that, in a situation of cultural pluralism, all groups, theoretically, have equal rights. In Kenya and the Philippines not only is there inequality, but also an unstable type of ethnic relationship, since it is possible that eventually discrimination may reach the point at which the minority is unable to function or is either massacred or deported. These are not just academic possibilities, but actions which have occurred in the past and could take place again. The Chinese in the Philippines had been nearly wiped out by massacres in previous centuries. In Kenya, after independence in 1963, thousands of Indians left the country fearing that they would be unable to make a living under the restrictions imposed by the Kenya government, and a few were actually deported. A similar Indian minority in Uganda has been deported en masse.

In addition to a preference for limiting the number of ethnic patterns we are using, there are three reasons for considering marginal trading peoples such as the Indians in Kenya and the Chinese in the Philippines as examples of cultural pluralism. First, there have been periods in the past when these commercially successful minorities did not experience discrimination to any great extent. Second, the majority refuses to acknowledge that the minority has suffered discrimination, since their average economic condition is usually better than that of the majority or dominant group. Finally, many societies face the question of determining their policy toward nonassimilable minorities which constitute marginal trading peoples. As we mentioned earlier, our ethnic patterns are "ideal types" and there are no situations which fit the definitions perfectly. Since the marginal trading peoples have an identity which is expected to persist for a relatively long period, since they usually experience at least some intervals when they enjoy equal rights, since they often prosper to a greater extent than the majority in spite of discrimination and are found in countries both with and without formal discrimination, it seems justifiable to include them under the cultural pluralism rubric.

General issues in cultural pluralism. An examination of these varied instances of cultural pluralism will raise many questions. For instance, is it possible for minority groups to be secure in a country in which democratic procedures allow the majority to take whatever repressive measures it sees fit? Related to this is the question whether a peaceful type of pluralism requires the acceptance by minorities of the dominance of one particular group which will serve as a core group in the society. An issue already mentioned is whether the course of intergroup adjustment is easier in a country in which the social ownership of the means of production has lessened the rivalries which are alleged to be inherent in a capitalist economy. A final question which occurs in all examples of cultural pluralism is the extent to which it is possible to maintain a separate ethnic identity while giving allegiance to a common society. These and still other issues will emerge in our analysis of these pluralist societies.

Temporary accommodation

The Peace Corps of the United States has been seen by some as a humanitarian endeavor to spread the benefits of Western technology, and by others as a sugar-coated tool of American imperialism. In our perspective it is looked at as an example of one technique of adjustment by an ethnic group engaged in a temporary sojourn on foreign soil. The usual pattern of temporary foreign groups has been to develop enclaves where they can restrict contact with the local inhabitants to the minimum basis essential for their mission while maintaining, to a high degree, a miniature society and culture which may be termed a "Little America," "Little England," or whatever country is represented.

The Peace Corps has taken the opposite tack of trying to avoid the development of enclaves while its representatives acquire to the greatest possible degree the culture of the country in which they live. No one would maintain that the Peace Corps has been completely consistent in these policies or that the policies have been completely successful even when faithfully carried out. Nevertheless, the Peace Corps approach does offer an interesting variant of the usual practice and one that may indicate patterns which will be more widely followed in the future.

CONCLUSION

In this chapter we have attempted to describe briefly the various patterns of intergroup relations and some of the results which occur in countries which attempt to follow them. In one sense, every experience is unique; in another sense, every human experience is an aspect of the universal situation. It may well be that we shall not only learn something about the factors involved in integration, segregation, and cultural pluralism, but that we shall also become aware of universal requirements which affect the course of human associations in all the varied patterns which may develop.

QUESTIONS

1. What are the major social structural patterns discussed in this chapter and are there other major patterns that could have been included?
2. What are the assumptions of segregation and integration and in what sense are these assumptions refuted by cultural pluralism? Discuss fully the implications of this issue.
3. What is the basis given by the authors for using the general term "ethnic" rather than some other term like religion, nationality, or race when speaking of significant group classifications? Do you have a preference?
4. Can you think of any countries other than the United States and Mexico where integration is the dominant pattern of intergroup relations? Discuss fully.
5. How do you account for the fact that in a culturally plural society it is virtually impossible for the various groups to feel that they have equal privileges?
6. Why did the Soviet Union adopt cultural pluralism and what was the attitude of the Czarist regimes?
7. Why have ethnic loyalties and differential assimilation of European cul-

ture often functioned to impede nationalism in Africa? Defend your answers and cite examples.

8. Why, do you suppose, does a commercial minority group function best under a colonial power whose major concern is economic development?
9. In order to have a peaceful type of pluralism do you think it is essential that several minorities accept the dominance of one particular group as a core group?
10. In what crucial way does the Peace Corps of the United States differ from other temporary foreign groups?
11. What is meant by ethnic equality? Why is this difficult to define?

Chapter 2

Cleavages within cleavages: Belgium and Northern Ireland, with a brief look at Switzerland

At least since the downfall of Napoleon, one of the common remedies for difficult intergroup relations has been the partition of territories into smaller units. Major examples of this are seen in the breakup of the Hapsburg and Ottoman empires. Other examples include the tripartite division of the subcontinent of India and the partition of Palestine into an Arab and an Israeli area.

In this chapter case studies of Belgium and Ireland are presented to illustrate processes of dealing with majority-minority relationships through partition. More specifically, the major generalizations generated in this chapter are as follows: (1) the creation of pure ethnic enclaves is virtually impossible in the modern world; (2) ethnic discontent is likely to increase with an increase in the level of living; (3) identification with group interests, not individual relationships, is a salient factor in ethnic conflict; and (4) cultural pluralism operates more effectively when the federal level recognizes ethnic distinctiveness at the local level.

The creation of the nation of Belgium through territorial partition dates back to 1830, when a revolt headed by Charles Rogier enabled Belgium to separate from the Netherlands. Rule by the Protestant Netherlands was disturbing to the Flemish people even though they were similar to the people of the Netherlands in language and in many other cultural characteristics. It was even more repugnant to the French-speaking section, which was different in these traits as well as in religion. Irish partition took place

24

in 1921, when predominantly Protestant Northern Ireland asked to remain a part of the United Kingdom so that it would not come under the rule of the predominantly Catholic, Irish Free State.

Partition in Northern Ireland united people similar in national background but different in religion, since there was a large Catholic minority. In Belgium, partition united peoples of two national strains who had a common religious affiliation. The pattern of religio-ethnic demarcation in the two territories is almost precisely opposite, but the course of historic development is strikingly similar. The partition of the Netherlands led to the creation of a Belgian state in which the unity based on identification with a common church is threatened by conflict stemming from ethnic and linguistic differences. In Northern Ireland unity on the basis of a common language is threatened by a cleavage based on differences in religious identity. To the outside observer such differences of language or religion may not appear to be major issues, but to the people involved they represent values which often seem superior to that of loyalty to the existing national state. Religious and linguistic cleavages are reinforced by patterns of economic stratification and of traditional prestige. These patterns are not as rigid or as uniform as segregation in South Africa or caste in India but past and present economic disparities are a potent force in maintaining group feeling.

In Belgium, the Walloons were traditionally the economically dominant group. This dominance is fading as industrialization in the Flemish districts has outstripped that in the Walloon areas and favored the growth of a successful Flemish middle class. Both the traditional prestige of French and its status as a world language, however, limit the social effect of economic prosperity in the Flemish regions. Not only have socially mobile Flemish usually found it necessary to be fluent in French for internal usage, but Belgium's role in world commerce and politics is another reason that the ambitious Flemish find French an almost indispensable language. To Flemish nationalists, these arguments for French are merely additional reasons that they need to construct further barriers and to limit their contacts with French institutions. In the meantime the situation is further complicated by demands that the wealthier Flemish districts subsidize a revitalization of the now depressed Walloon areas.

Northern Ireland also has lines of economic stratification which, to some extent, reinforce the cleavage based on religious differences. Generally, the Protestants are disproportionately represented in the higher strata of business, agriculture, government, and the professions. This does not, of course, mean that all Protestants are upper class or that no Catholics have achieved wealth and prominence. Further, Northern Ireland in general has been more prosperous than the Irish Free State, and Catholics share in the higher wage rates and social security payments.

The economic differences are well known, and perhaps even exaggerated, but their effect should not be overemphasized. Both in Belgium and in Northern Ireland there is much overlapping in economic status which finds many people from each group at a common economic level. Nor are the issues which excite popular passions usually economic in character. In other words, there is little justification for referring to Catholic or Protestant, or Flemish or Walloon, as disguised labels for bourgoisie and proletariat. Similarly it would be a mistake to assume that economic reform will lead to the elimination of ethnic conflict. Economic grievances exacerbate the Belgian and Irish ethnic quarrels, but the basic tensions are the result of a concern for ethnic prestige and survival to which economic concerns appear to be secondary. This does not mean that economic matters do not get into the fray. It is perhaps to be expected that the Irish Catholic leader, Bernadette Devlin, prefers a socialist to a religious image and that her Protestant opponent, the Reverend Ian Paisley, refers to himself as an anti-Communist spokesman. The trouble with their personal definitions is that there is little evidence that their followers see them as anything but leaders of religiously identified factions.

Similarly, *The Economist* cited the statement of a militant Flemish leader as indicating the primacy of economic concerns: "In almost any Brussels office," said the young Flemish zealot, "you will find a Flemish-speaking porter, a bilingual secretary and a boss who speaks only French. We are going to change all that."[1] This seems like a persuasive argument for economic determinism except that the current economic rise of the Flemish appears to have worsened rather than ameliorated their relationship with the Walloons and we have no reason to think a growth in the proportion of Flemish speaking bosses would change the trend. This is especially true since both language communities are insecure and neither is powerful enough to run the country alone.

The Flemish are a growing and prospering majority with a language which has little utility in the outside world whose trade and international associations have so much effect on Belgian prosperity. The Walloons are a minority whose relative economic status is declining but whose language is a link with the greater world. The communal problem is not so much economic as it is that many features of Belgian life; government, religion, and education, as well as economics, have been interpreted in communal terms. Economic changes may be essential but, without a reordering of communal attitudes and relations, such economic changes may still further exacerbate intergroup conflict.

HISTORICAL PATTERNS OF BELGIAN DEVELOPMENT

Belgium has had a mixed population consisting of Walloons, who in culture identify themselves with the French; the Flemish, who speak

---

1 "Squaring the Loop," *The Economist*, 208 (July 12, 1963), p. 137.

a dialect of Dutch; and a small minority of Germans. For centuries the area has been contested between various monarchies, and at times it has been dominated by one or another of the European empire builders. While it is difficult to pick any place for a beginning, perhaps it is best to look at the period of the Napoleonic regime, when Belgium prospered as a part of the French empire, using the free trade market which Napoleon had established. The end of Napoleon's regime led to a breakup of his dominions; in the case of Belgium, this was accomplished by formation of a Kingdom of the Netherlands, which combined Holland and Belgium, with King William of Orange as the monarch. King William, a man of Dutch descent, utilized the twin capitals of The Hague and Brussels, attempting thereby to govern a country which at the time included approximately 3.9 million Belgians, and 2.3 million inhabitants of what is now Holland.

The basis for both King Williams's initial success and his ultimate failure lay in a complex mixture of nationality and religious loyalties. The Flemish, who in many ways are close to the Dutch, were separated from the inhabitants of Holland by a Dutch tendency to look with disdain on the Flemish dialect, and also by religious differences, since the Flemish were staunch Roman Catholics while the majority of the people of Holland were Protestant. The French-speaking Walloons were separated from the Flemish in language, but might be thought to be united with them in religion, since both were of Roman Catholic background. However, the Walloons were close to France in sympathy, and many of them identified with the anticlerical ideals of the French Revolution. The anticlericals regarded themselves as Catholics, but they considered the influence of the Roman Catholic Church a menace in political, economic, and educational matters, and hence found it fairly easy to make a common front with the Dutch Protestants, who also desired to limit Roman Catholic power.

King William was an astute advocate of economic development and laid the financial and technical foundations of the Belgian economy, which still is one of the world's leading industrial establishments. However, he encountered several difficulties, one of these being the fact that his authoritarian rule was contrary to the spirit of the French Revolution, which still remained alive in the hearts of many of the Walloons. This led them to identify opposition to the King as consistent with dedication to liberty. Specific policies compounded his difficulties when, in 1825, he made Dutch the administrative language throughout Belgium; and when, in order to stifle the opposition of the Roman Catholic clergy, he endeavored to take over government control of the Catholic schools and seminaries.

Resentment at these policies brought the Flemish Catholics and the Walloon anticlericals together in opposition to what they considered an authoritarian and unjust type of rule. The gravity of the situation was compounded by an economic depression, which bore especially hard on the working-class population and led to various proletarian uprisings. Attempts to suppress these uprisings by Dutch troops only served to polarize the situation; the European powers eventually decided that a division of the Netherlands between Holland and Belgium was inevitable. A final attempt by King William to invade the Belgian area with a Dutch army was defeated by the intervention of the French, and, except for occupation by the Germans during the two world wars, Belgian independence has remained unchallenged since that time.[2]

While the regime of King William represented, to some degree, Dutch domination of the area, this relationship was reversed when Belgium became independent. Most of the nobility and industrialists were Walloon, while the peasants were predominantly Flemish. The result was a binational state with pronounced Walloon dominance. Perhaps the rather ill-fated motto of the country, *l'Union fait la Force* ("There is Strength in Unity") expresses the reverse of what has happened, since the union of Walloon and Flemish shows little sign of strength.

Complete dominance of the Walloons was modified in the succeeding period of nearly a century and a half by gradual concessions to Flemish sentiment. One of the first concessions was made in 1850, when the teaching of Dutch was allowed in the primary schools in the Flemish area. This was followed by the adoption of bilingual instruction in Flemish districts in 1860, although Flemish did not become the medium of instruction in secondary schools in Flemish districts until 1932, the same year that it was recognized in the University of Ghent. In 1962, Belgium was divided into two main linguistic areas with Brussels as a mixed area. This was the formal recognition of a territorial language policy which has made the language boundary lines literally a fighting matter. The culmination of the trend came in 1968, when it was agreed to move the French-speaking sections of the University of Louvain out of the Flemish areas. The same trend has been evident in politics. In 1873, the first Flemish judges were appointed in Flanders, and not until 1900 was the first speech in Parliament given in Flemish. Since then there has been a steady erosion of political ties across language lines and a growing tendency to divide along language lines with gradual gaining of ascendancy by the Flemish.

International events have complicated Belgian politics; especially the two world wars and the loss of the Congo, which in some ways accentuated Belgian divisions and yet temporarily increased the unity of the country. The Germans in both world wars were quick to exploit Belgain cleavages and to seek, with some success, the aid of Flemish collaborators. The situation was complex because some French Fascists in the Second World War, who considered themselves spiritually one with the Nazis, were also pro-German. The Belgian Resistance and the ultimate victory of the Allies had the temporary effect of welding the country together and of strengthening

---

[2] Adrien Meeus, *History of the Belgians*, translated by G. Gordon (New York, Frederick A. Praeger, 1962), pp. 255–84.

Belgium unity. The loss of the Belgian Congo in 1960, although it did not prove to be an insuperable economic handicap, was a blow to Belgian pride which weakened identification with a united country.

Since 1960, divisions have deepened along linguistic lines and political parties have faced a constant struggle in maintaining any kind of cooperation between their Walloon and Flemish components. Most major governmental positions are divided into two parts so that one may be held by a Walloon and the other by a Flemish. In spite of the shared symbols of church and monarchy there is a real question as to how long Belgium can survive as a nation. Usually cleavages in European nations are classified as national or ethnic, and perhaps it is indicative of the bitterness of the Belgian scene that the *London Economist* refers to it as a "tribal" type of conflict.[3] There has been much talk of federalism, but so far the parties advocating this are a minority of the Belgian Parliament.

On the other hand, the Liberals, Socialists, and Christian Socialists frequently find themselves split into Flemish and Walloon wings. Huggett comments: "the basic trouble is that governments are forced to preserve the semblance of a unitary state, while governing their country as if it were a federation."[4]

Language divisions have cracked the apparent facade of religious unity. For a long time, the Flemish priests were accustomed to denounce the godless French, and the leading Flemish daily carries on its masthead the motto, *Alles voor Vlaanderen, Vlaanderen voor Kristus* ("All for Flanders, Flanders for Christ"). Catholics do not hesitate to walk out of mass when it is said in the wrong language, a practice which has prompted one observer to remark, "In Belgium, there is much to be said against Pope John and the vernacular."[5]

Every area of Belgian life is riddled by ethnic division. Specific conflict may arise whenever a French speaking Belgian gives orders to a Flemish subordinate. Such matters as redefinition of linguistic zones, strife over policies in Brussels, the supposedly bilingual capital, and the relationships of the French- and Flemish-speaking sections of the University of Louvain, are the main points of friction.

Nearly 100,000 Flemish workers commute daily between Brussels, a city in which business is largely conducted in French, and their Flemish homelands. On the other hand, the expansion of adjacent suburbs finds people of French-speaking ancestry in zones that have been legally dedicated as Flemish, where they are compelled by law to send their children to Flemish-speaking schools. This was partly rectified by the inclusion

---

[3] "Tribal Troubles," *Economist* 205 (Oct. 20, 1962): 220.

[4] Frank E. Huggett, "More Troubles in Belgium," *The World Today*, 25 (March 1969): 93.

[5] Vivian Lewis, "The Belgian Linguistic Crisis," *Contemporary Review*, 208 (June 1966), p. 297.

of six boroughs in a French-speaking area, a move bitterly resented by the Flemish, but the battle over dominance in Brussels still goes on.

The controversy over the University of Louvain is one which has seemed almost incredible to outsiders. This is an ancient university, under Roman Catholic auspices, which is almost evenly divided between Flemish- and French-speaking students. The University has two faculties, so that a student has no need to be bilingual in order to complete his work. However, it came to be regarded as an affront to Flemish patriots that the French-speaking portions existed inside the Flemish language frontier, and a series of riots and demonstrations resulted in a decision to move the French-speaking parts out of the town of Louvain. Flemish opposition was apparently based on a fear that their position was eroding. This fear has produced opposition to anything that might be interpreted as "ground loss," or to the intrusion of any French institution which might support the influence of the French language.[6] The riots, demonstrations, and strikes which have been provoked by the language quarrel have had their influence in other types of controversies as well, so much so that Belgian political institutions have difficulty in functioning under any kind of a due process procedure:

The political machine in Belgium is short-circuited by anyone who feels his needs are pressing. Once, it was only linguistic extremists who tried to wield power directly, but the habit has now become widespread. . . .

To force the socialist union's insurance companies to change the payments system in their hospitals, Belgian doctors threaten to go on strike. To get modern guns to fight criminals, the police set up barricades and block traffic in Brussels. To protest the closure of their uneconomic collieries, miners tear down trees and attack the gendarmes in Limburg.[7]

The factors which have produced the extreme bitterness in the Belgian language quarrel may be attributed to a feeling by both the Walloons and the Flemish that only the most violent effort can prevent the forces of history from wrecking their language communities. French has a claim, both in its traditional ascendancy in Belgian aristocracy and business and in the fact that it is a world language; in contrast, even if Flemish and Dutch are considered identical, they are spoken only by a few million people. Belgium has a tremendous stake in world affairs; 30 percent of her industry goes into the export trade, and Brussels is the home of many international organizations. All these activities tend to increase the value of French, and one of the grievances of the Flemish is that one anxious for social mobility finds it almost imperative to become fluent in the French

---

6 Czeslaw Jesman, "A Note on Louvain University," *I.R.R. Newsletter* (May 1967): 220–21.

7 "Belgium Strangled in its Coils," *Economist*, 218 (March 26, 1966): 1216.

language. On the other hand, shifts in population and industry are working unfavorably for the Walloons. This change is described by Huggett:

The Flemish claims to equality of treatment have been strengthened by their transformation in this century from a derided peasant minority of the population into a majority group. A study carried out by a group of Belgian and French demographers in 1962 showed that the population of Flanders (excluding the Brussels area) had risen from a minority of 47.2 percent in 1910 to a majority of 51 percent in 1960, while the population of Wallonia had declined from 39 percent to 33.6 percent during the same period. By 1964, the population in the north had risen further to 54.8 percent, while that in the south had declined to 33.2 percent, with 12 percent in Brussels. The birth-rate in Wallonia as a whole is 15.5 per thousand—and for Walloons themselves only 13.5 per thousand—much lower than the 18.5 per thousand birth-rate in the predominantly Catholic north. It is estimated that by 1975, something like 60 percent of the Belgian population will be Flemish.

These changes in the population structure have been accompanied by changes in the economic sphere. . . . Since the end of the war, industrial development, particularly that of the big international companies has tended to be concentrated in the north, which is favored by better communications. This is symbolized in the postwar growth of Antwerp, now the fourth largest port in the world.[8]

The Flemish are a socially mobile group long considered subordinate, with a memory of ancient grievances aggravated by the fear that worldwide trends are working against the adequacy of their language. The French-speaking Belgians are a still powerful minority, who see their proportions in their country dwindling and their economic power disappearing. Rather than dominating the economy of the country, they are now in need of economic aid, which a non-French majority in the parliament is reluctant to give.

It would seem that some type of federalism, either openly acknowledged in Parliament or at least operational in practice, is almost inevitable in the Belgian situation. A country already divided into linguistic zones, with a dual apparatus of government, with violent conflicts over every issue aggravated by linguistic implications, is hardly a viable unitary state. Whether it will be possible to forge the minimum type of cooperation needed to enable the Belgian nation to survive at all is still an open question.

THE TWO IRELANDS

The senior author recalls that when he was a small boy his idealistic fantasies were stirred by newspaper accounts of the desperate and violent

---

[8] Frank E. Huggett, "Communal Troubles in Belgium," *World Today*, the monthly journal published by the Royal Institute of International Affairs, London, 22 (October 1966), p. 447.

struggle which the Irish Republicans were waging for independence from Great Britain. The pitched battles in the streets, the martyrdom of Roger Casement, and the eloquence of Eamon De Valera all made a tremendous appeal. All this was tied in with Woodrow Wilson's emphasis on the self-determination of peoples and the aftermath of the war "to make the world safe for democracy."

The Irish struggle was by no means new; rather it had been waged for at least 500 years, during which time the Britons had sought unsuccessfully to find a way in which Ireland could be incorporated into the British domains. Independence for Ireland did not constitute a complete solution of this conflict, and, as in the case of the division between the Netherlands and Belgium and between Pakistan and India, it was decided that an area which had been regarded as one country would have to undergo partition in order to have a regime of peace. In Ireland, the peoples were not separated, except in a rather vestigial sense, by language or by nationality, although a few differences might be discerned in these realms. The major distinction was one of religion, and when the question was posed as to how Roman Catholics and Protestants could live together in the same country, the answer came quickly that there was no conceivable formula by which Irish adherents of these two branches of the Christian faith might live under the same rule.

The result was a decision to divide the island of Ireland into two areas; the major portion was to constitute the Irish Free State, with a heavy Roman Catholic majority. The bulk of the Protestants were found in the six counties of Northern Ireland, compromising about two thirds of Ulster, and it was decided that these counties would gain a degree of self rule but would retain their link with the British empire.

As is usually the case, however, partition did not succeed in enforcing a complete separation between the contending parties. A very small minority of Protestants continue to live in the Irish Free State, while a still larger proportion of Catholics are found in Northern Ireland. In the territory of Northern Ireland which was linked to Britain, about one third of the inhabitants were Catholic as compared to perhaps a five percent Protestant minority in the rest of Ireland.

Northern Ireland was to be a Protestant enclave. This did not mean that Roman Catholics were hindered from engaging in worship, but it did mean that the Protestant majority was determined to maintain its dominance in all areas of life so that it would retain its separation from the much larger Irish Free State and guarantee that, within the enclave, Protestant rule would never be threatened.

Many results flowed from this determination to maintain a type of Protestant homeland in Northern Ireland. One was that, rather than having a hereditary hostility toward the British crown as the oppressor of the people, the people of Northern Ireland saw the link with England as a guarantee of freedom. Another distinction was that there was no move to restore the Gaelic language which had been the traditional speech of the Irish people and which still survived in a few isolated pockets of the country. Again, in legislation, no concession was made at all to Roman Catholic ideas on such subjects as birth control, censorship, and divorce. Catholics were allowed to maintain centers of worship, and a separate Catholic school system was supported by government funds. In some localities the Catholic population was so concentrated that a local Catholic majority might have been obtained, and in these areas various types of gerrymandering preserved Protestant rule.

The Protestants have traditionally been the wealthier settlers and they have maintained their economic dominance. In part, this may have been because of deliberate discrimination in which Protestants and Catholics both gave economic preference to their fellow religionists, with the Catholics coming out on the short end of the deal. Probably, to a larger extent, the situation of the Catholics, to some degree an oppressed proletariat, was a result of their lag in educational achievement and in commitment to a modern industrial type of society. The sense of oppression on the part of the Catholics and the continuing fears of the Protestants led to an unstable situation in which Catholics continually smarted under a feeling that they were second-class citizens. Protestants, on the other hand, felt that the Catholics' complaint about individual grievances were insincere and merely represented a step toward a time when the partition could be abolished and Northern Ireland could be absorbed within the predominantly Catholic Irish Free State.

Although the unrest of recent years has discouraged foreign (and also domestic) investment, Northern Ireland is still somewhat more prosperous than the Irish Free State. Part of this prosperity is due to the subsidization of social services in Northern Ireland by the United Kingdom—a subsidy which would be difficult for the Irish Free State to maintain if the two realms were united. This means that a union proposal would require either a major increase in governmental expenditures of the whole territory or a cut in the amount of money received by old-age pensioners, orphans, unemployed workers, and other beneficiaries of welfare payments. It is estimated that bringing social services in Ireland up to the level now maintained in Northern Ireland, without a British subsidy, would require an Irish tax increase of approximately 50 percent. Another way of looking at the picture is to compare levels of living in the three areas. It is estimated that while Northern Ireland is 20 percent below the British level, the Irish Free State is 40 percent below.[9] Catholics in Northern Ireland feel

---

[9] Discussion of the comparative economic status of Northern Ireland and the Irish Free State is based on Brian Crozier et al. *The Ulster Debate* (London, The Bodley Head, 1972), pp. 110–11. Personal per capita income in Northern Ireland in 1970

that they have been discriminated against in jobs and in the provision of government services. However justified the Catholic complaints may be, it is doubtful that separation from Britain and merger with a relatively poorer Irish Free State would ameliorate the economic situation of Northern Irish Catholics.

It would seem that the economic advantages of Northern Ireland as well as a simple desire to maintain peace would stimulate efforts to establish a reconciliation between Catholics and Protestants. Some attempts of this kind have been made. There have been occasional gestures toward friendship and unity. These include ecumenical conferences between Protestant and Catholic clergy and a few conferences between political leaders of Northern Ireland and the Irish Free State. Such gestures, however proved inadequate to bridge the gulf of mutual suspicion. Through the years occasional riots and protests have erupted, culminating in the extremely violent situation in 1968 and extending into the 1970s. In this situation a tenuous degree of order was maintained only by the presence and activity of substantial numbers of British troops.

Perhaps symptomatic of the extent of the differences between the two groups was the emergence of two intransigent figures who served to polarize the extreme factions. One of these was the Reverend Ian Paisley, a militant Protestant fundamentalist who established his own version of the Presbyterian church. The inflammatory oratory of Mr. Paisley produced an enthusiastic response in many Northern Ireland Protestants. At a time when religious fervor had been generally declining, his own church flourished, and he frequently preached to meetings of thousands of people. He was bitterly critical of what he considered the compromising tendencies of the Northern Ireland government. The Archbishop of Canterbury and other Protestant leaders of an ecumenical mood were also frequent targets for barbed criticism on the grounds that they were selling out to Rome.

On the Catholic side the most widely publicized leader was a militant spokeswoman typical, in many ways, of protest leaders in the late 1960s in the United States. Young, female, and attractive, she utilized American civil-rights techniques in the Irish setting. Bernadette Devlin was regarded by some of her followers as practically an Irish Catholic Joan of Arc. Perhaps a brief description of a speech she made in the English parliament may give some idea of the emotional tone which Miss Devlin conveyed. *Newsweek* described it as follows:

> Bernadette Devlin, the ardent 22-year-old M.P. from the Catholic Bogside district of Londonderry rose from her seat and delivered a blistering attack on Parliament. "It is your fault, your blame, your shame," cried the trembling,

---

was $1,958 as compared to $1,248 in the Irish Free State. This statement is based on data in *Digest of Statistics for Northern Ireland*, Belfast, 1970, table 109, p. 79, and in *U.N. Statistical Yearbook* (Statistical Office of the U.N., New York, 1971), p. 596.

diminutive Bernadette. From the greenleather benches across the floor came a chorus of incensed Tory voices. "Rubbish, rubbish, absolute rubbish," they shouted. But Miss Devlin was not to be shouted down. "It is not rubbish—you know it is not rubbish. You have been in this house a damned sight longer than I have and you know it wasn't rubbish a year ago. You said it was rubbish on Oct. 5 [the date of the first bloody civil-rights demonstration last year] and you also say rubbish when people complain who have never had the vote and will never have it now."[10]

The historical roots of the bitterness in Northern Ireland may be illustrated by two expressions often used in intergroup conflict, which the Irish have contributed. "Beyond the pale" refers to the days when territories in which the English had colonized in Ireland were referred to as the "pale." These were areas in which the Irish could live only on sufferance and beyond which Englishmen ventured at peril of life. Another example is that of the unfortunate Captain Boycott of County Mayo, a land agent in the 19th century whose activities led the Irish to refuse any kind of relationship with him, whose name now denotes this form of conflict through noncooperation.

The situation in Northern Ireland is probably most directly traceable to the plantation period in which British nobleman were granted large tracts of land which they endeavored to farm with the aid of Scotch and English settlers. These settlers have intermarried to a considerable extent with the local population, so that it would be somewhat questionable to refer to them as a Scotch and English element, but they have, for the most part, retained their Protestant religious affiliation and the tradition of pro-British sentiment. Superficially it wuold seem that the people in Northern Ireland are divided only by religion, but the religious mantle covers differences of political tradition, ways of life, and economic status.[11]

It would be a mistake, accordingly, to look at the quarrel in Ulster as one produced solely by a divergence in religious beliefs. With the exception of the Reverend Mr. Paisley, a few other Protestant clergy, and a few militant Catholic priests, most of the clergy have attempted to play down the religious aspects of the conflict and have been influenced to some degree by the current trends toward a more ecumenical position. Clergyman have often urged moderation, and at times those of different faiths have walked together through riot torn areas in an attempt, usually unsuccessful, to stem the fires of conflict. Rather than partisans for competing beliefs, Protestants and Catholics represent different communities. Regardless of the reconciliation which may be obtained between systems of belief, the

---

[10] "Backlash in Belfast," *Newsweek*, Oct. 27, 1969, p. 54. Copyright by *Newsweek*, Inc. 1969, and reprinted by permission.

[11] Robert W. Schleck, "Ireland's Clash of Colors," *America*, 121 (Sept. 26, 1969): 134–36.

differences between communities persist. Religious affiliation is not so much a symbol of contrasting beliefs as it is a badge by which hostile communities may be identified.

It is frequently argued that ties of personal friendship will be sufficient to overcome intergroup barriers. In Northern Ireland personal relationships are inhibited by school and residential segregation. Nevertheless the graduates of both Catholic and Protestant schools are citizens of the same country and, although residential areas may be segregated, the blocks which Catholics and Protestants inhabit are frequently contiguous. Catholics shop in Protestant-owned stores and Protestants usually find it necessary to resort to Catholic-operated taverns if they wish to quench their thirst for alcoholic beverages. Nor is the discrimination in employment complete; Catholic employers frequently have Protestant employees and vice versa.[12] Friendships often occur between Catholics and Protestants, but the evidence is tragically clear that such friendship is not strong enough to survive intergroup conflict. A tragic example is given in the following news item:

By Hugh A. Mulligan

BELFAST (AP)—Just after dark on the wildest of the wild nights the doorbell tinkled in a Roman Catholic greengrocer's shop in the Crumlin Road.

"Tommy, come in," said the woman behind .he counter, recognizing her Protestant neighbor and good customer of longstanding.

The man ignored the greeting. "I lost my home on Agnes St. tonight," he announced bitterly. "You have five minutes to get out before you're burned out."

"Sure, I had nothing to do with that," cried the woman, bursting into tears.

"I can't help that," the man said. "None of us can help anything any more." And he disappeared in the crimson glow of the crossroads where already a double-deck municipal bus, symbol of Protestant political power, was a burned skeleton and just behind it a public house, the symbol of Roman Catholic riotousness and rebellion, was leaping into flames.[13]

It has long been the dream of those who espoused an economic interpretation of history that, in the words of the "Internationale," "the universal party shall be the human race," meaning that men of different ethnic backgrounds will come together when they realize common economic interests. The Labour party in Great Britain has been able at times to express friendship toward ultimate union of all parts of Ireland, but the Labour party of Northern Ireland has never been an effective force of reconciliation. Rather, in the effort to keep some degree of unity between various components which may be predominantly of one religion or another, it

---

[12] W. T. Freeman, *Ireland* (London, Methuen & Co., 1969), p. 155.
[13] *Kalamazoo Gazette* (Aug. 24, 1969), p. 7.

has been forced to abstain from taking any effective position on intergroup conflict and has never become an effective opposition party to the Union party, which has been the vehicle of Protestants for maintaining domination.[14]

Along with common economic interests, citizens of all religious connections have a common need for the maintenance of a society in which at least a minimum of law and order provides for the protection of life and property. In a situation in which the state is regarded by approximately one third of the population as fundamentally illegitimate, it is probably impossible to look upon the police as a neutral agent guaranteeing the safety of all. The police have been exposed to inevitable charges of partisanship, and the militia, which most countries call on for situations which the police are unable to handle, consists of B squads, which are regarded as Protestant forces and therefore as instruments of domination. Even though the British troops in 1969 and the early 1970s brought some degree of order, and therefore of security, to all parts of the population, they were regarded by Catholics as another evidence of interference by Britain and its effort to obstruct the logical forces of history which should lead to a unification of Ireland.

In summary, all the forces of society which are usually regarded as bridging intergroup differences seem to have failed in this situation. The common emphasis of religious leaders on the virtues of brotherhood has been helpless before the folk definition of religion as the basis for separate communities. The solidarity of laboring men versus other elements in the society has proved less salient than ethnic loyalties which divide members of the labor movement. Finally, the very forces of law and order which represent ideally the monopoly of force by an impartial state are regarded by the minority as simply agents of their repression.

Prospects for the future

One question of obvious significance is whether or not demographic trends will permit the prolonged continuance of a Protestant majority. At the present time slightly more than one third of the population are Roman Catholic, but Catholic pupils constitute slightly over one half of the total enrollment of children in the schools; thus a higher Catholic birthrate may, over the long run, change the demographic balance. This is far from certain, since a variety of influences may produce a differential emigration by either group. In the period from 1901 to 1926 the Catholic population dropped by one half, but since that time it has been by all odds the most rapidly increasing group, and if this trend continues Northern Ireland may face a situation in which a stigmatized Catholic population is at least

---

[14] Deborah Lavin, "Politics in Ulster, 1968," *The World Today* 24 (December 1968): 530–36.

equal in size to the Protestant overlords. Such a possibility makes it difficult for either side to decide that they must work toward a reconciliation in which the strength of the two parties is reflected by the present population ratio. Catholics may well assume that ultimate victory in theirs, while Protestants may struggle for governmental privileges which would give them the power that a potentially declining superiority in numbers might not be able to sustain on a democratic basis.

Pressures for moderation are, of course, not absent in the area. In fact, G. F. Johnston, writing in 1965, stated: "In all, there is room for more optimism regarding a solution of the Northern Ireland 'problem' now than ten years ago. It is heartening to record that, apparently, the responsibility for finding this solution has been assumed by some of the leaders from both sections of the community here."[15] Less than a year later, however, Mr. Johnston was compelled to admit that his earlier optimistic forecast had been misleading and the tensions seemed to be increasing rather than subsiding.[16]

On the other hand, there are many factors which might be expected to favor those who hope for a modus vivendi which would at least avoid the extremes of conflict. In spite of a rate of unemployment of about 5 percent as of the late 1960s, Northern Ireland is an industrial and agricultural area which, under the best of conditions, would seem to have an economic potential somewhat greater than the rest of Ireland. Even though the Catholics look upon the government of the Irish Free State as an ally and talk frequently of unification, they nevertheless have been separated governmentally for 50 years from the rest of Ireland and cannot avoid considering whether or not unity with the Free State might bring them serious problems. Under the pressures of events the Protestant government of Ireland has been compelled to make concessions with respect to specific grievances. Chichester Clark, a prime minister who was appointed as a reaction against the alleged compromising tendency of Captain O'Neil, the previous Prime Minister, announced that he favored the "one man, one vote" principle in local government; an ombudsman was appointed to investigate complaints against government and efforts were made to administer welfare provisions in the allocation of housing in a way which would end Protestant favoritism.[17]

Such moves are looked upon by Catholics as forced concessions, and may be interpreted by them simply as indicating the type of success which violent tactics achieve. On the other hand, it is possible that the remedial

---

    [15] G. F. Johnston, "The Northern Ireland Situation," *I.R.R. Newsletter* (October 1965), p. 14.

    [16] G. F. Johnston, "Recent Developments in Northern Ireland," *I.R.R. Newsletter* (September 1966): 35–38.

    [17] G. F. Johnston, "Ulster's Misery," *Economist*, 230 (Jan. 11, 1969): 14–15.

measures for specific grievances may undercut the drive to revolt. Finally, the British government, although reluctant to abandon its common ties with Ulster, has no desire to perpetuate a situation in which Britons and Irishmen often seem to be cast in the role of enemies. The Irish Free State also has much to gain from a peaceful solution. Ireland's trade is greater with Britain than with any other country, most Irish migration goes to the British Isles and, with the prospects of British entry in the common market, the economic factors pulling British and Irish together would seem to be very strong.

Against trends which would seem to favor some sort of solution of the conflict must be set the ability of demagogic leaders to inflame passions that make difficult any kind of concession from either side. Catholics who would accept government reforms in good faith risk being branded as traitors by Bernadette Devlin and others of her ilk, while any sign of moderation shown by the Ulster government is immediately denounced by the Reverend Mr. Paisley and his followers as a sellout to "violence in the streets." The prospects of moderation should not be underestimated, but its victory is by no means certain.

Although the personal charisma of Bernadette Devlin and Ian Paisley have served as rallying points for the contending forces, it would be a mistake to overestimate the importance of personal leadership. Suspicion and fear are so deeply imbedded in both Protestant and Catholic groups that it seems easy for any leader to arouse a militant response. The same factors make it difficult for more conciliatory leaders to get a following. Catholics distrust governmental reform measures and regard these as tactical moves which might never be really carried out and which, in any event, are inadequate. Protestants, on the other hand, tend to look at any compromise as a threat to their security and to the continuance of separation from the Irish Free State.

One interesting aspect of the leadership pattern is the type of reference group utilized by the respective leaders. Miss Devlin has seemed to be somewhat embarrassed by being cast in the role of a sectarian religious leader and prefers the image of a socialist fighter for social justice. Thus, when an illegitimate pregnancy threatened her political role, she defended it in terms of social class rather than of ethnicity based on religion: "Whatever they think of my being pregnant it ought not for a moment to distract them from facing up to the real menaces of bad wages, exploitation, slum houses and oppressive landlordism."[18]

The Reverend Mr. Paisley was not averse to talking about the evils of Roman Catholicism, but much of what he has said seems to have been an effort to project his image as an opponent of Communism. Both Paisley and Devlin made tours in the United States. Devlin was supported by such left-

---

[18] *Newsweek*, July 12, 1971, p. 52.

wing groups as Students for a Democratic Society (SDS), The American Young Socialist Movement, and the Peace and Freedom Party. Paisley, on the other hand, was sponsored by right-wing fundamentalists such as Dr. Carl H. McIntire and the Reverend Bob Jones of Bob Jones University.[19] These ideological positions would seem to have more relevance to the international stature of the leaders than to the Irish conflict. If the battle lines shifted from religiously based ethnicity to right- and left-wing factionalism, the new cleavages would crisscross traditional alignments in Northern Ireland and perhaps present some hope of resolution. However, there is no evidence that the rank and file are greatly swayed by their leaders' international image or that social class interests are perceived as cancelling out traditional Catholic-Protestant rivalries. In other words, regardless of their social and economic viewpoints, both Paisley and Devlin were perceived as the leaders of religiously identified factions. If the present militant leaders pass from the scene, it should be easy to replace them with new personalities. For a moderate to attain similar leadership would appear to require political acumen of a very rare type.

While prophecy is always dangerous, four possibilities seem to be apparent. With wise leadership and effective action by the Ulster government, it is at least conceivable that, if Catholics are reassured on what is termed their civil rights, they might become reconciled to a continued existence in an Irish enclave which is not a part of the Free State. Some support of this possibility was given by Eddie McAteer, then leader of the Nationalist Party, when he suggested that perhaps aggrieved Catholics could look toward Belfast, the capital of Northern Ireland, rather than Dublin, the capital of the Irish Free State, for a solution to their grievances.[20] In spite of all the tensions, there is some warrant in saying that the movement toward a dissolution of Northern Ireland and unification with the Irish Free State had seemed to have lost impetus in recent years, up to the new "time of troubles" in the late 1960s.

The incorporation of Northern Ireland in the Irish Free State apparently would not be opposed by the British government if acceptable to Ulster Protestants. It is difficult to see such a solution in the short run, but a declining demographic majority of Protestants, if coupled with conciliatory moves by Catholics in the government of the Irish Free State, might eventually render a Protestant population unable to oppose such a move effectively.

A suggestion which seems sensible but which has drawn little support is that tension in Northern Ireland might be lessened by a change in the boundaries:

---

[19] Emma Layman, "Ulster's Paisley and His American Friends," *Freedom Institute Newsletter,* Fall 1969, pp. 1–3.

[20] Levin, "Politics in Ulster," p. 535.

While the six county area as a whole is two-thirds Protestant, Catholics comprise local majorities in certain districts: the counties of Tyrone and Fermanagh and Derry City. Redrawing the borders to attach these areas to the Irish Republic would reduce substantially the Catholic minority under Protestant rule and thus, perhaps, serve to dampen inflamed emotions.[21]

Such a compromise solution should appeal to moderate men but will probably draw little support while emotions are inflamed. Those who wish total unification of Ireland would not be satisfied, while many Protestants take the view that Northern Ireland's boundaries were fixed permanently at the time of partition. However, if the conflict appears deadlocked, it is possible that sheer weariness may make such a compromise feasible.

Unfortunately, the most obvious indication is that a state of tension will continue. If this is true, it means that Northern Ireland will erupt into violence at rather frequent intervals and will be kept a viable society only by the intervention of British troops. Neither side welcomes this type of outlook, but the stormy history of the last 50 years and the rising trend of intergroup conflict since 1965 make it an altogether too likely type of outcome.

THE SWISS EXAMPLE

In contrast to the rather unhappy situation in Belgium and Ireland, Switzerland is often cited as a successful example of cultural pluralism. In spite of a Catholic-Protestant split, along with three national and four linguistic groups, the Swiss nation has enjoyed comparative peace.

The majority of Swiss are German by background and language and Protestant in religious affiliation. There are minorities of French and Italian and a small pocket of people who still speak the ancient Romansch. In addition, there are poor but haughty mountaineers, sophisticated urbanites, an industrial proletariat and traditionally minded peasants—more than enough differences to cause virulent intergroup conflict.[22]

Various policies have prevented potential ethnic conflicts from coming to a head. Perhaps most significant is the circumstance that there is literally no Swiss language and that all the major tongues are given equal status, with consequent avoidance of the problem of choosing or developing a national language. Europe's intermittent wars could easily have torn the country apart, but a rigid policy of neutrality has minimized the internal effect of international tensions. Religious toleration is the rule, and both

---

21 Schleck, "Ireland's Clash of Colors," p. 136.

22 K. Mayer, "Cultural Pluralism and Language Equilibrium in Switzerland," *American Sociological Review*, 16 (April 1951): 157–63. H. de Torrente, "Role of Language in the Development of Swiss National Consciousness," *Pub. Mod. Lang. Assoc.*, 72 (April 1957): 29–31.

Catholic and Protestant churches receive state support. Although Switzerland has highly developed government welfare services, its economy is primarily capitalist, and there is relatively little opportunity for government decisions to affect the role of ethnic groups in the market place.

Perhaps more important than these policies is a federal system of government which allows local homogeneity to blend with national diversity. Switzerland is divided into 22 cantons (districts whose average size is about that of an American county), and each canton into several communes. The formation of Switzerland is traced back to a defensive league of four cantons in 1292, and the cantons, and even the communes, have retained a good deal of autonomy. Switzerland did have a civil war in 1847; a north-south and Catholic-Protestant conflict, and successive constitutions have strengthened the role of the federal government while still leaving the local units with more authority than is true in most countries.

Barber describes the local allegiance of Swiss citizens: ". . . for many citizens the decisive element in political life remains cantonal and communal citizenship. Ask a Swiss where he is from, and his initial answer will be 'Basel' or 'Lucerne' or 'Glarus,' rarely 'Switzerland.'[23]

This system of local self-rule, coupled with a high ethnic concentration in various cantons, allows most Swiss to live in relatively homogeneous ethnic enclaves, even though they are citizens of a highly diversified nation. One of the cantons is Italian, three are almost completely French, three are mixed French and German, and the rest, primarily German. Religiously, most Italians are Catholic, while both Germans and French are religiously divided. Thus, those united by religion are often divided by language, and vice versa.

When the canton has a heavy majority of one group, its language will dominate the area. When there are significant minorities in the canton, they are still usually concentrated in relatively homogeneous communes (villages) and thus maintain an ethnically oriented style of life.

This harmonious arrangement does not always work out, however, as is indicated by the unrest among the French minority in the Jura region of the predominantly German canton of Berne. The French population was incorporated in this canton in 1815, and separatist sentiment has manifested itself intermittently since that time. In 1947 a French-speaking candidate for cantonal director of public works was rejected by the cantonal legislature, apparently because of his French background. This incident sparked a separatist movement which reached a violent stage in the 1960s and early 1970s. At this time a "Jura Liberation Front" was engaged in terroristic activities directed against both the Swiss government and the antiseparatists in the Jural populace. Along with other disruptive activities,

---

[23] Benjamin R. Barber: "Switzerland: Progress Against the Communes," *Transaction* 8 (February 1971), p. 28.

youthful Jurassians dynamited munition dumps, invaded the hall of parliament and staged a sit-down in the Swiss embassy in Paris.

What is the explanation of such behavior in the supposedly tranquil country of Switzerland which so often has been pictured as one of ethnic freedom? How did the dissident Jurassians develop this sense of outrage in a country which prides itself on providing full freedom of expression for nationality, language, and religious groups?

The answer to these questions seems to be that two of the factors responsible for ethnic peace in the rest of Switzerland are absent in the northern Jura region. These are: (1) the voluntary nature of membership in the Swiss nation and (2) the presence of crosscutting affiliations which moderate the effect of any one type of social distinction.

The first factor finds expression in the manner in which various territorial units became a part of Switzerland. For most regions this was a voluntary action of seeking the protection which came through affiliation with a larger entity. For the northern Jura, however, it was a forced annexation by foreign powers which took this region from France and made it a part of Switzerland in 1815 after the defeat of Napoleon. Thus, there was a historical basis for connecting Swiss citizenship with at least a partial loss of national identity.

The presence of crosscutting variations is a second factor which moderates the intensity of ethnic conflict in most of Switzerland. The three main social categories involved are economic, religious, and linguistic. Some districts in Switzerland are wealthy while others are poor; some are industrial and others are agricultural; some are predominantly Catholic and others largely Protestant; linguistic differences are manifested by adherence to one of the four languages previously mentioned. There is no set pattern which joins these three categories together. Thus two areas may be united on the basis of their economies but separated by religious affiliation or language. Or they may be united in language but separated by religious affiliation, or vice versa. Thus separatist tendencies on the basis of one of these categories will be countered by unifying tendencies on the basis of common interests in one of the other categories.

The Jura itself manifests these crosscutting tendencies. It has approximately 147,000 inhabitants most of whom are French-speaking. However, various elections have produced a clear-cut majority for separatism only in the northern Jura. Presumably this is because the cross cutting pattern of social categorization present in the southern Jura and the rest of Switzerland is absent in the Northern Jura area. The three northern districts are relatively poor, primarily agricultural, Catholic, and French. They have about 60,000 inhabitants who give heavy support to separatist movements which usually stress points associated with the prestige of the French language. French language usage in the southern Jura does not produce a separatist majority. Presumably this is because the southern

Jura is more prosperous and industrial and is primarily Protestant. Similarly districts in the Jura, or in the rest of the Berne canton, which might be sympathetic to the Jura separatists on the basis of Catholic religious affiliation are differentiated because of German language usage. It is only in three northern Jura districts that people are united by economic, religious, and national ties, and here separatism is strong.

The Swiss government has been anxious to appease the Jura separatists but this is no simple matter. However, if territorial boundaries include only the separatist group and exclude others, then this is regarded as the alienation of territory which was historically Jurassian and hence belongs to the separatists even if the majority of the present residents disagree! It seems impossible to satisfy the Jurassian separatists completely without violating the wishes of others who live in the territories they claim; nevertheless, the Swiss have tried to reach a settlement which would at least reduce the points of contention. The Berne canton has been divided and a new canton formed. The new canton is designed to give autonomy to the French Catholic Jurassians, while the other canton will be a mixture of German, Swiss and non-Separatist French Swiss. Elections were held commune by commune to allow each commune to determine with which canton it wished to be affiliated.[24]

Whether this adjustment will satisfy the Jurassian separatists is doubtful. They do not feel that communes historically Jurassian should be allowed to separate from the new canton and, in any event, they probably would prefer either independence or annexation to France. The new canton will at least give the rebellious Jurassians a base of operations they can call their own and this may modify their discontent. In any event, the Jura situation is a "deviant case" in the idyllic Swiss practice of cultural pluralism. The difficulty of solving the Jura problem indicates that no nation is immune from ethnic conflict and that no system, such as cultural pluralism, will necessarily solve all aspirations.

Aside from the Jura problem, there are other factors which may bring intergroup trouble into the Swiss paradise. Urbanization has made ethnically homogeneous communes a less significant factor and has mixed industrial workers from different backgrounds. Trains and automobiles have promoted migration from one canton to another even though, in 1960, some 60 percent of Swiss still lived in the canton of their birth. Industrial expansion in Switzerland has brought foreign labor into Switzerland so that, in 1970, one person in six was an alien. Presumably, the alien was a short time resident who would soon return home and in the meantime, contributed to Swiss prosperity without seeking to change the country's social patterns. On the other hand, even with current moves to restrict immigation, it is more likely that Switzerland will have to adjust to a

---

[24]"Switzerland: Third Jura Referendum,"*Keesings Archives,* October 20–26, 1975, p. 27404.

group of permanent aliens whose traditions are not those of the country. The Swiss pattern of local ethnic homogeneity mixing comfortably with national heterogeneity may prove to have been an adjustment possible only in a small country in a period of history which is almost past.

CONCLUSIONS

While the preceding observations on ethnic trends are in some ways unique to these situations, they suggest generalizations which may apply to other intergroup relationships. Such generalizations should not be characterized as "sociological laws" comparable to the predictive power obtained, for instance, by Boyle's law on the pressure and volume of gas at a constant temperature. Ethnic relations never occur in a situation in which only one factor is operating, and these generalizations therefore represent influences or tendencies rather than any invariable pattern of relationships. Perhaps the vital phrase in their interpretation is "other things being equal"—a situation which never obtains.

The empirical method is valuable in gathering facts and in checking out hypotheses, but it seldom, if ever, yields results which can be used mechanically. Your authors feel that empiricism must be combined with a *verstehen* (understanding) approach in which sociology is an art as well as a science. The sociologist is one who has become sensitized to factors which may influence the behavior of human groups. Empirical investigation will reveal the extent to which these factors appear to be operating but only social wisdom based on an understanding of the total milieu can reveal the relative influence of various factors at any given time and place. Such wisdom is difficult to obtain or even to demonstrate. The limitations of the empirical method in sociology indicate that sociological inquiry is as complex as it is fascinating and that both the limitations of our data and the subtle, usually unconscious, influence of our own values may distort our analysis.

There is no guarantee against cultural myopia, but one partial protection is to enlarge our focus through the comparative study of situations in other societies. There is probably no society anywhere which is an exact replica of the Belgian, Irish, or Swiss situation, but there are enough common elements in all societies that these patterns will have some applicability everywhere.

In this analysis we shall discuss briefly some of the factors which seem to have been salient in Belgian, Irish, and Swiss situations and then proceed to offer some generalizations which, hopefully, have pertinence beyond these particular countries.

The history of both Belgium and Ireland offer mainly negative hypotheses about the course of intergroup conflict. The most obvious of these is that partition is a dubious remedy for ethnic quarrels. The division of the Netherlands and Belgium produced unity of a religious type in Belgium which, in turn, was sundered by the linguistic and national differences of the inhabitants. Similarly, the division in Ireland gave Protestants a state in which they were not under the authority of a Catholic government, only at the price of producing a society in which Catholics regarded themselves as oppressed and discriminated outcasts. Any suggestion for a realignment of boundaries intensifies the fire of conflict, since the population is so mixed that it is impossible to have a complete separation, and a readjustment of boundaries inevitably means that a territory which one group or the other regarded as its own will be lost.

Economic prosperity is frequently offered as a solvent for ethnic conflict on the theory that people who can realize their aspirations in a monetary sense will not jeopardize their status through destructive conflict. Belgium has been one of the world's most prosperous countries, and the Flemish group particularly has profited through the industrialization of recent years. Rather than moderating with prosperity, the Flemish claims increased. Industrialization seems to have raised their expectations and increased their resistance to whatever degree of economic influence is still wielded by French-speaking Belgians. Ireland has been less prosperous and Northern Ireland is faced by real economic problems, but the somewhat higher level of economic activity in Northern Ireland has failed to produce in Catholics a willingness to trade ethnic pride for economic advantage.

Finally, one of the favorite theories of intergroup relations is that intimate contact, especially if it is on the basis of equal status, tends to produce friendship and assimilation to a common viewpoint. For large groups of people, economic contact can never be on a completely equal basis, and the evidence is strong that, as minority groups rise in economic status, their expectations, and therefore the level of their demands, seem to rise. It is true that often an economic depression aggravates ethnic conflict, but it apparently is easier for a completely submerged ethnic group to accept subordinate intergroup situations than for a rising group to feel that an accommodation in terms of economic privilege is really adequate recognition of its true importance in society.

To summarize: competition and contact on the basis of equal status may accentuate bitterness, while rising economic status increases resentment at a subordinate ethnic situation.

One of the widely held beliefs is the notion that ethnic conflict is moderated when people who differ in one category are united in some other category. The Irish situation concerned people who were the same in nationality but differed in religion, and the nationality tie was not an adequate guarantee of peace. Belgium offered the opposite phenomenon; a people who differed in national background but were the same in religious affiliation. In actual practice categories of this type are never independent. Thus the connotation of Irish meant hostility to Britain for one classed as Irish Catholic but not for the Irish Protestant. Similarly in Belgium there were not just Catholics but Flemish Catholics and Walloon Catholics, each of whom could be very upset if mass were said in the other's language. Presumably if the total area of Ireland were threatened by disaster or if all Belgian Catholicism were under attack, cooperation and unity might emerge; although it is still possible that one group might minimize the common danger and seize a chance to overwhelm its local ethnic rivals. In the circumstances prevailing in the 1970s, however, there was little prospect that either Belgian Catholicism or Irish national identity required the cooperation of rival groups.

A federal system which combines ethnic control of regions with national control by a coalition of diverse ethnic groups is often suggested as a solution to problems of ethnic conflict. The Swiss experience indicates that, in some circumstances, such an arrangement is viable. From the standpoint of the central government this means that it will not seek to impose an unwelcome uniformity on the country. This is a price which many regimes are unwilling to pay. Today most governments would be willing to accept religious diversity, but how many are willing to forgo a national language or to allow the market to dictate the economic position of ethnic groups?

Even religious tolerance is not easy to achieve, since religious groups often support mutually antagonistic values. Thus religious groups may disagree on food tabus—pork for Muslims or beef for Hindus; or they may have very different views on family behavior—the acceptance of divorce by Protestants while Catholics press to have the government forbid divorce actions.

Most countries have taken the position that a common language is required for ease of communication throughout the land and as a symbol of national unity. Language carries both substantive content and emotional overtones so that it is hard for most people to conceive of a common national loyalty without a shared language.

Finally, in these days, when the whole world seems to be moving toward increasing governmental intervention in the economy, it is hard for any nation to refuse to make the attempt to alter the economic position of ethnic groups. The action may be to improve the lot of a group regarded as disprivileged or to restrain and penalize the groups which are over their proportionate quotas in favored economic positions. Whatever the rationale, government decisions in these matters tend to widen the area of potential conflict. The allegedly disprivileged, whether Catholics in Ireland, Flemish in Belgium, or blacks in the United States, never feel that governmental intervention in their favor is strong enough. On the other hand, the privileged groups are seldom happy in a situation in which preference for other groups means that the children of the current elite have decreased chances for success. Government assumption of the task of allocating economic awards thus transfers the rivalry from the market to the political arena with obvious danger to social unity.

If federalism requires a restraint by the central government which few regimes are willing to accept, it also imposes difficult requirements on local units. Supposedly, such local units are ethnic enclaves within which both laws and social customs reflect the culture of a particular ethnic group. Actually, economic development seems almost inevitably to lead to changes in the ethnic composition of the population. Natives leave to seek opportunity elsewhere, while development within the area brings in foreigners (or at least fellow nationals of a different ethnic group). The adjustment required is a type of moving equilibrium which reflects the changing ethnic scene. Either the area must be subject to frequent review and change of boundary lines and the natives must be willing to allow their influence to diminish and to see strangers, with peculiar ideas and odd customs, gain increasing power, or some device must be found which allows the maintenance of ethnic cohesion without reference to territorial concentration. Either of the first two choices are difficult, while the third choice would seem to abandon the territorial identification which has been regarded as the very essence of federalism.

In summary, two conclusions appear to develop from our examination of federalism along the Swiss lines: (1) in a federal system the central government must abandon the effort to impose cultural or economic uniformity; (2) probably local units cannot long expect to be bastions of ethnic homogeneity and must be willing to accept changes either in boundary lines or in ethnic composition, and possibly in both.

This examination of intergroup relations in three small countries yields little which might provide a basis for optimism. Belgium and Northern Ireland have been in a state of tension for many years. Switzerland, often looked upon as a success model, is not without problems and may be experiencing diminution of the viability of its federal system under the impact of modern industrialism. The fact that in these countries all the major groups are of the same race and are identified with Western civilization, as well as being close together in cultural development, darkens the outlook. It is indeed difficult for governments of pluralistic states to satisfy the interests of their various ethnic components and, even with partition and repartition, it is hard for the ethnic group to gain the security it seeks. In looking for a hopeful viewpoint one might suggest that perhaps governments should cease their concern for the rights of ethnic groups and regard themselves only as guardians of individual rights. Such individual rights would include the privilege of any desired type of ethnic association and the free competition of languages, ideologies, economies, and religions. This is not a solution easily reached, and its ramifications will be studied in a later chapter.

GENERALIZATIONS

Although all the areas to be considered in this book are important in themselves, their experience is also valuable in providing insight into comparable situations in other countries. The main feature which distinguishes the sociologist from the journalist in his interest in recurring uniformities in behavior.

The journalist may employ many of the techniques of investigation used by the sociologist, while the sociologist in turn may utilize journalistic accounts as data in his analysis. The difference between the two is their goal. The journalist is impelled to investigate by an interest in the particular situation. The sociologist is also interested in the particular situation, but he hopes to learn from the specific example of social interaction something about the nature of social interaction in a wider context. Thus we have looked at intergroup relations in a variety of countries to improve our understanding not only of these specific countries, but also of the nature of intergroup relations in general. For that reason in each of these chapters we shall list a number of patterns of behavior in specific situations and the implications of these specific behavior patterns for ethnic relations in general.

Irish-Belgian pattern. Partition left language minorities in Belgium and a religious minority in Northern Ireland.

Generalized pattern. The effort to construct pure ethnic enclaves in the modern world is doomed to failure.

Irish-Belgian pattern. Economic development in recent years has favored the Flemish in Belgium and has given both Protestants and Catholics in Northern Ireland a higher level of living than in the Irish Free State. At the same time that economic improvement has been taking place ethnic discontent has been mounting in both Belgium and Northern Ireland, and grievances are often expressed in economic terms.

Generalized pattern. A generally rising level of economic return will not diminish and may exacerbate ethnic discontent. Aspirations tend to grow more rapidly than improvement can be made.

Irish pattern. Patterns of friendship between Catholics and Protestants in Northern Ireland did little to diminish group hostility.

Generalized pattern. Ethnic conflict is based on identification with group interests, and individual relationships play little role in either the adherence to group norms or in the definition of group interests.

Irish-Belgian experience. A common religious faith in Belgium was redefined so that language differences were reflected, and one speaks of

Flemish Catholics and of Walloon or French Catholics. In Ireland a common language was less effective in ethnic identification than religious differences.

Generalized pattern. Sharing one of the characteristics often used in ethnic classification does not indicate that a common ethnic identification will develop.

Irish-Belgian experience. Socialist parties in Belgium and the Labor Party in Ireland which appealed to a common class-identification were unable to bring about unity between different ethnic groups in political matters.

Generalized pattern. Both organized groups and ideologies tend to be functionally specific rather than to determine the ethnic orientation of the individual. Acceptance of a political or economic viewpoint augments rather than displaces ethnic identification. One is not simply a socialist or a conservative but one is an ethnic socialist or conservative.

Swiss experience. A federal system in an ethnically heterogeneous country has worked well where the cantons and communes themselves were fairly homogeneous.

Generalized pattern. Cultural pluralism works well as long as integration at the federal level can be combined with ethnic distinctiveness at the local level.

Swiss experience. The Swiss have minimized the occasions for ethnic conflict by refraining from establishing a national language, by tolerating different religions and by allowing most economic roles to be determined by the market.

Generalized pattern. Minorities may be willing to remain in a pluralistic state if they feel that they can protect both their way of life and their economic welfare by individual efforts without harrassment by the majority.

Irish experience. Ian Paisley projects the image of one who is an anti-Communist leader, while Bernadette Devlin represents herself as a crusader for socialism.

Generalized pattern. Ethnic leaders will seek a universalistic frame of reference which places their demands on a broader basis than that of ethnic group preference.

Irish experience. British troops sent to Northern Ireland to maintain order have been attacked as invaders by Catholics and, conversely, have been charged by Protestants with being "soft" on Catholic terrorism.

Generalized pattern. Intervention by third parties often leads to charges that the intervening party is not really neutral but is an ally of one of the parties in the conflict. Since the moral credentials of the intervening force are always questionable, only massive force will enable it to restore peace.

QUESTIONS

1. How did the origin of Switzerland differ from that of Belgium and Northern Ireland? What significance does this have for intergroup relations within the country?
2. Both Belgium and Northern Ireland were formed as the result of an effort to minimize intergroup conflict. Would further partition end the conflict which remains? Why or why not?
3. How have Flemish and Walloons in Belgium evaded the implication that a common devotion to Roman Catholicism should bring about unity?
4. Is the ecumenical movement within Christianity likely to bring Protestants and Catholics in Northern Ireland closer together? Explain your answer.
5. Is it correct to regard Bernadette Devlin not as a Catholic leader but as a Socialist leader? Why or why not?
6. Is it correct to regard Ian Paisley primarily as an anti-Communist leader? Why or why not?
7. How do you explain the fact that both Paisley and Devlin have emphasized nonreligious issues?
8. Would a greater measure of equality of treatment by the Northern Irish government calm Catholic agitation?
9. Why has Flemish discontent increased as their economic situation has improved and discrimination decreased?
10. What is the role of Swiss federalism in keeping interethnic peace in that country? Is this method applicable elsewhere?
11. Would a federal system along the Swiss lines solve the ethnic problems of Belgium and Ireland?
12. Why are British troops in Northern Ireland not accepted as impartial guardians of law and order?
13. What is meant by the choice between a concern for individual rights and a concern for group rights? Which attitude has characterized the United States?
14. Why was it more difficult to impose the French language in the Flemish part of Belgium than it has been to persuade all Americans to use English? Should American emphasis on English be modified?
15. Why does equal-status contact sometimes lead to increased conflict?
16. Is interethnic peace compatible with the maintenance of ethnic identity and cohesion? Why or why not?
17. What is meant by partition and why is it viewed as a potential solution for hostile populations living in the same area?
18. What role have the religious leaders played in the Protestant-Catholic struggle in Ireland?
19. Would the conflicts between the Catholic and Protestants be resolved or

minimized if Northern Ireland were to become a part of the Irish Free State? Discuss fully the ramifications of this issue.

20. What are some of the implications of the statement that religious affiliation is a badge by which hostile communities may be identified? Specifically, how does this apply to Northern Ireland?

21. Do you agree that any "effort to produce pure ethnic enclaves in an independent world is doomed to failure?" Discuss fully.

22. What prospects do you think that the future holds for Belgium and Northern Ireland, two countries created by partition?

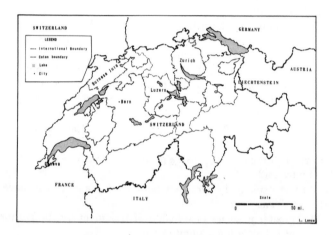

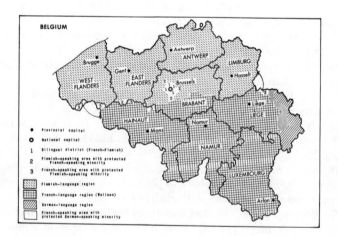

Map adapted from Eugene K. Keefe in *Area Handbook for Belgium,* Supt. of Documents, Washington, D.C. 1974.

For location of Northern Ireland, see map on page 327.

Chapter 3

Minorities in the Soviet Union: Pluralism or assimilation?

To many people in the United States the population of the Soviet Union is ethnically homogeneous, and "Russian" is simply the term applied to people living in the Soviet Union. Actually, Russians comprise only about half of the population, the balance of which includes as varied a collection of peoples as can be found in any country on the globe.

This fact is brought out rather strongly in a letter to the editor of a midwestern American newspaper protesting the indiscriminate application of the term Russian in a news story about an international chess match:

To the Editor:

A friendly warning to the *Gazette* editorialist who wrote "Chess Summit in Moscow" about the forthcoming match between Bobby Fischer, the American, and Tigran Petrosyan, the "Russian"; don't ever show that article to a citizen of Soviet Armenia. Not unless you'd like an inmate's view of an Armenian morgue.

When Petrosyan, the Armenian, beat Botvinnik, the Russian, Soviet Armenians staged their wildest celebrations since the death of Joe Stalin, the Russ ... er ... Georgian dictator.

I know you know, but just for the record: while every Russian living in the USSR is a Soviet citizen, not every Soviet citizen is a Russian. Knowledge of this

53

fact will enhance survival prospects as one travels about the Soviet Union. (Signed) John Gorgone, 434 Creston, Kalamazoo.[1]

Armenians, like other ethnic groups, came under the sway of a Russian-dominated country, but this did not make them Russian. A large part of the history of both the Czarist regime and the USSR concerns the relationships of Russians with the minority peoples. Thus, one of our aims in this chapter is to show the following principles of majority-minority relations: (1) ethnic conflict can occur in virtually any type of socioeconomic order; (2) recognition and tolerance of minority culture may prevent national disloyalty; and (3) the nature of intergroup relationships is often altered by significant social changes.

The history of the Soviet Union and of the Russian Empire which preceded it has been one of continental expansion with advances toward the Pacific, on the one hand, and toward the Atlantic via the Baltic Sea, on the other hand, alternating with periods of defeat and retreat. The total process has brought into being a sovereign state which is the largest in the world from the standpoint of area and is third, behind China and India, in size of population. An idea of the extent of the country may be gleaned from a brief description by Anna Louise Strong, one of the first Americans to write at length about the Soviet minority policies.

The USSR is the world's largest country; it includes about one sixth of all the dry land of the earth. It is about the size of all of North America; it is more than twice as large as our United States. The summer sun never sets on the great extent of it. When the long June days draw to a close in Leningrad at nine o'clock in the evening, it is already seven o'clock next morning in Kamchatka on the Pacific and the sun of the next day has been up for several hours. Each New Year, arriving, is greeted ten times as it travels across the country. The Far Eastern Express takes nine days from Moscow to Vladivostok. In the Vladivostok station stands a post marked "9329km" (5789 miles); there is no such figure on a milepost anywhere else in the world.[2]

The conquest of this vast area and its peopling and development has been a continuous struggle extending over many centuries. Unlike the experience of the Americans who also entered into a vast land mass and proceeded to conquer it, the Russians did not find that the indigenous inhabitants could be swept aside. At one time, indeed, the Mongol conquerors had invaded most of the territory now included in the Soviet Union, and it is probably true that the genetic stock of Genghis Khan is a part of Russian ancestry today. In part, the conquest of the land represents a struggle with people who were at least as "advanced" in technology

---

[1] Letter to the editor of the *Kalamazoo Gazette* (Aug. 27, 1971), p. A-7.

[2] Reprinted with permission of The Macmillan Company from *Peoples of the USSR*, by Anna Louise Strong. Copyright 1945 by Anna Louise Strong.

and political organization as the Russians themselves, if not more so. Over a period of many centuries, conflict was waged with the Swedes, the Germans, and the Baltic peoples in the struggle to move toward the west. Expansion toward the east has been going on for a similar period of time, and it was certainly a significant moment in Russian history when Ivan the Terrible captured the city of Kazan on October 2, 1552, marking the end of Tartar rule in European Russia.

ETHNICITY AND NATIONALITY

The territory occupied by the Soviet Union is inhabited by various ethnic groupings which have interacted in a long association involving both friendship and enmity. In addition to the distinctions kept alive by historic memories, they differ in culture—in some instances, quite sharply. Rather than ethnicity, the preferred term for such groupings is nationality. Soviet writers have made a number of efforts to define nationality; of these, the treatment by Stalin is the basic point of reference: "A nation is a historically constituted, stable community of people, formed on the basis of a common language, territory, economic life, and psychological makeup manifested in a common culture."[3]

A nation is not necessarily independent and it may or may not be a soverign political unit. It is not easy to identify either in territorical or qualitative terms. Many of the categories used in Stalin's definition of nation are themselves somewhat difficult to delineate in anything approximating precise terms. For instance, how much variation may exist in subgroups within a "common" culture and how much does such a culture have to differ from other cultures? Or, how many of the group can live outside of the "homeland" and still claim a "national" territory? In matters of language how much difference is required before a mode of expression is classified as a separate language rather than a mere dialect? In economic matters, is there a degree of economic interdependence which vitiates any claim to a distinct "common economy"? These and other questions frequently give rise to dispute as to whether or not specific groupings are "nationalities" or something else. Nevertheless, most of the groupings which are sometimes called "ethnic" are classified as "national" in the Soviet Union and, for that matter, in several other countries as well.

In terms of nationality policy two extremes are possible which are indicated by the terms "multinational state" and "nation-state."[4] "State" in this sense refers to an independent political entity, not a governmental

---

[3] J. V. Stalin, "Marxism and the National Question," in J. V. Stalin: Works (Moscow, Foreign Languages Publishing House, 1953), 2:307.

[4] Hans Kohn, "Soviet Communism and Nationalism: Three Stages of Historical Development," in Edward Allworth (ed.), Soviet Nationality Problems (New York, Columbia University Press, 1971), p. 43.

subdivision as in one of the "states" of the United States. The multinational state is one in which many "nations" live inside the boundaries of the same sovereign state. The nation-state, by contrast, is one whose national and political boundaries are approximately coterminous. The rationale of the "Russification" policy sponsored during the Czarist regime was that cultural assimilation would enable the Czarist Empire to become a nation-state in which previous particularistic nationalisms were obliterated by adherence to Russian culture. This policy was defended on idealistic as well as pragmatic grounds, and many of the Russian intellectuals viewed the movement as a way of uplifting lesser groups as a part of the civilizing mission of "Mother Russia."

The Soviet regime saw the Russification policy as neither expedient nor idealistic. Instead, the Soviets have tended to opt for a multinational state in which different nationality identities are maintained within the same sovereign state.

In line with this policy the Soviet regime developed as a federal state consisting of a number of political subdivisions whose boundaries correspond, to some extent, to the territories inhabited by particular nationalities. The basic units are the 15 "union republics" of which the largest is the Russian Soviet Federated Socialist Republic (RSFSR). Within these union republics are other ethnically (nationality) oriented units which include, according to size: autonomous republics, autonomous oblasts (provinces), autonomous krais (territories), and nationality okrugs (districts). In theory, at least, even the smallest nationality may thus exercise a measure of self-government within its own territory.

These republics, and also the lesser types of districts, lack inherent powers of taxation and are dependent on delegated taxing authority or appropriations from the central government. The republics and other districts do not control the use of their economic resources, have only the economic powers delegated by the central government, and have no control over foreign policy. They are thus subordinate to the central government in practically every field but still have a certain degree of cultural autonomy. This cultural autonomy is manifested in the use of the ethnic language in government offices, in the language of instruction of the school system, in the production of literature, in programs of mass communication, and in the performing arts. Through this combination of centralized control from Moscow and cultural expression indicated by the traditions of the group, it is hoped that the USSR can become a collection of nationalities which are, to use a favorite phrase, "socialist in content and national in form."

This type of cultural pluralism is frequently offered as an ideal pattern for the solution of problems of ethnic conflicts. For instance, the approach of the Communist Party to black Americans in the 1920s and 1930s emphasized the idea of a "Black Republic" which would be established in

TABLE 3–1

Soviet nationalities, 1970
(extract from preliminary report, Soviet census, January 1970: in thousands)

Nationality in USSR as a whole		Nationality: Number in titular administrative unit	
Russians	129,015	RSFSR	107,748
Ukranian	40,753	UkSSR	35,284
Uzbek	9,195	UzSSR	7,734
Belorussian	9,052	BSSR	7,290
°Tatar	5,931		
Kazakh	5,299	KazSSR	4,161
Azerbaijan	4,380	AzSSR	3,777
Armenian	3,559	ArmSSR	2,208
Georgian	3,245	GSSR	3,131
Moldavian	2,698	MSSR	2,304
Lithuanian	2,665	LitSSR	2,507
Jewish	2,151		
Tajik	2,136	TajSSR	1,630
German	1,846		
Chuvash	1,694		
Turkmen	1,525	TurSSR	1,417
Kirgiz	1,452	KirSSR	1,285
Latvian	1,430	LatSSR	1,342
Dagestan	1,365		
Mordvin	1,263		
Bashkir	1,240		
Polish	1,167		
Estonian	1,007	EstSSR	925

° Data concerning the nationality composition of titular administrative units below the union-republic level are not yet available.

Minor nationalities in the USSR (in thousands)

Udmurt	704	Ingush	158	Khakass	67
Chechen	613	Gagauz	157	Balkar	60
Mari	599	Nationalities of		Altay	56
Ossetic	488	the North,		Cherkess	40
Komi	322	Siberia, and		Dungan	39
Komi-Permyak	153	the Far East	151	Iranian (Persian)	28
Koryak	357	Karelian	146	Abazin	25
Bulgarian	351	Tuvin	139	Assyrian	24
Greek	337	Kalmyk	137	Czech	21
Buryat	315	Rumanian	119	Tat	17
Yakut	296	Karachay	113	Shor	16
Kabardin	280	Adyge	100	Slovak	12
Karakalpak	236	Kurd	89	Other nationalities	138
Gypsy	175	Finnish	85		
Uyghur	173	Abkhaz	83		
Hungarian	166	Turk	79		

TOTAL NATIONALITIES OTHER THAN RUSSIAN 112,717

Source: Preliminary reports based upon the Soviet census taken in 1970 and printed in *Pravda*, April 1971. Reprinted in Edward Allworth (ed.). *Soviet Nationality Problems* (New York, Columbia University Press, 1971), pp. 282–83.

the southern states with the heaviest black population. In this fashion, black Americans could have the same type of national self-determination which had been granted to ethnic groups in the Soviet Union. People who objected to this type of program on the grounds that the industrialization of the South and the movement of black labor to the North were destroying the possibility of such an ethnic base were classified as "white chauvinists" and their leader, Jay Lovestone, was officially read out of the ranks of the party faithful.[5]

The Communist platform did not prove attractive to black Americans, who for the most part considered it as, at best, far from their immediate concerns, and at worst a program which might confine them to the geographical areas in American life that offered the most restricted opportunities. It is one of the ironies of history that Southern industrialism on the one hand and black migration on the other hand have more than confirmed the objections of the Lovestonites and yet that black separatism in the 1970s is more fashionable among militant blacks than was true in earlier years.

CZARIST MINORITY POLICY

Communist critics described the Czarist regime as being "a prison of the minority peoples." In the words of *The History of the Communist Party of the Soviet Union*, "Tsarist Russia was a prison of nations . . . and tzardom a hangman and torturer of the non-Russian peoples."[6] Another way of describing this situation is to say that the Czarist policy was one of promoting assimilation under the dominance of the Russians, who comprised approximately one half of the population of the empire. The Czarist regime was quite candid about its policy and did not hesitate to require Russian to be the only language in official circles and to assist the Orthodox church in its attempt to establish a religious as well as a political and linguistic unity of the Russian peoples.

Two factors, however, moderated the Czarist policy. One factor is that there had been among the Russian people some tradition of racial and ethnic tolerance and acceptance of occasional intermarriage across ethnic lines. There was a frank assumption of Russian superiority over subject peoples, but this did not preclude social relations and intermarriage. Another moderating factor was the matter of the strategic considerations. Most of the Russian minority peoples were located near a border with nationalities similar to their own. Thus the policy of Russification might be restrained and local customs tolerated in the effort to avoid inflaming

---

[5] Wilson Record, *The Negro and the Communist Party* (Chapel Hill, The University of North Carolina Press, 1951), pp. 62–63.

[6] *History of the Communist Party of the Soviet Union*, Bolshevik Short Course (Moscow, Foreign Languages Publishing House, 1951), p. 17.

the conationals or coreligionists of Russian minorities who occupied countries beyond the Russian border. Finally, the Russian empire was so vast and the bureaucracy so comparatively inefficient that, through sheer inertia, the policy of Russification probably seemed more severe in theory than it proved in practice. Nevertheless, Russification had been pushed rather vigorously from the end of the 19th century until the outbreak of World War I in 1914, and there were smoldering resentments among the various minority groups.

COMMUNIST MINORITY POLICY

While the collapse of the Czarist armies in the middle of World War I was perceived by the Communists as their opportunity to come to power, it was seen by the minority groups in the empire as their opportunity for freedom. Thus at the same time that there was a struggle by the Communists against the democratic government which had succeeded the Czars, there was also evidence of a desire on the parts of minority groups to break away from any connection with Russia at all, under any kind of government. The Ukrainians, the Georgians, and the various Baltic peoples, to name only a few, were in the process of taking up arms and establishing their independence. If the Communists wished to seize power and to take over the territory belonging to the Czar it was necessary for them to appease the nationalistic sentiments of minority groups. This situation had long been recognized by the Communist leaders as a probability and the Czarist repression of minority self-determination had been denounced on numerous occasions. Thus, it was entirely in character when Lenin addressed a dramatic appeal to minority groups, asserting his respect for their desire for freedom.

Moslems of Russia, Tatars of the Volga and the Crimea, Kirgiz and Sarts of Siberia and Turkestan, Turks and Tatars of Transcaucasia, Chechens and mountain Cossacks! All you, whose mosques and shrines have been destroyed, whose faith and customs have been violated by the Tsars and oppressors of Russia! Hence forward your beliefs and customs, your national and cultural institutions are declared free and inviolable! Build your national life freely and without hindrance. It is your right. Know that your rights, like those of all the peoples of Russia, will be protected by the might of the Revolution, by the councils of Workers', Soldiers', and Peasants' Deputies![7]

This statement, which specifically mentioned the peoples who differed most from the Russians, was followed by a "declaration of the rights of the peoples of Russia" which was issued on November 16, 1917, and was signed by Lenin as head of the Soviet government and by Stalin as Peoples'

---

[7] Collection of Decrees and Regulations of the Workers' and Peasants' Government, No. 2 (1917) Article 18, cited in Robert Conquest, *The Nation Killers* (London, Macmillan & Co. Ltd., 1970), p. 32. Copyright by R. Conquest, 1960, 1970.

Commissar for nationalities. The statement supported minority rights in the strongest possible manner, including even the right of secession:

1. Equality and sovereignty of the peoples of Russia.
2. Right of the peoples of Russia to self-determination, including the right to secede and set up independent States.
3. Abolition of all privileges and restrictions based on nationality or religion.
4. Free development of national minorities and ethnic groups inhabiting Russian territory.[8]

The purpose of this statement was both to strengthen the position of the Communist faction at a time when it was engaged in civil war and to establish a nationality policy.

SECESSION AFTER THE COMMUNIST REVOLUTION

At first glance the mentioning of the right of secession would seem to be a surrender of the right to maintain a regime of any kind governing diverse peoples. Actually, this was only a recognition of reality. In areas bounded by western countries able to give military aid, the Soviets could not prevent the secession of dissident minorities. On the other hand, minorities in the eastern areas of Russia which did not have the potentiality of calling on western powers for support, such as the Armenians and the Georgians, were forcibly brought back into the Soviet Union in spite of attempts to maintain their independence. Watson describes the Russian policy toward secession as being one of "opportunism."[9] This characterization is probably not greatly different from what was meant by Stalin's statement that the right of secession was subordinate to considerations of the welfare of the proletarian revolution.[10]

The extent of the desire to break away from Russian rule can be seen on page 61 in the list of independent republics established shortly after the coming to power of the Communist Party in Russia in 1917.[11]

Since the Communists had proclaimed the right of secession as well as their respect for the autonomy of the various nationalities, the problem was to reconcile the verbal affirmation of the freedom of choice of affiliation with the USSR with a determination to hold together as large a part of the old Russian empire as possible. On a verbal level, this dilemma was

---

[8] Compendium of the Laws of the RSFSR, 1971, No. 2, Article 18, cited in I. P. Tsamerian and S. L. Ronin, *Equality of Rights between Races and Nationalities in the USSR* (Paris, UNESCO, 1962), p. 25.

[9] H. Seton Watson, "Soviet Nationality Policy," *The Russian Review* 15 (Jan., 1956), p. 4.

[10] Conquest, *The Nation Killers*, p. 117.

[11] Roman Smal-Stocki, *The Captive Nations: Nationalism of the Non-Russian Nations in the Soviet Union* (New York, Bookman Associates, 1960), p. 37.

Independence proclamations

1.	Idel Ural (Tatars)	Nov. 12, 1917
2.	Finland	Dec. 6, 1917
3.	Ukraine	Jan. 22, 1918
4.	Kuban Cossacks	Feb. 16, 1918
5.	Lithuania	Feb. 16, 1918
6.	Estonia	Feb. 24, 1918
7.	Belo-Ruthenia (Belo-Russian)	March 25, 1918
8.	Don Cossacks	May 5, 1918
9.	North Caucasians	May 11, 1918
10.	Georgia	May 26, 1918
11.	Azerbaijan	May 29, 1918
12.	Armenia	May 30, 1918
13.	Poland	Nov. 11, 1918
14.	Latvia	Nov. 18, 1918
15.	The Democratic Republic of the Far East (Siberia)	April 4, 1920
16.	Turkestan	April 15, 1922

resolved by Stalin in the following statement, which gave obvious preference to the interest of the Communist regime as opposed to the rights of
nationality.

The rights of nations freely to secede must not be confused with the expediency of secession of a given nation at a given moment. The party of the proletariat (the Russian Communist party) must decide the latter question quite
independently in each particular case from the standpoint of interests of the
social development as a whole and of the interests of the class struggle of the
proletariat for socialism . . .[12]

The implementation of the "expediency of secession" seemed to depend
very largely upon the military situation. Finland was able to establish its
independence after Russian sympathizers were defeated in a civil war.
After a considerable period of fighting, the Poles and the Baltic Republics
of Latvia, Lithuania, and Estonia were also allowed to go their separate
ways. The other independent republics soon lost any right of independence
and became incorporated in the Soviet Union as the Communist armies
emerged victorious against the various military efforts to defeat them. By
1922, peace had been established throughout most of the country and the
USSR emerged as a state considerably smaller than the Czar's empire but
still in command of a gigantic land mass with a diverse collection of
peoples.

PROBLEMS OF MAINTAINING SOVIET UNITY

Before trying to assess the success of the Soviet nationality policy it is
best to see what problems were involved in salvaging the territory of the

---

[12] J. Stalin, *Marxism and the National and Colonial Question* (London, Lawrence
and Wishart, 1936), pp. 269–70.

Czar's empire which remained. The minorities included a wide variety of types. Largest in number were groupings such as the Ukrainians and the Belorussians, whom Armstrong[13] has characterized as a "younger brother" type who were linguistically different from the Russians, who were not as urbanized and educated as the Russians, but had been in interaction with them for years and had come under the influence of the Russian Orthodox Church (or, in some cases, the Uniate Church, which is in communion with Rome although Orthodox in ritual). Somewhat similar to this type were the "state-nations"—groupings whose social progress was comparable to the Russians and which maintained a strong national consciousness; this type included the Georgians as well as the Baltic peoples who seceded from the Soviet Union at the time of the Revolution and who were brought back in 1940 during World War II. There were also the groupings classified as the "mobilized diaspora," so called because they were advanced in education and technology, were largely urban in their residence, but to a great extent were distributed throughout the Soviet Union. The two minorities most conspicuous as examples of this type were the Jews and the Armenians, although the Armenians had a greater concentration of population in a traditional area.

The final type which Armstrong labels "colonials" were comparatively small groupings differing drastically in culture as well as physical appearance from most of the other peoples in the Soviet Union. They were mostly Asiatic in origin and Muslim or Buddhist in religion. Most of their people were illiterate, and economic development had been extremely slow among them. While they had a high birth rate, the mortality rate was also high and most of the areas which they inhabited were lightly populated. There were also many diverse groupings which lived on an extremely low economic level and which lacked a written language.

The success of the Communist minority program required the maintenance of peace both among the territorially based groups and between the mobilized diaspora and the rest of the population, as well as the modernization of those groups furthest from standards of Western culture. All the needed adjustments had to take place at a time of great economic hardship and of threat of invasion from abroad.

THE CONCEPT OF HISTORICAL STAGES

The tolerance enjoined on various groups might be considered to represent not only a concession to cultural pluralism but also an acceptance of the idea of equality of all ethnic groupings or peoples. Nothing could be

---

[13] John A. Armstrong, "The Ethnic Scene in the Soviet Union: The View of the Dictatorship," in Erich Goldhagen (ed.), *Ethnic Minorities in the Soviet Union* (New York, Frederick A. Praeger, 1968), pp. 14–32.

further from the truth. The leadership of the Soviets was very largely Russian and could hardly escape the myth of the civilizing mission of the Russian people. This myth was compounded by a belief in the inevitability and desirability of communism as a social system for all peoples and all places. As Vucinich points out, "the doctrine of cultural relativity is incompatible with Soviet ideology."[14] However written languages were constructed for nationalities which lacked them, schools were developed which taught in the indigenous language and artistic expression was encouraged.

Why, then, this willingness not only to permit cultural diversity but in some ways even to foster it? The answer to this question lies in the Marxian concept that history inevitably moves by stages. The present condition of the minority peoples might be definitely backward as compared to the Russians, but this does not mean that sudden change should be introduced. Every society has to go through a somewhat similar series of stages from a primitive type of organization to a national identity and then to a kind of fusion which will make it an integral part of the Soviet state. Further, the minority groups had committed themselves to oppose modernization when this was presented as "Russification."

Moving from illiteracy to literacy in the Russian language would be considered a type of imperialism, but moving toward an expression of literary forms in the indigenous language would be an expression of the national ethos which in turn would prepare them for the next step, one of fusion with the general culture pervading the Soviet Union. Thus the Soviet nationality policy was justified on pragmatic grounds, both as an aid to gaining power at the time of the Revolution and as a long-term program for cultural advance.

The end of secession from the Soviet Union was accompanied by a move toward the establishment of nationality territorial districts which were supposed to safeguard cultural pluralism. Actually the Communist leaders were not as fully committed to the autonomy of nationalities as they appeared. While following many procedures to limit the dominance of the Russian ethnic group and provide more freedom for minorities, they simultaneously developed a number of techniques designed to promote the assimilation of all peoples in the Soviet Union in a common culture. Cultural pluralism was both immediately expedient and a desirable type of bridge toward a more homogeneous society, but it provides a potential threat to Communist unity, and the Soviets utilize a number of measures to curb what they regard as "excessive local nationalism."

Methods of Weakening Minority Nationality Adherence. In his book

---

[14] Alexander Vucinich, "Soviet Ethnographic Studies of Cultural Change," *American Anthropologist,* 62 (October 1960), p. 871.

on the peoples of the Soviet Far East, Kolarz makes an outline of measures taken to restrict nationalism in that area:[15]

1. Industrialization and de-tribalization which is linked with migration of natives to big urban centers.
2. Destruction of the native economy through state interference such as the fostering of class struggle and the confiscation of cattle.
3. Mass colonization of "national territories" by Europeans.
4. "Liquidation" of the native upper class and of the intellectual elite.
5. Persecution of religious beliefs peculiar to minority nationalities.
6. Prohibition of cultural and political integration of kindred tribes and nationalities.
7. Imposition of an alien ideology, of a foreign language and culture.
8. Suppression of historical and cultural traditions which are essential to the survival of the national consciousness of a given ethnic group.

Perhaps the most significant of these methods are those related to economic development. They need not be billed as antinational and yet are far more effective than any direct attack on national allegiances. Most ethnic social organization has clustered about some mode of economic activity, such as cattle herding by the nomads, and, when this is disrupted, social relationships are inevitably changed. Further, the drive for industrialization or the development of agriculture or of mining leads to a twofold dispersion of population. Managers, scientists, and laborers, most of whom are Russian, Ukrainian, or Armenian, are sent throughout the land, and at the same time numbers of the indigenous people are brought to the cities to serve as laborers. In each case, the effect is to break up the homogeneity of the society and to weaken local ties. This, in fact, was foreseen by the early Communist leaders, who did not hesitate to proclaim that assimilation was an eventual and desirable result of the nationality policy.

Khrushchev as Soviet premier from 1953 to 1964 removed many of the restrictions that Stalin had placed on Soviet nationalities and ushered in a period more congenial to cultural pluralism. It is interesting, though, that even he regarded national diversity as a transient phase soon to be replaced by a Socialist uniformity:

We come across people, of course, who deplore the gradual effacement of national distinctions. *We reply to them: Communists will not conserve and perpetuate national distinctions. We will support the objective process of increasingly closer rapprochement of nations and nationalities* proceeding under the conditions of Communist construction on a voluntary and democratic basis.

It is essential that we stress the education of the masses in the spirit of proletarian internationalism and Soviet patriotism. Even the slightest vestiges of

---

[15] Walter Kolarz, *The Peoples of the Soviet Far East* (New York, Frederick A. Praeger, 1954), pp. 179–80.

nationalism should be eradicated with uncompromising Bolshevik determination.[16]

Certain policies have been consistently followed by the Communist authorities in the effort to limit what they consider the excesses of nationalism. One of these is opposition to "federalist nationalism." Many of the nationalities in the Soviet Union are too small to be very powerful by themselves but when grouped with similar nationalities might make a bloc of some strength. A federation of the three Baltic Soviet republics, for instance, would be unthinkable under the working of Soviet policy. Similarly, the few federations which did develop, such as those in the Volga regions and in Central Asia, were suppressed after a very short period of existence. The motivation here is obviously to avoid the building of ethnic blocs which may be able to resist the central government.

Another consistent characteristic of Soviet Communism is opposition to religion. Since religion and ethnicity are frequently related, the attack on religion may be an indirect attack on nationalism. Thus the Soviet official does not attack Ukranians but he may attack Catholics. He does not criticize Chechens but he may attack Islam. He will not condemn Jews but he may castigate Judaism and Zionism. This attitude means that ethnicity is, to some extent, divorced from religious support and thereby weakened.

As far as language is concerned, the official attitude and practice is one of tolerance but the matter of linguistic nationalism is far more complicated than it appears. It is true that the Communists have encouraged the development of many languages, some of which did not even have a written tongue, and have fostered publications and artistic expressions in these languages. The question is whether such language autonomy is an end result or a transitional step toward the widespread use of Russian as the lingua franca of the Soviet Union.

In the development of languages, care is taken to intensify the differences between languages of the same family and also to increase the similarity with Russian by the use of Russian expressions wherever the local language is weak in modern vocabulary. Further, there is an obligatory teaching of Russian in all minority schools, and in many areas mixed schools are set up in which parents may opt for the education of their children in Russian. Thus, without waging a direct war on linguistic autonomy, the Soviets may still be channeling the Soviet Union toward a greater degree of linguistic homogeneity. This is born out by statistics which show an increase in the speaking of Russian and a decline in the speaking of languages of the nationality groups.

---

[16] Khrushchev's Report, *Pravda*, Oct. 19, 1961, cited in Alfred D. Low, "Soviet Nationality Policy and the New Program of the Communist Party of the Soviet Union," *The Russian Review*, 22 (January 1963), p. 10.

Even more pragmatic and devious than language policy is the use of history as an ideological weapon. History is by no means a static subject, since it contributes to current attitudes and thus the "truths" of history shift with the ideological needs of the regime. One interesting case of this is that of the history of the resistance to Czarism by the Chechen leader Shamil. In the early days of the Soviet Union, its publications had praise for Shamil as an outstanding political leader and military commander who emancipated the slaves, was against the local feudal lords, and was also democratic and progressive. His movement was described as having been aroused by the exploitive character of Czarist policy. In 1950, however, it was discovered and reported by *Pravda* that such historical teaching was anti-Marxist.[17] From that time on, Shamil was described as a reactionary Turkish agent who had no popular support. This change came about because, by this time, the Kremlin ideologists had decided that the Czarist annexation of the Caucasus was a progressive move and therefore not to be criticized, whereas before they had been anxious to paint every Czarist deed in the worst possible colors. After Stalin's death the emphasis on the inherent virtue of Russian expansionism changed somewhat, and it was no longer necessary to protray Shamil as a reactionary feudal despot. Even though Shamil had been in opposition to Russian power, he was no longer to be treated as a corrupt reactionary and his motives were admitted to be honorable.[18]

Perhaps a bit of content analysis here would indicate that the first view of Shamil was an effort to identify the Communists with the anti-Russian sentiments cherished by the Chechen people. The vilification of Shamil under Stalin was in accord with the theory of Russian patriotism and with the need, for the sake of national unity, of putting the best possible presentation on all Russian actions; while the final partial restoration of Shamil was consistent with the repudiation of Stalinist methods. Thus local traditions and history do not exist for themselves but for the value they have in serving the Communist cause.

THE UKRAINIAN AND BALTIC EXPERIENCE

The Ukraine, with over 44 million inhabitants in 1964, is the second largest union republic in the Soviet Union. Prior to the Revolution, education and industry were not as well developed as in the area of Russia itself, and West Ukraine had a strong Roman Catholic (Uniate) orientation as contrasted to the Orthodox church, which was dominant in the

---

[17] Conquest, *The Nation Killers*, pp. 84–94, and Lowell Tillett, *The Great Friendship: Soviet Historians on Non Russian Nationalities* (Chapel Hill, University of North Carolina Press), 1969, pp. 130–48.

[18] Ibid., pp. 164–68.

Russian portion of the Soviet Union. Nevertheless, Ukrainians and Russians were similar in physical appearance and had had a long period of association. This association brought some degree of cultural similarity and facilitated the Ukrainian adjustment under Communism which would be described by the apologist for the Soviet Union as following the trends which were appropriate in the industrialization of the country and the growth of the Communist party. The Ukraine was characterized by rapid urbanization (3.8 times as many Ukrainians were urban in 1959 as in 1926), growth in education, and a tremendous growth in the Ukrainian membership in the Communist Party (by 1965 the ratio in the Ukraine of Communist Party members to the total population was 77 percent of the ratio in the Russian area itself). Many Ukrainians were given important positions in Soviet enterprises, and many of them migrated to other sections of the Soviet Union. At the same time a great many Russian managers and workers made their way to the Ukraine. Ukrainian cultural development was encouraged: over 3,000 books, for instance, were published in Ukrainian in 1963, and Ukrainian was the language of instruction in most of the schools in that area.[19]

On the other hand, the Uniate Church was fiercely attacked,[20] the Russian language was promoted by the "mixed schools" in which children might receive instruction in Russian, and what was considered "excessive" Ukrainian nationalism was ruthlessly repressed. As compared to the Czarist regime, much greater cultural lattitude was allowed, but, at the same time, many programs which would facilitate assimilation were encouraged. In summary, the Ukraine may be said to have had a type of cultural life which was "socialist in form, but national in content," but the national content was being steadily diluted through the migration of the Ukrainians and the increasing presence of a large number of Russians in the Ukraine. Intermarriage between Ukrainians and non-Ukrainians, most of whom were Russian, grew from only 3.4 percent in 1927 to over 18 percent in 1959.[21] It would appear that the gradual assimilation of Ukrainians is well under way and that the cultural and economic differences between the Ukrainians and the Russians are steadily diminishing.

In the Baltic area, the formerly sovereign countries of Estonia, Lithuania, and Latvia are small in population but rich in their dedication to national integrity. For centuries they have been pawns in European power struggles—mostly between Russia and Germany, although at times other nations, including Sweden, were also involved. Germans had settled in large numbers in these countries and were well represented among the

---

[19] Armstrong, "The Ethnic Scene in the Soviet Union," p. 21.

[20] Walter Kolarz, *Religion in the Soviet Union* (New York, St. Martin's Press, 1966), pp. 227–44.

[21] Armstrong, "The Ethnic Scene in the Soviet Union," p. 17.

land owners and businessmen. By the latter part of the 19th century, the Russians had formally incorporated the three countries in the Czar's regime and had proceeded to a vigorous program of Russification directed against both the Germans and indigenous nationalism in the three countries.[22] All three nations secured their independence during World War I at the time of the breakup of the Russian empire and the defeat of the German armies, and proceeded to the task of national development. This national development included the emergence of a sizeable elite of intellectuals, the stimulus of cultural expression in their own languages, improvement in agriculture, and an increase in urbanization. The three countries were nominally dedicated to democracy, but internal conflicts made democratic functioning difficult. Lithuania, in particular, had periods of dictatorial rule.

World War II brought renewed difficulties to the Baltic nations. They were forced to ally themselves with the Soviet Union in 1939. This step, however, did not satisfy the Stalinist government, and in 1940 the Baltic states were formally incorporated in the Soviet Union. In 1941 they were invaded by the Germans, from whom, in turn, they were "liberated" by Soviet armies toward the end of 1944. More than a quarter of a million Balts, most of whom were probably of middle class status, fled these countries and refused to return after the war. Governments in exile still existed for the three countries in 1973, although any hope of their return to power seemed dim indeed. Sporadic resistance to Russian occupation did take place, but such resistance has been completely suppressed since 1952.[23]

Soviet policy since 1945 has included a massive thrust toward urbanization and industrialization which has brought many newcomers into the Baltic states and somewhat decreased the proportion of Balts in the several countries. For Lithuanians the drop was slight, from 80 percent in 1936 to 79 percent in 1959. During the same period Estonians and Latvians dropped both in absolute numbers and in the proportion of the population in their republics. Latvians declined from 76 percent to 62 percent and Estonians from 88 percent in 1934 to 75 percent in 1959.[24]

An important part of the cultural differentiation between the Baltic states and Russia was religious: Lithuania was primarily Roman Catholic and Latvia and Estonia, Lutheran. In recent times, the number of churches and clergy have been sharply reduced from the days of independence but religion is still regarded as a bulwark of objectionable (from the Soviet

---

[22] Emanuel Nodel, *Estonia: Nation on the Anvil* (London, Bookman Associates, 1963.)

[23] V. Stanley Vardys, "The Partisan Movement in Postwar Lithuania," *Slavic Review* 22 (September 1963): 499–522.

[24] Statistics from a variety of sources compiled by Jaan Penner, "Nationalism in the Soviet Baltics," in Goldhagen, *Ethnic Minorities in the Soviet Union*, pp. 200–202.

viewpoint) forms of nationalism. Thus Antanas SnieČkus states: "The remnants of nationalism are closely related to religious superstitions. This fact especially compels Party organizations actively to further atheist work as an integral part of the struggle against the ideology of bourgeois nationalism."[25]

Priests and ministers have been harassed, churches closed, the young denied religious instruction, and atheistic propaganda vigorously pushed. Priests have been arrested, exiled, and denied permission to function in their clerical roles. Resentment at these tactics led in 1972 to student riots and even the self-immolation (burning) of one protestor.[26]

The spectacle of unarmed students defying a monolithic dictatorship is a dramatic one which indicates that the nationalism of the Baltic states is deep-seated enough to survive a generation of propaganda even as Baltic national identity has survived centuries of foreign rule. Making resistance to that direct oppression more difficult, however, are the population shifts, which make the Balts a declining proportion of their own regions, and the attraction of Russian assimilation as an aid in securing desirable jobs.[27]

THE LIQUIDATED NATIONS

World War II brought to a peak the suspicions and fear with which the Russians regarded minority peoples residing in sensitive border areas. In spite of 20 years of Communist rule such potential nations had obviously not been completely assimilated and might easily be suspected of sympathy with foreign invaders who promised a greater respect for their national autonomy than had been given them in the Soviet Union. As a result, eight ethnically distinctive Soviet territorial units were abolished and large numbers of their people deported to distant areas in the Soviet Union. These included:[28]

Meskhetia	Balkars
Chechens	Kalmyks
Ingushi	Volga Germans
Karachai	Crimean Tatars

---

[25] Antanas SnieČkus in *Tiesa*, July 11, 1963. Cited in V. Stanley Vardys, "Soviet Social Engineering in Lithuania: An Appraisal," in *Lithuania under the Soviets: Portrait of a Nation, 1940–1965* (New York, Frederick A. Praeger, 1965), p. 248.

[26] "Protest in Lithuania," *Newsweek* (June 26, 1972), pp. 38, 39.

[27] Vardys, in *Lithuania under the Soviets*, p. 259.

[28] Conquest, *The Nation Killers*, pp. 64–66. Meskhetia was not organized as a republic but is a distinct area on the Soviet-Turkish border adjoining Georgia and Armenia. Its people, largely Turkish, were deported in November 1944 on grounds that they were in an area which might be reached by the enemy—information summarized from Conquest, pp. 48, 49.

The peoples in these territories varied in their cultural outlook, and were rather sharply divergent from the Russians. Some of them were largely Muslim and one, the Kalmyks, were Buddhist. Although in the early period after the Revolution, the Soviets ignored their religious institutions, the republics were soon all faced with antireligious propaganda. To the Communists all types of religions were competitive ideologies, and Islam and Buddhism were just as contrary to Communist doctrine as Christianity and Judaism. There were also attacks on their family life, which was usually polygynous, and on the subordinate position of women of the Muslim and Buddhist minorities.

The Volga Germans, on the other hand, were a highly westernized group who had been frequently praised for the efficiency of their collective farms. They had lived peacefully in Russia for nearly two centuries, having been invited to that country by Peter the Great, but they had retained the German language and it was suspected that they would be sympathetic to the German invaders.

Extreme military measures, including the deportation of peoples, are of course not unknown in other countries, and the American expulsion of the Japanese from the west coast of the United States might be taken as a parallel case, even though brief in duration. In any event, the breakup of these republics and the dispersion of their peoples marks the worst failure of Soviet minority policy. In 1957, an acknowledgement was made of the events which had transpired and five of the peoples were restored to their national status as autonomous republics but, as of 1971, nothing had been heard of political organization among the Volga Germans, the Crimean-Tatars, or the Meskhetians. A penetrating criticism of the whole affair appears in a speech by Khrushchev in 1957:

All the more monstrous are the acts whose initiator was Stalin and which are crude violations of the basic Leninist principles of the nationality policy of the Soviet State. We refer to the mass deportations from their native places of whole nations, together with all Communists and Komsomols without any exception; this deportation action was not dictated by any military considerations.

.   .   .   .

Not only a Marxist-Leninist but also no man of common sense can grasp how it is possible to make whole nations responsible for inimical activity, including women, children, old people, Communists and Komsomols, to use mass repression against them, and to expose them to misery and suffering for the hostile acts of individual persons or groups of persons.[29]

---

[29] Vardis, *Life under the Soviets*, p. 144. Report of a "secret" speech by Khrushchev in 1956 at the 20th Party Congress.

JEWS: PEOPLE OF THE DIASPORA

Prior to World War II, more Jews lived in the Soviet Union than in any other country of the world. The losses during World War II were catastrophic in proportions, amounting to possibly 2.5 million.[30] But in 1959 over 2.25 million Jews lived in the Soviet Union; they constituted about 1.1 percent of the population and were the eleventh largest group listed as a nationality.[31]

Under the Czars, the Jews were repressed in many ways. Jews in Poland and the Ukraine were confined to the region of their origin, which was known as the "Pale of Settlement." This meant that the population tended to increase in a restricted area with limited opportunities. Violent riots against Jews, termed pogroms, erupted on several occasions. Secondary schools and universities were restricted in the number of Jews which might be admitted. Quotas were given for Jewish entry into the legal and medical professions. Jews were restricted in government service and prevented from voting for the city Dumas (legislatures). In general, they were harried by popular prejudice, hampered by restrictive laws, and frequently victimized by prejudiced officials.

It is no accident that the earliest Zionists, under the leadership of Theodore Hertzl, based their operations in Russia. The need for some type of Jewish National Home must have seemed very great indeed under the conditions of persecution in the Czarist state.

The contrast between the official positions of the Czarist and the Soviet regimes toward Jews is quite striking. Jews were prominent in the Communist revolution and frequently occupied important government positions.[32] Jews have a proportion of scientific workers, writers, physicians, and university students far in excess of their proportion in the population. Armstrong, for instance, has estimated that Jews may constitute roughly one tenth of the skilled professionals in the Soviet Union as contrasted to being one one-hundredth of the population.[33] Anti-Semitism, which was practically a formal government policy under the Czars, is now forbidden by law and frequently denounced by government officials. Pogroms did

---

[30] A. Hove and J. A. Newth, "The Jewish Population: Demographic Trends and Occupational Patterns," in Lionel Kochan (ed.), *The Jews in Soviet Russia since 1917* (London, Oxford University Press, 1970), p. 142.

[31] William Korey, "The Legal Position of the Jewish Community in the Soviet Union," in Goldhagen, *Ethnic Minorities in the Soviet Union*, p. 319.

[32] Most Jewish Communist leaders did not identify with traditional "Jewishness." Trotsky, for instance, says, "In my mental equipment nationality [Jewish] never occupied an important place." Leon Trotsky, *My Life*, (New York, Pathfinder Press, Inc., 1970), p. 86.

[33] Armstrong, *The Ethnic Scene in the Soviet Union*, p. 10.

take place during the confusion of the revolutionary war when the Communists were seizing power but have not been known since that time (except during World War II in areas where the Soviets had lost control). In terms of freedom of movement and of occupational aspiration, it may be said that the Communists regime has changed Jews from a repressed and denigrated pariah group to one with nominally full rights as Soviet citizens. Certainly in terms of their proportion in prestige occupations, Jews have been far more successful in the Soviet Union than have other groups. Yet, in spite of these factors, the charges of anti-Semitism and accusations of persecution within the Soviet Union are frequently raised. Why is there so much dissatisfaction with the treatment of the Jews under the Communist regime in spite of the abolition of many of the abuses which took place under the Czars?

In the first place, there is another side to the story of Jewish life in the Czarist regime. Despite the obvious cruelties and limitations of that period, some liberties did exist which were lost under the Soviets. None of the charges of Czarist repression are false, but it is significant that during this same period, when the drive toward "Russification" was strongest and the restrictions on the Jews were most severe, there also emerged a flourishing cultural life among the Jews in Russia. This is described by Decter as follows:

. . . in the half-century before the October Revolution, alongside and despite the pauperization and persecution engendered by oppressive Tsarist policy, Jewish national-cultural life was experiencing a tremendous renascence.

There was an important Jewish labor and democratic socialist movement led by residues of the Bund on Russian soil. There was a burgeoning Hebrew theatre. There was a thriving and constantly expanding world of publication, with innumerable newspapers and periodicals and hundreds and thousands of Jewish books published in Yiddish, Hebrew and even Russian. There were many secular movements, institutions and organizations of every conceivable sort. There was, above all, a growing Zionist movement which had the support and sympathy of the vast majority of Russian Jews, and which imbued the renascence with moral, emotional and intellectual passion.[34]

The Communists had respect for the rights of Jews as individuals but, in spite of their professed concern for nationalities, they had little regard for Jewish cultural self-determinism. In part, this was because the Jews simply did not fit the definition of nationality afforded by the Russian leaders. A "nationality," in the Soviet view, not only had a unique tradition but also was found predominantly in a particular territory. While the largest proportions of Jews were in the Ukraine and Belorussia, they

---

[34] Moshe Decter, "Jewish National Consciousness in the Soviet Union," in Nathan Glazer, et al., *Perspectives on Soviet Jewry* (New York, Ktav Publishing Co., 1971), p. 10.

formed only a small part of the total population of these areas and the Jewish population itself was scattered over a considerable part of the Soviet Union. Hence there was no single district which could be labeled as Jewish territory. The Jews were genuinely a diaspora, a group which did not have a specific territorial base but were scattered throughout the population.

Since the Jews did not quite fit the Russian definition of a nationality, it was difficult to determine their treatment in nationality terms. Jews might be considered either as a nationality or a religion, but, in practice, neither of these classifications were particularly helpful in enabling them to find favorable treatment within the Soviet Union. Soviet authorities vacillated as to whether the Jews really had the status of a nationality, and Jewish religion, like all other religion, was under attack. The Jews suffered as a religious group and did not reap the full benefits which should have accrued to them as a Soviet nationality.[35] The skepticism about the existence of a Jewish nation expressed by Stalin in 1913 is a theme apparently frequently found in the thinking of Soviet leaders.

. . . what . . . national cohesion can there be . . . between the Georgian, Daghestanian, Russian and American Jews? . . . if there is anything common to them left it is their religion, their common origin and certain relics of national character. . . . But how can it be seriously maintained that petrified religious rites and fading psychological relics affect the "fate" of these Jews more powerfully than the living social, economic and cultural environment that surrounds them? And it is only on this assumption that it is generally possible to speak of the Jews as a single nation.[36]

In spite of the difficulties of classifying Jews as a nationality, it was impossible for the Communist leaders to ignore the fact that Jews did constitute a cultural group with some degree of cohesion, three fourths of whose members spoke the Yiddish language. Soviet Jews, like other Soviet citizens, are required to carry internal identification documents and their "nationality" is listed as Jewish.[37] In practice, the Communist leaders have varied between support of the cultural expression of Jewishness and repression of any interest in Jewish culture or Jewish religion as a manifestation of "cosmopolitanism" or of a counterrevolutionary bourgeoise ideology.

In any event, the policy of the Soviet government toward voluntary

---

[35] Joshua, Rothenberg, "Jewish Religion in the Soviet Union," in Lionel Kochan, *The Jews in Soviet Russia since 1917*, p. 162.

[36] J. Stalin, *Marxism and the National Question*, p. 10.

[37] In the 1897 census, 97 percent of the Jews claimed Yiddish as the mother tongue and only 24 percent could speak Russian. By 1959, however, only 20 percent of Soviet Jews were Yiddish-speaking. Discussion in Armstrong, "The Ethnic Scene in the Soviet Union," p. 11, and in S. Ettinger, "The Jews in Russia at the Outbreak of the Revolution," in Kochan, *The Jews in Soviet Russia since 1917*, p. 15.

associations meant the death knell of the network of Jewish societies which provided teaching, hospital care, orphanages, loan systems, and countless other social services. Such services were supposedly taken over by a governmental Jewish commissariat. The Jewish commissariat did not last very long, which is understandable, since the functions which it was called upon to supervise had been taken over by agencies administered on a territorial rather than an ethnic basis. Thus the voluntary network of services was largely liquidated and provision for Jewish communal life was left to the not always tender mercies of the Soviet government.

THE FANTASY OF BIROBIDZAHN[38]

Jews in Russia and elsewhere have often been the target of two types of charges: (1) they were rootless since they did not have any territorial base of operations that they could call their home; (2) they were too much an urbanized people and hence were not characterized by the rustic virtues which come from tilling the soil. In 1934 the president of the Soviet Union, Mikhail Kalinin, saw an opportunity to correct both of these deficiencies by the creation of a Jewish homeland within the Soviet Union. There had long been a feeling that more Jews should be colonized on the land, and even in the days of the Czarist regime a few Jews were placed in agricultural colonies. Shortly after the Communist government came to power, it formed two organizations to promote Jewish agricultural settlement, the *Kolmzet*, which means "Committee for the Agricultural Settlement of Jewish Toilers," and *Ozet*, the abbreviation for "Society for the Agricultural Settlement of Jewish Toilers." *Kolmzet* was an administrative arm of the government, while *Ozet* was an attempt to provide a mass organization. Some success had been obtained in settling Jewish farmers in the Ukraine in Belorussia, and in the Crimea; Kolarz estimates that there were 225,000 Jews employed in agriculture by the mid 1930s.[39] This figure was not considered enough, however, and there seemed to be strong obstacles to an expansion of settlement in already heavily populated areas. The fact that the Jews were farmers did not seem to diminish anti-Semitic prejudice against them but simply brought charges that they were competing unfairly for land with other peasants. If an underpopulated area could be located, this might serve as a basis for the settlement of Jewish

---

[38] This section is based on the treatment of this topic in the following works: B. Z. Goldberg, *The Jewish Problem in the Soviet Union* (New York, Crown Publishers, 1961), pp. 170–229; Chimen Abramsky, "The Biro-Bidzahn Project 1927–1959," in Lionel Kochan (ed.) *The Jews in Soviet Russia since 1917*, pp. 62–75; Salo W. Baron, *The Russian Jew under Tsars and Soviets* (New York, Macmillan, 1964), pp. 230–43; and Walter Kolarz, *Russia and Her Colonies* (Frederich A. Praeger, 1955), pp. 173–81.

[39] Kolarz, *Russia and Her Colonies*, p. 172.

farmers and also provide a geographically Jewish district which would afford the territorial basis required for Jewish nationality.

Such an area appeared to be found in the territory at the junction of two tributaries of the Amur River called Birobidzahn. This territory, 14,800 square miles in extent, was larger than the whole of Palestine and had a total estimated population in 1928 of only 34,000, or about three people per square mile. It was located on the Manchurian border, and, in addition to the advantage to the Jews, strategic interests would also be served if a greater population base could be established. Government assurances that the area was intended for Jewish settlement were expressed in 1928 in a decree of the Central Executive Committee of the USSR reserving Birobidzahn for that purpose and in a 1931 pledge that a Jewish territorial unit would be established if Jewish settlement were successful.[40] In 1934 Birobidhzan was proclaimed as a Jewish autonomous region. In the words of President Kalinin:

> The principles of Soviet national policy are such that each nationality is granted a autonomous political organization on its own territory. Hitherto the Jews lacked such a political organization, and this placed them in a peculiar position in comparison with other peoples. The Jews are now receiving what other nationalities possess—namely, the possibility of developing their own culture, national in form, socialist in content.[41]

In addition to the service of the strategic interests of the Soviet Union and the territorial interests of the Jews, it was also envisioned that Birobidzahn might become a type of Jewish homeland which would even attract the support, interest, and, perhaps, immigration of foreign Jews. And in 1931 and 1932 more than 1,000 Jews from other lands came to this new Soviet homeland for Jewish people. It was anticipated that immigration would start with a couple of thousand a year, rising quickly to 10,000 per year, and that, when the Jewish population reached 100,000, a Jewish republic would actually be proclaimed. Such immigration would not seem out of question with a Jewish population of nearly 3,000,000 people, but the desired quota was never obtained and in the year of largest migration, 1932, when 9,000 settlers came, half that number left the area for other parts of the Soviet Union.[42]

In 1959 the population of Birobidzahn had reached 163,000, but it was estimated that only eight percent were Jewish.[43] Birobidzahn was to be a home for Jewish culture, and Yiddish theatre, newspapers, magazines, and schools were to flourish. In the early days, such institutions were

---

[40] Ibid., p. 174.

[41] Goldberg, *The Jewish Problem in the Soviet Union*, p. 173.

[42] Ibid., p. 175.

[43] Abramsky, "The Biro-Bidzahn Project 1927–1959," p. 73.

established and a certain facade of Jewishness was maintained. However, foreign Jews were prohibited from coming after 1932 and Soviet Jews did not respond to the lure of the Soviet Jewish homeland in any large numbers. Jewish culture has practically died out and is said to be best represented by the fact that street signs are still seen in both Yiddish and in Russian. The situation was described by a *New York Times* reporter in 1959:

> No Yiddish is taught in schools, no Yiddish films are shown, no Yiddish books are printed. A well-stocked bookstore had not heard of a commemorative Yiddish edition of some works of Sholom Aleichem, published in Moscow this year. At the library there are said to be 12,000 old Yiddish volumes among the 100,000 books. Three times a week a two-page Yiddish newspaper, the *Birobidjaner Shtern,* appears. Soviet reference books list its circulation as 1,000.[44]

Controversy rages as to responsibility for the failure of Birobidzahn. Khrushchev admitted its failure and attributed this to the reluctance of Jews to engage in agricultural enterprises, particularly those of a collective nature. Other authorities maintained that the Soviet government never made adequate provision for the services needed in a pioneer community and hence, not even the most idealistic Jews could find Birobidzahn a very attractive setting.

In any event, Birobidzahn did not escape the hysteria of the Stalin period. In 1948 there was the "discovery" of an alleged Crimean plot, by leaders of the Jewish antifascist committee, to detach Birobidzahn from the Soviet Union to turn it over to Japan. This alleged plot formed the basis for the prosecution of anyone engaged in what could be described as Jewish activity. As Goldberg describes it: "Any Jewish activity—indeed, any item on the regional cultural program, any act of Jewish character, even if it had had formal official sanction at the time—constituted a crime or incriminating evidence. The official charge ran from artificially implanting Yiddish culture in order to impose it on the rest of the population, to treason and foreign espionage."[45]

The result was that much of the leadership of the territory was arrested and imprisoned and that Russian Jews were discouraged from any idea that Birobidzahn was a colony in which Jewish cultural expression could be safeguarded.

To be sure, the physical and economic difficulties of settling Birobidzahn were formidable, and few Russian Jews had the agricultural skill or interest which would have been required. However, the difficulties are not necessarily greater than those encountered in Palestine, and one won-

---

[44] Report of New York Times Correspondent Max Frankel cited in Goldberg, *The Jewish Problem in the Soviet Union,* pp. 222–23.

[45] Ibid., p. 206.

ders whether there was any real commitment by Russian leaders, apart from Kalinin, to implement the project.

As a propaganda symbol, Birobidzahn was an attractive prospect. As a reality, however, it would give support to Jewish nationalism in a manner hardly compatible with the assimilative policies of the Soviet Union. The Jews were not a backward people who needed to develop their own language in order to come to the place where they could appreciate the language of Russia. Nor were they a people whom history had cast in a compact geographical area. The Communists were interested in controlling and channeling toward their own objectives the national development of peoples where such considerations existed. Why should they conjure up support for a Jewish homeland inside their own country which ran completely counter to the assimilative ideal?

ISRAEL AND THE SOVIET JEWS

Although anti-Semitism is a crime in the Soviet Union, anti-Zionism is the theme of many tirades in *Pravda* and of many statements by Soviet leaders. Zionism represents a counterutopia to Soviet Communism; it proclaims a national idea which has greater vitality than that of social class; it allies individuals with the enemies of the Soviet Union and hence is a major crime. Opposition to Zionism has been a fairly consistent aspect of Soviet Jewish policy, but the specific attitude toward the state of Israel has shifted drastically.

In 1948 the Soviet Union was the first nation to give political recognition to the newly created state of Israel and posed as its major friend in the United Nations. Within a year, however, policy shifted, and since that time Soviet Russia has become a major supplier of munitions to the Arab countries in their efforts to overturn the state of Israel, has been a frequent critic of that nation, and sometimes has refused to allow Soviet citizens to migrate to Israel.

Two explanations, which are not necessarily mutually exclusive, are offered for the change of Soviet policy. One focuses on foreign policy objectives, and the other on domestic concerns. In terms of foreign policy, an independent Israel was seen as one method of diminishing British influence in the Mediterranean, which has been a long-term objective of both Czarist and Soviet diplomacy. After the British departure, however, the Middle East was seen as a power vacuum which the Soviets could best fill by cooperation with the Arabs.[46] Under terms of this latter viewpoint, pro-Israel Soviet Jews were supporting a power whose interests were seen as contrary to the objectives of Soviet policy.

---

[46] Hans J. Morgenthau, "The Jews and Soviet Foreign Policy," in Glazer, et al., *Perspectives on Soviet Jewry*, pp. 88–89.

On the domestic front the repercussions of pro-Israeli attitudes were a challenge to the whole tenor of Soviet ethnic policy. If Jews were permitted to retain ties with a homeland outside of the Soviet Union, how could other nationalities be denied the same privilege? If a revival of Jewish nationalism—a nationalism the legitimacy of which the Soviet Union had never acknowledged—was encouraged, then what nationalistic movement could be opposed? If Jews were permitted to reject a long-term goal of assimilation, then what would prevent other nationalities from following the same course? Add to these considerations a lingering anti-Semitism and the need for scapegoats for foreign and domestic frustrations, and the anti-Israeli shift becomes explicable.

The depth of the feeling that Israeli sympathies make the Jews an internally divisive force in the Soviet Union is seen in the following excerpt from a book published in the Ukraine:

propagating the creation of [a] . . . Jewish State, the leaders of Zionism are trying to prove that Jews of all countries are allegedly "one Jewish nation," are propagating class cooperation and are distracting the attention of working Jews from a joint class struggle with the peoples of the countries in which they live against their own and foreign oppressors, and from the struggle for democratic freedom and peace.[47]

Anti-Semitism might be outlawed but anti-Zionism provided a justification for the harassment of many Jews and for the elimination of Jewish cultural activities. Thus it is in the nation which has the second largest number of Jews of any in the world that Jews are denied an opportunity to learn either Hebrew or Yiddish; they have found their voluntary associations disbanded; their religious practices are discouraged and a request to migrate to the state of Israel is taken as being close to treason.[48]

Even the Jews who are most free from Zionist taint or religious affiliation are subject to suspicion because of the supposed Jewish tendency toward cosmopolitanism. Jews make scapegoats which are just as useful in the Soviet Union as elsewhere, and the troubles of the Communist Party in 1956 in Poland or in 1968 in Czechoslovakia or elsewhere in eastern Europe were often described as due to Zionist intrigue.

One of the best summaries of the reactions of at least some Jews

---

[47] T. T. Kichko, *Judaism and Zionism* (Kiev, Society Znannia of the Ukranian SSR, 1969), excerpted in William Korey, "Selections from Soviet Publications and Mass Media," in Glazer, et al., *Perspectives on Soviet Jewry*, p. 60.

[48] This policy is subject to change, and, after being adamant for several years, the Soviets relented somewhat in 1971 and began to allow Jews to go to Israel. Probably not all who wish to will be able to leave, but the number of emigres may reach 50,000 a year—*Newsweek*, Jan. 31, 1972, p. 30. Considerable protest was aroused in 1972 when the Soviets demanded compensation for the loss of professional men through immigration. The suspension of the Soviet demand for this kind of compensation in 1973 was attributed to the desire for a detente with the United States.

comes in a statement by Paul Lendvai on the attitude of the Jews who were accused of hijacking a plane in order to go to Israel.

But it has been impossible for Soviet propaganda to shift the focus from the fact that people are on trial for their convictions, and that Jews are being persecuted as Jews. They had no desire to criticize, attack, change, subvert or overthrow the Soviet system. On the contrary, their only desire was to leave that system altogether, and to exercise their elementary human right to leave their country of origin and settle in Israel, which they now regard as their ancestral homeland and as the sole place where they will be able to live as Jews.[49]

Whatever the persistence of Jewish identity there is no doubt that Soviet policies have made an impact. Certainly Jewish assimilation has proceeded a long way. By all reports Jewish religious observances are feeble reminders of a more vigorous past with congregations comprising, for the most part, a few old people of the population; Jewish cultural institutions have been largely destroyed and the speaking of Yiddish characterized only 18 percent of the Jewish population in 1969 as compared to 73 percent in 1917. Granting all the evidence of an eventual Jewish assimilation which may exist, yet the very animosity of the regime against Zionism or against Jewish nationalism, as well as the eagerness of thousands of Jews to migrate to the state of Israel, gives indication that a satisfactory modus vivendi between Jewish identification and the Communist ideal of the classless society has still not been achieved.

In spite of the excesses and crimes which have been committed against Jews, both by individuals and by the Russian government, it is hardly fair to charge the Communist regime with the type of anti-Semitism which characterized Nazi Germany or Czarist Russia. In a review of the book *The Russian Jew Under Tsars and Soviets* by Salo Baron, Stephen P. Dunn makes the following comment:

. . . Soviet government policy is not, properly speaking, anti-Semitic. Rather, the regime has found itself forced, for historical, cultural, and political reasons, to adopt certain measures which from an American perspective look anti-Semitic. The Soviet nationality policy, as first outlined by Lenin and developed by Stalin, embodies certain inherent contradictions and difficulties of application.[50]

The statement that one is "forced" to do certain things because of "historical, cultural, and political reasons" might be used to justify any possible type of ethnic discrimination. Perhaps it is more accurate to say that Soviet authorities are not deliberately anti-Semitic, but that they find it difficult to adjust to any group whose national allegiances, religious faith,

[49] Moshe Decter, "The Terror That Fails, A Report on the Arrests and Trial of Soviet Jews," in Nathan Glazer, et al., *Perspectives on Soviet Jewry*, p. 103.

[50] Stephen P. Dunn, "A Turning Point in the Discussion of Soviet Jewish Policy," *Slavic Review*, 24 (Fall 1965), p. 705.

or ideological premises challenge the notion that Communist theory is absolute truth and that the Soviet state is the embodiment of that truth. In a challenge to Dunn's conclusion that Soviet policy is not, "properly speaking, anti-Semitic," Weinryb lists a series of actions which might give rise to that charge in many minds:

. . . there is no question that during the last decade of Stalin's life, or at least after 1948, the policy became expressly anti-Jewish and led to such actions as closing down the last vestiges of Jewish cultural institutions, 'unmasking' Jewish writers as 'homeless cosmopolitans,' constructing a plot against Yiddish writers and intellectuals which led to the arrest and deportation of many and the subsequent execution of some.[51]

He concludes that while there may be a difference "between the policy toward the individual Jew and the policy toward the Jewish group," "Jews in Russia are under pressure from a policy of 'denationalization' and at least some Jews feel that this infringes on their rights and creates an anti-Jewish climate."[52] Such a statement certainly seems warranted by the course of events during the Communist regime and, given a past history of Jewish suffering, the fear that an anti-Jewish climate may encourage direct anti-Semitism is surely understandable.

NATIONALISM OUTSIDE OF THE SOVIET UNION

Soviet Jews are often criticized for alleged "cosmopolitanism," meaning that they are influenced by cultural currents outside of either the Soviet Union or the Communist party and are therefore not to be trusted. Both Jews and other ethnic groups in the Soviet Union are under constant suspicion of "excessive local nationalism," presumably meaning that they place too much emphasis on their particular national group and not enough on the Soviet Union as a whole. Similar charges are likewise applied to the satellite East European nations outside of the boundaries of the Soviet Union. They too are tempted to think too much of the interests of their own nation and not enough of that of world communism (i.e., the Soviet Union) and they too may neglect true Communist principles when they hear the siren call of the West. Such nations may seek profitable commerce with capitalist countries rather than barter trade with the Soviet Union on unequal terms. They may dilute their dogmatic devotion to Marxism because of a fascination with the way in which literature and science are pursued in Capitalist countries. They sometimes are tempted to moderate Socialist control of their economies in order to get greater efficiency. Finally, they may even wish to relax military relations with the Soviet Union.

---

[51] Bernard D. Weinryb, "A Note on Anti-Semitism in Soviet Russia (Post-Stalin Period)," *Slavic Review*, 25 (September 1966), 526–27.

[52] Ibid., p. 527.

Such heretical actions beyond Soviet borders receive the same kind of treatment as "cosmopolitanism" or "excessive local nationalism" by ethnic groups which are integral parts of the Soviet Union.

Cases in point are the Soviet invasions of Hungary and Czechoslovakia in 1956 and 1968, respectively. These invasions enabled the Soviet regime to overturn governments which were considered to have deviated too far from Communist policies. Hungary was the scene of heavy fighting and, when defeat was apparent, over 100,000 Hungarians fled the country. Czechoslovakia was overawed by a heavy military expedition and no fighting took place, although, as of 1973, Soviet troops were still stationed in both Hungary and Czechoslovakia. Conquest cites a *Pravda* editorial as indicating the Soviet view of the limits on freedom of action of supposedly independent countries: "*Pravda*, on 26 September 1968, said that nations do have the right to decide their own development, but added that 'none of their decisions, however, must harm socialism in their country, the basic interests of other socialist countries or the whole world workers' movement,' adding that 'world socialism is indivisible.'"[53]

One might question the relevance of these incidents in a discussion of ethnic policy on the grounds that these invasions were political matters which had nothing to do with ethnicity or cultural pluralism per se. The Soviets were not interested in destroying Hungarian or Czech culture but only in the preservation of a Communist type of socioeconomic system.

Such a view assumes that matters of ethnicity can be separated from the rest of social life, an assumption which experience seems to contradict. Whatever the rationale, the fact remains that the people of Czechoslovakia and Hungary are not free to determine their own manner of life. They are under the dictation of a government imposed by the armies of the Soviet Union—a country in which Russians are the dominant ethnic group. In this situation it is impossible to separate the category of "Russian" from the category of "Soviet Communist." Conversely, the veneration of Czechoslovak and Hungarian national heroes and the traditions of national culture may easily (and perhaps legitimately) be viewed as an indirect attack on the Soviet domination of the country.

It is certainly not true that the Soviet Union is attempting to "Russify" Czechoslovakia. Rather, it is maintaining a puppet regime in power in the hope that eventually a popular government will emerge which accepts the Soviet version of communism. In the meantime, Soviet troops are kept in isolated garrisons to be called out only in emergencies. A similar policy has been followed in Hungary and, presumably, might be adopted in other satellites if Moscow felt it necessary. This policy, though, does not quiet the fears of cultural pluralists. However pure the ethnic intentions of the Soviet authorities, they may have trouble in keeping the distinction clear

---

[53] Conquest, *The Nation Killers,* pp. 200–201.

between ethnic autonomy and politicoeconomic submission to Moscow. As the imposition of Communist orthodoxy is seen as a Russian act, a doctrine which began with a stress on proletarian internationalism may end with a classification as "Russian dogma" forcibly imposed on subject peoples. If so, it is an ironic, but, perhaps, inevitable outcome for a regime whose leaders speak of their society as being "national in form, socialist in content."

COMMUNIST ETHNIC POLICIES REVIEWED

The leaders of the USSR have tried to thread their way between what they describe as the danger of "Great Russian chauvinism" and "local nationalism." Great Russian chauvinism harks back to the Russification policy of the Czars and an effort to attain ethnic homogeneity by forced draft. Such a policy stimulates separatist trends in minority groups and splinters Communist energies into unnecessary battles over cultural and linguistic concerns. Communism itself is conceived of as an international doctrine, and presumably it can be expressed in many ways within the Soviet Union as well as abroad. On the other hand, devotion to local nationalism may bring disunity by emphasizing the virtues of one group and the defects of another and may turn the thoughts of the people away from the dream of a Communist society and toward the construction of nationalist homelands. Supposedly, in the organization of a large number of ethnically autonomous regions, the Soviets had sought to avoid both the image of a dictatorship by the Russian nationality and disruptive fragmentation by minorities. While this chapter has indicated many of the difficulties which arise in that process, perhaps the first thing to say is, that in comparison with other large countries of diverse populations, the Soviets have achieved a measure of success. This success has been greater with some minorities than with others, and the Soviets have certainly not worked out a method by which minority aspirations and national integration can be harmonized. However, as Godhagen points out, Soviet ethnic policy has important achievements:

Yet one should not underestimate the symbolic satisfaction that the trappings of autonomous "statehood," however insubstantial, have given to the ethnic pride of the minorities. Beyond this, the Communist regime during the 1920s encouraged the use of the native languages in local administrations and in the schools. It greatly expanded the educational systems of the minorities and launched a campaign to abolish illiteracy, widespread among most of them. It devised alphabets for unlettered peoples whose languages had never been written down. In short, it began to equip each of the non-Russian peoples with a cultural apparatus intended to transmit to them scientific knowledge and technical skills, as well as to serve as a means by which the new ideology could be implanted in the minds and hearts of its people. The statistics on the growth of schools, the increase of literacy, the numbers of educated persons and of trained engineers, scientists, and holders of academic degrees offer an impressive picture of cultural ascent of the minorities under Communist rule. The Soviet dictatorship surrounded the nationalities with an iron hedge, ruthlessly suppressing all endeavor for independence, but within these confines the national identity was given considerable freedom of scope.[54]

It is probably not fair to cite every example of a restriction of minority activity by the Soviet authorities as manifesting inconsistency or hypocrisy in their nationality policy. Even before the days of the revolution, the Communist leaders had tried to reconcile the needs of Soviet integration with minority nationalism. In doing this they had never denied that the needs of the Communist movement should always be paramount to the rights of any particular nationality. Stalin, for example, clearly indicates that while the Soviets will foster nationalistic movements when they are directed against capitalist states, they will oppose them when they fragment socialist organizations.

. . . support must be given to such national movements as tend to weaken or to overthrow imperialism, and not to strengthen and preserve it. Cases occur when the national movements in certain oppressed countries come into conflict with the interests of the development of the proletarian movement. In such cases support is out of the question.[55]

There is no nation which can claim a complete consistency, and the achievements of Soviet ethnic policy would be more impressive and the restrictions on the freedom of nationalities perhaps less disturbing were it not for the perfectionist claims made by Communist writers. On many occasions, the statement has been made that intergroup frictions, like most other societal ills, were a result of capitalism and would disappear in a Communist society. Consider for instance this statement by Soviet authors in a UNESCO publication dealing with ethnic policies:

Thus in Tsarist Russia the inequalities between national elements, and the oppression of national minorities and colonial peoples, were consequences of a reactionary social system based on Tsarist absolutism, capitalism and landlordism. Only the revolution of October 1917, which overthrew this regime and instituted the Soviet system enabled the peoples of Russia to achieve genuine equality of rights and freedom of development.[56]

In line with this proclamation that the Communist revolution gave freedom to the non-Russian peoples, it is worth while, as Al Smith used to

---

54 Goldhagen, *Ethnic Minorities in the Soviet Union*, p. ix.

55 J. Stalin, "Problems of Leninism," cited in Robert Conquest, *The Nation Killers: The Soviet Deportation of Nationalities* (New York, Macmillan, 1970), p. 117.

56 Tsamerian and Ronin, *Equality of Rights between Races and Nationalities in the Soviet Union*, p. 11.

say, to "look at the record." In doing this, one would find the "younger brother" nations moving in fair cooperation with the Russians, he would find the Baltic states, which attempted to separate, forcibly brought back into the fold; he would see the more primitive groups being rapidly brought into modernity with a consequent change toward assimilation of Russian culture in the process, even while their own culture is supposedly being developed; and finally, he would find greater freedom for individual Jews than was true in the Czarist era, along with a frustration of Jewish ethnic and cultural aspirations. These actions have been accompanied by the deportations of peoples during the war period, by the occasional use of Jews and others as scapegoats for national failures and by a suppression of any activity which might be considered excessive local nationalism.

The problems of Soviet ethnic policy have not brought any sense of humility to their publicists who not only proclaim that cultural pluralism has been an unqualified success in the Soviet Union, but also urge the adoption of similar policies in the rest of the world. Thus a Soviet book on the United States bears the title, *Land without Nationality Rights,* emphasizing the fact that the American legal system confers rights on individuals rather than on ethnic groups. Allworth cites this book and comments:

In addition to projecting Soviet nationality policy militarily into an independent neighboring state, Russian leadership has also persistently spread the notion farther afield that its own earlier solution to domestic nationality problems in the USSR (administrative division of the country according to the nationality principle) has proved superior to other formulas. Now Moscow pushes hard for the assimilation of all Soviet nationalities with the Russians, and for eventually erasing internal nationality boundary lines. The leaders at the same time promote the contrary idea abroad—especially in states with a mixture of nationalities in their population—of the need for separation or segregation into nationality units.[57]

According to the reader's preference, the apparent inconsistency between the Soviet restriction of minority peoples and their advocacy of cultural pluralism may be explained in one of two ways. Skeptics would say that no society is perfect, while orthodox Communists would reply that a capitalist society in inevitably flawed and that the Soviet Union has not yet reached true communism. Probably a more rewarding topic, and one which we now address, is whether or not there is a basic consistency between the necessary practices of a Communist society and the maintenance of a pattern of cultural pluralism.

There is no doubt of the verbal contrast between the Czarist policy of Russification and the Communist proclamation of devotion to the freedom

---

[57] Edward Allworth (ed.), *Soviet Nationality Problems,* p. viii. His comments are based on *Land without Nationality Rights* (Moscow, Politizidat, 1966).

of the non-Russian nationalities. Likewise, one must acknowledge the spur to the development of many nationalities given by the Communist policy of establishing territorial ethnic units of government. However, it is still possible to question whether the long-term operation of Communist policies really favors the retention of cultural pluralism.

Recognition of the legitimacy of ethnic claims minimizes national tensions, but it does not eliminate problems of intergroup adjustment. As far as the rights of ethnic minorities are concerned, the general thrust of the Communist regime may be as great a threat to their ethnic identity as its specific minority policies. The concern of the Soviet government with every aspect of the life of the individual brings the freedom of all types of activity into question, including those related to ethnic identity. Similarly, the intense concentration on economic development necessarily breaks up the homogeneity, and therefore the cohesion, of ethnic groups. On these grounds, Communism would have been expected to engender more rather than less ethnic friction. On the other hand, the Czarist regime frankly proclaimed and pursued a Russification policy, while the Communist regime talked about the freedom of the peoples and, to a considerable extent, followed cultural policies consistent with this goal. Certainly this type of overt policy has diminished the conflict between loyalty to the nationality anl loyalty to the USSR and thereby diminished the tendency toward ethnic friction, but there is another side to the story. This is that the monopoly of all activities of collective life by a totalitarian state eliminates the ethnic group's base of operations.

The abolition of voluntary associations weakens ethnic cohesion. Mutual aid societies, fraternities, churches, political and labor groups, organized on an ethnic basis allow the group to maintain its cultural identity. When these functions are taken over by the state, all ethnic questions become matters of government policy. This places all ethnic groups at the mercy of government functionaries and also expedites the processes of assimilation. If voluntary organizations are forbidden, the usual way to organize the services they offer is on a territorial basis which ignores ethnic identity. History suggests that it is the inability of the government to homogenize its citizens rather than its benevolence which is the best guarantee of ethnic pluralism.

Just as the devotion to Communist hegemony threatens the autonomy of adjacent countries in spite of a professed respect for their independence, so the internal application of Communist practices weakens Soviet cultural pluralism. It is not ethnic bigotry but Communist principles that stimulated the attack on many parts of the social fabric linked with ethnic culture. Judaism, Roman Catholicism, and Islam were not attacked because of their association with specific ethnic groups but because religion is condemned in Communist theory. Voluntary associations were regarded as unnecessary and diversionary in a country where the government provides all services. Petty traders or nomadic herdsmen were not restricted because of ethnic antagonism but because they too did not fit into the Communist framework. The intent of these and other moves may have been divorced from any intention of attacking ethnic pluralism, but the purity of the intention makes no difference in the character of the result.

An ethnic group which is deprived of the religious structure which has sustained its ethos, robbed of the voluntary associations through which mutual aid and the training of the young were carried on, and forced into economic activities foreign to its basic values is obviously a group operating in circumstances which weaken its cohesion.

One may look at any particular action and argue either for its justification on a pragmatic basis, or that it may be explained as an individual aberration. However, a fundamental question arises from the nature of Soviet Communism itself. Is it possible for a regime which makes the demands for conformity in many spheres to tolerate the type of diversity which genuine ethnic pluralism provides? The abolition of most forms of private business, the elimination of voluntary mutual aid societies, the monopoly of education by the public sector, the one-party political system, and the attack on religion, are moves certainly consistent with a drive for uniformity and conformity. Cultural pluralism, on the other hand, by definition implies variety. If the private organizations which might provide this variety are to be suppressed, cultural pluralism can only be carried on through governmental instrumentalities. Is it possible for a highly centralized Soviet state to tolerate the type of deviations which are likely to arise if ethnically delineated governmental units actually follow the values implicit in the traditions of the nationalities that they supposedly represent? Or is the Soviet revision of cultural pluralism doomed to a continued conflict with "local nationalism," frequent purges of nationalist leaders, and growing pressures toward complete assimilation? To put it more concretely: does the Lithuanian student who attempted to burn himself to death in defense of Lithuanian nationalism symbolize a transient phase of bourgeoise nationalism or is he an indication of inevitable tension between national identity and the Soviet design of a unified society?

Summary. The Soviets proclaimed that not only were they changing the policy of the country from "Russification" to cultural pluralism, but that ethnic conflict was basically a result of capitalism and would disappear in a Communist society. Such a view is regarded as applicable beyond the Soviet Union, and any reluctance to foster development of separate nationalities within a sovereign state is regarded as imperialistic oppression. Experience indicates that while the Soviet version of cultural pluralism has mitigated some forms of ethnic conflict, it has fallen far short of producing a harmonious society. Indeed, the elimination of voluntary ethnic organizations threatens the vitality of all non-Russian societies in the Soviet Union. Similarly, the drive for economic development alters existing cultural patterns and jeopardizes the maintenance of ethnic enclaves. Tension is manifested by unrest in the Baltic states which were forcibly returned to the Soviet Union after World War II, by the dissolution of some ethnic territories and the dispersion of their inhabitants, by continual concern that ethnic groups are engaged in "local nationalism," by a continued protest by Jews against the restriction of Jewish cultural activities, and, finally, by the military overthrow of governments in satellite countries which had overstepped the party line. Further, the consistency of the Soviet commitment to cultural pluralism is clouded by occasional statements that the cultural autonomy of nationalities is merely a transitional step on the path toward a homogeneous socialist society.

In spite of all its problems it may be true that intergroup relations are no more tense in the Soviet Union than in most other large countries. On the other hand, the evidence does not indicate that ethnic conflict is absent in a Communist society or that the Soviets have developed a blueprint for the creation of model multiethnic societies in the rest of the world.

SOVIET ETHNIC POLICIES IN RELATION TO GENERALIZED INTERGROUP BEHAVIOR

Soviet pattern. The Soviet experience since the announcement of their nationality policy includes a variety of intergroup tensions. Several of the smaller ethnic territorial units were completely eliminated and their people deported to other portions of the USSR. In practically all the nationality districts, leadership has been purged on the ground of excessive nationalism; Jews are requesting permission to emigrate to Israel and, in turn, are denounced as enemies of the state; foreign students in Moscow complain of prejudice and segregation. Lithuanian students demonstrated against alleged repression of Lithuanian nationalism.

Generalized pattern. The generalized pattern deduced from this specific example is simply this: Intergroup tensions may be found in any type of socioeconomic order.

This conclusion may be dismissed as commonplace or even banal, but it is listed first because it directly contradicts the main tenet of Marxian interpretation of ethnic conflict. This is, briefly, that such conflict is due to a faulty social system (capitalism) and will disappear when a Communist society develops.

Even while giving due recognition to the very important accomplishments of Soviet minority policy, it is impossible to claim that the onset of Communism wiped out intergroup problems. It is even possible to argue that the creation of a Communist state leads almost inevitably to an attempt to crush all non-Communist groups and thus represses the expression of ethnic diversity. The forms that ethnic tensions take may vary with changes in social systems, but no system yet devised appears to offer a sure cure for intergroup conflict.

Soviet pattern. The Soviet authorities have encouraged expression of the indigenous culture of minority peoples in art, dance, music, theatre, and literature. In some cases, a written language has been formulated for groups which lacked such a medium. This process has not been regarded as an end in itself but as a stage through which groups must pass in the development of culture. The illiterate learns to read and write in his own language and then it is easier for him, or for his children, to take the next step and acquire Russian language and culture. The development of indigenous culture is thus seen as a part of the process of developing a unified culture for the entire USSR. On the other hand, when the indigenous culture becomes competitive with Russian culture this is likely to lead to charges of "excessive nationalism."

Generalized pattern. The development of the culture of minority groups is compatible with national integration. Folk and primitive peoples, especially those living in a traditional territory, usually change most easily by moving to a related culture rather than to something totally strange. Thus it is easier for a people to become literate in their own language than in a foreign language. Similarly, it is easier to expand and modify traditional social institutions than to fit into the totally new. Eventually, though, progress is likely to move toward the assimilation of the dominant culture without the need for direct coercion. Once literate in his own tongue, one can grasp the principle of literacy easier and can see the advantage of literacy in a language whose usage is more widespread. Once the inadequacies of traditional social institutions have been demonstrated it is easier to move toward new forms whose utility has been tested in the greater society. The difficulty with this premise is that indigenous cultural progress may provide a goal in itself which thereby threatens ultimate assimilation and strengthens separatist tendencies; so, in terms of ultimate assimilation, the development of the indigenous culture is at best a calculated risk.

Soviet pattern. The Communist regime has passed through two crisis periods; the initial revolution in 1917 and the German invasion in World War II. In each period, actions were taken to assure minorities of their status. In the revolutionary period, minorities were assured of autonomy and even of the right to secede from the Russian state. In World War II, these assurances were repeated and hitherto restricted Jewish cultural activities were given a new lease on life.

Generalized pattern. Tolerance of minority culture may promote national loyalty. Dual loyalties can only be maintained when the one is not seen to threaten the other. A drive against minority culture in the name of national uniformity produces resistance and division. Reassurance that citizenship in a larger state does not threaten ethnic identity enables the individual to be loyal to both the minority group and the larger state.

Soviet pattern. During the World War II period, at least eight nationalities were deported from their homes to remote parts of the Soviet Union and their ethnically defined governmental units were destroyed. These were groups in border regions who were linked by ethnicity to actual or potential enemies.

Generalized pattern. Wartime strains may diminish tolerance for minorities ethnically linked to enemies. Whether this action is wise or necessary military strategy is doubtful. Khrushchev's condemnation of the Soviet actions as without justification has already been mentioned (page 70). Americans took similar action against mainland Japanese-Americans while a much larger Japanese population in Hawaii remained undisturbed. The point is not that such actions are wise or even expedient, but that wartime perils diminish the confidence which governments have in suspect minorities and thereby seem to justify an abridgement of peacetime freedoms. In addition to the Soviet and American actions of this type, one might cite the demand for the removal of German minorities from European countries after World War II, the Ottoman Empire's suspicion of Christian subjects when it was embroiled in conflict with Christian countries, and the flight or expulsion of Arabs from Israel and of Jews from Arab countries.

Soviet pattern. The teaching and publication of history in the Soviet Union has followed a zigzag course in order to furnish historical justification for current policies. Minority leaders of revolts against Czarist rule such as Shamil (see page 66) were first eulogized as fighters against tyranny, then denigrated as reactionaries who resisted beneficent Russian rule in order to exploit their people, and, then, when the party line shifted again, partially restored to their earlier image as freedom fighters. The question has not been what is objectively true but what interpretation serves to advance the current party line.

Generalized pattern. Historical teaching and writing tend to reflect ethnic viewpoints. While the changes are more heavy-handed and abrupt in a totalitarian state, the phenomenon is nearly universal. Every faction in society is hopeful of using the "lessons of history" for its own purpose, and this desire finds expression in writing and teaching. In the United States, the 1960s and the 1970s saw a great emphasis on Black History. All historians had been at least dimly aware that blacks in America had a history, but this became increasingly important when an effort was made to redefine the place of black people in American life. Similarly, historians were aware that the delegates to the American constitutional convention were men with various types of property interests. This fact, however, did not become emphasized until the rise of a school of thought which identified economic interest as the major cause of social action. Likewise, histories written in imperialist countries tend to speak of the contributions of colonial rule, while those written in former colonies dwell on the mistakes, cruelties, and injustices of colonial rule. Sometimes the emphasis is made consciously in an effort to attract popularity or to support a specific policy. More often, the emphasis is the result of an unconscious tendency to be in harmony with the spirit of the times. In either case, the result is the same and the emphasis in question is often related to the interests of ethnic groups. This does not mean that history should not be written as objectively as possible, but is simply a recognition of the fact that such writing is difficult in any circumstances and in the totalitarian state it is impossible.

Soviet pattern. Efforts to implement Communist theory have produced many changes in the Soviet Union. These include a restriction on the number and activities of churches and clergymen, the abolition of most voluntary (private) organizations, the monopoly of education by the state, and the abolition of most types of private business. None of these changes were justified on ethnic grounds, but all have had an influence on the cohesion of ethnic groups. When an ethnic group has specialized in a certain type of business, the elimination of that business disrupts the group's pattern of life; when religious bodies identified with an ethnic group are restricted, this handicaps one method of maintaining cohesion. Attacks on the Uniate Church were indirect attacks on Ukrainian identity; attacks on the Armenian Orthodox Church threaten Armenian social structure; Islam as a religion is virtually inseparable from the social structure of Islamic nationalities; and, although many Jews are nonreligious, it is hard to attack Judaism without attacking the very basis of Jewish identity. Whether they are secular or religious, voluntary associations afford avenues of ethnic expression and their elimination means that ethnic activities are dependent on the support of governmental machinery usually dominated by ethnic Russians.

Generalized pattern. Any important social change may alter the pattern of intergroup relationships. Whether such changes are introduced with the intention of affecting intergroup relationships is unimportant. Thus a major influence in producing intergroup changes in the United States was the mechanization of southern agriculture which forced millions of blacks to leave the farm and move to the city. Southern agriculture was not mechanized because of a desire to intensify racial conflict in northern cities, but it certainly had this long-range effect. In the Soviet Union much of the impact of a commitment to at least temporary cultural pluralism has been diminished by homogenizing tendencies inherent in the effort to build an industialized Communist society. In the Republic of South Africa, a burgeoning industrialism produces pressure to upgrade black labor to fill industry needs. In any society, changes which are put into effect without any intention of altering the relationships of ethnic groups may have results which are even more important than those produced by overt ethnic policies.

QUESTIONS

1. How did Czarist policies toward minorities differ from those of the Communist regime?
2. Does anti-Semitism exist in the Soviet Union? If so, how does it differ from Czarist policies?
3. If there had been a more enthusiastic Jewish response to Birobidzahn would a Jewish Republic have been established?
4. Why was the right of secession acknowledged for Finland but not for Armenia?
5. Is the Soviet regime inconsistent when it condemns both "Russification" and excessive minority nationalism?
6. Since the Soviet authorities have encouraged the development of national languages, how can their language policy be classed as "assimilationist?"
7. Is it possible for a policy which is equally hostile to all forms of religion to be antiminority in its consequences?
8. Is there any connection between the rationale for Soviet nationality policy and the invasion of Czechoslovakia?
9. Has the Soviet Union been guilty of genocide? If so, how?
10. How does the treatment of history in the Soviet Union reflect nationality policy?
11. Why is Zionism viewed as incompatible with Communism? Would this still be true if a peace treaty were negotiated between the Arab States and Israel?
12. Is the greatest threat to the existence of distinct minority groups in the Soviet Union the direct restriction of nationalistic activities or the indirect measures which grow out of Communist ideology? Explain your answer.
13. Is the repression of minority culture necessary in order to maintain national unity? What wartime examples are relevant to this question?
14. Do the Soviet nationality policies furnish a suitable model for black-white relations in the United States? Why or why not?
15. How many nationalities attempted to secede between the end of the Czarist regime and 1922? How would you account for the failure of some and the success of others?
16. When the Soviet government destroys nationality territorial units or restricts nationality expression it is often accused of being inconsistent with earlier pronouncements of Communist leaders. Is this charge justified?
17. In general, do ethnic groups have the best chance of maintaining their identity in a Communist or a capitalist society? Why?

18. Should nations which feel that they must "contain" the Soviet Union and stop its territorial expansion, promote the independence of minority peoples of the Soviet Union?

19. Both the Soviet Union and the United States of America are the result of the populating and conquest of a continental land mass. Why has Americanization been more successful than Russification?

20. In what ways can the Soviet Union claim that its minority policies have been successful? How do you account for the minority difficulties which still exist?

21. Compare Communist minority policies with policies during the Czarist regime. Consult Samuel P. Oliner, "The Non-Russian peoples in the U.S.S.R.: an Unsolved Problem." The UKRANIAN QUARTERLY XXXII, No. 3 Autumn, 1976, pages 261–285.

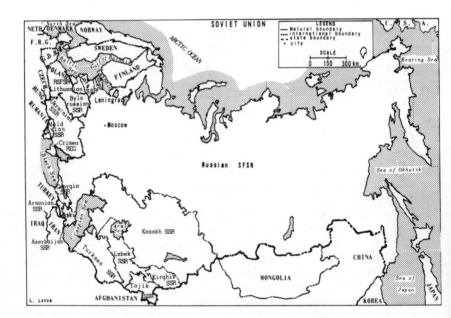

Chapter 4

Marginal trading peoples: Chinese in the Philippines and Indians in Kenya*

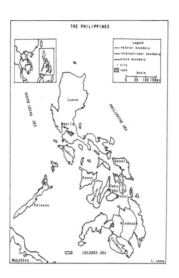

Tourists in the Philippines find that one of the fascinating sights of Manila is the Chinese cemetery. Here, enormous mausoleums, equipped with kitchens for the days when the Chinese offer food to their decreased ancestors (and themselves), give convincing evidence of Chinese wealth and achievement. Spaniards ruled the country for 350 years and Americans for nearly half a century, but neither nationality is as prominent in business as the Chinese. Indeed, in rural areas, *Chinese* is almost a synonym for *businessman.* In Nairobi, the capital of Kenya, the majority of the population is African, the government, until recently, was British, and the impact of a minority Indian population is inescapable. Hindu temples and Muslim mosques rise above the Christian churches, and turbaned Sikhs are conspicuous in the shops and factories.

Commercial success, skilled labor, and professional activity (to the extent it is allowed) are far more prevalent among these overseas Chinese and Indians than in the indigenous population. As a result, these Chinese and Indians are both admired and scorned. They contribute greatly to the commercial life of these countries, and yet discrimination against them grows steadily more severe. By most indices they have made a successful

---

*For location of Kenya see map on page 206.

adjustment in their host countries, but conditions for their existence are increasingly difficult and it is altogether possible that both the Philippines and Kenya may follow the lead of Uganda and forcibly expel this portion of their alien population.

ROLE OF OVERSEAS CHINESE AND INDIANS

What is the role of the overseas Chinese and Indians? How did it arise? Why is their situation now so precarious? To answer these questions, let us look at some general features of interethnic relations and their operation in Kenya and the Philippines. Probably the most relevant feature is the relationship of social class, occupation, and ethnicity.

Social class, occupation, and ethnicity are closely linked. There are few, if any, countries in which the occupational distribution, and therefore the social class rank, are proportionately equal in all ethnic groups. A particular form of this ethnic-occupational syndrome is found in many of the developing countries where specific minority groups occupy a role in which they function as intermediaries between European powers and the traditional society. European penetration in such societies usually began on the basis of fairly casual trade. The profits from such trade stimulated still further contacts and a greater demand for goods; a demand which was not easy for the traditional society to meet. Usually the economic surplus was not great, nor was increased production easy to stimulate. The local rulers may have appeared to be complete autocrats with the power of life and death over their subjects, but even such absolute rule had to be exercised along traditional lines. Efforts to increase the amount of produce given as tribute or to change the customary types of production usually met with resistance which quickly established the limits of royal power.

The European traders, either in the form of company enterprise or in the form of imperialist rule, then proceeded to set up their own direct agencies for securing the needed trade goods. This meant the establishment of a permanent group of Europeans who would require certain services for themselves and, in addition, the construction of roads and harbors to facilitate commerce. The European adventurer was usually able to defeat the armies of the native king, but he too found that it was difficult to reorder the economy. His powers of coercion could be resisted by withdrawal into the countryside, and the inducements he could offer as rewards were usually insufficient to stimulate the type of changes he had in mind. Further, the Europeans were few in number: enough to man a small army and some of the major posts in government but insufficient to establish a network of close relationships with the people of the country.

One of the first reactions in these circumstances was to bring in other peoples who could be depended upon to furnish plantation labor, to build railroads and other public works, and to provide a nucleus of artisans.

Frequently the laborers were indentured, meaning that they were committed to work for a nominal amount of pay for a period of years until the charges for their passage had been reimbursed and that then they were allowed to sell their services on the open market.

Chinese and Indian workers often came to colonial areas as indentured servants, and they formed a high proportion of those who eventually filled the role of intermediaries between the Europeans and the traditional society. They usually formed only a small percentage of the population, but were prominent in economic life. For the most part, the members of the traditional society had little desire to engage in wage labor and had no experience or motivation which might provide the stimulus and patterns needed to becoming a trading people.

The indentured workers frequently came from an area in which there had been some development of a wage system and, in any event, since they had been torn away from the land, had no choice but to enter into economic relationships set by the Europeans. The indigenous people, on the other hand, had already established a network of economic activity which provided for a combination of subsistence and minor exchange. They saw little to be gained from participation in the European-dominated export trade and their resistance or indifference was often a massive barrier to economic development.

In several different parts of the European overseas territories, the indentured Chinese and East Indians not only provided needed and dependable contract labor, but quickly perceived the profits to be gained from participation in the cash economy. The result was that, as their period of service ended, they looked about for opportunities as traders. Frequently these trading possibilities were found in bringing manufactured goods to the farmer and in moving farm goods to the export markets. The Chinese and Indian populations in many instances were greater in numbers than the Europeans, willing to accept a lower standard of living, and far more emancipated from traditional values than were the natives. Their culture and appearance distinguished them from both the European and the native population. A quick adaptation was made in terms of learning the local language, although usually efforts were made to set up a school system to preserve Chinese or Indian culture. Most of the migrants were men and miscegenation took place on a large scale. On the other hand, Chinese or Indian brides were preferred when available and enough migration of women occurred to make it possible for the group to be perpetuated as a recognizable entity.

Both the European and the native reactions to these marginal trading groups were somewhat ambivalent. The Europeans welcomed them as laborers and also as petty traders and agricultural middlemen. However, their culture was disdained, intermarriage was frowned upon, and social interaction, apart from business affairs, was discouraged. As a few of the traders expanded their operations and accumulated small fortunes, this aroused the jealousy of some of the Europeans, who began to look at them as competitors.

The native population at first saw the newcomers as people of an inferior culture who were performing a type of work which had some value to the native population and in which the natives themselves had little desire to engage. Gradually, however, the export market expanded, westernized education increased, the wealth of the middleman contrasted with the poverty of the peasant, and friction arose. Since the middleman was viewed as a person who paid too little for produce, who charged too much interest on the loans he made, and who was accused of selling his retail goods for too high a price, he was an obvious target for the resentment of a peasant population whose desires rapidly expanded beyond their economic resources.

Whatever might be the individual European's reaction toward these marginal groups, the colonial governments usually appreciated the role that the migrants played in the economy and afforded them a measure of protection. When independence came to countries in Asia or Africa, the development of the export economy had indicated pretty clearly the possibility for wealth from the middleman type of role. The European government was primarily interested in economic development per se, while the independent government was interested, not only in the total economy, but also in the role played by various ethnic groups. The independent government had come into power promising both political freedom and also economic advance. Since economic advance was never as rapid as promised, a scapegoat was needed to relieve social tensions, and the marginal middleman served that role in exemplary fashion. He was regarded as being rich, culturally inferior, and politically powerless. He represented a group wealthy enough to arouse envy, but not powerful enough to sustain its position, and hence he was a safe outlet for the aggression produced by the frustrations of the society.

While these general processes could be elaborated at greater length, it is probably more helpful to see them in concrete detail, and for this purpose we propose to examine the role of the Chinese in the Philippine Islands and of the Indians in Kenya. In this chapter we are interested in illustrating several important generalizations concerning ethnic relations; namely, (1) that similarity in cultural practices and/or physical appearance tends to facilitate intermarriage; (2) in a colonial situation a minority may function better in certain areas than either the colonial or the indigenous population; (3) a developing society may engage in extreme forms of discrimination in an attempt to protect or augment the welfare of the indigenous population; and (4) contractual obligations with a minority are not likely to be honored by a government that perceives a conflict between such obligations and the wishes of the majority.

CHINESE IN THE PHILIPPINES

Although pottery finds indicate that occasional Chinese traders had visited the Philippine Islands at least as far back as the Sung Dynasty (A.D. 960–1270), Chinese settlement probably only goes back to the 15th century, or about 100 years before the Spanish occupation, which may be said to have begun with the visit by Magellan in 1521.[1] Chinese settlement was not numerous until after the Spaniards had stimulated the export trade. For some time the Spanish did very little in the economic exploitation of the resources of the Philippines. Their motivations were rather to establish a strategic military outpost, to carry on missionary activity, and to profit from the China trade. There were practically no Spanish laborers and very few traders, so that the Chinese found a profitable field for their activities.

From an early date Chinese worked as artisans in Manila, transported the food which provisioned the Spanish forces, and carried on a lively trade between China and the Philippines. It is estimated that by the beginning of the 17th century there were more than 30,000 Chinese in the Manila area, which was several times the number of Spanish settlers at the time.[2]

Chinese in the Spanish period

The fact that Chinese and Spanish relations were mutually profitable did not prevent conflict from arising. The Spanish considered the Chinese to be heathens who resisted the Christianizing work which had been a major Spanish goal. They also feared their potential political power, a fear which found justification in the attempt of the Chinese "pirate" Lim-Ah-Hong to capture the city in 1574. The Chinese, for their part, accused the Spanish of extortion and feared that the Spanish might launch a preventive attack and justify it on the grounds of potential Chinese aggression. The result was alternating periods of acceptance and persecution for the Chinese. A period of prosperity would be followed by a massacre and official restrictions or even expulsion, after which the Chinese would again be invited to return to the country.

Somewhat of an equilibrium was reached during the middle of the 18th century when the Spanish government followed a policy of trying to limit the total number of Chinese to about 5,000.[3] This was regarded as

---

[1] Hubert Reynolds, "Why Chinese Traders Approached the Philippines Late—and from the South," in Mario Zamora (ed.), *Studies in Philippine Anthropology (in Honor of H. Otley Beyer)*, (Quezon City, Alemar-Phoenix, 1967), pp. 466–68.

[2] Shubert S. C. Liao, "How the Chinese Lived in the Philippines from 1570 to 1898," in *Chinese Participation in Philippine Culture and Economy* (Manila, Bookman, Inc., 1964), p. 32.

[3] Edgar Wickberg, *The Chinese in Philippines Life*, (New Haven, Yale University Press, 1965), pp. 24, 53.

adequate for the commercial functions which the Chinese served and yet small enough to prevent any threat to Spanish interests.

Most of the records of the earlier days talk mainly about relationships between Spaniards and Chinese and say little about Chinese and Filipinos. This is partially because the Chinese tended to live on the edge of the Spanish settlements and to relate their activities to the supplying of the Spanish in the Philippines and to making contributions to the galleon trade between the Philippines and Mexico.

With the passage of time, a considerable part of the work of the early Chinese agricultural middlemen had been taken over by Filipinos, many of whom were Chinese mestizos. The 19th century saw a considerable expansion of commercialized agriculture in relation to a growing export trade. The Spanish government was aware of the role the Chinese played in such an enterprise and, presumably because of a desire to accelerate economic growth, removed the restrictions against Chinese immigration. The result was that between 1864 and 1886 the number of Chinese grew from 18,000 to 90,000.[4] This should be seen in the context of a Filipino population of only 6,000,000, most of which was rural. Chinese laborers not only were employed as artisans but also were preferred as stevedores and warehouse laborers, and the city of Manila began to use them for public work projects. The Chinese traders were instrumental in stimulating a greater production of such export crops as abaca, coconuts, and tobacco. On the domestic scenes, they became the leading processors of rice and corn. Much of the agricultural marketing activity was carried on through the *cabecilla* system, which is described by Wickberg as follows:

... A *cabecilla*, or *towkay*, to use a comparable Chinese word, was usually a Chinese wholesaler of imports and exports who was established at Manila or another port where he dealt with foreign business houses. He usually had several agents scattered about the provinces, who ran stores as retail outlets for the imported goods that he had acquired and advanced to them on credit. At the same time, the agents bought up crops for the *cabecilla* to wholesale to the foreign business houses. ...

The establishment of the Chinese agent store, usually a miscellaneous goods or *sari-sari* store provided a systematic wholesale-retail agency of great economic potential. In the hands of a Chinese agent, the *sari-sari* store became a retail outlet for local food and household products as well as imported goods, and a source of credit and crop advances to local farmers. In a sense, it could be said that the *sari-sari* store, used in this fashion, was a basic frontier institution —a device for opening up new areas to Chinese economic penetration.[5]

---

[4] Ibid., p. 61.

[5] Edgar Wickberg, "Early Chinese Influence in the Philippines," *Pacific Affairs*, 35 (1962), 280.

Chinese in the American period

The economic role of the Chinese in the Philippines continued under the American regime. By the advent of the Americans, local feeling against the Chinese among the Filipinos had increased. Originally it was based mainly on cultural prejudice, which saw the Chinese as people of an inferior culture speaking a strange tongue and worshiping false gods; men who wore pigtails and women who bound their feet and who were suspected of all sorts of immoral and vicious practices. This in itself might be enough to generate animosity, but the Chinese were also seen as picking up the best fruits of economic enterprise and thus as economic competitors, and finally as an alien element which ran counter to nationalistic strivings. In deference to these feelings, the American regime ended Chinese immigration but placed no other restrictions on Chinese activity. When a Philippine legislature was established there were occasional attempts to adopt discriminatory legislation against the Chinese, most of which were vetoed by the American authorities.

Chinese social adjustment

According to the 1961 registration of aliens in the Philippines, there were 137,519 Chinese.[6] This number did not include those of Chinese ancestry who had become Filipino citizens or illegal immigrants who escaped the registration procedure. Estimates on the total number of Chinese in the country go all the way to 750,000, and it is impossible to arrive at any exact figure. Even the highest estimate, however, would place Chinese at less than two percent of the population. The great majority of the Chinese live in the city of Manila, with smaller numbers in various provincal urban areas. Manila's Chinatown gradually merges into the rest of the city, and the more prosperous Chinese have scattered to the city's outskirts and suburban areas. No exact figures are available, but the majority of Chinese appear to have converted to Christianity. There are only two Buddhist temples in the country, one in Manila and one in the city of Cebu. The proportion of Chinese who are Protestant is higher than that of the general Philippine population, and they tend to be members of exclusively Chinese congregations. The Chinese Protestant congregation acts in the fashion of a typical ethnoreligious grouping and often has a large and enthusiastic membership. Catholicism offers only one exclusively Chinese parish, although a few Chinese priests, mostly exiles from mainland China, labor in various parts of the Philippines.

The distinctive institutions of the Filipino Chinese are the Chambers of Commerce and the Chinese schools. Every important city has a Chinese

---

[6] *Journal of Philippine Statistics,* vol. 15, no. 1, 1962. A 1959 registration of aliens by the Bureau of Immigration found 138,457 Chinese (Liao, in *Chinese Participation in Philippine Culture and Economy,* p. 428).

Chamber of Commerce which is a meeting place for businessmen and a sponsor of economic activities for the total community. The Chamber of Commerce is also responsible for raising funds for the support of the Chinese schools as well as for charitable enterprises of many kinds of a non-Chinese character. In some Philippine cities there is no Chamber of Commerce apart from the Chinese Chamber, reflecting the extent to which those of Chinese ancestry predominate in the business life of the community.

The Chinese schools offer both a Chinese and a Philippine curriculum. This double burden does not seem to be too great for the students, who stand well in examinations on the regular Philippine subjects as well as absorbing a portion of Chinese culture. The Chinese schools come under the control of the government bureau of private schools and are compelled to hire a certain proportion of Philippine staff. Along with Chinese students, they usually include a few Filipinos because of the generally good academic reputation of the schools as well as the feeling on the part of some parents that a Chinese education is good preparation for a commercial career. The schools are often considered a divisive institution in the community but are protected under a treaty with the Republic of China, which at this writing meant the Taiwan regime.

In the public mind the terms *Chinese* and *businessman* are practically synonomous. So much is this so that cooperative organization among farmers is advocated, not as a device to eliminate the middleman, but as a way to get rid of the Chinese. Incidentally, the cooperatives have a very dismal record with repeated failures in the Philippines in spite of a good deal of government encouragement. Probably one of the reasons for their difficulties is that the exclusion of Chinese personnel from management positions in the co-ops means that they are shut off from the greatest source of managerial talent.

Relations between individual Chinese and Filipinos are tolerable but seldom friendly. There have been no large-scale riots for many years, but there is a tendency for social relationships to be segregated; Chinese tend to live in neighborhoods with other Chinese and to attend religious and educational institutions which are Chinese in character. Ethnic stereotypes about the unscrupulous character of the Chinese are a part of the Philippine folklore, and the social distance ranking of the Chinese is rather far down the scale. Table 4-1 shows the reaction of a sample of Philippine university students to various nationalities in a number of specific relationships. It will be noted that usually Chinese are rather far down the list, with a much more unfavorable rating than Spanish or American. The one exception is in the role of business partner, where higher acceptance is a tribute to Chinese commercial abilities.

There are two types of interaction which bring Chinese and Filipino together; namely, business and intermarriage. The business stereotype is a rather complicated one. The Chinese is frequently regarded as being unscrupulous and as one who gives bribes. On the other hand, he is regarded as more likely to repay his obligations and to carry out the

TABLE 4–1

Philippine university students social distance scale
(sample size 444)°

	Percent who indicate:			
Nationality	Desirable in this relationship	Indifference	Mild hostility	Extreme resistance to this relationship
As husband or wife:				
American	31.98	43.69	14.14	9.91
Japanese	21.62	38.74	22.07	17.57
Spanish	20.27	45.05	19.82	14.64
Chinese	18.02	33.11	23.65	25.23
Indonesian	16.22	47.75	21.35	14.19
As roommate in the dormitory:				
American	51.80	34.88	9.46	4.05
Japanese	43.24	34.68	14.41	7.66
Spanish	38.29	41.67	13.06	6.76
Indonesian	38.06	38.96	16.44	6.53
Chinese	34.46	35.59	17.34	12.61
As business partner:				
American	41.22	30.18	18.24	10.66
Chinese	39.64	26.80	16.67	16.67
Japanese	36.94	31.98	20.50	10.59
Spanish	14.19	44.37	26.13	15.09
Indonesian	13.51	49.77	25.23	11.26
As important Government officials:				
American	21.4	23.42	23.42	31.76
Japanese	11.04	28.60	24.77	35.46
Indonesian	8.56	33.78	25.68	31.98
Chinese	8.33	27.25	24.77	39.64
Spanish	7.88	31.53	26.35	34.23
As citizens of the Philippines:				
American	29.73	33.33	21.40	15.54
Spanish	23.43	33.33	23.65	19.59
Indonesian	21.62	38.06	20.95	19.14
Chinese	18.47	29.50	25.45	26.58
Japanese	18.02	36.49	23.87	21.62

° Based on a sample of classes in the University of the East, The University of the Philippines, and Silliman University, taken in March and April 1970. Questionnaires were distributed by Socorro Espiritu, Ofelia R. Angangco, and Luis Lacar at the request of Chester L. Hunt. Cf. Chester L. Hunt and Luis Lacar, "Social Distance and American Policy in the Philippines," *Sociology and Social Research*, Vol. 57, (July 1973) pp. 495–509.

terms of a contract than might be true of Filipinos in a similar position. Both the alleged vices and alleged virtues of the Chinese businessman serve as a justification for discrimination, since they render him a more formidable type of competitor.

It may be surprising in view of mutual prejudice between Chinese and Filipinos, that the intermarriage rate is fairly high. The explanation for this is social and demographic. The demographic factors refer to a distorted sex ratio. In 1918, there were 13 times as many Chinese men as women; in 1948, the ratio had dropped to two to one, and, although current figures are not available, the assumption is that it is approaching an equal distribution, particularly at the age levels below 40.[7] In the past this sex ratio has meant that Chinese men necessarily turned to Filipino women for mates, with the result that a large Chinese-Filipino mestizo contingent was formed; Beyer estimated that at least ten percent of the Philippine population had some degree of Chinese ancestry.[8]

The line between Chinese, mestizo, and Filipino is a rather indefinite one. It relates to degree of Chinese ancestry and to extent of participation in Chinese or Filipino social groups. One with mixed parentage who speaks Chinese, lives in a Chinese section, sends his children to a Chinese school, and, in general, identifies with the Chinese group is considered Chinese. The reverse is true for the individual who separates himself from Chinese contacts and identifies with Filipino society.

The move toward a greater equality in the sex ratio does not seem to have diminished the tendency toward intermarriage. Thus, in 1958, 61 percent of the marriages of Chinese men were with Filipino women, while 30 percent of the marriages of Chinese women were with Filipino men. Since there were nearly twice as many marriages involving Chinese men as Chinese women, this would indicate that by 1958 the sex ratio had not yet reached equality. In these circumstances, it is interesting that even 30 percent of the marriages of Chinese women were with Filipinos.[9] Presumably, Chinese women are highly valued as brides by Chinese men and the fact that as many as 30 percent were married to Filipinos indicates that the value system is changing to the extent that in Chinese eyes a Filipino may be not only an available marriage mate, but also one to be preferred.

It is not only demographic but also social class factors which favor the acceptance of Chinese mates by Filipino brides and grooms. Social dis-

---

[7] Data for 1948 from *Census of the Philippines, Summary of Population and Agriculture* (Manila Bureau of the Census, 1954), p. 67. Data for previous years taken from Victor Purcell, *Chinese in Southeast Asia* (Oxford Press, London, 1950), pp. 575–77.

[8] H. Otley Beyer, Table of Philippines Racial Ancestry, cited in Marcelo Tangco, "The Christian Peoples of the Philippines," *Natural and Applied Science Bulletin,* 11 (University of the Philippines, January–March 1951), p. 110.

[9] *Philippine Journal of Statistics,* Vol. 12 (April–June 1959).

tance tests indicate a high degree of aversion to intermarriage, and the popular interpretation of such marriages is that economic advantage has outweighed ethnic prejudice. A survey of some 30 Chinese-Filipino couples indicates that the popular stereotype may have considerable validity.[10] In each case, the Chinese groom was in an income bracket which would place him in the top one percent of the Filipino population and also was at an income level considerably higher than that occupied by members of his wife's family.

The Chinese community tends to be viewed by Filipinos as a cohesive, clannish group with a low opinion of Philippine culture and, therefore, as a self-perpetuating foreign irritant in the body politic. If one looks at such Chinese institutions as schools and chambers of commerce and notes the survival of the use of the Chinese language, this view is certainly understandable. However, the evidence is strong that, given opportunity, the Chinese both assimilate Philippine culture and intermarry, with the result that the Chinese population is probably declining rather than increasing.

One example of this tendency toward assimilation is furnished by the experience of the Chinese school in Cotobato. Cotobato had a Chinese Mestizo association which had a fairly complete list of those of mestizo ancestry in the community. Trends in school attendence of mestizo children should indicate the degree to which this group is swinging from Chinese to Filipino identification. Table 4–2 shows that the proportion of

TABLE 4–2

Proportion of mestizos in the Chinese School[*]

Academic level	Pure Chinese	Mestizo
Kindergarten	35	65
Primary	50	50
Intermediate	70	30
High school	80	20

[*] Estimate furnished by Chen, Liesch Fu, principal of the Cotobato School. Cited in Socorro C. Espiritu and Chester L. Hunt, *Social Foundations of Community Development, Readings on the Philippines* (Manila, Garcia Publishing House, 1964), p. 222.

children of mestizo ancestry in the Chinese school diminishes as the academic level progresses. In kindergarten, a majority of the children were mestizo, but by high school their proportion had fallen to 20 percent. Presumably, this indicates that the children find Filipino society to have a strong attraction and place pressure on the parents to transfer them to a school in which Philippine identification will be facilitated.

----

[10] Belen Tan-Gatue (Medina), "The Social Background of Thirty Chinese-Filipino Marriages," *Philippine Sociological Review*, 3 (July 1955): pp. 3–13.

Similar trends were found in a study of assimilative trends among college students of Chinese ancestry made by Hubert Reynolds in 1968.[11] Reynolds found that the Chinese students had little interest in Chinese language or culture, desired to be recognized as Filipino, and had at least as many contacts with Filipino students as with students of Chinese ancestry. These two studies suggest that, in spite of high Chinese economic status and pride in Chinese culture, the attractions of assimilation are overwhelming and it is only the exclusionist policies of Filipinos which enable the Chinese to survive as a distinct and separate group.

In spite of barriers between Filipinos and Chinese, intermarriage has been going on so long that a large part of the Filipino population is of mixed ancestry. In the words of one Filipino writer:

Up to the present time there are numerous Filipinos who do not only have Chinese blood but also carry Chinese surnames. The surnames Yangco, Lim, Dee, Lee, Locsin, Tan, and numerous others are Chinese Surnames. The Philippine national hero, himself, Dr. Jose Rizal, was part Chinese, so was former president Sergio Osmena Sr. And so is General Emilio Aguinaldo, president of the first Philippine Republic, and a number of the revolutionary leaders such as General Manuel Tinio, Severino Tainio, Maximino Hizon, Mariano Limjpa, Telesforo Chuidian.[12]

In summary, the Chinese present the paradox of a successful group with strong ethnic institutions and a deep pride in their culture which, at the same time, is susceptible both to intermarriage and cultural assimilation. This tendency to biological amalgamation and cultural assimilation keeps down the size of the group identified as Chinese and facilitates their cooperation with the rest of Philippine society. It does not, however, seem to lessen prejudice or to weaken the popular image of the Chinese as a cohesive group with little concern for outsiders. Nor does the high proportion of people with mixed ancestry lead to greater acceptance of Chinese by Filipinos. In fact, one might argue that the need of people with mixed Chinese ancestry to prove their identification as Filipino rather than Chinese is one motive which leads to the expression of anti-Chinese feeling.

Independence and discrimination

The change of sovereignty from Spanish to American hands seems to have enhanced the position of the Chinese. Both the Spanish and Americans viewed the Chinese question primarily in terms of economic development. The Spanish pattern may be described as one in which "squeeze" was widely practiced by Spanish authorities and the Chinese

---

[11] Hubert Reynolds, "Overseas Chinese College Students in the Philippines: A Case Study," *Philippine Sociological Review,* 5 (July–Oct. 1968): 132–34.

[12] Alejandro R. Roces, "For Closer Chinese-Filipino Cultural Relations," in Liao, *Chinese Participation in Philippine Culture and Economy,* p. 49.

were viewed as sources of both illicit taxation and illegal bribes. The American regime reduced the practice of bribery and continued to recognize the Chinese as an important element in economic progress.[13]

By the time the Commonwealth regime was inaugurated in 1936, giving limited independence under American tutelage, the Chinese had at least 20 percent of the Philippine foreign trade, a virtual monopoly of the rice and corn milling business and at least half of the retail trade. The Chinese were also strong in manufacturing and in contracting. The statements of Chinese influence were probably actually an underestimate, since many people who were Chinese by ancestry were Filipino citizens, and thus their properties were not listed as Chinese held. Informal estimates indicate that the control of the retail trade, for instance, may have been as much as 70 to 80 percent Chinese.[14]

Philippine governments may have been even more concerned with economic development than were the Spanish or American regimes, but they tended to give greater emphasis to Filipino participation than to the expansion of the economy as such. Chinese business was regarded as a necessary evil rather than an economic boon, with many indications that very critical attention was being given to the definition of "necessary." Independence in the Philippines not only produced the usual disparity between expectation and realization, but was undertaken shortly after the end of massive destruction and social disorganization consequent on World War II. The Chinese formed a natural lightning rod to attract the dissatisfactions of the populace. American prestige was too high among the Philippine masses for Americans to be the likely scapegoat, and American political, financial, and military influence was also thought to be too strong to be openly challenged. On the other hand, the Chinese formed a minority which was relatively powerless, which was culturally despised, and which was unable to call on either Taiwan or Mainland China for effective support. The result might be summarized by saying that the greater the duration and the extent of Philippine control, the greater the economic discrimination which has been enforced against the Chinese.

Chinese rights came into focus at the time of the formation of the Commonwealth regime in the definition of citizenship. The American regime had followed the practice of *jus soli* under which all people born in the country acquired citizenship automatically. Under the Commonwealth constitution, the basis of citizenship was changed to *jus sanguinis* (citizenship on basis of parentage). This latter doctrine meant that Chinese were

---

[13] Khin Khin Myint Jensen, "The Chinese in the Philippines During the American Regime: 1898–1946," unpublished Ph.D. thesis, University of Wisconsin, 1956, pp. 45, 65, cited in Sheldon Appleton, "Overseas Chinese and Economic Nationalization in the Philippines," *Journal of Asian Studies*, 19 (February 1960), p. 153.

[14] Amry Vandenbosch, "The Chinese in Southeast Asia," *Journal of Politics*, 9 (February 1947), p. 84.

required to make formal application for citizenship regardless of their place of birth and that even a Filipino mother did not constitute automatic grounds for establishing Philippine ancestry.[15]

The effect of this switch in rules for citizenship is, of course, fairly obvious. Under the *jus soli* doctrine, with the elimination of immigration, all people of Chinese ancestry would soon have become Philippine citizens and thus immune from any discriminatory laws. Under the doctrine of *jus sanguinis,* which required naturalization application by Chinese born in the Philippines, many Chinese would fail, for one reason or another, to make the more or less automatic application before age 21 and after that might find acceptance as citizens rather difficult. Further, citizens admitted under naturalization can always have their citizenship taken away from them on the grounds either that citizenship was attained by fraud or that their conduct had made them undesirable as citizens.

Other constitutional provisions of the Commonwealth were similar. These were provisions which excluded the Chinese from owning land, exploiting Philippine natural resources, or operating public utilities. Chinese could rent land for periods of up to 99 years or they could invest in legally designated businesses where 60 percent or more of the stock was Philippine owned. Similarly, in 1941, the Manila Municipal Board decided to accord priority for stalls in the common market to Philippine citizens; the implementation of this measure was delayed by the war, but it was put into effect at the end of hostilities in 1945.

For some years, legislation concerning the Chinese provoked a conflict between the executive and the legislative branch. Presidents Quezon, Osmena, and Quirino felt that nationalist progress could be served better by strengthening the position of Filipinos than by directly damaging the activities of the Chinese. They favored laws to assist Filipino businessmen but tended to oppose legislation restricting Chinese economic activity. The presidential position was somewhat similar to that of the American and Spanish regimes in that it considered economic development to be a prime goal and felt that Chinese capital and enterprise were indispensable.

The presidential stand against Chinese discrimination collapsed with President Magsaysay in 1954. He acceded to frantic pleas of Filipino congressmen "not to deprive us of our nationalism" and signed the Retail Trade Nationalization Law. The law provided that, within six months after the death of the original owner, Chinese had to leave the retail trade business. The effect of the law was expanded by decisions of the Filipino Supreme Court which, in effect, meant that wholesale and retail became almost synonymous terms. Thus corporations which bought large quan-

---

[15] Cornelius J. Peck, "Nationalism, 'Race' and Developments in the Philippine Law of Citizenship," *Journal of Asian and African Studies,* 2 (January and April 1967): 128–43.

tities of raw material for processing or shipment overseas were considered to be in the retail business and subject to the law.

The Supreme Court decisions expanded the constitutional provision against the Chinese ownership of agricultural or mineral land to include also urban land. The establishment of import control laws likewise provided an opportunity to favor Philippine importers and to exclude the Chinese. Later, legislation was passed which had the effect of driving Chinese out of the rice and corn trade. Earlier legislation had prohibited Chinese participation in most professions, while nationwide attitudes made it impossible for Chinese to be employed by government bodies.

Thus by 1965, administrative, judicial, and legislative decisions had made Chinese participation illegal in the rice and corn business and in a very broadly defined retail trade. Chinese could not own any kind of land, could not engage in agriculture and found public employment and most professions closed to them. A 15 percent preference for Philippine contractors made it impossible for Chinese firms to compete for public awards in the construction business. A very limited amount of importing was still authorized, and Chinese firms were allowed to participate in manufacturing. In spite of the relatively narrow scope of activity legally permissible to the Chinese, they still continued to be an important factor in economic life.

Perhaps the basic reason for Chinese economic survival in face of discriminatory action is that the Chinese ability in business operations proved to be strong enough to enable them to surmount many handicaps. This may be seen in the attitude of foreign firms which are often charged by Filipinos as preferring to do business with Chinese. Appleton cites the experience of one firm in this matter:

The head of a large American business firm in Manila agreed that all the banks in the Philippines showed favoritism towards Chinese and Americans immediately after World War II, but maintained that in the light of his own experience this was merely sound banking. His firm, in business in the Philippines for almost fifty years, had done 70 percent of its 75,000,000-peso business with Chinese and Americans losing less than 25,000 pesos in bad debts in the process. But in the remaining 30 per cent of the business which had been done with Filipinos, about 2,000,000 pesos in bad debts had been lost, despite the fact that the firm had screened the Filipinos much more closely than it had the Chinese.[16]

Various loopholes existed which enabled Chinese merchants to evade the effect of restrictions to some extent. The government tried to close these loopholes, but Chinese are so thoroughly integrated in Philippine society that this is an extremely difficult process. The major device for obtaining exemption from anti-Chinese measures has been the acquisition

---

[16] Appleton, "Overseas Chinese and Economic Nationalization in the Philippines," p. 157.

of Filipino citizenship, which has become much more popular with Chinese since the onset of independence. Gaining citizenship is not an easy type of procedure, since Chinese have to have proof of economic viability to an extent far greater than the average Philippine income and also have to produce character references certifying that they have not been guilty of any types of anti-Filipino actions. Usually the Chinese find that action on citizenship tends to be rather slow, but is expedited by the payment of bribes. Bribe payment in turn subjects the Chinese to continual blackmail, since citizenship may be withdrawn if there is a proof that bribery played a part in its acquisition.

Another device which is quite common is the use of a Filipino "dummy." This device is illegal, but one which is very difficult to detect and to prove in court. The "dummy" is a Filipino front man who has nominal ownership of the business, but permits the real operations to be carried on by Chinese. The Filipino secures a fee for the use of his name and, since the Chinese have greater capital and expertise, this arrangement is beneficial to all concerned. It has been especially prominent in the foreign trade field, where Chinese have the experience and the existing outlets but Filipinos had been given a legal advantage in securing import quotas. Thus a Filipino might become a businessman only for the purpose of securing a quota, and turn goods over to a Chinese for ultimate sale to the consumer.

This dummy setup, of course, means that costs are higher and that the consumer pays more, and does not have very much effect on ethnic occupational composition. Such a process even occurs in the case of goods imported by government agencies supposedly for direct sale to consumers. A situation described by Appleton on the basis of a news story in the Manila Times indicates how the dummy process operated with one government agency:

A like fate befell the National Marketing Company (NAMARCO) set up to import commodities duty free and sell them to licensed Filipino dealers for distribution. Again, instead of retailing the goods themselves, some Filipino purchasers resold them to Chinese retailers. In the summer of 1958 Philippine Constabulary and Bureau of Internal Revenue officials raided a Chinese store in downtown Manila and reported that it contained between 2,000,000 and 4,000,00 pesos' worth of illegally procured foodstuffs, including large quantities of NAMARCO goods from which the labels had been removed and replaced with the labels of the Chinese firm. At that time the General Manager of NAMARCO announced that his own investigation had disclosed a similar situation in another store nearby.[17]

These examples of the evasion of the law do not mean that the legislation was of no effect. Even the Chinese who were able to stay in business one

---

[17] Ibid., p. 160.

way or another found that their costs had heavily increased and that they faced the constant threat of criminal action. Some shifted to permissible investments in manufacturing or wholesaling, and many others moved capital outside of the country. Capital removal is illegal under Philippine currency restrictions and the amount involved is hard to estimate, but it does occur. The American Chamber of Commerce in 1958 estimated that something over $200,000,000 of Chinese capital had moved to Hong Kong and that undetermined amounts had gone to Borneo, Singapore, and elsewhere.[18]

Prospects for future relationships

Although the Chinese have been extraordinarily resilient, it is very difficult to be optimistic about their future in the Philippines. If one piece of legislation is circumvented, a more stringent law is usually in the offing. If one official may be neutralized by bribery, an official from another bureau will soon be around. The political climate is such that a formal pledge of an anti-Chinese attitude is almost a prerequisite for election of any politician. The honest politician promises to discriminate against the Chinese, and he carries out these policies when in office. The dishonest politician uses the threat of anti-Chinese legislation as a lever for bribery.

Even citizenship is not a guaranteed way out of the dilemma. Philippine courts tend to make the granting of citizenship as difficult a process as possible, and there is increasing argument that legislation should discriminate against naturalized citizens.

There are some factors that work in the opposite direction. The end of Chinese immigration means that as the older Chinese die off, they are replaced by a group which still may gain citizenship more or less automatically by making a request before the age of 21. This means that the number of Chinese aliens against whom discrimination legally applies should be rapidly diminishing in the future. However, as long as Chinese make the most acceptable scapegoat, their actual number or influence in society is somewhat irrelevant, since any incident is sufficient to justify discriminatory legislation and the definition of Chinese can always be expanded to include citizens as well as noncitizens.

One feature which may reduce pressure on the Chinese is the reversal of attitudes toward Americans on the part of the younger generation. For the Philippine masses and, to a great extent, all parts of Philippine society, the Chinese represented a backward, Oriental, destructive type of influence, while the American image was one of honest, benevolent, Western democracy. The younger and more militant Philippine generation of students is more likely to view America as an imperialist power. In fact, this

---

[18] "Philippine Capital Prospering Hong Kong," *American Chamber of Commerce Journal* (Manila), 24 (February 1958), p. 54.

charge of imperialism seems to grow in intensity even as vestigial privileges are being abandoned.[19]

As with other symbols, the appeal of propaganda against anti-American imperialism seems to be inversely proportional to the reality of the process. Now, when the American proportion in Philippine trade is declining and when the exemptions of Americans against alien discrimination procured at the time of independence are running out, the resentment of Philippine intellectuals against continued alleged American domination seems to be at white heat. Concessions do not allay this resentment but simply indicate that American power is a "paper dragon." It is interesting that the student riots in Manila, which almost paralyzed that city in 1970 and parts of 1971, included frequent attacks on the American Embassy but were not directed against the Chinese. For Filipino college students, Americans seem to be moving into the scapegoat position.

Some Filipinos have urged that a greater acceptance of assimilation by the Chinese involving the abandonment of Chinese schools and Chinese Chambers of Commerce might procure increased Philippine acceptance.[20] This, however, would constitute a major retreat by the Chinese without any guaranty of reciprocal action by Filipinos. If Chinese were granted free access to Philippine society, it seems evident that such assimilation would move at a rapid pace, but current prejudice and discrimination tends to throw Chinese back more and more into an ethnically defined society. It is perhaps more likely that a shift in popular attitudes from anti-Chinese feeling to anti-Americanism may give the Chinese at least a temporary respite from further political pressure against them.

The two cultures, Chinese and Filipino, have much in common. The bulk of the Chinese have become affiliated with Christian churches and tend to be influenced by the value system expressed therein. In spite of their devotion to Chinese culture, they cannot escape the force of the westernized, Filipino cultural milieu. Chinese have been active in economic development to the extent that they cannot disengage without great loss both to themselves and to the Philippines. On the cultural side as well, Chinese influence has been extensive. Some of the most popular Filipino foods such as pancit, siopao, lumpia, and lechon are Chinese in origin. A Philippine anthropologist, Arsenio Manuel, estimates that about 3.5 percent of words in the Tagalog language are of Chinese origin.[21]

When, by reason of Philippine citizenship, Chinese young people have

---

[19] Filipino anti-Americanism should not be exaggerated. Americans in 1972 were still the most popular foreigners. The existence of a pro-statehood organization claiming 6.5 million members indicates the tenaciousness of the "good" American image. ("The Philippines: The 51st State?" *Newsweek,* July 24, 1972, p. 50.)

[20] *Constructive Channeling of Tensions in the Philippines* (Manila, Institute of Economic Studies and Social Action, Araneta University, August, 1961).

[21] Arsenio E. Manuel, *Chinese Words in the Tagalog Language* (Manila, Philippinians Publications, 1948), p. 117.

been able to escape occupational restrictions, they tend to enter occupations such as law and education, rather than the traditional Chinese field of business enterprise. In 1975, President Marcos, who was a virtual dictator in the Philippines, reversed government policy and provided easy naturalization for Chinese living in the Philippines. Most of the Chinese living in the Philippines have become naturalized, which means that they now have essentially the same rights, including the right to engage in business, as other Philippine citizens. Marcos regarded economic improvement as an urgent need and presumably felt that freeing Chinese businessmen from restrictions would improve the economy. The Chinese situation has improved under a government which placed top priority on economic growth. No democratic government could have made changes favorable to the Chinese and whether the changes will survive the advent of a new regime is open to question.

OVERSEAS INDIANS AND AFRICAN NATIONALISM: KENYA

Between 1896 and 1902 the British imported some 32,000 Indian indentured laborers to work on railroad construction in East Africa. The assumption was that Indians would perform the railroad work and then return to the Indian subcontinent. Most of them did, but some 6,000 remained.[22] These were joined by their families and augmented by additional Indians who had heard of opportunity in Kenya. Opportunity beckoned first in work as contract laborers or artisans, since this was work which Africans had neither the training nor the inclination to perform. Most Africans lived in tribal locations eking out a living in subsistence agriculture and saw no reason to forsake this life for the regimented routine of wage labor.

The Indians, by contrast, came from an area where expanding population made it difficult for them to get a toehold in agriculture. They lived in a society in which centuries of European rule had stimulated the introduction of large-scale labor-employing enterprises in which wage labor was looked upon as an opportunity to gain a supply of capital rather than simply as dependence on the bounty of a foreign overseer.

Commercial opportunities in Kenya soon presented themselves to the Indians in the form of acting as petty retailers in selling European manu-factured articles to the Africans as the railroad was built into the interior. Tiny shops, known as *dukawallas,* were set up. These were shops which required a minimum of capital and operated on far too small a scale to attract European businessmen. However, they did form an entering wedge into commerce and the Indian proprietors quickly began to be the agents for the procurement of raw materials which were shipped to Europe as well as to the growing cities of Kenya. The dukawalla operator had to

---

[22]J. S. Mangart, *A History of Asians in East Africa* (Oxford, Clarendon Press, 1969), p. 39.

take a good deal of abuse from his customers who constantly charged him with overpricing his manufactured goods and underpaying for farm products. He was also an object of derision from European businessmen for his apparently primitive methods, but neither African traders nor European businessmen were able to displace him in a competitive struggle.

Some of the Indians were English-speaking, and many of them took advantage of the educational facilities which were developing in Kenya. As a result they were able to fill jobs as clerks in the government and in business establishments. They worked at a discriminatory scale which gave them less than half the income of a Briton occupying the same job, and they seldom rose to a high position either in the civil service or in European-owned business. Nevertheless, the money obtained was far in excess of the average income available to Africans and did allow for the acccumulation of a minor amount of savings as well as the gaining of valuable experience.

The stories of the early years of the Indians in Kenya are replete with tales of conflict between Indians and British, with relatively little attention paid to the African population which comprised the overwhelming majority of the country. This tension centered around political participation and on rights to purchase land.

Questions of political participation originally hinged on the decision of the colonial office in London as influenced by the opinion of the European settlers. As the colonial office gradually yielded a greater degree of local autonomy, the Indians also pressed for a voice in the governmental process and were eventually given a limited franchise which at first meant a majority of seats for Britons, a minority for Indians, and for Africans, none at all. Indians pressed unsuccessfully for representation on the basis of their population, which was three times that of the Europeans. As far as Africans were concerned, the assumption of both Europeans and Indians was that Africans had not reached the stage of development at which they could be safely entrusted with the franchise.

The European position was even more adamant in the matter of land tenure. The Kenya highlands were a sparsely populated area with vast agricultural potential. In spite of Indian protest, this area was reserved for European land ownership and eventually became known as the "white highlands." The exclusion of Indians from land ownership meant that they were diverted from agriculture and that their aspirations for social mobility would be found in education which led to clerical and professional employment; in work as artisans, and in commerce, mainly as a link between large-scale British interests and the Kenyan African farmers and consumers. While most of the Indians were of modest means, a number were able to expand their commercial establishments to the point where they had considerable wealth.

A survey in 1962 found that over 68 percent of the Indian taxpayers had incomes of 400 pounds a year or more, while an examination of the accounts of a Nairobi bank in 1967 showed that more than 50 percent of the savings were held by Indians as contrasted to 15 percent by Europeans and 34 percent by Africans. Abbott reports that a land survey in central Nairobi indicated that the major part of privately owned Urban land in that area was Indian.[23] It is not possible to get an exact approximation of Indian wealth, and some Indians undoubtedly lived at a low income level. However, the conclusion is inescapable that practically no Indians lived at the typical African subsistence level and that a fair number had managed to accumulate substantial holdings of money or real estate. Thus when Kenyan independence came, the Indians, although a small minority of the population—only about 182,000 in a country of six million—constituted a very substantial part of the commercial middle class as well as of the minor government employees.

To Western observers who are familiar with industrialized societies which have only a small proportion of the population in agriculture with a very large proportion in professional and technical as well as industrial occupations, it may seem amazing that there could be so much concern over the economic position of the Indian minority. In 1962 there were only something like 40,000 economically active Indian males.[24] The reason for this concern lies in the underdeveloped state of the economy and the strategic position of the Indians in a society which offered relatively few professional or managerial posts.

In 1962, there were estimated to be only 69,000 positions which required secondary or university education, and over 20,000 of these were held by Indians. In addition to being prominent in commerce and in skilled manual work, Indians had a majority of the physicians and lawyers in the country, and approximately one third of the employed Indian work force was in government service. These were occupations in which qualified personnel was scarce and in which the Indian's superior educational background placed him in a favorable position compared to that of the bulk of the African population.

A rapidly expanding African educational system was turning out an increased number of graduates, but these graduates were still insufficient for the country's needs for skilled personnel. They tended to concentrate in a few white-collar occupations and, even if employment might be open, they regarded the middle-range positions held by Indians as a barrier to African advancement.

In the field of commerce, where Indians were alleged to conduct 80 percent of the business, the Indian position had even less legitimacy in the African mind. Since commerce did not necessarily require university or secondary degrees, it was hard to demonstrate any relationship between

---

[23] Simon Abbott, "Profile of Kenyan Asians," *Institute of Race Relations Newsletter* No. 1 (February 1968): 125–29.

[24] Ibid., p. 127.

the wealth of the businessman and his ability or training. Most observers would have explained the Indian business success in terms of a culture which encouraged hard work, thrift, discipline, and entrepreneurial activity. To the African, the explanation was more likely to lie in the "clannishness" of the Indians, which gave them access to credit and to supplies of goods on more easy terms than African merchants could get, and to their "unscrupulousness," which enabled them to take advantage of African customers.

In the eyes of many observers, the Indian civil servant or professional was holding posts which had not attracted sufficient British and for which Africans were not qualified. The businessman was one who, at great risk to himself, undertook the bringing of European manufactured articles to the remote parts of the country and the collection of crops to pay for these items, and thus was a major agent in the development of the economy. While the more sophisticated Africans may have been aware of this Indian contribution, it was difficult for most to resist the dominant stereotype of the Indians as exploiters and unfair competitors.

Indian social strata

The Indian population was characterized by social divisions within the group as well as a general separation from the African population. There were divisions by religion and also by caste. The largest group, the Hindus, comprised over half of the population, but were split into four caste groups. The Roman Catholics were mainly from the Goan area of India, for a long time controlled by the Portuguese. The largest group of Muslims were the Ismailis, the followers of the Aga Kahn, but there were also three other smaller Muslim groups. The various Muslim groups had little interaction with each other and practically no common activities with African Muslims except their participation in the annual pilgrimage to Mecca. The Sikhs, constituting about 12 percent of the Indian population, were mostly skilled craftsmen and tended to be quite separate from any of the other Indian groups. All of the Indian groups tended to maintain rules of endogamy within the subgroups and particularly within the general Indian category. Their children were either educated in Indian schools in Kenya or sent to India or Britain.

Indian separatism was encouraged by a concentration of population (nearly half of the Indians lived in Nairobi), separate religious and educational institutions, the persistence of Indian languages, a distinctive style of dress for the women, along with an occupational concentration in certain lines of business and craftsmanship. It was thus possible for an Indian to live in Africa in a situation in which his contacts with Africans were only those between merchant and customer or between employer and unskilled employee.

It was true, of course, that long residence in Kenya tended to change the Indian perspective and cultural attitude. This change was not so much an assimilation of African customs, although the Indian usually learned to speak Swahili, as it was a turn toward the European model. Europeans as the dominant group in the society held great prestige in both African and Asian eyes, and the general direction of cultural change was toward an acceptance of European practices. The following statement is probably a fair summary of cultural drift among Asians:

To sum up, Asians living in East Africa have probably tended, like all *emigré* communities, to preserve their own customs even more strongly than they have been preserved at home. They have thrived in business, have adopted superficial Western customs and values, and are moving into industry and large-scale agriculture. Change is only now beginning to reach into the homes and touch the women, so that it will be more than a generation before it is really felt. As a group, the Asians are moving into many former European preserves, but from the Africans they remain socially divided as much by family organization and a certain lack of leadership as by any feelings of racial superiority.[25]

Either the Indian was becoming acculturated along the British lines or he remained a steadfast adherent to Indian practices. In either case, he was viewed as being culturally alienated from the African. The African might give a grudging respect to Indian ability in commerce, but Indian culture in general, although exotic, was hardly attractive. The African considered himself either as a westernized person who was heir both to British culture and to British prestige, or a nationalist reviving the lost glories of his people. Not infrequently both ideals coexisted in the mind of the same individual.

Whatever the African orientation, though, the Indian cultural stance was at best irrelevant and at worst a threat. The Indian had little interest in African culture aside from acquiring a proficiency in the language which was adequate for trading purposes. Insofar as he acquired European culture, he was hardly even a second-class model. Further, his social exclusiveness and endogamy tended to arouse African resentment. This attitude was graphically expressed in a statement by a leading African nationalist, Tom Mboya:

At that same meeting it appeared I had put a cat among the pigeons by telling the Indian Congress that "cocktail integration is not enough. You must be prepared to revise some of your long-established conceptions. For instance, an integrated community can lead to intermarriage between the members of that community—and why not?"

There was widespread reaction from Asians against these remarks, but I was not disappointed in that. The more people speak publicly about such matters, the better. There will be more intermarriage during the next twenty years or so, and I welcome the prospect. We have to break the myth that there is something wrong with different races marrying each other, that intermarriage leads

---

[25] "Asians in East Africa," *Institute Race Relations Newsletter* (February 1965): 13–17.

to an extinction of values and civilized standards. The example of the West Indies should be enough to convince us that this is a false argument. On the other hand, intermarriage is not intended to be a goal or policy or a subject on which to legislate. It remains a matter for free and voluntary and natural decision. What is in fact referred to is that group of people who pretend to be Kenyans but want to live in social and racial compartments. Such people are hypocrites.[26]

Indian and British relationships

Indians and Africans shared a common situation in the fact that they were both colonial subjects under the control of a white British government. Resentment at this situation developed much more rapidly among Indians than among Africans, and they very early made a demand for representation in governmental circles. The Indian demand was seriously considered by the British government, whereas Africans were regarded as being so restricted in education and so concerned with tribal affairs that their participation in the Kenya government was regarded as hardly a real issue.

Thus, in 1923, there was a legislative council whose elected representatives consisted of 11 Europeans, 5 Indians, 1 Arab, and 1 unofficial member nominated by the governor to represent African interests. At the time, Indians in Kenya greatly outnumbered the British, and they demanded a common voting roll which would have resulted in Indian domination of the council. British political ethics required that they come up with a convincing rationale to oppose this supposedly democratic proposition. The opposition to the common roll could not be based on property requirements, since enough Indians could meet any requirements put into effect to outweigh the Europeans, and, for similar reasons, it could not be based on requirements of education or literacy. The required rationale was found in the statement that Britain could not consent to a system which meant Indian rule of Kenya because the British were primarily there as trustees for the African population and could not turn over this trusteeship to any other group. The position is frankly expressed in the British government white paper of 1922:

Primarily Kenya is an African territory, and His Majesty's Government think it necessary definitely to record their considered opinion that the interests of the African natives must be paramount and that if, and when, those interests and the interests of the immigrant races should conflict, the former should prevail . . . in the administration of Kenya, His Majesty's Government regard themselves as exercising a trust on behalf of the African population, and they are unable to delegate or share this trust, the object of which may be defined as the protection and advancement of the native races.[27]

---

[26] Tom Mboya, *Freedom and After* (Boston, Mass., Little, Brown and Company, 1963), p. 109. Copyright © 1963 by Tom Mboya.

[27] Marshall A. MacPhee, *Kenya* (New York, Frederick A. Praeger, 1968), pp. 73–74.

Kenya had a considerable settler population, and there were forces in Britain sympathetic to the idea of increasing white immigration and making Kenya a white man's development. MacPhee credits the need for a rationale against Indian voting power as the force that prevented a settler-dominated Kenya from emerging:

this battle between two immigrant races may have done more than anything to safeguard African interests. It provoked the British Government to maintain, as a compromise, and way out of a difficult situation, that the interests of the African people were paramount in any conflict between the three races. So, without the Indian question, Kenya might well have followed Southern Rhodesia and become a self governing colony ruled by a white minority.[28]

African and British relationships

Africans, of course, had mixed emotions toward the British. In many cases, they had very little contact, since the British were generally either large farmers or government officials who had relationships with only a limited circle of Africans. On the other hand, the Indian commercial interests brought them into frequent contacts, often of a somewhat abrasive nature. The British population in Kenya usually ran about one third that of the Indian, which further decreased the frequency of contact as well as diminishing the picture of the British as an economic exploiter or competitor of the African.

Tension between the British and Africans did arise on the question of governmental authority and land tenure. A high proportion of government officials were British, and about one fourth of the arable land of the country had been reserved for British cultivation. This situation was mitigated both by the extent of British participation and by British policies. The role of the British in government and in university education had been so prominent that it seemed obvious that activities in these areas would collapse if there was a sharp and immediate withdrawal of British personnel. Even if such a withdrawal did take place it offered no threat to the personnel involved, since the British had assured civil servants and educators of generous compensation if they lost their position because of Africanization.

The position of the British farmers was quite different. Their land seemed to be a rich prize, and it was obviously the target of African aspirations. On the other hand, the economic viability of the country appeared to depend on exports produced by British farmers. MacPhee summarizes the situation as follows:

For the time being, the European settler was absolutely essential to the economy as Kenya's wealth was wholly agricultural. Rainfall and soil conditions

---

[28] Ibid., pp. 61–62.

allowed intensive production over a fifth of the country—about 41,600 square miles. African agriculture occupied 34,000 square miles, the rest was farmed by Europeans. The settlers produced 80 percent of Kenya's exports, which in 1962 were worth £38 million, and disbursed about £10 million in wages, Kenyatta knew that he could not upset the balance of an already shaky economy. He also knew that even if he had the money to buy out all the settlers, the fact that each square mile of European farming produced £4,150 as against £1,180 from African farming would have been enough to deter him from forcing any sudden change in the settlers' position.[29]

As with the civil servants, the British government recognized the possibility of Africanization and had provided money for the purchase of 1,000,000 acres from British settlers to be turned over to African farmers. This provided for a relatively painless transfer of as much land as the Africans could absorb in a short period of time. Even these concessions were not enough to altogether reassure the British settlers, and a fairly large exodus prompted the Kenyan government to make reassuring statements and promises about the security of the British in the future in the country. Other instances of British-African collaboration were found in continued investment by British firms, grants-in-aid by the British government, and the use of British troops to put down a revolt in the early days of the independent Kenya regime.

Indians at first regarded themselves as being in competition with the British for a dominant position in the nation. Later they recognized the inevitability of African nationalism, and Indian businessmen often financially aided African leaders. However, the effort to form an Indian-African alliance foundered on suspicions on both sides. The Indians were obviously fearful of what might happen to their status under Africanization, while the Africans were smarting under past and present snubs and inclined to criticize the Indian role in the society. The differential in interpretation by Africans of the British and Asian contribution is born out by attitude surveys:

TABLE 4–3

Reactions of 653 Africans to the following statements: Europeans (a) and Asians (b) "don't like Africans to learn anything that will help them to get a job."

	(percentages)	
	a	b
True	32	78
(Completed primary education)	(40)	(73)
(Some secondary education)	(24)	(77)
(Completed secondary education)	(29)	(82)
(Elders)	(34)	(92)
False	65	18
No opinion	4	4
Total	101	100

Source: Donald Rothchild, "Ethnic Inequalities in Kenya," *Journal of Modern African Studies*, 7 (December 1969), p. 703.

[29] Ibid., pp. 173–74.

The question of citizenship

The fears and hopes of Asians, British, and Africans came to a focus when the date for Kenyan independence was set. Both British and Indians were minority groups who had been living under the protection of the United Kingdom. How would they fare when an African majority was in control of the government?

The Indians had been given British citizenship and passport privileges, which meant that, both for the Indians and British, the United Kingdom could, supposedly, be a place of refuge if life in Kenya became too difficult. On the other hand, in many cases both Indians and British had either been born in the country or had been brought there at an early age, and Kenya was considered their native land. Both their associations and their economic interests were deeply rooted in Kenya and not easily transferable. As far as the Africans were concerned, the aliens were both colleagues and competitors. Their capital and skill would be constructive in a nation lacking in both and anxious for economic advance. On the other hand, their entrenched position in government, business and education might be seen as a roadblock to African aspirations.

Existing jobs and businesses occupied by aliens were obvious targets of African nationalism. Yet the issue was far from clear-cut, for the question remained how to accommodate the millions of Africans who were leaving subsistence agriculture and seeking wage employment. This wage employment could only be provided through industrialization and economic development, which, in turn, required massive injections of capital. The obvious sources, both for entrepreneurial leadership and for capital formation, were the Indian and British businessmen already in the country. Their cooperation was not likely to be forthcoming if the incoming independent regime regarded Africanization as an excuse to throw aliens out of jobs and to confiscate their economic holdings.

The fears of the aliens of hostile acts by an African government were to some extent countered by the gains from remaining in a familiar area in which they already had a large investment. For Africans, the gain from seizing economic assets, or by replacing alien workers with Africans, were countered by the damage which might result from an indiscriminate withdrawal of alien capital and business talent. This question may be highlighted to some extent by a manpower analysis in the government of Kenya development plan for 1964 to 1970 which indicated a shortage of over 47,000 in the highest categories of skilled manpower, a shortage which would be aggravated if the nation were deprived of European and Asian talent.[30]

The point at which conflicting motives were supposedly resolved was

---

[30] Government of Kenya, *Development Plan* 1964–1970 (Nairobi, Government Printer, 1964), p. 136.

in the granting of citizenship to non-Africans. Before independence the question of Kenyan citizenship had not been important. The colonial government maintained the rights of everyone in the country, while a United Kingdom passport gave the needed facility for international travel. However, it was apparent that any African government would soon make a distinction in its treatment of aliens and citizens and the question whether and on what terms aliens or non-Africans could become citizens of the new country was obviously important. On the surface, the provision for citizenship appeared to be quite liberal. A Kenya-born non-African with one parent born in Kenya could qualify automatically for citizenship if he foreswore allegiance to other countries. Others could qualify for naturalization if they made application within two years after independence or by December 1965.[31]

For all concerned, the matter of citizenship was a test of good faith. As far as Africans were concerned, they looked with a good deal of suspicion upon applications for citizenship, since they felt that such applications might be motivated by personal interest rather than a desire to identify with the Kenyan nation. Nevertheless, the fact that an application had been made was one indication of Kenyan identity whereas rejection of citizenship was definitely interpreted as a desire to remain out of the mainstream of the country.

For aliens, citizenship meant trading the degree of security represented by a British passport for the uncertain protection of an African government. Aliens were afraid that there might be two classes of citizens and that citizens of non-African origin would become second-class nationals. They feared that even citizenship would not be a safeguard against policies to take over alien privileges in the name of African improvement. If one opted for Kenyan citizenship, would this guarantee him an equality of rights in Kenya or would he still find that his business might be taken away or his employment terminated on the grounds of his national origin? Or even worse, was it not possible that his citizenship, once granted, might be rescinded and he might become a stateless person, deported from Kenya and without rights in any other land?

Such questions were responsible for a rather considerable hesitation in applying for citizenship. In 1963, there were approximately 180,000 Indians in Kenya. Of these, 50,000 were qualified for citizenship by virtue of birth, while 20,000 more applied. The European response was even more hesitant, since only 2,000 out of a population of 60,000 made application for citizenship, although some 4,000 others were eligible under the birthright provisions. Approximately 10,000 of the applications for citizenship were made in the last few weeks of time alloted and were very

---

[31] D. Rothchild, "Kenya's Minorities and the African Crisis over Citizenship," *Race*, 9 (No. 4, 1968).

slowly processed by the Kenyan government, leading to additional doubts, in the minds of the Indians particularly, as to the good faith of the offer.[32] The Asian attitude toward Kenyan citizenship is indicated in responses to a survey undertaken by Rothchild and Marris:

> From the way the government is handling the matter, I don't think there is any advantage of citizenship for non-Africans . . . The biggest disadvantage is that a non-African can be deprived of his citizenship—but not an African.
>
> There is no promise of getting jobs and if they are thrown out they will be stateless.
>
> Even citizens are deported . . . The people are not treated according to their citizenship, but according to their colour.
>
> For some time preference (for citizens) will be given in civil service and other high posts. But if an African is available the non-African citizen will be left in the cold . . . In times of trouble the country might not regard the non-Africans as full fledged members of the country and that would spell trouble. Moreover it is difficult to go overseas or to send children overseas for further education.
>
> There is no future. The government prefers *black* Africans only.[33]

Post-independence developments have confirmed to some extent the fears of the Asians. Kenyan citizens of Asian, and a few of British descent, have been thrown out of employment to make places for Africans or have been denied a permit to do business. Also a few Kenyan citizens of both Asian and British background have been deprived of citizenship and deported. Thousands of noncitizen Asians have been denied a permit to engage in trade or have been dismissed from governmental or private employment. Britons, by contrast, have received fairly good treatment and, in 1970, the number of Britons entering Kenya actually exceeded those who were leaving.

The panic among Asians became so great that there was a mass rush to escape to Great Britain while that possibility remained open. This migration, in turn, stimulated anticolored feeling among Britons and resulted in the British government's also deciding that perhaps citizenship had one meaning for natives and another for those considered aliens. This led to a restriction of immigration among Asian holders of United Kingdom passports, a topic which is discussed in the chapter dealing with intergroup relations in France and Great Britain.

The process of Africanization is a continuous one with no end in sight. Asian firms have put their stock up for public sale and even awarded stock without payment to longtime African employees, while other Asian busi-

---

[32] Vincent Cable, "The Asians of Kenya," *African Affairs,* 68 (July 1969), p. 223.

[33] Donald Rothchild, "Citizenship and National Integration: The Non-African Crisis in Kenya," *Studies in Race and Nations,* University of Denver, Vol. 1, Study No. 3, 1969–1970, p. 16.

nessmen have gone into partnership with Africans. These steps, however, seem ineffective in gaining more than a temporary respite from the demands for Africanization. An indication of the process involved may be seen in a story in the *New York Times* in January 1970.

Special to the New York Times

Nairobi, Kenya, Jan. 10—Nearly a thousand Asian traders in Kenya have been ordered by the Ministry of Commerce and Industry to close their businesses by June. The ministerial notices informed the traders that their licenses would not be renewed.

Many of the traders affected are noncitizens, although of 400 in Nairobi, a large number claim to have Kenyan citizenship.

One Asian shopkeeper with Kenyan citizenship noted Government assurances that all citizens would be treated alike in their applications for trading licenses. But he added Kenya appears to be treating Asians as second-class citizens.

Last year 730 Asian traders were ordered to close their businesses and leave Kenya, according to a ministry spokesman. More than half of those businesses —mostly retail shops—have since been taken over by Africans. The Government has established a financing organization to provide loans for African traders to enter business.[34]

The Indian resident in independent Kenya is indeed a "marginal man." If he decided against citizenship and held his United Kingdom passport, he has few legal rights in Kenya and has a wait of several years before his number will be reached on the British immigration quota. If he opted for Kenyan citizenship, it is possible that his application still may not have been acted upon or that citizenship may be revoked once it has been granted. Even if citizenship remains intact, this is no guarantee of equal treatment and the permanent secretary of the Kenyan Ministry of Commerce and Industry has reminded Indians that the government has an absolute right to issue trading licenses as it pleases whether the applicants are citizens or noncitizens.[35] In these circumstances, it is perhaps surprising that the Kenyan exodus has not been even greater than it has been; the answer to that may be that the unfortunate Indian has no place to turn, since neither India nor the United Kingdom will give him unrestricted entry. Table 4–4 gives a picture of the non-African population of Kenya which indicates that there has been a drop of only a thousand Indians between 1964 and 1969. This, of course, is partially explained by the fact that normal population growth would have probably produced an increase of around forty thousand Indians in the same period and thus

---

[34] *New York Times* (Jan. 11, 1970).

[35] Lawrence Fellows, "For Kenya, It's an Economic Purge," *New York Times* (Jan. 19, 1968), p. 8, IV. Copyright © 1970 by The New York Times Company. Reprinted by permission.

TABLE 4–4

Population
(mid-year estimates in thousands)

| Year | African | Non-African | | | | | Total |
		Asian	European	Arab	Other	Total	
1964 ..	8,832	183	49	36	4	272	9,104
1965 ..	9,097	185	42	37	4	268	9,365
1966 ..	9,370	188	43	38	4	273	9,643
1967 ..	9,651	192	42	39	4	277	9,928
1968 ..	9,941	182	42	40	4	268	10,209
1969 ..	10,239	182	38	41	4	265	10,504

Source: Statistics Division, *Kenya Statistical Digest*, 1969, Vol. 7, p. 4.

in spite of the apparent stability of numbers, there has been a very considerable migration.

African and Western views of citizenship

To one viewing the question of citizenship in legalistic terms, the Kenyan tendency to create two classes of citizens seems to be a gross breach of faith. This, however, is apparently a concept which only a nation with a comparatively secure position for its indigenous inhabitants can accept, and it should be noted that not even Great Britain was able to maintain this position in the face of what seemed to be a threat of rather massive Asian immigration. For the African to accept the notion that citizenship gave non-Africans equal status with Africans would be to deny the meaning of independence, which is seen not just as gaining political power but as regaining a patrimony almost lost to alien exploitation.

Both Asians and Europeans in Kenya have been criticized for their hesitation in applying for Kenyan citizenship, but this reluctance may have been a saving grace. There is at least a fighting chance that Kenya can absorb most of those who did apply, but a larger number might have been impossible to absorb in a manner compatible with African expectations. One authority makes the dire comment: "If most of the Kenyan Asians had responded to the offer of citizenship they could have provided the fuel for a pogrom of the 1970s."[36]

The tragedy of the situation is that the Africans were probably misguided about their own interests both from a short-run and a long-run viewpoint. No country has an excess of dynamic, venturesome, productive, hard-working people. The capital and the enterprise of the Indian community, if left free to operate, could have increased prosperity for Indian and African alike. Two hundred thousand Indians would not have

---

[36] Vincent Cable, "The Asians of Kenya," p. 219.

been a large enough group to have filled all the desirable economic niches, but it would have been large enough to have greatly facilitated Kenyan economic development. However, this is a lesson which has been hard for the West to learn, if indeed it has, and one that could hardly be expected to impress a newly independent people with a still fresh memory of historic racial inequities.

One of the fortunate aspects of development in the United States was that enterprising foreigners could come to America freely for more than a hundred years before immigration barriers shut off the flow. The newly independent countries do not have this long a time span to allow the infusion of fresh elements in the body politic and will no doubt pay the price in a more slowly developing economy. Arguments for the justice or even the wisdom of citizenship policy are largely irrelevant. The formal provisions for Kenyan citizenship ran against popular prejudice, and in this kind of contest the formal provisions usually have less effectiveness than their wording would indicate.

CONCLUSIONS

The Indians in Kenya and the Chinese in the Philippines were both marginal trading peoples acting as intermediaries between native peoples and European colonial powers. In the Philippines, first the Spanish, and then the Americans found the Chinese valuable in exchanging Western manufactured goods for export crops, while in Kenya the Indian traders served the same function. The Indians and the Chinese far outnumbered the British in Kenya and the Spanish (as well as the Americans) in the Philippines and sought to challenge their control. Neither group was supported in this effort by its home government, and both had to concede dominance to the Europeans. The British justified their dominance in terms of protecting African interests. The Spaniards, having little commitment to democratic forms, did not find this necessary but operated in terms of frank self-interest. The American regime restricted Chinese immigration on the basis of protecting Filipino rights. The controversy in Kenya between Briton and Indian forced a declaration of African priority from the British which may have been a major factor in preventing Kenya from becoming a settler controlled area like Rhodesia. The Spaniards at intervals engaged in the massacre or expulsion of the Chinese but, for the most part, all the colonial powers protected the commercial activities of the marginal trading peoples. As the growth of the export crops increased both the Chinese and the Indians flourished; several in each group accumulated sizeable fortunes, and the average occupied an economic status midway between the representatives of the colonial power and the indigenous population.

The Chinese had much similarity to the Filipinos, both in culture and in physical appearance, and assimilation and intermarriage were rapid in spite of ethnocentrism in both groups. At the same time, Chinese culture had less prestige than Spanish or American, and, while the Chinese were respected for their economic abilities, they never acquired the prestige of the colonial powers. In fact, the tendency of the Filipinos to be somewhat Hispanicized or Americanized increased the attraction of Filipino culture for the Chinese and diluted feelings of superiority. The Indians found a sharp contrast between themselves and the Africans in both physical appearance and culture, and neither assimilation nor intermarriage was very widespread. Both the Africans and the Indians were drawn to British culture, but neither regarded the other as a very good representative of British culture nor did the two groups have mutual respect for their indigenous cultures. Separate schools and chambers of commerce were maintained by both the Chinese and Indians. The Indians maintained separate, mostly non-Christian, religious establishments. The Chinese had few non-Christian centers of worship and, for the most part, were either Protestant or Catholic, although usually in parishes separate from the Filipinos. Both Chinese and Indian faced charges of being clannish and conspiring against the indigenous population.

Independence brought the question of citizenship to the forefront for both Indians and Chinese, since the new governments had scant concern for the rights of "aliens." In the Philippines the doctrine of *jus soli* was succeeded by the more restrictive doctrine of *jus sanguinis,* while naturalization became difficult and there was a tendency to consider the naturalized citizen as a second-class citizen. In Kenya, the processing of citizenship applications was slow and citizens of non-African origin might be denied jobs or business permits or might even be deported from the country. Many of the Kenya Indians had British passports, but British restrictions made these virtually worthless when the British were alarmed by what seemed like a mass rush from Kenya to Britain. Both the Philippines and Kenya enacted drastic curtailments of the economic activity of aliens which were more restrictive on Asians than on British or Americans.

Future indications are that restrictions will continually be increased on both Chinese and Indians. The Chinese have literally no place which they see as an alternative to Philippine residence, while the 1,500 Indians allowed to enter Britain each year are less than the natural increase of the Indian population. Both groups are natural scapegoats and both may suffer in time of severe social tension. The Indians are a highly visible group and seem fated to lead a marginal existence for a long time. It is somewhat easier for the Chinese to amalgamate with the Filipino population, and with the restriction of immigration they may ultimately disappear as a distinct group. The fact that anti-Americanism is currently the more popular slogan of the young Filipino nationalists may diminish the scape-goat role of the Chinese and facilitate their assimilation in Philippine society.

KENYA INDIAN AND PHILIPPINE CHINESE BEHAVIOR PATTERNS IN RELATION TO GENERALIZED BEHAVIOR PATTERNS

Indian and Chinese pattern. Indians and Chinese quickly took over a middleman function as collectors of export crops and distributors of European trade goods. These were functions which neither the colonial power nor the indigenous people seemed able to assume.

Generalized pattern. Especially with functions such as making loans, or buying crops which involve potential conflict, members of a minority may be more successful than either the colonial or the indigenous group.[37]

Indian and Chinese pattern. High rates of intermarriage between Chinese and Filipinos and low rates between Indians and Africans paralleled the greater physical and cultural similarity between Chinese and Filipino.

Generalized pattern. Intermarriage is favored by a similarity in either cultural practices or physical appearance.

Indian and Chinese pattern. Both Indians and Chinese fared better under colonial than under independent governments.

Generalized pattern. Governments of industrialized societies are likely to be more interested in the overall rate of economic development, while those of developing societies are more concerned about the role of their nationals in existing economic enterprise. Either type of society may engage in discrimination in behalf of its nationals, but this is likely to be more extreme in the developing society with fewer rewards to share.

Indian and Chinese pattern. In spite of Indian conflict with the British and Chinese aid to Filipinos in the revolt against Spanish control, the Indians and Chinese are not regarded as allies of nationalistic movements.

Generalized pattern. Nationalistic movements will avoid any ethnic alliance which dilutes their identification with the ethnic majority.

Indian and Chinese pattern. Both Filipino and Kenyan governments have been accused of making naturalization difficult and of treating naturalized citizens differently than others.

---

[37] See discussion on this point in Hubert M. Blalock Jr., *Toward A Theory of Minority-Group Relations* (New York, John Wiley & Sons, 1967), pp. 83–84, Also, Edna Bonacich, "A Theory of Middleman Minorities," *Am. Soc. Review,* Vol. 38, No. 2, (October 1973), pp. 583–94.

Generalized pattern. Governments are not likely to honor contractual obligations to minority ethnic groups when these conflict with majority sentiment.

QUESTIONS

1. What is meant by the term *marginal trading people?* Why are nations often ambivalent in their reaction to members of this group?
2. How do you explain the alternating policies of hostility and protection of the Spanish toward the Chinese in the Philippines?
3. What evidence is there of the assimilation of Chinese in the Philippine society? Does this indicate an easing of tensions between Chinese and Filipinos?
4. What is meant by *jus soli* and *jus sanguinis?* Why was the latter concept more appealing to Filipinos?
5. What was the effect of Philippine independence on the status of the Chinese?
6. Compare the suitability of Americans and Chinese for the role of scapegoat in the Philippines. Why is there more anti-American feeling now than when the United States held a more powerful and privileged position in the Philippines?
7. How does the situation of the Chinese in the United States compare with that of the Chinese in the Philippines? Is there any group in the United States whose situation is at all similar to that of the Chinese in the Philippines?
8. What is the role of the Chinese schools? Would their elimination lead to improved Chinese-Filipino relations? Why or why not?
9. In Kenya what was the attitude of Africans, British, and Indians toward each other?
10. How did conflict between the Indians and the British affect the position of the Africans?
11. How do you account for the difficulties that arose in regard to Kenyan citizenship? Would there have been less friction if all resident Indians and British had applied for citizenship immediately?
12. Is there any tendency for the assimilation of the Indians in African society? If Indians were less ethnocentric would this increase their acceptance by Africans?
13. What was the affect of Kenyan independence on the status of the Indians? Which nation do you feel discriminated most against the Indians, Kenya or Great Britain? What does that indicate about the level of racism in each country?
14. Did Kenyan and Filipino society make a net economic gain by discriminating against the Indians and the Chinese?
15. How would you explain the economic success of the Chinese in the Philippines and of the Indians in Kenya?
16. Is Kenya guilty of genocide? If not, what further steps against the Indians would justify this allegation?

Chapter 5

Mexico: A successful case of amalgamation

Frequently, the description of intergroup adjustments is one of mounting conflict in which moments of peace and tranquility are transient and fleeting, while the underlying tensions seem to be continually growing. Fortunately, there are a few examples of countries which give promise of a happier intergroup relationship. None has a perfect situation, but each has some degree of harmonious adjustment. One is Switzerland, where peoples of diverse religion and national background have been able, in spite of occasional friction, to live cooperatively and peacefully in a federally organized society which is under a common government. Another, and greatly different, sign of promise is the record of assimilation and Americanization in the United States. This is a process which has enabled a great many people, particularly those of European background, to minimize differences of national origin and to find unity in a common allegiance to the American nation. Another situation is found in the Republic of Mexico, where both cultural assimilation and biological amalgamation are making one people from a varied collection of blacks, Indians, and whites.

In a world in which ethnic separatism appears to be growing, the movement of the peoples of Mexico toward a common culture and a common sociobiological classification is a situation worthy of notice. This does not indicate that the Mexican development is the result of deliberate planning. It would have been difficult to have predicted the current harmony on the Mexican ethnic scene from a survey of events of the last 400 years. Indeed, almost all the deliberate policies undertaken in the society were of an ethnocentric character which might reasonably be expected to have intensified ethnic divisions. The tendency toward amalgamation to a common physical type and assimilation to a common culture is a classic illustration of the fact that human actions may have entirely unintended consequences.

The territory we now know as "Mexico" was occupied, before the Spaniards entered, by many Indian peoples speaking different languages, occupying separate regions, and varying greatly in the complexity of their culture and social organization. Some of the Indian ethnic collectivities were organized as simple tribal societies; others had developed highly complex states, including multi-ethnic empires. The Spanish entered the country as white overlords and, when the Indians proved to be not altogether satisfactory as slaves, introduced thousands of blacks from Africa to take the role of slave labor. The Indians were demoralized through their defeat by Spanish arms, were divided by internal conflicts between themselves, and except for a few tribes in remote regions, found many important aspects of their culure completely shattered. The blacks were powerless slaves and were apparently as brutally treated as slaves in Brazil or in the United States. The Spaniards, for their part, were ethnocentric in both their biological and their cultural attitudes. A campaign of systematic cultural destruction was inaugurated by the conquering armies which destroyed many of the temples and city residential dwellings erected by the more advanced Indian tribes.

Actual genocide was approached in the imposition of conditions of servitude so harsh that the Indian population decreased to a mere fraction of its size before the Spanish entry. Biologically, the ideal was the Caucasoid physical type. This was an ideal considered so important that the population of colonial Mexico was divided along minute biological classifications so that a slight variation in the proportion of Spanish ancestry would place people in an entirely different type of category.

It is difficult to conceive of a society which was more ethnocentric in the attitude of its governing classes or in which the minority had been more completely subdued than colonial Mexico. The two agencies which made some effort to ameliorate the situation, the Roman Catholic Church and the central Spanish government, proved to be ineffective. Both church and central government made many pronouncements in favor of a humane treatment of Indians and, to a lesser extent, of the blacks, but neither was in a position to enforce this viewpoint on the Spanish settlers. Hence, there was no power in the society under which blacks and Indians could expect protection. The movement from an emphasis on precise and exclusive racial definition to a mestizo physical type and from cultural conflict to assimilation and accommodation is certainly one that ran against the intentions and desires of many of the people in a dominant position in Mexican society.

There are six tendencies in intergroup relations which emerge rather clearly from a study of the Mexican situation: (1) deliberate policies are often altered by crescive (unplanned) developments; (2) elaborate classifications based on heredity tend to collapse because of their own cumbersomeness and complexity (also noted in Chapter 7); (3) movement from one ethnic classification to another is facilitated when biological and social criteria are mixed; (4) legal institutional equality facilitates the social mobility of an ethnic group even when it has limited power and status; (5) the status of a once denigrated ethnic group is enhanced when it becomes a symbol of nationality; (6) the rate of sexual activity involving members of a subordinate and a dominant group tends to be higher when there is an unequal sex ratio in the dominant group.

In this chapter we will trace how the shift from arrogant racism to amalgamation and assimilation occurred, and perhaps the place to begin is with the Indians before the Spanish Conquest.

BEFORE THE CONQUEST[1]

The history of the Indians in Mexico is characterized by frequent warfare, which at times escalated into major and prolonged battles and sometimes involved several tribes simultaneously. It appears that few, if any, tribes were left in peace for any prolonged length of time; for many of them to have created and maintained an advanced culture under such adversity speaks highly of their industriousness, creativity, and perseverance. Cultural diffusion, often a latent function of conflict, did occur among the warring factions; and, as most of the larger tribes in the valley were Nahuatl-speaking people, the borrowing process was made easier. This is not meant to imply that cultural distinctiveness was eradicated and that we should look upon the Indians as constituting a homogeneous cultural entity. On the contrary, most of the tribes, even those conquered and forced to pay tribute, struggled to maintain their own uniqueness. Tribal ethnocentrism was a major prop for unity; hence fierce pride in their own culture may be viewed as directly contributing to their intense contempt and hostile attitude against outsiders. Such attitudes made it extremely unlikely that conflicts would diminish in frequency and scope or that intertribal unity could be developed.

Most of the Indian tribes showed little differentiation in physical fea-

---

[1] This section is based to a great extent on Charles Gibson, *The Aztecs under Spanish Rule* (Stanford, Stanford University Press, 1964), and Alma M. Reed, *The Ancient Past of Mexico* (New York, Crown Publishers, 1966).

tures, but biological resemblance was not strong enough to counteract the cultural differences and tribal rivalries leading to conflict. The presence of conflict among biologically similar Indians is one of the many indications that the presence of observable racial differences is not a necessary precondition for human conflict. The Indians fought among themselves even as whites had struggled in Europe. When the Spanish came to Mexico they found it possible to make alliances with many of the Indian tribes that felt oppressed by the Aztecs; 20 years after the capture of Cauhtemoc, the Aztecs joined the Spanish to crush a revolt by the Mixtecs.

Cultural and not racial differences can be blamed for many of the conflicts, and sheer desire to exercise control over certain territory and its inhabitants cannot be dismissed as an important motivating force among the Indians. The latter desire became an overriding fact when a "native bureaucracy" became an institutionalized pattern among the more politically sophisticated Indians. This pattern was an oppressive system that destroyed self-rule and placed the conquered people in a subordinate status in which they were forced to pay tribute to the conquerors.

The tribe which instituted this bureaucratic type of organization and which had hegemony over all nearby tribes was the Aztecs. They had come into the area known as the Valley, the district around Mexico City, in the 13th century when it was already occupied by other tribes. They managed to resist subjugation and to expand their area of influence. Eventually, the valor of their armies and the skill of their diplomacy so increased their power that many of the Indians in Mexico had to acknowledge their supremacy. The Aztec administrative apparatus was designed to draw tribute of gold, rubber, corn, and feathered plumes from a wide area. They were also an urbanized people and in Tenochtilán (now Mexico City) had developed an urban complex of over 300,000 population with a canal system for transport, tremendous markets, and impressive palaces and temples. Aztec dominance was designed to get not only tribute, but also victims for human sacrifice, a custom which had apparently been growing in the years immediately preceding the Spanish invasion and one which rendered real reconciliation with subject tribes impossible.

THE SPANISH CONQUEST OF MEXICO

The story begins on February 10, 1519—over a century before the Pilgrims landed on the eastern coast of North America. On this date Hernando Cortez, a 34-year-old Spanish adventurer, sailed west from Cuba with 11 small ships and 633 men. He eventually landed on the coast of Mexico, and in a period of about 20 years conquered this vast area, including several Indian peoples, on behalf of the King of Spain. The odds against him were tremendous. The numbers of his men were small, they had practically no protection against the health hazards of this strange land, they were totally ignorant of the terrain and of the culture of the society, and were overwhelmingly outnumbered. They did have certain advantages operating in their favor: one was that the Mexicans, who had never seen Europeans before, were for a long time confused about whether the European intentions were malign or benevolent. There was, of course, the legend of Quetzalcoatl, the blond god whose return had been foretold by the priests, and one could hardly be sure whether these Spaniards with their white faces were really humans or gods. Furthermore, the Spaniards were able to literally breathe thunder and lightning by the use of guns, and their mobility had been greatly accelerated by the horse. The Spanish contingent was small, but it had a semidivine aura about it; it was far more mobile than anything the Mexican Indians had been able to discover and its muskets and cannons gave it a major death-dealing power.

Nevertheless, the odds against the Spaniards were formidable, and time and time again the little band of men barely escaped annihilation. Their final victory is perhaps accounted for, in large part, by the determination of Cortez, who burned his ships behind him, making retreat impossible, while Montezuma, the Aztec head of state, vacillated between resistance and conciliation. At one time, Cortez was nearly overwhelmed by the superior numbers of the Aztecs, but he was able to raise allies among other Indian tribes, who welcomed this opportunity to throw off the Aztec domination, and he eventually assembled an army of Indian allies who may have actually outnumbered the Aztecs. In the meantime Montezuma had died in Spanish captivity and had been replaced by the legendary Cauhtemoc, who led a valiant but futile resistance to Spanish domination. The ensuing battles resulted in the defeat of Aztec armies, after which the Spaniards turned on their Indian allies and quickly brought a major part of the country under Spanish rule.[2]

There was a short period of indirect rule through the Indian chiefs, whom the Spanish designated as *caciques,* but this quickly gave way to a system of direct rule in which the land was partitioned in *repartimentos,* which were great grants of land alloted to individual Spaniards but supposedly under the supervision of representatives of the Spanish Crown. The *repartimento* was a minor modification of the *encomienda* system. The distinction sought by the *repartimento* was that the Spaniard to whom a grant was made was acting as an agent of the Spanish Crown rather than as a proprietor. This distinction gave the legal basis for government protection of the Indians, but the de jure protection seldom resulted in any action which challenged the serflike condition of the Indians. The deed authorizing *encomiendas* read as follows: "Unto you, so and so, are given in trust [*se os encomiendan*—hence these distributions were called *en-*

---

[2] Our account of Cortez follows Caesar C. Cantus, *Cortez and the Fall of the Aztec Empire* (Los Angeles, Modern World Publishing Co., 1966).

comiendas] under chief so and so, with the chief so many Indians, for you to make use of in your farms and mines; and you are to teach them the things of the holy Catholic faith." The Spanish Crown occasionally tried to protect Indians, as in the order of Philip II that the clergy should not whip Indians or confine them in stocks, or the command of Queen Isabella that no one should destroy the native's personal liberty. The laws, however, had to be carried out by those opposed to its intent and the frequent reaction, was, *obedzco pero no cumplo* ("I obey but I do not carry out").[3]

Toward the Indians, churchmen such as Bartolmé de las Casas felt a paternalistic concern. Spreading Christianity had been a major part of the rationale of Spanish conquest and was hardly compatible with a wholesale destruction of Indian life and society. Las Casas made many petitions to the Crown for better treatment of Indians and is said to have refused absolution to Spaniards who owned Indian slaves. Las Casas was joined by other priests who became advocates of Indian liberty but they were a small minority within the church itself and had very little influence on the general society. In fact, Las Casas was even under fire by other clerics who advocated the usual treatment for troublesome priests—recall to Spain and assignment to a monastery.[4]

The church did not escape the dilemma between planting the cross and finding gold. Both individual churchmen and religious orders became involved in agricultural developments and in the erection of monasteries and churches in which the church was taskmaster and the Indian the laborer. The situation is thus described by the second archbishop of Mexico:

Some check should be put upon the extravagant expenditures, excessive personal services, and sumptuous and superfluous works for which the monastic brotherhoods are responsible in the villages of these Indians, entirely at the cost of the latter. Some of the monasteries in places where there are not more than two or three monks would be inordinately superb even in Valladolid. The Indians are driven there like beasts of burden, five or six hundred of them, without pay or even a mouthful of food, and compelled to come four, six and twelve leagues to work. I have seen two monasteries, one of which must have cost eight or ten thousand ducats, the other a little less; both were finished inside of a year, by the money, sweat, and personal labor of the poor. Some Indians die of the scant food and of this work to which they are not accustomed . . . and if the Indians do not come they are thrown into jail and whipped. Moreover it is entirely common to see richer ornamentation . . . than may be found in the chapel of Your Majesty. The personal service of these Indians in the monasteries is excessive; they serve as gardeners, porters, sweepers, cooks, sextons,

---

[3] Ernest Gruening, *Mexico and Its Heritage* (New York, Greenwood Press, 1968), pp. 24–25.

[4] Fr. Bartolmé de las Casas, *Historia de las Indias*, Vol. 3, Chapter 3, cited Ibid., p. 14.

and messengers without receiving a penny. . . . And the cost of all these edifices and of the rich and superfluous adornment is secured by assessments levied upon these wretched people.[5]

Many of the Indians were enslaved and the rest were grouped in small nucleated villages where they had local self-government subject to the supervision of higher Spanish authority. They were required to give a certain number of days of labor as tribute, but were otherwise considered to be fairly free. This situation resulted in a continued conflict between the colonists and the representatives of the Crown, and sometimes, of the Church. The colonists almost invariably won out in such fashion that increasingly the Indian population became regarded as a subservient group with few rights of any kind. Some estimate of the effect of these measures may be gained from the population statistics which indicate that, while the population of Mexico at the time of the Spanish entry was estimated at 13–20 million, by 1646, a little over a century later, it had diminished to under 3 million—a point from which it began gradually to rise, but it did not reach the 20 million figure until 1940.[6]

ROLE OF THE BLACKS

Both the Crown and the Church took a different attitude toward black slavery than they did toward Indian slavery. Royal decrees throughout the latter part of the 16th century prohibited the use of Indians in such activities as sugar processing and crop production, which were considered inimical to their health, and recommended their replacement by black slaves, who were also the recommended source of labor for the mines. Beltran estimates that at least 120,000 slaves were brought into Mexico in the period between 1519 and 1650.[7]

There is an apparent inconsistency between the acceptance of African slavery by state and church and the condemnation of Indian slavery. Slavery had been known in the Mediterranean area for centuries, and it is doubtful that the slavery of any group would necessarily have been shocking to Spanish feelings. Morner comments on the matter as follows:

The question is an intricate one, but I think Charles Verlinden provides the basic explanation by stating that Indian enslavement was a threat against

---

[5] Anacona, "Historia de Yucatan," Vol. 2, p. 71, Obregon, "Los Prescursores de la Independencia," p. 133, 194; Rivera Cambas, "Los Gobernantes de Mexico," Vol. 1, p. 159; cited in Gruening, *Mexico and Its Heritage,* p. 174.

[6] Howard F. Cline, *Mexico* (New York, Oxford University Press, 1963), p. 11, suggests that the 20 million figure is too high and that 13 million might be more realistic for the period immediately preceding the Spanish conquest. The 1970 census reported a total population of 48,313,428.

[7] Aguirre Beltran, "The Integration of the Negro," in Magnus Morner, *Race and Class in Latin America* (New York, Columbia University Press, 1970), p. 25.

"colonial peace," whereas the enslavement of Africans, brought from regions where Europeans did not exercise colonial responsibility, did not present a similar threat. If, instead, Africa had first been colonized, perhaps Indian slaves would have been brought to its plantations! In any case, it is historical fact the Negro slave became the labor force of the plantations in the New World.[8]

In spite of the attitude that blacks were less important than Indians, they were still regarded as having souls, being persons, and having certain rights such as family solidarity and marital privileges. Theoretically, there were methods by which a slave could gain his freedom, such as purchasing his freedom or marrying a freed person. Whatever good intentions the Crown and Church might have toward African slaves, however, were generally frustrated in practice by the slave owners, who saw them only as a source of labor. Davidson summarizes the situation as follows: "That many Negroes were tried and punished in courts and not by their masters seems to have made little difference regarding slave treatment. Repeated evidence reveals that cruelty and mistreatment were as much a part of slavery in colonial Mexico as they were in most slave regimes in the New World."[9]

Another method of controlling the slaves was by separating those who came from the same or nearby tribes in Africa. Those who came from the same linguistic groupings were also separated. They were forced to learn Spanish, and often an Indian language as well.

Even in the absence of complete documentation, one would assume that under similar conditions, the responses of slaves in Mexico did not differ significantly from slaves in the United States or other parts of the world. For example, conduct which would be termed malingering by owners, was a form of protest by slaves. Slaves engaged in passive protest, feigned sickness, broke or hid tools, developed numerous mechanisms to slow down production, "planned" accidents, etc. One of the most overt forms of protest took the form of running away. Escape was a threat to the colonial order because other slaves might be induced to follow the pattern of the runaway. Militia and owners were anxious to capture and return runaways, in order to put down mutinies and rebellions among the slave population.

Over a period of time enough slaves had run away to form sizeable rural communities, which were large enough to attack farms and caravans. Often the authorities would attack these communities and survivors were returned to their owners. Beltran, however, mentions two *palenques* (com-

---

[8] Morner, *Race and Class in Latin America*, p. 112.

[9] David M. Davidson, "Negro Slave Control and Resistance in Colonial Mexico, 1519–1650," *Hispanic American Historical Review*, 56 (August 1966), p. 241. Copyright 1966 by the Duke University Press.

munities of *cimarrones*—runaway or escaped slaves) which were able to wrest some important concessions from the colonial government:

On several occasions the colonial government sought to sign treaties with the *cimarrones*. The most notable efforts occurred in 1608 when San Lorenzo Cerralvo was founded and in 1768 when the Pueblo Nuevo de la Real Corona was established on the banks of the Tonto River. In both cases the *Cimarrones* obtained rights to the land and to municipal self-government along the lines of the Indian republics. The *cimarrones,* unlike the Indians, never formed corporate groups; had this been possible, they would have gone from the slave caste to the Indian caste, instead of remaining in a middle position between the two castes.[10]

The freedman was in a better position than the slave, but he, too, was not accorded full citizenship: he was held responsible for all the duties of a citizen without receiving all the rights and privileges of a citizen. He was forced to pay taxes, and serve in the military but was not allowed to own land. Moreover, he was discriminated against in jobs. Beltran states that the Europeans organized themselves into "feudal-type guilds" which barred "colored persons" from entrance.[11] Thus the latter were forced to seek out unskilled tasks and hire themselves out at subsistence or below subsistence wages. Many of them were unable to find employment and joined the *cimarrones* in the mountains, fought the Europeans, or settled down to eking a living from the soil in agricultural pursuit. The mulattoes were in a position similar to that of the freed black persons in Mexico during colonial times. They were not allowed to own land, but had to pay taxes and serve in the militia. Even in the military the blacks and mulattoes were not allowed to use guns and wear certain uniforms until the militia was replaced by the regular army in 1765.[12]

The slave status of the black inhibited his movement in search of pleasure while denying him the satisfaction of a secure place in a settled community. On the other hand, a sex ratio estimated at three males to one female meant that many of the men had to look for sexual companions outside of the group. Although the black's prestige suffered from the slave stigma, his association with the Spaniards tended to raise his status and to make him a desirable mate in the eyes of the Indian women. The black women for their part were subject to the sexual whims of the slave owners and soon began to bear mulatto offspring.

In spite of the restrictions which surrounded them, the number of slaves of pure African origin tended to decrease and the number of hy-

---

10 Beltran, "The Integration of the Negro," pp. 20–21.

11 Ibid., p. 18.

12 Rolando Melaffe, *Methods y resultados de la politica indiginesta en Mexico* (Memorias de Instituto Nacional Indiginesta, VI) p. 45, cited in Morner, *Race Mixture in the History of Latin America.* Copyright © 1967 by Little, Brown and Co., Inc.).

brids of some African ancestry showed a dramatic increase. Thus, in 1570 there were 20,000 Africans and only 2,500 mulattoes, while in 1646 the number of Africans had grown 50 percent to 35,000 and the number of mulattoes had multiplied 36 times to over 116,000.[13] Eventually, the pure Africans were to practically disappear from the population, while the number of people with some African ancestry became very large indeed.

The number of African slaves who managed to escape from their masters and to find places of refuge became a considerable problem to the Spanish authorities. Davidson summarizes the situation:

It is apparent that officials and slave owners found it extremely difficult to prevent or contain slave resistance. Few in numbers, they were forced to rely on the scarce royal troops in Mexico aided by untrained and undisciplined bands of mestizos and Indians. These haphazard military operations faced serious strategic and tactical problems, especially in campaigns against distant hideaways in the frontier regions. Mexico's rugged terrain compounded the difficulties for fugitives could establish settlements in the mountains and isolated barrancas which afforded excellent defensive sites. Moreover, Indian cooperation seems to have been instrumental to the success of various revolts and made the job of repression all the more difficult. With such a weak system of control, the flight and insurrection of slaves continued into the eighteenth century, and it was only the abolition of slavery in the early nineteenth century that put an end to slave resistance in Mexico.[14]

This ease of flight was one of many factors which rendered black slavery in Mexico a different institution from black slavery in the United States. In essence the difference between the two systems was that the American pattern of slavery was a reasonably stable system until ended by emancipation. In Mexico it was so hard to keep blacks in slave status that most of them had merged into the general population even before the abolition of slavery in 1810.

MESTIZATION

The Spaniards brought very few women with them and sexual relationships, resulting in a mestizo population, began very early in the period of first contact. In fact one female slave, Malinche, presented to Cortez by the Tabascan Indians shortly after his arrival in Mexico, proved a valuable aid in the Spanish operations. She served as interpreter, advised Cortez about the strength of various tribes and is credited with persuading Montezuma to trust himself to Spanish hospitality—an action which soon led to his death. Her relationship with Cortez produced one of the first

---

[13] Beltran, "The Integration of the Negro," p. 18.

[14] Davidson, "Negro Slave Control and Resistance in Colonial Mexico, 1519–1650," p. 252.

mestizos, her son Martin, whose acceptance in Spanish society in indicated by his appointment as a *comendador* of the Society of St. Iago.[15]

In the early days of the Spanish period, Mexican society was characterized by a dualism of conqueror and conquered, Indians and whites. But a society with few Spanish women was also characterized by widespread miscegenation, which eventually brought the end of the dual system because too many people failed to fit either the pure Spanish or the pure Indian category. For the Spanish male, sexual expression became a form of athleticism in which the number of Indian maidens he had impregnated was proof of his virility. Although the Spanish saw race and culture as linked, acculturation did not keep pace with miscegenation. Usually the children of mixed unions remained with their mothers and had only casual contact with their fathers. The Crown permitted interracial marriage and the church encouraged it, but permanent wedlock was a rare phenemenon and most Spanish-Indian liaisons were casual relationships in which the father assumed little responsibility for his offspring. Although the church frowned on concubinage, priests, as well as soldiers, were involved in the miscegenation which produced a mestizo populace. In fact, clerical activity of this kind was so widespread that it was necessary to draw up rules concerning the status of their offspring:

As the slave condition of the mother dictated the bondage of the offspring, mulatto children also became slaves as a matter of course. But there were at least two kinds of legal escape for them; a royal decree, addressed to the officials of the exchequer in Cuba in 1583, considering that some Spanish soldiers there had sired children with slave women owned by the state and now wanted to purchase their freedom, ordered that the fathers be given preference at the auction where their children were to be sold.[1] The other exception dealt with the children of ecclesiastics with slave women. At least the first Mexican Council decreed that "if it so happens that an ecclesiastic . . . has had or maintains lustful relationship with his slave . . . he should be punished according to law, and the Bishop dispose of the slave woman as he sees fit, and the children, if there are any, be set free[2]. . . ."[16]

The mestizo part of the population increased so rapidly that it was estimated to be nearly as large as the European population in 1570 and to surpass the European population by 1646. The Spaniards moved toward a hybrid type of racial situation and, in an effort to assume the proper def-

---

[15] Lucas Alaman, Historia de Mejico, 1849, Vol. 5, No. 1, p. 23, cited in Gruening, *Mexico and Its Heritage*, p. 24.

[16] Magnus Morner, *Race Mixture in the History of Latin America* (Boston, Little, Brown and Co., 1967), p. 42; Copyright © 1967. Interior footnote 1 indicates that statement is based on *Coleccion de documentos para la formacion social de Hispano-america 1493–1810*, II (Madrid 1953–1962) p. 547. Interior footnote 2 indicates a statement taken from Aguirre Beltran, *La poblacion negra de Mexico, 1519–1810: Estudio etnohistoricao* (Mexico, 1946).

erence to people possessing qualities of white ancestry, arranged an elaborate classification system which was said to have had, at times, as many as 46 possible categories. Roncal says that the Parish registers which kept track of births, deaths, and marriages recognized ten different castes:[17]

1. Espanol (habitually entered in special books along with "indios noblis")
2. Indio
3. Negro
4. Mestizo (Spanish and Indian)
5. Castizo (Spanish and Mestizo)
6. Mulatto (Spanish and Negro)
7. Morisco (Spanish and mulatto)
8. Lobo (Indian and Negro)
9. Coyote (Indian and mulatto)
10. Chino (Indian and Lobo)

There were many problems in maintaining an accurate list of the castes, the chief of which was the difficulty of establishing ethnic identity. The ten categories were obviously both close together and overlapping. Also, the belief that social traits and biological heritage were linked could only be maintained by imputing higher ethnic status to those who were socially mobile. Further, the only escape from an impossible bureaucratic tyranny was to accept ethnic self-classification, for, as one administrator reported, "to classify the 'castas' would involve the gathering of odious information, and if rigorously done, very dark stains already eased by time would be uncovered in well-accepted families."[18]

The ideal of a "pigmentocracy" was not given up easily, but even the most zealous administrators found it difficult to enforce. This difficulty is the basis of the complaint of the crown attorney of Mexico to the viceroy in 1770:

The liberty with which the plebs have been allowed to choose the class they prefer, insofar as their color permits, has stained the class of natives as well as that of Spaniards. They very often join the one or the other as it suits them or as they need to. . . . A Mulatto, for instance, whose color helps him somewhat to hide in another "casta," says, according to his whims, that he is Indian to enjoy the privileges as such and pay less tribute, though this seldom occurs, or, more frequently, that he is Spaniard, Castizo or Mestizo, and then he does not pay any (tribute) at all. . . .[19]

By the end of the 18th century, the caste system which included slavery was becoming increasingly unworkable. There were too many marginal men who were difficult to rank within the numerous gradations of that

---

[17] Joaquin Roncal, "The Negro Race in Mexico, *Hispanic American Historical Review*, 24 (Aug. 1944), p. 533.

[18] Aguirre Beltran, *La Poblacion negra de Mexico* (Mexico, 1946), quoted in Morner, *Race and Class in Latin America*, 1967 p. 70.

[19] Jose Antonio de Areche, *Representation hecha ael Exmo Senor Marques de Croix.. June 23, 1770.* Latin American mss. Mexico, Lilly Library, Indiana University, Indiana.

system, and when the successful movement for independence brought an abolition of slavery and of the *castas* system, there was little protest.

Another complicating feature of Mexican racial classifications was the distinction between Spaniards born in Spain, known as the *Peninsulars*, or *Gachupinos,* and those born in Mexico, the *criollos.* The highest positions in church and state were reserved for the Spanish-born—a situation which often made it impossible for a son to achieve the status of his father! Mestizos born in wedlock, for long a small minority of the mestizo group, were accepted as *criollos,* and thus recognized as part of the second highest stratum in Mexican society. While the intention of the preference for the *Gachupinos* was to make a rigidly stratified society in which place of birth as well as race was involved, the effect was to produce in Mexico an alliance between the legitimate mestizos and the Spanish born in Mexico. Eventually this alliance was to spread to the illegitimate mestizos as well, in order to diminish the white-mestizo differentiation.[20]

MEXICAN INDEPENDENCE

The revolution of 1810, which ended Spanish rule and brought independence to Mexico, made some difference in the relations between whites but very little between that of whites and Indians or hybrid groups. The abolition of the *castas* was merely a formal recognition of the collapse of a system; the real change was an alteration in the power position of two groups of whites. The revolution was sparked very largely by a longtime competition for power between the *Gachupinos* and the *criollos.* The royal policy, probably in an effort to maintain a greater degree of control, of favoring the *Gachupinos* became increasingly resented by the *criollos,* and when the Spanish government was weakened by the Napoleonic Wars, they took the opportunity to break the ties with Spain and to establish an independent nation in which the *criollos* would be the dominant element.

Another measure which had considerable effect was the abolition of the *repartimentos* and also of the laws protecting the Indian communities. The *repartimentos* were succeeded by the haciendas, which were private land holdings granting direct ownership of land to one individual who was also permitted to have direct control over the labor force in the locality. The impact of these changes is described by Wolf:

The hacienda, however, proved admirably adapted to the purposes of the colonists who strove for greater autonomy. Unlike the encomienda, it granted direct ownership of land to a manager-owner, and permitted direct control of a resident labor force. Its principal function was to convert community-oriented peasants into a disciplined labor force able to produce cash crops for a supra-community market. The social relationships through which this was accom-

---

[20] Ibid., p. 55.

plished involved a series of voluntary or forced transactions in which the worker abdicated much personal autonomy in exchange for heightened social and economic security.[21]

Through their need for occasional seasonal labor, the haciendas helped to provide small amounts of cash which, in turn, stabilized nearby Indian communities. Since both the Indians and the hacenderos resented the intrusion of any outside forces, they combined forces to preserve a status quo which slowed down, although it did not eliminate, Indian assimilation. The need for a labor force with a complete commitment to the hacienda was met through debt peonage, which tied Indians to the hacienda nearly as securely as slavery or the forced labor required by *repartimentos.* In theory, the hacienda meant the end of special burdens on Indians; in practice, it destroyed what little protection the government had provided for Indian communities.

While Mexican independence and Mexican nationalism were first stimulated to serve the interests of the *criollos,* they had implications for the Indians and mestizos as well. Mestizos, as early as the 18th century, had begun to assume an important position in Mexican social life, and they found that an emphasis on identification as Mexican and a commitment to nationalism tended to legitimate their position. They were working for a society which was based upon achievement rather than ascription by racial category, and hence the process of mestization and Mexican nationalism moved hand in hand. Even for pure-blooded Indians, the barriers to moving into Mexican society in important positions were not insurmountable, and in 1857, the presidency was won by a Zapotec Indian, Benito Juarez, who is sometimes considered the Abraham Lincoln of Mexican history. Juarez announced a reform administration and proceeded to seize Church lands and stop payments on foreign debts. The seizure of Church lands was a part of a long term anticlerical (meaning anticlergy) trend in Mexican politics which involved both the resistance of Spanish colonists against efforts of the Church to ameliorate the lot of the Indians and a protest against the power of the Church in its role as landlord and as director of education. The Church was, at one and the same time, an institution which tried to afford some degree of protection to Indian communities and, on the other hand, the largest landowner, and thereby employer, in Mexico. Any revolutionary or reform movement tended to become anticlerical, but any movement to limit the power and wealth of the Church also weakened the part it might play as a protector of Indian communities.

Financial problems forced Juarez to suspend foreign debt payments; this brought about a tripartite intervention from France, England, and

21 Eric R. Wolf, "Aspects of Group Relations in a Complex Society: Mexico," *American Anthropologist,* 58 (December 1956), p. 1069. Reproduced by permission of the American Anthropological Association.

Spain, who sent troops to Mexico, and ended the Juarez regime. The other nations withdrew when it became apparent that France proposed to become the dominant power in Mexico. The French-appointed ruler, Maximillian, lasted just long enough to give a Parisian appearance to Mexico City and to stimulate nationalistic feeling against foreign influence. At the end of the civil war, diplomatic pressure from the United States caused the French to withdraw their troops, and in 1867, Maximillian was captured and executed. Juarez returned to power until his death in 1872, but the major changes in Mexico during the 19th and early 20th century were brought about by a dictatorial ruler, Porfirio Diaz.

In 1875, Porfirio Diaz became the Mexican president—a post he was destined to hold, with one interruption, until 1910. Diaz was a follower of a Darwinian positivist philolosophy which placed a great deal of faith on free competition and deprecated the possible role of deliberate social reform. During his regime foreign capital was welcome, banditry suppressed, the budget balanced and internal customs duty abolished. The mileage of the railroads increased almost 50-fold, the total values of exports became five times what they were at the time of his inauguration, free schools were established, and public improvements of many kinds were undertaken.[22] In spite of the success in economic development, most of the people felt that prosperity had passed them by; the revolution of 1910 toppled the Diaz regime and led to a period of confusion for several years until a stable and much more nationalistic government emerged.

It is, however, worth looking at some of the racial attitudes which developed in the Diaz regime. The idea that the white man was the end product of evolution was rejected, and the assumption was made by several thinkers that the gradual biological domination of the mestizo was both an inevitable and a healthy type of process with which the state should not interfere. One of the favorite intellectuals of the Diaz regime, the historian and sociologist Andres Molina Enriquez, gives a reluctant admission that the Darwinian hypothesis seems to favor the mestizo:

The mestizo element is the strongest. It is beyond doubt that the mestizo element is the strongest since in a long history they have lasted more than three centuries in the face of immense difficulties, and in the struggle with other groups have achieved preponderance. Their strength comes from indigenous blood and they are in intimate contact and constantly mixing with the indigenous element which is still numerous, they can renew their energies incessantly. Neither the indigenous races nor the mestizo are distinguished, as we have had occasion to say, by either beauty or culture, or, in general by the refinements of the races of very advanced evolution. but by its incomparable adaptation to the environment by the qualities of extraordinary animal strength.[23]

---

[22] James Creelman, *Diaz, Master of Mexico* (New York, Appleton Co., 1911).

[23] Andres Molina Enriques, *Los Grandes Problemas Nacionales* (Mexico A. Carranze, 1909), pp. 42, 262–63; cited in Martin S. Stabb, "Indigenism and Racism in Mexican Thought," *Journal of Inter-American Studies*, 1, (October 1959).

The works of the racist thinkers such as Houston Stewart Chamberlain and Arthur De Gobineau were rejected and, as Stabb indicates,[24] one would have to consider that the emphasis on indigenism in the revolution of 1910 really has roots that go back to an earlier period. The Diaz regime was generally regarded as one of privilege for the propertied interests in Mexico, but this did not mean that it espoused a racist philosophy.

THE REVOLUTION OF 1910

With the fall of Diaz, Mexico entered into what is perhaps the first successful socialist type of revolution in the 20th century. This was a revolution which described itself as being anticapitalist, antiforeign, and anticlerical. It was allied with an Indianist movement to protect Indian rights, although most of its adherents equated mestizo background with a truly Mexican type of nationality. This revolution brought the final seizure of the Church estates and thereby the end of any semblance of communal protection for the Indians. The Indians were regarded on the same basis as other Mexicans with no special protection and with no disabilities. The temper of the times and the turmoil of the revolution favored an increase in internal migration which in turn led to a still greater blending of racial groups, an increase in the proportion of mestizos, and a further drop in the percentage of pure Indians. The revolution of 1910 brought an attack on the haciendas, the remaining Church-owned lands, and the communal holdings of the Indians. Indians were thus freed from the bonds of debt slavery (peonage) and gained more mobility, while outsiders found it easier to buy land within the Indian communities.

On the other hand, legal provision was made for the formation of *ejidos*, cooperative communities owning land in common. The *ejidos* were supported both on the basis of land reform and on a commitment to Indian cultural values. Supposedly the *ejidos* would end the exploitation of Indian peasants, increase production, and be a training ground for democratic participation. Unfortunately these goals required more than land reform; they involved, management, and capital. The management was often both venal and incompetent and capital was in short supply so that, in general, the *ejidos* have failed to reach their objectives. They probably also have the effect of stabilizing an agricultural proletariat which is not really geared to link itself with a modern economy.[25] However, the *ejidos* do represent a concern for Indians and Indian values. Even though their record has been disappointing, one can expect a continual push for expansion and improvement of the *ejidos* with an incidental effect of providing a base for cultural pluralism in the relations of Indians and mestizos.

---

[24] Ibid., p. 6.

[25] Cline, *Mexico*, p. 212; Wolf, *"Aspects of Group Relations in a Complex Society: Mexico,"* pp. 172–73.

Such a base for indigenism will not embrace more than ten percent of the population and whether the *ejidos* will be really viable in either a cultural or an economic sense remains to be seen.

The pattern of land operation has had a great effect on the development of intergroup relations. The original ideal of the development of the two republics; the republic of Spaniards and the republic of the Indians, was vitiated by the failure of attempts to separate the two groups economically. The *repartimento* system was a modification of the *encomienda* whereby the Indians in their labor were to be directed by royal functionaries and the Spanish also were to be dependent on the Crown. Indian communities were organized for the payment of tribute, the provision of forced labor, and the maintenance of churches. The failure of the *repartimento* to preserve Indian communities was only partly due to the remoteness of the Spanish Crown and the corruption of its officials. Another factor in the situation was an unequal sex ratio which led to miscegenation to such an extent that some authors have referred to the subjugation of the Indians by the Spaniards as "the conquest of the women." Economic relationships also tend to break down Indian isolation as permanently employed Indian workers became acculturated to a Spanish model, while the same process worked in reverse as mestizos and mulattoes invaded Indian villages.[26]

Although the maintenance of corporate villages did not prevent miscegenation it did, however, stabilize a poverty-stricken Indian group only lightly touched by modernization and usually speaking an Indian language. On a limited level such Indian villages were complete social units operating in a relatively self-sufficient situation with only limited contact with outsiders. Wolf describes the situation as follows:

> Thus equipped to function in terms of their own resources, these communities became in the centuries after the Conquest veritable redoubts of cultural homeostasis. Communal jurisdiction over land, obligations to expend surplus funds in religious ceremonies, negative attitudes toward personal display of wealth and self-assertion, strong defenses against deviant behavior, all served to emphasize social and cultural homogeneity and to reduce tendencies toward the development of internal class differences and heterogeneity. . . .[27]

Stavenhagen points out that, while the trend in the chaotic periods which made up much of the 19th century was for retreat and isolation of Indians in the more remote and inaccessible parts of the country, this trend was reversed in the latter part of the 19th century.[28] Then increased demand

---

[26] C. E. Marshall, "The Birth of the Mestizo in New Spain," *Hispanic American Review*, 19 (May 1939): 161–84.

[27] Wolf, "Aspects of Group Relations in a Complex Society: Mexico," p. 1067.

[28] Rodolfo Stavenhagen, "Further Comments on Ethnic Relations in Southeastern Mexico," *American Anthropologist*, 66 (Oct. 1964): 1156–1158.

for such cash crops as coffee and sugar and the increased private ownership of land changed the situation. Peasants now produced for an overseas market and ladinos (mestizos) formed the intermediary link between
farm and export market. In one sense, this was a continuation of colonial
relations with function ascribed by race[29] and the Indians were, for the
most part, illiterate peasants while mestizos carried on trade. However, an
increasing number of Indians became acculturated and thus left the Indian classification, while increasingly there was a social class rank, based
on wealth, which categorized Indian and non-Indian alike.

Current statistics indicate that less than ten percent of the population
speak a language other than Spanish as the mother tongue,[30] and apparently Mexican nationality has been built upon a racial blend of European, Indian, and Negro. Many authorities claim that there is no racial
problem or racial consciousness in Mexico at the present time. This statement would have a high degree of truth if one takes race as being
biologically defined. However, the distinction in Mexico is not so much
race as culture. Thus, one authority states that an Indian who is living in
the city or employed in a factory is accepted as a mestizo.[31] However,
those who are culturally Indian may still be an exploited part of the
society, and a nation which expresses its nationalism in terms of a legendary Indian hero, its Catholicism by its adoration of the Indian virgin of
Guadelupe, its artistic values by Diego Rivera and the school of painters
which followed him emphasizing the Indian aspect of the Mexican tradition, may still denigrate those who are culturally Indian at the present
time.

In her analysis of the current place of Indians in Mexico, Iwanska distinguishes between the image of the Indian in Mexican national ideology,
the stereotype of the Indian held by the rest of the population, and the
self-concept of various linguistic groups of Indian tribes.[32] The national
ideology has adopted Cauhtemoc as a symbol of traditional greatness and
a rallying point for a historically based ego structure. Cauhtemoc, the
proud conqueror and legendary hero of past glories, whose real nature is
only vaguely perceived, has become a Mexican cultural hero. However,
the historic image of the Indian has little relationship to stereotypes

---

[29] Pablo Gonzales Casanova, "Internal Colonialism and National Development,"
Studies in Comparative International Development (St. Louis, Social Science Institute, Washington University, Vol. 1, No. 4, 1965), pp. 34–36. Casanova argues that
the position of the Indians versus the mestizos is essentially that of colonial subject
to imperialist, although he admits that the Indian can change his status by assimilating
the dominant culture.

[30] Cline, *Mexico*, p. 96.

[31] Ralph L. Beal, "Social Stratification in Latin America," *American Journal of
Sociology*, 58, (January 1953), p. 338.

[32] Alicja Iwanska, "The Mexican Indian: Image and Identity," *Journal of Inter-
American Studies*, 6 (October 1964): 529–36.

about contemporary Indians. Some of these stereotypes are similar to those traditionally held by white southerners in the United States about blacks, except that the permanence of biological barriers is denied and assimilation is the ideal. In Iwanska's words:

This image of the Mexican Indian held by the average Mexican bears some similarity to the image the white Southerner in the United States has of the so-called "good Negro." But the differences are much greater than the similarities, since the "Indian problem" is supposed to disappear in Mexico through assimilation of Indians while the Negro problem is to white Southerners and to many other Americans as well not a problem at all as long as the Negro "keeps his place" in a segregated society and does not try to merge with "the white race."[33]

In looking at the Indian self-concept, Iwanska refers to a group she regards as somewhat representative, the Mazahuas of central Mexico. First, she notes that they seldom refer to themselves as "Indians," since this has somewhat the same connotation among them that "nigger" has in the United States. They are not much interested in their historic position but are quite proud of their tribal identification. Their self-concept is somewhat similar to the stereotype held of them by other Mexicans. "They think of themselves as primitive, lazy, uncivilized, and often even stupid." On the other hand, they claim such moral virtues as being better Catholics and more trustworthy spouses and parents.

Insofar as they are committed to a governmental allegiance, it is not to the state and local governments, which they regard as either indifferent or controlled by exploitative interests, but to the national government, which was responsible for land distribution and from whose agents they learned that Mazahuas had rights as well as duties. They have thus adopted the rational egalitarian aspects of the Mexican revolution without really being greatly affected by its glorification of a mythological Indian past.[34]

The image of the Aztecs and the Mayans serves to legitimate the notion that Indians are inherently capable people who can be assimilated to mestizo status. It has not led to a vigorous pan-Indian movement, a justification of separatism, or a glorification of the present character of the Indian peasant. The greatness of the historic culture thus becomes an emotional symbol of national greatness but one seen as hardly relevant to current values and concerns. One might summarize the Mexican definition of the situation by saying that the Indians established a great culture which was overthrown by the Spanish, who brought in a culture more adapted to modern needs. The Indians are today a backward element which is a drag on Mexican progress, but by acculturation they can become mestizo and thereby enter the main stream of Mexican life. Differ-

[33] Ibid., p. 533.
[34] Ibid., pp. 534–35.

ences in pigmentation and facial features are recognized and caucasoid traits are preferred. This preference is associated with the predominance of the lighter-skinned among the upper class, but a darker skin is not an absolute barrier to social acceptance. Stratification is on class lines and race as such is said not to matter.

With the remaining Indians, though, class differentiation is reinforced by cultural differences. Speaking a different language and responding to the mores of a subsistence agricultural society rather than to the relentless pace of urban industrialism, the remaining Indians are, in many ways, a group apart. It may be culture rather than race which sets them apart, but the distinction is none the less real. On the other hand, Indians currently do not constitute more than ten percent of the populaion and while they may have been bypassed by modernization they do not challenge it. There is no strong "Indianist" movement in defense of a separate society, and presumably the process of "mestization" will continue as more and more Indians are drawn into commercialized agriculture or industrial employment. Whether distinct Indian communities will ever completely disappear may be doubtful. Those that remain, however, will certainly be small and seem more likely to be passive enclaves in isolated areas than to be the nuclei of dynamic Indian cultural groups.[35]

Color prejudice did play a role in the formation of a distinct racial population—mestizos, in the sense that the offspring of Indian-white unions were viewed differently from so-called pure-blooded Indians. But Mexican ethnic relations operated on a set of premises different from those in the United States or in South Africa. First, in Mexico the Indians were not dehumanized to the same extent as blacks in the United States, and they were viewed as persons with a soul. Moreover, in the development of the country, identity was not simply based on phenotypes, but a preponderance of weight was placed on culture, and the racial identity of parents did not carry the same significance as it does in the United States. A mestizo could readily admit to his Indian ancestry without fear of being ostracized or of being regarded by others as an Indian. This is impossible in the United States among black Americans, even for those with a high amount of Caucasoid genetic heredity. Turner gives the following historical summary of the process "mestization":

The process of miscegenation by which the Indian and white races inter-

---

[35] As Harris analyzes the trend toward assimilation, "Many idealists in Mexico and abroad look upon this outcome with distaste. Quite rightly they argue for the right of the Indians to maintain their own culture and their own language . . . But . . . the isolation of the Indian communities has been broken . . . with few caste-like barriers around him, the Indian will continue with ever-increasing speed to be assimilated by the Mexican majority." Marvin Harris, "The Indians in Mexico," in Charles Wagley and Marvin Harris, *Minorities in the New World* (New York, Columbia University Press, 1964), p. 85.

married to form the mestizo group greatly changed the racial composition of Mexico during the nineteenth century. In 1824 Humboldt estimated that 1,860,000 mestizos made up 27.3 per cent of the Mexican population, while Ramon Beteta estimates that on the eve of the Revolution 8,000,000 mestizos comprised 53 per cent of the population. According to Humboldt's and Beteta's figures, the number of white Mexican citizens fell from 1,230,000 in 1824 to 1,150,000 in 1910, and the proportion of white citizens decreased from 18 per cent of the total population to only 7.5 per cent. Although the number of Indians rose from approximately 3.7 million to 6 million, the Indian portion of the population fell from 54.4 per cent to 39 per cent. Even if we accept Ramon Beteta's opinion that a larger number of Mexicans were mestizos in the early nineteenth century, the proportion of mestizos still rose from 38 per cent to 53 per cent in the hundred years before 1910. The biological miscegenation of the Mexican population was a gradual and irreversible process, because both the union of whites and Indians and that of mestizos with either of the other groups produce mestizo offsprings. This process had reached such a point by 1908 that Frederick Starr, a contemporary anthropologist from the University of Chicago, stated that "in some parts of Mexico, it almost seems as if what white-blood once existed is now breeded out."[36]

Mestizo in the early days of colonial domination meant *bastard* or *illegitimate offspring;* this was one of the stigmas that youngsters in the mestizo population had to carry, and it served as a major impetus in the thrust for nationalism in Mexico as the mestizo population increased. Because they were economically and culturally inferior to the whites they became part of the vanguard for nationalism, a move to bring the rival factions into a national community based upon their contribution and not on racial distinctions or socioeconomic position in the society.

THE CHINESE IN MEXICO

Amalgamation may be diminishing conflict between the major groups in Mexico, but this does not mean that Mexicans are immune from the forces leading to intergroup conflict in the rest of the world. A case in point concerns the relationships of Chinese and Mexicans.

Chinese migration to Mexico began in 1893, when Mexico and China signed a treaty of amity and commerce. Starting in the northwestern area the Chinese spread throughout Mexico, with a particular concentration in the state of Sonora. Beginning as farm and rail construction laborers, they rapidly made their way into various types of business enterprise. As wholesalers of agricultural commodities, grocers, and money lenders, they soon became a ubiquitous part of the commercial scene. In addition, they began to buy up agricultural land in small but noticeable quantities.

---

[36] Frederick C. Turner, *The Dynamics of Mexican Nationalism* (Chapel Hill, University of North Carolina Press, 1968), pp. 72–73.

The predictable result of their position as marginal commercial middle-men was that they became scapegoats for the tensions in Mexico. One point, made much of by revolutionary propaganda, was the toleration of the Chinese by the Diaz regime. As a commercial middle class the Chinese were a valuable part of the Mexican economy, but as a source of both cheap labor and commercial competition they were a natural focus of ethnic antagonism. Since they were neither native Mexicans nor a part of the "colossus of the North," they were in an exposed position with no one to protect them.[37]

The Chinese suffered not only from discriminatory legislation but also from occasional riots and even massacres. One such incident at Torreon in 1911 caused the death of 300 Chinese. The virulence of anti-Chinese feeling contrasts with the supposedly more benign pattern of ethnic relations in Latin countries and indicates that, with groups outside of their traditional orbit, Mexicans are subject to the same tensions as are people of other areas. Morner's comments on this situation are much to the point:

> Thus the Chinese, a hard-working, only partly assimilated group faced almost identical kinds of persecution in the United States and northern Mexico. Such episodes show that, under certain conditions, latent ethnic prejudice may produce discrimination and racial violence in any ethnic environment. It is not a phenomenon unique to Anglo-Saxons, Germans and South Africans.[38]

Antipathy toward the Chinese led to the elimination of immigration by restrictions effective in 1927, but this step did not end anti-Chinese agitation. Feeling ran highest in the state of Sonora. Here a series of restrictions against the Chinese had been put into effect over a period of 20 years. Restrictions on landholding, requirements that accounts be kept in Spanish, prohibition of entry into various occupations, and discriminatory taxation were all used by the state government at various times. Much of the legislation was evaded by the Chinese, but heavy taxation and rules restricting commerce in 1931 were too severe to be endured and, in the fall of 1931, the Chinese residents of Sonora left the state, some to return to China, others to migrate elsewhere in Mexico, and the state Governor could boast that the "Chinese problem has been completely terminated in Sonora."[39]

Animosities against the Chinese and against such "gringo" groups as the Mennonite and Mormon settlers have served to strengthen nationalism by defining the outsiders. Within the groups considered Mexican, ethnic distinctions have diminished; Africans have virtually disappeared as a

---

[37] Charles C. Cumberland, "The Sonora Chinese and the Mexican Revolution," *Hispanic American Historical Review*, 40 (May 1960), p. 192.

[38] Morner, *Race Mixture in the History of Latin America*, p. 138.

[39] Jose Angel Espinoza, *El ejemplo de Sonora* (Mexico, 1932), cited in Cumberland, "The Sonora Chinese and The Mexican Revolution," p. 203.

recognizable group, whites have diminished as a proportion of the population, and many Indians have crossed into the mestizo category. All the major groups which make up the Mexican population seem to be in the process of merging into one population which increasingly represents both a common culture and a common physical type.

CONCLUSIONS

Mexico is a society which began with an extreme exposure to domination and ethnocentric social distinctions as a result of the Spanish Conquest, but in which consciousness of racial distinctions has been greatly reduced. Clashes may occur with those considered alien, but among the populace accepted as "Mexican" there seems to be little ethnic conflict. Cultural distinctions still survive, both in a fairly pure Indian culture in the more remote parts of the country and in some degree of tension between those who retain a degree of Indian identification and the rest of the population. However, the proportion who can be identified as other than mestizo is rapidly shrinking. There is greater concern for the welfare of the Indian minority and Mexico appears to be a society in which widespread racial amalgamation has minimized group conflict.

Although some degree of racial intermixture seems to have been a result of every colonial situation, this has been more true of the French, Spanish, and Portuguese colonies than those controlled by Anglo-Saxon nations. Among all of the large countries which have seen intermixture as the result of the colonial experience there is none in which this has progressed to a greater extent than Mexico. Both in the extent of racial intermixture and in the psychological attitude toward the mestizo population, Mexico occupies a unique place.

In looking at the probable reason for the Mexican outcome it may be worth while to refer to the sociological distinction between crescive and enacted change. Enacted change is that which comes as a result of deliberate planning, while crescive change refers to developments which occur without any conscious design. It would seem that the course of Mexican intergroup relations has certainly not been due to the deliberate type of design which we associate with enacted change. There was nothing in the Spanish policy, or for that matter in the Indian reaction, which was deliberately designed to produce racial amalgamation. Rather, there was considerable racism on both sides of the fence and one would attribute amalgamation to a failure of enacted change and to the operation of crescive forces whose significance was not really discerned at the time. What are these crescive factors and how do they operate? Let us look at some of them and analyze their effect on the pattern of Mexican ethnic relations.

Effect of cultural homogenization

Perhaps the first, and possibly most paradoxical factor, which comes to mind is the very ruthlessness of Spanish rule and the intolerant ethnocentrism of Spanish attitudes. Most of the Spanish colonists had no appreciation of the magnificence of the Aztec and Mayan cultures and viewed them only as perversions which were to be destroyed. Spanish architecture was the only legitimate form of architecture, the Catholic religion was the only true religion, the Spanish language was the only language which could be spoken by civilized men. While some of the indigenous culture such as foods, agricultural practices, and clothing managed to persist, yet in language, religion, government, architecture, and family life, Spanish influence was all-pervasive. This tended to homogenization and, therefore, to assimilation. The fact that the society was dominated by a single culture meant that persons of diverse racial backgrounds still had a common cultural orientation and could interact with some degree of ease.

Symbolic value of Indian culture

The ruthlessness of the Spaniards was matched against the vigor and development of the more advanced Indian cultures. While the Indian societies became an easy prey to Spanish military prowess and political intrigue, their influence did not completely fade away from the earth. Even the destructive Spanish could not demolish all the pyramids and temples; so the legends, and some of the material evidence of great and advanced civilizations, managed to survive the Spanish Conquest. Thus the Mexican was a person with a double ancestry—an ancestry in both lines of which he could take pride. From his Spanish ancestry he inherited what would become the dominant cultural values of Mexico, but on the Indian side he could identify himself with the glories of a past civilization which in many ways rivaled that of medieval Europe. Thus, it is perhaps to be expected that the favorite images in Mexico—the statue of Cauhtemoc, the Indian defender of Mexico City, and of the Virgin of Guadelupe, the Indian girl who has become a symbol of Catholicism—were expressions of this double heritage. The fact that the Indian heritage was so largely destroyed made it easy for people of Indian ancestry to accept the cultural aspects of mestization, while the historical glory of their ancestral culture allowed them to participate in the common nation without a historic badge of shame or inferiority.

Local versus centralized rule

The hierarchy of both the Roman Catholic Church and of the Madrid government in Spain endeavored to protect, to some degree, the Indians against the rapacity and cruelty of Spanish colonists. The government attempted to avoid the abuses found in other countries in the *encomiendas* by providing that the Spanish settlers would be subject to the rule of a government official concerned about the salvation of the Indians' souls, about their material welfare, and about their rights as human beings. It was probably as a result, at least in part, of Catholic pressure that Indian slavery was abolished after a relatively short period of time. However, many of the priests and bishops faced a different type of situation than that envisioned by the more remote members of the hierarchy, and in any event they had little influence upon the practices of individual Spaniards. Further, the Catholic Church became the biggest landowner in Spain and therefore was tempted to view the Indian peons as a labor source to be exploited in a backward but monopolistic agricultural situation. Actually, there was little difference between the church estates and the privately owned haciendas, and in either situation the Indians occupied a subordinate role where his culture was attacked, while the only defense of his personality was his being freed from slavery. For various reasons the Catholic church was less concerned about African than about Indian slavery. It agreed to the extension of African slavery as a means of preventing the exploitation, and even the extermination, of Indians under conditions of slavery.

This inability of either state or church to protect the Indians from the Spaniards meant that the Indian population of Mexico, to a great extent, was forced to interact as a part of the general society. The demise of the Spanish regime in 1810 ended any possibility of interference from the Madrid government. Similarly, the extreme anticlericalism which came with the revolution of 1910 deprived the Catholic Church of any opportunity to protect a separate Indian society.

If either church or government had been successful in its Indianist policies the result would have been a realization of the ideal of the two republics—Spanish and Indian, existing in distinct societies and maintaining distinctive cultures. In such a case Indian communities might have had greater protection against exploitation, but this protection would also have kept them more isolated and would have slowed down both miscegenation and acculturation. Neither the Church nor the Madrid government was able to enforce its ideals, and Indian exploitation proceeded at both the sexual and the economic levels. The initial result was a decline in the Indian population but the long-term effect was amalgamation of African, Indian, and Spaniard in a largely mestizo population.

Influence of multiple racial classification

It is possible to argue that the Spanish were even more concerned about the importance of race than were the Anglo-Saxons in the sense that the

Anglo-Saxons had only a dichotomous relationship of white or black, while to the Spanish it was extremely important to distinguish the degree of white ancestry and to provide the "proper kind" of social treatment in accord with the exact classification of the individual involved. This was the purpose of the *castas* system with its numerous social and ethnic classifications. The extreme detail of this classification, however, was its own undoing. As Mexico became a more mobile and populous society, it became impossible to identify with any precision the varying ethnic categories, and it was impossible to keep ambitious mestizos with limited white ancestry from achieving social prominence. As a result the whole process of ethnic categorization tended to break down. There is still a lingering degree of pride in an allegedly pure white ancestry, but most Mexicans find that a mestizo classification implies acceptable social status.

Legalization of intermarriage

Prejudice and discrimination were certainly rife for many years in Mexico, but intermarriage was never illegal and, with the proclamation of independence in 1810, came the end of any restrictions of a legal nature placed on individuals by the virtue of ancestry or place of birth. This, of course, did not destroy discrimination or necessarily weaken prejudice. It did mean, however, that the exceptional individuals who for one reason or another departed from the norm and engaged in formal mixed marriages, rather than in illicit unions, could find a degree of acceptance in the society. Their example was followed by others and eventually produced a large number of people of mixed white, Indian, and African ancestry who had a respectable social status. This again contrasts with the more rigid pattern in Anglo-Saxon countries, in which the offspring of mixed parentage tended to be classified as a member of the colored group, and frequently a mixed marriage was legally prohibited.

Linkage of cultural and racial superiority

While the Spaniards had concern for the importance of biological background, this was also linked with ideas of cultural superiority and social position. The very description of the *castas* implies that social status and biological background were expected to go together. The combination of this bio-social classification and a society which had legal provisions of equality enabled adjustments to be made. For instance, the *criollos*, the Spaniards born in Mexico, many of whom had some degree of Indian ancestry, were allowed to retain the "fiction" of pure white ancestry. Since they had the social position which was consonant with the white ancestry, it was easy for society to allow the circumvention of a purely biological classification. Under these circumstances the distinction between *criollo* and mestízo tended to break down, a process which still further favored amalgamation.

Mestization and Mexican nationalism

Nationalism has frequently meant that the claim of being a "national" of the country was linked to a certain type of ethnic ancestry. In the case of Mexico, the development was somewhat different. Obviously, neither the Indian nor the Spanish could claim to be the true representative of Mexican nationality. The Spaniard had his primary links with European society, while the Indian was associated with an era before the formation of the national state. The Indian, and, to the degree to which he was recognized, the African, were attempting to escape from a servile status, while the Spaniard needed protection from Indian resentment. All groups could find a claim to identity which validated their Mexican nationalism in the mestizo classification. If Mexico is a product of the union of two cultures, then the individual who is the biological product of the "two bloods" is certainly the true Mexican.

The revolution of 1810, which brought independence to Mexico, is often viewed as primarily a movement of the *criollos* against the Peninsulars, the Spaniards who were born in Spain and immigrated to Mexico. The Socialist revolution of 1910 represents the culmination of forces which had been bringing the mestizo into a more favorable position and which made him the true representative of Mexican nationality. The Indian was accepted primarily as a historical figure, and some concessions were made to isolated Indian societies. Primarily, however, the program for the Indian was one of mestization, and as he moved to a city, took a factory job, and learned Spanish he, too, was considered to be a mestizo regardless of his racial ancestry. Thus, the two forces of mestization and Mexican nationalism moved together.

Effect of universalistic religion

While the Catholic Church has a very mixed record in its own relation to Indians and was never able to impose its ideals completely upon the Spanish colonists, its influence did make a difference. First, since the salvation of Indians was important, the prevention of their massacre was a Christian virtue. Secondly, the church gave support to the ideal of monogamous marriage in a situation where an unequal sex ratio made it impossible for most Spaniards to marry Spanish women. This support of a monogamous institution facilitated what was really a deviant type of action in the initial tendency of a few Spaniards to marry those of colored ancestry. Finally, the association in a common religious institution is a bond of culture and of participation which has brought various elements of Mexico together.

GENERALIZATIONS FROM MEXICAN EXPERIENCE

Mexico is a society which is pluralistic in the biological background of its people but "essentially homogenous" in terms of culture. There are, it is true, many survivals of Indian civilization, but these are not seen as offering competition to the dominant culture which is an amalgam of Spanish and Indian with the Spanish element predominant. For the individual moving ahead in modern society in terms of social mobility there are few possibilities of cultural alternatives and therefore few possibilities of cultural conflict. Hence the Mexican situation is quite in contrast to patterns in Ireland, where there is a possibility of religious differentiation, or in Belgium, where language identity serves as a focus for group separation. Whether it is similar to the United States depends upon the way current trends are analyzed. If skin color is being downgraded and a large number of middle class blacks are seen as entering an essentially homogenous society then the similarity is obvious. If, however, black separatists and white segregationists are successful in their effort to maintain and extend color cleavages, then the United States will diverge from the Mexican pattern even more in the future than it has in the past.

MEXICAN BEHAVIOR PATTERNS IN RELATION TO GENERALIZED BEHAVIOR PATTERNS

Mexican pattern. It may be considered the essence of a "racist" point of view to assume that physical features are correlated with various social traits, but this theory may have unexpected results in practice. The Spaniards regarded pure Spanish ancestry as indicating the possession of the type of traits which make for mobility in a modernized society. While this may be considered unbridled ethnocentrism, it did facilitate a certain degree of passing from one ethnic category to another. If virtue is associated with a particular biological category, then those who manifest social virtue tend to be assigned to the correlated biological category. The very cultural homogeneity of the society facilitated this type of movement, since there was rather general agreement as to which traits were socially desirable.

Generalized pattern. Mixing of biological and social criteria for ethnic classification facilitates movement from one classification to another.

Mexican pattern. The difficulty, in a mobile society, of keeping track and of classifying people in from 10 to 46 different types of categories is so great that the whole procedure breaks down. Once the finer distinctions have been blurred there is a tendency to classify everybody as mestizo except those who are culturally Indian or members of distinctive alien minorities such as the Chinese. By contrast the Anglo-Saxon practice of making only a dichotomous separation between white and colored would seem to be less racially fanatical, although in the long run it is probably more effective in preserving racial separation. In a biomodal system any-one with known colored ancestry is classified in the subordinate group; there is little possibility of movement from one group to another, and racial distinctions can be maintained with relative ease. The tendency to blur racial distinctions in Latin cultures and to maintain them in Anglo-Saxon cultures does not come because the Latins were unconcerned with race but because in the height of their concern they established an edifice impossible to maintain.

Generalized pattern. Multiple biological classification yields over a period of time to a blurring of biological distinction. The maintenance of very fine gradations for the classification of biological identity is a type of "racism" which not only is absurd but is self-defeating.

Mexican pattern. The initial stand of the Roman Catholic Church in favor of the human qualities of all men, including Indians and blacks, was largely ignored by the Spanish settlers who took an instrumental view of ethnic minorities. Similarly, the declaration, at the end of the revolutionary movement which inaugurated independence, that ethnic designations would no longer have social effect, was hardly taken seriously by any element of the Mexican population. These formal gestures toward a recognition of equality had little effect in themselves in ending ethnic discrimination, but they did facilitate change with relatively little friction as the colored groups progressed in social mobility. There were no legal barriers against intermarriage or citizenship or any type of economic ac-tivity. This meant that when the basic social condition had changed and the mestizo group became more mobile there was no institutionalized way of stopping them. Hence the legal provisions, even though from a stand-point of enforcement they were ineffective, did provide a gate through which socially mobile minorities could pass.

Generalized pattern. Legal institutional equality, even though seem-ingly ineffectual, minimizes frictions as changes occur in the relationships of ethnic groups.

Mexican pattern. Throughout the history of Mexico since the Spanish Conquest the pure Spanish ancestry and the white skin have been con-sidered prestige traits. In contrast to this type of evaluation, the Nation-alists urged that Mexico should be developing a population which was genuinely "Mexican." Such a population could not be Indian, since the Indians were divided into separate numerous tribes, nor could it be Span-ish, since this label was identified with aliens. The logical type of ethnic identity for the true Mexican was the mestizo category, comprising as i did the contribution of all groups which had made up the Mexican population. The acceptance of this type of mixed ancestry as comprising the genuine Mexican identity tended to validate the position of the mestizo in comparison with either the Indian or the pure Spanish population.

Generalized pattern. When a once denigrated ethnic group becomes the symbol of nationality it raises the status of the group.

Mexican pattern. The identity crisis of the Mexican Indian is certainly a bit different from that of the American black or the North American Indian. It is true that the Mexican Indian occupies a servile position and is constantly reminded of his humble status. On the other hand, he is the heir to the empires of the Aztecs, the Mayas, and others, and he can boast of an ancestral culture which compared favorably with Spain at the time of Cortez. The pyramids and temples are symbols which the person of little Indian ancestry is compelled to accept and respect and they are also symbols to which the Indian may look for ego gratification. It may be true that they have relatively little effect on the position of the Indians today, but their contributions to psychological adjustment are certainly significant.

Generalized pattern. Appreciation of indigenous achievements may support both minority self concept and respect from the outgroup.

Mexican pattern. The influence of the sex ratio is a point which needs very little laboring. The Spaniards brought only a very small proportion of women to the New World with them. Since sexual activity was bound to take place, it necessarily involved the Spanish and the Indian population. It took place in terms under which the Spanish were dominant and the Indian maiden not only was unable to resist the advances of the Spaniards but frequently found that bearing a child of mixed ancestry was a matter of positive advantage. In these circumstances the Spanish contribution to Mexican physical heredity was far greater than the comparatively small number of Spaniards might indicate.

Generalized pattern. Unequal sex ratios favor amalgamation.

Mexican pattern. Neither the central government at Madrid, the government of the province of Mexico as such, nor the smaller subdivisions were particularly strong. They were able to rule only insofar as their authority was accepted by the Spanish settlers. Their efforts to protect the interests of blacks or Indians as separate groups ran counter to the settler desire to utilize Indians and blacks primarily as sources of labor. Hence there was little protection of Indian or black society, and Indians and blacks had to find their way in a society dominated by whites. The result of this was a society in which, for the most part, the superordinate positions went to whites and the subordinate positions to the people of color.

However, it was a common society with a common culture which featured the cooperation and interaction of people of different ethnic groups even though on a stratified basis.

A strong central government might have been able to enforce a stronger stand for the preservation of indigenous culture and society. Strong regional governments might also have emerged as the spokesmen for indigenous interests of people in their region. Since government on either level was relatively ineffectual, the driving part in the organization of society was played by the hacenderos and, eventually, by the industrialists of the city, whose need for labor overrode respect for the distinctive ethnic background of any group. To generalize from the Mexican experience one might observe that, in the absence of governmental restraints, a socioeconomic system develops which does integrate various ethnic groups in a common social system. Probably they will not be integrated on an equal basis, but at least they will become mutually interdependent and thus will lay the basis for a society which involves the interaction of those from different ethnic groups.

Generalized pattern.   In a country with a weak government the interaction of alien and native ethnic groupings fosters the growth of a common ethnic system.

Mexican pattern.   The laws and regulations of colonial society in Mexico provided for a caste system with differential privilege based on the degree of white, Indian, and black ancestry. Thus the Spaniards sought to enact an ethnically stratified society with the top privileges going to those of lightest skin. They failed in this effort because the forces working for miscegenation produced a population which it was impossible to classify in these terms.

This specific situation may not often be repeated, but history is full of instances when enacted change was defeated by unplanned crescive developments. For instance, American communities have enacted laws against housing segregation only to find such laws ineffective as a major urban migration of blacks expanded the segregated areas. Examples of this kind could be multiplied. The point is not that enacted changes never succeed but that they are more likely to be successful when they work with prevailing social trends.

Generalized pattern.   Crescive developments may undercut attempts at enacted change.

QUESTIONS

1. What factors were responsible for the movement toward a common culture and a common biological classification, since there was no deliberate design to achieve this goal?

2. How do you explain the failure of the Spaniards to completely strip the Indians of their cultural heritage?

3. Why did the Spaniards develop an elaborate and complex ethnic classification scheme? How would you account for its eventual failure?

4. Do you see any reason to believe that the Spaniards were less concerned about the importance of biological distinctions than the Anglo-Saxon? Defend your answer.

5. How do you account for the intense intertribal conflicts in Mexico before the conquest? What, if any, role did biological differences play in these conflicts? Defend your answer.

6. What major factors helped subdue the Indians who overwhelmingly outnumbered Cortez and his men?

7. What part did centuries-old intertribal hostilities play in the conquest of the Indians?

8. How would you explain the fact that fierce battles and competition existed even among linguistically related tribes?

9. What is the difference between the following systems used to control Indians: *repartimento, encomienda, caciques* and *hacienda?* Which system would you say was more oppressive?

10. During the early days of conquest what were some of the attitudes of the Catholic Church toward the Indians and what were some of the consequences?

11. In what way did the attitudes of church and state differ toward black slavery and Indian slavery?

12. What were the attitudes of the colonists toward the Indians and what impact did they have on the life style and life chances of the Indians?

13. How would you account for the fact that the population of the mulattoes increased much more rapidly than that of the blacks in Mexico?

14. In what way did the rigidly stratified society in Mexico produce an alliance between the mestizos and the *criollo* (Spanish born in Mexico)?

15. Why did Benito Juarez further restrict the power of the church when he became president? Defend your answer.

16. For what major reasons did the mestizos assume a vanguard role in the promotion of nationalism in Mexico?

17. How do you explain the fact that, although Mexico has made great strides toward assimilation and amalgamation, the Chinese were not accepted?

18. Are there any developments in Mexico that can be applied to the analysis of ethnic relations in the United States? Discuss fully.

Chapter 6

Herrenvolk Democracy:
The Republic of South Africa

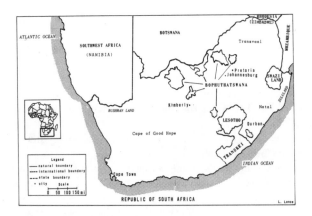

REPUBLIC OF SOUTH AFRICA

At the beginning of World War II, in 1939, most of Africa was ruled in colonial fashion by European powers. Even Egypt, which might be cited as the major exception, was compelled to allow the British to occupy the Suez Canal and to be in charge of Egyptian defense. This situation changed drastically in the postwar years, which brought a massive shift away from colonialism. By 1963, when Kenya gained its independence, decolonialization had taken place in a majority of African countries. Although a few small territories did not achieve independence until the latter 60s or early 70s, the year 1963 marked the end of colonial regimes for most of Africa. The most striking exception to this pattern is found in the Republic of South Africa which stands alone as an African country ruled by Europeans.

Its singular position has made the Republic of South Africa the target of world criticism. The white South Africans often feel persecuted and unjustly accused. They point out that, in spite of some restrictions, their press is the freest in Africa, their courts the most impartial and their democratic institutions the most controlled by popular vote. Further, although most black

160

Africans make only a fraction of the wages of whites, their economic status is still better than that of Africans in most other countries. In addition, the South Africans speak of their expenditures on education and health for Africans, the gradual upgrading of African labor and the loosening of segregation. South Africans even resent criticism of white privileges and argue that the income of whites living in black controlled African countries are even higher than white incomes in South Africa. When they are denounced for restricting political activity by Africans, they argue that the rulers of black controlled countries do not hold free elections or permit the existence of a political opposition. All of these points are true to some degree and worthy of consideration, but they fade into insignificance beside the central fact that the Republic of South Africa is now the only country in the world where a white minority forcibly maintains rule over a non-white majority. As long as this is true, the Republic of South Africa will be a center of controversy, regardless of the virtues or defects of particular policies.[1]

Unlike the French, Spanish and Portugese, the European settlers in South Africa have been reluctant to accept the idea of racial merger so that there is a sharp distinction between white and colored. Thus, unlike Mexico, there has been little racial blending, although in the Republic of South Africa about ten percent of the population are of mixed ancestry, the result of miscegenation in earlier years.

Important generalizations in this chapter include the following: (1) the removal of certain ethnic limitations may be facilitated by a need for skilled and technical workers as a society becomes more and more industrialized; (2) when a permanent commitment to the land is made by a white "settler" population a desperate struggle will be made to maintain its dominance; (3) a subordinate group that is not allowed to assimilate and whose culture is greatly weakened may expect a high degree of social disorganization among its members; and (4) when an opportunity is available a biologically mixed population has the tendency to identify with its more prestigious ancestry and not the denigrated ethnic element.

If one were to ask why the Republic of South Africa has pursued a course so different from the rest of the continent, the answer is simply that this is the effect of "white settler" dominance. As van den Berghe remarks, "Race relations in the Union of South Africa is more a white problem than a black problem."[2] A settler population produces a demand for continued European dominance, whereas the typical colonial pattern is a rather transistory phenomena. Colonialism is usually based on the

---

[1]Leonard Sussman, "From Basskap to Pluralism," *Freedom At Issue*, No. 42, September–October, 1977, pp. 5–8.

[2]Pierre van den Berghe: *South Africa: A Study In Conflict* (Middletown, Conn. Wesleyan Univ. 1965). (Berkeley, University of California Press, 1970), p. 13. This is the first of several references to Professor van den Berghe's works, which are major sources for one writing on sociological aspects of South Africa.

desire for trade and for strategic advantages. Frequently, these economic and strategic concerns may, after a period of development, be as well served by a relationship with an independent country as with a discontented colony. Even if there is some loss in trade preferences or in military alliances, the mother country is forced to balance this loss against the expense of maintaining a political dominance which tends to become more and more difficult as the subject population becomes assimilated to the standards and aspirations of a technological culture. Thus the African nationalists of the 50s and the 60s found that there was often suprisingly little European opposition to independence and discovered that a comparatively slight resistance to colonial domination was enough to end European rule.

By contrast, the settler is one whose life and fortune are committed to the adopted country. Frequently he, and perhaps even his parents and grandparents, were born in the country; they know of no other life and see no other possibility of a satisfactory type of existence. To the European settler, African independence is not simply a matter of trade policies and strategic concerns, but is quite literally a question of life and death. For him, it involves placing his life and fortunes under the rule of a people whom he regards as being, on the one hand, anxious to revenge ancient wrongs and, on the other, incapable of carrying on a modern state either because of inherent limitations in intelligence or because of their lack of cultural development.

Many of the white settlers feel that the only real choice is either to continue white domination or to leave the country. For the missionary, the educator, the government official, or the soldier, this is not really a major problem. He may, over a period of time, have developed bonds of real affection with an African people, but he has always regarded himself as being somewhat transient in the country and it is comparatively easy for him to resume his career in another area. The situation is quite different for the farmer or businessman, whose career is tied to the ownership of capital and whose capital is difficult to move from its territorial setting. This individual, if he remains, fears what he thinks are the possibilities of capricious, vengeful, or, at best, incompetent government; and, if he leaves, he may face the loss of most of his savings and the necessity to start a new career in a new land without the capital to support his efforts.

In the long run, one may feel that the white settler is simply refusing to face the inevitable, and, even in the short run, his reactions may be shortsighted, since the independent government, if allowed to make a free decision, may choose a partnership with Europeans whose lives are also committed to the country. However mistaken the viewpoint of the white settler may be, it is one that is firmly held and which prompts him to vigorous exertions to maintain white dominance in spite of changes which have made this concept outmoded in most of Africa.

The South African doctrine of apartheid is not simply an aberration of racial prejudice. Rather it is a desperate effort to maintain white dominance when both South African and world trends seem to be going the other way. The independence movements which have swept most of the rest of Africa have been blocked in South Africa, but they have certainly had an effect on black thinking. Nor are internal social changes necessarily moving to shore up white supremacy. Black population is increasing more rapidly than white and increasing technological sophistication enables blacks to confront whites on a more nearly equal basis. While the conflict seems to be intensifying at the present time, it has its roots in the past and it is to a delineation of the historical factors which produced the multi-ethnic state of the Republic of South Africa that we now turn.

EUROPEAN SETTLEMENT

The first settlements of South Africa took place not so much from the lure of African riches themselves as from the needs of trade. The first recorded European to notice the advantages of the area for navigation was a Portuguese, Bartholomew Diaz; in 1486 he named the southernmost end of the continent "The Cape of Storms," a name which, in terms of history, seems to have been more justified than the term applied later by King John of Portugal, "The Cape of Good Hope".[3] Portuguese discovery, however, did not lead to permanent settlement, which waited until 1652, when the Dutch East India Company sent a small group of employees to establish what was called "a cabbage patch on the way to India."[4]

The purpose of this settlement was simply to serve as a station for refreshments, which were vitally needed, since fresh vegetables helped Dutch sailors on the long voyage between Holland and the East Indies to fight off scurvy, a constant menace on long voyages. The area was sparsely populated. To meet the need for a labor supply the company began to import slaves from Madagascar, Mozambique, and the East Indies, so that, before long, the number of slaves exceeded the number of whites.[5] The Cape of Good Hope soon became a thriving agricultural colony whose fertile farms produced the provisions which made the long East-West voyage more practicable.

The original African peoples of the Cape area, the Hottentots and the

---

[3] Allan Paton, *Hope for South Africa*, Frederick A. Praeger, New Edition, 1958, p. 11.

[4] Cornelis W. De Kiewitt, *A History of South Africa* (Oxford, Clarendon Press, 1941), p. 4.

[5] John Fisher, *The Afrikaners* (London, Cassel & Co., Ltd., 1969), p. 36.

Bushmen, either retreated or were pushed out as whites came into the area, so that the population consisted largely of Dutch immigrants and their slaves. The system of slavery that developed had paternalistic characteristics, with close contacts and extensive miscegenation between whites and the slaves. The fact that such a society was paternalistic did not mean that it could be considered equitable or that it was a society which offered any degree of hope for real improvement in the condition of the slave population. The subordination of the slave group to the white owners was unchallenged, and the custom of concubinage served to emphasize the essential inferiority of a slave group unable to insist on any degree of regularization of family patterns. Nevertheless, the conclusion of van den Berghe that it was a system of stable and integrated race relations quite different from that present in South Africa today[6] seems a reasonable one.

Agricultural work in the Cape area was, however, necessarily a restricted field, and many dissatisfied settlers looked for opportunity in the interior of the country and began the practice known as "trekking," a custom which endured in South Africa for centuries. The Boers, as the whites of Dutch descent became known, who were looking for an economic niche, found this as herders of sheep and cattle, and they plunged into the interior of the country where vast expanses of untouched land could be found. Movement into the interior, however, brought active conflict with the native population. This expansion was not promoted by the Dutch East India Company. Indeed, the expansion made it harder for the company to maintain a monoply of cattle raising; the trekkers were involved in constant warfare, which was a cause of expense to the company and a threat to safety in the entire area.

Some idea of the extent of conflict between the Boers and the Bushmen is indicated by the compilations made in 1836, as reported by Marais. The figures covered only one district, the Graaf-Reinert frontier, but are nonetheless impressive. They indicate that between 1786 and 1795 over 2500 Bushmen and 276 colonists were killed. In the same period, colonists reported livestock losses that included 19,161 cattle and 84,094 sheep.[7]

The trek became a tradition in the life of the Dutch in South Africa and was a type of movement which took place whenever there was a desire to flee from some force which was considered oppressive. In some ways, it acted as a safety valve for social discontents in much the same way as the American movement toward the West. However, the population of whites involved was smaller than in the United States and eventually the native resistance became stronger.

---

[6] van den Berghe, *South Africa*, p. 20.

[7] D. Moodie (ed.), *The Record; or, a Series of Official Papers Relative to the Condition and Treatment of the Native Tribes of South Africa, 1838–41*, p. 5. Cited in J.S. Marais: *The Cape Coloured People, 1652 to 1937* (London, Longmans, Green & Co., 1939), p. 17. Reprinted in 1957 by Witwatersrand University Press.

The favorite comparison of the Dutch themselves was with the conquest of Canaan by the children of Israel. In this analogy, the Dutch were regarded as the children of God, the land in the interior became the Promised Land full of potential milk and honey, and the natives whom they displaced assumed somewhat the same role that the Philistines had for the Israelites. This interpretation of history made European expansion seem in harmony with the plan of God and the Dutch appear as those establishing the rule of righteousness for the chosen people in a dark and heathen land.[8]

The next impulse for the trek came as a result of a change in international politics; namely, the effect of the Napoleonic wars, which enabled the British to acquire the Cape area in 1795. Although the British were Europeans, they spoke a different language and held ideals which seemed hostile to the prevailing settler culture. The British were not so much farmers as traders and businessmen, and they looked with a suspicious eye on the institution of slavery. In the British viewpoint, the potential equality of mankind was admitted, and slavery was a basic affront to the human condition. In 1828 the British emancipated the slaves; subsequent policies gave the natives the right to vote, to own land and even to hold office.[9]

To the Dutch, all of these ideas were abhorrent components of a heretical philosophy—a denial of what they saw as the essential basis of Christendom. Further, the Dutch viewed racial superordination as the only way to maintain the labor force required by their farming needs. As a result, there took place the Great Trek of 1836. The Dutch who remained under British control became known as Afrikaners, while those who took part in the Great Trek were cattle farmers and sheep herders and known as Boers. In their effort to escape British rule, the Boers took an even stronger position toward the separation of European and non-European peoples than had been true when a paternalistic slave regime was relatively unthreatened.

The trek led the Boers directly into the interior, around the mountains of Basutoland and eventually into Natal. The entry into Natal brought a series of battles between Boers and Zulu ending in the Zulu defeat at Blood River in 1838. This Boer victory, which is commemorated by a national holiday in South Africa, enabled the Boers to found the short-lived republic of Natal in 1838. When the British countered this action by annexing Natal as a Crown Colony in 1843, the majority of the Trekkers recrossed the mountains and expanded into the territory which later be-

---

[8] Fisher, *The Afrikaners*, p. 352. Local Africans were not enslaved and many of the imported slaves were Malays.

[9] Douglas Brown, *Against the World: A Study of White South African Social Attitudes* (London, Collins, 1966), p. 23.

came known as the Orange Free State and the South African (Transvaal) Republic. The Boers, by this trek, escaped British influence and entered an area in which conditions were conducive to the rugged individualism which they favored. A population which could not have numbered more than 40,000 was scattered over territory of more than 100,000 square miles. All roads and towns had to be built from scratch, and the Boers were constantly engaged, until at least 1880, in wars with African tribes. Some of these tribes were protected by the British and, as a result, Lesotho (formerly Basutoland), Swaziland, and Botswana (formerly Bechuanaland) became British protectorates and today are independent black enclaves surrounded by Republic of South Africa territory.[10]

The British policy of "liberalism" was not unrelated to the struggle for control between the British and the Dutch. In 1853 a qualified franchise was granted to all in Cape Colony regardless of color. This was a grant which Cecil Rhodes justified on the grounds of "equal rights to all civilized men."[11] This franchise had the obvious effect of increasing British political support. At other times, the British were capable of taking a somewhat different attitude. Natal, which the British took over from the Boers in 1843, was also the locale of the development of the first large-scale scheme for the segregation of the races in South Africa: the system of native reserves established in the late 1840s by the British administrator, Theophilus Shepstone.[12] Various dispersed tracts were set aside for the exclusive occupation of Africans. The ostensible reason for these actions was to protect the land rights of Africans against European settlers. On the other hand, the tracts made the Africans more accessible for labor than they would have been if concentrated in one area; at the same time, the tracts, by breaking up population concentration, minimized the threat inherent in growing African numbers. The system of reserves was expanded in the native land act of 1913 and the Native Trust and Land Act of 1936.[13]

Another event of outstanding importance in African ethnic relations, which took place also in Natal, was the importation in 1860 of indentured Indian laborers to furnish cheap workers for the sugar cane industry. Most of the Indians did not return to India when their period of indentured service was over but remained in South Africa, where they became a minor commercial middle class which has functioned as middlemen between the Africans and the Europeans.[14]

---

[10] Fisher, *The Afrikaners*, p. 348.

[11] Vindes F. Verschoyle, *Cecil Rhodes: Political Life and Speeches 1881–1899*, (London, Chapman and Hall, 1900), pp. 160–61.

[12] Fisher, *The Afrikaners*, p. 88.

[13] van den Berghe, *South Africa*, p. 31.

[14] Fisher, *The Afrikaners*, pp. 3, 99, 307–10.

The efforts of the Boers to escape British rule were rendered futile by the impetus given to the British desire for territorial control by the discovery of the great mineral wealth of the country—first, of diamonds and later, of gold. The diamond fields around Kimberly were simply annexed to the British-controlled Cape Colony, a step which the Orange Free State was in no position to resist. An attempt to extend British territory to the Transvaal in 1877 led to the first Boer War and to a British withdrawal from that territory. The fate of the Transvaal was sealed, however, with the discovery of gold in 1886 near what was to become the city of Johannesburg.

The discovery of gold brought the building of railroads and an influx of non-Boer miners, who quickly began to contest the political supremacy of the Boer settlers. Arguments over the rights of the non-Boer miners eventually led to British intervention and the Anglo-Boer War of 1899–1902. This was a conflict in which larger British forces fought against the Boers, who used guerilla tactics. The guerilla tactics were broken by interning the Boers, including women and children, in concentration camps where 26,000 of them died of disease.[15] The British use of African troops against them was considered by the Boers as a final insult. The British won the war and established political control of South Africa, but at the cost of a legacy of anti-British feeling which has persisted to this day.

In one sense, the British victory represented the triumph of racial liberalism. In another sense, it was simply an exchange of masters as far as the native population was concerned. British power was helped by antipathy between Africans and Boers, but, at the same time, the growth in number of the mixed population (the Coloured) and of the African tribes (known generally as Bantu)[16] was a threat to white dominance to which the British responded in much the same fashion as the Boers.

The various African tribes have different traditions, languages, and customs which present-day South African policy, in one sense at least, encourages them to preserve. However, in spite of tribal differences they all occupy a similar status relative to whites. On the one hand, they are a source of cheap labor and essential to the industrial development of the country. On the other, they are regarded as being destined for a different type of life, so that the tribal development rather than integration in the total society is the ultimate goal.

When the British were in control of South Africa their commitment to some type of liberalism and equality clashed with a determination to

---

15 Brown, *Against the World*, p. 26.

16 Bantu is sometimes used by anthropologists to refer to related groups of tribes. In reference to South Africa, however, it usually refers to all of the population of African descent except the "coloured," who have mixed African and European background. Some of the larger tribes included in the term Bantu are Xhosa, Zulu, Bapedi, Sotho, Tswana, and Tsonga.

maintain white control at all costs. Africans were given the vote but the franchise was restricted by property qualifications. Nor did a theoretical concern for African rights prevent the development of "pass" laws to restrict the movement and conduct of Africans. The "pass" laws set up a curfew time for the natives, required that they carry an identification book with them at all times, and indicated the parts of the country to which they were allowed to move. These laws were justified on the grounds that they were needed for control and also for preventing the overcrowding of urban areas. They seemed to have had some effect in preventing the urban concentrations of unemployed Africans which have plagued other cities in the continent, but they are a continual source of humiliation and tension and, even in a police state, it has been impossible to completely enforce compliance.

When coalition political control gave way to that of the extreme segregationists in 1948, whatever compromise there was between liberalism and white supremacy yielded to a single-minded policy of repressing all native rights and maintaining white supremacy in its most naked form. The British won the Boer War but lost the eventual struggle for hegemony in South Africa. For many years this was not apparent, as South Africa was governed by a coalition of British and Afrikaners. The basic principle upon which this cooperation was founded was that, although the British Empire's sovereignty was recognized along with certain basic rights of the Africans, nothing would be done which might seriously jeopardize white supremacy.

"Pass" laws restricted the movements of Africans, and a dual wage system under which a white man might be paid ten times as much as an African doing the same work was frankly recognized. The Afrikaner leader in this arrangement was Field Marshal Smuts, who had been a military hero on the Boer side during the war. Smuts always had to contend with a right-wing opposition from Afrikaners who still smarted under the humiliation of the Boer War and who regarded the very modest privileges afforded the native population as a dangerous liberalism which was likely to undermine white superiority. Smuts's military prestige and political astuteness enabled him to keep a cooperative policy with the British in force for many years, but eventually the right-wing opposition won out.

EMERGENCE OF APARTHEID

In 1948 this opposition arose to power in the form of the Nationalist Party, which advocated apartheid, a form of separate development for white and nonwhite which theoretically amounted to segregation in all walks of life. This was hardly a radical change from previous practice in South Africa, and many of the critics of apartheid argued that white supremacy was so firmly bulwarked that a formal policy of apartheid was "unnecessary." The difference between the adherents and the opponents of apartheid lay in their interpretation of social change and in their vision of an ideal solution to the "native problem," but did not imply any conflict over white supremacy. As Field Marshall Smuts remarked at one time, "There are certain things about which all South Africans are agreed, all parties and all sections, except for those who are quite mad. The first is that it is a fixed policy to maintain white supremacy in South Africa."[17]

The more liberal school regarded the Bantu as an attractive but backward race who were in need of tutelage for an indefinite period of time. It was essential that control of the government should be in white hands, but some degree of participation might be allowed to the Bantu and this could be expected to increase gradually over a period of time. The economic and social conditions of the Bantu and the Europeans were so far apart that a high degree of segregation was considered advisable. Segregation, however, was modified by the interaction of whites and Bantu as participants in economic enterprise, and integration could be allowed where it favored such enterprise. There was also a small, highly educated group of Coloured and Indians emerging, and these could be safely allowed to mingle with whites on roughly equal terms.

To most of the world, South Africa during the Smuts regime constituted a "Herrenvolk democracy"[18] with a frank recognition of white supremacy and only token gestures toward any degree of equality for the nonwhite populations. To the Nationalist Party, which assumed power in 1948, the apparently feeble concessions toward equality and integration constituted a hole in the dike which would eventually be enlarged and would endanger the entire structure. As they saw the situation, the four to one numerical predominance of nonwhite over white meant that any concession to integration or political participation had potential danger. Thus the aim of society was not a benevolent partnership with the white man as the senior and guiding partner, but frank recognition of the white man as boss for eternity. The nationalists at times spoke of the benefits which the civilizing mission of the whites had brought to the Africans but assimilation was not their aim.

In fact, European acculturation was seen as a major danger to the African:

Not only is the culture of the whites slavishly imitated, without any con-

---

[17] J. C. Smuts, Prime Minister, speaking in the Union House of Assembly, Cape Town, March 13, 1945, cited on title page of Oliver Walker, *Kaffirs are Lively* (London, Gollancz, 1948).

[18] The Herrenvolk democracy concept is developed by Pierre van den Berghe in *South Africa: A Study in Conflict*, pp. 29, 64, 201. It designates a society in which the ruling ethnic groups operate democratically within group lines but dictatorially in reference to subordinate groups.

sideration of its merits or demerits, but the Bantu is exposed to evils of a different kind, evils which were formerly unknown to him. He becomes acquainted with crime and confusion and subjected to ethical, moral and spiritual decay.

Since these phenomena are alien to the traditional Bantu way of life, he tends to degenerate, and if the process continues unabated it can result in a rootless, urbanised and semi-Westernised Bantu society that is a danger to itself.[19]

Grave dangers were seen in the effort to encourage development of the Bantu along European lines, and it was assumed that, for a group of their particular condition and mentality, the only fruitful road was the one toward the development of indigenous culture. Rather than being Europeanized, Africans should be aided in "revitalizing" their own language and tradition. The following statement is typical of many expressed along this line:

The Bantu has his roots in the tribal system, and for centuries has been governed by its laws and conventions. To cut those roots in one blow would mean the crippling of the Bantu's soul and render him impotent to draw from his own cultural heritage. In developing the Bantu's governmental institutions a start is made with that which they know. There will naturally be adjustments and adaptations in accordance with the claims of modern civilization. These will be effected by themselves and with the assistance of the Europeans.

The allegation that South Africa is retribalizing the so-called "detribalized" Bantu is void of truth. Very few Bantu are completely detribalized. There is, for instance, not a single Zulu who cannot speak Zulu or who does not cling to certain Zulu customs. Where tribalism is revitalized and modernized and developed into a progressive force, it does not imply that the literate Bantu would be expected to go back to the kraal and the mud hut; it means the spiritual return to his fold so that he is not lost to his own nation but may serve his nation and help uplift his people with his newly acquired skills. In this way they too will be led from darkness to light.[20]

The Nationalists saw apartheid as a realistic approach to the racial problems of South Africa and were determined to wipe out any lingering vestiges of assimilationist or integrationist practices. Thus intermarriage was outlawed and interracial sexual relations were made a serious crime for either Africans or whites. African representation in the legislature was completely eliminated, the "pass" laws were strengthened and, with minor exceptions, the education of Africans in European universities was prohibited.

Since Africans form an important part of the industrial labor force, it is impossible to enforce complete separation at all times. Instead a number

---

[19] M. D. C. De Wet Nel, "Bantu Policy In South Africa," in James Duffy and Robert Manners, (eds.), *Africa Speaks.* Reprinted by permission of Van Nostrand Reinhold Company. (Princeton, Van Nostrand, 1961), p. 199. Copyright © 1961 by Litton Educational Publishing, Inc.

[20] Ibid., p. 201.

of policies have been devised for different situations, which allow economic cooperation while still minimizing association. Van den Berghe categorizes these in the following classification:[21]

1. *Micro-segregation*, i. e., segregation in public and private facilities (such as waiting-rooms, railway carriages, post-office counters, washrooms etc.) located in areas inhabited by members of different racial groups.

2. *Meso-segregation*, i. e., the physical segregation resulting from the existence of racially homogeneous residential ghettos within multiracial urban areas.

3. *Macro-segregation*, i. e., the segregation of racial groups in discrete territorial units, such as the 'Native Reserves' of South Africa, now being restyled as 'Bantustans.' [officially called Homelands.]

Micro-segregation would not be needed if the complete separation had developed, since there would then be little occasion for white and nonwhite to use common facilities. As in the American South of the pre–civil-rights period, the maintenance of separate and usually unequal facilities is a constant reminder of white dominance in a multiracial situation.

Meso-segregation is an effort to keep economic mixing from spilling over into non–work-related contacts based on common residence. Meso-separation included an effort to eliminate mixed residential districts by the evacuation of the nonwhites and even a ban on nonwhite domestic servants remaining overnight in white households.

Macro-segregation was held to express the true ideals of apartheid and was to be attained through geographical separation, envisaged as the development of semiautonomous, but probably not independent, states called Bantustans. The Bantustans were to be areas in which primarily agricultural blacks would be able to maintain and perfect a tribal culture; the language of the schools would be the indigenous language and the officers of the local government would be African. It was also envisioned that some Bantustans might border European industrial establishments so that Africans could commute to the white industrial areas for employment during the day and go back to the Bantustans after working hours. The project is described in South African terms as follows:

the central aim of apartheid is eventually to develop the reserves set aside for African occupation into self-governing states, colloquially known as "Bantustans". The Whites will retain exclusive rights in their own part of the country, where Africans are regarded only as visitors. In return . . . Africans (officially

---

[21] Pierre L. van den Berghe, "Racial Segregation in South Africa: Degrees and Kinds," in Heribert Adam (ed.), *South Africa: Sociological Perspectives* (London, Oxford University Press, 1971), p. 37; reprinted from *Cahiers d'Études Africaines*, Vol. 6, No. 23, 1966.

known as "Bantu") will be free from white interference in the Reserves, each race developing separately in harmonious disjunction. . . . In other words, South Africa's answer to the world's hatred of apartheid is to push it to its logical conclusion, which is complete separation of the races, both territorial and social.[22]

The advocates of apartheid regard the Bantustans as a benevolent device that will enable the Africans to achieve self-determination without white interference. The opponents claim that the amount of land allotted is so small in proportion to the population that it is unrealistic to feel that the Bantustans can ever be economically viable. Further, they contend that the major items of control are still in the hands of white government and that, rather than real self-determination, the Bantustans represent a repressive direction of African life by white supremacists. Other critics claim that the Bantustans have been ineffective in reducing African urbanization and charge that the main function of the Bantustans is not to develop African separatism but simply to serve as a propaganda device. Frank Taylor, for instance, in a 1968 statement, charges that the development of the Bantustans has had no success in reducing African urbanization: "After twenty years of apartheid . . . the hard fact is that the ratio of Africans to whites outside the home-lands—that is in the urban centers of 'white' South Africa—is rising every year instead of falling. In these so-called "white" areas there were 14 Africans to every 10 whites when a survey was taken last year."[23]

INDEPENDENCE FOR THE BANTUSTANS

According to the white South African view, the ultimate destiny of the Bantustans is independence which will enable each major tribal group to control a separate country. In 1976, the most developed Bantustan area, the Transkei, was awarded independence and, in 1977, similar independence was granted to BophutoTswana. To date, most of the rest of the world has refused to recognize these countries. South Africans, however, argue that eventually they are bound to win international acceptance. When all Bantustans receive their independence, South Africa will no longer be a country with a black majority. Instead, whites will be the majority and separate parliaments will be set up for the Indian and colored populations. The majority of black

---

[22]Christopher R. Hill: *Bantustans: The Fragmentation of South Africa* (New York, Oxford University Press, 1964), p. 1.

[23]Colin Legum and John Drysdale, *African Contemporary Record: Annual Survey and Documents, 1968–1969* (London, African Research Limited, Africa House, 1969), p. 288.

Africans will no doubt live in the white areas, but they will be citizens of independent countries who will have the same status in the Republic of South Africa as do the *Gastarbeiters* (guest workers) from Yugoslavia, Italy and Spain who work in Switzerland or Germany. The most rigid rules of segregation are being abolished, but the black workers in Johannesburg will have no more political rights in the South African Republic than an Italian working in Lugano has in Switzerland.

BophutoTswana and Transkei have government buildings, legislatures, executives and all the trappings of independence. They are not under the direct control of the Republic of South Africa and they can, and have, taken opposing views. On the other hand, it is difficult to see how they can be economically viable and their territories are not contiguous. BophutoTswana, for instance, is comprised of six segments, none of which are connected. At the moment, their governments could not exist without a South African subsidy.

The idea of independent Bantustans is really another form of apartheid or separate development. The theory is that black Africans are not only too different from whites to form a common nation, but the various tribes are too different from each other to get along in the same political unit. Therefore, nations erected on a tribal basis will not only allow black and white Africans to go their separate ways, but will also avoid the tribal rivalries which have bothered other African nations. Independent Bantustans, or apartheid with African equality recognized, represent the application of cultural pluralism to South Africa. This may, indeed, be more feasible than majority rule based on the integration of a very heterogeneous population. The question is whether independent Bantustans can possibly develop a self sustaining economy.

From the outset, the development of an internal domestic structure that will afford the Transkeians a chance to earn a living was one of the biggest tasks facing Transkei. This problem still plagues the area. Because the province is unable to provide the necessary number of jobs, very large numbers of Transkeians are forced to seek employment outside of the "homeland" as domestic servants, mine workers, and migrant farm workers. Hill describes the condition of the province and appraises the prospects for the future:

Vast numbers of Africans in the Transkei cannot make a living off the land and must seek employment outside. According to figures given to the Parliament in May 1962 there was only 20,592 in paid employment within the Territory in 1962, and of these over 8,000 were in domestic service. Earlier in the year the Minister had said that 115,000 Transkei Africans seek work in the mines every year, 28,000 to 30,000 on European farms, and 1,000 or more in other industries.[23]

---

[23] Hill, *Bantustans,* pp. 85–86.

Neither argiculture nor industry is conducted on the scale which would enable the majority of the labor force to earn a living within the Transkei. As far as agriculture is concerned, the amount of land is simply inadequate. The potential of industry is harder to evaluate, but it seems doubtful that adequate funds for the massive capital investment required would be available under the present policies of separate development. All financial institutions are under the control of South Africa, and it is unlikely to give priority to the needs of the Bantustans.

The other Native Areas are worse off than Transkei. They have yet to achieve even so-called self-government. Zululand is still in the hands of Chiefs and their headsmen or councilors, who jealously guard the last vestiges of traditional power.[24] In the Natal Province there are 11,808 square miles designated as African land, with over a million people trying to eke out a living on it. The land is overpopulated and, as in Transkei, many of the inhabitants must seek employment in the border areas because of the surplus rural population. In all these areas, education is falling farther and farther behind that of the whites and even behind that of many of the newly independent nations of Africa, especially Zambia. Housing is an ever present problem with little relief in sight in the near future for millions of Africans.[25]

The conclusion, therefore, is inescapable that under the present policy of separate development the Bantustan Areas cannot succeed. Sir de Villiers Graaff, right-wing leader of the Official Opposition, speaking before the United Party in August 1968, answered the question on the success of the Bantustans: "Who is there who would dare to claim that the National Party is today closer to a solution of the race question than 20 years ago? . . . The truth is that where there was separation there was no development; and where there was development there was no separation."[26]

Rather than a realistic proposal for cultural pluralism, the Bantustan program appears to be a technique for channeling African protest into

---

[24] A *New York Times* dispatch for Dec. 4, 1971, quotes the minister of Bantu administration as promising that the 4,000,000 Zulus of South Africa would eventually receive independence. The statement was made at the installation of a new Zulu Paramount Chief and promised a "fully fledged, self governing and independent nation." No date was set for "independence" and no indication given as to the powers that might be reserved for the Republic of South Africa, but the fact that such a possibility is even mentioned may be significant.

[25] Many of these problems, especially housing, could be greatly reduced if the economic picture would improve for Africans. According to Legum and Drysdale (*African Contemporary Record*, p. 289): "The White national income per head was R1,400 to R1,500 a year—more than 10 times that of the other three races combined. The national income per head for urban Africans was R120 to R130 a year, and for Bantustan Africans R30 to R35 a year. The non-white population was doubling itself twice as fast as the whites . . . to reach 26 millions in the 1990s."

[26] Ibid., p. 289.

unrealistic dreams of separate nationalistic development. The Bantustans occupy only about 13 percent of the South African land, although the Bantu people comprise 70 percent of the South African population. They contain few of the country's mineral resources, no ports, and none of its major cities or industrial areas. They are scattered into 260 separated areas which there is no plan to bring together. The economic handicaps of the plan are highlighted by the fact that since the establishment of apartheid in 1948 over 1,000,000 Africans have moved from the reserves to the cities.[27]

There are some signs, however, that the Bantustan brand of black nationalism may not be so innocuous as it seems. While the intellectuals have usually taken the position that the stress on indigenous culture was merely a device to shut Africans out of influential positions in the modern society, there may be another side to the coin. Currently there is an effort to make the apartheid-fostered tribalism a vehicle for race pride and signs reading, "I'm black and I'm proud" are starting to appear in black settlements.[28] The whites in South Africa may yet find that Africans are taking African identity in a way that challenges white supremacy.

THE COLOURED POPULATION

In South Africa the term "coloured" refers to one of known mixed European, Malay, Indian, and African ancestry. They were estimated to number about 2,300,000 in 1971.[29] They are most numerous in Cape Colony where, in earlier days of an unchallenged slave society misceg-enation was widespread. Criticism of mixed unions arose only gradually as the Boer-English clash over slavery drove the Boers into a segregated stance in defense of white superiority. As long as white superiority was unchallenged, sexual access to the non-European group was seen as one of the aspects of white privilege. When the British challenged this system, the Boers felt themselves compelled to establish a color line which pro-tected the purity of the master race. The turn to sexual segregation was a gradual one, miscegenation continued to be fairly frequent, and even intermarriage occasionally took place, until the apartheid legislation of 1948–1949 forbade interracial sexual relations either in or outside of marriage.

It is the situation of the Coloured which is responsible for the notorious race classification boards of South Africa, which give identity cards classi-

[27] Based on summation in Colin and Margaret Legum, *The Bitter Choice: Eight South Africans; Resistance to Tyranny*, (New York, New World Pub. Co., 1968), pp. 21–22.

[28] Peter R. Webb, "South Africa's Black Mood," *Newsweek* 77, (May 10, 1971), p. 47.

[29] Ibid., p. 47.

fying indivduals as white, Coloured, Indian, or African. The "Coloured" vary in complexion from white to very dark, they are almost totally detached from indigenous African culture, a majority speak Afrikaans (the language of the settlers of Dutch ancestry) and about 30 percent are members of the Dutch Reformed Church.[30] Wolheim provides the following portrait:

> The Coloured people of South Africa are by no means a homogeneous group. They range in skin colour from people indistinguishable from Whites to people indistinguishable from Africans; they speak a variety of languages, mainly English and Afrikaans; they belong to all the churches to which White people belong; they range from a small number of extremely wealthy persons to a large number of very poor ones.[31]

Some of the actions of the Race Classification Appeal Boards and of the courts in deciding cases under the Immorality Act give an idea of the bizarre nature of South African racialism. Since descent is often mixed, appearance and acceptance by whites are the deciding factors under the racial Immorality Act, although under the racial classification act these factors may be ignored in favor of genealogical data. The difficulty of racial classification is indicated by a Supreme Court ruling that the Department of the Interior has the right to alter a person's racial classification more than once!

Racial classification may be made either by Race Classification Appeal Boards or directly by the Department of the Interior. No information was available concerning actions by the Department of the Interior, but board action in 1969 resulted in the reclassification of 91 persons from Coloured to white and 61 from Bantu to Coloured with no action in the opposite direction.[32] The Immorality Act, which bars sexual relations between those of different racial categories, is often invoked because of confusion over racial classification.

A brief synopsis of two of the cases tried under the Immorality Act indicates the vicissitudes of racially marginal people:[33]

> Mr. W.B.L. and Miss B.S. lived together in Johannesburg as a white married couple and were generally accepted as such, for seven years and had five children. He was white; she is stated to have had a white father and a Mauritian mother. As she was officially classified as coloured they could not marry. During June, they were charged under the Immorality Act: as a result of the publicity the man lost his job. The magistrate acquitted them: he found that the woman was coloured in appearance but generally accepted as white.

---

[30] van den Berghe, *South Africa*, p. 40.

[31] O. D. Wolheim, "The Coloured People of South Africa," *Race*, 2 (October 1963), p. 25. Published for the Institute of Race Relations, London, by the Oxford University Press; Copyright by the Institute of Race Relations, 1963.

[32] Muriel Horrell, *A Survey of Race Relations in South Africa* (Johannesburg, South African Institute of Race Relations, 1970), p. 29.

TABLE 6-1

Immorality Act
(statistics July 1968–June 1969)

	Charges		Convictions	
	M	F	M	F
White	591	21	336	9
Coloured	11	234	5	121
Asians	9	12	6	10
Africans	6	300	4	188

Source: Muriel Horrell, *A Survey of Race Relations in South Africa* (Johannesburg, South African Institute of Race Relations, 1970) p. 29.

Mr. A.P.J. van V., classified white, fell in love with a coloured girl. As he was dark skinned, he applied several times to be reclassified as coloured so they could marry but without success. They lived together for six years in his parents' home and had two children. Eventually someone reported them to the police. A magistrate at Meyerton found them guilty but imposed no sentence, ordering them to appear in court for sentence if called upon to within the next twelve months. Shortly afterwards, Mr. van V. won a further appeal to be reclassified Coloured: the appeals cost him about R2000.

The foregoing cases, although causing the parties involved great difficulty, had apparently happy endings, but such is not always the case. Whether or not one is convicted the mere fact that a charge is brought may be so threatening that life no longer seems worthwhile as indicated in the following cases:

... Mr. Z.E.B. a married man with four children was found hanging by his shirt in a police cell at Vanderbijlpark. He was facing charges of incitement to contravene the Immorality Act. Another married man Mr. H.D. also with four children was found in the same cells on November 6 in similar circumstances. Mr. J.C. of Excelsior shot himself while on bail after having been charged under the Act.[33]

While some of the cases arising under the Immorality Act concern individuals who are marginal in racial category and may not have been aware that they were violating the law, others undoubtedly realized that their actions were a contravention of both the law and strong social feeling. Sexual relations in these circumstances testify both to the degree of common understanding reached by the different racial groups and to the difficulty of forcing human relationships to follow the lines of official policy. The divergence between group viewpoints and personal behavior is indicated by the fact that Afrikaan-speaking whites outnumbered the English-speaking whites in the immorality cases. While the greatest amount of

---

[33] Ibid., p. 30. These cases are based on reports in South African newspapers.

miscegenation undoubtedly occurred in Cape Colony in the slavery period, the passing of slavery did not eliminate the power of sexual attraction across racial lines. Both the number of cases still arising under the Immorality Act, and the extent of intermarriage while it was legal, indicate that, at one time at least, the development of a biologically mixed society in South Africa was a real possibility.

A glance at the arrests for violation of the Immorality Act and the marriage statistics from 1926 until intermarriage was outlawed in 1949 indicate the effect of two factors: a pattern of hypergamy and the central position of the Coloured population. Hypergamy is a form of marriage in which the male is of a higher status than the female. This pattern is borne out in the record of arrests under the Immorality Act, which indicated a high proportion of white males and of African and Coloured females. A similar pattern may also be discerned in the record of mixed marriages, which indicated that approximately three fourths of all mixed marriages between 1925 and 1946 were hypergamous.[34]

Both the racial classification of offenders under the Immorality Act and the mixed marriage statistics demonstrate the acceptability of the Coloured as marital partners for other groups. While they are a minority of the offenders against the Immorality Act, the Coloured representation was several times its proportion of the South African population. The position of the Coloured in intermarriage is even more striking, as over 95 percent of the interracial marriages between 1926 and 1949 involved a Coloured person. Since the Coloured population was intermediate to both white and black, they might, in different circumstances, have played the same role in South Africa that the mestizos played in Mexico.

The Coloured population were the last of the nonwhites to lose the privileges which the British had extended in 1856 to the indigenous inhabitants of the Cape Colony.[35] This electoral equality was later diluted by waiving property and income qualifications for whites but not for others, and by giving the vote to white females but not to other women. Eventually the Bantu lost all right to vote and the Coloured were only allowed to vote for whites who represented them in Parliament. Even this limited franchise drew Nationalist criticism, and in 1972 all parliamentary voting by the Coloured was ended; this completely nullified the last vestige of the political rights obtained in the Cape Colony in the 19th century.[36]

As Coloured people had long lived and worked with whites they were especially affected by the Group Areas Act of 1950, which proposed to

---

[34] Pierre L. van den Berghe, *Race and Ethnicity* (New York: Basic Books, Inc., 1970), p. 231.

[35] Marais, *The Cape Coloured People*, pp. 156–57.

[36] Horrell, *A Survey of Race Relations in South Africa*, pp. 174–75.

TABLE 6–2

Number and Percentage of Interracial Marriages
by Race, 1925–1946

Racial combination	Number of marriages 1925–1946	Percent of total	Expected percent[*]
White-Coloured	1,766	13.33	7.60
White-Indian	116	0.88	2.53
White-African	277	2.09	56.51
African-Coloured	9,255	69.87	24.22
African-Indian	170	1.28	8.07
Indian-Coloured	1,662	12.55	1.08
Total	13,246	100.00	100.01

[*] The expected proportion for any given combination is:

$$P = \frac{p_j \cdot p_j}{\Sigma p_i \cdot p_j}$$

where p_i and p_j are proportions of the groups in the total population. The same assumptions
are made as in computing the exact proportion of intermarriage.
    Source: Pierre L. van den Berghe, *Race and Ethnicity* (New York, Basic Books, 1970), p.
232, table 13.

eliminate the so-called black spots, or areas in which blacks, Coloured, or
Indians were surrounded by whites. Its psychological impact was particularly severe among the Coloured, since it reversed policies nearly 300
years old and drove the Coloured from property in which they and their
ancestors thought they had secure tenure. It often meant a complete disruption of community life as well as a threat to employment. Schools,
churches, hospitals, shopping centers, and other community amenities
all had to be developed from scratch. An idea of the frustration involved
may be gleaned from the following description of one such removal
in 1969:

About 100 African families who lived at Macleantown, some 24 miles to the
northwest of East London, were, after about five months' warnings, moved
during March to Chalumna, about 30 miles from the city, on the other side of
the main railway to the interior, along the road to Peddie. They had to demolish
their previous homes, some of which were brick houses and others mud huts,
and sell or take with them useable building materials. Compensation was paid
to those who had title-deeds.
    Those who had owned land were given plots at Chalumna measuring about
one-half hectare. They were each allowed to take two head of cattle: many had
owned more. The others had to dispose of all their livestock at whatever prices
these would fetch, and were given residential stands only in the resettlement
area.
    A four-classroom school had been built in advance. Tents were available for
temporary accommodation: these were said to have been too small for some of
the families, and furniture had to be left in the open. The people had to dig

their own latrines. For the first three days the Department of Bantu Administration provided rations of mealiemeal.[37]

In spite of the erosion of the rights of the Coloured they still occupy a privileged position compared to that of the Bantu. The pass laws have not been applied to them and, while the Industrial Conciliation Act has shut them out of some occupations, it has given the Coloureds some protection against competition from the Bantu. Rex summarizes their position as follows:

The Cape Coloureds, however, have clearly been divided from the Afrikaner worker, not by their language and culture, which is simply a variant of Afrikaner working-class language and culture, but by the difference in the economic functions assigned to them and the rights which they enjoy. In economic terms the Coloured have established themselves in a range of skilled trades, in factory work and other minor roles and have succeeded in defending some of these positions against white competition. At the same time the fact of this competition has led to a continuous process of deprivation of political and social rights and to increasing segregation so that a niche has been found for the Coloured population, which, while it is a state of almost complete rightlessness compared with the white settler population, is nonetheless a position of great privilege when compared with that of the Bantu.[38]

That the Coloured's standard of living is generally higher than that of the indigenous African is undoubtedly true, but, since the government has become increasingly restrictive along color lines, there is little reason to believe that the Coloureds will continue to make significant progress in the republic. On the contrary, various Acts have already caused setbacks, and it is likely that opportunities will be lessened. Africans are asking for more lower-level jobs formerly occupied by Coloureds, who are trying to move up the economic ladder; the latter, in turn, must compete with whites who are not anxious to see their position occupied by nonwhites. Hence much of the progress that the Coloureds have experienced over the years may be wiped out or their future opportunities may be seriously impeded by an increasing number of structural barriers resulting from the apartheid policy. Because of these recent developments:

The relationship of co-operation and common loyalty has been changed for one of suspicion, distrust and dislike. More and more Coloured people are turning inward to themselves for their salvation and the numbers who look towards the African for future help are increasing. It seems incredible, but it is true, that the present regime representing only 3⅓ million White people should introduce legislation and take action which would deprive them, should a clash occur

---

[37] Ibid., pp. 132–33.

[38] John Rex, "The Plural Society: The South African Case," *Race,* 12 (April 1971), p. 411; published for the Institute of Race Relations, London, by the Oxford University Press. Copyright by Institute of Race Relations, 1971.

between White and African, of 1½ million stauch and loyal allies almost as sophisticated as themselves.[39]

The Coloured population still occupies an essentially marginal position in South African society. Light skin is prestigious and, in spite of the many rebuffs from the ruling party, there is still a tendency to reject African identity and to emphasize the relationship to the whites. A continuance of the drive to place all nonwhites in a frankly subordinate category may drive the Coloureds into identification with the Bantu. On the other hand, some of the more moderate Nationalists still advocate a policy of economic, cultural, and political assimilation for the Coloureds.[40] Such a policy would probably have the effect of cementing an alliance between the Coloureds and the white population and would do something to redress the white numerical inferiority. This policy gets no support from the present government, but it is not impossible in the future. Certainly a country which can make the Japanese "honorary whites" is capable of reassessing its attitude toward the mixed population.

THE INDIAN POPULATION

Indians in 1970 numbered about 600,000 and constituted three percent of the population. Indian population first appeared in South Africa when brought to Natal as indentured laborers for the sugar cane industry. For the most part, they have now left agricultural labor and constitute a middleman population serving primarily African customers. Most Indian enterprises operate at a marginal level, but a few individual businessmen have been strikingly successful and have accumulated rather considerable wealth. Indians have become an almost completely English-speaking group but have retained native dress, particularly for women, and have resisted conversion to Christianity. They are totally excluded from the Orange Free State and their residence and activities are restricted elsewhere. The current government option is for separate development for the Indians, although, up to the present writing, they are without even a vestige of representation, since Indian affairs are conducted entirely by Europeans appointed by the South African government.

The middleman position of the Indian has often produced the expected friction between them and the African population. This friction was highlighted in 1949 in riots by Zulus against Indians in Durban in which more than 142 were killed and over 1,000 were injured. Antipathy between the Bantu, the Coloured, and the Indians is one of the factors weakening the possibility of a united nonwhite resistance. Thus van den Berghe, in speak-

---

[39] O. D. Wolheim, "The Coloured People of South Africa," *Race*, No. 5 (October 1963), p. 33.

[40] Brown, *Against the World*, p. 174.

ing of the Pan-African Congress, describes it as not only militantly anti-European, but also anti-Indian and anti-Coloured.[41]

Although not identifying with Africans, the Indians have rather consistently struggled for a high status within the South African community. Mahatma Ghandi practiced law in South Africa and developed his doctrines of nonviolent resistance in campaigns for Indian rights within that country.[42] Like the Coloureds, Indians are a marginal group, oppressed by white discrimination and, at the same time, fearful of black nationalism. Black nationalism led to the exclusion of Indians in Uganda and might be expected to take the same form in South Africa if the Bantu ever assumed control.

FACTORS IN FUTURE DEVELOPMENT

The Republic of South Africa is often depicted as a country in which the forces of white domination and black nationalism are girding for a battle of annihilation sometime in the indefinite future. Indeed, this kind of feeling is not confined to outside observers and one can frequently talk to staunch nationalists of the apartheid persuasion who will say that, in their feeling, all they are doing is "buying time," meaning that before long the inevitable growth in numbers of the African population and their increasing sophistication in modern technology will lead to a bloody overthrow of white rule. These prophecies of an inevitable conflict with consequent suffering to the society may be fully warranted, but it is seldom true that societies take the most obvious course and it may be worth while to consider the factors which could be expected to affect long-term developments.

Value Clashes

The majority of the people in the Republic of South Africa are Africans whose values are molded by traditional social norms somewhat eroded by contact with Western culture but still viable to a great extent.[43] The nominal standard for the society, however, is set by the values of the whites. These are values of a different character than traditional African norms and are imposed by the white military and economic power. Such values meet rather considerable passive resistance from Africans, and their effect is diluted by various value conflicts within the white community.

Culture contact usually leads to some degree of cultural diffusion and a consequent modification of values. In South Africa we have the paradox

---

[41] van den Berghe, *South Africa*, p. 168.

[42] Fisher, *The Afrikaners*, p. 308.

[43] In this topic we are indebted to van den Berghe, *Race and Ethnicity*, pp. 216–46.

of an ethnocentric white group which is firmly convinced of the value of its own customs and ideals and yet, at the same time, resists the assimilation of Africans into the total social fabric. The result is that traditional African norms are not considered legitimate and that the lack of social acceptance deprives Africans of the support that might encourage a whole-hearted acceptance of western culture.

Several examples of this type of conflict may be given. One, for instance, is the attitude toward work. African cash incomes for those working in mines range around 200 Rand (about $280) a year.[44] This enables Africans to subsist and to purchase a few manufactured goods, but does not enable them to have anything like full participation in a modern economy. The result is that the African tends to view his work, not as a major commitment which will carry him ever more deeply into an expanding economy, but simply as a necessary evil that permits him to return afterward to the village and to live for a few months at a subsistence level without the grueling labor of mine or factory.

Europeans thus argue, and perhaps with partial justification, that higher wages tend to reduce the labor supply, on the theory that the minimum amount needed for subsistence living is earned more quickly, and thus Africans are less committed to the labor force. Insofar as this rationalization is true, it reflects a major barrier to upward social mobility by the Africans and also indicates the consequence of a partial rejection of African economic integration.

Somewhat similar is the situation in regard to cattle. Cattle represent the favorite means of establishing the prestige and status of a family and also the most acceptable form of payment for *lobola* or bride price. The emphasis is on the gross number of cattle rather than their contribution in milk, meat, or hides. African population has been growing and the land available to Africans has been shrinking with the result of overgrazing, eroded lands, and scrawny herds. The South African government has endeavoured to introduce a culling of the herds and a reduction of their total size, only to meet with resistance from the African population to actions which are undertaken "for their own good." Cattle retain their place as being intrinsically valuable among the Bantu in almost the same way that gold holds a position of a medium of exchange in the Western world. Africans, when confronted with the difficulties which this stand permits, are likely to reply that the trouble is not too much cattle but too little land.

Family customs are also a basic source of cultural misunderstanding. In South Africa, the ideal African family system was polygyny (plural

---

[44] The Peace Commission of the National Catholic Federation of Students estimate the African miner to average 18.3 Rand per month—*Race Relations News* 33 (December 1971), 3. In 1971 the Rand was about $1.40.

wives) rather than monogamy, and the emphasis was on the extended rather than the nuclear family. The *lobola,* or bride price, is not so much a form of barter as it is a method of symbolizing the obligations of the respective families. Thus the bride price symbolizes the investment in the marriage and, in case of adultery, this investment is damaged and the readjustment is made by payment of fines. To the whites, this seems like a gross commercialization of marriage and an evidence that the sexual impulses of the Africans are unrestrained. African values are reflected in the native law which presumably regulates affairs on the reserves, or Bantustans, but this is a law which has been codified and frequently administered by whites who lack an understanding of its basic premises.

Many South African whites would deny the charge of ethnocentrism and would say that they recognize the value of the indigenous social system. These are not values which would be expected to stand up in comparison with those of a modern society, but they do represent a form of social control suitable for a people of limited development. South African whites would point to the fact that they have tried to maintain the system of chiefs and have encouraged native languages, ceremonies, and cultures. The difficulty with this argument is that the real authority of native institutions has been blunted. Strong societies such as the Zulu nation have been dispersed, and the chiefs are obvious puppets who can be appointed and replaced at will by the European authorities. In these circumstances traditional society loses its prestige and power of social control, and white support only serves to erode still further the legitimacy of the traditional rulers.

The migration to the cities, with incomplete assimilation, has led to real social disorganization among the African population. This social disorganization takes the form of violence, alcoholism, divorce, and family irregularity. These phenomena are viewed by the whites as evidence of the instability and weakness of African character and of inability to adjust to the standards of a Western type of society. Since the growing needs of industry for labor make a policy of "retribalization" impossible, the answer has been more repressive laws and administration, which seem to aggravate the evils they are designed to heal. This is another situation in which industrialism has destroyed the traditional culture while racial discrimination prevents African assimilation of the European value system.

Cultural conflict takes a different form among the minority of educated persons of the nonwhite population. This group is rather thoroughly committed to an acceptance of the superiority of a Western value system. Consequently, they find communication with the masses difficult and become marginal men who are accepted neither by those still close to the traditional society nor by the whites. Their adjustment is handicapped by white rejection, on the one hand, and a feeling of "cultural shame" in regard to their background, on the other. It should be stated, however, that this group of educated Africans represent a "petty bourgeoisie" who are assuming economic leadership and who, under more favorable conditions, might also assume political leadership.

The white value system is hardly a consistent one. The first and most obvious discrepancy is in the interpretation of Christianity. One faction—probably the dominant grouping—in the Dutch Reformed Church views the Afrikaaners as the chosen people who have been selected to bring civilization to the wilderness and to subdue the savages. While they were called on to bring light to the heathen, the heathen, since they are of another race, are regarded as destined by God for a separate type of existence. They are doomed to a subordinate role as "hewers of wood and drawers of water" in penance for the sins of their ancestors who looked without shame upon the naked form of their father Jacob when he lay drunk. Thus there is a paternalistic drive to bring the native population into the Christian fold, but this is not accompanied by any feeling of brotherhood or equality.

On the other hand, there is the stream of Christian thinking, which has not totally escaped the Dutch churches and is largely reflected within the English churches, which emphasizes the brotherhood of man and the fatherhood of God. This type of thinking sees the role of white as only temporarily that of trusteeship and feels that Christian brotherhood means an ultimate equality of all the races of mankind.

The two viewpoints are sharply divergent, and the expulsion or imprisonment of dissenting clergymen has been one of the most frequent actions of the Nationalist regime. Even within the Dutch Reformed Church, occasional questions are asked and criticisms raised, but, as of yet, these seem to be the expression of an impotent minority. Ferment in the Dutch Reformed Church surfaced in the 1960 conference at Cottesloe, which proclaimed that no one who believed in Jesus Christ should be excluded from any church on the grounds of race and that there were no scriptural grounds for the banning of mixed marriages. These conclusions were repudiated by the Afrikaans churches but were supported by some clergymen, among them Byers Naude, who was dismissed from the ministry when he became the head of the Christian Institute, an organization which aims to cut across barriers of race and social distinctions to foster Christian unity. In 1967 Beyers Naude and an associate, Albert Guyser, sued for libel when a newspaper charged them with being Communists and were awarded $37,500 damages.[45]

Such dissent in the Dutch Reformed Church is that of a small minority, and the significant thing is not that it is widespread but that it exists at all.

---

[45] C. Legum, *The Bitter Choice*, pp. 127–34. M. Brown, *Against the World*, pp. 176–95, has an incisive account of the position of the churches in which he credits the Afrikaans churches with having the greatest potential as change agents.

Views of this type are more common among British clergymen and may represent a majority sentiment but not one that is salient enough to be a driving force against apartheid. Probably the main significance of this split in attitude among Christians is that it threatens the unity of the Nationalists, since it throws open to question the basic ideological premises upon which their policies are based.[46]

Another conflict which will be dealt with more at length later is that between white supremacy and economic rationalization. As long as the primary need of economic development was cheap labor, there was no clash between these objectives, but the rapid development of industry has meant a growing need for skilled and technically trained labor which makes the restrictions on the use of Africans seem anachronistic to the profit-motivated entrepreneur. This dissension is related to the cleavage between whites of English and Dutch ancestry.

The British whites have a higher income with more advantageous positions in industry and the professions. They are more open to change and hope that the pattern of race relations in South Africa can be rephrased in a way which will bring less conflict with the rest of the world. The Dutch, on the other hand, even though they are a majority of the whites in the country, have the "siege mentality" of a minority. They see themselves as the chosen people who have the superior value system but one not understood either by those outside the land or by the British in the country. They represent the conservatism of the farmer and the small shopkeeper and the laborer. Hence the winds of change seem to them a threat and their racial conservatism is a part of a general world view which sees virtue in the maintenance of the past and only danger in opening South Africa freely to the forces of change.

Bantustan and African pride

The obvious interpretation of the Bantustan policy is that it is a device to segregate the Africans and to keep them from the kind of exposure to Western culture which would make them competitive with the whites. Presumably Western culture is the "white man's culture," which is good for him but which is bad for the African. The African who is exposed to Western culture becomes socially disorganized (and certainly there are many examples of this). On the other hand, the African who lives in a situation where he can see his own immediate authorities and feels that he shares in making the decisions which immediately concern him will have a feeling of satisfaction and peace. If he is educated in his native language and trained in his native crafts, his ambitions will move along

---

[46] Adjustment is possible for the regime. In 1973 a Billy Graham evangelistic meeting in Durban attracted 45,000 people, half of them nonwhite. It was the first integrated meeting to have been held in the stadium. *The Church Herald*, April 13, 1973, pp. 5, 6.

lines which do not make him a subversive force in regard to the European control of South African society.

The other side of the coin, of course, has not been overlooked within South Africa itself. This is that the African may develop an increased pride in his culture and in his race. This pride may lead to separate development, but it may also lead to a questioning of the legitimacy of white dominance. For the most part, African nationalist leaders have viewed tribalism and tradition as something which the whites are trying to impose upon them. However, the prospect that even a modest development of Bantustans may lead to a very real revival of nativism, in a way which will be hard for the South African government to challenge and yet threatening to the basis of its rule, is a real possibility.

White South Africans have spoken ambiguously as to whether or not independence might be the ultimate goal of the Bantustans, since the promise of independence might seem, on the one hand, to justify their policy and, on the other hand, to threaten their continued security. Africans themselves are divided, and some have attacked the Bantustan idea on the very basis that it is opposed to eventual African integration in South African society. Still other Africans have taken hold of the opportunity to use native ceremonies to express nationalistic feelings along tribal lines. This is a type of "retribalization" which may ultimately issue in forms far different from those desired by white segregationists.

Demographic trends

One of the defenses against the charge that a white-dominated South African government is based on conquest is the assertion that the area was largely unpopulated at the time of initial European settlement. Since the ancestors of most people were migrants, there is no large group which can claim historic occupancy of the land, and the descendants of the early European settlers have as much claim to be considered "indigenous" as the blacks whose ancestors came from other parts of Africa. However this claim is evaluated, there is another population aspect which is more important and that is the demographic trend at the present time. Obviously, population proportions are one factor in the continuation of white dominance. There are many factors other than population size which have more immediate importance, but, in the long run, if whites are a decreasing minority, this will affect their relative power position.

Between 1960 and 1970, the white proportion of the South African population declined from 19.29 percent to 17.75 percent. This may seem like a small decline but, considering the fact that the Asian and Coloured birth rate was more than 50 percent higher than the white rate (no accurate figures are available for Africans) and that the comparatively high nonwhite death rate is declining, this trend may accelerate in the coming years. Thus the supporters of apartheid face the prospect of becoming a proportionately smaller numerical minority inside South Africa at a time when world opinion is becoming increasingly critical of the apartheid position. This does not mean that apartheid will collapse at any predictable date, but it certainly bodes ill for the long-term prospects.

TABLE 6–3

Population trends

Group	1960	1970	Percent increase
Africans	10,928,000	14,893,000	36.3
Whites	3,088,000	3,779,000	22.4
Coloured	1,509,000	1,996,000	32.3
Asians	477,000	614,000	28.7
Total	16,002,000	21,282,000	32.9

Source: Adapted from Muriell Horrell, *A Survey of Race Relations in South Africa* (Johannesburg: Institute of Race Relations, 1971), p. 24.

Economic aspects

The Marxist viewpoint is that apartheid represents the exploitation of black labor by white capital. This would certainly seem to be true if one looks at the wages of black labor, which are only a fraction of those paid to whites. According to the Secretary of the Johannesburg Chamber of Commerce, in 1969 white workers in industry and construction averaged 3,124 Rand per year, while Bantu averaged 566 Rand, or a ratio of 5.5 to 1.[47]

There are, however, at least two criticisms of this policy from a strictly economic standpoint. One is that African labor is not really as cheap as it might appear, and the other that racial policies prevent the recruitment of the type of labor which is needed. A great deal of African labor is of a migratory character in which the men leave their homes in the reserves and come to work for a period of time in mines, mills, and factories, and then return to the reserves. This means that for approximately half of the time, the worker is living in the native reserve where his labor is relatively, and almost absolutely, unproductive. Further, the enforcement of this type of system requires an enormous expenditure on police. Finally, cheap labor is usually unproductive labor because of the physical condition and the lack of motivation of the laborers. It also limits the extension of a consumers' market and therefore the possibility of an outlet for manufactured goods.

Even more serious than these considerations has been the development of a need for skilled and technical labor. This is an almost invariant tendency in an industrializing society. South Africa is definitely in the class

---

[47] Horrell, *A Survey of Race Relations in South Africa*, p. 80.

of industrialized nations with a high per capita income which produced a 46 percent increase in real income (allowing for price changes) for whites between 1939 and 1953.[48] Even at a time when there is a great deal of unemployment of Africans, industrialists are constantly complaining about the shortage of skilled, technical, and professional personnel.

There are elaborate schemes to lure Europeans to South Africa for these functions. An obvious alternative to this practice is the upgrading of black labor. This upgrading is now forbidden by laws, custom, and union practice, which declare that any kind of service work which is primarily for whites must be performed by whites, including such low-status jobs as taxi driving and bus driving; and that most jobs of a skilled or technical character are automatically white jobs. This policy has been challenged by Harry Oppenheimer, a gold mining magnate, and by various other industrialists, mostly British.

There has been a small increase in the proportion of Africans in more skilled and responsible jobs and a change of policy to permit the open extension of such utilization of African labor is a continuing point of debate within South Africa. Indeed, it may be possible to argue that restrictions on the use of African labor impede industrial development in the total community and that whites as well as blacks are paying a heavy price for the economic policies of apartheid.

There is a continual argument over the upgrading of African labor to allow them to enter skilled occupations. Usually employers favor such upgrading, while it is opposed by labor unions (Africans are not allowed to belong to registered unions), and by the more extreme advocates of apartheid. Typical of the employer attitude is the following statement by the chief technical advisor to the Chamber of Mines:

Time and time again the industry has had to stand by and see its reasonable endeavors to make everyone take one step up the ladder frustrated either by short sighted union policy or political expediency. . . . This is a time when men, not only of good will but of common sense should get together and examine methods for using all the manpower in South Africa to the best possible advantage.[49]

He added another blow to South African racial stereotypes by stating that aptitude testing had proved many Africans capable of doing jobs held by whites.[50]

---

[48] F. P. Spooner, *South African Predicament* (London, Cape (J) Ltd., 1960), p. 284. Evidence that this growth is continuing is seen in a report of the South African Reserve Bank that the gross domestic product, at constant prices, increased over 12 percent in 1970. Horrell, *A Survey of Race Relations in South Africa*, p. 79.

[49] Statement of Vic. Robinson, cited in Horrell, *A Survey of Race Relations in South Africa*, p. 114.

[50] Ibid., p. 114.

Some idea of the problems involved in attempting to restrict certain jobs to whites is illustrated by the reports regarding railway and postal labor in 1970:

Replying to questions on 28 and 31 July the Minister (of Transport) said that 88 Coloured, 101 Indians and 1,299 Africans were then temporarily employed on work normally performed by white graded staff—mainly as flagmen, trade hands, shed attendants, and stokers and deck hands on tugs and dredgers. In addition 1,371 Coloured, 140 Indians and 12,698 Africans were performing work formerly done by unskilled and ungraded white railworkers.[51]

Although most of the postal employees were whites, a number of others had been added in posts normally occupied by whites including:

     783   Coloured postmen and messengers
     243   Indian postmen and messengers
   1,068   African postmen and messengers[52]

In the rest of Africa, one of the marks of white prestige is that manual work is usually performed by blacks. Thus the visitor who comes to South Africa after a sojourn in other African countries will perhaps be surprised to see whites driving taxis and buses, carrying mail, doing routine factory work, and working at a number of tasks which, in Africa, are usually considered to threaten white status. In South Africa, this indicates that the general white prestige has been shared by the white laborer, who has marked off as his own a number of occupations which in other countries are carried out by African laborers.

The idea of "white jobs" is an exclusionary device which preserves a section of the labor market for whites and enables them to draw wages which are sometimes ten times as high as those paid to Africans. Such high labor costs are obviously a handicap to business, but the color bar has not been directly challenged since the 1920s, when a large-scale strike of white workers in the Witwatersrand district prevented the admission of African workers to certain semiskilled classifications.[53] Union labor has the power to prevent any direct challenge to the color bar, and the gradual upgrading of nonwhite labor has been disguised by circumlocutions or justified as a temporary expedient.

An example of the kind of casuistry often employed in deciding questions of occupational upgrading is seen in the following summary of an argument over the racial composition of construction labor:

Early in 1970 the Department of Labor intervened when Roberts Construction Company was using African building workers to do block laying in a low

---

[51] Ibid., p. 122.

[52] Ibid., p. 122.

[53] Sheila T. Van der Horst, "The Effects of Industrialization on Race Relations in South Africa," in Guy Hunter (ed.), Industrialization and Race Relations (London, Oxford University Press, 1965), pp. 97–140.

cost housing scheme for whites at Pietermaritzburg at lower wages than those payable to artisans of other racial groups. Work was held up for three months while the company tried to recruit other artisans and sub-contract some work; but these efforts were unsuccessful. Eventually, with the knowledge of the Department, the company re-employed the Africans, overcoming the reservations contained in the job reservation determination by not issuing specialized tools. The Africans were provided with gardening trowels instead of builders trowels, used the handles of axes instead of hammers, and made use of jigs instead of lines and levels to lay blocks.[54]

The racial classification policies affect the relations of nonwhite groups with each other as well as the relations of all groups and the whites. Thus it was announced in March 1970 that the government had reaffirmed its refusal to allow Indians to employ Africans as domestic servants or nursemaids.[55] Apparently an African domestic servant was a prestige symbol suitable only for whites.

Within the Bantustans the racial classification of jobs still continues. Even government plans to allow for the gradual training and upgrading of Bantu miners within their own areas runs into union opposition: "Following talks with the Minister of Mines, the executive committee of the Mineworkers Union issued a statement saying that it had decided not to support the Government's plan for the gradual advancement of Africans in the Homelands. The committee called upon members of the union to refuse to train African miners."[56]

This kind of conflict represents a refutation of some interpretations of South African racial policies. Evidently it is usually the capitalists who favor the upgrading of African personnel and the white workmen who resist such changes. This means that, at the present stage of industrial development, apartheid is repugnant not only to liberal and humanitarian sentiments but also to business interests.

International pressures

Most of the rest of the world has looked upon South African policies of apartheid, or, as it is currently called, "separate development," with a critical eye. The Afro-Asian block particularly has been vigorous in its criticism of South Africa. In October 1958 the General Assembly of the United Nations adopted by a vote of 70 to five with four abstentions a resolution expressing "regret and concern" over policies which impair the rights of all racial groups to enjoy the same rights and freedom.[57] Another resolution with similar character carried the United Nations in

---

[54] Horrell, M., A Saving of Race Relations, pp. 115–16.

[55] Ibid., p. 125.

[56] Ibid., pp. 152–53.

[57] Africa, Special Report, Vol. 3, No. 12, p. 6.

1961 by a vote of 97 to 2 with only one absention, and, in 1962, a boycott resolution received the necessary two-thirds majority to go into effect.

The effects of the boycott resolution have not been encouraging to those who view economic sanctions as a method of altering national policies. Boycotts on imports or exports by one country have frequently been violated by other countries, so that South Africans have been able to maintain and to increase their world trade without any serious embarrassment. Similarly, foreign investment in South Africa has increased through the years: thus one has a record of verbal condemnation of South Africa by the rest of the world along with an economic cooperation which has actually been increasing.

The basic assumption of the South African boycott has been that, if the restriction of trade would bring a slowdown, or perhaps reversal, of economic development, the South African whites would be willing to change their policies. It is equally possible to argue that a slowdown of economic development would bring a tendency for an even more rigid attitude toward African economic advance. The current spurt in economic development has brought the economic color policies into very serious question. The more rapid the pace of economic development, the greater the need for skilled manpower and the greater the tendency to upgrade the African labor force. In point of fact, the efforts at international boycott have been unsuccessful, but it is quite possible that they would have been counterproductive even if they had been carried out efficiently.

From a psychological standpoint, the effect of such world condemnation is more difficult to appraise. It is apparent that condemnation from the outside has tended to unite the South African whites in their resistance to external pressure, but that is not the whole story. While South Africa takes a militant and almost monolithic stand in opposition to criticism from political or religious bodies, it is nevertheless embarrassed by being considered a pariah among the world's nations. The South African reaction has included some degree of flexibility, to allow, for instance, open competition for representation on athletic teams and a welcome to integrated teams from other countries.[58]

There have been attempts to break the solid front of African countries against South Africa. South Africa has exchanged diplomatic representation with the countries which are largely surrounded by its borders (or those of the Portugese colonies) such as Lesotho, Botswana, Swaziland, and Malawi, and has afforded black diplomats exemption from the segregative rules of apartheid. Further, the South African government has announced its willingness to support the development of African economies.

---

[58] Sports policies are not always consistent. Integrated sports events are sometimes allowed but usually prohibited. Prominent nonwhite athletes have competed in South Africa and have also been banned, as in the case of American tennis star Arthur Ashe.

Trade and aid relationships were established for a while with the Malagasy Republic, and countries as far away as the Ivory Coast and Ghana (some 14 in all) have indicated that they might be willing to consider some kind of economic association with South Africa.[59]

This evidence of flexibility in South Africa did not indicate a definite change of direction. Confronted with criticism by the right and a cooling by African countries indicated by Malagasy's breaking off aid and trade discussions after a coup, the government began to abandon *verligheit* ("enlightenment") and return to a harder line. In the summer of 1972 one of the more moderate cabinet ministers resigned and was subjected to bitter criticism, student demonstrators were attacked with dogs and clubs, and "70 clergymen were arrested, placed under house arrest or prevented from preaching."[60] Certainly the brief period of slight relaxation of apartheid indicates that a South African government can make at least minor adjustments, but the switch back to a more repressive regime demonstrates the persistent power of the most rigid nationalist elements.

Going back to the matter of external criticism and pressure, its effects seem to be mixed. On the one hand South African whites tend to take a solid stand against foreign criticism, but, on the other, they are obviously disturbed by their growing isolation. The effort to impose sanctions has apparently not affected the economy and seems to have been a futile gesture. There has been some effort to change the South African image, but this is evidently less important than internal political considerations. In summary, external criticism of South Africa has solidified internal support for the government, has not seriously affected the economy, and has stimulated efforts of South Africa to present a more acceptable image to the rest of the world without making any basic alteration in apartheid policies.

Internal politics

One aspect of internal politics is the ability of the South African government to contain opposition to its policies. Throughout the years there have been, in the mining fields, occasional large-scale strikes, most of which have been completely crushed without concessions. There have been demonstrations, and there have been some efforts at guerrilla activities. At the time when Chief Luthuli received the Nobel Peace Award in 1961 there was a major emphasis on nonviolent methods of resistance. The reaction of the South African government has been so repressive that it has been nearly impossible to carry on any kind of nonviolent political opposition, and occasional ineffective bursts of guerrilla terrorism have been the only outlets for African opposition. Militancy among African revolutionary

---

[59] "Money Has No Color," *Newsweek*, November 30, 1970.
[60] "South Africa; Back to the Dark Ages," *Newsweek*, July 24, 1972, p. 52.

groups has been rising in the Portuguese colonies, and the "freedom fighters" received aid from the independent African states and possibly from outside the continent as well. The South African reaction has been to step up the size of the police and the army and to repress any sign of protest—a tactic which has been highly effective.

Legum and Drysdale presented figures to show that South Africa has the dubious distinction of having the highest hanging rate of any country in the world.

In 1967, 106 Africans, 8 whites, 12 Coloureds and 1 Asian were sentenced to death. Of the 8 whites, only 2 were executed; 81 of the Africans were hanged.[61]

The Pass Laws and various acts (e.g., Sabotage, Suppression of Communism, and the Unlawful Organization acts) are all used to imprison individuals or groups of individuals viewed as enemies of the state. Although all racial groups are represented among the so-called political prisoners, the vast majority are Africans.

While it would be incorrect to call the Republic of South Africa a police state, it certainly is a close approximation. Vaguely worded and very general laws make it possible to arrest practically anyone whom the government considers an annoyance. Individuals may be detained without trial, and, on occasion, people acquitted by a court have been remanded to prison by the Minister of Justice without any new charges being filed. During 1969, seven whites, 11 Coloured, 15 Asians, and 769 Africans were serving sentences under various subversive activities acts.[62]

The general criminal laws, especially those concerning pass regulations, also serve to harass the African population and to help to repress any kind of dissent. Mrs. Helen Suzman, the lone Parliamentary representative elected by the Progressive party, describes the South African prison population as the highest proportionate prison population in the Western world.[63]

But, in spite of the passage and rigid enforcement of stringent laws, the government is keenly aware of the fact that silence among the masses does not mean consent and that it cannot afford to ignore the scattered incidents in the last few years in the form of demonstrations, rioting, terrorism, mob violence, and guerilla activity.[64] As a result of the more violent forms of activities, and perhaps to forestall an Algerian type of confrontation in South Africa, the government has augmented the number

---

[61] Legum and Drysdale, *African Contemporary Record*, p. 305.

[62] Horrell, *A Survey of Race Relations in South Africa*, p. 54.

[63] Ibid., p. 47.

[64] Although banned in South Africa, the South West African People's Organization and the African National Congress are among the major groups that are of concern, because of their guerilla activities, in Southern Rhodesia as well as the Republic of South Africa.

TABLE 6-4

Criminal sentences

| Sentence | 1968–69 | | | | | 1967–68 |
	White	Coloured	Asian	African	Total	Total
Death	1	20	2	84	107	115
Life	—	1	—	12	13	34
Indeterminate and for prevention of crime	211	610	12	2 046	2 879	3 707
Corrective training, and 2 years and longer .	477	1 912	44	8 407	10 840	9 549
Over 4 months to under 2 years	1 394	7 483	231	48 290	57 398	50 101
Over 1 month to 4 months	1 692	13 943	381	142 465	158 481	145 456
Up to and including 1 month	3 959	38 217	937	222 600	265 713	276 745
Periodic	122	31	4	44	201	217
Corporal (cane)	26	59	—	354	439	336
Totals	7 882	62 276	1 611	424 302	496 071	486 260

Source: Muriel Horrell, A Survey of Race Relations in South Africa (Johannesburg, South African Institute of Race Relations, 1970), p. 42.

of men in the army, navy, and air force and increased the funds for the Secret Service.

Thus, by combining the regular armed services, the police, and the "citizen force" (persons who have had some military training), South Africa can marshal a sizeable force of fighting men. One account estimates that within a few days South Africa could field 120,000 troops supported by an air force carrying napalm bombs. Added to this is an ever ready complex of missile bases strategically located in the country. Hence, the prospects of an Algerian type of encounter is most unlikely at the present time, and the likelihood of a successful blow from external forces is also remote.

The blacks in South Africa are at least as divided as the whites. Tribal loyalty is still strong, and many Africans still look at life primarily from the viewpoint of Zulus, Bapedis, Tsongas, etc. Indians and Coloured are quite distinct from Africans, and the antipathy between the three groups often is as strong as the feeling between whites and nonwhites. Probably the intellectuals are the ones least swayed by divisions among nonwhites, but they too are divided between the militants, who favor violent action, the remnant of the followers of Chief Luthuli, who hope that nonviolent resistance may be possible, and those who feel that any effort at resistance would only provoke South African repression and worsen the position of the nonwhites.

There are some indications of a degree of flexibility in the white controlled South African government. The question of the upgrading of blacks occupationally is continually being agitated and, although no favorable governmental pronouncement has come forth, there is evidence that some industries have taken steps in this direction. Other situations also indicate that the South African stand is not always completely rigid. In Natal, white physicians failed to schedule their annual dinner in 1970 until they received official permission to include the Indian physicians. When the World Council of Churches made an appropriation for welfare activities by African "Freedom Fighter" groups, the government denounced the action but did not attempt to force churches to break ties with the Council.[65]

CONTRASTS TO THE LATIN AMERICAN AND
NORTH AMERICAN MODELS

It is natural to attempt to judge South Africa in the light of the racial experience of other countries. Thus one may ask why it has been impossible to achieve the rather low level of racial consciousness which exists in much of Latin America or the swing toward equal rights which is taking place in the United States. It is true that the segregation pattern in the American South resembled the apartheid pattern of South Africa in its general acceptance of segregation and white supremacy while it still used an African population as an unskilled labor force. At this point, however, the similarity stops.

In the United States, the African population was a small minority of the total, varying from 20 percent in Revolutionary days to approximately 11 percent in 1971, while in South Africa nonwhites have a four to one majority. In the Republic of South Africa, tribal groups have retained their language, and some degree of tribal organization. In the United States, slaves were so dispersed that it was impossible to carry on their languages, and social customs. In South Africa, tribal authorities were maintained and utilized for administration, while in North America, tribal authorities were nonexistent for the black population.

Thus in North America, the descendants of the African slaves are a minority population whose culture is a southern, rural, lower-class, version of the dominant American culture and who share in the African heritage only to the extent to which that heritage has penetrated the total American society. In these circumstances, integration posed little threat to the continued white character of the society and indeed, is sometimes criticized by black nationalists as a threat to any type of black cultural identity.

Since miscegenation has been widespread in both Latin America and in the Republic of South Africa, one may well question why the

---

[65] Horrell, *A Survey of Race Relations in South Africa*, pp. 15–18.

results in the two areas have been so different. The story of Mexico, for instance, is that of a society in which the mixed racial element has become dominant and in which open racism is almost unknown. This process has extended further in Mexico than in most other Latin American countries, but race is far less of a factor throughout this entire area than it is in many other places of the world.

Here it should be noted that the history of the Cape Province is rather different from the rest of South Africa. In the Cape Province, a fairly stable slave regime was the scene of rather considerable miscegenation which, with the end of slavery, saw the emergence of a distinct mulatto population with a social status somewhere between that of the pure whites and the Africans. The further development of this process was arrested by British-Afrikaner rivalry and the fact that the Europeans, although a minority, were still numerous enough to dominate the area without a consistent use of nonwhite allies.

In most of South Africa, the main source of labor was not slavery but migratory forced labor. The African women remained at some distance from the Europeans in native reserves and the men lived in semi-prison conditions where they were cut off from social interaction with the whites. Similarly, tribal governments were seen as convenient administrative mechanisms, and the perpetuation of tribal regimes together with the frequent return of workers to the native reserves meant that acculturation was only partly accomplished. Opportunities for miscegenation were decreased, and eventually the white population was able to completely outlaw intermarriage while making few concessions to the mixed population already formed. Van den Berghe describes the differences between the Africa and other areas:

In Africa, the European impact has been much milder, both genetically and culturally, because the circumstances of conquest were less devastating, because migratory labor rather than slavery or peonage followed conquest, because christianization was largely on a voluntary rather than forced basis, and because traditional structures were retained largely for administrative convenience rather than deliberately destroyed as in America.[66]

In Mexico a repressive slave-holding regime facilitated miscegenation, which in turn led to the rise of a mestizo class that now dominates the country. In South Africa the same initial events took place but were followed by an influx of Europeans massive enough to govern the country without making consistent use of their natural allies—the Coloured population. Hence the cycle went from white entry to miscegenation to still greater white dominance, a ban on further miscegenation and a complete subordination of the nonwhite population.

---

[66] Pierre van den Berghe, "Racialism and Assimilation in Africa and the Americas," *Southwestern Journal of Anthropology*, 19 (1963): 431.

PARTITION—A POSSIBLE WAY OUT

While many voices have been raised in condemnation of apartheid, there have been very few suggestions for other approaches. Presumably, the liberal opposition in South Africa would prefer a regime which continued essential features of white supremacy while giving at least token political representation to Africans and increasing their prospects for social mobility. Such a development is bitterly resisted by a majority of whites, and it is hard to see how it could be satisfactory to the Africans for any considerable period of time. The history of all other nations indicates that the aspirations of suppressed peoples grow with concessions, and it is impossible to dismiss the Nationalist fears in this regard as being either exaggerated or unrealistic.

Nor does the experience of other African countries offer much basis for a hope that the acceptance of the "one man, one vote" principle would produce a society in which the white minority could sustain any substantial proportion of its present privileges. In Algeria, for instance, nearly 80 percent of the French settlers had left the country within two years after the end of French rule. South African whites do not consider that they have a homeland other than South Africa, and both their economic interests and their concept of nationality would impel them to a diehard resistance to rule by an African majority.

It may be argued that, regardless of the interests of the white population, justice requires majority rule and that the consequences are a small price to pay. In making this assumption, it may be best to consider the nature of the price involved. A military overthrow of the South African regime would necessarily be a bloody process resulting in the total demolition of the existing society. That society has many shortcomings, but it also has a virtue of being economically the most dynamic part of Africa.[67] It is not unique in its resemblance to a police state; this is true of several African countries, and the degree of democratic control in South Africa is greater than that allowed in the African military dictatorships. Nor are discrimination and repression on the basis of ethnic background absent in other African countries. Examples include the treatment of the Indians in Kenya and Uganda, the bloody civil war between the Ibos and the rest of the Nigerian population, and the long period of strife between Arabs and blacks in Sudan. Probably the most dramatic example of ethnically based strife and cruelty in recent years is the slaughter of an estimated 100,000 Hutu in Burundi by their Watutsi overlords. The slaughter was in reaction to an unsuccessful revolt by the Hutu in which 5,000–10,000 Watutsi civilians were slain. Reporters indicate that the Watutsi counter

---

[67] South Africa has 24 percent of the continental GNP while making up only six percent of the population—van den Berghe, *South Africa*, p. 86.

action was a deliberate effort to exterminate all potential Hutu leadership, and charge that even school children were among the victims.[68]

Although South Africa is the most frequent target of criticism because of its ethnic policies it certainly has no monopoly on ethnic repression and discrimination. It is also true that in spite of many difficulties in South Africa there is no effort of Africans to migrate to other areas nor does South Africa have difficulty attracting workers from adjacent African countries. As depressed as living conditions of Africans are in South Africa, they are still substantially better for the average man than is true in the rest of the continent. It is hard to see any net gain to humanity in the destruction of the most successful economy in Africa.

One suggestion for a way to avoid the seemingly inevitable bloody conflict has been proposed by Edward Tiryakian.[69] He has suggested that, although successful integration seems unlikely and a violent destruction of the society is too costly to contemplate, a partition might not be impossible. His plan for partition would divide the present Republic of South Africa into two countries. One would be a nation ruled by Africans and the other a nation ruled by a combination of Europeans, Indians, and Coloured, with the Europeans dominant. The African nation would include the present Bantustans and reserves along with a good deal of land not included in these categories.

The European country would take in the areas with the heaviest European population, which would include most of the cities and ports. No boundary lines of this type would satisfy everyone, and it is difficult to imagine a pattern which either whites or Africans would accept. Its appeal does not lie in its positive attraction so much as in the dread of the evil consequences of all conceivable alternatives. Such a solution would give an outlet to African nationalism while still enabling most whites to live under their own rule. Self-interest would motivate a cooperation between the African and the white-dominated sections of the country in a way which would work to mutual benefit.

The examples of partition elsewhere indicate that territorial division does not necessarily solve all problems but still may have been the most practical step for the countries concerned. It is at least conceivable that, in the peculiar circumstances of South Africa, a partition of the type envisioned by Tiryakian might be a way of avoiding both the continuing scandal of domination by a European minority and the fearful destruction likely to accompany any forceable termination of European rule.

---

68 "Burundi: Slaughter of the Hutus," *Newsweek*, June 26, 1972, pp. 39–40. Roger M. Williams, "Slaughter in Burundi: A First Hand Account," *World*, 1 (Nov. 21, 1972): 20–24.

69 Edward A. Tiryakian, "Sociological Realism: Partition for South Africa?", *Social Forces* 46 (December 1967): 209–21.

CONCLUSIONS

The Republic of South Africa is a modern industrialized country peopled by a varied group of Europeans, Africans of many tribes, mixed bloods, and Indians, with whites outnumbered four to one. Since European settlement it has been plagued by conflict between settlers of Dutch and British ancestry, with those of Dutch ancestry eventually gaining political dominance in spite of having lost a supposedly decisive war. Their dominance has led to an attempt to wipe out any vestige of equality or integration and to impose a segregated pattern known variously as apartheid or separate development. Ideally, this pattern assumed that Africans would live in separate semiautonomous states known as Bantustans, would be shielded from European culture, and would lead an existence entirely cut off from European contact.

Because of the relatively small size and undeveloped character of the Bantustans, as well as the demand for African labor in European-controlled industry, this segregation has been far from complete, but the apartheid principle has been implemented to the extent that it deprives Africans of any opportunity to resist white domination. Occasional protests have been brutally suppressed, and the Republic of South Africa has been able to resist the type of movement which led to the end of colonization in most of the rest of Africa.

The differences of the Afrikaners and the British with respect to racial policies are not so much a matter of type as of degree. Both groups acknowledge the need for maintaining white supremacy. The British would accomplish this through a regime which makes minor concessions and allows some rise in African status. The Afrikaners, feeling that any concession may represent a case of the camel's nose under the tent, would enforce as rigid a brand of segregation as it is economically possible to maintain—and perhaps would even be willing to sacrifice some economic growth in the process.

If race relations in Africa are defined as a "white problem," the differences in the racial patterns of various African countries must be ascribed to the differences in the European populations in the various countries. In most of the British colonies (and the French colonies as well, except for Algeria) the Europeans were small in number, and found occupational roles as traders, government officials, soldiers, missionaries, and business executives. In Rhodesia and the Union of South Africa, most of the whites were either farmers or businessmen, or workers who regarded their post in industry or government as a permanent assignment. Such a "settler" type of population is far removed in attitude from the typical colonial representative, who still retains his ties with the imperial country.

The transient colonial representative can still return home whenever he feels unwelcome in the former outpost. Similarly the colonial government may feel that granting independence to unruly colonies represents a net gain to the treasury and a lessening of governmental problems. In any event the interests of local representatives of the colonial power are only one item, and frequently a minor one, in the overall calculation of national interest. If the imperial government remains it regards itself as a trustee of the interests of the native population, which it must protect against exploitation by foreigners—and if independence comes it is not regarded as a catastrophe.

The settler sees the situation far differently. The imperial trusteeship idea is seen as a yoke of bureaucratic regulation which blocks the development of the country, while rule by a native majority is considered an intolerable evil which would make life unbearable for the European. The different viewpoints held by settler and transient European populations can be seen in the divergent attitudes which develop toward the role of the British Empire. In parts of Africa where European settlers were either few or nonexistent the empire was regarded by British residents as a necessary guardian in a period of transition toward self-rule. African nationalists tended to think that this role was outgrown and that the empire had become an imperialist threat to their interests. Independence came when the nationalists felt they had mustered enough strength to go on their own and the British decided that the effort required to maintain a continued guardianship was too great. For white men in Rhodesia and the Republic of South Africa, the empire was not so much of a guardian as an outside force which threatened to impede the maintenance of white superiority through a concern for the privileges of the African population. On the other hand, the blacks saw the empire as a means of defense against the rule of white settlers and demanded that Britain refuse to give Rhodesia independence and force the Union of South Africa to abandon apartheid.

Thus it is that in some countries the black nationalists demanded independence and the end of British suzerainty, while in other countries they demanded that independence be blocked and the influence of the empire be continued. Conversely, the white settlers, for the most part, favored independence not as a means of promoting African nationalism but as a means of suppressing it more ruthlessly than was possible under the policies of the colonial office.

The dominance of "Herrenvolk Democracy" in both the Republic of South Africa and Rhodesia further illustrates the dynamics of power in a settler area. Rhodesia did not have a large Boer population, and British liberalism, which regarded both African and European as members of a common society, was the official doctrine. Indeed, one of the Rhodesian leaders, Todd, strove mightily, though unsuccessfully, to correct some of the racial imbalances. Rhodesia did not glorify a doctrine of apartheid, and, even after the unilateral declaration of independence, African students continued to attend the predominantly white university. Probably the main difference between Rhodesia (now Zimbabwe) and the Republic of South Africa is that Rhodesia had a smaller settler population—only five percent white as contrasted to 20 percent in South Africa. Hence, Rhodesia never had complete segregation and eventually the whites accepted majority rule.

Neither Rhodesia nor the Republic of South Africa were dictatorships in the sense of an absolute rule by a small oligarchy. Rather they were "garrison states" which sought to maintain democratic choice and at least some freedoms for the white populations while keeping the nonwhites in subjection. Political action by Africans was either minimized, controlled, or repressed completely, and whites who disagreed too sharply with the prevailing ethos might also face repressive action. In both countries divergent political parties competed for votes and some open critics of the government were allowed their freedom, but in each the need for presenting a solid front against a hostile world was a factor leading toward increasing lack of tolerance for dissent from either blacks or whites.

One of the rather curious features of the South African experience is that the brand of separatism imposed on blacks by the South African government closely parallels many of the demands made by black militants in the United States. The Bantustans set up separate states within South Africa which, even though they have limited powers, still act as centers for the preservation of indigenous culture. Schools are segregated with black pupils and teachers, and instruction is in the native languages. In every way except in the employment of labor, blacks are excluded from the dominant society and forced back on indigenous African culture. In the circumstances it seems that white South Africa itself is doing much to make any kind of unified country impossible and is reinforcing in the minds of blacks the idea that they have no common destiny with the whites.

On the other hand, economic developments are operating against the basic labor principles of apartheid. In brief, these were to eventually force blacks out of industry and back onto the land and, while they remained in industry, to keep them in an unskilled status. The current difficulty with this formula is that South Africa has become a highly industrialized nation in which the demand for industrial labor is increasing rather than decreasing and in which the labor shortage is greatest in semiskilled, skilled, and technical categories. Industry has a decreasing need for a reservoir of cheap unskilled labor and a rising demand for workers in fields which in the past have been considered white men's jobs. Upgrading the educational background and occupational skills of the black population may soon be essential if industrial leadership is to be maintained. The economic motivation, which at one time led to the black man's being confined to the lower reaches of the occupational hierarchy, may soon force a break with the whole system of racially sanctioned economic discrimination. Minor concessions are already being made, wages have lifted

slightly, and blacks are already employed in such previous white preserves as engineering, railroads, and construction.[70] Economic equality
is still far away, but the day when the skilled black worker is important
as a part of the labor force and his purchasing power is a major part of the
total market may be fast approaching.

Experience in other countries gives us little clue as to the eventual
outcome in Rhodesia and the Republic of South Africa. In Algeria a native
revolt ended French rule and most of the French settlers have left the
country. In the United States and Australia the indigenous inhabitants
were outnumbered and pushed back by a horde of European immigrants
who greatly outnumbered them. In Mexico widespread miscegenation led
to the blurring of racial distinctions and the dominance of the mestizo.
At one time it looked as if such a development might take place in South
Africa, since there was a rapid growth of a mixed population which had
adopted European culture; however, a gradual hardening of economic
and social stratification along racial lines aborted such a development

There is no possibility that the whites will become numerically dominant in South Africa, and, at the moment at least, there seems little
chance that they will be pushed out by Africans or that their behavior
will be modified by the notoriously ineffective campaign of external
sanctions. Genuine apartheid with complete racial separation seems like
a fanatical dream with little chance of realization, and integration on a
level of equality certainly faces difficult hurdles.

In the meantime the government is combining conciliatory gestures
with continued repression. Thus, integrated athletic contests may be permitted, African diplomats may be exempted from the segregative rules
of apartheid, and their countries may be promised South African economic
aid. Such concessions do indicate an interesting change in what had often
been considered a completely inflexible regime, but it is hard to see that
they offer much hope for an ultimate solution. One of the more interesting
suggestions is that of partition, which would attempt to divide the territory into two nations, one white and the other black. It is difficult to see
how satisfactory boundary lines could be drawn and the history of partition elsewhere is not encouraging. Nevertheless, it is one possible way of
avoiding the seemingly inevitable holocaust and it may yet be tried.

PATTERNS OF SOUTH AFRICAN ETHNIC INTERACTION IN RELATION TO GENERALIZED INTERGROUP BEHAVIOR PATTERNS

South African pattern. The advance of industrialization has resulted
in a gradual upgrading of some portions of the African labor force to-

---

[70] Marvin Howe, "Blacks in South Africa Developing a New Awareness," *New York Times,* July 12, 1970, p. 1.

gether with a growing demand for a reduction of restrictions on the use of labor by color.

Generalized pattern. Industrialization is inconsistent with a society in which occupation is assigned by ascription. Industrialization reduces the demand for unskilled labor and increases the need for semiskilled, skilled, and technical workers. The production of such workers will result in higher wages, a more competitive assignment of jobs, and pressure to remove ethnic limitations on social and geographic mobility of the work force.

South African pattern. South Africa's white population is a "settler" type with a permanent commitment to the land and a determination not to submit itself to the rule of an African majority.

Generalized pattern. Transient populations of officials, soldiers, and traders will rather easily give way in the face of nationalist demands for independence, while a fairly large, permanently rooted population will fight desperately to maintain its dominance.

South African pattern. The racially bigoted Boers engaged in widespread miscegenation, while the comparatively liberal British were more nearly racially endogamous.

Generalized pattern. The degree of racial prejudice bears little relationship to miscegenation, which may, in fact, be a symbol of the subordinate status of the minority group.

South African pattern. The urbanized African population has a high incidence of crime, alcoholism, and family disorganization.

Generalized pattern. A nation which destroys or greatly weakens the culture of a subordinate group without allowing assimilation may expect to see a high degree of social disorganization resulting.

South African pattern. International boycotts have been ineffective and the South African economy has continued its growth.

Generalized pattern. International relationships are usually not determined by approval or disapproval of internal ethnic policies.

South African pattern. The efforts to restrict Africans have also resulted in laws and administrative practices which restrict the freedom of white politicians, academics, clergymen, and businessmen.

Generalized pattern. Freedom is indivisible, and it is not possible to maintain a society in which a subordinate group is heavily restricted without applying some of these restrictions to members of the dominant group as well.

South African pattern. The "Coloured" population tends to identify culturally with the whites in spite of many rebuffs.

Generalized pattern. Biologically mixed populations will identify with the more prestigious element of their ancestry if given any opportunity at all to separate themselves from a denigrated ethnic group.

South African pattern. Under the auspices of apartheid, the Bantu are discouraged from what is considered "European imitation" and encouraged to develop a culture and a language separate from those of the Europeans. To the extent that this policy is carried out, the effect is to restrict the Bantu prospects for social mobility in South African society.

Generalized pattern. Efforts to retain a nativistic style of culture will be a handicap in the competition for advancement in an industrialized society.

South African pattern. The white population comprise about one fifth of the total and is too small to operate the country's industries by itself and yet is large enough to resist the type of efforts which have led to the end of European rule in most of the rest of Africa.

Generalized pattern. Demographic patterns play a major role in shaping the pattern of intergroup relations. Even if it has wealth and technological superiority, a small minority will usually soon be overthrown by a majority. A larger minority may not be overthrown for a considerable time, but the legitimacy of its rule will become increasingly suspect, and eventually it will reach the stage where its position can be maintained only by naked force.

QUESTIONS

1. Why do the "settler" type of colonies tend to be the most resistant to the end of white rule?
2. What is the difference between the Portuguese and the South African attitude toward blacks? Why might blacks find the Portuguese attitude unsatisfactory?
3. What was the nature and cause of the "trek"? What effect did the trek have on race relationships?
4. What is the difference between Boers and British on race relations? Why did the British lose dominance after their success in the Boer war?
5. Why was miscegenation between whites and Bantu higher during the period of slavery than later?
6. How do you explain the difference in the status of the Coloured in South Africa and the mestizo in in Latin America?
7. What are the similarities and differences in black-white relationships between the Republic of South Africa and the United States of America?

8. How does economic development threaten apartheid?
9. Assuming that the vigorous enforcement of a boycott is possible, would this persuade the South African whites to modify apartheid? Explain.
10. Do you think there is any chance that the Bantustans will enable the objectives of apartheid to be achieved?
11. On what basis are both the defenders and the critics of apartheid able to cite Christianity as a justification for their beliefs?
12. Why was it deemed necessary to establish racial classification boards? What does the existence of such boards indicate about the racial composition of the people of South Africa?
13. Most white workers are for racial discrimination in jobs, while many industrialists would like to upgrade African workers. What does this indicate about the Communist theory that racial conflict is due to capitalism?
14. Do you think the whites in South Africa will be able to maintain their dominance indefinitely? Would partition be the road to racial peace in this area?

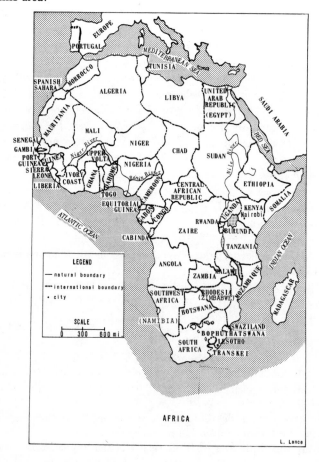

AFRICA

L. Lance

Chapter 7

Political integration of overseas territories: Martinique and Guadeloupe

Since the 20th century has seen the breakup of empires and the near elimination of colonialism, it is often assumed that detached overseas territories are necessarily headed for independence. This notion is challenged by a number of distant territories which have voluntarily maintained their relationship with a larger country. Sometimes their action is inexplicable to outsiders, as in the case of Puerto Rico. To the United Nations' Committee on colonialism it seemed obvious that Puerto Rico was being held in colonial status by the United States. However, in an election which occurred in 1972 a few weeks after the U.N. committee's statement, the main division came between Puerto Ricans supporting the Commonwealth regime and those seeking statehood, with less than four percent of the voters supporting the Independence Party.

American readers will also think of Hawaii, 3,000 miles from the nearest United States mainland, which received the status of statehood without major internal opposition or agitation for independence. Hawaii has a largely Oriental population which has generally assimilated American culture, while, in Puerto Rico, Spanish culture is still strong and Spanish is the major language. The fact that two territories, so different both from the mainland and from each other, could each welcome an American governmental link indicates that a variety of circumstances may lead overseas territories to reject separation from a mainland power.

207

While an extensive analysis of the relation of the United States with overseas territories would make an interesting story, this is not the major concern of this chapter. Instead we have turned to former French possessions, since of all former colonial powers it is the French who were the strongest assimilationists and had the greatest hopes for the continued association of the overseas territories with the "mother country."

The focus of this chapter will be on Guadeloupe and Martinique, two territories located in the West Indies and commonly included under the term French Antilles.[1] In our discussion of these two territories we advance the following generalizations of intergroup relations: (1) tendencies toward political separatism often vary directly with the degree of ethnic economic competition, (2) there is an inverse relationship between the intensity of ethnic conflict and the number of ethnically distinct groups, and (3) the viability of a group's original culture often determines the extent to which it can be influenced by another culture.

These territories, which seem relatively content with their status as departments of France, will be contrasted with two other areas in which continued association with a stronger power was rejected. One of these areas consists of various territories in the former British West Indies and the other is the African country of Senegal. The point at issue is why Guadeloupe and Martinique cherished the ties with the one time imperial power when the other territories opted for independence. The British West Indies were selected for comparison because in size, socioeconomic development, and, geographical location they are similar to the French Antilles. Senegal was also selected for comparison because it is often cited as one of the countries in which the French gave most support to the ideal of assimilation. Now let us take a closer look at the French Antilles.

Martinique and Guadeloupe each have a population of around 300,000; Martinique, with an area of 425 square miles, had a population density in 1966 of some 766 per square mile and Guadeloupe, with a slightly larger area, of 686 square miles, had a population density of 487. In relation to arable land these population densities are among the highest in the Caribbean. Martinique is 40 miles long and 21 miles wide at its broadest point, and about two thirds of the land is mountainous territory. Guadeloupe consists of two major islands and a number of little ones. One of the main islands, Basse-Terre, is flat and well adapted to sugar growing.

Since 1946, Martinique and Guadeloupe have been departments of France. In this status, their government is exactly like that of French departments on the Continent. They vote for members of the French Chamber of Deputies, they are governed entirely by French law, and some of

---

[1] French Guiana and such islands as St. Pierre and Miquelon are also included under the rubric French Antilles. They are excluded from this discussion: Guiana because of its extremely underdeveloped character, and the islands because of their small size.

the officials in the territory are selected directly by Paris. There have been occasional agitation for independence and a few minor riots which seem to have an anti-French character, but, in general, while the inhabitants may have specific grievances, they seem to look forward to a continued relationship within the French nation.

The words of a recent French writer gave a picture which is often presented as the dominant reaction in this area. "The Antilles cannot and do not want to be anything other than French," states a Martinican, "they are French in spirit, in heart, in blood."[2]

EARLY HISTORY

Martinique and Guadeloupe were first occupied by the French in 1635. An early interest in the role of the islands as fishery bases soon gave way to realization of their potential value in sugar production. The islands were sparsely inhabited by the Carib Indians. The Caribs were soon eliminated, in part through warfare and the disruption of their economic life and, in part through interbreeding with the French and with African slaves brought to the islands as a labor force for sugar cultivation. Thus the indigenous inhabitants have completely disappeared as an identifiable group, although they have contributed some of their physical character-istics to the general population. The islands were subject to occasional attacks by the English and the Dutch, but except for short intervals, French hegemony has been maintained since the date of first settlement.

African slaves were effectively cut off from contact with African culture and, while a number of East Indians were brought over as laborers on sugar plantations in the early part of the 20th century, their number has been too small to enable them to have a decisive impact on the general population. Ethnic statistics are not available. The usual estimate is that about 5 percent of the population are French whites, another 5 percent are Indian, 10 to 20 percent are "mixed bloods" who are classified as colored, and the balance are Negro who have little or no ancestry other than African.

The early history of the French Antilles saw slave revolts which were brutally suppressed and the emancipation from slavery which was revoked by Napoleon I, followed by a subsequent emancipation which became effective in 1840. From the time of the second emancipation of the slaves, there was a gradually growing effort to extend the rights of French citi-zens to all the inhabitants of the islands. Thus, racial discrimination and segregation are not recognized in the formal law and universal suffrage has prevailed since 1871.

---

[2] Victor Sable, *La Transformation des îles d'Amerique en departements francais* (Paris, 1955), p. 176.

During most of World War II, the islands were ruled by Admiral Robert in the name of the collaborationist Vichy government. He brought to the island 10,000 French sailors who were unwilling residents of a place they considered one of exile and who took few pains to conceal frankly racist attitudes. Britain and the United States imposed a blockade on the islands which brought commercial activity to a halt and caused real hardship to the residents. The blockade was lifted after the "Free French" took over the area.

When the Free French, as the followers of de Gaulle were termed, took over the island, they were greeted with great enthusiasm by the bulk of the population. The Free French were regarded as representatives of the "true" France who embodied the paternalistic type of concern which was presumed to prevail in relations between the colonies and the mother country. Thus the World War II experience, which brought disruption and nationalism to many territories, served to reinforce the ties between the metropolitan French government and the French Antilles.

General de Gaulle himself was apparently even more of a charismatic figure in the Antilles than he was in mainland France and in elections on a national basis de Gaullist parties usually received 90 percent of the vote cast. The extent of de Gaulle's popularity is indicated by the *New York Times* story on a visit by the General in 1964:

The tour has had considerable effect on General de Gaulle himself, enhancing, if possible, his confidence in the mission of France and himself.

The general has been delighted by the evident loyalty of the people of the three departments. "Mon Dieu, Mon Dieu," he told a crowd yesterday, "how French you are."[3]

ECONOMIC PATTERNS

The economic development of the islands followed a typical colonial pattern in the local production of raw materials and the purchase of manufactured products from the mainland country. Trade has been primarily with France although, in recent years, efforts have been made to attract American and British capital. In 1969, 93 percent of the exports were represented by sugar, bananas, and pineapples. The sugar plantations are handicapped by the mountainous contour of the islands, which makes large-scale cultivation difficult and by general technological backwardness. Sugar, the main crop, would not be economically viable on the world market and survives only because of a French preference which affords a price not only higher than that in world trade, but 20 percent higher than the preferential price given by the United States to its favored sugar suppliers. Land ownership is heavily concentrated and it is reported that

---

3 *The New York Times*, Tuesday, March 24, 1964, p. 8, col. 4.

ten *Beke* (whites born in the islands) families own 80 percent of the arable land in Martinique.

However, the rather dismal poverty which would be assumed in such a system is moderated by very heavy expenditures by the French national government. Martinique and Guadeloupe receive more government money per inhabitant than any of the other 89 French departments and, in spite of heavy unemployment, have an average per capita income of about $500 per year.[4] It is estimated that direct government aid and investment from France, which was $106,000,000 in 1966, amounts to about two thirds of the combined gross product of the departments. French minimum wage schedules apply, French social security payments, including family allocations, prevail, although some of the family benefits have been diverted to educational expenditures. Immigration to the French mainland is permitted and about 5,000 islanders a year leave to search for work in France.[5]

Thus, while there is uncertainty of income for many people and real poverty for some, many of the islanders are working at jobs paying far above the average in the Caribbean and there is a growing array of housing projects, roads, airports, schools, hospitals, and electric power grids. The system may support a privileged position for the white elite, but it also gives real benefits to the bulk of the population.

The economic dependency of the departments upon mainland France is so obvious that few of the island leaders contemplate a separate economy. Murch, in a survey of 60 of the leaders of Martinique and Guadeloupe, found that 87 percent believed that economic reasons rendered independence unfeasible.[6]

RACIAL PATTERNS

Racial patterns throughout the Caribbean contrast rather sharply with the dichotomous distinctions between white and Negro which have been maintained in the southern part of the United States. This is not to say that whites in the Caribbean have been free of prejudice or are egalitarian in their attitudes. Rather, because of a combination of cultural and demographic factors, "race" is viewed as a continuum represented by several shades of skin color in which the dominant position is held by the "pure white" and the lowest rank by "pure black."

The dominant economic group are the whites, who have lived for several generations in the islands and constitute the landowning group.

---

[4] Barry Lando, "de Gaulle's Outpost in the Caribbean," *The Reporter* (March 7, 1968), p. 31.

[5] Ibid., p. 32.

[6] Alvin W. Murch, "Political Integration as an Alternative to Independence in the French Antilles," *American Sociological Review* 33 (September 1968), p. 549.

As a small minority, they take pains both to safeguard family lines ("racial purity") and to avoid public expression of racial attitudes which would be objectionable to a majority of the population. Intermarriage between the Bekes and the nonwhite population is almost unknown, and the occasional participants in such mixed unions usually find life so uncomfortable that they leave the islands. However, public behavior such as participation in religious, governmental, or commercial activities is carried on without open reference to color lines. The behavior of the indigenous whites contrasts with that of representatives from metropolitan France in that the former both have a greater ease of association with the colored population, as a result of long years of experience, and also are more determined to maintain a color line in the sphere of private relations.

Illicit relationships have long been common between male Bekes and colored females, and occasional intermarriage takes place between whites born in metropolitan France and the colored Martinicans but not between the latter and the indigenous whites. People of all shades mix at religious and civic events, with the Bekes maintaining a fairly complete segregation at private social events.

Tensions which might be expected from such a policy are deflected by the presence of a group of mixed racial ancestry which acts as a buffer between the Bekes and the darker-hued inhabitants. While there is no perfect correspondence between color and economic status, the lighter-colored group has benefited more from education than has the darker-skinned element, is more likely to be found in commercial and governmental positions, and has some representation in landholding. The colored group strives to maintain a distinction between itself and the black majority, while the blacks, in turn, tend to stress any possible claim to identification with mixed ancestry.[7] So much is this true that the claim is sometimes made that the whole thrust of social aspiration is a claim to a light skin.

Similarly in Guadeloupe *mulatre* is used less to refer to a person of half-white and half-black ancestry than to a fair-skinned quadroon or octaroon with straight or wavy hair . . . Martinicans claim that they have no 'pure' Negroes at all—that they all have at least one white ancestor . . .

In . . . Martinique today the whole population is visibly light-skinned.[8]

The darker-skinned populace is more heavily represented among agricultural workers and, where an occasional black is economically successful, the tendency is to classify him also as mulatto. The obviously mixed part of a population, while it may be jealous to some degree of the Bekes, is more

---

[7] Charles Wagely and Marvin Harris, *Minorities in the New World* (New York, Columbia University Press), pp. 109–18.

[8] David Lowenthal, "Race and Color in West Indies," *Daedalus* 96 (Winter-Spring 1967): 580.

directly in competition with the darker-skinned inhabitants. The result is a symbiotic relationship in which the Bekes and the colored part of the population work together to reinforce mutual privilege and to keep the darker-skinned inhabitants in their place. Friction, in turn, comes primarily between the obviously dark-skinned people of low economic status and the mulatto elements from whom most of the island leaders have been drawn: "If the interests of the white plutocracy and the people . . . . clash outright," writes an observer on Martinique, "the mulatto has no doubts as to where he stands, he is on the side of the whites."[9]

One of the best general description of racial relationships in the French Antilles has been made by Leiris. The following summary of his statements is by Hoetink.

Among mulattoes, as among the native whites, class and racial considerations coincide in the determination of social status. The higher the economic level of the coloured family, the more important racial considerations seem to be. Thus in families of the *haute bourgeoisie mulatre* contempt for the Negro appears to be greatest, even more than among the white aristocracy. In these circles it is certainly regarded as desirable to have a more caucasoid partner in marriage, *pour sauver la couleur*, as the phrase is in Martinique.

In spite of this strict exclusiveness pursued by the white group, some members of these groups are barely distinguishable from the very light-coloured mulattoes (*mulatres blancs*). Such marginal physical types are classified on the basis of their genealogies, which are generally known in these small islands; he is a white who is by descent 'in principle' exclusively white, and he is coloured who is of 'double' descent.

The dividing line between Negroes and coloureds is vague. Coloured marriages sometimes result in very dark coloured offspring; the poor mulatto is little superior or different from the Negro; and the well-to-do Negro, an exception, may without great difficulty join the intermediate category and is then called ironically, *gros-mulatre*.[10]

Since the dominant whites maintain endogamy as well as the exercise of economic privilege, it might be thought that there is really little difference between race relations in the Caribbean and in the continental United States. While the objective variation in racial practice between the American and the French approach may be slight, the variation in psychological result is very great indeed. It has often been remarked that West Indians in the United States are especially upset by the tendency to classify them as Negro and therefore definitely in the most subordinate category. Lighter-

---

[9] Daniel Guerin, *The West Indies and Their Future* (London, D. Dobson, 1961), p. 75.

[10] H. Hoetink: *The Two Variants in Caribbean Race Relations*, published for the Institute of Race Relations, London, by the Oxford University Press, New York, 1967, p. 42. Based on M. Leiris, *Contacts de civilizations en Martinique et en Guadeloupe* (Paris, UNESCO 1955), pp. 122 ff. Copyright by Institute of Race Relations, 1967.

skinned people in the West Indies would never face such indignity, since their mixed characteristics would give them an intermediate position. One with a darker skin would find his sense of injustice kindled to an even sharper degree as he observed the open discrimination against those labeled Negro in the United States.

Thus it is not surprising that some of the most militant leaders of American Negro protest have been migrants of West Indian origin, such as Marcus Garvey, who launched the back to Africa movement in the 1920s, and Stokeley Carmichael, who has been identified with "Black Power."

Much has been written to proclaim the theory that the racial attitudes of those of Latin background are more benign than the attitudes of the Anglo-Saxon. The nature of the difference between Latin and American attitudes is aptly summarized by Cahnman, who, while commenting on the book *Negroes in Brazil,* by Pierson, points out that the main practical difference between Anglo-Saxon and Latin-American racial practice is found with the mulatto rather than the Negro.[11]

Classifying racial groups into multiple categories with intermediate privileges and status, rather than simply white and Negro, tends to blur racial distinctions rather than to sharpen them. Since the light-skinned are "almost white" they may avoid a feeling of frustration and sustain their ego by contrasting their own situation with that of the "lowly" black. He, in turn, may find justification for considering himself "practically mulatto" in a self-identification process which diminishes a recognition of physical traits associated with low status. If the acknowledgement of his blackness and hence of low position is inescapable, then his rage is more easily kindled against the uppity mulatto than against the white man from whom he is more distant both in physical appearance and in social position. Classification by fine points of appearance and ancestry may indicate more rather than less racial consciousness, but by fragmenting the nonwhite group it avoids a complete polarization and thereby produces a society which is more tolerable psychologically for many of the nonwhites.

CONTRAST WITH BRITISH WEST INDIES

The islands in the British West Indies, of which Jamaica, Barbados, and Trinidad are the largest, are nearly identical in their economic resources with the French Antilles. Both areas are primarily producers of tropical raw materials and consumers of industrial goods produced by the metropolitan society. While neither area could be classed as developed, the British West Indies are less backward in the technology used in sugar plantations and have attracted a rather considerable tourist trade.

---

[11] W. J. Cahnman, "The Mediterranean and Caribbean Regions: A Comparison in Race and Culture Contacts," *Social Forces* 22 (October 1943–May 1944): 210.

Although reference is sometimes made to an allegedly more permissive social relationship between racial groups in the French Antilles, this is hard to document and the differences, if any, are slight. Slavery was a brutal affair in both regions, with final emancipation coming at about the same time in each (1838 in Jamaica and 1841 in Martinique). Americans have long been impressed with the apparent lack of racial social distance in Jamaica. Broom cites an 1851 statement by John Bigelow as a case in point:

. . one accustomed to the proscribed condition of the free black in the United States will constantly be startled at the diminished importance attached here to the matter of complexion. Intermarriages are constantly occurring between the white and colored people, their families associate together within the ranks to which by wealth and color they respectively belong, and public opinion does not recognize any distinctions based on color.[12]

For a more recent analysis of racial interaction in the West Indies, we turn to a discussion of ethnic stratification in Trinidad by Lloyd Braithwaite.[13] His analysis is strikingly similar to the pattern which Leiris described as prevalent in Martinique (see page 213). Thus both Braithwaite and Leiris write of distinctions on the basis of fine shades of color, the relations between color and social class, and the endogamy of the Creoles (whites born in the country).

As similar as the British West Indies and the French Antilles may be in economic structure and racial attitudes, they diverge sharply in politics. The British Islands opted for independence, but the French Antilles sought only a better status within the French nation. Five reasons are adduced for this difference in viewpoint: (1) the influence of French assimilationist policy, (2) the greater homogeneity of the French Antilles, (3) the attraction of French romanticism, (4) the extension of social services by the French on a scale comparable to that in the metropolitan area,[14] and (5) a French colonial policy of democratic centralism as contrasted to the British trend toward island oligarchies.

While the British Commonwealth may seem as attractive to former colonies as the French Union, it is formed on a different basis. The British saw their empire, not as an extension of Britain, but as complementary control over inherently and permanently different areas which had a symbiotic relationship with the mother country. Although educational experience at Oxford and Cambridge or at the military school at Sandhurst might

---

12 John Bigelow, *Jamaica in 1851*, cited in Leonard Broom, "The Social Differentiation of Jamaica," *American Sociological Review* 10 (April 1954): 18, 119.

13 Lloyd Braithwaite, "Social Stratification in Trinidad," *Social and Economic Studies in the Caribbean*," Vol. 2 and 3 (October 1953), pp. 90–98.

14 These factors are based on Charles C. Moskos, *The Sociology of Political Independence: A Study of Nationalist Attitudes among West Indian Leaders* (Cambridge, Mass., Schenkman, 1967), pp. 548, 562.

produce common cultural bonds, this was an incidental result rather than a main concern. The British Empire, and later the Commonwealth, existed not so much because of a common culture as because historical accident and present interests brought a measure of cooperation in economic and political areas.

The "civilizing mission of France," on the other hand, was seen as the beneficent extension of French culture to the underdeveloped areas under French influence. While racial traits often coincided with cultural orientation and racial prejudice was evident, it was still a way of life rather than ancestry which was regarded as the ultimate criterion of French nationality. Similarly no nonsense about cultural pluralism or self-determinism was allowed to dull dedication to the proposition that French culture represented the highest level man could attain.

Rupert Emerson expresses this distinction cogently:

> By native inclination the French have always tended to find the true inspiration for assimilation . . . the ideal of the French colonial vocation is to bring less fortunate peoples within the fold of French culture and a single all-embracing France . . . It has fitted the French genius in the past to assume that the people of their colonies could become Frenchmen and to aim at their integration into the homogeneous society of a single greater France revolving around Paris. The British on the other hand work toward the creation of a looser Commonwealth made up of diverse and independent peoples.[15]

The assimilation policy in the French Antilles was aided by the comparative homogeneity of the population, consisting mainly of French and Africans, with only a small minority of East Indians, and little influence from other European nations. The British colonies, on the other hand, were imposed on regimes already established by Spain or Holland and had a larger East Indian and Chinese population; Trinidad, for instance, is over one-third East Indian in population.

Along with limited ethnic variation a common religious institution was also an assimilating factor. Catholicism in the French Antillies, nominally at least, embraced practically all the population. In the British West Indies the sizeable Indian population was a formidable barrier to the spread of Christianity. Mission work was split between the Anglicans, and Roman Catholics and the Free Churches (mostly Methodist and Baptist). British institutions did have a major influence, especially on the culture of the middle and upper class groups, but ethnic and religious diversity with concessions to local autonomy, limited their impact.[16]

British and French practice in the extension of social services reflected

---

[15] Rupert Emerson, *From Empire to Nation: The Rise to Self Government of Asian and African Peoples* (Cambridge, Mass., Harvard University Press, 1960), p. 69.

[16] Murch, "Political Integration as an Alternative to Independence in the French Antilles," pp. 553–56.

their differing views on assimilation. While British trade unionism seems to be an export item, general social legislation was framed in terms of Caribbean conditions without any effort to make wage scales or welfare payments follow British models. Similarly, educational policy sought to provide a trained elite and a literate group of trained workers but sharply restricted secondary and higher education while leaving a large part of the population outside of the school system entirely. The French applied metropolitan standards of social legislation, sought universal literacy and supported a comparatively large program of secondary and higher education.

TABLE 7-1

A Comparison of School Attendance at the Primary, Secondary and University Levels in the French Antilles (1966) and in Jamaica (1960)

Level of education	French Antilles	Jamaica
Total primary school age population (7 to 14 yrs.)	138,249	307,222
Percent of total attending primary school	96	60
Total secondary school age population (10.5 to 19)	113,514	310,003
Percent of total attending secondary school	31	5
Number of students attending universities	3,038	4,021
Ratio of students to total population ..	.0048	.0025

Source: Alvin W. Murch, "Political Integration as an Alternative to Independence in the French Antilles," *American Sociological Review* 33 (September 1968), p. 549.

Perhaps the major difference lies in governmental policies. The French granted universal suffrage to Martinique in 1870, while the British did not adopt a similar policy in Jamaica until 1944. For the French, political development meant increasing participation in the affairs of France itself: representatives of the Antilles were members of the Chamber of Deputies and local officials were appointed from Paris. For the British, political development was seen as increasing local self-rule. First, a shift from crown colonies with direction from London to semiautonomous units dominated by a local oligarchy of white and colored, then a wider suffrage and greater power exercised by the blacks, and finally independence. The French policy of democratic centralism meant that greater democracy resulted in more participation in the French nation, while, with the British policy, greater democracy led to greater absorption in local affairs.

Perhaps a logical culmination of these trends was a decision in 1968 by the British government that Commonwealth migration must be curtailed, while France continued to welcome migrants from the Antilles. If a romantic attitude toward metropolitan French dominated the thinking of the inhabitants of Martinique and Guadeloupe, this is an understandable consequence of a chain of circumstances which led to the strengthening of the tie between Paris and the West Indian islands. If the inhabitants of the French West Indies felt that economic ties bound them to Paris and made independence unfeasible, this conviction was related to French subsidies and the inclusion of the Antilles in French social legislation.

A rather elaborate study of the basis for different political attitudes in French and British West Indian areas has been made by Murch. He interviewed a sample of 62 Antillean leaders and compared their attitudes with a similar group of leaders interviewed by Bell and Moskos in the British West Indies, as shown in Table 7–2.

TABLE 7–2

Leaders' Attitudes toward Political Independence in the French Antilles, 1966, and the British West Indies, 1961–62 (percentages)

Status desired:	French Antilles dimension of attitude		Status desired:	British West Indies dimension of attitude	
	Ideal status	Best possible status		Ideal status	Possible status
Independence	70	2	Independence	50	53
Other	76	98	Other	50	47
Autonomy	10	19		—	—
Adapted			Total	100	100
Department	48	61	(N) ....(112)		(112)
Status Quo	18	18			
Total	100	100			
(N)	(62)	(62)			

Source: Alvin W. Murch, "Political Integration as an Alternative to Independence in the French Antilles," *American Sociological Review* 33 (September 1968): 550.

Murch also found that there was no relation between degree of enlightenment (commitment to egalitarian viewpoint) and desire for independence in the French Antilles, while in the British West Indies the most "enlightened" leaders were almost invariably the most desirous of independence. This led him to the conclusion that in the British West Indies the search for a better life led to a demand for independence, whereas in the French Antilles human betterment and attachment to metropolitan France were seen as compatible. In brief, not only was the desire for independence a small minority viewpoint in the French Antilles but independence was seldom seen as an essential step in a wider social program.[17]

---

[17] Ibid., pp. 559–60.

NEGRITUDE IN THE CARIBBEAN AND IN AFRICA

What has been said about the general acceptance of the prestige of a light complexion and of metropolitan France as a frame of reference may seem rather odd in view of the fact that the poet Aimé Césaire, who is one of the fathers of the concept of negritude, was a resident of Martinique, and Frantz Fanon, whose writings on the Algerian situation sparked a general wave of color consciousness, spent his early manhood on the island of Martinique.

Fanon traces his own awakening to his experience in Martinique during World War II, when the Vichy forces under Admiral Robert held sway in the island and French sailors expressed their uninhibited scorn of everything of local origin.[18] Later, Fanon practiced as a psychiatrist in Algeria and he came to believe that nothing white or French could be trusted and that only in an absolute, brutal, and violent repudiation of colonial heritage could the man of color find his self esteem.

For others who remained in the West Indies and did not participate in the Algerian struggle, it was easier to assume that the Vichy regime was a perversion of the true France, which had a benevolent concern for the welfare of the inhabitants of the French Antilles whatever their color. Césaire was not bemused by French paternalism, but his political career has been characterized by a plea for autonomy rather than a demand for independence. Césaire and Léopold Sédar Senghor, first president of Senegal, were students together in Paris and are both associated with the literary formulation of the concept of negritude. With both men, negritude involved an exaltation of Negroes and the culture associated with them and a rejection of the superiority of whites and the culture associated with them. Between Césaire and Senghor, however, there are subtle but important differences, which to some extent, foreshadowed the differences in their political careers.

Césaire's negritude is less a glorification of the Negro past in Africa or of its potential contribution than it is an unabashed acceptance of the current posture of the black man in the French Antilles and his life in a society which, however assimilative its ideals, is still perceived as racist. As Reed and Wake point out, Césaire's negritude was "at origin an existential act of self-affirmation, a decision to affirm and take pride in those things for which the Negro has been despised . . . principally and symbolically, in his black skin, but aslo in his uninventiveness, his irresponsible gaiety before life. Césaire accepts the white man's myths about the Negro and glories in them."[19]

---

[18] Frantz Fanon: *Toward the African Revolution,* translated by Haakon Chevalier (New York, Grove Press, 1967), pp. 22, 23.

[19] John Reed and Clive Wake, *Senghor Prose and Poetry* (London, Oxford University Press, 1965), p. 10.

I know my crimes; there is nothing to be said in my defense. Dances. Idols. Backsliding. Me too.

. . . .

I have assassinated God with my laziness with my words with my gestures with my obscene songs.

. . . .

I have exhausted the patience of the missionaries, insulted the benefactors of humanity.

. . . .

My negritude is neither a tower nor a cathedral

. . . .

it digs under the opaque dejections of its rightful patience

. . . .

Eia for the royal Kailcedrat!
Eia for those who invented nothing
for those who have never discovered
for those who have never conquered
but, struck, deliver themselves to the essence of all things, ignorant of surfaces,
but taken by the very movement of things not caring to conquer, but playing
the game of the world.[20]

Césaire became a political leader, which indicates that, however little his poetry may be understood by the masses, his demand for an acceptance of Negro dignity registered. He at first was a Communist and as such was elected both to the French Chamber of Deputies and as mayor of Fort-de-France, capital of Martinique. After breaking with the Communist Party, he was again returned to office by an overwhelming vote. He has not demanded independence, but rather has asked for a stronger type of autonomy within the French union, comparable to that of Puerto Rico's status as a Commonwealth associated with the United States. Even this demand does not seem to have been pressed, and the survey by Murch indicates that most leaders in Martinique are satisfied with department status.[21]

Senghor makes little effort to defend the African proletariat. His main theme is the merit of both traditional and current African culture and its potential contribution to the total society. Senghor's affirmation of the worth of African culture is far more pertinent to the type of cultural myth needed by an independent state than is Césaire's paean to the existential personality traits of black individuals living in a white-dominated society.

---

[20] These extracts are taken from Aimé Césaire's *Return to My Native Land* (*Cahier d'un retour au pays natal*), translated by Emile Snyder (Paris, Présence Africaine, 1968), pp. 59, 101–3.

[21] Murch, "Political Integration as an Alternative to Independence in the French Antilles," p. 554.

Contrast for instance this 1950 statement by Senghor with the verses of Césaire:

Negritude is the awareness, defence and development of African cultural values . . . However the struggle for negritude must not be a negation but an affirmation. It must be a contribution from us to the people of sub-saharan Africa, to the growth of Africanity and beyond that to the building of the civilization of the universal.[22]

While Senghor's writings support a tradition which can be the basis for a separate national culture, this was not at first realized by Senghor himself. Wake and Reed describe his sentiments as follows:

Senghor himself does not praise his people for what they have not done. Nor does he characteristically justify the African by the glories of a past . . . Senghor is concerned less with what the African has lost than with what he still has . . . This idea of a contribution, that the African not only has something of his which is not to be found elsewhere but something which he can offer to others, is fundamental to Senghor's thinking. The French policy of assimilation, although it was in reaction against this that African self-assertion springs up, profoundly influenced the reaction against itself. Senghor's answer to the French policy of turning Africans into Frenchmen was not to stress the eternal and unabridgeable differences between African and French culture, but to say "assimilate, but don't be assimilated". . . . African culture is not then an end in itself. Its ultimate justification is the contribution it can make, what it can give to the rest of the world.[23]

THE SENEGALESE EXPERIENCE

One might well ask why Senegal is taken as a point of comparison in view of many obvious differences from the Antilles. From the standpoint of the economy, natural resources, and geographic situation the island of Madagascar (name changed to Malagasy after independence), for instance, would seem far more comparable. The answer is that, while the French professed the ideal of integration in all their colonies, it was in Senegal and in the Antilles that the most vigorous steps were taken to implement this ideal, while in other colonies racial segregation was allowed to develop fairly freely in spite of formal policies of assimilation.[24] Hence

---

[22] *Chants pour Naett* (Seghers, Paris, 1950) excerpted in Léopold Sédar Senghor, *Prose and Poetry*—translated and edited by John Reed and Clive Wake (London, Oxford University Press, 1965), p. 97.

[23] Ibid., p. 11.

[24] Paul Alduy, "La naissance du nationalisme outremer," in *Principles and Methods of Colonial Administration.* (London, Butterworths, 1950), p. 127. Translated and summarized in Harold Mitchell, *Europe in the Caribbean* (London, W. & R. Chambers Ltd., 1963), p. 34.

Senegal and the Antilles afford a case study of two French colonies in which the policies were uniquely comparable.

The first European outposts in Senegal were established by the Portuguese in 1445, and it was 185 years later when the French set up their first trading post at the mouth of the Senegal river. For some time conflict with the British prevented much interior penetration, and it was not until 1783 that the French cleared the area of British occupation.

After the turbulent period with Britain was over and troubles at home subsided, the French set out to promulgate throughout Senegal a policy of assimilation. Assimilation did not mean a bilateral approximation of the fusion of the indigenous culture with that of metropolitan France, which would imply that the indigenous culture of the African in Senegal was equal to that of France or at least had some traits worthy of acceptance. Instead, assimilation as practiced by the French was for the most part a coercive process whereby the indigenous population accepted the "superior" French culture—politically, economically, and educationally. In many ways the fruition of this policy is seen in the capital city, Dakar.

Dakar, the capital of Senegal, presents to the incoming visitor very much the image of a modern European city. Such features as an elaborate airport, with direct flights to Brazil, the port with many ships, and skyscraper office buildings, give every impression of a community which is completely dominated by European culture. This European appearance is not surprising, since it is estimated that in 1962 over 60,000 French and other foreigners lived in this country whose population was little more than 3 million. Most Europeans lived in the city of Dakar and constituted at least 10 percent of that city's population,[25] making it, next to Abidjan in the Ivory Coast, the largest French community in Africa.

One who came to Dakar would be surprised to see the extent to which many of what the British call the "subaltern" types of positions were still occupied by Europeans. If he were attending a conference of the type which it has been popular to hold in Dakar for some time, he hight join the delegates at a party at the presidential palace, where he would be served cocktails by a French barman. He would find French stenographers, French clerks in the bank, even French waitresses and French taxi drivers. In the high ranks of government he would learn that two of the Senegalese officials were men who were French by birth, but Senegalese by naturalization, and hence, at least temporarily immune from the Africanization laws. In the heart of the city he would find stores and apartments which bear much more resemblance to a French provincial town than to any architecture of African origin.

---

[25] Michael Crowder, *Senegal: A Study of French Assimilation Policy* 2d. Ed. (London, Methuen & Co., 1967), p. 82.

The bulk of the inhabitants of Dakar and of Senegal are, of course, Africans native to the country. Like all African communities, it has internal cleavages, with the Wolofs the most numerous grouping, accounting for about 35 percent of the population. Observers feel that tribal rivalries are less virulent than in most African nations and that the major divisions in the Senegalese population are those between town and country residents and between members of different castes. Looking first at the caste system, we find this is comprised of several strata ranging from nobles to liberated slaves, with artisans as an intermediate group and with the *griots* or minstrels in a position close to slaves. Castes are endogamous and most of the political elite come from the two top castes.[26] Quarrels between castes occasionally involve mob violence, but relations are usually amicable and the claim is made that caste consciousness is decreasing among the younger generation.[27]

Perhaps even more difficult to overcome than the cleavage between castes is that between town and country. In the cities one finds both the intellectuals, impatient for modernization, and an urban proletariat working for wages in the factories and warehouses of a commercial city. The population of the countryside has entirely different interests. It tends to be traditional in outlook, it is largely illiterate and is practically untouched by wage employment. Europeans are rare and the facade of modernization found in Dakar and other cities is almost completely absent. The peasant is not protected by wage laws or by labor unions and must gain his living from the sale of groundnuts whose price is dictated by world markets (although the French support it a bit) and, which as a main export crop, has to bear the bulk of expenses for the urban sector of society. These mixed modern and traditional characteristics of Senegal may give some clue, both as to the progress of assimilation with the French nation, and its ultimate failure in social policy.

ASSIMILATION POLICIES

Whether history is the story of great men who act as catalysts to bring to fruition the possibilities of their times, or whether the supposedly great men are themselves simply creatures of circumstances, is a perennial topic of academic discussion. Whatever the inclination of the reader on this question, there is no doubt that some individuals stand out as apparently personifying the trends of their era. For Senegal, under French auspices, the

---

[26] Richard Adloff, *West Africa: The French Speaking Nations* (New York, Holt, Rinehart and Winston, 1964), pp. 34, 64. C. Wesley Johnson, Jr., *The Emergence of Black Politics in Senegal,* published for Hoover Institution on War, Revolution and Peace by Stanford University Press, Stanford, Calif., 1971, pp. 13–17.

[27] Crowder, *Senegal,* pp. 110–11.

ethos of colonialism was represented best by Governor Faidherbe, who took office in 1852.[28]

Faidherbe not only extended the military domination of the French into the hinterland; he also laid the basis for much of the institutional development that was to follow in later years. He began the work which was to make the city of Dakar one of Africa's leading ports. He established banks, schools, and even a newspaper. He promoted the cultivation of groundnuts, which were to become the principal export crop and the mainstay of the economy. In the cities, he accepted local autonomy and worked with those of African background. In the rural areas, he used forced labor and authoritarian rule to bring about the changes which he felt were essential. He has often been compared to Lord Lugard, who brought Northern Nigeria under the sway of the British. Like Lugard, he relied on an alliance with the chiefs, based on a respect for Islamic institutions, as a mainstay of his rule. During his administration the decision was made against European agricultural settlement. Faidherbe certainly represents the epitome of the "civilizing mission of France," and his decision against agricultural settlement meant that this civilizing function was not going to involve a large and socially indigestible mass of French citizens with a permanent attachment to the land.

In 1871, after the close of Faidherbe's regime and the end of the second empire in France, the right of Senegal to send a representative to the French Chamber of Deputies was reaffirmed, and, while there were many arguments within metropolitan France, this right remained valid except during the short-lived Vichy regime from 1940 to 1943.

While governmental relationships are important, they operate in a social environment which does much to determine their effectiveness. A policy of assimilation on the governmental level is more effective when it is promoted by activities on the interpersonal level which are compatible. These include a type of personal relationships which promotes amalgamation, a religious network which gives the two peoples a scheme of shared values, educational progress which produces common ways of looking at life, and economic integration which gives a vested interest to all groups in the continued association and assimilation of the peoples involved. It is to these topics which we now turn.

Personal relationships

The early French settlers, government officials and soldiers found a tremendous cultural gulf between themselves and the indigenous population which rendered a relationship with any degree of equality seemingly impossible—with one exception. This exception, as might be assumed, was a

---

[28] Richard Adloff and Virginia Thompson, *French West Africa* (Stanford, Stanford University Press, 1957), p. 20.

type of relationship based on sexual needs. The first Frenchmen remained in the colonies for many years, and came to Africa without their wives. The inevitable result was a considerable number of unions with African mistresses (*signaries*) which resulted in the production of a small mulatto (*Metis*) population. For a time, many of these relationships had a somewhat permanent character, and becoming a mistress of a Frenchman was for the Senegalese girl a realistic road toward social mobility and eventual assimilation. Hargreaves describes the early 18th century situation as follows:

> Since white women were virtually unknown in the eighteenth century (though one Director General brought his wife and children out in 1731), mulatto children soon began to appear. Some French authorities in Senegal (though not their superiors in France) were glad to encourage inter-racial menages as likely to produce a more stable community; French men provided with comforts were less likely to desert and set up as private traders. So, when marriage according to Catholic rites was not possible or expedient, unions *à la mode du pays* were celebrated with some formality, constituting family relationships of recognized status which often endured happily until the man returned to Europe. The children were usually educated, sometimes in France, and provided with career opportunities within the settlement. Their mothers also acquired something of the wealth and social status of their consorts; *signares*, as the often formidable women were called, acquired property, entered trade, and became respected members of the community. In 1786 Governor de Boufflers, an aristocratic litterateur, gave a ball for the ladies of Goree; it is doubtful whether any of them had been born in Europe.[29]

This somewhat idyllic pattern proved to be short-lived. As the French interests in Senegal expanded, the total French population, including women, increased, and terms of service became shorter. The result was that sexual unions became transitory affairs, in which, oftentimes, the Frenchman took little responsibility for the support and education of the offspring. A *Metis* population did emerge which provided some of the assimilated leaders in Senegal society, but the numbers involved were always small and there is little indication that this group came to be regarded by either Frenchmen or Africans as essentially a bridge between the two. Rather than being a bridge of marginal men engaged in the transaction of interpreting Africa to France and France to Africa, it was more nearly an outcropping of one group of Africans of mixed background who had somewhat greater access than the average to French culture. Thus the *Metis* did provide a number of auxiliaries for the work of French colonial development without any major change in the French-African relationship.[30]

---

[29] John D. Hargreaves, "Assimilation in Eighteenth-Century Senegal," *Journal of African History* 6 (1965): 177–84.

[30] Johnson, *The Emergence of Black Politics in Senegal*, pp. 106–23, 196–212, describes the elimination of the *Metis* as a political force in Senegal.

Crowder remarked in 1967 that the relationships between French and Africans in Dakar were "negatively good."[31] By this he meant that there was little evidence of open friction, and no official policy of segregation, but also there was little personal mixing between African and French personnel except on the official plane. The French personnel were frequently assigned to Senegal for a period of five years or less and had annual summer vacations in France. They brought their families with them and, while in Senegal, they associated primarily with members of the European community. Illicit sexual relationships were probably less common than in earlier days and, although marriages were occasionally contracted between French girls and Senegalese students in Paris, their number was small. The restaurants and clubs of the cities were theoretically open to all, but limitations of African income and variations in taste limited the participation of Africans in these activities. The French population included a number of the *petit blancs* (poor whites) who were holding laboring or clerical jobs to which the upwardly mobile Africans might easily aspire. Between this group and the Africans was a rather considerable bitterness which was only partly masked by the official policy of equality. In general, one would conclude that the relationships were formally equal and socially stratified, officially friendly, but seldom intimate.

Religious development

While French colonial rule brought the introduction of Christian missions, especially Roman Catholic, their work had only a limited influence. The activities of Catholic missionaries were largely restricted to educational and philanthropic services, so that the number of actual converts was small. Islam offers obvious obstacles to conversion, and the French government has frequently been anticlerical, with the result that the proselyting activities of missionaries have never had full support. Some converts have been made, and many of these have played a leading role in Senegalese political, educational, and economic development, but the total number is small and the country remains overwhelmingly Muslim.

Probably the French rule actually did more to expand the sway of Islam than to extend Christianity: it facilitated the conversion by the Muslims of a considerable portion of the pagan population. French rule improved communication and thereby Islamic propaganda, and the official recognition given to Islamic law and Muslim dignitaries served to convince the pagans that Islam was an important religion and therefore a profitable path to follow.

---

[31] Crowder, *Senegal*, p. 83.

Not only did the persistence of Islam mean that a unified religious outlook could not be a basis for assimilation, but a distinctive Muslim culture limited the degree to which many Africans were willing to accept French standards. Thus, the inhabitants of the four communes who were granted French citizenship were also given the *Statut Personnel,* which allowed them to follow Muslim practices of polygamy, informal divorce, and equal division of inheritance.[32] Unlike the situation in the Spanish areas in South America or in the French West Indies, Catholicism has been simply a factor in the education and conversion of a few of the elite rather than a widespread popular religion.

Education

Education was seen by the French as the main vehicle of the policy of assimilation and, for the most part, was as faithful as possible a copy of the French educational system. The teachers were either French or Africans trained in French schools; the curriculum followed that of metropolitan France, gave little attention to African traditions, and sought not only to give literacy in the French language, but also to justify the French policy in Africa. In addition, some Senegalese students found their way to higher education in France. By 1939, only about 17,000 students, overwhelmingly males, were enrolled in school.[33] While after independence this number sharply increased, illiteracy is still widely prevalent, and the effect of French education has been to provide an elite group rather than to penetrate the mass of the population with French culture.

Economics

The groundnut cultivation encouraged by Faidherbe has continued to increase and groundnuts remain the principal export of the country, but they are subject to price fluctuation which makes the income of the growers something less than certain. In addition, the port of Dakar has flourished as an *entrepot* (distributing and warehousing) center, and there is the beginning of some manufacturing. As in all former French colonies, French aid in the forms of roads, schools, and medical service has been generous, and, in recent years, French industrial investments have been increasing.

The modern sector of the economy is largely operated by the French, with the Lebanese serving as the shopkeepers and commercial middlemen. To date, the educated Africans have been fairly well absorbed in government and in the operation of the schools with relatively little entrance into business. Economic activity in the modern sector is dependent to a

---

[32] Phillip Neres, *French Speaking West Africa* (London, Oxford University Press, 1962), p. 22.
[33] Crowder, *Senegal,* p. 34.

great degree on relations with France without being interlocked in a way that the individual Senegalese can interpret as having a direct effect on his own pocketbook. In recent years, non-French capital has also been welcome and efforts have been made to interest the industrialists of other nations in economic development, although industry and commerce remain overwhelmingly French.

Political development

The coastal cities were the first points of intensive French settlement and were also the first points where Senegalese participation in the Western type of political bodies became apparent. In 1831, the free inhabitants of the communes were granted French citizenship, and the right of municipal rule, as well as the right to vote for a delegate to the Chamber of Deputies. Later a grand council for the country was established which had limited financial powers, although many of the expenditures were regarded as mandatory and, therefore, beyond the power of the legislature to control. While French colonial policy in general gives considerable weight to the value of assimilation, Senegal was unique in African countries in this respect. French citizenship was theoretically open to all Africans, but, in 1936, Senegal had 78,000 French citizens as compared to only 2,400 in all the rest of Africa.[34] Other French African colonies were not given the right to send deputies until a much later date, and municipal self-rule was practically unknown.

Assimilation was always a somewhat controversial policy. On practical grounds, it brought obvious difficulties to the French colonial officials who, even though they frequently controlled the municipal and national councils, still felt constrained by the necessity to gain Senegalese consent for their measures. On the other hand, assimilation was defended as a means of enlisting the loyalty and facilitating the cooperation of Senegalese people with France. On the ideological plane, there is also a controversy which is represented by the perennial split in France between the ideals of the French Revolution and of an authoritarian paternalistic regime which has never accepted the legitimacy of the norms that the Revolution sought to establish. Policies have wavered at various times; assimilation received its chief setbacks during the Second Empire, 1852–1870, and during the Vichy regime, 1940–1944. With these exceptions, however, it is still true that measures for Senegalese participation in political life have been maintained and gradually extended. The Vichy regime scrapped all elective institutions in Senegal, and, even though it followed a paternalistic and benevolent policy toward individual Senegalese, did so on a basis of segregation. The postwar period, however, saw the end of forced labor and the extension of the franchise.[35]

---

34 Ibid., p. 34.
35 Ibid., pp. 47, 48.

One major step which was not taken was the application of the French social security system to Senegal. This would have meant that welfare standards would have been identical in the much poorer African territory and in metropolitan France, a measure which would have involved enormous cost to the French taxpayer and was never seriously considered by the French Chamber of Deputies.

In the 1930s, debate within France over the desirability of assimilation was also matched by a growing uncertainty among the Senegalese themselves. This questioning of assimilation came among the very Senegalese who had been most exposed to French culture, among whom was the historian Cheikh Anta Diop, who gave an extremely idealistic picture of Africa's contribution to world situation, claiming that Pharonic Egypt was essentially a Negro civilization and, therefore, that the world owed the same debt to Negro peoples that it did the Graeco-Latin cultures. Diop also stressed the essential unity of black Africa and thus helped to give birth to the concept of Pan-Africanism.[36] He was joined in this by Léopold Sédar Senghor, who contributed especially the idea that the African personality and outlook on life was one that was holistic rather than fragmented, and, therefore, distinct from that of the West and was one of unique value.

For the French, doubts about the feasibility of assimilation gave rise to the idea of "association." This was to be a system whereby French and colonials worked together in a cooperative relationship without trying to repress ethnic differences or to insist that French practices be the invariable norm throughout the French-controlled portions of Africa and Asia. The direction to which the Senegalese intellectuals were turning in their rejection of assimilation was somewhat less certain. They, themselves, were the most Gallicized of their nation, and had no desire to cut the ties with France. They seemed to be groping for a basis on which they could accept both French and indigenous culture and to be insisting upon a more nearly equal relationship in which the value of African cultural contributions was given equal weight with the "civilizing mission" of France. From the beginning of French colonial occupation, to the middle 1950s, there was a steadily increasing participation of Senegalese in local political decision–making; conversely, a steadily decreasing weight was being given to French authority itself, and, therefore, there was a waning pattern of political integration.

In retrospect, the obstacles to assimilation seem to be quite evident. Intimate personal relationships were decreasing, and no large group of mixed bloods emerged which blurred the distinction between French and Senegalese ethnic identity. Religion failed to be a basis of unity, while religious distinctions preserved barriers in customs and legal interpretations. Education was too restricted to bring the bulk of the population

---

[36] Ibid., p. 55.

under the influence of the French culture, and, while the economy was closely linked with that of France, the individual African did not see his immediate income as dependent upon his ties with the French metropolitan area.

Although by the middle of the 1950s there had been complete participation by the Senegalese in French institutions nationally, as well as in their own local government, this participation had come so much by fits and starts that it had aroused irritation and resentment which led to the questioning of the sincerity of French intentions. On the other hand, none of these difficulties in the path of assimilation were necessarily insuperable, and it is possible to argue that, had the course of history been more favorable, the dream of assimilating at least the Senegalese portion of French Africa to the French nation might have materialized. Probably its failure was due less to the defects of the basic structural pattern of assimilation than to the pattern of events which promoted the growth of nationalism in French colonies during the decade of the 1950s.

THE FAILURE OF ASSIMILATION AND INTEGRATION

Many of these events can be summed up in the life of Léopold Sédar Senghor, professor, poet, grammarian, and first president of the Republic of Senegal. Turning again to the great man theory of history, it is certainly no exaggeration to say that Senghor played as important a role in Senegalese independence as Faidherbe did in its colonial development. Senghor was born in 1906 in Joal, a small town south of Dakar. He was a member of a minority tribe, the Serer, which had accepted Christianity. Senghor attended a Catholic elementary school and eventually finished a university education in Paris. He became a member of the French Chamber of Deputies and was renowned for his intellectual as well as his political accomplishments. His writings in poetry and prose, largely in defense of negritude, have acquired a world fame; he is a member of the French Academy, and at one time was the official grammarian, solving questions of language usage for the Chamber of Deputies. He was a member of the French army during World War II, was taken prisoner by the Germans, was released, and later became a member of the resistance movement. His first wife was the daughter of Felix Eboue, a Negro native of French Guiana, who became governor-general of French Africa.[37] Later he married a French woman, the former Collette Hubert. He spent many of his adult years in France, and, even as Senegalese President, made a practice of taking his summer vacations at his residence in Normandy.

It might be argued that the necessity of reconciling the African and the French aspects of his background forced Senghor to a rejection of assimi-

---

[37] Reed and Wake, Senghor Prose and Poetry, pp. 3–5, 14.

lation; it might also be argued that perhaps it was the exigencies of political life which compelled him to differentiate his own stand from that of his
French mentors. Whatever the case may be, Senghor has had a variety
of attitudes and expressions toward assimilation. From first being the eager
schoolboy, he became a bitter critic of things French and, in his own
words, says, "As Negro students in the years 1930–1934, I admit that we
were racialist: we were intoxicated by the banner of negritude. At that
time, no intercourse was possible with Europeans."[38] This completely
negative phase was apparently a passing element in Senghor's life, and
later he came to speak of assimilation as something that was essentially
bilateral, involving the acceptance of both African and French culture.
He was not an early advocate of independence, and, even when he criticized French actions, he proclaimed the unity of French and African
peoples, saying, "The peoples of Africa do not intend to cut themselves
off from metropolitan France: they want to be able to construct side by
side with her their own buildings which will construct and extend French
territory."[39]

Senghor's dream of co-assimilation and integration of African and
French nationality was based on the idea of a West African federation,
embracing a population of 20 million people, which would be an equal
partner with metropolitan France. West African politics in the 1950s was
largely the story of the wreckage of that dream. It floundered on French
ambivalence toward a large federation as a part of the French nation, the
ambitions of particular African territories, and vendettas by one political
leader against another.

To understand the effect of French vacillation and African leadership
rivalries, it is necessary first to look at some aspects of the political picture.
As in every emerging country, the competition for political power in
Senegal was intense. One of the earliest opponents of Senghor was Lamine
Gueye, who was a leader of the Socialist Party branch in Senegal. Senghor
effectively broke Gueye's power by leaving the Socialist Party and charg-
ing it with being concerned only with metropolitan France and ignoring
the real needs of Senegal. In this way, he consolidated the support of
tribesmen outside of the cities and their traditional leaders, a base of
operations on which he relied from that time on.[40] However, when the
Loi Cadre, giving a universal franchise to Africans and a major degree of
self-government in internal affairs, was passed, it did not provide for an
effective West African Federation with its own executive. There were two
reasons why the federal dream of Senghor was frustrated at this particular

---

[38] Crowder, *Senegal*, p. 49.

[39] Michael Crowder, *Senegal: A Study in French Assimilation Policy* (London, Oxford University Press, 1962), p. 51.

[40] Reed and Wake, Translation of Senghor, *Prose and Poetry*, pp. 16, 17.

time. One was that his opponent, as a leading member of the Socialist Party, was able to persuade the French members of that party that federalism would give an undeserved boost to Senghor, who had been their opponent. Another reason is that the French, themselves, were uneasy about what would happen in metropolitan France if 20 million Africans were to have a proportionate say in French politics. In any event, the passing of the *Loi Cadre* without making provision for an effective West African Federation indicated that the tide was running against the formation of a strong, united French West Africa.

The dream of federalism, however, was still not dead, and Senghor continued to proclaim its necessity. In this policy he came up against Houphouet-Boigny, a capable politician of the Ivory Coast, who felt that Federation would mean a drain on the resources of the wealthy Ivory Coast in favor of the poorer nations, and, at the same time, was able to outmaneuver Senghor for political support within the Federation. His maneuvers were aided by the exigencies of French politics, which gave near independence to Togo in 1956, as a counterweight to the grant of independence made by the British to Ghana, at the same time.[41] When de Gaulle in 1958 decided on a new policy for the French, he indicated that national autonomy for the French African territories was to be given more weight than the strengthening of the Federation.

Senghor thus saw his French Federation becoming a mere shadow, and also found himself outvoted in political maneuvering; his reaction was to withdraw from a dream of French West Africa and to unite in the only remaining possibility of federation, one with Mali. The Mali Federation itself was a short-lived situation. Sharp rivalry soon emerged between Mali and Senegal politicians, and it became apparent that the more Marxian and militant leaders of Mali would hardly go along with the Gallicized leaders of Senegal.[42] Consequently, Senghor ended the Mali Federation and proclaimed Senegal an independent nation, thus tolling the death knell to the dreams of a West African federation, as well as marking the end of centuries of attempted assimilation and integration between Senegal and metropolitan France.

In the early days of Senegalese independence the influence of French culture within Senegal seemed unchallenged, but later developments indicate that this, too, is under question. A student strike which closed the University of Dakar in 1969 demanded the Africanization of both cur-

---

[41] The analysis of the demise of the idea of The French West African Federation is based largely on Crowder, *Senegal*, pp. 65–74, and John D. Hargreaves, *West Africa: The Former French States* (Englewood Cliffs, N. J., Prentice Hall, Inc., 1967), pp. 155–59.

[42] Richard Folz, *From French West Africa to the Mali Federation* (New Haven, Conn., Yale University Press, 1965), pp. 184–85.

riculum and staff:[43] Obviously French cultural influence in some form will survive the passing of the dream of political union between France and its African possessions, but even among the elite we may expect to see a greater divergence from the pattern indicated by the mission *civilisatrice*.

CONCLUSIONS

Any type of political prediction is dangerous, and it is quite possible that the trends depicted as operational in the Antilles and in Senegal may be reversed. It seems unlikely that Senegal will ever become an integral unit of France as part of a West African federation, but such a development is not inconceivable. It is far more probable that changes in the Antilles may lead to a greater separation from metropolitan France. Problems of employment and economic development still remain, and some of the younger generation of intellectuals no longer find French nationality a satisfactory form of cultural identity. It is by no means impossible that either Césaire or one of his intellectual heirs may yet emerge as the leader of a successful movement for independence in the Antilles.

Pattern in Senegal and the French Antilles. History has no examples of permanent political structures but, regardless of how transient the Senegalese and Antillean situations may be, their differences still offer some intriguing hypotheses in the field of intergroup relations. Perhaps the first and most obvious hypothesis is derived from a general comparison of the formal French policy of assimilation with policies of a more pluralistic nature. The professed objectives and methods of the British made it impossible for integration to be accepted by their Caribbean or African colonies. Similarly, the American discouragement of statehood aspirations in the Philippines made ultimate independence of that country a certainty, while the opposite policy allowed Hawaii to become fully integrated with the mainland United States. Vacillation between assimilation and pluralism in Puerto Rico has favored the emergence of an intermediate type of policy in the form of the Commonwealth government. A formal policy of assimilation may fail to reach its objectives, but without it the triumph of separatist tendencies appears inevitable.

General pattern. Centrifugal tendencies often lead to segmentation along ethnic lines unless countered by a manifest policy of assimilation.

Pattern in Senegal and the French Antilles. Closely related to the effectiveness of assimilationist policy is the extent to which such policies actually provide a common situation for two or more ethnic groups rather than being an invitation to different groups to accept a common allegiance

---

[43] "Senghor's Emergency," *West Africa*, June 14, 1969, p. 666.

on the basis of unequal privileges. In Senegal assimilation was primarily a matter of rhetoric, marginal cultural activity and political participation. In the Antilles, assimilationist policies led to the extension of French social security benefits to residents of the Antilles, heavy French expenditures for welfare purposes, and commitment to a common pay scale for natives and migrants from metropolitan France in comparable positions. Economically, the status of the Antilles was guaranteed by its relation to a relatively prosperous France while the Senegalese economy was subsidized rather than guaranteed and the individual Senegalese had no claim on the French treasury. The average man in the Antilles found his total life situation directly affected by his residence in a French department; for the Senegalese, French sovereignty had only a peripheral relationship and French subsidies were actually greater after independence than before.

General pattern. The effectiveness of assimilationist policies varies directly with the proportion of the total life situation they encompass.

Pattern in Senegal and the French Antilles. Another fairly obvious factor is that cultural similarity between the minority and majority ethnic groups facilitates political integration. Again, similarity by itself does not guarantee successful political integration, as can be seen by one of the first colonial revolutions, that of the United States against a culturally similar Britain. Before allowing the American example to vitiate this hypothesis, however, we would remember that the British rule of the colonies lasted for over 150 years, that there was much disagreement in the 13 colonies about the revolution, and, that when independence finally came, several thousand loyalists left the country. Insofar as cultural homogeneity is helpful, it is certainly a trait which applied more to the Antilles than to Senegal or to the British colonies in the Caribbean. In the Antilles French was practically the only language used, Catholicism was the religion of the bulk of the inhabitants, the monogamous family was accepted by all as the ideal pattern, and nearly universal education of a French character had provided a common life view for most of the inhabitants.

General pattern. Acceptance of political integration varies directly with the degree that cultural homogeneity allows the government to be a symbol of shared values.

Pattern in Senegal and the French Antilles. Since, by definition, some differences will exist between ethnic groups, the character of their relationships determines whether these differences will be considered variation on a common theme or a focal point for tensions. Here we would observe that cooperation promotes unity, while competition may lead to conflict. As long as the relationship between two ethnic groups is a symbiotic one, with each group performing generally acceptable yet noncompetitive roles, unity is enhanced. When the roles become competitive, especially when total opportunity is limited, conflict may result.

Frequently the basis for conflict is competition between colored citizens and "poor whites" for jobs with an intermediate prestige ranking. In the Caribbean the migration back to the homeland of many of the descendants of the white settlers left a vacuum in this area which was filled by the people of mixed ancestry. In Senegal, on the other hand, the importation of Frenchmen as laborers and clerks led to competition with literate Senegalese and to an advocacy of independence as a means of "Africanization." The *petit blancs* were perceived as occupying the rungs on the occupational ladder to which Senegalese might aspire, and hence their presence was viewed as a barrier to Senegalese social mobility.

General pattern. Tendencies toward political separatism vary directly with the degree of ethnic economic competition.

Pattern in Senegal and the French Antilles. A major factor in the intensity of ethnic conflict is whether cleavages are seen as dichotomous or multiple. When they are seen as essentially polarized, there is little doubt that eventually the majority group will view a dominant minority as the enemy. All the Caribbean countries tended toward a multiple classification of color differences which avoided a simple black versus white confrontation. In Senegal, however, the *Metis* became a small separate group rather than a bridge between Europeans and the Africans. Their existence blurred the sharpness of color identification, but did not alter the essential division of interests along lines of African versus Europeans.

General pattern. The intensity of ethnic conflict varies inversely with the number of groups classified as ethnically distinct.

Pattern in Senegal and the French Antilles. The attraction of acculturation is affected by the value given competing alternatives. In Senegal the non-European looked at Christianity and French culture from the vantage point of Islam and a cohesive tribal culture. In the Antilles, only vestiges of tribal culture and animistic religion remained, and the non-European had no apparent alternative to the religion and culture proffered by the French. It is easier to maintain an ethnic identity than to construct one; hence individuals separated from their cultural tradition are far more open to acculturation and assimilation than those whose links with a cultural background are unbroken.

General pattern. The appeal of another culture varies inversely with the viability of the original culture.

Pattern in Senegal and the French Antilles. One reason the wave of nationalism passed relatively lightly over the Antilles is the comparative isolation of the area, another situation shared by Hawaii. Senegal was so close to nationalistic African states that it would have had difficulty in remaining a French enclave even if other circumstances had been more propitious. By contrast, the non-Europeans in the French Antilles were separated from similar groups in the Caribbean by language and from Africans by both culture and distance.

General pattern. The probability of integration with a larger political unit comprised primarily of another ethnic group varies directly with the social and geographic distance from other members of the original ethnic group.

All of these various propositions relate to the extent of the benefits the integrative situation offers to the minority group as contrasted to the disabilities involved and the alternatives available. This does not mean that the terms of national identity are achieved in some sort of sum—zero calculation, or, if so, that the variables involved are easily calculated. The salience of various factors is often as emotional as rational and as frequently affected by chance events as by an inevitable logic of history. Without the charisma of a de Gaulle the French Antilles might still have gone the way of other colonies, and if Senghor had been on better terms with other African leaders a French West Africa domain might have been constructed. The variables described in our sundry propositions indicate the ground of combat, but the issue of the battle is still determined by the men in the fray.

QUESTIONS

1. What are the political arrangements of Martinique and Guadeloupe with France and how are they regarded by the inhabitants of the two islands?
2. What is the ethnic composition of the French Antilles and what role did the Free French play in cementing the ties between France and the islanders?
3. To what extent are the inhabitants of the Antilles economically dependent upon France? Could this be a factor which makes independence undesirable?
4. Is there any association at all between skin color and socioeconomic status among the populace of Antilles?
5. What role does the mulatto play in the scheme of race relations in the French Antilles and, should a clash occur, which side is the mulatto most likely to be on? Why?
6. Why does racial blurring tend to occur in a society when racial groups are classified in multiple categories with intermediate privileges and status? What are some of the psychological implications of this process?

7. How does the French view of assimilation and of their "civilizing mission" differ from that of Britain?

8. How do you account for the fact that in the British West Indies independence is viewed as necessary for human progress but for the Antillians attachment to metropolitan France seems essential for human betterment?

9. What are the important differences between Césaire's and Senghor's concept of negritude?

10. What factors were responsible for the emergence of a small mulatto (*Metis*) population in Senegal and what role, if any, did it assume in the assimilation process?

11. How would you characterize the relationships between the poor whites and blacks in Senegal?

12. Why were the Christian missions unsuccessful in achieving a stronghold in Senegal? In what way did Islam impede assimilation?

13. In what sense was it true that education was the main vehicle of the French assimilation policy in Senegal?

14. What were the important points of contention during the 1930s debate which increased the uncertainty over the desirability of assimilation in Senegal?

15. How would you account for the fact that by the mid-1950s it was evident that the French assimilation policy in Senegal was doomed to failure?

16. Do you think that, had Senghor been able to realize his dream of federalism, this would have significantly altered the socioeconomic conditions of Senegal? Defend your answers.

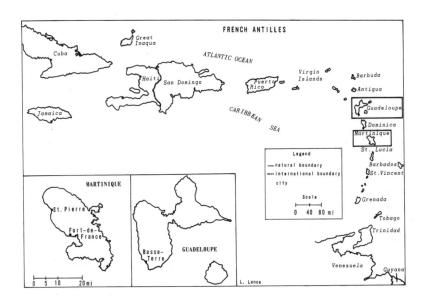

Chapter 8

Minorities in Islamic States

When the armies of the followers of Mohammed advanced through the Arabian Peninsula, the Middle East, northern Africa, and parts of the Far East, they encountered people foreign to them in both ethnicity and religion. The promises of Allah were open to all and a large part of the population became converted to Islam. However, Christians and Jews, as those already "people of the book," were resistant to conversion and many so-called pagans also clung to the ancestral faith.

While the ideal situation was one in which all inhabitants of the state were Muslim and hence equally under the rule of a common religion, Islam was not unprepared for minority problems. The teachings of the Koran and the pronouncements of early Islamic theologians dealt frequently with this topic. The result was that a definite body of principles was developed to govern the relations of the faithful with the infidels.

Like other groups, Muslims have not always lived up to their professed ideals and the formal pattern was occasionally marred by massacres, riots, and persecutions. Nevertheless, the Islamic treatment of minorities compares favorably with the record of other groups. Islamic culture has endured for centuries and has enabled people of distinct identities to live together in a relatively peaceful atmosphere. Some of the policies adopted by Islamic societies were conditioned by particular circumstances, but others reflect enduring aspects of the relationships of different peoples inhabiting a common territory. Certainly the student of intergroup contacts cannot ignore the Muslim experience. In this chapter, then, we offer the following generalizations of interethnic relations: (1) the existence of several ethnic groups within a given political regime will be accepted if defined in ways which avoid a clash between political loyalties and ethnic identities, (2) it is difficult for a minority with an invidious status to gain acceptance through participation in nationalist activities, (3) the gulf between minorities and the majority group is often widened when a minority receives foreign protection, (4) the degree of discrimination against minorities tends to vary directly with the scope and nature of activity by the state, and (5) cohesion in a multi-ethnic state requires the acceptance of the dominance of an ethnic group or of an ideology.

IMPACT OF RELIGIOUS PRINCIPLES

The simplicity and directness of Islamic monotheism has produced an attitude toward minorities which is more definite and more consistent than that found among groups with other religious affiliations. Allah is the one true God and no other deities are allowed to share in his glory. Mohammed is the prophet of Allah and other prophets only proclaim truth when their teachings are interpreted in harmony with those of Mohammed, although Christians and Jews, as people of a partial revelation, may be tolerated under certain conditions. No being, either human or supernatural, shares in the divine charisma, and there is no official religious hierarchy, although individual religious teachers, the *ulami,* may at times have significant prestige and influence.

Along with the proclamation of the one true God, the principal teaching of Mohammed was the Law of God. The duty of the faithful is to learn and observe the law, and the state exists to enforce the Islamic law and expand its sway. The law makes definite provision for the treatment of various categories of unbelievers, and the minority policy of the state is to enforce, so far as circumstances permit, the minority policies proclaimed in the Koran and elaborated by later sages in the *Hadith.* Reciprocal obligations, such as between master and slave, teacher and pupil, one who has seen the light and one who has not, form the major content of the *Hadith.*

State and church in the Middle East are intertwined to a degree which seems almost incomprehensible to a western observer. The following statement by an Arab writer gives some idea of the nature of the situation: "Islam is not merely a body of religious doctrine and practice; it is also a form of social and political organization . . . Most of the Christian sects

. . . are also governed by religious law. In the Middle East there is no clear distinction between religious and secular life.[1]

Since law had a religious basis, the minority communities could not be expected to be governed by the law of Islam but by their own religious law. Thus the very philosophy which gave a prominent place to Islamic law (with concessions to the customary law of the locality) also supported the maintenance of other religiously based legal systems applying to the various Christian and Jewish settlements. The fact that the enforcement of the law was a major Islamic justification of political organization does not mean that all—or even most—Islamic states were theocracies. In spite of the ideal tenets, the same variations existed in practice that are found in states with Christian religious affiliations. At times religious and political leadership were merged, and something close to a general theocracy developed. At other times secular considerations were paramount, and the supposedly Islamic states were as free from specifically religious controls as their Christian neighbors. Nevertheless, the primacy of the Islamic law is a recurring theme with an attraction for the faithful, even if not always followed by the rulers.

Since the main function of the state was to enforce the Islamic law, the most salient characteristic of minorities was their rejection of the principle which was considered absolute truth by the state. Hence the question as to how deviant religious groups might be treated was the main issue in determining minority policy. Minorities were classified in two types, "People of the Book" and "pagans." The pagans were entirely outside of the true faith and as idol worshippers deserved no consideration from the Islamic authorities except that which their military power might dictate. Christians and Jews as People of the Book shared in part in the revelation of religious truth. However, they have rejected the supreme prophet Mohammed, and Christians are guilty of committing the sin of "association," which means that through acknowledging the divinity of Christ they had associated another figure with that of Allah.[2]

Another classification was made on the basis of the nature of the capitulation of the minority to the Islamic state. If the capitulation had been a surrender which avoided a test of arms, the lives of the minority could be spared. If, however, dominance had been won in actual combat, it was the duty of the Muslim to put the enemies of the Faith to death. These precepts, like all principles, were difficult to observe in complete purity. Either the power of the minority groups or the laxness and loss of will of the Islamic rulers might force the acceptance of a compromise situation.

---

[1] Ibrahim Abdulla Muhy, "Women in the Middle East," *Journal of Social Issues* 15 (1959): 51.

[2] Pierre Rondot, "Islam, Christianity and the Modern State," *Middle Eastern Affairs* 5 (November 1954): 341.

Under extreme conditions it might even be necessary for an Islamic minority to live under the rule of the infidels as in the Philippine Islands, Yugoslavia, and Kenya today, and this was true even for majorities in much of the Islamic world during the colonial period in the Middle East following World War I. Usually, though, the Islamic group was dominant in the state and, according to the degree of its power and its doctrinal purity, fashioned the government after Islamic tenets. One practice was practically inconceivable, that religious affiliation might be disregarded so that nonbelievers and Muslims could participate in the state on equal terms.

MILLET SYSTEM OF THE OTTOMAN EMPIRE

The system reached its most perfect expression during the days when the Ottoman Caliphate dominated the Middle East, including considerable portions of North Africa and Europe. The Ottoman Caliph not only was a Turkish Sultan, but he also claimed to be the Defender of Islam and the Ottoman Caliphate was the governmental organization of the faithful. The Empire had included, from the time of its origin in 1231 until its demise in 1924, a fair proportion of minorities. These minorities had two distinctive, frequently overlapping attributes, religion and a sense of nationality. The Islamic community was identified with the sovereign state and, as Hourani expressed it, not only was the dominant element Muslim, it was this element alone which constituted the political community.[3] The Empire was the community of believers living in common under the authority of the sacred law; and the Sultan's role was to administer the law, to extend its sway in the world, and to protect the Muslim community from external dangers.

The minority religious groups were organized into communities of their own, or millets. Each millet regulated its life according to the terms of its own religious law under the authority of its supreme religious leaders, a patriarch in the case of Christian groups or a Grand Rabbi for the Jews. Thus the Islamic viewpoint dictated not only the essential nature of sovereignty but also the type of adjustment which minority religious groups made. While the organization of millets did provide a certain security for minority religious entities, it in no way implied equality. Rondot delineates the subordinate-superordinate relationship of the Muslims and the Infidels in the millet system.

The most characteristic features of this structure are the following: a member of a non-Muslim community may always be converted to Islam, but a Muslim may not, on pain of death, embrace a new faith; Muslims maintain their form

---

[3] A. H. Hourani, *Minorities in the Arab World* (London, Oxford University Press, 1947), p. 17.

of worship and may proselytize; not so Christians and Jews, whose places of worship must not open into public thoroughfares and whose ritual must be subdued; Christians and Jews may not erect new sanctuaries or repair old ones without special permission; in matters of personal status (concerning marriage, divorce, inheritance, etc.) Christians and Jews are ruled by their own religious law, but they may always change over into the sphere of Muslim law; they may not exercise functions of authority in the state; a Muslim may marry a Christian or Jewish woman, but a Christian or Jew may not marry a Muslim woman.

Thus, tolerance is early identified in Islam with a system of separation and subordination of non-Muslim communities under the "protection" of Islam, while the latter, fusing the spiritual and temporal, permeates the state. Step by step, humiliating measures (prohibition of floating garments, introduction of a distinctive badge, etc.) crystallized and reinforced this system of inequality which, by its very foundation, is devoid of any possibility of evolution.[4]

RELIGION AND ETHNICITY

While religion was the essential basis for the organization of the millets, ethnicity could not be ignored. Ethnic tensions came about in three ways: (1) not all of the Muslims themselves were of the same ethnic background; (2) the religious groups tended to become not so much communities of "believers" as ethnic groups whose ancestors had at a previous time held a common faith; (3) within the Christian group there was a struggle for supremacy of one or another ethnic group both within and between the various Christian denominations.

The Ottoman Empire itself, while in one sense a manifestation of the universal Caliphate, in another sense was regarded as simply the Turkish state. The Arabs, although they were the ones to whom Mohammed came first and therefore in a certain sense were a people "set apart," were nevertheless, a subject people within the Ottoman Empire. Their rights were not curtailed, but elections were practically unknown and the major officials were chosen by the Turkish government. Similarly, the Kurds felt they too were a suppressed minority without a national state of their own. As the bounds of the Ottoman Empire shrank in the last days of the "sick man of Europe," Muslim minorities, which at one time had been loyal, manifested the same nationalistic urges as the Christians. The Albanians, for instance, who had long been a pillar of the empire, sought and obtained their independence in 1912. Distinctions between Islamic sects also, at times, played a role in the ethnic relations between Muslims. Thus the other Muslim empire, the Persian, adhered to the Shi'i sect, while the Turks were Sunni.

In this delineation of relationship between Muslim peoples, it should

---

4 Rondot, "Islam, Christianity and the Modern State," pp. 215–16.

be emphasized that no Muslim peoples as such were regarded as subordinate. Rather, the government was autocratic and the government within the Ottoman Empire was Turkish; therefore the leading officials were usually Turkish, or at least responsible to a Turkish Sultan. Tensions between Muslims came to the ultimate point during World War I, when the Arab-speaking world sided with the Christian French and English against the Muslim Caliph of the Ottoman Empire in a successful push for freedom from Turkish rule.

Within the Christian communities millets were divided along nationality as well as along religious lines. Roman Catholics, Orthodox, and Protestants competed for the adherence of the Armenians and the Greeks, and a variety of other nationalities. Within the Orthodox hierarchy each group preferred to be represented by its own patriarch, although the prestige of the Greeks gave them almost exclusive control for a time and the Greek Patriarch in Constantinople became the leading Christian prelate in Muslim areas. Hourani summarizes the situation as follows:

> The religious communities were shut off from one another on the levels of belief, personal law, and close personal relations, but on that of economic life they were closely intertwined. There were no legal restrictions on movement within the Empire; even before it came into existence the greater part of its territory had formed a single trading unit for hundreds of years; and its religious sects had grown up within a community which was already united, and of which the constituent elements were already inextricably mixed. For all these reasons, the different religious and racial communities were not sharply divided from one another geographically. Some of them (for example, the Arabs) were compact, possessing some region in which they formed the vast majority; others (for example, the Armenians) were in a minority in all their regions of settlement.[5]

Spiritual and temporal duties and privileges of the patriarchs were so intertwined that it was difficult to distinguish their religious and secular functions. The patriarchs were interpreters of the law and religious celebrants, but the religious law embraced civil concerns and the act of worship was also a manifestation of community patriotism. Perhaps the recent role of the Greek Orthodox Patriarch, Makarios of Cyprus, as political leader of the nation may illustrate the double scope of community religious leaders within the old Ottoman empire. Religion had become largely a matter of ancestry rather than of personal conviction. The Christain or Jew lived in a particular millet and was governed by its rules; he might or might not have a firm conviction of the validity of the articles of his faith.

Frequently a double religious and nationality tag was required for

---

[5] A. H. Hourani, "Race and Related Ideas in the Near East," in Andrew W. Lind (ed.), *Race Relations in World Perspective* (Honolulu, University of Hawaii Press, 1955), p. 121.

identification. Thus a sharp line was drawn between Christian and Muslim Arabs. When the young Turks decided to eliminate the Armenians, this decision applied to those of Orthodox faith and exempted Protestants and Catholics, who evidently were not considered true Armenians. In the exchange of populations in 1925 between Greece and Turkey, the Turkish-speaking person living in Greece who was a member of the Orthodox Church was not sent back to Turkey, whereas if he had been a Muslim, transfer would have been automatic. Similarly, in Asia Minor, Greeks who were of Protestant or Catholic affiliation were not included in the exchange, although those of Orthodox faith were deported in wholesale fashion.[6]

MINORITY TENSIONS IN THE OTTOMAN EMPIRE

For many years the essentially symbolic nature of the relationship between minority and majority operated to relieve tension and to promote cooperation. The various millets as well as the Muslim minority groups and the ruling class in the empire were separated by the type of law, a high degree of marital endogamy, differential rights as citizens, and differences of religious beliefs. However, their economic activities were inextricably intertwined. Most peasants as well as military[7] and political officers were Muslims of Turkish background, while Christians and Jews were disproportionately active in commerce and in the professions. Some ethnic groups lived in relatively compact geographical regions; others were scattered throughout the Empire; and at times even villages might be mixed in their religious and nationality composition. While the Ottoman Empire usually required taxation of the minorities greater than that imposed on the dominant group, there were compensations such as the exemption from military service for Christians and Jews.

The Ottoman Empire lasted for nearly 700 years and during that time maintained a degree of peace between the various Muslim groups, between Arab and Jew and between Christian and Muslim. This is no mean achievement, especially when considered in the light of the internal feuds and the ethnic quarrels which have pervaded the Middle East in recent years. Nevertheless, it would be a mistake to view the Ottoman Empire as an idyllic period of contentment in which the military dominance of the Turks brought to their unwilling subjects an era of peace and tranquility.

---

[6] Ibid., p. 30.

[7] Occasionally individual Christians or Jews were trusted with high office on the assumption that they would be less inclined to intrigue against the Sultan than his fellow Muslims. For a time the elite corps of the Ottoman army, the Janissaries were recruited from Christians. The Jannissaries were eliminated after an unsuccessful revolt in 1826. See Lewis A. Coser, "The Alien as a Servant of Power: Court Jews and Christian Renegades," *American Sociological Review* 37 (October 1972): 578–81.

The maintenance of order was marred by massacres, and even in peaceful years the minorities experienced discrimination.[8]

One of the indications of difficulty is found in the existence of groups known as crypto-Christians. These were people who espoused a double faith, being openly Muslim and yet secretly of Christian persuasion. They came from both Orthodox and Roman Catholic wings of Christianity and were found throughout the Ottoman realms. Apparently, the motivation was a desire to cling to Christian beliefs while gaining privileges reserved for Muslims. In periods of stress and persecution the number of crypto-Christians increased, while in periods of relatively calm tolerance they declined, although the Islamic rule against conversion from Islam to any other religion made it difficult for the crypto-Christians to formally admit their Christian beliefs.

In lands which were only tributary to the Ottoman Empire there was relatively little pressure against nonbelievers, but when these areas were incorporated into direct rule, the pressure was likely to become intense and the growth of crypto-Christianity proceeded. Since Christians and Muslims have a common heritage in their respect for considerable portions of the Old and New Testament and have lived together for many years, it was not unnatural that certain elements should have passed through religious boundaries. Perhaps an extreme example of this type of accommodation is in the case of the Vallakhads, a Greek group living near Gervena, among whom were persons who actually espoused both faiths without concealment, including individuals who might go to the mosque on Friday and Church on Sunday.[9] Other groups which include a mixture of Christian and Muslim elements in their faith would include the Druzes in Lebanon and Syria and the Subbah in southern Iraq. Lines of doctrinal separation are not always as clear to the laity as the clergy might wish and it is not surprising that, where differential privilege was accorded religious affiliation, conversion for convenience might occur.

As the Ottoman Empire declined and strong nation states emerged in Europe, Christian nations tended to assume the role of protectors of the various millets. The ultimate consequence of this intervention was independence; for Serbia, Greece, Bulgaria, and Roumania, this arrived in the 19th century.

Berkes describes the Christian intervention in the millet system:

Two great contending forces (the Western powers and Russia) had become intensely interested in the question not only in respect to their relations with the Ottoman Empire but also in respect to their relations with each other on every

---

[8] Cecil Roth, "Jews in the Arab World," *Near East Report* (August 1967), pp. B–17, B–20.

[9] Stravo Skend, "Crypto-Christianity in the Balkan Area under the Ottomans," *Slavic Review* 26 (June 1967): 226–46.

front. Furthermore both religion (Catholicism and Orthodoxy) and race or nationality (in consequence of the French revolution and the rise of Russian pan-Slavism) had become complicating factors. And there was a third factor newly entering upon the scene—the emerging British Near Eastern diplomacy with its Protestant coloring as personified in the Ambassador Stratford Canning. The millet system began to emerge in international diplomacy as an inviolate system that was no longer a unilateral grant of status and privilege to non-Muslim communities; they were seen as having rights as *nationalities* guaranteed by the Christian powers of Europe.[10]

The most severe examples of minority dissatisfaction were found in the experience of the Greeks and the Armenians. A growing nationalism in Greece eventually led to the formation of a separate Greek kingdom but this did not settle the issue, since both Greeks and Turks had a claim to Asia Minor and Constantinople (Istanbul). The resulting war in 1921–1924 ended in a Turkish victory and an agreement that populations would be exchanged. Those identified as Greeks but living in Asia Minor were to be returned to the Kingdom of Greece, and those identified as Turks but living in European Greece were to be returned to Turkey, with Constantinople and Asia Minor remaining under the rule of the Turks. In this fashion people were forced to leave homes which their ancestors had inhabited for centuries.

The geographical dispersion of the Greeks meant that their problems were not solved by the formation of a Greek nation. The dispersion of the Armenians and their division into a number of competing religious groups meant that neither the millet system nor national independence was a feasible solution to their relationship to the Turks:

In the Ottoman system, the Armenians constituted a millet that did not have a territorial base and was, therefore, incapable of being transformed into a nation state. In addition, the schismatic struggles since 1847 among the Gregorian, Catholic and Protestant churches not only shattered the Armenian millet but also severed it from its traditional status in the Ottoman system. The desire of the Armenian nationalists to establish an independent Armenia was frustrated hopelessly by the conflicts among the churches, the geographical and occupational distribution of the Armenians within the Ottoman Empire, and also the rivalries between Russia and Great Britain, who alternately supported and dropped the Armenian nationalist aspirations.[11]

The case of the Armenians was especially tragic because the reforming zeal of the young Turks led to an effort to "purify" the Turkish nation by the elimination of these "troublesome outsiders"; through civil conflicts,

10 Niyazi Berkes, *The Development of Secularism in Turkey* (Montreal, McGill University Press, 1964), p. 96.

11 Ibid., p. 318.

massacres, and deportations, the Turks practically destroyed the Armenian population of Asia Minor between the years of 1894 and 1922.[12] In general it may be said that any period of stress for the Ottoman Empire was a period of difficulty for minorities, since they were suspected of involvement with similar religious or nationality elements in other countries and thus were regarded as an internal force subversive to the Empire. When the Turks were in their full vigor the system of millets continued on a tolerable basis, but when the Ottoman Empire became a declining power every move to extend its life seemed to result in some type of minority repression.

BEYOND AND AFTER THE OTTOMAN EMPIRE

The defeat of Turkey in World War I led to the end of the Ottoman Caliphate even inside Turkey itself. For a brief period most of the Middle East was a colonial area under the domination of Western powers who endeavored to apply the rule of secular law on an approximately equal basis to all the people in their possessions. This colonial era, however, was destined to be short lived, and by the end of the decade of the 60s all of the Muslim territories had been liberated from colonial rule,[13] although the Arab world was divided into many different states, some of which were comparable to feudal principalities.

The newly independent countries inherited the communal institutions of the millet, but the spirit of the new nationalism was hardly compatible with the pluralistic tolerance of the old empire. Some of the leaders of the newly independent Muslim states were essentially traditional princes who regarded the Islamic law as a bulwark of their regimes. Other rulers were modern nationalistic leaders who were thoroughly secular in their viewpoint and who saw Islamic law more as an obstacle than a bulwark. Their regimes stressed modernization and national loyalty rather than religious uniformity but, while sometimes eliminating traditional discrimination against minorities, they also attacked the communal system. Perhaps the prototype of such nationalist leaders was Mustafa Kemal Ataturk, who sought the modernization of Turkey. Muller describes his program as follows:

Thus he did away with the 6000-year-old sultanate, in its stead establishing a republic. With it and the caliphate he scrapped the Sacred Law of Islam, substituting the Swiss civil code. While beginning to modernize the economy, he forced Turks to learn how to manage the commerce and industry that had been

---

[12] Robert H. Hewsen, "The Armenians in the Middle East," *Viewpoints* 6 (Aug.–Sept. 1966): 3–10.

[13] For a description of postcolonial developments from a Christian point of view see Max Warren, "Christian Minorities in Muslim Countries," *Race* 6 (July 1964): 41–51.

left to Greeks and Armenians. He started a system of public schools to provide a purely secular education. He replaced the Arabic by the Latin script, changed the alphabet, and began purging the Turkish language of many Arabic and Persian words. Likewise he replaced the Islamic by the Gregorian calendar and made Sunday the day of rest. He put his people into Western clothes, requiring men to wear hats instead of fezzes. He conferred complete equality upon women, including the rights to vote and to divorce; long degraded as women had been in no other civilization, they soon had proportionately more representatives in the Grand National Assembly than American women have in Congress today. And so it went—on every social front, all within half a generation.[14]

His attack on Islamic social controls made it necessary to shift from identification as a Muslim to identification as a Turk, and the new order was even harsher on minorities than the old. Most minorities were deported at the end of the Turko-Grecian war in 1925, and those who remained found their privileges steadily eroding as non-Muslims came to be regarded as non-Turks and hence as aliens to be eliminated from profitable business activities.

No other Muslim nationalist leaders have been quite so ruthless in their attack on Islamic customs, but most of them have tried to enhance the power of the secularly based state apparatus and have interpreted nationalism as implying control of economic enterprise by those regarded as nationals. The result has been both a curtailment of the power of Islamic law and a restriction of self-rule by the religious officials of minority communities. Members of religious minorities were thus deprived of communal protection and subjected to the civil rule of those who regarded non-Muslims as being close to nonnationals. A decline of the observance of rigid Islamic law has meant an erosion of minority safeguards rather than a liberation from discrimination.

With the new nationalism came the question of what it meant to be a national of a given country. The answer to this was not just a matter of judicial procedure, birth in a particular area, or habitation within national boundaries; rather it was a question of whether one "belonged" to the nation. "Belonging" was established by ties both of nationality and of religion. The man who claimed identity with the national state but came from a different nationality background or a minority religious creed was one of doubtful loyalty who might easily be suspected of collaboration with a foreign power whose religious or national background was similar to his own. Further, the minority was also a convenient scapegoat for nationalistic governments which were long on promises and short on performance.

The breakup of the Ottoman Empire produced a need for boundaries of the new states and provoked a series of quarrels between the Muslim

---

[14] Herbert J. Muller, *Freedom in the Modern World* (New York, Harper & Row, 1966), pp. 463–64.

states themselves as well as between individual states and the great powers. Frontier questions, however, proved to be more amenable to solution than relations with non-Muslim groups within the newly independent states.

There remained the question of minorities. While in a supranational Empire several ethnic groups could live side by side in the same territory without asking whose it was, once the nation-state was set up, those who did not belong to the nation in whose name the state was established also did not belong in the full sense to the political community. However long their ancestors had lived there, they were now regarded as strangers. At best they lived on sufferance; at worst they might be looked on as economic rivals by the new indigenous bourgeoisie, or as potential traitors by the new government, dangerous either because of their own strength or else through the use to which they might be put by a Great Power.[15]

THE EXODUS OF THE JEWS

Among the areas ruled for centuries by the Ottoman Empire was the land of Palestine, which was sacred soil both to Jew and to Muslim. The end of empire signaled a fresh opportunity for national states to be developed by Arabs, but it also brought encouragement to Jewish Zionists, who had long been talking about a "national home." Palestine at the end of World War I was less than ten percent Jewish, but it occupied a pivotal point in Zionist thinking and it seemed the logical location for some type of national Jewish state. Hitler's persecution of the Jews in Europe, which sent approximately 4.5 million out of 7 million European Jews to their death,[16] stimulated Zionist sentiment. A Jewish state had been considered by many Jews as the messianic dream of an extremist minority; now it was seen as essential to Jewish physical survival.

When the Turks left Palestine the country was taken over by Great Britain under a mandate from the League of Nations to prepare it for self-government. The British strove to discover a formula under which Jews and Arabs could live together but finally gave up the task and left in 1948 without having reached a settlement, and the United Nations recognized partition of the area between Jordan and the newly created state of Israel. The result was a short-lived war in which the Arabs, who hoped to liquidate the state of Israel, were defeated.

The establishment of a Jewish state provided a place of refuge for Jews throughout the world who now had a homeland which could speak for

---

[15] Hourani, "Race and Related Ideas in the Near East," p. 128.

[16] Gerald Reitlinger, *The Final Solution* (South Brunswick, N. Y., Thomas Yoselof, 1968), p. 546. At an earlier date the figure of six million was often given. Reitlinger, on the basis of a thorough analysis of more complete data, feels the 4.5 million estimate is more accurate. Needless to say, either figure is a shocking indication of the depths of human depravity.

Jews in international organizations and which could offer asylum to Jewish refugees. It also meant the exodus of about 900,000 Arabs, who had left the area which became Israel during the time of war and who neither desired to come back under a Jewish state nor were welcomed by the Israeli authorities. This situation quickly led to an informal exchange of populations in which the Arab refugees became a semipermanent ward of the United Nations, living in the districts surrounding the state of Israel, while in turn over 600,000 Jews fled from Arab lands where they and their ancestors had been living for centuries.[17] In some cases Jews were forcibly expelled; in most, they fled, fearing renewed discrimination and more oppressive burdens, but in all Arab countries the Jewish community was reduced to a tiny fraction of that which had existed in previous years. Jewish and Arab nationalism had brought to an end a type of coexistence which had existed for hundreds of years. It was a coexistence which was not altogether satisfactory from either standpoint and one which denied the Jews full freedom of movement or full status of citizens, but it had proved both more tolerable and more durable than the situation of Jews in most countries in the West.

In all Arab countries the situation of the small Jewish community which remained has become precarious at best. In spite of resolutions against Zionism and protestations of loyalty to the Arab cause, they continue to be objects of suspicion. Iraq's large Jewish community has shrunk to 3,000, mostly elderly people. These live under a cloud of suspicion and are required to carry identity cards; several have been arrested and a few hanged as alleged spies. Life for the approximately 7,000 Jews still remaining in Syria, Egypt, and Libya is nearly as severe as in Iraq. Whereas in Saudi Arabia and Jordan all Jews have left, in Morocco, Lebanon, Algeria, and Tunisia open persecution is rare and life, at last report, was still fairly tolerable. About 75,000 Jews still remain in Arab lands as contrasted to nearly 600,000 before the creation of the state of Israel. In some countries life is relatively calm; in others it is a constant nightmare, and, in all Arab lands, Jews live in constant fear that the next crisis may bring intensified persecution.[18] In general, only a vestigial remnant of once flourishing Jewish communities remain and even this remnant lives under the constant harassment and the constant fear of extermination. The creation of the state of Israel furnished a haven for European Jewish refugees, most of whom had no other place to turn, but it also meant the creation of a very large population of Middle East refugees, both Jewish and Arab.

---

[17] To Israel 498,677 Jews immigrated from Europe between 1948 and 1963, while 618,763 came from Asia and Africa in the same period. Israel Office of Information, *Facts about Israel* (Jerusalem, 1967).

[18] "Jews in Arab Lands," *Near East Report* (August 1967), pp. 15–16; "The Other Victims in the Middle East's Long War," *Economist* 230 (Feb. 1969): 21; "Jews in the Arab World," *Time* (Feb. 7, 1969), p. 23.

SOCIALISM AND MINORITIES

In the 18th and 19th centuries nationalism was usually seen as the establishment of a political government controlled by residents of a particular territory. In the 20th century, nationalism has been joined by socialism, and programs for group advancement and development have largely replaced demands for individual freedom. This means that a nationalist movement goes far beyond the establishment of a particular form of government and seeks to alter the economic relationships of groups within the political state in a way more favorable to those who are considered genuine members of the national group.

Socialism offers an obvious tool, and private enterprise, a hindrance for this type of process. If economic activities are left to the determination of the market, nationality is of little consequence and success will go to those who have most developed the qualities which make for vigorous competition and the type of capital goods and strategic trading positions which are useful in commerce.

Since commerce by its very nature is a risky proposition, it tends to be shunned by those who have any traditional claim to status. In the days before socialism, this traditional claim to a livelihood found expression in land ownership or in a claim to government positions. The socialist replacement of the free market, however, makes it possible to reap the rewards of commerce and still avoid the threats of bankruptcy, since the government treasury provides a bulwark against losses resulting from incompetence, corruption, or miscalculation.

In the free market, minorities frequently come to the fore. In a socialist economy, where the government rations goods and decides which individuals are to be active in economic enterprises, minorities at best are rationed according to their proportion of the population and at worst are excluded completely. The best possible treatment, proportionate quotas, is difficult for minorities, since usually they have been excluded from other aspects of the economy and a proportionate quota may mean that only a fraction of the group will be able to make a living in the occupations which had supported many in previous years.

THE EGYPTIAN COPTIC CHRISTIANS

The Coptic Christians in Egypt may be taken as a prime example of the plight of a minority group in a country committed to nationalism and socialism. Copts were residents of Egypt for centuries before the Muslim era, and the term Coptic itself has been taken as equivalent to Egyptian. Copts have served in high government office and have been prominent in the nationalist movements. They have many customs in common with the Muslims; they observe a taboo on the eating of pork, follow the practice of circumcising their sons, and usually veil their women in areas where this is the Muslim practice. In fact, the similarity between the Copts and the Muslims appeared so great that to Lord Cromer they seemed essentially different sides of the same coin.

The only difference between Copt and Muslim is that the former is an Egyptian who worships in a Christian church, whilst the latter is an Egyptian who worships in a Mohammedan mosque.[19]

To be a Copt in the early part of the 20th century in Egypt meant that one was an Egyptian who shared the traditions of his Muslim fellow citizens but whose aspirations for upward mobility, devotion to education, and activity in business were far above the average. As a result, many Copts were found in the employ of foreign businesses, a larger number were rural land owners and the government bureaucracy was at least 45 percent Coptic.

Socialism led to an expropriation of the large agricultural estates and foreign businesses as well as large domestic concerns, so that for most educated Egyptians the only possible type of occupation was government employment. At the same time, a growing nationalism tended to equate Muslim with Egyptian and to demand that Muslim citizens have their proportionate share of government employment. As early as 1937 the proportion of Copts in the Egyptian civil service had dropped to about 9.1 percent and new appointments are usually made on a Muslim-Copt ratio of about nine to one. Many Copts thus find their fortunes have been confiscated and their career avenues closed. Egyptian census figures state that Copts are about 7.1 percent of the population of Egypt, but the Copts feel that these figures are biased, that their actual representation is 16–20 percent of the population and that a nine to one quota is grossly unfair.

At the same time, the Coptic community is under threat from a nationalism which clothes itself in terms of a secular state and, on this basis, is steadily eliminating all privileges of separate religious communities. Thus the Coptic courts have lost most of their power and the minority must turn to the civil courts where they face Muslim judges. Similarly, the Coptic community has lost the lands the rent from which once gave substantial support to religious and charitable enterprises. The Copt is thus deprived of the protection of his special community status and governed in all the details of his life by a state which is primarily committed to the welfare of the Muslim group. In these circumstances, it is perhaps not surprising that the current Patriarch has apparently turned from a concern for the Coptic community to an effort at reinvigorating the Coptic church in a struggle to make religious faith a vital matter at a time when the re-

---

[19] Earl of Cromer, *Modern Egypt* (London, 1908), Vol. 5, II, pp. 295–96, cited in G. Baer, *Population and Society in the Arab East* (New York, Praeger, 1960), p. 98.

ligious community is losing its power and cohesion. The success of this effort is still in doubt, although it appears that even if the church becomes a more committed type of fellowship, it is likely to be smaller in numbers, since it is estimated that about 5,000 Copts per year are converting to Islam.[20]

Minority groups tend to have more difficulty when frustrations develop in the country in which they live and the 1972 reports on the situation of the Copts bear out this assumption. It is probably more than a coincidence that as the Egyptian government and people find it difficult to fight Israel, the lot of the Copts appears to be worsening. Press reports list the burning of a Coptic church in Khanka together with a riot in that city after Coptic protests.[21] The Khanka incident is the eleventh such incident during 1972 and Copts are understandably nervous. The current head of the Coptic church, Pope Shenouda, is credited with an activist attitude and, in addition to trying to revive Coptic religious zeal, also seeks greater employment of Copts in government positions. The government is apparently trying to maintain order and protect minorities, but may find this difficult in a time when a frustrated nationalism is seeking scapegoats.

COLORED AND PAGAN MINORITIES

When Malcom X, a black militant leader in America, visited Mecca in 1965 he was somewhat shaken in his racial views. In Mecca he observed what was truly a case of racial integration in which men of all shades of color mingled together in the pilgrimage to the holy places of Islam. Contrary to the teachings of the Black Muslims in America, which he had embraced at an earlier stage, he realized that Islam embraced white as well as black and was truly a religion which stood above human divisions both in its formal teachings and in the nature of its membership.[22] Christian observers might say that the same impression could have been gained by a visit to the World Council of Churches, The Vatican Council, or other international Christian gatherings, but there is still no religious activity in the world involving as large and diversified a group of people as the Muslim pilgrimage.

The major interracial contact of Islam along white and black lines has come in North and East Africa as the Arab traders and their converts have gradually moved north of the Sahara Desert. Usually, when we think

---

[20] Edward Wakin, "The Copts in Egypt," *Middle Eastern Affairs* 12 (Aug.–Sept. 1961): 198–208; also his book, *A Lonely Minority: The Modern Story of the Egyptian Copts* (New York, William Morrow, 1963).

[21] "Copts and Moslems," *Newsweek*, Dec. 4, 1972, p. 47.

[22] Malcolm Little, *The Autobiography of Malcolm X* (New York, Grove Press, 1965), pp. 367–68.

of the white population of Africa, we are considering scattered groups of visiting experts in various countries and the settler populations in South Africa and Rhodesia. Actually, approximately one person in five in Africa is "white," and most of this white population is represented by the Arabs north of the Sahara in the area that the French refer to as *Afrique Blanche*.[23] This region has been the scene of constant exchange between Europe, Africa, and the Asian Middle East since before the time of the Roman Empire and, consequently, has long been an area of interracial contact.

Formal doctrines of integration or exclusion certainly affect the course of such a relationship, but equally important is the nature of the specific contacts. In this case, the contact was frequently between conqueror and conquered and between slave trader and slave. Further, the contact was not between Muslims and other "Peoples of the Book" but between Muslims and pagans. Slave raiding and trading was conducted by the Arabs in East North and Central Africa before the demand for slaves arose on the American continent and continued after the end of slavery in the Western World. Slaves moved in one direction across the Sahara in great caravans, while cargos of salt and textiles moved in another. Although slaves were used in the salt beds and in other forms of public works, their major work was as household servants. Hence there was intimacy, and frequently interbreeding, which made this slavery assume a somewhat different character from that of the plantation slavery in the New World. Notwithstanding the more personal character of this relationship, a dark skin still became a stigma of inferiority. Miner's description of attitudes in the ancient city of Timbuktu would apply to some degree in much of Northern Africa.

Men in Timbuktu feel that lighter skinned women are more attractive. Aesthetic values, as always, are status linked. Light skin color is associated with the high status groups—Tuareg nobles, Arma, and Arabs. Conversely, the slaves are the darkest skinned and the serfs—Daga and Gabibi—are intermediate. While there may be a few Negroid persons of status, slaves almost never show Caucasoid traits.[24]

Muslim principles dictate that children of Muslim fathers should be accepted with full rights of inheritance regardless of the race or religion of the mother. In Timbuktu, this type of marriage seems to be the occasion for cultural conflict in which the children of a mixed union were often rejected by their siblings who came from a pure Arabic type of parentage and the legal rights of darker skinned children were sometimes not honored in practice.[25] Arabic and Islamic culture tolerated intermarriage between

---

[23] Leon Carl Brown, "Color in Northern Africa," *Daedalus* 96 (Spring 1967): 465.

[24] Horace Miner, "The Primitive City of Timbuctoo," *Memoirs of the American Philosophical Society* 32 (1953). Published for the American Philosophical Society by the Princeton University Press; Copyright by the American Philosophical Society.

[25] Ibid., p. 265.

those of different color and allowed an intimate relation between master and slaves. It also produced, to some degree, the usual type of color consciousness, even though this was not followed by practices of segregation or legalized discrimination.

One reaction to the Arab invasion was for the black Africans to flee further south, and in this manner, most of the Sahara and northward gradually became a white, Arab type of country. However, flight was not always possible and many black groups went through an experience of defeat and subsequent Islamic conversion. In this manner, the Hausa and Fulani became dark-skinned converts to the Islamic Creed and their loyalty in many cases was as staunch as that of their Arab tutors.

INTERACTION BETWEEN MUSLIM AND NON-MUSLIM BLACKS

The contacts of the black Muslims were not so much with the Christians and Jews as with pagan tribes. Since there was no religious basis for the toleration of the pagan group, the Islamic obligation was simply one of conversion in which the might of the sword and the usual techniques of propaganda were equally acceptable. On the other hand, the pagan tribes were frequently too strong to be overcome by Muslim military strength; thus an uneasy period of coexistence emerged which was not sanctioned by any of the norms in Muslim society but was made necessary by a relative balance of power.

It was in this kind of situation that Uthman dan Fodio became both a preacher and a military leader in the area now known as Northern Nigeria. More than a century after Cromwell had engaged in a similar purification of allegedly decadent practices in England, Uthman dan Fodio sought to purify, strengthen, and enlarge Islamic conformity among his people. Not only had the coexistence of many of the pagan tribes been tolerated but this toleration had had the inevitable effect of "contaminating" the Muslims themselves. Some of the chiefs would take more than the allotted four wives; the laws of inheritance were disregarded and a favored son might receive the entire estate in an effort to keep holdings intact; women went around without any type of facial coverings; and prohibitions against usury or excessive prices in the market place were disregarded.

Uthman dan Fodio first gained renown as a preacher and teacher and collected about him a number of other Ulami (teachers of Islamic law) to expound the true tenets of Islam and to urge a vigorous adherence regardless of the cost to the privileges of the powerful. This type of teaching naturally aroused the resentment of those who profited from the existing order. The new leader soon found himself the object of military attack. He responded by calling for a jihad (holy war) against both infidels and renegade Muslims. He had such military and political success that the formal structure of societies in this part of Africa became that of the Islamic state.[26] The leading chieftains were defenders of the Faithful who governed according to Islamic law, a pattern so well established that when the English conquered the area in 1900 they continued to utilize these governmental structures through the technique of indirect rule.

As is usually the case, the later followers of the charismatic leader— Uthman dan Fodio—were less concerned with living up to his ideals than they were with maintaining their privileges. The jihad lapsed and the pagan tribes, which today make up perhaps 30 percent of the population of Northern Nigeria, were allowed to exist under the rule of their own chieftains but without any direct political power in the larger state. With the coming of British rule they joined the larger nation of Nigeria, in which a secular state dominated the political order.

In this situation, a pattern of forced tolerance has developed and the law is a mixture of Islamic code, an English type of legislation, and pagan customary law, administered by judges according to the type of situation covered and the religion of those involved. This practice has been generally accepted by the more modern of the Muslim leaders, and yet the Muslim who perhaps was the most influential in recent years, the Sardauna of Sokoto, Sir Ahmadu Bello, launched a vigorous Islamization campaign. In this campaign, he spoke to tremendous rallies in which he pledged himself to give a *riga* ("cloak") and five pounds to any man who converted to Islam as well as to shake his hand personally. In spite of these promises, coming from a man with the prestige of the Premier of Northern Nigeria, the crusade had only limited success and his successors seem more likely to settle for coexistence than to maintain an apparently futile effort to restore a dominance, which, in any event, had never been complete.

Northern Nigeria contrasts with Africa further south of the Sahara, since, in this part of Nigeria, blacks developed Islamic states which, under secular auspices, are still carriers of Muslim culture. It is also an area in which Muslims have learned to coexist with other beliefs, first with pagans and later with Christians as well. Uthman dan Fodio's jihad did not exterminate either paganism or heresy, but it did lay a basis for Muslim influence in this part of Africa.

EPILOGUE

The post–World-War-II era has seen the end of colonialism in Muslim countries and also the continual decay of the historic pattern of majority-minority relationships. The end of western colonialism has not brought either the revival of the Caliphate or the formation of an effective Muslim or Arab federation. Rather, there has been the establishment of small national states whose rulers strive to incorporate the institutional practices

---

[26] Thomas Hodgkin, "Uthman dan Fodio," *Nigeria Magazine* 9 (October 1960): 129–36.

of the West even as they turn out propaganda against its alleged iniquities. The propaganda is not so much directed against Christians or Jews as against capitalists, Zionists, and imperialists. The leaders of the new states are usually Muslim by background, but they have no desire to establish an Islamic state in the traditional sense and regard the most fervent Muslims as reactionaries who are a barrier to modernization. Thus Indonesia and Egypt proclaim themselves to be secular governments although each has a heavy Muslim majority. Even countries such as Pakistan, which do claim to be Islamic states, provide for formal freedom and equality of all citizens regardless of religious adherence.

The extent to which the secularism of the leaders is shared by the masses is difficult to determine. The fact that today's leaders avoid the frontal attack of Mustafa Kemal Ataturk and praise Islam in rhetoric, while curtailing it in practice, indicates a belief that popular religious loyalty is still strong. On the other hand, nationalistic and socialistic beliefs exercise popular passions more frequently than religious dogmas. Likewise, militant right-wing Muslim movements such as Dar ul Islam in Indonesia or the Muslim Brotherhoods in Egypt seem to have been contained fairly easily. It still remains true, however, that a westernized dictator always faces the possibility of a Muslim reaction and hence tends to avoid, if at all possible, a direct confrontation with traditional Islam.

The nature of the Islamic legacy which remains seems to depend upon the type of interaction between religion and nationalism that is taking place in various countries. As far as Jews are concerned, there appears to be little variation in the Middle East and North Africa. The appearance of the state of Israel means that Jews are now not only unbelievers but also enemies of the national state and hence doubly despised. In other areas such as Africa south of the Sahara or the Far East, Jews are not numerous and the Israeli issue seems remote. In these circumstances, diplomatic relations may be maintained with Israel and Jews living in the nation are a tolerated and numerically insignificant minority.

Patterns of interaction with Christians and pagans are more diversified. In Sāudi Arabia, Islamic law is still maintained in the rigid austerity of its traditional interpretation and minorities have no rights except those granted by the indulgence cf the majority. In Morocco, Algeria, and Tunis constant pressure is maintained against the rights supposedly granted to Christian minorities, and Christian missions are giving up landholdings and considering whether or not proseletyzing should be completely abandoned. Here the cry of the nationalists against western imperialism is joined by the traditionalists' fear of Christian influence or conversion.[27] Egypt is an avowedly secular state in which the cry of "Egypt for Egyp-

---

[27] Pierre Rondot, "Islam, Christianity and the Modern State," pp. 341–345. John K. Cooley, *Baal, Christ, and Mohammed: Religion and Revolution in North Africa* (New York, Holt, Rinehart and Winston, 1965).

tians" was first raised by a Christian journalist. In Egypt a secular government has formally abolished many of the privileges of religious communities while nationalizing business and regulating the civil service on a quota system. The result is that identity as a Muslim tends to be part of identity as an Egyptian and the Coptic minority is deprived of communal institutions while being subjected to civil authorities predominantly Muslim and being squeezed out of traditional occupations.

Let us now look again at the millet system as it developed under Arab and, later, the Ottoman empires. The millet was a communal organization in which identity was based on religious adherence and the community in turn was governed by the religious law of the group. This system is somewhat more adapted to the religious genius of Judaism, in which the law was the basic component of the faith, than to Christianity, in which, although canon law developed, legalism has always been somewhat suspect. Notwithstanding these difficulties, it did provide a system in which various groups could be ruled in most aspects of their lives by those with whom they shared common values.

Further the millet system institutionalized minority status in a tolerable even if not egalitarian manner. Minority identity was not threatened and the millet had rights which the majority group had obligated themselves to respect.

The effective operation of the millet system rested on four basic premises: (1) a state with limited powers which would allow minorities to make an economic adaptation on the basis of skill and interests, (2) the dominance of the territorial claims of the empire over those of individual nationalities, (3) priority for religious rather than racial or national identification, and (4) priority of Islam over other religious beliefs. To the extent that any of these were weakened the system was in jeopardy.

As long as religion was the major criterion of identity, Arabs, Albanians, Turks, and Kurds could dwell together under the same government. When the religious definition of the empire lost salience and the Sublime Porte (Ottoman Caliph) became a symbol of Turkish hegemony rather than Islamic unity, Arabs, Kurds, and Albanians became susceptible to nationalistic impulses. Likewise, when European powers began to assert the right to protect those associated in religion or nationality, the minority was seen as an actual or potential threat to the empire and often became a victim of persecution.

The acceptance of the dominance of Islam rendered the religious situation noncompetitive and therefore removed the fears of the majority group while it allowed minorities to trade an acknowledgement of subordination for the right to continue a separate existence. The Muslim might feel that the coexistence with a group of unbelievers was a compromise, but his society was secure because conversion of Muslims or even conspicuous minority religious activities were forbidden and his ego was salved by having certain privileges in government such as a lighter burden of taxation. On the other hand, members of minorities were free to pursue their own customs, maintain their own worship, operate their own schools, and try cases in their own religious courts.

When the nationalistic state succeeded the polyglot empire and a planned society with much government activity replaced a laissez faire economy, the millet system was doomed. Now only those who were "nationals" deserved the protection of the state and religion became identified with nationalism. Further, the national state was committed to improving the economic lot of its nationals and hence was obligated to displace aliens from positions they had won in a relatively free market economy.

Now that the empire is dead, nationalism triumphant, the free market subordinate to socialistic planning, and the autonomy of religious communities replaced by all-inclusive secular legislation, the millet system would seem to have lost every major item on which it depended for survival. It does have historical value as a demonstration that there is an alternative to nationalistic particularism and that different groups can live together in the same nation for centuries even though their experience may include occasional massacres and constant discrimination.

Some authorities feel that a modified millet system may be the only way to restore peace to one part of the old Ottoman Empire. Palestine has been the scene of three wars since 1948, based on the refusal of the Arabs to acknowledge partition and a separate Jewish state. Donald Grant suggests that an independent Arab state could be set up in Palestine which would share sovereignty of Jerusalem and would have trade ties with Israel and Jordan.[28] This would seem a far cry from the millets subordinate to the Ottoman Empire, but it does contain the idea of a certain amount of joint relationship together with separate communities under the rules sanctioned by their own culture. Ethnic loyalties are slow to fade whether under benign integration or brutal oppression, and it may be that some aspects of the millet idea will prove viable in the modern age.

The historic Muslim pattern of ethnic relationships was one of cultural pluralism in which the minority had to give definite acknowledgement of the rule of the majority. It flourished in an age when empires were able to contain nationalistic animosities, religious creeds were regarded as the basis for community government, and private enterprise allowed the individual to compete freely in the economic sphere regardless of his ethnic identity. The Muslim pattern of ethnic relations is obviously hard pressed in an age of rampant nationalism, increasing secularism, and expanding socialism. It had no acceptable criteria for dealing with pagans who were not People of the Book, and, even for those with whom kinship was recognized, its rule was often harsh. Notwithstanding these strictures, its sur-

---

[28] Donald Grant, "After Empires—What?" *Vista* 5 (July–August 1969): 42–49.

vival through the centuries testifies to the fact that a system can be devised under which different groups dwell in the same national territory. It may be that the millet idea is a historical relic, but its past is not without statesmanship and it may survive in altered form in the future as a recognition of the need for respect of subcultural identities within a larger national framework.

IMPLICATIONS FOR INTERGROUP RELATIONS

Certain trends in the Ottoman Empire and in the nations which emerged after its demise are significant for the general field of intergroup relationships. There follows a listing of these specific trends together with an interpretation of their more general application.

Muslim pattern. The Ottoman Empire could survive only as long as it was regarded as more a religious than a secular political regime. This statement is based on the premise that the non-Turkish Muslims would accept Ottoman rule only when the Sultan was viewed more as the Defender of the Faithful than as a Turkish monarch.

General pattern. A political regime which includes several ethnic groups will be accepted if defined in ways which avoid a clash between political loyalties and ethnic identities.

Muslim pattern. The Copts' effort to identify with Egyptian nationalism failed in spite of the fact that many Copts were active in nationalistic struggles. On this point Hourani observes:

> Egyptian nationalism had two faces. On the surface it was a lay movement which linked together Copts and Moslems and was much influenced by ideals of French liberalism . . . there was however a difference between the articulate leadership and the inarticulate spirit of the movement; the latter was much more Islamic than the former.[29]

In other words, the popular definition of Egyptian nationalism tended to exclude the Copts even though this was contrary to the statements of nationalist leaders. The Copts not only were a religious minority, but they also had a degree of social mobility which drew envy from other Egyptians, and it was this factor which made it most difficult for them to be accepted as genuine nationalists.

Generalized pattern. A minority regarded as having invidious status will not be able to gain acceptance through participation in nationalist activities.

Muslim pattern. Efforts by foreign countries to protect minorities in

---

[29] Hourani, *Minorities in the Arab World*, p. 32.

the Ottoman Empire had only temporary effect and frequently backfired by helping to stereotype the minorities as tools of foreign powers.

Generalized pattern. Foreign protection of minorities often deepens the gulf between them and the majority and its effect is proportionate to the power of the foreign government and the weakness of the majority ethnic group.

Muslim pattern. The millet system was based on a recognition of Muslim hegemony by the minorities. Since it is difficult to establish a regime in which each ethnic group has equal power, this leads to the following hypothesis:

General pattern. The functioning of a multiethnic society requires acceptance (whether by force or by inner conviction) of an ethnic group or an ideology as dominant in the society.

Muslim pattern. The expansion of state activity in the nations now occupying the territory of the former Ottoman Empire has threatened minority educational enterprises and economic activities. Any expansion of state functions obviously makes it more feasible for people to gain their ends through state action. Since one of these ends is preference for the ethnic majority, we make the following conclusion:

Generalized pattern. Discrimination against minorities tends to vary directly with the scope of activity by the state. This proposition applies particularly to economic successful minorities which fare well in the private sphere on a competitive basis. It does not apply so well to the proletarian type of submerged minority which has occupied the bottom rung of the competitive ladder. Thus expansion of state enterprise has been accomplished by a diminution of opportunity for the Copts of Egypt and the overseas Chinese in the Philippines and by a heavy onslaught on communal organizations in the case of the Jews of Russia. For the blacks of the United States, expanded enterprise has accompanied an expansion of opportunity and increased social mobility. Similarly, the expansion of state enterprise and concern has probably improved the position of the lower castes in India. We might conclude that the expansion of government roles will probably result in the restriction of a group characterized by a fair-sized successful middle class element but may enhance the position of groups with a large lower class element.

QUESTIONS

1. What was the millet system?
2. Why did the millet system invite intervention by foreign powers in the Ottoman Empire?

3. Why did either the millet system or national independence prove less of a solution for Armenians and Greeks than for other groups in the Ottoman Empire?

4. How did the jihad of Uthman dan Fodio enable the British to govern northern Nigeria by indirect rule? Was the Muslim character of this region an aid or hindrance to the ultimate formation of a Nigerian nation?

5. Was Malcom X correct in stating that Islam represented an interracial religion? How would you explain elements of racism which may be found in Islamic groups?

6. Does the millet system offer any suggestions which may be applicable to the conflict between the state of Israel and the Arab nations?

7. Muslim hegemony was considered an essential part of the millet system. Is there any similarity between the function of Muslim hegemony and the function of Anglo-conformity in the United States?

8. Why would even a fairly administered quota system be regarded as detrimental to the Copts? Is there any alternative to quota systems in the maintenance of harmonious intergroup relations?

9. What were the four situations considered as prerequisites for the efficient functioning of the millet system? Do any of these apply to other patterns of intergroup relations?

10. What effect does socialism have on the welfare of ethnic minorities?

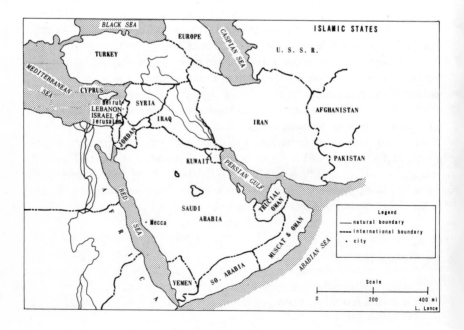

Chapter 9

Nigeria: Secession, civil war, and reunification in a multi-ethnic state

During the period 1968–1970 the mass media were featuring the story of the Nigerian civil war. The southeastern part of the country, taking the name "Biafra," tried to secede, while the Federal government strove to "Keep Nigeria One." The resulting warfare included savage battles and a campaign of attrition which reduced Biafra to near starvation before its final collapse. The Biafran suffering stimulated foreign interest and volunteers from many nations came to its aid, while American senators, McCarthy and Kennedy among others, proclaimed their sympathy for the secessionist regime. Even churches were involved as both Catholic and Protestant agencies organized airlifts to ward off Biafran starvation. Among the major powers, the United States and Great Britain tried to maintain a neutral stance while recognizing the Federal government. France was the principal support of the Biafrans. The Soviet Union became the chief arms supplier for the Federal government.

What was the cause of this bitter warfare in the country of Nigeria, which had seemed to have such a promising future at the time of its independence a few years before? Were the issues at stake unique to Nigeria, or are they found throughout the African continent? Was the struggle, with its numerous charges of atrocities, a case of good guys versus bad guys or was something else at stake? What are the problems of political unity which emerge as we examine the African scene?

ETHNICITY IN AFRICAN COUNTRIES

Most of the recently independent African countries are faced with the problem of welding together diverse peoples who had little or no sense of a common destiny before the colonial period. In many ways, Nigeria is well suited to serve as a case study of this type of multi-ethnic state. Nigeria, from a standpoint of population, is the largest country in Africa, having over 67 million people according to a 1970 estimate. Several countries cover a greater expanse of territory, but its area of 356,669 square miles gives it a respectable territory mass. It is made up of a considerable variety of ethnic units which vary in language, history, and economy. Although the bulk of the country's colonial experience has been with Great Britain, the British followed different policies in various parts of Nigeria, and thus a variety of colonial experiences further contributed to the diversity of the country. In addition to other types of diversity, the area has been a point of contention between two universalistic religions, Islam and Christianity, as well as a number of territorially based animistic faiths.

Especially in Africa, many countries face the task of welding into one nation a collection of peoples usually known as "tribes." Since the usage of the tribal designation has itself become controversial, it is perhaps worth while to look at this topic before plunging directly into the Nigerian situation. The term "tribe" is as vague and as subject to different types of definitions as any collective label. Groups classified as tribes may vary in size from a few hundred people to several million. Some of them have, at one time, been the masters of fair-sized empires with elaborate administrative structures, with a written history which recounts the glorious deeds of their ancestors. Others are small groups of illiterates whose time perspective is limited to the oral tradition conveyed by the elders. The formal definition used by the British administration in Nigeria presents an effort to formulate a statement sufficiently broad to cover the many meanings sometimes involved in tribal classification: "...one or more clans descended from one legendary ancestor, though the legend may have been lost; originally observing one common shrine, though the memory may have been lost; speaking one language, though perhaps not the same dialect, and enlarged by assimilated peoples."[1]

In this usage, there is no implication that the term "tribe" applies to any particular degree of cultural development. The British definition allows for the inclusion of groups of a wide variety of social and technological complexity. Nevertheless, the stereotype that "tribe" refers to primitive bands is still widely accepted. In this view, a "tribe" is a small relatively primi-

---

[1] James S. Coleman: *Nigeria: Background to Nationalism,* originally published by the University of California Press; reprinted by permission of the Regents of the University of California.

tive, very cohesive, band of relatives, while "nationality" or "people" refers to large, less cohesive, and more technologically advanced groupings.

Thus, it may be held to be a denigration of African society when Yoruba and Hausa are termed "tribes," while Flemish and Irish are described as "nations" or "peoples." Since words have only the meaning which people attach to them, it is futile to fight a popular stereotype, and in this discussion we will try to avoid the word "tribe" except when referring to literature or customary African practice which uses tribal terminology. In designating significantly differentiated territorially based groupings, we shall use the term "ethnic" as we do in other chapters. Also in this chapter we set forth several generalizations, among them are the following: (1) a solution for ethnic conflict is not solely found in the constitutional guarantees of individual rights, (2) the mere development of a democratic government does not mean that there will be an elimination of ethnically based conflicts, and (3) ethnic groups often question the legitimacy of rules, even supposedly universalistic ones, that are perceived to work against their welfare.

Now let us turn to the substantive problem of incorporating Nigeria ethnic groupings in a modern state. It is hardly fair to blame all of these problems on the British, but, in view of the fact that it is the British who brought Nigeria into being as a sovereign state, a brief discussion of Nigerian-British interaction is perhaps the place to start.

COLONIAL DEVELOPMENT AND REGIONAL DIVERSITY

British contact with the area which eventually became Nigeria dates back to 1553, when vessels under the command of Captain Windham visited Benin harbor.[2] In the 16th and 17th centuries, slaves became the main export of West Africa and the British eventually became the chief suppliers. In the 19th century, the British did an about-face, outlawed the slave trade, and attempted to suppress it through patrolling the coast and influencing African chiefs. Expanded trade in the interior became more feasible with the exploration of the Niger by Richard Lander in 1830. The initial efforts to establish stable relationships between the British traders and the African rulers were made by private trading companies, notably the United African Company and, later, the Royal Niger Company. These companies waged war, drew up treaties, and acted as veritable governments, but eventually surrendered their political functions to the British Crown.

Direct British control in Nigeria was expanded gradually over about a 60-year period. The first instance of governmental takeover occurred in

---

[2] T. O. Elias: *Nigeria: The Development of Its Laws and Constitution* (London, Stevens and Sons, 1967) p. 4.

1861, when Lagos was declared a British protectorate. Shortly thereafter, trading companies had contacts with the Yoruba-speaking people in the area which became known as Western Nigeria; contacts extended in the latter part of the 19th century and the early part of the 20th to the Ibo-speaking people in Eastern Nigeria. Finally, the northern portion of the country, which comprises more than two thirds of the land area, was brought under British control by the conquest by Lord Lugard around the turn of the century.

None of these various regions are entirely homogenous. The Hausa and Fulani are dominant in the Northern Region, and this area was known as the home of the six Hausa states, yet more than a third of the population do not speak Hausa as their native tongue. In the West, about three quarters of the population are Yoruba-speaking, and, in the East, about two thirds may be classified as Ibo-speaking. To some extent, Hausa, Ibo, and Yoruba are spreading as second languages; on the other hand, variations of dialect are sometimes so great as to make it difficult for people who speak the same basic language to communicate with each other. This is especially true in the Ibo-speaking regions.[3] Hausa, Yoruba, and Ibo have contended for influence in Nigeria and have also been plagued by problems concerning their relationship to minority peoples within the areas where they predominate. In the southern portions of the Northern Region is an area known as the "middle belt," whose ethnic groups include the Nupe, Tiv, Igala, and Idoma, along with a number of very small tribes; as contrasted to the Hausa and Fulani who are a majority in the rest of the old Northern Region. This so-called "middle belt" has also seen a much greater exposure to Christianity than have the Hausa-Fulani areas and thus represents a minority religious group within the North. In the Western Region, a feeling of distinction between Yorubas and such groups as the Bini, Ishan, and Ibos was strong enough to stimulate the creation of still another region, the Mid-West. Also major internal splits among the Yoruba sometimes made intragroup rivalry nearly as severe as that be-tween ethnic groups. The Ibos, the smallest of the major ethnic groups, have been forced to deal with a number of smaller groups who, in a sense, form a minority within a minority. Thus, the North, the West, the East and later, the Mid-West, frequently conceived of themselves as distinct regional groupings which were contending for power, but each of these was riven by divisions within its own borders. It is estimated that there are approximately 248 distinct languages within Nigeria, most of them spoken by small tribes, but a few by several million people. Although the Hausa-Fulani are the largest ethnic grouping, they do not comprise

---

[3] K. M. Buchanan and J. C. Pugh, *Land and People in Nigeria* (London, University of London Press, 1965), p. 94.

more than a third of the Nigerian population and there is no "majority" group.[4]

Having looked briefly at the ethnic composition of the regions let us now turn back to the topic of British penetration. The annexation of Lagos served as a stimulus to further expansion of British governmental control. Lagos had been depicted as a stronghold for slave holding and slave trading which the British were committed to suppress. It was also extremely important as a shipping center for other types of commerce. British annexation of Lagos thus served a dual function of helping to suppress the slave trade and, at the same time, of protecting British commerce. British commerce soon demanded expansion of government protection into the interior of the country. British Consuls were established in various places and, in 1885, the British established the Oil Rivers Protectorate, which in 1893 was changed to become the Niger Coast Protectorate and eventually became the Protectorate of Southern Nigeria, after the charter of the Royal Niger Company was revoked.

In the meantime, the British traders had been penetrating into northern Nigeria, but were finding resistance from native chiefs as well as competition by French trading companies. British control moved north in 1900, when Sir Frederick Lugard, after defeating the Sultan of Sokoto, proclaimed the protectorate of Northern Nigeria. In 1906, the Protectorate of Lagos was amalgamated with the Southern provinces and, in 1914, for the first time, the North and South were amalgamated under a common administration. This common administration still kept two lieutenant governors, one responsible for the North and one for the South, and did not end the separate development of the Northern and Southern areas.

The last two areas to come under British rule were the North and Iboland. The North was late in coming under British influence because British traders at first worked through African middlemen in the Niger Delta rather than penetrating the region themselves and also because a string of fairly substantial monarchies constituted a seemingly formidable barrier to British incursion. The Ibos in the Southeast had been on the periphery of British influence until trade expansion pushed in their direc-

---

[4] The following estimate of regions and tribes in 1963 was made by Robin Luckham, *The Nigerian Military: A Sociological Analysis of Authority and Revolt 1960–1967* (London, Cambridge University Press, 1971), p. 208.

Region	Population (millions)	Major constituents (millions)
North	29.8	Hausa-Fulani, 16,
East	12.4	Ibo, 10
Mid-West	2.5	
West	10.3	Yoruba, 9, plus
Lagos	7.0	Northern Yoruba, 1.9

tion. Their incorporation in the British domain was delayed for exactly the opposite reason of that of the North; they had no large kingdoms and, hence, no leaders with whom the British could make treaties and thus bring large areas under their domain. The result was a gradual extension of British rule, village by village, until it was firmly established by the end of World War I.

British Rule in the North

Looking first at the Northern invasion, we find Lord Lugard racing with the French to establish contacts for trade in this area in the 1890s and finally, without the formal approval of the British colonial office, waging a war against the Sultan of Sokoto which had the effect of bringing the whole Northern area under the British domain. It was in the North that Lugard established his famous principle of governing by "indirect rule." It was his policy, while bringing in the "Pax Britannica," to rule through the traditional authorities. The Sultan of Sokoto and the leading Emirs were provided with British advisors who were charged with the twofold duty of maintaining a respect for the authority of the local rulers on the one hand and establishing a regime safe for British commerce on the other. The two duties were not regarded as incompatible and in a very short time, the British came to be regarded as bulwarks of the native aristocracy. In fact, in 1907, a revolt against the British was crushed with the aid of the Sultan of Sokoto.

Not only did the British respect the governmental system of the North; they also strove to leave the social life and customs of the people as untouched as possible. Some change was unavoidable, however, when the extension of commerce in the North led to the planting of groundnuts and cotton and their shipment to southern ports. This required the aid of a small army of middlemen whose services were necessary but not rewarding enough to justify the importation of a sufficient number of British.

The need for middlemen, clerks, and semiskilled laborers was met, to a great extent, by southern Nigerians who migrated north. The usual pattern of residence in Nigerian cities was for migrants who were not of the local ethnic group to live in quarters on the periphery of the old city, known as *Sabon Gari* (or simply *Sabo* in the South) which means literally "new city." The migrants could thus maintain their own customs, and even have their own "chiefs," while at the same time they interacted economically with the total community. This residential segregation was seen as a device whereby the group could retain its own culture and be a member of the host society in only a symbiotic sense. It was occasionally breached in practice, and people who had long been in residence in the area or whose culture resembled that of the local majority might live in the nuclear city. Both Ibos and Yoruba were found in the *Sabon Garis*, but the Muslim Yoruba occasionally lived in the old city.

This pattern was thought to facilitate the existence of migrants in all regions. In the North, it promoted economic development (and at the same time exacerbated ethnic jealousies) by bringing in from the South, Nigerians who had acquired a European type of education. In this fashion, northern economic development took place without a massive expansion of European-style educational facilities.

The lack of educational progress in the North did not particularly distress the British administrators. Indeed, Lugard regarded the rapid expansion of education in English as being a threat to colonial rule: ". . . the premature teaching of English . . . inevitably leads to utter disrespect for British and native ideals alike, and to a denationalized and disorganized population."[5]

Lugard's reluctance to make provision for a western type of education was aided by the Muslim character of the Northern Region. In his communication to the traditional Muslim rulers, Lugard promised that the government would not force the introduction of Christian missions upon them. Since at that time the great bulk of educational activity was carried on by missions, a ban on missions meant in effect a ban on the Western type of education. There were two exceptions to Lugard's anti-missionary policy which did allow the growth of a small number of educated men in the Northern Region without altering the essential character of the area. Missionaries were allowed to work among the pagan tribes of the North, and several missions of this type were established. They were also allowed to come in under specific invitation by one of the Emirs, which happened in at least two places. However, the general barrier to missionary advance was strong enough that when the Western Region proclaimed universal primary schooling in the 1950s (universal schooling was more a formal aim than a real condition, but the gap between West and North was still tremendous) the North had only about six percent of its children in some type of school, although, by that time, missions had been expanded and government schools had been opened as well.

British colonial rule in Northern Nigeria had meant the building of roads and railways, the suppression of wars between local chiefs, an increase in agricultural production, and an expansion of commerce. None of this development involved a violent break with Islamic or tribal customs. The Emirs still kept their palaces and the right to hold court, including imposition of the death sentence. The predominant mode of education remained the Koranic schools in which a small proportion of the children of the area absorbed enough Arabic to enable them to participate in Islamic services. Most of the elements of commerce were carried on either by aliens, or by Nigerians from other parts of the country, and, although

---

[5] F. D. Lugard, *Annual Reports, Northern Nigeria, 1900–1911*, cited in Coleman, *Nigeria*, p. 137.

groundnuts, cotton, and tobacco provided cash crops, the life of most of the Hausa and Fulani went on pretty much the same after the entry of the British as it had before. The alliance between the British colonial authorities and the traditional rulers seemed to be strengthened by all these developments. British rule increased the security of the rulers' realms and the receipts of his tax collectors. If it also meant the erosion of the Emir's power, this was so gradual a process, and the interim benefits were so great, that little protest was aroused. The limitation of education meant that there was no clamorous group of natives with a western education who were frustrated by a lack of opportunity; rather, the few educated Northerners were quickly absorbed in positions in government. The British were not only the strongest power, to whom no viable alternative was seen; they were also protectors of the North against the South. On occasion, this was quite frankly acknowledged as in the statement attributed to one Emir to the effect that he greatly preferred the white Britons as teachers and government servants to southern Nigerians.[6]

Northern traditionalism did not make fertile ground for the spread of nationalist sentiment. This came out very clearly in 1953 when the Northern delegates to the Nigerian Parliament refused to support a request to the British to establish a definite date for the granting of independence. The reason for the Northern attitude was a fear that the departure of the British might simply lead to the domination of the North by the South. It was taken for granted that an independent government required an educated personnel to carry out government activities. Since the North lacked an educated personnel large enough to staff government offices, this was interpreted as meaning that, in the words of Coleman, "in a self-governing Nigeria the North would, in effect, be a backward protectorate governed by Southerners."[7] The editor of the Hausa paper *Gaskiya Ta Fi Kwabo* expressed the situation thus:

. . . Southerners will take the places of the Europeans in the North. What is there to stop them? They look and see it is thus at the present time. There are Europeans but, undoubtedly, it is the Southerner who has the power in the North. They have control of the railway stations; of the Post Offices; of Government Hospitals; of the canteens; the majority employed in the Kaduna Secretariat and in the Public Works Department are all Southerners; in all the different departments of Government it is the Southerner who has the power.[8]

In summary, a half century of British occupation had left the Northern part of Nigeria peaceful and commercially developed to the extent of maintaining an export agriculture. The region had a government which

[6] Coleman, *Nigeria*, p. 360.

[7] Ibid., p. 361.

[8] *Gaskiya Ta Fi Kwabo,* Feb. 18, 1950, cited in *Report on the Kano Disturbances,* p. 45, and in Coleman, *Nigeria*, p. 362.

was an efficient agency for maintaining order, raising taxes, and operating a nucleus of schools and social services. At the same time, the core Hausa-Fulani society was only lightly touched by westernization. Through support of the traditional rulers, the British had obtained the support of the Northern area, and by the same policies had fostered, often unwittingly, a policy which lent itself to a maximum of suspicion between the North and the South. The British policy had, it is true, brought in a nation which had not previously existed, but for the North, the price of any degree of cooperation in national affairs was a jealous insistence on its own autonomy as well as a veto power in all national decisions. The history of the period before and immediately after independence is very largely the story of the struggle of the North to protect itself against feared Southern domination and the effort of the South to win a greater degree of control of governmental machinery.

DEVELOPMENT OF THE IBOS

In many ways, social conditions in the Ibo district were exactly the opposite of those in the Northern areas. While much of the North was uncultivated; the Ibos had one of the most densely populated rural areas of any place in the world; meaning that, as Ibo population increased, it was more and more difficult for the sons to earn a living on the farms which had occupied their fathers. The North was characterized by strong hierarchial regimes, the Ibo territory by smaller, mostly village types of governments in which there was no chief in the sense of one who had recognized authority over his people, but a variety of more democratic types of decision making. The Ibos were regarded as individualistic and competitive; the Northerners as regimented and cooperative. Although the Hausa traders linked Nigeria with northern Africa and the "cattle Fulani" would drive their herds 500 miles to Southern ports, the bulk of the Northerners found it possible to earn a living within their ancestral villages. For the Ibo, even subsistence status often meant moving away from his traditional area. The North thus provided a relatively stable type of social system offering a fairly satisfactory life to its inhabitants, while for the Ibos mere survival, not to speak of improvement, necessitated either a change in occupation or a movement to a new area.

The Ibos relation to Christian missions helps to pinpoint this type of difference. While the Ibos had oracles whose fame spread over a considerable region, the bulk of their religious practices consisted of animistic ceremonies which varied from village to village and which did not have the effect of imposing a common religious loyalty over a large area. Christian missions in Iboland had to compete with traditional beliefs, but they were competing with a fragmented type of native religion which could not boast of a systematic type of theology comparable to either Islam or

Christianity. Further, the schools offered by the Christian missions were not seen as a threat to the society, but as a means of social mobility. The Ibos responded eagerly to the approach of Christian missions and were converted in large numbers, so that, within a short time, the East had the highest percentage of Christians of any area in Nigeria.

Not only did strong Christian institutions develop rapidly in the Eastern region, the homeland of the Ibos, but frequently both Protestant and Catholic churches in the Northern areas were primarily supported by Ibo adherents. The acceptance of Christianity, was, of course, coupled with an acceptance of the western mode of education. While the Yorubas had the most extensive early contacts with the British and therefore were, for a long time, the leaders in English literacy, the Ibos rapidly closed the gap, and, by the time of independence in 1960, had probably exceeded the Yorubas in the proportion of educated persons. Their relation with the Yorubas was a highly competitive one as they each sought places in the government bureaucracy and in the school systems.

Although the Ibos have been characterized as competitive, they have also developed certain means of tribal cooperation. These included the formation of age groups, which were especially effective in binding the young men together in various types of voluntary societies, and an elaborate development of markets. This type of voluntary group and trading relationships gave rise to complaints among other Nigerians that the Ibos were clannish people who worked together for their interests. In contrast, the Yorubas were notorious for intragroup quarreling.

The achievement ethic of the Ibos has been documented in a rather unusual way by LeVine,[9] who used the analysis of patterns found in schoolboy dreams to supplement data gained from public opinion polls. The public opinion polls showed that on such questions as desire for self-government and commitment to progress through technological advance, the Ibos were the most achievement-oriented, with the Hausa last and the Yorubas in an intermediate position. On the other hand, a questionnaire designed to test social compliance and obedience, which would presumably indicate acceptance of traditional status, showed Hausas first, Ibos last, and the Yorubas again in an intermediate position.

This is a type of result that even a casual observer might expect if one assumes any relation at all between achievement motivation and social mobility. The sample was chosen in such a way that it might easily have exaggerated the extent of achievement motivation among the Hausa, since school attendance might be assumed to represent more of a mobility orientation than is present in the general population. However, the findings showed the greatest amount of achievement imagery in dreams among the

---

[9] Robert A. LeVine, *Dreams and Deeds: Achievement and Motivation in Nigeria* (Chicago, University of Chicago Press, 1966).

Ibos, with the southern Yorubas, northern Yorubas and Hausa following in that order.[10]

This achievement ideology had some political repercussions, since it served to condemn the non-Ibo part of the population as backward people needing some drastic type of reconstruction. Thus Chike Obi, an Ibo university lecturer and politician, writes in favor of military dictatorship in 1962 because it would: "succeed in persuading the illiterate, ignorant, lazy, individualistic and undisciplined natives of Nigeria to make great physical and mental sacrifice . . . for the defense of their country and for the common good."[11]

The Ibos and the Yorubas occupied a similar position in the Nigerian social structure. Both of them were found in rather large numbers in Northern cities, where they served as mechanics, merchants, and clerks for government and business. Both were regarded by the Northerners as somewhat exploitive outsiders; the Ibos were recipients of the greater degree of animosity as a conspicious group which had most recently moved into the area. Many of the Yorubas were Muslim, which may have lessened Hausa hostility.

Certainly the evidence from riots bears out the idea that greater hostility was expressed against the Ibos. One of the first examples was the Kano riot in 1953.[12] At this time Southern-Northern relations were extremely tense because of political controversies which included the refusal of Northern representatives to endorse a request that the British establish Nigerian independence in 1956. It is especially significant that all the dead and most of the injured were Ibos, since the riot was touched off by reports that a Yoruba political leader was going to speak in Kano. Kano was the largest city in the Northern region, and the Yoruba leader had denounced Northern representatives as "despots and British stooges." The speech was cancelled at the request of the British resident, but resentment still touched off a riot in which Ibos were the principal victims. This pattern of greater Ibo vulnerability also held in the riots in 1966, when the victims were Easterners, mostly, but not exclusively, Ibo.[13] In fact Yorubas were even able to move into jobs in the North which had been vacated by fleeing Ibos.[14] This immunity of the Yorubas from Hausa-Fulani pres-

---

10 Ibid., p. 78.

11 Chike Obi, Our Struggle (Yaba, Pacific Printers, 1962), cited in LeVine, Dreams and Deeds, p. 76.

12 John N. Paden, "Communal Competition, Conflict and Violence in Kano," in Robert Melson and Howard Wolpe (eds.) Nigeria: Modernization and the Politics of Communalism (Lansing, Mich., State University Press, 1971), p. 132. Michael Crowder. A Short History of Nigeria (New York, Frederick A. Praeger, 1966), p. 284.

13 Luckham, The Nigerian Military, p. 272.

14 Stanley Meisler, "The Nigeria Which Is Not at War," Africa Report 15 (January 1970): 16–17; reprinted under title "Report From the Federal Side," in Nancy L. Hoepl (ed.), West Africa Today (New York, H. W. Wilson, 1971), p. 83.

sure was neither secure nor complete, and after the Ibos had been expelled from the North, especially during the civil war, rivalry between the northern Yorubas and other Northerners increased. In the competition for civil service or university positions, for instance, northern Yorubas were preferred to Nigerians outside the region, but had little chance in competition with non-Yoruba Northerners. On occasion, Yorubas would be passed over and positions left vacant in the hope that non-Yoruba Northerners would soon become eligible. As the war progressed, there were even rumors of further riots in which the northern Yorubas might be the next victims:

A year ago rumors swept through Kano and Kaduna that the Hausas intended to slaughter the Yorubas just as the Ibos were slaughtered three years ago. Firm talk by the emirs and the military governors, however calmed the Hausas, and the massacre never materialized.[15]

THE MINORITIES COMMISSION

From a chronological viewpoint we have jumped ahead of the script, since we have left the colonial period and followed interethnic relations in the North into the period of independence and civil war. Perhaps we should now turn back again to the British period and assess ethnic relationships at the time when the British were getting ready to abandon their suzerainty. Warfare had been a rather constant feature in precolonial Nigeria and its enforced cessation during the colonial period is often referred to as the "Pax Britannica." The British had indeed prevented traditional rivalries from flaring into open warfare, and they had also maintained freedom of movement throughout the territory and had inaugurated a national administration which gave those living in the territory some sense of common status.

On the other hand, the regions corresponded, in some degree, to ethnic divisions, and democratic politics often exploited ethnic rivalries and fears. Further, the economic development induced by the British brought new struggles for a favorable position in the modern economy. In 1957, three years before independence, ethnic antagonisms were sufficiently intense that the British organized a Minorities Commission to see what could be done to allay fears of ethnic groups who anticipated trouble once the British had withdrawn.

One of the first issues the Commission faced was the demand that the existing regions be divided into smaller units. This demand was based on the belief that the ability of one major ethnic group to dominate each region stimulated ethnic conflict. It was argued that this occurred because the ability of the Ibos, Hausa-Fulani, and Yoruba to dominate their re-

---

15 Ibid., p. 84.

spective regions both crushed the smaller ethnic groups and increased the influence of the major ones. The creation of additional and, therefore, of smaller regions would both provide a shelter for some of the smaller minorities and also be a way of limiting the voice of the larger groups in the national government.

The Minorities Commission recognized that some of the fears of the smaller minorities were justified, but refused to recommend the creation of additional regions; rather they proposed that human rights clauses be inserted in the constitution so that members of minority groups would be protected by guarantees affirming the rights of individual citizens.

The Minorities Commission drew on the United Nations Convention on Human Rights. The following excerpt dealing with discrimination is interesting, since the note concerning the Northern Region indicates that even drawing up general principles for the Nigerian situation was not a simple matter. The proviso referred to was to allow a period of grace for the Northern Region's policy of "northernization" under which Nigerians from other areas were discriminated against in government jobs. This was a relatively minor issue at the time but one which foreshadowed increased tensions still to come.

Group E. Discrimination

(14)   The Enjoyment of Fundamental Rights without Discrimination

The enjoyment of the fundamental rights set forth in the Convention shall be secured without discrimination on any ground such as sex, race, colour, language, religion, political or other opinion, national or social origin, association with a national minority, property, birth or other status . . .

Note: It may be necessary to make provision for an exception in times of war or other public emergency.

(15)   Protection against Discrimination

(i)   No enactment of any Legislature in Nigeria, and no instrument or executive or administrative action of any Government in Nigeria shall (either expressly or in its practical application)

(a) subject persons of any community, tribe, place of origin, religion or political opinion to disabilities or restrictions of which persons of other communities, tribes, places of origin, religions or political opinions are not made subject; or

(b) confer on persons of any community, tribe, place or origin, religion or political opinion any privilege or advantage which is not conferred on persons of other communities, tribes, places of origin, religions or political opinions.

(ii)   Nothing in this provision shall prevent the prescription of proper qualifications for the public service.

Note: It may be that in the Northern Region some proviso to the prohibition[16] *in this clause may be necessary for a limited period.*

The commission evidently proceeded by analogy with the American and the British practice which was to guarantee not group rights, but individual rights, on the theory that a government committed to the protection of individual rights would also be committed to the protection of minorities.

The recommendations of the Minorities Commission did influence the framers of the Nigerian Constitution, and a whole chapter of that document is devoted to a bill of rights. These are taken from the United Nations Universal Declaration of Human Rights. Not only are such rights listed but machinery is provided for their enforcement through appeal to the regional High Courts.[17]

These provisions have been criticized[18] on the grounds that they exempt prevailing practices such as employment preference within regions for natives of those regions and the use of caning (beating) as criminal punishment in the North. There is also criticism that the social rights of the Universal Declaration of Human Rights, such as the right to education and the right to work, were excluded. Finally, in addition to specific exceptions, most of the the rights listed are followed by wording which provides, "Nothing in this section shall invalidate any law that is reasonably justified in a democratic society."[19]

The preceding criticisms of the constitutional provisions for human rights should not be exaggerated. Indeed, they do not even touch on the principal defect of this type of approach to minority protection. The chief difficulty was not of wording or of subject matter, but rather that no kind of constitutional guarantee of individual rights could have protected minority individuals in the face of constantly mounting civil strife. No constitutional guarantees would have enabled a weak government to maintain domestic tranquility when confronted with growing ethnic tensions expressed in riots, massacres, and expulsion. In effect, the Minorities Commission sought to protect Nigeria from the slashing wounds of ethnic conflict by applying the Band-Aid of constitutional guarantees of individual rights. It was a remedy directed to individual privileges when major

---

[16] Henry Willinck, Gordon Hadow, Philip Mason, J. B. Shearer, *Report of the Commission Appointed to Enquire into the Fears of Minorities and the Means of Allaying Them* (London, Her Majesty's Stationery Office, 1958), p. 102.

[17] Oluwole Idowu Odumosu, "Constitutional Development," in L. Franklin Blitz (ed.), *The Politics and Administration of Nigerian Government* (London, Sweet and Maxwell, Ltd., and Lagos, African Universities Press for the Institute of Administration, Zaria, Nigeria, 1965), p. 54.

[18] Obafemi Awolowo, *Thoughts on Nigerian Constitution* (Ibadan, Oxford University Press, 1966), pp. 120–22.

[19] Ibid., p. 121.

structural changes in the government were required. Such criticism is easy to make in retrospect, but in all fairness, it must be added that there is no assurance that recommendations for structural change would have been adopted by the Nigerians or that they would have been successful if put to the test. In fact, ethnic cleavages were so deep, and support for a united Nigeria so limited that it is doubtful if any specific changes could have prevented the eventual civil war.

REGIONAL POLITICS AFTER INDEPENDENCE

Nigerian nationalists were often torn by the question whether nationalism meant a concern for ethnic identity and regional independence or for a united Nigeria in which their region would share sovereignty with several others. There were obvious advantages to being a part of a larger country, and Nigerians could not escape the pressure toward nation building which was manifested in other parts of the continent. Nevertheless, they were painfully aware of the fact that the creation of Nigeria had been much more the result of British than of Nigerian efforts. Perhaps the extreme form of the statement along this line is the utterance in 1947 of Obafemi Awolowo, a leading politician of Yoruba background: "Nigeria is not a nation. It is a mere geographical expression. There are no "Nigerians" in the same sense as there are "English," "Welsh," or "French." The word "Nigerian" is merely a distinctive appelation to distinguish those who live within the boundaries of Nigeria from those who do not."[20]

Nevertheless, in spite of all the reservations felt by politicians, independence did come to a united Nigeria in 1960. The pattern was one in which the North, by virtue of its dominance, with respect to population, was given (in practice) control of the House of Representatives and, therefore, the government. On the other hand, the three regions, with the Midwest added later, were given a high degree of autonomy relative to the federal authority. They had a major voice in education, agricultural policies and health services and kept "residual control" of all powers not specifically given to the federal government. They had the right to levy their own taxes and to share in those collected by the federal regime.

The federal government was given some taxing power, control of foreign relations, and the right to maintain an army. So powerful were the individual regions that they were sometimes each represented by individual missions abroad. For instance, all of the regions maintained offices in London for the hiring of expatriate personnel who, at this time, were still considered essential for the manning of Nigerian business and governmental institutions.

---

[20] Obafemi Awolowo, *Path to Nigerian Freedom* (London, Faber and Faber, 1947), pp. 47–48.

Whatever the difficulties ahead it looked as though Nigeria could expect a bright future. Its government was a democratic organization bringing together the largest number of people of any country in Africa. Independence had come with the blessing of the British and the promise of substantial aid, which was augmented by the United States International Aid Program, as well. The first years of independence saw a rapid expansion of education and transportation facilities along with a minor beginning of industrialization and the discovery of large supplies of oil. In spite of reports of widespread corruption and inefficiency, there was an undoubted quickening of economic life and there was much to be said for the viewpoint that Nigeria represented a dynamic and democratic type of state which in many ways might be setting a pattern for Africa.

The other side of the coin was that the political parties soon found that they were primarily based on regional support. There were essentially one Northern party and two Southern parties, one of which was stronger with the Ibos and the other with the Yorubas. The Northern party governed the nation with the aid of one of the Southern parties amid constant complaints of regional and ethnic discrimination. At the same time, the ostentatious living of the leaders of government, the padding of government payrolls which increased many fold from the time of British suzerainty, and the generally accepted practice of adding 10 percent to all contracts to provide loot for prominent officials, brought the government into disrepute. Numerous crises arose, and in the fifth year of independence, in 1964, indications of coercion and fraud in the election were so evident that the President of the Republic was reluctant to accept the election figures as the basis for a new government. The first five years of Nigerian independence produced some degree of progress, but they also saw the increase of ethnic animosities and a general decline of faith held by the educated portions of the Nigerian public in leading government figures.

The escalation of regional and tribal animosities and the loss of confidence in political leaders soon led to the overthrow of the civilian government. Coup was followed by counter coup and then by the Biafran attempt at secession. Since the military played a major role in these events, we now turn to a discussion of the armed forces in relation to ethnic conflict.

THE MILITARY

To a great extent, it might be said that the more slowly the British handed over a part of the governmental apparatus to Nigerian control, the greater was the national influence and the less the regional. This was because Nigerian control invariably meant the emergence of regional rivalries which the British held in check as long as they were in power. The army was one of the last departments of government to become free o

British control. Probably this was because a colonial government fears that its authority would be threatened if the armed forces came under indigenous authority and therefore hangs on to the armed forces until the eve of independence. Even under British control, regional rivalries, although suppressed, were nonetheless present. With Nigerian control, these rivalries became a major problem for the army.

Under British control, the regional and tribal composition of the armed forces could be disregarded because the ultimate authority was so obviously removed from ethnic intrigue. When the military came under Nigerian authority, however, the potential role of the armed forces in ethnic rivalry was so great that carefully developed plans to keep the military removed from ethnic conflict proved ineffectual.

When, in 1958, the army finally came under Nigerian authority, most of the commissioned and noncommissioned officers were British, a majority of the enlisted men were of Northern origin, and the few indigenous officers were mostly from the South.[21] The events between 1958 and 1965 saw the complete replacement of British officers by Nigerians and an effort to equalize regional distribution both in the enlisted and in the officer ranks. Supposedly, both for officers and enlisted men, recruitment was to proceed on a basis of 50 percent from the North and 25 percent from each of the Southern regions. Exact information on the composition of the enlisted personnel is not available except that the Western region was quite underrepresented, with only 700 soldiers at the end of 1966, while the North continued to have a predominance in the number of common soldiers. Information on the officer ranks reveals a gradual shift from South to North with a continuing majority of Southern officers as seen in Table 9-1.

The question whether or not the army was really national in character depends upon attitudes as well as upon the composition of various ethnic groups. In this respect, it is significant that a Northern prime minister appointed General Ironsi, an Ibo, as the first Nigerian general to replace the British commander who left at the end of 1964. Ironsi's appointment was not recommended by the departing British commander and might easily have been avoided if the prime minister had desired to do so. Apparently, however, the prime minister felt that passing over an Ibo officer's claim to seniority would promote friction and insecurity among Ibo officers and thus undermine army cohesion. The army also followed a policy of frequent transfer of both enlisted men and officers from one region of the country to another, partially to prevent the cementing of local and, therefore inevitably, tribal ties.

The size of the army was felt to be an insurance that it would be the defender rather than the master of the country. Since the army comprised

---

[21] Discussion in this section is heavily indebted to Robin Luckham, *The Nigerian Military.*

only 7,000 at the time of independence and by 1965 had increased only to 10,000, it was thought that the threat of a coup by so small a group in so large a country would be minimal. At the same time, the pay of both soldiers and officers was approximately doubled between 1958 and 1960 so that it could be regarded as being at least the equivalent of the pay of other government employees.

TABLE 9-1

Regional/Ethnic Composition of Officers Commissioned 1958-61 (combat officers only)

Year of commission	North	Yoruba	Ibo	Other from South	Percent Northern
Before 1958	5	6	11	5	20.0
1958	1	0	6	1	12.5
1959	0	3	9	1	0.0
1960	4	3	8	4	21.0
1961	16	9	14	3	36.0

Sources: *Federation of Nigeria, Official Gazette,* plus estimates of ethnic/regional distribution as given in Chapter 9, subject to small margin of error. Luckham, *The Nigerian Military,* p. 245.

One feature which made the national image of the army somewhat difficult to preserve was its involvement in essentially political disputes in the first five years of independence. These included intratribal conflicts among the Tivs, a middle belt group; in 1960 and 1964, an internal political crisis of the Action Group in the Western Region of Nigeria in 1962 and conflict over the election in same region in 1965. Even the participation of Nigerian troops in the United Nations Congo operation in 1961 seemed to many Nigerians essentially a political type of operation. In the federal election crisis in 1964, the use of troops was considered, but was decided against on the ground that it would encourage politicization of the army, although earlier, during that year, the army had been utilized in an attempt to maintain some essential services during a general strike. Luckham summarizes the impact of political concern on the army as follows:

After one major political crisis occurred in Nigeria after another from the suppression of the Action Group in the Western Region in 1962 onwards, the talk in officers messes became increasingly political. By 1964 at the latest several groups of officers thought military intervention "to stop the political mess" was likely, though this is not to say they necessarily thought then of staging a coup themselves. Major General Gowon says that he twice had occasion to warn military colleagues (then at the Lt. Colonel level) to desist from talking about the seizure of political power.[22]

---

[22] Robin Luckham, "The Nigerian Military: A Case Study in Institutional Break down" (Ph.D. Dissertation, University of Chicago, 1969), p. 119.

The concern of army officers for essentially political issues does not mean that their attitudes were ethnic rather than national; rather, it indicates that in any discussion of Nigerian politics, national and ethnic concerns become intermingled, both in the eyes of the participants themselves and in the appraisals which others make of their action. Perhaps this interplay of ethnic and nationality sentiments is best seen in the military coup which ended the first civilian Nigerian government on January 15, 1966. This was a coup which proclaimed the death knell of tribalism[23] and yet was later alleged to be an Ibo attempt to take over the government for ethnic aggrandizement.

BACKGROUND OF THE COUP

Tranquillity and unity in a democratic state depend on the willingness of contending forces to accept the results of the election process even if this means their removal from seats of power. In Nigeria, the enmity between the leading ethnic groups was so strong that it was not possible for them to take this view of the electoral process. Instead, every election was fought as though it was setting the terms of political life for eternity and every aspect of the process was questioned. Even the allocation of seats in the legislature on the basis of population became an issue almost impossible to resolve. Charges of fraud in the census in 1962 were so widespread that the census was never officially sanctioned and another census was taken in 1963. This census was not accepted by all the government officials, it was also widely regarded as designed to artificially boost the supremacy of the North, and its legitimacy was never accepted by the Southerners.

Charges of fraud in the counting of votes or in the certifying of candidates were so serious that the Eastern Region refused to participate in the 1964 election and the government was formed without its votes.[24] The president of Nigeria, Dr. Nmandi Azikiwe, an Ibo, asked for army support to annul the results of the election and order new polls. This army support was refused by the expatriate commanding officer, Major General Welby-Everard, on the grounds that the powers of the president were formal in nature and only the prime minister had the kind of authority which the president had attempted to assume. The prime minister was a Northerner and in sympathy with the results of the election, and hence no action was taken.

In the fall of 1965, another electoral crisis erupted in the Western Re-

---

[23] Based on initial proclamation of the coup leaders, cited in S. K. Panter-Brick (ed.), *Nigerian Politics and Military Rule: Prelude to the Civil War* (London, Ahlone Press, 1970), pp. 184–86.

[24] Polls were eventually held in the East early in 1965, so that it finally did have an influence on the federal government, although the abstention from voting of Ibos in other regions caused the defeat of some candidates.

gion. At this time, Chief Akintola, an ally of the leading Northern politicians, was attempting to maintain the position of the newly established NNDP party and therefore his position as premier of the Western Region. Charges were made that boxes were stuffed with fraudulent votes, that the votes were miscounted, and that opposition candidates were not allowed to run. Although Chief Akintola's party supposedly received a heavy majority, resentment was so great that widespread rioting ensued in the Western Region. The rioting was beyond the power of the police to suppress and it seemed that restoration of peace in the West required either a political compromise or the restoration of order by the action of the Nigerian army. A political compromise would have been considered a defeat, both for Chief Akintola and for his Northern supporters. They were reluctant to call in the army and not altogether certain of its reliability, but rumor had it that this step was under consideration in January 1966.

By November 1965, there were many rumors of possible attempts at a coup by discontented officers who felt that only decisive action by the army could end what they felt had become a scandal of political corruption and ineffectiveness; such reports were apparently ignored, possibly because there were so many of them. Luckham[25] asserts that there may have been as many as four different hypothetical plots reported.

At least one of these plots was far from hypothetical. A group of army officers, mostly majors and mostly of Ibo origin, who had come to know each other through association as students in training schools and in the sharing of posts in the army, had been making definite plans for a drastic move. Three of the officers most active in the coup occupied highly strategic positions. Major Nzeogwu was small arms instructor at the military academy in Kaduna, the capital of the Northern Region, Major Ifeajuna was Brigade Major of the Second Brigade, stationed at Apapa near Lagos, and Major Okafor was commander of the Federal Guard in Lagos, which was charged with the responsibility for the defense of officials of the federal government. These men, together with several other majors and some lower officers, and with the possible tacit collusion of one or two higher officers, had been planning a coup for some time and anticipated that it would take place in February 1966.

However, it seemed to them, in mid-January, that there were two factors which favored the immediate launching of the attempt. First was the fear that a strong military intervention in the Western Region might make it difficult for their coup to succeed. Second, on January 15, a combination of circumstances called many of the men who might have been their opponents away from their posts. The president of Nigeria was in London. Several leading officers were either on leave or in Lagos for a conference, and two battalions lacked commanders because of changes in post-

25 Luckham, *The Nigerian Military*, p. 19.

ings. Thus it was that most of the combat units of the Nigerian army either were not under the direct control of their designated commanders or were under the command of men sympathetic to the coup. Therefore January 15 seemed to be an ideal time to eliminate the entire upper echelon of political and military leadership in Nigeria in a clean sweep of the elements that were alleged to have corrupted the country. Preparations were hasty, but first reports indicated that the coup was a success. The leading politician of the North, the Sardauna of Sokoto, Sir Ahamadu Bello, had just returned from Mecca and was killed in his official residence by Major Nzeogwu. Meantime, in the South, other conspirators had captured and later killed the federal prime minister and the finance minister, the premier of the Western Region, and a number of the senior army officers.

Plans for a total liquidation of the country's leading politicians did not completely succeed. The premiers of the Middle-West and the East were not assassinated but merely held as captive, and the general of the Nigerian army, Ironsi, and one of his chief assistants, Lieutenant Colonel Gowon, managed to escape. The result was that, although the conspirators had indeed altered the government beyond recognition through the slaughter of many of the leading officials, in the final analysis they failed to obtain control of the country. General Ironsi and Colonel Gowon managed to rally the armed forces, and a council of the remaining ministers of the republic authorized General Ironsi to form a military government. Seeing that he had failed to destroy the command structure of the army, Major Nzeogwu agreed to surrender on promise that his life would be spared, while Major Ifeajuna fled to Ghana, returning later to face arrest and imprisonment. Thus, the conspiratorial majors ended the period of civilian rule in Nigeria, but were forced to hand over rule to a group of officers not involved in the plot.

RATIONALE OF THE COUP

The leaders of the attempted coup proclaimed that their motives were a desire for the regeneration of Nigeria, the ending of unrest in the West and other regions, the elimination of imperialist influence, and the purging of the country of such social evils as "bribery, tribalism, bureaucracy, nepotism, and feudalism."[26] Their opponents charged that this was a conspiracy by a group of Ibo officers to seize control of their country for sectional and personal motives. The fact that men who proclaimed their opposition to tribalism should themselves be accused of tribalistic tendencies is paradoxical, to say the least. An understanding of this paradox will do much to illuminate the nature of Nigerian ethnic conflict.

---

[26] Arthur Agwuncha Nwankwo and Samuel Udochukwu Ifejika, *The Making of a Nation: (Biafra)* (London, C. Hurstin Co., 1969), p. 137.

First, a look at the ethnic origin of the officers most actively involved in the revolt leaves no doubt of the Ibo influence. Six of the seven majors involved were Ibo, and 19 out of 23 of the other active participants as well. None of the active participants were Northerners, although some Northern noncommissioned officers had supported the revolt under orders from superior officers. One prominent Northerner, Lieutenant Colonel Hassan Katsina (then a major) cooperated with the conspirators, apparently under coercion. In these circumstances, it is easy to conclude that the attempted coup was an Ibo conspiracy and that the broader objectives proclaimed by its leaders were mere window dressing. It seems, however, that the real explanation is not quite this simple.

The seeming paradox between the common ethnic identity of these coup leaders and their condemnation of Nigerian tribalism may be resolved by an appreciation of the meaning which tribalism held for different sectors. For the North, tribalism appeared as a threat by Southern Nigerians to utilize their superiority in educational and economic attainments to make the North a sort of Southern colony. According to this view, the insistence upon the "northernisation" of personnel in the Northern region, and to a significant extent in the federal government, was not tribalism. Rather, it was a defense against exploitation of the North by other elements.

To the Southerners, and especially to the Ibos, the definition of the situation was entirely different. First, it was in the South that radical intellectuals were developing an ideology which was a compound of Marxism and nationalism that called for radical reconstruction of the government. They saw their principles in opposition to the program coming from the power of the North, which, as they saw it, not only promoted Northern ethnic interests, but also opposed radical, political reconstruction. The North tended to be friendly to private enterprise and suspicious of socialism. Most of the leaders in the North were friendly to the British and trusted them to a far greater extent than they did any stripe of Southern politician. Finally, the social structure of the North had been preserved with relatively little change over a period of at least a hundred years and Northern leaders saw their sectional interests and the retention of much of the traditional structure as being entirely compatible.

It is extremely difficult to sort out Ibo self-interest from adherence to a modernizing, political ideology. Overpopulation in the Eastern Region meant that sectionalism alone would not protect the interest of the Ibos. For their own survival and prosperity, they needed the opportunity to work and live in other areas. Further, they did not need any particular kind of quota preference in the process. The superior education of the Ibos, their openness to modernizing ideas, and their acceptance of the achievement ethic made them formidable competitors in the race for prestige. A Nigerian nation in which there was no formal recognition of ethnic identities and in which all Nigerians were able to move freely and to work freely with equal rights in all regions was one friendly to Ibo aspirations. On this basis, Ibos became the most fervent nationalists in the country and the strongest advocates of a united nation. At times they frankly linked the situation of Ibo advance and a united Nigeria as in a politically unfortunate statement in 1949 by Azikiwe:

... it would appear that the God of Africa has specially created the Ibo nation to lead the children of Africa from the bondage of the ages. The martial prowess of the Ibo nation at all stages of human history has enabled them not only to conquer others but also to adapt themselves to the role of preserver. . . . The Ibo nation cannot shirk its responsibilities.[27]

While the chief conspirators in the January coup did not hold power for more than a few hours and never formulated a coherent political program, it is impossible to accuse them of any desire for secession. In fact, even after the outbreak of the Nigerian civil war, Major Nzeogwu wrote a letter published in a Nigerian paper in which he deplored the failure of efforts to build a united nation.[28] There is some evidence that Nzeogwu and two other leaders of the conspiracy who eventually joined the Biafran armed forces found the Biafran devotion to the breakup of Nigeria an uncongenial viewpoint. Nzeogwu was killed in rather strange circumstances which indicated a possibility that he might have been considering defection to the federal army. Two other officers who had participated in the coup, Lieutenant Colonel Banjo and Major Ifeajuna, were executed by the Biafran authorities on the charge that they had been conspiring against the Biafran leader, Lieutenant Colonel Ojukwu, and plotting a surrender of Biafra. It was, indeed, a curious set of circumstances which led them into a coup designed to forge a more united country but which eventually paved the way for an attempt at secession in which some of the chief conspirators of the coup were, in turn, killed by soldiers from their own region. Their difficulties probably followed from the problems of a mobilized minority that was attempting to become the chief support for a united nation. Many of these problems became highlighted in the brief regime of General Ironsi which followed the coup.

THE IRONSI REGIME

There is considerable discussion as to whether General Ironsi, after his almost miraculous escape from assassination, seized power or had it thrust upon him. Those who accused him of ambition argued that the correct course would then have been for him to have supported the appointment

---

[27] *West African Pilot*, July 6, 1949, cited in Coleman, *Nigeria*, p. 347.

[28] *Advance: The Nigerian Worker's Own Newspaper*, Aug. 13, 1967. Cited in Luckham, "The Nigerian Military," p. 40.

of a civilian prime minister and to have used his authority to maintain a civilian government. On the other side, the argument may be made that the armed forces had become so disillusioned with the civilian government that they would have refused to follow their commander in chief in this kind of effort and that only an assertion of the dominance of the army could have united the military forces of the country. At any rate, this seems to have been the rationale upon which Ironsi relied when he formed a government of national unity with the military in power. As commander in chief, he himself was also supreme leader and essentially dictator of the nation, and he appointed military governors to be the supreme authority in each of the regions. Although Ironsi himself was an Ibo, most of his staff were not. Another Ibo, Lieutenant Colonel Ojukwu, was named as military governor of the East, but the command in other regions was given to non-Ibos.

One of the most perplexing questions faced by Ironsi, the punishment of those responsible for the attempted coup, was never clearly faced. The culprits were removed from military command and held in protective custody but were never prosecuted. Not only was there a failure of prosecution but the lack of publicity on the detailed events of the coup led to all sorts of rumors and speculation; presumably pressure from radical intellectuals in the East and the West on the one hand, and from Northerners on the other, made it impossible to arrive at a clear-cut decision on this matter. Discontent at the vacillation of the government in dealing with the leaders of the January coup was aggravated by the fact that Ibo officers in many cases had moved into the vacancies left by the killings of the senior military commanders.

Ironsi, on the other hand, expressed himself publicly as being thoroughly committed to a government in which there was no recognition of tribe on any basis. He proclaimed tribalism as a deadly sin and his famous "decree 34," which abolished the regions and the federation, declared that only a united Nigeria existed, and created a group of provinces.

As might have been expected, Ironsi's unification decrees did not bring tranquillity, but a resurgence of ethnic suspicion and animosity. Riots broke out in Northern cities in May 1966, and many Ibos were beaten or killed by Northern mobs. Military authorities attempted to pacify the situation but unrest remained. In July, another coup broke out, this time led by Northerners, and General Ironsi was seized by Northern soldiers and shot. Another coup had taken place, the unity of the army and the government had again been shattered, and the question came, what next for Nigeria?

PREPARATION FOR SECESSION

The senior army officer, Brigadier Ogundipe, a Yoruba, would seemingly have been the logical person to have assumed control. Apparently he doubted his ability to unify dissident elements of the army, and Colonel Gowon, who had been Ironsi's chief of staff, was sent to negotiate with the rebels. Gowon was a member of a small minority tribe from the middle belt. He was identified as a Northerner, but was not a Hausa or Fulani and was a Christian. Thus, he embodied in his own person identification with the Northern Region on the one hand, and a minority tribe and the Christian faith on the other, a combination of traits which tended to make him acceptable to more different ethnic groups than might have been true of most of the other officers.

Gowon's own career may indicate the basis for his emergence as a leader of Nigerian unity. As a non-Southerner, he could hardly have been expected to be sympathetic toward an ideal of Nigerian unity which, in practice, seemed to mean Ibo domination. By the same token, he would not have shared the bitterness and frustration of Ibos who saw their dream of leadership of a Nigerian nation fading away. On the other hand, there would probably have been no place for a Christian minority tribesman in a separatist North.

It is apparently true that some of the Northern military leaders, in their resentment at Ironsi, desired to withdraw from the federation and hoped that Gowon would be their leader in this move. Nwanko credits Gowon's change from separatism to unity to the influence of foreign advisors who feared the effect of a divided Nigeria on the stability and security of foreign interests.[29] It seems likely that other considerations were more influential. These would include his awareness of the fact that it was only in a united country that members of small minorities could find a scope for action on the national scene. This feeling was supported by the Tivs, who made up a large percentage of the enlisted men of the Nigerian army. The Tivs, a middle belt group, were a minority in the Northern region and had no enthusiasm for a Northern secession which would doom them to minority status without any redress from a supraregional source. Finally, one should not discount Gowon's sense of loyalty and obligation as an officer of the Nigerian army.

In any event, Gowon sought to assemble a government of reconciliation which would make unity possible in spite of the many conflicts which had occurred. His dream of reconciliation was rather rudely shattered by new disturbances in the North and West which led to the slaughter of 6,000–8,000 Ibos living in those areas[30] and the expulsion of between one and two million Ibos from Northern and Western areas where many of them had lived for a generation or longer.

---

[29] Nwanko and Ifejika, *The Making of a Nation*, p. 161.

[30] There is a controversy about the actual number, varying from a police figure of 3,300 to a maximum Ibo claim of 30,000. The 6,000–8,000 figure is the estimate of Professor O'Connell, and is based on "careful interviewing and some knowledge of the police reports." James O'Connell, "Authority and Community in Nigeria," in Melson and Wolpe, *Nigeria*, p. 672.

This expulsion apparently ended, for many, the association between Ibo identity and Nigerian nationalism. The massacres were widespread and featured an almost casual type of brutality. Prominent Ibos were tortured and humiliated before being slain, hospital patients were killed in their beds, and refugees were pulled from trains as they were fleeing. For a period of a few days, the worst phases of mob violence had complete expression. In Kano, elements of the Nigerian army killed fleeing Ibos.

The riots were deplored by all the leaders of the country including Northerners, but, to many Ibos, it seemed that the only place of security for them was in the confines of their own region. Ojukwu, who had become the head of the Eastern Region military government, welcomed back the refugee Ibos and then made every effort to make the Eastern Region a viable, separate establishment. There were many attempts at conciliation between the regions, and one of these, the ill-fated conference at Aburi, Ghana, in January 1967, led to supposed agreement. The agreement, however, which would have provided practically complete autonomy for the regions with an extremely weak central government, was never carried into practice.

Subsequent efforts at conciliation failed because of seemingly irreconcilable differences. Ojukwu was unwilling to come to any kind of agreement which would not allow the existence of the Eastern Region as a virtually independent nation, and Gowon was unwilling to commit himself to a program which would make the federal government completely dependent upon unanimous agreement of the regions. At the urging of Awolowo, the Yoruba leader, Gowon agreed to a peace formula under which all the measures the federal government had taken against the East were withdrawn. Even this measure failed to appease the East; the two sides gradually consolidated their forces and drew further apart. In May 1967 Gowon, in exasperation, decided to force the pace by changing the composition of Nigeria from four regions to twelve states in which the "minority tribes" were no longer under the control of either the Ibos in the East or the Hausas in the North. This was interpreted as a move to weaken Ojukwu's control in the Eastern Region, and almost immediately the latter region proclaimed its independence as the nation of Biafra. Six weeks later, after claims and counterclaims as to which side was shooting, federal forces attacked the border towns and the civil war was under way.

THE COURSE OF THE WAR

The onset of the war saw a peculiar reversal in regional attitudes. The East, which had been the home of Nigerian nationalism, was leading the forces of secession. The North, which frequently had threatened secession and had tried to shut itself off from national influence, proclaimed its determination to "Keep Nigeria One." Gowon had followed a policy of conciliation toward Awolowo and other Yoruba leaders which kept that section of the country safely on the federal side. From the standpoint of population, there were up to 40 million people on the federal side and not more than 16 million in Biafra, including five million non-Ibos of very doubtful loyalty to Biafra. From a standpoint of economic resources, the picture was more mixed. Oil had been discovered, mostly within the Biafran territory, and offered an enormous boon to that region. The Ibos were confident that the oil resources, their own human resources in trained personnel, and the sympathy of much of the world would allow Biafra to become a viable, economic unit. From a military standpoint, there seemed to be few outstanding advantages for either Biafra or the federal government. Neither side had a large stockpile of arms. The Biafrans profited from the high proportion of Ibos in the officer corps of the army, while the majority of the enlisted men were from the North. At the time the conflict began, there were probably 10,000 soldiers in the federal army and probably a slightly smaller number on the Biafran side. It was a small-scale affair from any perspective, and it seemed quite possible that the conflict might end in a standstill. The long military campaign saw occasional Biafran victories, but more meaningful was a steady buildup of federal strength to the point where, at the end of the war, Biafran forces were compressed in a territory hardly a tenth the size of that nation at the beginning of the struggle.

One of the most interesting features of the war was the propaganda campaign between Biafra and Nigeria for world sympathy. The Biafrans claimed that their secession was the exercise of self-determination by a nationality which had in reality been cruelly expelled from the rest of Nigeria and could hope for nothing in the future in union with that country. Biafra was proclaimed as the home of Christian, progressive peoples who were resisting the tyranny of the fanatical Muslim emirs who sought to extend their domination.[31] The efforts of the federal government to suppress secession were described as cruel repression. Claims were made that the federal government sought to exterminate all Ibos through a process of starvation and bombardment. Biafra was portrayed, by talented publicity men, as a gallant struggling little nation fighting to save the lives of its people from genocide practiced by Nigeria.

General Gowon strove to suppress any anti-Ibo elements in the propaganda of the Nigerian government. He proclaimed that the war was not being waged against any particular tribes and announced that the Ibos could expect good treatment if they rejoined the union. Ibos who had remained in Lagos and were federal employees retained their jobs and were personally secure during the war. As soon as the first bit of territory was wrested from Biafra, an Ibo, loyal to Nigeria, was appointed governor

---

[31] "Dateline Africa," *West Africa* (June 7, 1969), p. 661.

of the region and Ibo refugees from Biafra were welcomed. Further, the Nigerian government restructure, in which 12 states replaced the four regions which had comprised the nation previously, meant that the North was broken up into six states whose diversity in ethnic composition would probably cause them difficulty in presenting a united front; thus the spectre of domination by a monolithic Northern area was eliminated. The East was also broken up into three states, which was a clever bid for support of minority groups in that region. Ibos would be the dominant element in the East Central State, but the other two Eastern states were formed in such a way that non-Ibo elements would probably have control. The Lagos area became a state, as well as the West and the Mid-West. By these measures, General Gowon was able to present Nigeria to the world as a country which guaranteed the rights of all peoples and which had been structured to make the continued domination by any one group more difficult than had been true in the previous regime.

Gowon's efforts to present the federal government as a humanitarian regime concerned for Nigerian unity but anxious to protect the individual Ibos were partially nullified by the memories of the massacre of Ibos in 1966 and by occasional outbursts of cruelty during the war. Federal troops were under order to protect Ibo civilians, and the ultimate surrender of Biafra did not lead to a blood bath. However, feelings were high and federal troops did not always follow the orders of the supreme commanding officer. One example of such difficulty took place in the reoccupation of the city of Benin in the Midwestern area by federal troops. This area had been captured only six weeks before by Biafran forces in a ruthless surprise attack which involved the defection of several federal officials of Ibo background. When Benin was retaken by federal troops reporters in the Midwestern capital counted 989 Ibo corpses.[32] *Time* reports the incident as follows:

> Benin's non-Ibo residents went on a rampage, looting and wrecking businesses owned or managed by Ibos. Many Ibo civilians were handed over to Northern soldiers, who competed with each other for the fun of shooting them. Hundreds of Ibo bodies, many stripped and full of holes, were scooped into dump trucks and carted off to common graves, or to the nearby Benin river. Others were left to rot in the blistering sun.[33]

The federal forces were also accused of attempting to starve the Biafrans. The Biafran region had been a food-importing area and the exigencies of wartime made food production even more difficult than before. The consequent result was much hunger and malnutrition, if not actual famine. The Nigerian government, on the other hand, may claim credit for being

---

[32] *International Herald Tribune*, Oct. 23, 1967.

[33] *Time*, Oct. 6, 1967. Reprinted by permission from TIME, The Weekly Newsmagazine; Copyright by Time Inc., 1967.

one of the first wartime governments in history to allow food to go to a hostile region. In principle, the Nigerian government favored sending relief supplies to Biafra, but formal agreement on the circumstances in which relief could be sent proved to be difficult. The Biafrans, while sending out horror stories of the extent of malnutrition and kwashiokor, a debilitating disease especially affecting children, were reluctant to allow any restrictions on the shipments of relief which might affect their military advantages. Planes which brought relief were subject to taxation, and any efforts to inspect relief shipments to insure that munitions were not also included were bitterly resisted. The suffering of the Biafran people became, in effect, a military weapon, which could be used to gain sympathy and support from the rest of the world.

The Biafran tactics seemed to be successful in the publicity sphere. Biafran relief efforts raised an enormous amount of money, some of which was apparently channeled into nonrelief expenditures. Many foreign statesmen criticized Nigerian policy and urged help for the suffering Biafrans. In response to the appeal to end suffering, aid was organized under both Protestant and Catholic auspices; at times, as many as 50 planes a day came into Biafran airports laden with supplies.

The Biafrans had also hoped for recognition, along with diplomatic, and possibly military, support from foreign countries. But this did not come, at least not in the form which they had expected. For a period of several months, no foreign government extended diplomatic recognition to Biafra. The American government maintained recognition of the Nigerian government but refused to sell arms to either side. The British, after some vacillation and much debate in the House of Commons, continued recognition of the Nigerian government and allowed a small quantity of armaments to be shipped. Nigerian needs for armaments were met to a great extent by the Russian government, which gave wholehearted support to Nigeria and which provided, on a cash basis, the bulk of Nigerian armament.[34]

Biafra, at first, had sympathy from several quarters without official recognition from any. Eventually, recognition came from two countries in French West Africa, the Ivory Coast and Gabon. Later, these countries were joined by Tanzania, Zambia, and Haiti. These five nations were the only ones to extend recognition. Toward the end of the war, Biafrans received effective aid from the French, who, while not affording diplomatic recognition, proclaimed their sympathy with Biafra and shipped substantial amounts of arms via former French colonies. A varied group of foreigners, including Frenchmen, South Africans, Swedes, and others, at one time or another fought with the Biafran forces. Rallies, to express sym-

---

[34] For an authoritative discussion of the role of various countries in supplying arms to both sides see *The Arms Trade with the Third World* (New York, Humanities Press, Stockholm Int. Peace Institute, 1972), pp. 630–32.

pathy, to raise funds, and to denounce the alleged cruelties of the Nigerian army, were staged in many countries. The international efforts provided some help for Biafra but failed to tip the military balance. The Biafrans won the war in the newspapers but lost it on the battlefields, an indication that it is not true in all cases that the pen is mightier than the sword.

Sympathy for Biafrans on humanitarian grounds and a tendency to identify with the underdog were countered by many other factors. As far as Great Britain was concerned, it would be difficult for a country which had literally created the nation of Nigeria to give official support to those who sought its breakup. The United States followed an ambivalent policy which brought criticism from both sides, but it was reluctant to take a position which would be seen either as threatening African unity or as completely yielding influence in Nigeria to the Russians. The African nations themselves were also ambivalent. Many of them had, no doubt, been jealous of Nigeria and had feared its power. Others were horrified by the bloodbath which seemed to be involved in the civil war and were inclined to interpret the insistence on continued Nigerian unity as a vestigial remnant of imperialism.

However, every African nation was aware that it, too, was made up of a variety of ethnic units and, therefore, was vulnerable to the same divisive forces which had brought about the Nigerian civil war. As sympathetic as they might be to the claims of the Biafrans, they could not ignore the fact that each nation had many potential Biafras within itself. The fear was continually expressed that success for Biafra might be the key to the disintegration of other African nations. The Organization for African Unity made many attempts to end the conflict, but told the Biafrans that the only way they were authorized to mediate was on the basis of preserving Nigerian unity. In summation, the suffering of Biafran civilians brought world sympathy, and the courage of its soldiers evoked admiration, while the skill of its public relations, and the clumsiness of Nigerian efforts of the same type, limited the effects of Gowon's conciliatory moves. On the other hand, even though the world might be swayed by Biafran propaganda, most nations were reluctant to take any step which might be seen as encouraging secession and thereby promoting the further fragmentation of a continent which had already been divided into far more nations than could be justified on an economic basis.

The war did not end on the basis of negotiation, which General Gowon had frequently offered, but by the flight of Ojukwu and the surrender of the Biafran military. The guerilla resistance, which many people had predicted, failed to develop and the Ibos were gradually incorporated in the nation of Nigeria. The immediate postwar policies of the Nigerian government are portrayed in an article in *West Africa* under the title "Reconciliation in Nigeria!"

With astonishing resilience the Ibos are now applying themselves to the task of becoming Nigerians again. Many hundreds have remained Nigerians all the time; millions more, when they came under Mr. Asika's administration, learned long before the collapse of the rebellion the falsity of their leaders' propaganda against the Federation. That falsity is now completely exposed, not only because there has been no murder of civilians or destruction of the Ibo community, but also because the Federal Government is carrying out its pledges to the people of the East-Central State.

They are being reinstated in the public services, rehabilitation of their education is being planned, their property abandoned elsewhere in the Federation has been looked after and money due to them has been desposited in banks. The Federal army, in which misbehaviour has been speedily restrained, so far from engaging in massacre is assisting relief. The Nigerian police are re-establishing an all-Ibo force in the state, and Mr. Asika's administration for the State, again all-Ibo, is being expanded and is recruiting officials of the former secessionist regime. No wonder that in the worthless "debate" in the House of Commons this week (Mr. Hornby, the Conservative former Minister, commented aptly: "We should congratulate General Gowon on his magnanimity and beyond that mind our own business.") turned into a chorus of praise for the almost unparalleled generosity of the Federal leader.[35]

Many problems, of course, will remain for a long time, but there are also many assets. The oil discovered in Nigeria has become a major source of revenue and is helping to relieve the economic strains and inflation produced by the war. The government, which continues to be a military regime, at least until 1976, has been able to maintain order, and Ibos have begun again to move to the parts of Nigeria from which they were expelled in the massacre of 1966. The reintegration of Ibos into the Nigerian nation is not a simple process, since many of them had been replaced in their jobs and businesses by other Nigerians and certainly the feelings of tension stimulated by the war cannot be immediately quieted. Nevertheless, the issue seems to be settled that, in spite of ethnic conflict, secession is not a viable alternative and that Nigeria, for the indefinite future, will be a united nation. Not only is this outcome significant in Nigeria but it may also be taken as possibly a turning point from the tendency which had prevailed throughout much of the world since the end of World War I to break up larger nations into smaller entities on the grounds of self-determination. It appears that the already tiny states of Africa will not be again fragmented and that, on one basis or another, people from numerous ethnic backgrounds and speaking different tongues will continue living in the same national boundaries.

In Nigeria, the abolition of the regions and the creation of twelve states have created a different pattern of ethnic relationships. On the one hand, the defeat of the Biafrans in the civil war and the abolition of the

---

[35] "Reconciliation in Nigeria," *West Africa* (Jan. 31, 1970), p. 125.

regions have eliminated the principal challenges to the idea of Nigeria as a unified sovereign state. On the other hand, ethnic rivalries are by no means over and the replacement of regions by states in some ways intensifies the conflict. Tribes which were too small to hope for major influence in a region may seek power in one of the states. Conversely, the larger groups which still had to compromise in the region may be able to dominate a state with few concessions to those outside the ethnic fold. Presumably, both a greater loyalty to Nigeria as a sovereign state and the stronger powers of the federal government should help to reduce ethnic discrimination. In the meantime, effort to reintegrate the Ibos into all sections of the country is at least mitigating some of the wartime hostilities. The future will not be free of ethnic problems but does offer hope that a system will emerge which combines features of cultural pluralism with a common Nigerian loyalty.

SUMMARY

Nigeria was a collection of diverse ethnic groups brought into being as a state by the fiat of the colonial power. The ethnic differences were exacerbated by unequal development in the various regions of the country which produced a significant differential in modernization. In the Northern section illiteracy and a traditional society were the norm, while other sections of Nigeria were moving into a literate, modern type of social organization. The removal of colonial rule set the stage for increasing ethnic conflicts through democratic processes which were badly subverted in practice. Later, competition in the political arena was abandoned for the attempt at secession, leading to a triumph of the forces favoring a continuation of a united Nigeria on a stronger basis than before the war began. The story of Nigeria illustrates both the tensions which can develop in ethnic adjustments and some of the possible avenues for amelioration.

CONCLUSIONS

Nigerian pattern. The formula of the 1957 Minority Commission, one which totally failed in practice, was a reliance on the protection of the rights of individuals. As long as large and bitterly antagonistic ethnic groups were unrestrained, it was futile to expect the constitutional guarantee of individual rights to have a significant effect.

Generalized pattern. Constitutional guarantees of individual rights are not by themselves a solution for ethnic conflict.

Nigerian pattern. National unity and a disregard of tribal origins favored Ibo mobility at the expense of gains by other Nigerians. Such a situation means that ethnic feelings are directed against the national entity as well as against competing groups. It is natural that a modernized minority should be attracted to the idea of a strong national government in a pluralistic state. Such a minority, however, will have to give convincing evidence of its willingness to share with other groups the gains which come from national unity if it is to achieve a national consensus.

Generalized pattern. Pleas for national unity may be considered simply a mask for strengthening exploitation when national unity is viewed as a device to facilitate the dominance of a particular ethnic group.

Nigerian pattern. The theory of the small army is that it would be unable to maintain its rule over a large population. The difficulty with this theory is that as long as any group has a virtual monopoly of force, the smallness of its numbers is not an appreciable factor. On the other hand, a small army is easily subject to conspiracy, since the removal of a comparatively small number of officers will change the power structure of the military forces.

Generalized pattern. Limiting the size of the army does not guarantee civilian control.

Nigerian pattern. Through decisions made on the criteria of education, achievement, and test performance, Ibos in Nigeria were getting a disproportionate quota of positions in academia, business, and government. To the minority, this procedure seems to be only fair, to the excluded majority, it seemed to be a technique by which their efforts at advancement were frustrated. Thus, we may expect any group handicapped in open competition to insist on quotas or similar devices, to assure its members what is considered a proper share of the rewards.

Generalized pattern. Ethnic groups will not accept the legitimacy of supposedly universalistic rules which appear to work to their disadvantage.

Nigerian pattern. The experience of Nigeria and many other African states has indicated that the politician seeking office may find that the best political base is ethnic affiliation. Thus, it is possible that modernization and democratic government may actually intensify ethnic loyalties and tribal identification rather than lead to their demise. The natural process of evolution cannot be expected to end tribalism, at least not within a short time. Multi-ethnic states will have to deliberately foster areas of cooperation which cross ethnic lines and afford new methods of identification.

Generalized pattern. Ethnically based conflict does not necessarily diminish with development of democratic government.

Nigerian pattern. At the time of independence Nigeria was divided into three regions, each of which was dominated by one ethnic group. Later one additional region was added, and shortly before the civil war the regional divisions were scrapped in favor of a twelve-state arrangement. The regional arrangement increased the power of major ethnic groups because control of the region increased their influence on the federal government. It also meant that smaller ethnic groups were minorities on both the regional and the national scene. The Hausa-Fulani-dominated North, for instance, comprised more than half of both the population and the land area of the country. It included sizable minority tribes who had little influence on either the regional or the federal government. Breaking up this region into six states meant that at least two of the states would not have a Hausa-Fulani majority and thus would be controlled by those with another ethnic affiliation. Similarly, since it would be hard for the Hausa-Fulani to dominate more than four of the states, they would probably have less influence on the federal government. The Eastern Region, which had been dominated by Ibos, was divided into three states, only one of which had an Ibo majority. Presumably this will mean less Ibo control in this area and less Ibo influence on the federal government. The three states created from the Mid-West, the West, and Lagos may not directly decrease Yoruba influence at either level, since they represent a less drastic change from the earlier pattern than the division of the other regions into states.

All the new states are large enough to be respectable territorial units while small enough to enable some hitherto powerless ethnic groups to have a major voice at the state level. Likewise, the division of the North will make it impossible for the Hausa-Fulani to rule the country on their own through supposedly democratic processes. It is hoped that this will mean an end to the North-South dichotomy, which has so long bedeviled Nigeria politics and will lessen the likelihood of a two-way struggle for power. Earlier politics did involve coalitions, but the new state system should require a winning political party to be a still more inclusive organization which minimizes its identification with any one ethnic group.

General pattern. Territorial arrangements which limit the power of the major ethnic groups force broader coalition politics and decrease the likelihood of violent confrontation between the major groups while giving more expression to the desires of the smaller minorities.

QUESTIONS

1. What is meant by "indirect rule"? Why was this more feasible in the North than in the East?
2. Why did Lord Lugard feel that it was disastrous for Nigerians to learn English "prematurely"?
3. Why were the Ibos at first more ardent nationalists than the other tribes?
4. When the other regions wanted to ask the English to set a definite date for

Nigerian independence the Northern region blocked this action. How do you explain the Northern attitude?

5. The Minorities Commission recommended that individual rights be protected by constitutional guarantees. Why did these guarantees fail to protect minorities?

6. Was the action of Lord Lugard in agreeing to restrict the entry of missionaries in the North beneficial or harmful to that section of the country?

7. Why did the Ibos switch from support of a strong Nigerian nation to secession?

8. Is *tribe* a legitimate term for Nigerian ethnic groups? Why might some people object to it? Do you have a better category?

9. What is the danger of using the army to suppress disturbances which are the result of political controversies?

10. Will the creation of 12 states rather than four regions make it easier to deal with ethnic conflict in Nigeria? Why could not this step have been taken earlier by a civilian regime?

11. Was it neocolonialism to insist that Nigeria remain a united nation after the British withdrawal?

12. Why did the ably conducted public relations campaign of the Biafran government fail to win stronger support?

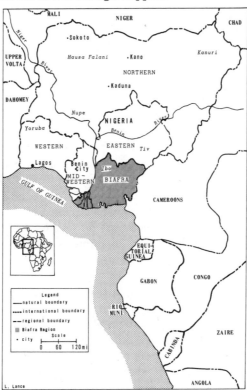

Chapter 10

Non-European minorities in France and Britain

Elsewhere in this book, we discussed the treatment of the natives in countries which were colonized by whites coming from France and Britain. We noted the attempt to assimilate the Senegalese and the Martinicans to the colonizer's way of life and we looked at the British role in South Africa and in Southern Rhodesia. Throughout this discussion it is evident that the French and British always established themselves as the dominant group and the indigenous people were placed in a subordinate position where their labor and natural resources could be exploited by the imperial power. In tracing these patterns, we saw how the French and British went about the process of governing their vast possessions, most of which are now independent and in the process of throwing off the last vestiges of colonial rule.

In this chapter we are interested in a reverse flow; the non-European immigrants who have come, on either a temporary or a permanent basis, to metropolitan France and Britain. With respect to this situation, then, we advance the following generalizations of interethnic relations: (1) major political conflicts combined with salient cultural differences may generate more antagonism between groups of similar physical appearance than exists between groups that are differentiated phenotypically, (2) the greatest endorsement of ethnic egalitarianism is most likely to be found among those in closest contact with agencies of communication and education, (3) low-status minorities seeking social mobility are most likely to meet with native resistance, (4) the rejection of minorities tends to be less severe in industrialized countries than in developing ones, and (5) the development of racist actions is not prevented by sentimental ties or legal guarantees.

What are the attitudes of the natives toward these outsiders? To what degree have they been accepted by the host societies? What success have the non-European minorities had in finding employment, securing housing, and educating their children? How do the non-European minorities respond to their treatment by the indigenous population of the host society? In general, what patterns of behavior have developed? What are the prospects for the future of these minorities who have taken up residence in the colonial mother country? Before we attempt to answer these questions, let us look briefly at the countries and groups involved.

Whereas France and Great Britain underwent colonial expansion at about the same time for about the same reasons, there are differences as well as similarities in their experiences. The French, with an empire much smaller in population, although possibly equal in area, were committed to the assimilation of their subject peoples. Their long-term objective was to incorporate the colonial territories into the French union on an equal basis. The British disdained long-term objectives and acquired a reputation for "muddling through." At first they regarded the empire as likely to remain on a colonial basis for the indefinite future. Later, the British accepted the inevitability of nationalist development and came to regard themselves as trustees who were preparing their colonial wards for self-government.

It is primarily because Arabs from northern Africa formed a high proportion of the migrants to France that we have used the term non-European rather than colored. The Arabs are sharply differentiated from the French in culture, but in physical appearance there is probably no more difference between Arabs and the average Frenchman than between those of darker and lighter complexion among the European French. Indeed, the French often speak of the Arab areas of Africa as *Afrique Blanche* ("White Africa"). There is no hard-and-fast color criterion for race, but the color contrast between Arabs and Europeans is so much less than between blacks and Europeans that it seemed unwise to lump them in the same color category. *Non-European* is a term which is neutral in regard to color and refers to all peoples whose recent origin is outside of the European continent.

The contrast between the situation of non-Europeans in Britain and France and the situation of the French and British in their colonies is brought out quite eloquently by Edgar Thompson in a review of a book

on the British situation.[1] His comments would apply equally well to the
French experience:

During recent years Britain has emerged as a minor but important race relations region. It is not a region such as is Northern Rhodesia exploiting native
labor in huge mining industries. It is not a region such as the South where a
master and a slave race together pushed the natives aside and occupied a territory by means of plantation settlement. It is not a region such as Hawaii where
white capitalists imported one racial labor group after another for large-scale
agricultural production. It is rather, a region where the "natives" are highly
civilized people. It is a "mother" country, and not a frontier as we have understood frontiers. It is a mother country to which her colonial and cultural children
of color have been returning from imperial possessions. It is a race relations region at the very center of what has been an expanding world community. If the
migratory movements which brought race contacts in the past have been centrifugal in character, this one is centripetal.

Most examples of racial contacts examined in this book have come about
because of the migration of Europeans to other continents. The two instances we are now reviewing, occur because of the migration of Africans
and Asians to Europe. The European migrants were usually able to enforce the submission of the native peoples. The Asian and African migrants find the natives difficult and must assume a subordinate rather than
a dominant status, although their subordination is modified by legal systems which seek to guarantee the rights of all individuals regardless of
race. Thus the migration of the non-Europeans to France and Britain
turns the previous patterns topsy-turvy and affords an example of intergroup relations in which the natives are more powerful than the migrants.

THE BRITISH EXPERIENCE

This chapter will treat separately the question of colonial immigrant
adjustment in France and Britain, but some similarities are worth noting.
Both France and Britain had a long-time colonial experience which involved intimate relationships between a small number of Europeans and
a great number and variety of other peoples. In both countries, the striking thing about large-scale migration to the empire homeland is that it
was so late in beginning; neither country saw very large immigration until
after World War II.

The British had been the rulers of the world's largest empire, one in
which the number of colonials far exceeded the number of native Britons.
As the seat of power of the world's largest and most diverse empire, Great

---

[1] Edgar T. Thompson, Review of Michael Banton, (*White and Colored: The Behavior of British People towards Coloured Immigrants*), in *Social Forces* 40 (October
1961): 94–95.

Britain, in general, and London, in particular, might have been expected to become a cosmopolitan mixture of peoples. Actually the picture is quite the reverse. It is true that the Soho district of London supports many foreign restaurants and that a collection of foreign students, diplomats, and traders has added diversity to London society. On the whole, however, Britain has been a remarkably homogeneous society with relatively little immigration from any quarter, and even that immigration represented people who usually have been assimilated in the society on a basis of "Anglo-conformity." As Michael Banton has said, "Britain is such a homogeneous society that it seems to rely heavily upon implicit norms and tacit modes of instruction."[2] This long tradition of homogeneity means that there is an intense suspicion of the stranger and that, since everybody is expected to pick up the social cues for proper behavior as a result of long exposure, there is no formal machinery for socializing newcomers in the society. It also means that, whatever success long-term assimilation may allow them to achieve, the initial role of newcomers is likely to be difficult. A comparison with some European immigration groups may be relevant at this point.

EUROPEAN IMMIGRANTS

Previous immigrants would include the Irish, who have been the principal source of immigration to the British Isles, Jews fleeing from the pogroms that occurred between 1880 and 1945, Huguenots seeking security and religious freedom, and many peoples displaced by the forces of World War II. The reaction to some of this early migration may be seen in a statement in a Tory election leaflet for 1900:

> The Radicals by their obstruction to the Aliens Bill, are evidently glad to see all foreigners who are criminals; who suffer from loathsome diseases; who are turned out in disgrace by their fellow-countrymen; who are paupers; who fill our streets with profligacy and disorder. The Unionist Government wants to keep these creatures out of Great Britain.[3]

Huguenots have assimilated to the point of disappearance as a recognizable group. Jews have been prominent in British life and have supposedly been almost completely anglicized, but there was still enough anti-Semitism in the country in the 1940s that agitators such as Sir Oswald Mosley could get a considerable following on the basis of anti-Semitism.

Although the Irish have been the most numerous immigrants to Great Britain and have amalgamated to a great extent through intermarriage,

---

[2] Michael Banton, *Race Relations* (New York, Basic Books, 1967), p. 371.

[3] Conservative Central Office, "Notes for Speakers, No. 325," cited in David Steel, *No Entry: The Background and Implications of the Commonwealth Immigrants Act, 1968* (London, C. Hurst and Company, 1969), p. 15.

their history has been one of considerable friction. Controversies over Irish independence affected relations between English and Irish, as did the Roman Catholic religious affiliation of the majority of Irishmen, although the major difficulty seems to have been contrasting life styles. In 1821 an English writer on moral and political problems expressed the sentiment that the effect of the Irish was definitely inimical to the British pattern of life. "Ireland, whose population, unless some other outlet be opened to them, must shortly fill every vacuum in England or Scotland, and reduce the labouring classes to a uniform state of degradation and misery."[4]

Occasional riots marred the relations between the British and the Irish and the naive and rural-oriented Irishman with his clay pipe became a stereotype of vaudeville humor on the British stage. In recent years open expression of hostility and prejudice has diminished, but the Chairman of the London Sessions in 1957 proclaimed "this court is infested with Irishmen who come here to commit offences and the more that can be persuaded to go back the better.[5]

The discussion of prejudice against the Irish should not lead to an exaggeration of their difficulties in Great Britain. The fact that heavy Irish immigration to Great Britain continued while the American quota of 19,000 Irish immigrants per year went for several years without being completely filled indicates that most Irishmen must have found the total picture in Britain attractive in spite of any discrimination which they may have faced. However, the fact that people with such a long relationship as the Irish and British, and with such a similarity in culture, could encounter this type of friction does underline the difficulty of immigrant adjustment to Great Britain.

COLONIAL IMMIGRATION

Large scale colonial immigration of permanent residents is usually dated from the arrival of the Empire Windship, which sailed from Kingston, Jamaica, in 1948 with 400 West Indian passengers. This immigration was regarded at first as being an isolated incident, but the new arrivals increased in volume until, in 1961, more than 66,000 West Indians arrived in Great Britain. During the same year, over 40,000 Indians and Pakistanis arrived. The numerical situation as of 1967 was summarized by Daniel as follows:

---

[4] R. Southey: *Essays Moral and Political* 2 (London, 1832): 275; reprinted in John Archer Jackson, *The Irish in Britain* (London, Routledge and Kegan Paul, 1963), p. 153.

[5] *The Manchester Guardian*, May 4, 1957, London; reprinted in Jackson, *The Irish in Britain*, p. 157.

Today, the total Commonwealth coloured immigrant population in Britain is estimated by the Home Secretary to be slightly over 1 million—or about 2 percent of the total British population of nearly 55 million. They include, according to the Ministry of Health, roughly 525,000 West Indians, 200,000 Indians, 125,000 Pakistanis, and 150,000 from Africa and other parts of the Commonwealth.[6]

The extent to which the non-European minorities in Great Britain will increase is dependent both on natural increase and immigration. Either of these may change, but the immigrant population is fairly young and in its home countries had a high birth rate. Immigration of adult workers has been sharply restricted, but the admission of dependents will bring in about 50,000 persons a year for the next few years unless this category too is further restricted. The British ministry of health in 1967 estimated that the non-European minorities might reach 3.5 million by 1985, which would make it about six percent of the population.[7] Such a prediction is probably high in view of the 1968 immigration restrictions, but there is no doubt that the non-European population will be more significant in size than in earlier years.

All the populations we have designated as colonials had a badge of color which distinguished them from the British. They had, however, rather considerable differences from each other. The colonials could be divided into three main groupings: the West Indians, the Asians, and the Africans. The West Indians, mostly from Jamaica and Trinidad, came from a society in which any indigenous cultural elements had been pretty well destroyed. Their language was English and their religion was similar to that of the British Christian churches. For them, England was much more the "mother country" and less the colonial overlord than for other groups. Their culture was a local variant of the culture which was best exemplified in the British Isles. Hence the West Indians came to Great Britain expecting assimilation and acceptance even though, for the most part, they regarded their sojourn as temporary and hoped to be able to accumulate capital and return to the Caribbean area.

The Asians were at the opposite end of the pole. Many of them were not English-speaking, their religion, Islam or Hinduism, separated them sharply from the British, and their mode of dress and ideals of family life were molded in a different culture. The Indians sought economic opportunity and access to public facilities, but it is doubtful that they either expected or desired assimilation.

Midway between these two groups were the West Africans. Most of the West Africans had had some exposure to a British system of education and

---

[6] W. W. Daniel, *Racial Discrimination in England* (London, Penguin Books, 1968), p. 9.

[7] Ibid., p. 10.

had at least a rudimentary grasp of the English language. However, they came from countries in which tribal society was still strong and in which British culture was an additional item rather than the basic ingredient of the life style. Religiously, many of the West Africans had moved toward the acceptance of a form of Christianity, although this had been a more recent, and therefore a more ambivalent, type of decision than was true with the West Indians.

Most of the colonials were poor and by British standards, inadequately educated. This does not mean that they formed a homogeneous social stratum, since they included over 70,000 Commonwealth students attending British universities, together with a considerable number of physicians, nurses, and businessmen. Kingsley Martin puts both the quality and the quantity of immigration into perspective with the following statement:

This inevitable increase of the coloured population will not be composed of immigrants but of British citizens, educated and often born in this country, who are for the most part treated as equals in schools, only to discover to their resentment when they are adolescent that they are second-class citizens. Actually, those who now come into this country are trained, professional people who are essential to our economy. They provide a high proportion of our nursing staff and nearly half the hospital doctors. How many people know that coloured immigrants—foreign and commonwealth—represent only a third of Britain's total immigrant population, that there are slightly fewer of them than there are Irish immigrants and considerably fewer than the total number of white immigrants from commonwealth and foreign countries?[8]

The non-European immigrants were primarily male and their traditional family pattern varied from British monogamy. The man who had left a wife at home might take a temporary mate and establish a family in Britain. When the Indian or Pakistani wife arrived, she usually retained her traditional sari and was often expected to observe purdah. The maintenance of traditional dress is, of course, visible evidence of her rejection of one aspect of British culture, and the effort to observe purdah necessarily limited her contacts with the British population, since purdah, by definition, is the restriction of women to the house. Immigrants tended to send for their relatives, and the flow of immigration, in recent years about 40,000–50,000, has consisted very largely of dependents.

The colonial immigration was not promoted by a deliberate government policy, and there were no plans set afoot by the national authorities to help the immigrants to adjust to their new environment. Some local authorities attempted to offer English-language classes or to foster interaction between the colored immigrants and the rest of the community, but their efforts were, for the most part, sporadic and ineffectual. The formal

---

[8] Kingsley Martin, "What Could Happen Here," *New Statesman* 75 (June 7, 1968), p. 759.

position of British mores was that, although the immigrants were strangers and hence somewhat ignorant of British customs, there was no need to treat them any differently from the native born white British. In any event, acquiring a real understanding of British culture was, as we mentioned earlier, thought to come about through informal rather than formal mechanisms and was not regarded as something to be accomplished by deliberate indoctrination.

PREJUDICE AND DISCRIMINATION

As the number of colonial immigrants increased and as various forms of tension occurred, considerable interest developed concerning the extent of prejudice and discrimination. A number of surveys were made which indicated that Britons were almost equally unwilling to admit to bigoted attitudes or to accept the colonial immigrants in what might be construed as intimate relations. The results of a series of attitude questions indicated a high degree of verbal tolerance as shown in Table 10–1.

TABLE 10–1

British racial attitudes

	Percent
Highly prejudiced	10
Prejudice inclined	17
Tolerance inclined	38
Tolerant	35

Source: Mark Abrams, "Attitudes of Whites towards Blacks," The Listener (Nov. 6, 1969), p. 623.

The expressions of prejudice did not seem to vary by proximity to the immigrant population and were approximately the same throughout the country. Generally the more prejudiced types were those who, because of age or social isolation, might be expected to have a more authoritarian view of life. Prejudice was lower among the better educated and among the youth. This tendency toward a greater tolerance among the youthful could be interpreted as a hopeful sign, but some observers have pointed out that the greater tendency toward violence among youth might counteract their lesser attraction to racial prejudice.[9] This means that, even though virulent racial prejudice might apply to only a small portion of the youth population, the youth so inclined might be disposed to enter into violent riots which in turn exacerbate the conflict and increase prejudice.

When one turns from the question of prejudice to that of discrimination the picture changes sharply. Discrimination included higher fees for auto-

---

[9] "Race and Generation Gaps," The Economist 233 (Dec. 27, 1969), pp. 11, 12.

mobile insurance, difficulty in securing housing, snubs and poor service from merchants, and bias in hiring. The flavor of discriminatory situations can be conveyed by the impressions of a white British girl who worked in a social research project concerning colonial immigrants in 1966:

> Apart from the question of discrimination, we have managed to get some idea of what it is like to be a coloured person in Moss Side. The majority when asked say that they are treated well, or more commonly that they "keep themselves to themselves." But my impression is that this is a front. Sometimes they say something like "It is a bit difficult but you get used to it," and it seems that after a time people do become almost immune to snubs. But occasionally we hear things like "You have no idea how bad it is to be black in this country," and we hear about people cutting them dead in the streets, serving white people before them in shops, refusing to sit next to them in the bus, and hundreds of petty little incidents that build up to make life unpleasant for people.[10]

It would be a mistake to conclude that every colored person is a victim of either overt or covert prejudice even though occasional examples can be cited. One of the authors chanced to talk with a neighbor of Emperor Hailie Selassie of Ethiopia during that monarch's World War II exile in London and was informed that his majesty's residence was regarded as "lowering the tone of the neighborhood!" However, the more highly placed colonial tends to be surrounded by people who seldom let raw prejudice come through. Kenneth Little's description of colonial professional men is to the point:

> The latter families generally have plenty of friends and acquaintances, and there is no apparent restraint on the grounds of color in this middle and upper-middle-class section of society. Contacts are made and friendships established through membership in various leftwing associations opposed to South African *apartheid* or in the course of professional work. In other cases, the white and the colored individuals concerned have met while the former was employed as a civil servant or as a university teacher in the latter's country. In social groups of this kind, use of the term "colored" is eschewed. Non-European people as well as non-European personalities are referred to as far as possible by their nationality. Although the parties concerned probably share a number of certain personal and intellectual interests, this practice implies a consciousness where "race" and "color" are concerned.[11]

DISCRIMINATION IN PRACTICE

Employment is a particularly controversial field. On the one hand, there were many British industries which were unable to attract white

---

[10] Dipak Nandy, *Race and Community* (Canterbury, University of Kent, 1968), p. 11.

[11] Kenneth Little: "Some Aspects of Color, Class and Culture in Britain," *Daedalus* 96 (Spring, 1967): 522–23.

workers for their jobs, and oftentimes textile mills, hospitals, and bus transportation were kept in operation only because of the work of colonial immigrants. While most of these colonials were in low status jobs, this fact is not unrelated to their qualifications, since many of them came from rural backgrounds with no experience in an industrial society, had very inadequate command of English, and had only a limited education. On the other hand, British workers were very afraid of competition with any kind of colonial workers. Employers expected colonials to be less stable and more difficult to supervise and there is little doubt that the colonials, for the most part, had to start at the bottom of the ladder and found social mobility far from easy.

This occupational structure is not atypical of the situation as a whole. By and large the immigrants have found ready employment whenever there has been a call for labor in semiskilled and unskilled capacities; professional and white-collar employment, however, tends to be another matter. . . . Some firms would take exceptional individuals; others, more liberal, were cutting back to stiffer quotas because they were being saturated with colored applicants and were afraid of getting a name as a "colored shop," still others were staffing whole departments, usually those with the heaviest and dirtiest jobs, with the colored workers.[12]

One of the best documented types of discrimination occurred in the purchase of insurance for automobiles. Some 20 insurance companies were visited by West Indian, Hungarian, and British researchers. They found that only three of the 20 firms gave the same terms to the West Indian as to the Hungarian or the British. There were three firms which refused to insure the West Indian at all, and the remaining 14 firms offered service but at sharply higher rates. There was relatively little difference between the terms offered the Hungarian and the Briton, although there were four firms which asked slightly higher rates from the Hungarian than from the Briton.[13] In defense of the insurance company practices, it should be mentioned that the West Indian did not have a proof of a record as a policyholder. Regardless of whether or not this might have justified the insurance company's hesitancy, there is no question how this treatment appeared to the colonials.

The housing pattern for colonials is somewhat different from that experienced by minorities in other countries. It is true that the colonials usually lived in the less favored sections of the town and that they occupied older houses under more crowded conditions than was true of the British generally. On the other hand, there were no solid ghettos, since there were few districts of any kind which had more than 50 percent of colonial

---

[12] Ibid., pp. 512–22.
[13] Daniel, *Racial Discrimination in England,* pp. 201–3.

population, and evidence between 1961 and 1966 showed some dispersal away from the central areas. A most peculiar feature of the situation is that the proportion of the colonials owning property actually appeared to be higher than for the British. Jamaicans, in central London, for instance, were three times as likely to be owner occupiers as were the natives[14] and a majority of the landlords brought up for housing code violations in cases involving colonials were colonials themselves.[15]

The explanation for the greater degree of home ownership is not the prosperity of the colonials, but discrimination against them in rental property. Most of the rental property (except furnished rooms) has simply not been available to colored or colonials, or not available except on exorbitant terms. This is especially true of public housing Council property in which British applications are usually filled before the colonials are even considered. Faced with this situation, many of the colonials have bought houses, and, in turn, financed them by overcrowding them with fellow colonials.

Education has also brought difficulties. The children of colonials are subject to the compulsory education laws applying to other residents of the British Isles and thus have the opportunity of public education available. They meet with hostility on occasion, however, from white Britons who feel that the presence of immigrant children lowers the quality of school work. This fear of the white Englishmen that the colonial children lower school performance may be exaggerated, since at least one analysis found that at the 11 plus stage there was no significant difference between them and the other pupils.[16] Most studies do not show such a result and whatever the long-term outcome, there are real problems for colonial children and the fears of British parents are at least understandable.

The British policy has been one of integration, and liberals tend to minimize the differences between colonial and native children. Whether this attitude is realistic, given the language and learning handicaps of the immigrant children, is questionable. Even the West Indians, who in many ways regard themselves as British, have language difficulties. On this topic Bell remarks:

Many West Indians especially those from country areas, speak a Creole which is admittedly based on English, but is not merely a dialect of it as say Liverpudlian or "broad Norfolk" are. It is a discrete language which varies from the

---

[14] Nicholas Deakin, "Race and Human Rights in the City," *Urban Studies* (November 1969), p. 394.

[15] Nicholas Deakin, "Residential Segregation in Britain: A Comparative Note," *Race* 6 (July 1964), p. 23.

[16] "The Education of Immigrant Pupils in Primary Schools," L.L.E.A. Report no. 959, December 1967, cited in Nandy *Race and Community*, p. 9.

standard English not only in accent but also in vocabulary and grammar. It is so deviant that it is now unintelligible to English people.[17]

Placing the colonial children in a standard British classroom means that they are simply bewildered, and, faced with academic defeat, are likely to become behavior problems and disturb school discipline. Thus there is a tendency to provide "reception classes" in which the colonial children can spend at least a part of the day in a class designed for their linguistic situation. Schools are also likely to assign colonial children to classes for retarded children in a pathetic confusion of cultural and genetic problems. Education authorities have stressed techniques for teaching English as a foreign language and have provided extra clerical and welfare staff for schools with a large proportion of colonial children.[18] Such efforts are no doubt helpful, but the fact remains that the entry of a large number of children whose English is either limited or nonexistent places major strains on the schools and educational difficulties become one of the more difficult aspects of race relations.

TABLE 10–2

British housing tenure by ethnic group
(percentages)

Ethnic category	Owner-occupiers	Renting furnished	Renting unfurnished	Council renting	Other	Number of households
English	3	7	53	24	3	9,604°
Jamaican	25	61	12	1	1	7,597
Other Caribbean	9	75	14	1	1	5,211
Indian	16	48	26	7	3	2,190
Pakistani	18	58	16	5	3	269
Irish	33	18	35	13	1	3,793
Polish	8	34	40	15	3	13,914
Cypriot	34	28	30	6	2	1,891

° 1 in 25 sample of English households.
Source: Full Census analysis cited in R. B. Davison: *Black British: Immigrants to England* (London, Oxford University Press, 1966), p. 53.

Language difficulty inevitably brings problems to the schools. Even Nandy, in arguing that these problems are exaggerated, asserts that 49 percent of immigrant children in British schools had no language difficulties. This is hardly a reassuring statement to anxious parents, since it means that at least half of the immigrant children did have some type of language difficulty and could be expected, therefore, to produce problems of communication in the school room.[19]

---

[17] Roger T. Bell, "Education," *Fabian Research Series 262: Policies for Racial Equality* (July 1967), p. 10.

[18] Henry Miller, "Race Relations and the Schools in Great Britain," *Phylon* 27 (Fall 1966): 254–55.

[19] Nandy, *Race and Community*, p. 9.

There are, of course, individual immigrant children who are good students and the average performance improves with the period of time in the country. Even with the passage of time, though, the average performance by native British children is still superior, and for the recent immigrant the difference is great indeed. Whatever the long-term adjustment, there can be no doubt that the initial school experience of immigrant children is traumatic for them and also disturbing to native children who are in the same classes. Table 10–3, based on a survey of 52 British schools, summarizes the situation.

TABLE 10–3

Achievement of Native and Immigrant Children in
London Primary Schools

| | Percentages in groups 1 & 2 (high) | | | |
| | Immigrants | | | |
	Recent	Long Stay	Na- tive	All
English	1–6	13	23	25
Verbal reasoning	1–9	12	25	25
Mathematics	2–3	14	24	25

| | Percentages in groups 3, 4, 5, (medium) | | | |
| | Immigrants | | | |
	Recent	Long Stay	Na- tive	All
English	23–3	50	52	50
Verbal reasoning	19–7	45	48	50
Mathematics	23–3	47	50	50

| | Percentages in groups 6 & 7 (low) | | | |
| | Immigrants | | | |
	Recent	Long Stay	Na- tive	All
English	75–1	38	24	25
Verbal reasoning	78–4	42	27	25
Mathematics	74–4	40	27	25

Source: Alan Little, Christine Mabey, and Graham Whitaker, "The Education of Immigrant Pupils in Inner London Primary Schools," *Race* 9 (April 1968) p. 452. Published for the Institute of Race Relations, London, by the Oxford University Press, Copyright by Institute of Race Relations, 1968.

EFFECTS OF THE KENYAN CRISIS

Racial difficulties within Britain were compounded by the effect of racial difficulties in Kenya, a former British colony. The difficulty in Kenya concerned the relations between Africans and Indians after the independence of the country in 1963. The Indians, for the most part, were descendents of railway workers who came in 1895 to help the British build the Uganda Railway. They comprised only two percent of the population, but they formed the middle class between the British and the Africans and were far more important in an economic sense than their numbers would indicate. For instance, at the time of independence, 695 of the 750 physicians practicing in Kenya were of Asian origin.[20] Their proportions in other fields were not as high, but they formed a considerable section of the government employees and of the commercial middle class.

British policies provided for a differential pay scale in governmental and commercial jobs, with Indians receiving about two thirds of the European salary but still more than twice the stipend given to Africans. A few of the Indians operated substantial businesses and had become wealthy. The Indian contribution to Kenya was recognized as early as 1908 by Winston Churchill, who wrote:

It is the Indian trader who, penetrating and maintaining himself in all sorts of places to which no white man would go, or in which no white man could earn a living, has more than anyone else developed the early beginnings of trade and opened up the first slender means of communication. It was by Indian labour that the one vital railway on which everything else depends was constructed. It is the Indian banker who supplies perhaps the largest part of the capital yet available for business and enterprise, and to whom the white settlers have not hesitated to recur for financial aid.[21]

One might argue that the Indians formed a valuable and practically indispensable element of the Kenyan population. They provided expertise, capital, and enterprise in a country in which these factors were in short supply. Although uncertain about the effect of independence on their status, they had, for the most part, not opposed the nationalist movement and frequently had been at odds with the British. The Indians were criticized for social exclusiveness, a superiority complex, and a reluctance to place Africans in management positions in their firms. Some effort had been made by Indians to be conciliatory on these points, but they were not convincing to the African masses or politicians.

To the Africans, the Indians did not appear as a population making a contribution, but as aliens occupying an economic niche which otherwise

---

[20] Steele, *No Entry*, p. 134.

[21] Sir Winston Churchill, *My African Journey* (London, Holland Press, 1964), pp. 33–34.

might be available to Africans. Consequently, disillusionment with the fact that independence failed to bring in the promised economic benefits for Africans stimulated hostility toward the Indian minority. Indian shop-keepers were blamed for rising prices and Indian civil servants were accused of holding jobs which might belong to Africans. The result was a policy of "Africanization" under which aliens had to receive specific government sanction to hold jobs or to engage in business. At the same time, if they wished to leave the country, they were restricted in the amount of capital which they might take with them.

The Indians were all classified as British subjects and holders of British passports. They were given an opportunity at the time of independence to opt for Kenyan citizenship if they so desired. Many of the Indians, however, felt that Kenyan citizenship would probably not protect them against discriminatory treatment and would deprive them of the one refuge to which they might look—escape to Great Britain. Others who did apply found that the process of gaining citizenship was unexpectedly slow and that years might pass before action was taken on a citizenship application. In the summer of 1967, the screws began to be tightened; permits for employment were frequently given for periods of only three to six months' time, schools were often unavailable for Indian children, and the slowness and uncertainty of action by the Kenyan government on Indian citizenship applications added to the confusion.

Immigration to Britain had begun to be noticeable at the time of independence in 1963; by the summer of 1967 it had reached 1,000 a month and, in September, had reached 2,631. In January 1966, the Kenya cabinet decided that the process of Africanization had been too slow and designated another 20,000 jobs held by Indians which were to be opened up to Africans. Job permits were restricted to three months, by the end of which time individuals were expected to be ready to leave the country, and a bond of 150 pounds was required to pay for deportation costs in case that should be necessary.

Within Britain itself, the arrival of the Kenyan Asians stimulated anxiety about the size and nature of the colonial immigration. Enoch Powell estimated that 200,000 Indians might come from Kenya to the United Kingdom, an estimate which most authorities felt was 150,000 too great.[22] He and many other leaders called for an end to all colored immigration into the United Kingdom. Both the Tory party and the Labour government bore responsibility for the situation which had allowed the Indians to have British passports originally, but both began to give in to the agitation. Evidence that changes in the Immigration Act might take place stimulated panic among Indian Kenyans who, in February 1968, began to leave

---

[22] Martin Ennals, "U.K. Citizens of Asian Origin in Kenya," in Steele, *No Entry*, pp. 248–51.

Kenya at the rate of 750 a day. Elaborate plans were under way to "beat the ban" and get to Britain by chartering flights and arranging mass exits. The plans did not materialize in many cases, and there were hysterical mob scenes at the Nairobi airport as thousands of Indians clamoured for passage. In the last week before the passage of the restrictive bill, some 10,000 Indians did succeed in leaving Kenya and arriving in Britain.

LEGISLATION

Framing a bill to discourage immigration of the Kenyan immigrants was a difficult job, since it meant the abandonment of promises made by the British government at an earlier date and the devaluation of British citizenship. Further, it was essentially a racist type of bill which had to be framed without racist designation. The problem was solved by special provisions referring to citizens of the United Kingdom and the colonies who desired to enter the United Kingdom without voucher or special permits. According to the law, this could only be done by those who themselves or whose fathers or grandfathers were either born in the United Kingdom or had become naturalized in the United Kingdom itself. For others entry was restricted to a limit of 1,500 heads of households and their dependents per year. Thus approximately 350,000 people who thought they held British passports became essentially stateless persons who had only very limited possibility of admission to Britain and who were fast losing any rights at all in the countries in which they lived.

The British passion for "fairness" meant that some gesture had to be undertaken to make amends for the restrictive immigration law. This measure was found in a 1968 Race Relations Act which was modeled after the civil rights laws in the United States. It established a Race Relations Board empowered to deal with discrimination in housing, public accommodations, and employment. Apparently the premise of the bill was that, while immigration restrictions prevented Britain from being overwhelmed by a tide of colonial immigrants, there was still need for efforts to improve relationships between the immigrants already in the country and the rest of the population. The bill places a heavy reliance on conciliation, especially the voluntary conciliation of employment complaints by industry. In the first year of its life, it received 1,562 complaints, which was about twice the number that the framers of the law had expected.[23] This act has removed such racial irritants as advertisements indicating that "no colored need apply," and should protect the colonial immigrants from the most overt types of discrimination. Obviously the act does little by itself to deal with tensions arising from different social customs or with poverty associated with limited education and a lack of systematic work habits. Per-

---

[23] "A Year's Law," *The Economist* (Nov. 29, 1969): 223–34.

haps the main value of the law is in a symbolic affirmation that the colonial immigrants do have the same rights as if born in the United Kingdom and that black or brown Britons must be regarded as first-class citizens.

FUTURE PROSPECTS

Probably the major question in looking at the future prospects of intergroup relations in the United Kingdom is in the definition of the situation. At least two interpretations are possible. One is that the difficulties of the colonial immigrants are comparable to those of the Irish and other minorities in the past and foreshadow a time of eventual assimilation and acceptance. Another viewpoint is that the United Kingdom has a race relations situation which is not going to lead to assimilation, but to a continuing pluralistic society. Arguments for the development of a pluralistic society included the feeling that the badge of color makes it impossible for non-Europeans to lose their ethnic identity, that the growing third world consciousness leads to a conscious resistance to assimilation and that communication with the home communities is strong enough to keep alive distinct cultural interests. On the other hand, it is argued that the Race Relations Act will reduce discrimination and that with the passage of time the immigrant will absorb the local culture and become a "black Englishman." Further, the number of immigrants is too small to keep alive a vigorous ethnic community. There is no absolute figure which must be reached to maintain a separate community, but this is obviously easier with a large growing minority population. The non-Europeans now comprise only a small proportion of the population, and it seems unlikely that they will ever become more than six percent of the total. Birth rates, which are now high, are expected to level off and the restrictions on immigration limit that source of increase.

Any weakening of the immigration ban seems to be exceedingly unlikely, since the response to the demands by Enoch Powell for a "Keep Britain White" policy was far too strong to be ignored. In fact, a public opinion poll, taken shortly after his speech in April 1968, found that 75 percent of Britons were in favor of stricter curbs on immigration and 71 percent were afraid of racial violence of the type seen in the United States.[24] Certainly, it seems unlikely that the United Kingdom in the foreseeable future will adopt a more open immigration policy or that the colored population will exceed six percent of the total, even at the most generous estimates.

One major aspect concerning the future of assimilation in Great Britain concerns the attitude of the younger generation. At present, most of the colonial immigrants are adults, but a generation of children are growing

---

24 "Now: Mounting Racial Trouble in Britain," *U.S. News and World Report* (May 6, 1968), p. 64.

up who will have been reared and educated in the United Kingdom. One possibility for their behavior is that they will repeat the second generation's syndome which has characterized many American immigrants and will react against the parental culture in an effort to secure complete identification with British society. As Banton suggests, if the major conflict becomes one between the immigrant fathers trying to hold onto the culture of the country of their origin and their children attempting to become more British, this conflict will probably weaken second generation demands for acceptance and give the British a little longer period in which to come to terms with the minorities in their midst.[25] Such a situation might most easily come to pass with the children of Indian and Pakistani immigrants, who have a rather cohesive and closely structured ethnic community in Britain against which they may revolt.

For the West Indian and African children, the prospects of this second generation revolt are more remote simply because their parents have not offered them a type of culture which contrasts sharply with that dominant in British society, and hence, for this group, there is little conflict between home and assimilation. It is also entirely possible that all groups may be influenced by "third world" demands for cultural recognition and rejection of the West as a model. Nor can we be sure that the Race Relations Act and similar reform measures will lead to an easy accommodation. Experience of the United States would indicate that, whereas discrimination and repression led to resentment and revolt, rapid social mobility may have the same effect. Rapid social mobility usually stimulates increased expectations, and these expectations are always in excess of actual attainments. In the interpretation of social phenomena there is very frequently the attitude which Banton defines as "majoritarian" and "minoritarian."[26] The majoritarian usually has a fairly comfortable conscience because he is a relativist. He tends to take a historical viewpoint and he can see an improvement over a period of time against which the remaining obstacles or inequities seem relatively trivial. The minoritarian, on the other hand, tends to be an absolutist. He does not compare the society in which he lives against the much more imperfect society of the past, but against a type of utopia in which there is no disparity between the real and the ideal. Thus the same society which seems to the majoritarian, progressive, and friendly to minority relations will, to the minoritarian, seen unjust, discriminatory, and racist.

So far the "black power" type of organizations which proclaim an allegiance to separatism and a distrust of white cooperation have been comparatively powerless in the United Kingdom. However, every speech by Enoch Powell concerning the menace of the colored immigrant pro-

---

25 Banton, *Race Relations*, p. 392.
26 Ibid., p. 388.

motes a counter truculence among at least some of the colonial immigrant population. As yet the number of militants is small, but the existence of even such a minority indicates the potential of this kind of reaction. Perhaps more to the point than occasional shrill statements from small groups, which may not have more than a dozen members, is the continued vitality of minority expression. This minority cultural expression indicates that the process of assimilation is far from rapid and the older loyalties are slow to die. Gordon Lewis describes the cultural scene as follows:

There are the novels of Andrew Salkey that document the idiocies of English social snobbery. There are the musical forms—the Jamaican "sound-beat," Trinidad calypsos, the Indian ceremonial dirges—that sustain the separate immigrant life-styles. There is the ghetto life, more psychological than physical in character, that builds up defence-mechanisms against the alien English influence; indeed, it is only in the last few years that the West Indian-Somali-Cypriot life of Tiger Bay, cut off from the Cardiff white citizenry by its railway barrier, has given way to assimilative processes precipitated by slum clearance measures. There is, finally, the intimate tie with the homeland, marked even in the most pro-English group, the West Indians, as the continuing open sale of the Jamaican paper, the *Daily Gleaner,* in the West Indian areas shows.[27]

In today's world, with the strident insistence on a separate identity by many peoples and tribes, the conventional theories of the social status of the colonial immigrants seem unsatisfactory. It is doubtful that the color-class theory of the British Communist party is sufficient to explain all ethnic differences, and it would be utopian indeed to argue that social mobility among the immigrant population and the elimination of alleged capitalist exploitation would lead to assimilation. Neither is the concept of the colored immigrant as the "archetypal stranger" altogether satisfactory. Indeed, it is possible that those experiencing social mobility will also be exposed to rising expectations which will increase social discontent. Further, it is possible that the increased association which diminishes the feeling of strangeness may also increase the competitive struggle, which can easily be defined in ethnic terms.

The United Kingdom is thus a country without a strong tradition of open racial discrimination, in which no major group espoused a racist ideology and which some of the colored immigrants regarded as their cultural homeland. Nevertheless, the ethnic conflicts and adjustments which have taken place appear strikingly similar to those in countries which have known a history of slavery and a racist ideology. The problems of ethnic adjustment seem strikingly similar regardless of the disparity of historical background.

---

[27] Gordon K. Lewis, "Protest Among the Immigrants: the Dilemma of Minority Culture," *The Political Quarterly* 40 (October 1969): 434–35.

The restriction of immigration may lessen the fears of the majority, while the increasing assimilation of the minority may make them seem less "strange" and therefore more capable of being accepted as an integral part of British society. On the other hand, the presence of over one million colored people, probably destined to increase to three million before the figure stabilizes, furnishes a recognizable and obvious scapegoat for all the ills of British society. Nor is it true that the problems of assimilation are altogether due to British resistance. The Third World has its own siren call which appears increasingly attractive to the young seeking recognition and impatient with the slow rate of progress in Western society.

NON-EUROPEAN MINORITIES IN FRANCE

While both France and Great Britain had colonial empires there were many differences in their racial attitudes and policies. Assimilation, which, to the British, was irrelevant, became a major theme of French colonial policy, although practiced more often in theory than in reality. The civilizing mission of France was not simply to spread French culture, but to bring the colonial peoples to the point of development at which they were worthy of full status as French citizens. French assimilation policy was never carried through consistently by the French Colonial office and, in the end, was rejected by many of the colonial peoples themselves, as we indicated in our discussion of Senegal; but, nevertheless, it left a residue of acceptance. The participation of a few black politicians in the Chamber of Deputies in their capacity as citizens of the French Union is a symbol of a degree of acceptance of men in spite of racial background. Between the French and the British Empires, there were differences in size as well as philosophy, since the French empire at its height probably numbered no more than 30 million people. It lacked such colossal populations as those of India, and the French had little fear that they would eventually be overwhelmed by the sheer number of the colonial subjects.

The similarities between France and Britain, however, may be even more striking. Both of them sought, for a time, to guarantee freedom of immigration between their past or present colonies and the metropolitan area, and neither of them experienced any large influx of non-European immigrants until after World War II. In spite of the allegedly greater tolerance of the French, the same complaints are made by non-European immigrants in France that have appeared in Britain, and the same kinds of tensions between the aliens and the French population have arisen.

One major difference when looking at the non-European minorities is that those who came to France include something over one-half million Arabs from Algeria, who come from what the French refer to as *Afrique blanche*, meaning that many of the Arabs are not recognizably darker than the Frenchman and that there is more difference between the Arabs and the African blacks than there is between Arabs and French in physical appearance.

Immigrant workers began coming into France when the reconstruction needs after World War II indicated the need for foreign labor. The greatest number of these came from Europe; mostly from Italy, but with considerable numbers from Spain, Poland, and Belgium, along with a few from Germany and Switzerland.

The Algerians formed the second largest group of migratory workers, next to the Italians. There were only 50,000 Algerians in France in 1947, but their population had increased to 400,000 by 1960.[28] French industry has been expanding faster than the increase in French population has produced new workers, and it is estimated that, in time, France could absorb as many people as the 1960 population of Algeria (8,000,000).[29] While the Algerian workers come from a country which has been under French rule for more than a century, most of them are illiterate and unskilled and occupy the lowest rungs of the French occupational structure. Like the non-European minorities in Britain, the Algerians for the most part came to France without families, regarding their stay as temporary, sending back the equivalent of a $100,000,000 a year to Algeria in remittances and hoping someday to return to the homeland. Unlike the British immigrants, few of them have sent for their families or give indication of a permanent residence. They are described as making "minimum demands on accommodations," and perhaps too typical is the following description of a hotel just outside of Paris:

> A long filthy corridor has on either side rooms in which the beds are run up the walls. These three-bunk-high rooms are just large enough for a pile of bunks against each wall, with room to walk between. The rooms are dark; between the rows of bunks the men's washing hangs from a string. A sink for hand and face washing, a kitchen for elementary cooking, and extremely primitive lavatories are crammed in the yard outside.
>
> The man who runs this "hotel" is an African, from Mali. He claims that he in his turn is exploited by the French owner of the building. He and his brother have three establishments, totalling a thousand beds, between them . . .[30]

That this situation was not unusual is indicated in an article by Marlene Tuninga, in which she states that it was not unusual to pack ten men into a single room and that cellars, attics, or old factories are frequently used

---

[28] Vernon Waughray, "The French Racial Scene: North African Immigrants in France," *Race* 2 (November 1960): 64.

[29] Ibid., p. 61.

[30] "The Black Side of Paris," *The Economist* 216 (July 3, 1965): 20.

as dormitories. Her estimate is that not even a fourth of the non-European workers had accommodations which could be said to even approximate decent housing.[31]

The situation of the Algerians in France was complicated by the revolt in Algeria which eventually resulted in independence for that country. This movement for Algerian independence was resisted bitterly by the French, since over 1,000,000 French *colons*, or "settlers," lived in Algeria and many French statesmen proclaimed proudly that "Algeria is France." The period of struggle did not leave the Algerians resident in France untouched, and there were frequent riots between rival factions of Algerian parties represented among those living in France. This, in turn, resulted in curfew restrictions for the Algerians by the French government, mass protest by the Algerians, savage repression of demonstrations by the police, and a general feeling of tension between the Algerians and many of the French population. The grant of independence to Algeria has minimized the political differences, but leaves many problems unsolved. Unemployment in Algeria is still very high, resulting in continuing migration from Algeria to France in search of jobs. The French and the Algerian government in 1964 reached an agreement to limit the Algerians to those workers who had been given a work permit, and who had passed a medical examination. This had the temporary effect of reducing the flow of migration. However, this measure soon became ineffective, since Algerians found they could get around the law by simply stating that they were coming to France as "tourists." Thus the migration continued unchecked at an increment of about 50,000 a year.

There were in 1965 perhaps 160,000 black non-European immigrants in France, including those from French West Africa and from the French departments of Martinique, Guadeloupe, and Reunion.[32] These latter areas, which are now departments of France, have unrestricted immigration privileges, but since their total population is small the number of immigrants they can send out is obviously restricted.

PREJUDICE: BLACK AND WHITE

It is perhaps both the comparatively small number of blacks eligible for migration to France and the bitter experience with Algerians during the revolt which have produced attitudes in France apparently unrelated to color. A survey in 1967 on the attitudes of the French toward blacks,

---

[31] Marlene Tuninga, "African New Wave in France," *Institute of Race Relations Newsletter* (September 1964), p. 12.

[32] John Guynn, "French without Tears," *Institute of Race Relations Newsletter* (November 1965), p. 16.

Arabs, and Jews found that, with various criteria combined, 34 percent of a sample of men holding professional positions in Paris were prejudiced against Jews, 52 percent against blacks, and 65 percent against Arabs. As in the United Kingdom, prejudice was less marked among the younger people and those with more education and higher incomes. Table 10–4

TABLE 10–4

Degrees of prejudice against Jews, Negroes, and Arabs
(percent)°

Having as a professional colleague:	Jew(s)	Negro(s)	Arab(s)
Situations			
Happy	22	22	15
Indifferent	67	69	52
Rather discontented	4	5	17
Very discontented	7	4	16
Having as a personal friend:			
Happy	26	26	18
Indifferent	65	66	57
Rather discontented	4	5	12
Very discontented	5	3	13
Having as a son-in-law:			
Happy	14	9	7
Indifferent	54	40	29
Rather discontented	18	26	26
Very discontented	14	25	38
Attributes of the prejudiced			
Age:			
20–29	25	36	51
30–39	30	49	62
40–49	36	62	72
50+	47	62	75
Salary:			
Up to Fr. 1,000	42	47	68
Fr. 1,000–Fr. 2,000	35	53	65
Fr. 2,001–Fr. 3,000	28	55	62
Fr. 3,000+	35	56	62
Education:			
Primary	41	54	70
Technical	26	53	64
Secondary	30	52	64
Higher	26	42	52
Religion:			
Catholic	40	58	73
Non-Catholic	19	33	43
Political affiliation:			
Extreme left	22	38	50
Left	28	48	62
Center	43	65	75
Right	53	73	82
Extreme right	48	55	81
Marais ("At sea")	37	52	65

Source: *Institute of Race Relations Newsletter*, N. S. vol. 2 (January 1968), p. 35.
° Based on sample survey of French men.

gives a summary of French attitudes which would seem to belie the stereotype that the French are relatively unprejudiced.

FUTURE PROSPECTS

It seems unlikely that the French will follow the British lead in sharply restricting immigration from Africa and from the remaining French departments outside of Europe. In part, this is because the populations, only about 1 million in the departments, 20 million in West Africa, and 8 million in Algeria, did not offer the potential immigration which was true of the former British possessions. It also appears to be unlikely because of a continuing need for immigration to France, which is probably threatened by industrial development in Spain, Italy, and Portugal, the prime sources of manpower in the past.

The French seem to have a higher proportion of temporary workers who leave their families in Algeria and return home after two or three years than has been true of the British. Temporary workers do not seek complete incorporation in the nation and are more willing to accept a relatively segregated type of social life. It may be that, in the future, an increasing number of these workers will remain in metropolitan France and that the problem of their identity as Arabs, blacks, or Frenchmen will become more pressing and will put to an increasingly severe test the viability of the French devotion to the principle of assimilation. So far the total number involved are relatively small and the majority of workers still leave their families in their original habitat. In the meantime the need for additional labor continues and migration is unimpeded. There will probably be an increasing struggle to maintain an identity which is at once French and something more; but it is doubtful whether the struggle will reach the pitch it has attained in Britain, where a group of permanent non-European residents waver between assimilation in Britain and identification with a homeland which has several times the population of the British Isles.

FRANCO-BRITISH NON-EUROPEAN MINORITY PATTERNS IN RELATION TO GENERALIZED INTERGROUP BEHAVIOR PATTERNS

French pattern. Verbal indications of prejudice showed a greater rejection of Arabs than of blacks.

Generalized pattern. Sharp political conflict combined with cultural differences may produce more antagonism between groups of similar physical appearance than exists between groups of more sharply differentiated physical appearance but less salient political conflict. In other words, in some circumstances, hostility against those of the same color can be greater than against those of a different color.

Franco-British pattern. The young, the better educated, and the more wealthy showed less verbal indication of ethnic prejudice than the aged, the poor, and the uneducated.

Generalized pattern. When the respectable morality endorses ethnic egalitarianism, this will be accepted most by those in greatest contact with agencies of communication and education.

Franco-British pattern. Professionals from former colonies were drawn to work in France and Britain, and found fairly good social acceptance.

Generalized pattern. High-status individuals, not regarded as too competitive by their local counterparts, are usually favorably received.

Franco-British pattern. The bulk of non-European immigrants are welcomed in low-status jobs but meet discrimination when they attempt to find better positions.

Generalized pattern. Efforts toward social mobility made by low-status minorities meet native resistance. Current patterns of development in the more industrialized nations lead to a demand for social mobility which makes nationals unwilling to take low-status jobs. Immigrants are welcomed for these positions but meet discrimination when their push for better positions makes them competitive with majority group citizens.

British-Kenyan pattern. Kenya has taken discriminatory measures which have caused large numbers of Indians to leave the country. Great Britain has passed legislation to protect minorities against discrimination and, even with the immigration restriction, still allows a small number of non-Europeans to enter the country.

Generalized pattern. Rejection of minorities tends to be more severe in developing countries than in those already industrialized. While industrialized countries are worried by prospects of mass immigration, they can usually tolerate an existing minority population. Developing areas, however, tend to regard all permanent aliens as competing with nationals and to drive aliens out of the economy and thereby out of the country.

British pattern. Despite a desire to maintain Commonwealth ties and despite the fact that some potential non-European immigrants held British passports, their entry into Great Britain was heavily restricted.

Generalized pattern. Neither sentimental ties nor legal guarantees are adequate protection against the development of racist actions when the minority is regarded as a threat to the majority.

Franco-British pattern. Despite the small size of the non-European minorities a few militant separatist groups existed.

Generalized pattern. When identity as a member of the host community is blocked or accorded on a subordinate basis, the minority, if it regards itself as permanent or long-term residents, will demand recognition as a separate entity. Since assimilation is seldom complete, some degree of separatist activity is probably to be expected in most mixed ethnic situations.

British pattern. Although the British have not discriminated against non-Europeans in the provision of school facilities, there is much criticism of the schools by both the majority and the minority group.

Generalized pattern. School achievement reflects the motivation and the home culture of the student as well as the quality of education facilities provided. Educational facilities which are "fair" or "equal" but which fail to take account of minority backgrounds will usually lead to disappointing results. The minority students fail to learn at the expected pace and their frustration leads to conduct which limits the usefulness of the classroom for all students. Highly motivated children from groups with a great respect for education, such as Jews or Asian Indians, may overcome these obstacles and make good academic progress. In most groups, however, the first or even second generation to be exposed to the American-European type of educational process will include a high proportion of low achievers. Whether efforts to adapt the school to minority culture will improve the learning process still remains to be demonstrated.

Franco-British pattern. The tendency was for non-European migrants to rent quarters owned by landlords of their own race. The rents charged were sometimes exorbitant in terms of prices which had existed before the migrants entered the district, and the accommodations were frequently overcrowded and lacking in sanitary facilities.

Generalized pattern. The rate charged for the provision of goods and services is determined by market conditions regardless of the ethnic relationship of parties involved. The rent charged for housing is not determined by considerations of ethnic solidarity or differences but by the supply and demand forces operating in the market. The native landlord will not be able to raise rents if the supply of housing is surplus; on the other hand, the landlord who is of the same ethnic group as his tenants is not likely to overlook a chance for higher rent when a short supply of housing tilts the demand-supply situation. In any economic situation, one can best make an analysis, not by knowing the ethnic background of contending parties, but simply by being aware of the forces which affect supply and demand. Frequently minority entrepreneurs may be accused of exploiting their own ethnic group. Whether the charge of exploitation is justified or not is doubtful, since they are providing a service which other businessmen have failed to provide. In any event, the minority person looking about for profit-making opportunities is likely to see those affecting his own people first. On the other hand, the needs of minority peoples are not as likely to be brought to the attention of the majority group of businessmen. Thus we find that the provision of services is often for the minority by their own members and at a rate which may seem excessive in terms of prices charged before a minority influx increased the demand.

British pattern. Housing surveys indicate that only about one to three percent of most of the non-European minorities have been able to find "Council" housing. This is government housing provided at a low cost by the municipal authorities. The presumed explanation of this situation is that there is a long list of applicants for housing and that they are selected in order of application. In addition, there are other requirements such as seniority in terms of residence in the area, in which migrants stand rather low. Supposedly, the lack of non-European minority representation in Council housing is simply a result of the impact of impartial regulations, but such a conclusion overlooks the fact that local administrative bodies usually find a way to favor the majority local group. John Rex of the Fabian Society concludes as follows:

There can be little doubt that there is systematic discrimination against immigrants in local authority housing, though it rarely occurs in the form of an explicit policy excluding colored people from housing. What is the case is that a system which does and must discriminate between one applicant and another is used in practice to discriminate against colored applicants.[33]

The mechanics of such discrimination may or may not result from the letter of the law. The refusal to consider the special needs of minorities or to change regulations to meet these needs simply underlines the fact that, whenever there is a restricted supply, the outsiders tend to find little help from local authorities.

Generalized pattern. Goods and services provided by local governmental units often discriminate against minorities. The very fact that the local government unit is close to the people and responsive to their needs and demands enables it to take somewhat narrow policies of group favoritism. This practice is more difficult on a national level, where rules and policies are usually framed in universalistic terms, and national bodies are reluctant to give overt expression to discriminatory attitudes. Another example of such a situation can be found in the relationship of American Indians to the federal government. While the Indians are frequently disappointed in their relationship with the federal government, they have learned to expect the worst possible outcome in their relationships with state and local governments, where rules of universalistic policy are much less binding. Consequently, American Indians have usually fought any

---

[33] John Rex, "Housing," *Fabian Research Series 262: Policies for Racial Equality* (London, Fabian Society, July 1967), p. 22.

attempt to reduce their rights as "wards" and place them under the control of state governments. There are, no doubt, exceptions, but, in general, minorities are likely to get greater consideration from national bodies operating on universalistic standards than from local authorities directly responsible to a vested local interest.

British pattern. A British politician, Enoch Powell, was able to attract a large following for a platform barring colored immigration in spite of ideological opposition from both major parties.

Although Britain had always been slow to accept strangers, there were no formal norms of ethnic discrimination or segregation. When the non-European population was extremely small, minority problems of education, housing, or employment simply did not arise on a noticeable scale. The British prided themselves on following the principle of fair play and thought that racial discrimination, prejudice, or conflict were phenomena of less enlightened breeds. The entry of over a million non-European immigrants in two decades' time, and the prospect of a still larger number yet to come, changed this situation and the British viewpoint. In the changed situation, the British perceived the new migrant as a noisy and unsanitary neighbor, a problem in the school, and a competitor in the labor market. In this set of circumstances, the older set of norms, in the opinion of many British, became irrelevant. As they viewed it, the non-European influx was a threat to the British way of life and the Enoch Powell proposals to end immigration, and even to deport non-Europeans currently in the country, found acceptance by a significant number of British.

Generalized pattern. A sudden change or threat of change in the pattern of intergroup relationships leads to defensive reaction in behalf of the older patterns. Changes in the population composition due to immigration are a prime example of this pattern. When Jewish immigration to Palestine threatened the position of Arabs, hostility increased to the point where some Arab leaders were threatening to drive the Jews out of the country. The initial acceptance of immigration restriction in the United States in 1920 also seems to have been based on a fear that the immigration of southern Europeans was threatening the continued dominance of a basically Anglo-Saxon type of culture. The old majority group may eventually decide that it has no choice except to come to terms with the newcomers, but some attempts to restore the *status quo ante* are likely to occur. Previous norms of egalitarianism or tolerance tend to be ineffective in meeting new intergroup situations.

QUESTIONS

1. Which is the more racist policy, Kenyan laws which forced Indians out of the country or British restriction of immigration? Defend your answer.

2. Some writers on French minority policy lump Arabs and blacks together as a "colored" group, while others distinguish between "colored" and Arabs. How would you explain this discrepancy?

3. On the basis of opinion polls, which are the most prejudiced, French or British?

4. Is fair play and nondiscrimination the answer to minority problems? If not, why are these inadequate?

5. Some small groups of non-European immigrants in both France and Britain reject assimilation. Can such a group maintain itself over a long period?

6. Is color the main criterion for sharp ethnic distinction? How do you explain the indications of greater French prejudice against Arabs than against blacks?

7. Can the civil rights legislation be expected to end friction between white Britons and the non-European minority?

8. Will the second generation of colonials born and educated in France or Britain make an easier adjustment? What factors might still generate friction?

9. Is the best answer to minority educational problems to be found in integration or in separate schools specifically adapted to minority needs? Can the two ideas be harmonized?

10. Youth is usually less inclined to express prejudiced opinions than older age groups. Does this indicate that there will be less ethnic conflict in the future?

11. Did the actions of the Kenyan government which forced many Indians out of the country help or hurt the prosperity of African Kenyans? If all the Kenyan Indians had opted for Kenyan citizenship immediately would this have solved the problem?

12. Will the long-term effect of the reduction of non-European immigration to Britain make for racial harmony or for increased conflict?

13. Both the Conservative and the Labour party in England have been accused of being false to their ideals in restricting the immigration of colonials with British citizenship. What would have been the result if the leadership of the two parties had stood firm and refused to restrict immigration?

14. Employment tension between non-European and others seems to increase as the non-Europeans seek better jobs. What is the best way to alleviate tension of this kind?

15. The landlords accused of "exploiting" non-Europeans are often of the same nationality as their tenants. What does this prove about the ethnic basis of such exploitation? Would the non-Europeans have fared better in a state in which all housing was government-owned?

16. Metropolitan France and Britain have never had the slaveholding system which characterized the United States. What difference has that made in current relations between non-European immigrants and the natives?

17. Would increased travel by French and British contribute to an improvement in relationships between natives and non-European immigrants?

18. In the past, highly trained professionals have been welcomed in France and Britain as well as in the United States. Do actions of this kind have

any effect on relationships between the natives and lower-class non-Europeans?

19. Would you expect France or Britain to have the most difficulty in assimilating non-Europeans?

20. Are the British simply repeating a cycle which has involved the initial rejection and ultimate assimilation of immigrant groups? State arguments on both sides of this issue.

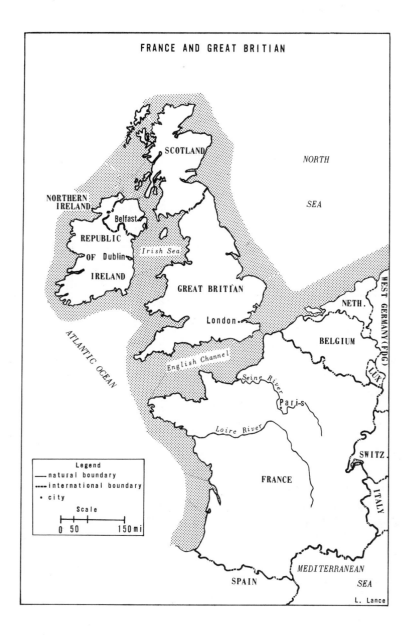

FRANCE AND GREAT BRITIAN

Chapter 11

Black America
at the crossroads

At one time or another the relations of blacks and whites in the United States have been shaped by each of the three major patterns of segregation, integration, and cultural pluralism. The first 60 years of black and white contact were a time of uncertainty and tentativeness which eventually led to the enslavement of the majority of American blacks, along with the existence of a number of "free Negroes" of rather marginal status. The period of slavery was one which combined the greatest possible degree of intimacy between races with the greatest possible degree of subordination of blacks to whites. This was a period in which miscegenation was widespread and, at the same time, one in which the slaves were "chattels" who were not regarded as having legal rights at all as persons.

The end of slavery introduced a brief effort at integration and "reconstruction," followed by a period of segregation and discrimination which might be dated roughly from the Hayes-Tilden presidential election controversy of 1876 until the school desegregation decision of the U.S. Supreme Court in 1954. The school desegregation decision marked the acceptance of integration as an official government policy. This acceptance of integration was a high point in a long struggle by blacks and white liberals and, supposedly, was resisted only by the segregationist whites.

By 1966, however, a number of spokesmen in the black community questioned whether integration was a feasible, or even a desirable, goal for American blacks and proposed various types of separatism or cultural pluralism. The emergence of a militant separatist black group was confusing both to integrationist blacks, who felt they were leading the wave of the future into a color-blind society, and to whites of almost all persuasions. Liberal whites who had been cooperating in the move toward integration now suddenly found themselves damned as enemies by the new separatists. Segregationist whites, on the other hand, found that some of the most militant blacks were suddenly speaking a language which sounded very similar to that of segregation.

The American racial picture in the 1970s suggests that, as far as blacks and whites are concerned, the old-style type of segregation is dead or dying. Whether the new pattern will be integration, cultural pluralism, or some relationship (autonomy, liberation, nationalism, etc.) to which these labels cannot be profitably applied, remains to be seen. At this juncture in the development of race relations in the United States, many black Americans find themselves at the crossroads wondering which way to go. Which will provide a richer and less oppressive life, the road of social integration or cultural assimilation, or the path leading toward separatism? Cultural pluralism has proved to be a viable alternative in places like Switzerland, but will it work for black Americans? Is black America's best solution one of voluntary segregation within the context of the larger American society, accompanied by fuller control by black people of the various institutions found in the black community? These are some of the major questions facing black America in its search for freedom, equality, and liberation.

The crucial issue of whether black Americans should move toward a new definition of integration, separation, or liberation cannot be fully understood without some knowledge of the historical developments and persistent problems that have brought them to this particular crossroad. Therefore, we shall provide a brief account of the black man's arrival in this country and his subsequent struggle for liberation. The following generalizations were derived from our discussion of this quest: (1) in a complex, modern society the chances of a cohesive, united front against oppression are hampered by intragroup cleavages, (2) often the culture of a subordinated minority is denigrated and the dominant group tends to force its culture on minority group members, (3) a desire for the elimination of socio-economic disparities tends to be greater after a subordinated minority has already experienced some measure of improvement, and (4) substantial change without complete success often creates a sense of alienation that undermines the likelihood that further change will occur through orderly procedures.

PRE-CIVIL WAR EXPERIENCE

The pattern of slavery in the United States proved to be an institution centered almost altogether in the South, with slave labor utilized mostly in plantation agriculture. The slaves had come from several different West African areas, and they varied in tribal affiliation, customs, and even, to some extent, physical appearance. They were scattered widely throughout the United States in such a fashion that they usually could communicate with other slaves only by means of the English language; except for a few vestigial remnants, African culture was almost totally destroyed. The slavery pattern was somewhat slow to emerge, though, and the first 60 years of experience in the United States witnessed a much more fluid pattern of racial relationships. In fact, the first blacks to be introduced to that part of the New World evidently were not perceived as lifetime slaves:

Even the first Negroes in the colonies, who happened to land in Virginia, were not treated as slaves, though they had been purchased from a Dutch man-of-war that had taken them off a captured Portuguese slaver. Possibly because English law did not cover slavery, possibly because they were Christians, these twenty Negroes appear to have enjoyed a status similar to that of indentured servants. Moreover, many of the other Negroes in Virginia during the next several decades had a similar status. After a stipulated number of years of service, they received their freedom as well as land and a few implements. Some even became masters of other men, even white men.[1]

The fact that the first blacks in America were at least potentially free men does not mean that they were accepted on a basis equal to whites. Even before the rise of a large-scale slave trade and the establishment of a definite system of slavery on the American soil, it was apparent that men of color were perceived as being different from those of white skin and therefore inferior. While this belief served later as a rationalization to justify the eventual slave status, it appears to have emerged even before such a status had crystalized. Thus Quarles states:

For, while it is true that slavery had its root in economics, it must not be overlooked that discrimination against the Negro antedated the need for his labor. In the early years of Virginia, the Negro population grew slowly, in 1648 numbering around 300 in a population of some 15,000 and in 1671 numbering 2,000 out of a population of 40,000. It was not until the turn of the century that Virginia's Negro population took a sharp rise. But long before that time, the distinction between the white and the black servant had become marked. From

---

[1] Eli Ginzberg and Alfred S. Eichner, *The Troublesome Presence—American Democracy and the Negro* (New York, Mentor Books, New American Library, 1966), p. 23. Copyright 1964 by The Free Press of Glencoe, a division of the Macmillan Company. Reprinted by permission.

the beginning Negroes were thought not to be assimilable; they were not considered fellow parishioners in the church or even fellow roisterers at the tavern.[2]

Such a statement should not be taken to indicate that a segregated social pattern emerged immediately. There was a period of discussion and gradual change in the legal and religious status of the black population. For instance, did they have the same rights in court as white men or were these rights to be modified in some fashion? Were they eligible for baptism as Christians and, if baptized, could they still be held as slaves? The settlement of these and other issues required a period of perhaps nearly a century and was never completely uniform in all areas, with blacks, and even slaves, having somewhat greater rights in New England than in the deep South.

Slavery itself was some time in emerging as a major issue. Many of the early settlers of North America were bondsmen of one type or another, and it is estimated that close to 80 percent of the colonists arrived under some form of servitude.[3] The most common form of servitude was that of the indentured servant who, voluntarily or otherwise, had agreed to serve his master without pay for a period of years in return for his passage to the New World. Both whites and blacks were classed as indentured servants, and many members of each race eventually found their freedom and became respected members of the community. The black indentured servant, however, tended to find that obstacles were placed in the way of his eventual freedom, and his position tended to merge with that of other blacks who had been bought or captured from Portuguese or Dutch traders and whose status was that of lifetime slaves. Eventually the category of indentured servant fell into disuse, and the population became divided into whites, all of whom were free men, and blacks, some of whom were free, but most of whom were lifetime slaves.

Two factors seem to have accelerated the trend toward the establishment of a definite slave system. One was the decision in 1698 by the British Parliament that threw the slave trade open to British subjects. The other was the perception by settlers in Virginia and elsewhere of the economic possibilities of the cultivation of tobacco. The expansion of tobacco cultivation produced a demand for labor which the indentured servant system could not satisfy, nor could adequate labor be secured by a straight wage payment. Indentured white servants were likely to flee before their period of service was over, and wage laborers were likely to leave their employment for independent farming or for businesses of their own. Slave labor might have many drawbacks, but at least it offered the planter a fairly permanent type of work force. Benjamin Franklin, for

---

[2] Benjamin Quarles, *The Negro in the Making of America* (New York, Macmillan Co., 1969), pp. 37–38. Copyright 1964, 1969, by The Macmillan Company.

[3] Ginzberg and Eichner, *The Troublesome Presence*, p. 22.

instance, found that slavery was a cumbersome and costly type of labor but admitted its advantages: "Why then will *Americans* purchase slaves? he asked. Because Slaves may be kept as long as a Man pleases, or has Occasion for his Labour; while hired Men are continually leaving their Masters (often in the midst of his Business) and setting up for them selves."[4]

By the time of the American Revolution, slaves comprised approximately 20 percent of the population. By this time the best tobacco lands had begun to wear out and the economic advantages of slavery had begun to come into question. The ethics of slavery were freely discussed, and slavery was openly condemned by many leading statesmen. The adoption of the American Constitution stimulated a debate between those who wished to abolish slavery completely and the interests which wished the constitution to protect slavery from any government interference at all. Eventually a compromise was reached which recognized the existence of slavery but provided that the slave trade could be outlawed after 20 years' time.

One of the arguments used by opponents of slavery to justify this compromise was the opinion that slavery was proving economically unprofitable and soon would be as rare in the South as it was in New England. This sentiment was typified by the statement of Oliver Ellsworth of Connecticut during the constitutional debates: "Let us not intermeddle. As population increases, poor laborers will be so plenty as to render slaves useless. Slavery in time will not be a speck in our country."[5]

There were many factors which supported the idea that slavery was a dying institution. In the areas of the South which had been settled earliest, tobacco was less profitable as the soil had apparently been exhausted. In newer areas, wheat and other cereals, which were less adapted to slave labor, seemed to be the most profitable crops. The price of slaves had fallen so low that many planters found it actually profitable to give them away, and between 1790 and 1820 the number of "free Negroes" in the South increased more than threefold.[6] There were a number of anti-slavery societies in the South, and it was not uncommon for Southern clergymen, journalists, and politicians to denounce slavery as an immoral and unprofitable institution.

Most of this was to change, however, as Eli Whitney's cotton gin, invented in 1794, came into wider use. The cotton gin broke a bottleneck in agricultural development, since it separated the seeds from the cotton fiber in an economical manner. As soon as the utility of the cotton gin

---

4 Leonard W. Labaree (ed.), *The Papers of Benjamin Franklin* (New Haven, Conn., Yale University Press, 1959), Vol. 4, p. 230.

5 Max Farrand (ed.), *The Records of the Federal Convention of 1787* (New Haven, Conn., Yale University Press, 1937), Vol. 2, p. 369.

6 Ginzberg and Eichner, *The Troublesome Presence*, p. 83.

was perceived, cotton became regarded as the most profitable crop and slavery was viewed as essential to provide the labor supply which made southern prosperity possible. By 1830 the South had become substantially unified in its defense of slavery and had silenced or expelled the critics in its midst. From that time on, slavery became a sectional issue, with the South committed to its support and the North either indifferent or hostile.

The favorite picture portrayed by the writers of the ante bellum South is of a paternalistic regime with happy slaves and indulgent masters. Supposedly an accommodation had been reached by which the slaves accepted their servitude in return for the security and protection afforded by paternalistic masters. There can be little doubt that frequently both slaves and masters regarded slavery as the only possible type of system and proceeded to make the best of the situation. There undoubtedly were many cases of real affection between slaves and owners, and there were many stories told of the faithful household servant or the "old Negro mammy" who had faithfully reared the children of her white master. Resentment against the system was apparently neither so deep nor so widespread that it became unbearably expensive to keep a slave force intact and, even during the Civil War, it appeared that most slaves continued to perform their customary duties.

On the other hand, this supposedly idyllic state was not so universal as to·prevent the emergence of occasional slave revolts. There is disagreement as to the type of incident which should be classified as simply a normal altercation between master and slave rather than a planned revolt. The estimate by Aptheker that there were over 250 conspiracies and revolts may be an overstatement; however, there is no doubt that many such revolts did occur and that their prevention or suppression was a fairly constant concern of the slave owners. Perhaps the best known revolts are those of Nat Turner, Denmark Vesey, and Gabriel Prosser.[7] Prosser led over 1,000 blacks in an effort to attack the city of Richmond. Denmark Vesey had similar designs on Charleston, South Carolina, and was frustrated because whites were alerted by a fellow slave. Probably the most spectacular revolt was one in South Hampton County, Virginia, led by Nat Turner. This revolt led to the killing of 55 whites in the first day of Turner's activities. Two months later he was captured and executed but not until his revolt had stimulated an almost paranoid type of anxiety among the slave owners which led to the killing of hundreds of slaves and even some free blacks.

The fact that the majority of blacks labored faithfully without planning revolts does not indicate that they accepted the status of slavery joyfully. In addition to revolts, there were also efforts to escape which led to the

---

.   [7] For description of these revolts see Thomas W. Higginson, *Black Rebellion* (New York, Arno Press and the *New York Times*, 1969).

establishment of the famous "underground railroads," consisting of a network of friendly whites and free blacks who would guide the escaped slaves from Southern plantations to safety in Canada. However benign the paternalism of the slave owner or however terrible his means of repression, the slaves never abandoned the dream of freedom.

THE AFTERMATH OF EMANCIPATION

When freedom finally came to the American slaves, it was as a result of a costly war which lasted for almost five years and nearly led to the demise of the American nation. Not only did the Civil War lead to emancipation, but the freed slaves were also given the right to vote, and their privileges in society as free American citizens were guaranteed by a variety of new federal civil rights laws prohibiting racial discrimination.

Immediately after the end of the Civil War, those active in support of the Confederacy were disenfranchised and the Republican Party, with the aid of both whites and freed slaves, captured the legislatures of most of the Southern states. In most of these states blacks were a minority among officeholders, but there were many blacks in state legislatures and a few were elected to the Congress, both in the House and in the United States Senate. The legislatures undertook the reconstruction of the South and endeavored to set up educational and governmental services which would enable the freed slaves to take a successful role in Southern society.

This activity was considered an outrage by most of the white Southerners and could only be supported as long as federal troops remained stationed in the South. Eventually, a rising Southern white resistance and a loss of interest on the part of the North led to the withdrawal of troops and the collapse of the Republican regimes. The political maneuvers involved were complicated, but it is perhaps sufficient to say that by 1876, after little more than a decade of effort at reconstruction, the Northern troops were withdrawn and the blacks were abandoned to the discriminatory rule of the Southern whites.

The Southern whites were compelled to accept the finality of emancipation but sought to restore a system which, as far as possible, would assure a permanent supply of cheap black labor. Their efforts to do this led to a system of segregation[8] which remained unchallenged in the South for many years and, to some extent, affected the North as well. Under this system of segregation, the rule was separate facilities in practically all walks of life. As far as government was concerned, black participation was completely excluded and, for the most part, blacks were prevented

---

[8] For a discussion of the development of segregation—a post–Civil-War phenomenon—see C. Vann Woodward, *The Strange Career of Jim Crow* (Fair Lawn, N. J., Oxford University Press, 1957).

from even voting. For schools, libraries, prisons, and practically all government services, separate, and usually inferior, facilities were set up for blacks. In the private sphere, the operators of hotels, restaurants, and transportation enterprises were legally prohibited from mixing blacks and whites in the same accommodation.

In economic life, the tendency was to classify all work as either white men's jobs or black men's jobs. By and large, the black men's jobs were those which were so poorly paid or so lacking in prestige that no white man desired to occupy them. The only exceptions were provided by the existence of black-operated private businesses and by the acceptance of black professionals for the service of a black clientele. Blacks were given a monopoly as clergymen in black churches, or as teachers and administrators in black schools. They were allowed to operate private enterprises with some degree of freedom, and there were occasional cases of blacks who became successful businessmen or large landholders. For the most part, however, segregation meant that politically the black was powerless, and socially and economically he was restricted to the least desirable aspects of society.

Changes in economic conditions have usually brought a change in the reaction to racial patterns, and the first major change to threaten the pattern of segregation was the labor shortage of World War I, which increased the demand for factory workers at the same time that it shut off the supply of European immigrants. As a result, hundreds of thousands of blacks left agricultural employment in the South for industrial jobs in the North. In the North, the black migrant found both opportunity and problems. The opportunity consisted of jobs which paid a much higher compensation than agricultural or service work in the South and of access to public facilities, such as education, without a color tag. The problems came from the difficulty of adjusting to a new and harsh environment and from the resentment felt by white workmen who feared competition for their jobs and by white householders who regarded their new neighbors as a threat to the community.

Labor agents were sent to the South to spread the news of opportunities in the North but, at the same time, the new migrant often found himself in the midst of riots that wrecked many Northern cities in the years from 1917 to 1920. The pace of the black migration North slackened briefly after the end of the war, but picked up again in the economic prosperity of the 1920s. By 1930, millions of blacks had moved from Southern plantations to Northern cities. Most of them occupied unskilled or, at best semiskilled jobs, but the general level of living was considerably higher than that provided by Southern agriculture, and at least a few of the group had begun to make their way into more rewarding types of occupations.

The dream of advancement which the wartime and 1920 migration had brought on was rudely shattered by the depression of the 1930s. This brought about mass unemployment that affected, in many areas, as much as a third of the working force. Blacks, as the last hired were often the first to be fired and the population movement from the South to the North almost ceased. A large part of the black population was enabled to survive at all only by the emergence of federal welfare measures.

The next change came with World War II, which produced an even greater demand for soldiers and industrial laborers than World War I. Wartime demands enabled migration from South to North to begin again; only this time the destination was Southern cities as well as the Northern metropolis. Blacks moved from service occupation to factory labor and, under the exigencies of wartime pressures, a small number of higher status jobs were open to black applicants. Again, there was a question as to black status after the end of the war, but the expected depression did not come and the prosperity which continued into the 1950s and mushroomed into dramatic growth in the 1960s provided for a substantial upgrading of large numbers of the black population. At the same time, Southern agriculture found less need for unskilled black labor because the tractor and the cotton picker enabled a farmer with two or three hired hands to cultivate as much land as had been worked by 20 sharecropper families two decades before.

Thus the growing demand for labor in the cities was matched by a decreasing need for labor in the part of the South which had insisted on the most rigid pattern of segregated race relations. The strong pressure to do away with enforced segregation was given legal recognition in 1954, when the Supreme Court declared that legal requirements for segregated education were a violation of the constitutional provision for the equal protection of all U.S. citizens. The court decrees were followed by state and national legislative enactments which have outlawed discrimination in employment, housing, government, and public accommodations.

In brief, the reconstruction civil rights measures which were passed at the end of the Civil War were revived again in the two decades following the end of World War II. The legal basis of segregation had been completely destroyed, the population distribution had changed from a picture of 90 percent of blacks living in the South in 1900 to a nearly equal distribution between the South and other sections in 1970, and, however much they disagreed on its meaning, the goal of equality of opportunity had received assent from a major proportion of the American people.

The spirit of the period was perhaps best exemplified by a biracial march on Washington led by the Reverend Martin Luther King, Jr., which brought over 200,000 people to a fervent pitch of excitement in an affirmation of interracial brotherhood. Admittedly, there were barriers which remained in the path of black social mobility, and different interpretations of the period soon began to emerge. To white liberals and integrationist blacks, the civil rights period was one of rapid progress which pointed the way toward a society in which whites and blacks would be able to co-exist on an equal basis. To critics, the period was one in which results had not lived up to promises and in which the black man was asked to trade his racial identity for a largely formal, and partly fictitious, equality as an assimilated American.

INTEGRATION AND PROGRESS

Any evaluation of the impact of the period since the end of World War II will be likely to reflect the influence of what Banton has described as the "majoritarian and minoritarian" viewpoint.[9] The majoritarian tends to look back at the past to describe the changes which have taken place and to conclude that satisfactory progress is being made. The minoritarian, on the other hand, does not use his past status as a frame of reference. Rather, he will compare himself either with an ideal standard or with the most favored group in the society. He then describes the disparity between his present status and his ideal and decides that progress has been negligible and that the society is essentially unfriendly to his aspirations. Both the majoritarians and the minoritarians can find data in the American scene to support their conclusions. The majoritarian will point to both absolute and relative improvement in the education, health, and economic well-being of blacks; while the minoritarian will point to the disparity which still exists between whites and blacks.

For the most part, those who are impressed by the progress of the last two decades of American interracial relationships tend to take the viewpoint that integration is a realizable ideal and that steps in this direction have already brought significant gains to American blacks. Those who might be classed as separatists tend to deny that any effective integration has taken place and to minimize the extent of any economic gains which may have occurred.

It is doubtful whether any discussion of trends will be satisfactory to all, but a factual analysis will at least illustrate the basis for different contentions. On the legal front, there would seem to be little room for argument on the changes in an integrative direction. The laws in the Southern states which once forbade intermarriage, on the one hand, and required a segregation of all types of facilities on the other, have been rendered inoperative. A vast apparatus of laws and commissions has been created whose objective is to see that no American is penalized because of race in his search for education, housing, or employment. Further, the right to vote has been safeguarded so that millions of blacks now vote in the South where only a few thousand voted before 1960, and blacks have begun to

---

[9] Michael Banton, *Race Relations* (New York, Basic Books Inc., 1967), p. 388. Compare the use of this concept in Chapter 10 pages 316–18.

hold political office in significant numbers. A black man sat in President Johnson's cabinet, another black man, Thurgood Marshall, was appointed as a justice of the Supreme Court and, in Massachusetts, a black politician, Senator Brooke, was elected to office in a state where blacks are a very small minority of the total population. In addition, there are more than a dozen black Congressmen and hundreds of blacks occupying appointive and elective positions in city and state governments. In federal employment, it is estimated that 15 percent of federal jobs may be held by blacks as compared to an overall proportion of 11 per cent of blacks in the total population. The United States Army, which, as recently as World War II, was openly and completely segregated, has now abolished all formal racial distinctions; the number of black noncommissioned officers is higher than the proportion of blacks in the army, and they are represented (although less than proportionately) in the upper ranks of the officers' corps.[10]

The state of Michigan furnishes several striking illustrations of black political advance. In 1972, in addition to holding two seats in Congress, blacks had won positions in statewide elections even though they are only ten percent of the state population. Black educators are in demand at predominantly white universities, and Michigan State University, in 1971, selected a black man, Clifford Wharton, as its president.

Critics of integration would contend that such examples are exceptional. They would point out that black office holders in government still represent less than one percent of the total of elected officials and that even in areas such as federal employment or the army, where numbers of blacks are close to their proportion of the population, they are underrepresented in the top spots. They would further contend that blacks in prominent positions have to conform to "white middle-class norms" and thus cannot really represent the black population.

Education is a field in which the black advance has been little short of spectacular. During the 1960s, the proportion of blacks in the 25–34 age bracket who had graduated from college increased more than 50 percent and the differential in average education completed by blacks and whites dropped from 3.5 years in 1959 to 1.1 years in 1969.[11] The elimination of segregative requirements has opened up all institutions of higher education to qualified blacks and, in addition, there has been a pronounced move toward lower entrance requirements and financial subsidy for members of minority groups.

In schools below the college level, the de jure integration orders were countered by a massive movement of blacks into the cities and of whites

---

[10] Charles C. Moskos, "Racial Integration in the Armed Forces," *The American Journal of Sociology* 72 (September 1966): 132–48.

[11] For source of statements on black socio-economic status see Tables 11–1 and 11–2.

TABLE 11-1

Black and white progress

Category	Year	Blacks	Whites
Percent above poverty level	1959	43.8	81.9
($3,743 in 1969)	1969	69.0	90.5
Median black income as	1965	54	
percent of white income	1969	64	
Family income $10,000 and	1947	3	11
over (1968 dollars)	1960	8	24
	1968	21	42
Families under $3,000	1947	60	23
income (1968 dollars)	1960	41	16
	1968	23	9
Unemployment rates	1969	6.5	3.2
Median years of school	1959	8.6	12.1
completed	1969	11.3	12.4
Percent 25–35 years old	1960	4.3	11.7
completed college	1966	5.7	14.6
	1969	6.6	16.2
Single-parent families	1960	25	8
(either male or female head)	1969	31	9

Sources: Bulletin No. 1511, *The Negroes in The United States: Their Economic and Social Situation*, U.S. Dept. of Labor, June 1966; Charles E. Silberman, "Negro Economic Gains Impressive but Precarious," *Fortune* 82 (July 1970): 74–78. U.S. Census Bureau Special Report, 1970, *Current Population Reports*, Series P-23, No. 29, BLS Report No. 375.

to the suburbs which left the actual proportion of blacks in predominantly black schools in the North greater than before the Supreme Court decision, and in the South provided only for small change. In the 1970s there has been a spate of court-ordered busing which has avoided the limitations of residential segregation and has drastically increased the proportion of students in schools which are racially "balanced" on about the same basis as the ratio in the surrounding population. Busing has aroused consternation among whites who fear the destruction of the neighborhood school and the lowering of academic standards. At the same time, there is little evidence of support from black parents, many of whom fear that their children may be placed in an unfriendly and harshly competitive atmosphere. Whether a large-scale busing program will survive is uncertain, but it certainly has been a major step in the desegregation of the common schools.

The attack from the other side is not so much on the reality of integration as it is on the nature of the education offered to black students. The claim is made that the schools, whether integrated or segregated, are creatures of a white society which does not recognize the ethnic needs of black students. Teachers are charged with being "racist" in failing to understand black students and in using methods and standards which make it difficult for the students to find relevance in education. Curricula have been modified to provide for the introduction of black history and similar subjects, but black students continue to have an average achievement rate in academic subjects about two years below that of the white average and to have a larger dropout rate.[12]

It was once assumed that desegregation would bring closer contact and therefore a greater degree of friendly understanding between black and white students. In recent years, however, desegregated schools have been the scenes of many battles along racial lines, often with an increase in suspicion among both blacks and whites.

Probably the crucial test of the degree of progress in recent years is seen in changes in economic status. There is no doubt that there has been an absolute improvement in the economic circumstances of blacks and also that there has been a relative improvement in comparison with whites. The grounds for dispute are whether such changes are mere tokenism or whether they indicate a major shift in the nature of black economic participation. The number of black families living in poverty has decreased and the number living in affluence has increased. In comparing the years 1947 and 1968, one finds that, in 1947, 60 percent of black families were living in poverty (defined as $3,000 in 1968 dollars) and that, in 1968, this had declined to 23 percent, which was the proportion of white families that lived in poverty in 1947. Taking an income of $10,000 a year or more in terms of dollars with the 1968 purchasing power as an index of affluence, the number of black families in this level is almost twice the proportion of white families in 1947—21 percent as compared to 11 percent—and represents a sevenfold increase in the proportion of black families above that level since 1947.

Naturally, the longer the period of years, the greater the degree of change, but even comparisions within the decade of the 60s show rather sharp and favorable changes. The greatest relative changes have come in the ranks of young families, which might be taken to indicate a trend which will eventually be more pervasive. For instance, in 1959 the median income of young black husband-and-wife families in the northern and western parts of the United States, with both mates working, was only 64 percent of similar white families; it had risen to 104 percent in 1970.[13] On an overall basis, the median income of black families, which was only 51 percent of that of white families in 1959, had risen to 59 percent in 1972.

---

[12] James S. Coleman, et al., *Equality of Educational Opportunity*, (Washington, D.C., Office of Education, U.S. Dept. of Health, Education and Welfare, 1969), pp. 274, 454–56.

[13] Department of Commerce, Bureau of the Census, *The Social and Economic Status of the Black Population in the United States, 1971* (Washington, D.C., United States Government Printing Office, 1972), Table 21, p. 34.

In the South, the black family had 55 percent of the white family income and in the North and the West, 68 percent.[14]

Looking at the other interpretation, there are obviously continuing problems for blacks and continuing disparities between black and whites. In 1968, there were still 2.5 times the proportion of blacks who lived in poverty as compared to whites, while whites had twice the proportion living in affluence.

TABLE 11–2

Median income for families with head under 35 years of age, by region, in 1959 and 1969

Area and type of family	1959				1969			
	Black	White	Differ-ence	Black as a per-cent of white	Black	White	Differ-ence	Black as a per-cent of white
United States	$	$	$		$	$	$	
All families	2,972	5,535	2,563	54	6,001	9,032	3,031	66
Husband-wife families	3,534	5,658	2,124	62	7,488	9,384	1,896	80
North and West								
All families	3,913	5,778	1,865	68	6,938	9,330	2,392	74
Husband-wife families	4,594	5,897	1,303	78	8,859	9,703	844	91
South								
All families	2,423	4,839	2,416	50	5,146	8,367	3,211	62
Husband-wife families	2,735	4,987	2,252	55	6,286	8,649	2,363	73

Source: U.S. Department of Commerce, Bureau of the Census from Monograph, *The Social and Economic Status of Negroes in the United States, 1970* (Washington, D.C., Bureau of the Census, July, 1971).

A major distinction along economic lines is in the impact of unemployment, which for several years has run about twice as high among blacks as among whites. The minoritarians would argue that such figures would indicate that in a time of enormous prosperity blacks have received only a few crumbs and that the relative condition of blacks has not really altered in an appreciable fashion. The majoritarian would argue that it is impossible to alter the economic position of a group completely in a few years' time and that blacks have done very well in recent years if their progress is compared with that of such groups as the more recent

---

[14] U.S. Dept. of Commerce, Bureau of the Census, The Social and Economic Status of the Black Population of the United States, 1972, Series P–23, No. 46. p. 17.

immigrants, who have also been moving from a low-status position to that more nearly equal to the median of the population.

They would also argue that some of the apparent inequities are due to special circumstances for which there is no immediate and simple correction. Thus a large number of the black families living in poverty, probably at least 66 percent, are families that have only a female parent living in the home.[15] Since the 1973 rate for the family with a female head was 35 percent for blacks as compared to nine percent for whites,[16] it may be argued that this aspect of poverty is related to a particular type of family life rather than to any general racial discrimination. Further, the increase in unemployment may be taken in some ways as a measure of progress rather than the reverse. There was relatively little unemployment when most blacks were engaged in agricultural or in service occupations. Since blacks have entered industry and have turned away from the service type of position, they are more subject to industrial fluctuations without having had time to gain the seniority which has partially protected white workers against this difficulty.

Compared to any previous decades, the period of the 1960s has afforded a time of economic progress among the blacks which is probably unmatched in the world's history for any group of any ethnic background. This statement does not, of course, mean that people will be convinced that such progress indicates the essential soundness of the integrative procedures which have been followed and that the future should be more of the same. The militant is likely to argue that past injustices have been so great that readjustment should be more rapid and more massive than has taken place. He would further argue that we cannot rely on the techniques fashioned in the civil rights controversy and in the war on poverty and must look to some new kind of structuring of society.

Several questions arise in predicting the effects of more drastic governmental efforts to equalize the racial income balance. One is the simple matter of feasibility. In the past, the greatest minority gains have come as general prosperity has increased the demand for labor, while, on the other hand, the returns from specific reform programs have been somewhat disappointing. Apparently, as the economic system now operates, blacks receive an increasing share of the economic gains of the whole society as national income increases. If there is a method by which more rapid proportionate gains can be made for blacks than occurred in the 60s, this method has not yet been demonstrated. Another problem is that, since blacks are a minority, comprising around 11 percent of the population, it is necessary to avoid programs which would cause a white backlash. Whites who are content to see black progress come through economic

---

[15] Ibid., p. 12.
[16] Ibid., p. 100.

growth might be quite hostile to programs in which black gains were perceived as white losses.

THE BLACK COMMUNITY

One of the very difficult policy questions is how to deal with the malaise of black communities as represented by unstable family life, drug use of almost epidemic proportions, and a high crime rate. The psychological cost of living in the black community has risen appreciably in the last few years, especially from the time that the drug problem assumed gigantic proportions. Many blacks, both men and women, are afraid to walk the streets at night for fear of being robbed and injured. One of the features of black crime is that, for the most part, it is likely to be directed against blacks rather than against whites. It is the black person who is the victim of a homicide rate much higher than that of whites. It is the black householder whose property is lost through theft, the black woman who is molested by rapists, and, to a great extent, the black youth who is demoralized by the drugs offered by the pusher.

In spite of the suffering of the black community from crime, there is a tendency to look upon the police as an outside agency representing a repressive power structure. The white policeman is often criticized as insensitive and brutal, and black police do not escape such criticism, either. Further, the poor image of police in black communities makes it difficult to recruit black policemen, since they are often regarded by fellow blacks as those who have "sold out to whitey." Police have often been criticized for a tendency to ignore criminal behavior or minimize their attention to it when both the criminal and the victim were blacks. However, attempts of police to engage in a closer surveillance of black criminals frequently bring community resentment. Thus departments are criticized because they do not send sufficient police into black communities, but are also criticized for excessive concentrations of police and harassment of black individuals. Crime is often attributed to institutional racism and to poverty, but recent years have seen an increasing attack on behavior which could be called racist and a mounting scale of material well-being, accompanied by a rising crime rate.

Apparently there is a major need for community cooperation with the police. Whether this can be brought about by "community control" of police forces or by more effective and wholehearted acceptance of blacks in the larger society remains a question. Banfield, for one, observes that similar phenomena occurred in immigrant colonies in the United States and that the situation did not improve until there was a substantial movement of these ethnic groups toward middle-class status.[17]

---

[17] Edward C. Banfield, *The Unheavenly City* (Boston, Little Brown & Co., 1968), p. 170.

Closely related to the crime situation is the difficulty of maintaining stable black families. Illegitimacy and divorce rates have been rising for both races. Although the illegitimacy rates for whites recently have shown a greater proportionate change than for blacks, there is still a significantly higher percentage of black families without a male parent in the household. This phenomenon is frequently attributed to the matriarchal pattern established in slavery, when the slave owner was often unconcerned about maintaining the family unit. This explanation, though, is hardly applicable to the present situation, since the number of families headed by women has been growing rapidly in recent years, rising from 17.6 percent in 1950 to 35 percent in 1973. Apparently the single-parent unit represents an adjustment to lower-class urban life rather than simply a hangover from days of slavery.

Not only is there a high percentage of single-parent families at any given time, but apparently a frequent reshuffling of mates through divorce and remarriage affects a much larger percentage of families sometime during their existence. For instance, in 1965, the proportion of blacks on Aid for Families with Dependent Children (AFDC) was 14 percent, but the probabilities were that 56 percent of black children would be in an AFDC family sometime during the childhood period.[18] Black families have many strengths including a resilience and a cooperation which has enabled them to meet difficult conditions. However, it seems hard to argue that the one-parent family is not handicapped both economically and in child discipline and that family instability is a part of the black community problem. The Black Muslims have opted for a strong patriarchial family pattern with an emphasis on male responsibility and female subordination. It might also be argued that the increase in the size of the black middle class would lead toward a more stable family life. The difficulty with this argument is that the white middle-class family is showing signs of increasing instability although at a considerably lesser rate than the black family.

BLACK REACTION TO SOCIAL CHANGE

Black reactions to social change in the United States may be said to have had three major components: (1) integration on an equal basis in the total society; (2) some type of separate development within the United States, and (3) the attraction of Africa. The latter alternative came to the fore relatively early with the formation of the African Colonization Society in 1816, which was a device to settle freed slaves on the African

---

[18] *The Negro Family: The Case for National Action* (Washington, D.C., Office of Policy Planning and Research, United States Department of Labor, March 1965), p. 12.

continent. It led to the development of the country of Liberia and the resettlement of a few thousand freed American slaves, who in turn became the aristocracy of the new country. However, the appeal of the Colonization Society was short-lived. The freed slaves protested that the United States was their true home and, meanwhile, the expansion of the cotton-growing area produced a demand for labor which made slave owners reluctant to see their slaves leave. The movement emerged again in substantial force after World War I under the leadership of Marcus Garvey. He was criticized by most of the intellectuals but drew an enthusiastic response from the black masses. His movement attracted immense crowds of followers until it foundered on the rocks of government hostility, fiscal difficulty, and internal rivalry.

A genuine "back to Africa" movement has not yet reasserted itself, but the 1960s saw a fascination with African culture and a growing interest in the newly independent African states. More militant blacks felt that wearing dashikis, learning to speak Swahili, and wearing the massive "Afro-American" hairdo were all a sign of black nationalism. Further, Africa was part of the "third world," which, it was assumed, would side with American blacks in their struggle for greater status.

One of the first separatist leaders, Booker T. Washington, emerged to prominence at a time when the blacks had lost all political power and an extreme segregation was unquestioned in the Southern part of the United States. Washington abjured the desire for social equality or political participation and proclaimed that by the acquisition of economic skills the black man could develop in a way advantageous both to the white South and to himself.

Washington was challenged by W. E. Burghardt DuBois, who deplored Washington's preference for vocational education and called for political action and first-class citizenship for blacks. Washington was accused frequently of being an accommodating "Uncle Tom" type of leader, while the activities of DuBois led eventually to the formation of the National Association for the Advancement of Colored People and a vigorous push for integration of blacks in American life.

In the 1930s, the integrationist leaders were able to forge an alliance with the liberal Democrats which paid off in a Democratic commitment to the abolition of segregation through administrative and legislative support for civil rights. Men like Whitney Young of the Urban League, Bayard Rustin, who had close connections with the labor movement, and Roy Wilkins of the NAACP, stood high in the councils of government and were able to secure a considerable measure of support, not only from liberal Democrats, but also from circles in business and in organized labor. However, in the mid-1960s, their analysis of the situation was challenged by another group of leaders, who not only were contemptuous of the progress made toward integration, but discarded it as a goal of black Americans. Since policy preference is related to one's view of the nature of American life, let us now turn to that topic.

MODELS OF SOCIAL CHANGE

This search for alternative ways to explain blacks in the American setting gave rise to at least two separate but related radical models: the marginal working class and the internal colony models. Many scholars view blacks as an underclass or a marginal working class that has been exploited for the benefit of the ruling elite. This exploitation came into existence during the "capitalism of slavery" and has been perpetuated until the present time by the "exploitive capitalists." During slavery the accumulation of wealth was achieved by exploiting some of the best human specimens produced in Africa. After slavery there has been a systematic attempt to keep black people in a low socio-economic status. According to Sidney Wilhelm:

> Some writers attribute the perpetuation of racism directly to the ruling stratum seeking to restrain wages, by instilling in white workers a racial prejudice against Negroes, the latter remain vulnerable to brutal exploitation while the former are rendered less competitive because they strive against the slave wages of blacks. In this manner, the ruling elite derives cheap labor from both black and white.[19]

Along the same lines, William K. Tabb states:

> If one group of workers are able to command higher pay, to exclude others from work, and if other groups of workers are limited in their employment opportunities to the worst jobs and lowest pay, then a marginal working class has been created which benefits the labor aristocracy and to an even greater extent the capitalist class.[20]

There is little question about the accuracy of such an interpretation for the period of slavery, but its usefulness as a model for race relations in the 20th century is more doubtful. For instance, an argument can be made that business has frequently operated in a manner which increased black opportunity. Thus, the Rosenwald Foundation was a principal proponent of the improvement of public education for blacks in the American South and Henry Ford was instrumental in introducing blacks to factory labor in Northern cities. Many businessmen either have contributed philan-

---

[19] Sidney M. Wilhelm, *Who Needs the Negro?* (Garden City, New York, Doubleday, 1971), p. 170.

[20] William K. Tabb, "Race Relations Models and Social Change," *Social Problems,* 18 (Spring 1971), p. 438. Published for The Society for the Study of Social Problems; Copyright 1971. Reprinted by permission.

hropic support to black movements or have pressed for the introduction
f black labor in areas of employment which previously had been white
reserves.

The thesis that the situation of the American black is really a form of
olonialism is perhaps best articulated by Robert Blauner, who writes,
the essential condition for both American slavery and European colonial-
sm was the power domination and the technological superiority of the
Vestern world in its relation to peoples of the non-Western and nonwhite
rigins.[21]

The colonial argument implies that blacks are kept as a permanently
ubjugated group which is denied both cultural autonomy and individual
dvancement. Unlike other Americans they came to the United States
nvoluntarily and are really subjects rather than citizens. Hence, the model
vhich they should adopt for planning strategy is not the other ethnic
roups that have been assimilated in American society, but the people in
underdeveloped countries who find political and economic freedom by
eparating themselves from the oppressive rule of the imperialist state.

A cogent counter argument to the colonial model as a proper fit has
een made by Nathan Glazer, who acknowledges that the "ethnic group
nodel" is on the decline but, upon examination of residential, economic,
nd political data, asserts that scholars like Blauner have exaggerated the
lifferences between black and white ethnic groups.[22] Glazer states:

Blauner has argued for understanding black development in terms of internal
olonialism, while white ethnic group development is to be interpreted in com-
letely different terms. However, in the Northern cities, differences between
lack and white ethnic group development are not as sharp as he believes,
vhere we examine residential segregation, economic development, and political
evelopment. In the South, the internal colonialism model fits the evidence bet-
er. In the North, blacks have a choice as to whether they interpret their expe-
ience by the internal colonialism or the white ethnic group model. The choice
vill have political consequences.[23]

Strong support for the ethnic group model also comes from Edward C.
anfield in his analysis of urban America, *The Unheavenly City*. Banfield
naintains that most of the behavior patterns which are considered racial

---

[21] Robert Blauner, "Internal Colonialism and Ghetto Revolt," in James A.
Geschwender (ed.), *The Black Revolt* (Englewood Cliffs, New Jersey, Prentice-Hall,
971), p. 236.

[22] For a fuller statement of this argument see Nathan Glazer, "Blacks and Ethnic
Groups: The Difference, and the Political Difference It Makes," *Social Problems*, 18
Spring 1971): 444–61.

[23] Nathan Glazer, "Blacks and Ethnic Groups: The Difference and the Political
Difference It Makes," *Social Problems*, 18 (Spring), p. 444. Published for The Society
or the Study of Social Problems; copyright 1971. Reprinted by permission.

could better be explained in terms of soial class. His thesis is that just as the European migrants to America were primarily lower class and manifested such lower-class behavior as higher crime rates, more unstable families, and inadequate school performance, so blacks are migrants from the rural South to the urban North and manifest the same behavior.[24] His argument is that blacks are going through the same sort of transition to higher-class status as the European migrants, and that this is a perennial type of process, beginning afresh with each new group to enter the city. One of the points which may be taken as backing his viewpoint is that the assumption that blacks always moved into the central city while whites moved to the suburbs is now being questioned. Each year since 1964, an average of 85,000 blacks have moved from the central city to the suburbs. In many cases, this may mean that they are moving toward predominantly black suburbs and do not escape segregation, but it is hard to deny the conclusion of Reynolds Farley of the University of Michigan, "Negroes, similar to European ethnic groups, are becoming more decentralized throughout the metropolitan area after they have been in the city for some time and improve their economic status."[25]

The debate between the proponents of the internal colonialism model and those of the ethnic group model cannot be resolved, because it is possible to marshall evidence to support either position. Perhaps a resolution is not the most important aspect of the debate, but rather a consideration of how these perspectives influence the outlook of black people and their leaders. Tersely, the consequences of the colonial model will not be the same as those of the ethnic group model because the latter assumes that, although there are black-white disparities, blacks can and will eventually overcome the structural barriers as the white ethnic groups have. Therefore, the strategies and tactics for social change will differ markedly from those called for in the internal colony model. It appears that the strategies and tactics in the internal colony perspective would lead in the direction of complete separation (a new nation) or to internal separatism. Parenthetically, while both perspectives caught the imagination of a significant proportion of black youth during the 60s and early 70s, there is evidence that the present generation is creating a new climate of race relations in which attitudes are more optimistic, materialistic and economically oriented. Although this orientation augurs well for the ethnic group model, it should not be interpreted to mean that the notion of decolonization; of achieving political and economic control over the black community, has been abandoned.

Stokely Carmichael was speaking to this issue when he said:

The colonies of the United States—and this includes the black ghettos within its borders, north and south—must be liberated . . . the form of

---

[24] Banfield, *The Unheavenly City,* pp. 66–87.
[25] *New York Times* (July 11, 1970), p. 221.

exploitation varies from area to area but the essential result has been the same—a powerful few have been maintained and enriched at the expense of the poor and voiceless colored masses. . . . For racism to die, a totally different America must be born.[26]

THE RACIAL TOWER OF BABEL: A CONFUSION OF VOICES

Thus far we have discussed only two perspectives, and one should not assume that these are the only viewpoints that are having an impact on the racial scene. If they are to play an important role in the development of Black America, they have to successfully compete with traditional as well as emergent models. Therefore, by looking at the various groups and organizations involved in the black movement, we are better able to understand that, at this juncture, no one perspective has gained the full endorsement and support from the black community. As a matter of fact, in the past few years, the newer perspectives have not caused a major shift of opinion among blacks with regard to the various black organizations. According to a recent Harris survey,[27] 73 percent of the rank and file of blacks have a "great deal" of respect for the NAACP, the Congress of Racial Equality (CORE) got 43 percent, and the Black Panthers received 23 percent from those surveyed. All the traditional civil rights organizations were respected by at least 50 percent of the blacks in the cross-sectional survey.

The new perspectives and new groups which grew out of the chaos created by the Black Power slogan have to compete with the established organizations for black members; new ideas must compete with old ideas; radical perspectives must struggle against traditional ones. Tersely, this has functioned to intensify intragroup fraction and conflict. To provide a clearer picture of what is involved in this development, we have provided an arbitrary scheme which takes into account the major groups and their orientations. We realize that there are dangers in any attempt to develop a typology of black organizations, but we do so in hopes of providing some meaningful way of specifying the various strident voices in the black community. The discussion which follows should be regarded as more illustrative and descriptive than analytic, since the latter seems a hopeless task at the present time.

The major black organizations may be viewed on an integrationist-separatist continuum, with the National Association for the Advancement of Colored People (NAACP), the Southern Christian Leadership Conference (SCLC), People United to Save Humanity (PUSH), and the National Urban League are at the integrationist end of the continuum, while the Black Muslims and the Republic of New Africa are placed at the separatist end. Groups like the Congress on Racial Equality (CORE), the Black Liberationist as

---

[26]Quoted by Sidney Wilhelm, *Who Needs the Negro?*, p. 170.
[27]*Kalamazoo Gazette* (Thursday, Jan. 13, 1972), Section A, p. 4.

well as the once highly visible Student Nonviolent Coordinating Committee (SNCC) and the Black Panther Party would fall some place in between the two poles (see below).

Separatist/Integrationist Continuum

Separatist tendency		Integrationist tendency
Republic of New Africa (now virtually defunct)	SNCC	NAACP
	CORE	National Urban League
Black Muslims (currently Moving to the right)	Black Panthers	SCLC
	Black Liberationist	PUSH

INTEGRATIONIST-REFORMIST TENDENCY

Although some significant shifts have occurred in the last few years, the integrationists essentially take the position that integration has been and still is the most viable goal for black Americans. They operate on the basic premise that it is still possible to transform the American system into one in which peoples of all hues can live harmoniously under the American flag. Once white racism and its various debilitating manifestations have been controlled, genuine integration is possible. Hence the integrationists are not attempting to bring about the total destruction of the American system, but rather the aim is to change particular aspects of it.

Roy Wilkins of the NAACP stated that "the overwhelming majority of the Negro-American population, ranging as high as 95 percent and as low as 78 percent, choose integration," and that "the anti-integrationists have forgotten that the siren song of separatism has fallen flat several times before in the history of American black-white relations."[28] He argues that integration is not the same as assimilation, in which the cultural heritage of black people is rejected for that of whites. People United to Save Humanity (Operation PUSH), under the leadership of the Reverend Jesse L. Jackson, is also opposed to the separatist tendency, and views the current goal of Black America as one of achieving educational and economic parity and equity with white America.

The late Whitney Young, Jr., of the Urban League, saw the tendency toward separatism as an attempt "for relief from the 'grueling struggle' with American racism" and claims that "there are no virtues to be found in segregation, whether imposed by white racists or sought out by our-selves."[29] Not unlike Wilkins, Young did not view integration as a process whereby blacks reject their blackness. Four Young there was a "need for an

---

[28] *Ebony*, 25 (August 1970), p. 55.
[29] Ibid., p. 90.

integrated society, not because of association with whites is, of itself, a good thing, but because it is through participation in the mainstream that full equality can be won."[30] Today many integrationists have embraced the concept of Black Power as a viable and relevant concept. Young's thinking is representative of other organizations of this tendency in the sense that "Black power can be—and should be—interpreted to mean the development of black pride and self-determination. It means that black people must control their own destiny and their communities. It means the mobilization of black political and economic strength to win complete equality."[31]

CORE and SNCC made a more drastic shift in their thinking and orientations than the NAACP, the SCLC, or the Urban League. In particular, CORE has remained basically a reformist organization rather than the champion of a revolutionary version of black separatism and feels that, at least for the moment, integration is irrelevant and meaningless. Therefore, for CORE, separatist programs are essential for the development of black progress and to any long-range plans for genuine integration. Greater control of the black community and its institutions is the drive behind the present plans of CORE.

SNCC broke with the traditional integrationist-reformist tendency and for a very brief time formed an alliance with the Black Panthers. After a power struggle in SNCC, Stokely Carmichael became the party's prime minister and, along with other members from the leadership of SNCC, helped the new group to get established on the West Coast. SNCC has failed to establish a national black political party and, according to Robert Allen, "thought the Black Panthers could become such a party . . . but this alliance was short-lived, if it ever really existed, and ended a few months later in angry verbal exchanges and near-violence."[32]

The SNCC emphasis was on self-determination, revolution, and anti-capitalism. It did not rule out alliances with any oppressed minority and also welcomed potential allies coming from the white population—the young white radicals with sufficient revolutionary zeal to help change the system. But with the ousting of Carmichael and his subsequent departure from the country, and with the loss of other national leaders, SNCC rapidly lost the attention it had in the late 60s. Before the decline in power, SNCC leaders, especially Carmichael, encouraged blacks to get guns and become prepared for the second American revolution.[33]

[30] Ibid., p. 94.

[31] Whitney M. Young, Jr., *Beyond Racism: Building an Open Society* (New York: McGraw-Hill, 1971), p. 238.

[32] Robert L. Allen, *Black Awakening in Capitalist America* (New York: Doubleday, 1970), p. 263.

[33] For a more comprehensive statement on Carmichael see Robert Allen, *Black Awakening in Capitalist America*, pp. 247–256.

BLACK NATIONALISM

The ideology and programs of the black nationalists are in direct opposition to those of the integrationists, but this schism is an old issue. For example, Martin Delaney in the mid-1800s espoused a brand of black nationalism (Africa for Africans) which was contrary to the thinking of Frederick Douglass, the abolitionist-integrationist. Thus, the integrationist-nationalist controversy is not a recent phenomenon on the American scene. What is basically a contemporary situation, however, is revolutionary nationalism, whose emergence comes out of a new interpretation of black-white relations nationally and internationally. Black nationalism, within the American context, is a drive for self-determination—a mechanism through which a new ethos and a sense of peoplehood can be sufficiently manifested. It is opposed to assimilation or any other process that threatens to weaken black solidarity and black culture.

At the moment, black nationalists view the white American society as a fossilized nation that is spiritually bankrupt and morally corrupted and whose institutions are without any redeeming features. Therefore, the nationalists accept as their task the creation of a social system that is not a replica of the white system.

In their drive for nationhood the black nationalists are forced to view those of the integrationist tendency as enemies who must be defeated if they are to attain their goal. They allege continued failures of the integrationists to achieve any major victories for the masses of black people; they charge that integrationists are unable to relate to the demands of blacks; and they declare it is impossible to eliminate racism and oppression by merely seeking to reform certain aspects of the American system. They claim that the black integrationists, especially the bourgeoise variety, are the only ones who have benefited from the system, not the masses. Even those few blacks who have made some economic gains are still exploited because of race; hence so-called progress is an illusion and therefore the integrationists, not unlike the white liberals, tend to block true black liberation.

BLACK NATIONALISM: FOUR TYPES

Strongly opposed to integration during the 60s and early 70s were four expressions of black nationalism: (1) black cultural nationalism, (2) black revolutionary nationalism, (3) black separatism, and (4) black liberationism. Each group advocated a drastic revision of the American system, although their strategies and tactics differ markedly, a situation which made them both compatriots and rivals.

The several cultural nationalist groups were perhaps best represented by such national spokesmen as Maulana Ron Karenga and Imamu Amiri Baraka, the former LeRoi Jones. At this stage in the development of Black America, revolution was not feasible and, according to the cultural nationalist, there were certain logical prerequisites that black people must achieve before they can realistically entertain thoughts of revolution. Accordingly, the cultural nationalists placed primary emphasis on the development of black cultural art forms as a mechanism of black liberation. Karenga and Baraka argued that there was a need for a cultural revolution before one may entertain the notion of a political revolution. In essence, black people must be culturally free before they can be politically free. Nationalism, then, was viewed in terms of a black cultural nation, and a common future based on their blackness. Accordingly blacks should be concerned with self-determination, race pride, and the pursuit of blackness.[34]

Through black culture, the collective consciousness of black people can be aroused to challege the "decadent culture of the oppressor." Moreover, and perhaps more importantly, a revolutionary black culture can function to specify the plan that will bring about the demise of black oppression.

As mentioned above, there was disagreement between the integrationists and black nationalists, there was also a cleavage between the various brands of nationalism, especially on how to achieve the goal of mass liberation. The main controversy between the revolutionary and cultural nationalists was over emphasis and strategy. The former (revolutionary nationalists) agree that the development of black culture is necessary but not sufficient; rather the attainment or seizure of power is more important. The cultural nationalists disagreed and placed strong emphasis on the cultural aspect of the struggle as a necessary adjunct of revolutionary nationalism.

The separatist nationalists, best represented by the Black Muslims and the Republic of New Africa, sought to set themselves physically apart from the larger white society. The Republic of New Africa wanted to take over five Southern states and build a black nation. They attempted to set up a campaign, with Mississippi as a base, to organize and attract more blacks for the building of the nation.

The Muslims, on the other hand, expressed an interest in obtaining a state or a parcel of land which would enable them to escape the oppressive influence of the white man. Both groups depended on membership affiliation and, although it is impossible to determine the size, it is doubtful that either group had over 100,000 members. To date, neither group has been able to separate completely from the larger society. As a matter of fact, the Republic of New Africa is virtually non-existent and the Black Muslims have made a drastic shift in their posture since the death of the Honorable Elijah Muhammad in 1975. For example, under the leadership of the Honorable

---

[34] Allen, *Black Awakening in Capitalist America*, pp. 165–66.

Wallace D. Muhammad, the son of the late Elijah Muhammad, the name of the group has been changed to the World Community of Islam in the West and whites are now eligible for membership. When the authors visited a Chicago mosque in 1978 they observed that there were some whites in attendance and a few of them played a prominent role in the prayer service.

Both groups, however, did call for the destruction of the American system, but they differed with respect to how this was to be accomplished. For the Muslims, the demise of the white society would come through the intervention of Allah, and, according to the late Honorable Elijah Muhammad, this downfall would take place within the next decade. The Republic of New Africa sought less mystical means to bring about the downfall of the system. With the help of Third World Allies they expected to wage a major battle against the United States.

Finally, there are the black liberationists, who advocate another direction for black America. Many of them see the need for a totally new social structure in which blacks and whites will cease to be enemies. One of the best articulated statements on this position has been made by Lerone Bennett, Jr., who cogently spells out some of the dilemmas confronting the integration-separation tendencies and clarifies some of the confusion surrounding such terms as *separation, segregation, integration, desegregation,* and *assimilation.*[35]

According to Bennett, when these terms are used the "standard reference is white, the orientation is white."[36] In such a context, then, *assimilation* implies absorption of blacks—culturally and physically—by white people; *integration* means interaction of blacks and whites within a context of white supremacy; *separation,* for many, remains the same as segregation and *desegregation* is often viewed as integration. But such connotations are not necessarily true if taken from a black perspective. This perspective suggests that *desegregation* is not the same as integration; *separation* does not mean *segregation; assimilation* does not mean the disappearance of black culture and physical traits; nor does *integration* mean the interaction of blacks with whites within a context of white supremacy.

To the liberationist, *integration* implies relating to another human being as a human being, regardless of color, race, nationality, religion, or culture. This relationship implies the absence of sub- and superordinate statuses. The argument is that desegregation cannot be viewed as integration because what is involved here is simply the elimination of structural barriers, legal and nonlegal, which heretofore prevented people from having equal access to public facilities and public transactions. Desegregation

---

[35]For a full statement on this position see Lerone Bennett, Jr., "Beyond Either-Or: A Philosophy of Liberation," in *The Challenge of Blackness,* copyright © 1972, Lerone Bennett, Jr., and Johnson Publishing Company, Chicago, Ill. pp. 293–312.
[36]Ibid.

may be a necessary first step, but it is not in itself integration. The fundamental difference between segregation and separation is that the former is forced while the latter is based on choice. So-called separatism in America, according to Bennett, "is not separation but regroupment. It is not separation for blacks to come together on matters of common policy. It is not separation for them to go on Sunday to a church which has never been closed to anyone. It is not separation for them to go into the closet and shut the door to hammer out a common policy."[37]

Bennett posits six major reasons why the either/or proposition of integration-separation is useless, namely:[38]

1.   The proposition is irrelevant and immaterial because it confuses means and ends, strategy and tactics. It makes a fetish out of mere words and offers a predetermined response for every place and time.

2.   The either/or proposition is irrelevant because it is based on false premises. It assumes that blacks are free to choose and that their only options are the two horns of a dilemma. . . . It ignores the infinite gradations between integration and separation and the fact that there is a third choice, pluralism, and beyond that a fourth, transformation.

3.   The either/or proposition is false because it is based on a misunderstanding of the modern world which is grounded on power, group organization and group conflict.

4.   The either/or proposition does not explicate the dialectics of development in which a negation is necessary for a synthesis; nor does it deal with American experience, which is an experience not of the melting pot but of fierce struggle for existence by organized national groups.

Bennett is suggesting that blacks must regroup (separate) to advance their own interests in the same way that other immigrant groups did when them came to America.

5.   The either/or dilemma contains neither heat nor light for this situation; more importantly, it fails to meet the concrete questions and demands of the black masses who pay little or no attention to the either/or arguments.

6.   Finally, the either/or dilemma is irrelevant and immaterial because it is a reaction instead of an action. As Robert Chrisman argued in a brilliant review of Harold Cruse's "The Crises of the Negro Intellectual" in *The Black Scholar* . . . "Neither truly challenges the racist structure of American society, instead, each accommodates it in different ways." Both integrationists and separationists are excessively preoccupied with the white man. The integrationists with sitting down with the white man; the separationist with the question of not sitting down with the white man. The liberationist says the presence or absence of the white man is irrelevant. What obsesses him is the liberation of black people.

---

[37] Ibid., p. 298.
[38] Ibid., pp. 298–307.

Accordingly, the liberationist calls for transcending the entrapments that currently plague those who advocate integration or separatism and to move toward transforming the total society into a system whereby racism, oppression, and exploitation will be eliminated. Achieving this goal calls for a critical appraisal of black-white institutional arrangements and the policies and practices that are used to govern them. It also calls for the formulation of new values and an advanced economic program which ensures a greater and more equitable distribution of wealth and power.

Bennett sees a role for whites in the liberation of black people, but the role will not be the traditional one in which the whites assumed the leadership roles. Whites can help by making financial contributions and by educating whites in their community about their prejudical attitudes, how they have benefited from a system that exploits and oppresses, and how they themselves are being exploited and oppressed by the same system. Finally, whites can help in the creation of a "new white consciousness"[39] that will facilitate transforming America into a society that is just for all peoples regardless of race, creed, or color.

CONCLUSIONS

In the foregoing paragraphs we have discussed the various groups and the historical background out of which they emerged. Because of the many factors involved it is difficult to predict accurately the road that the black masses will take toward liberation; therefore the following statements must be taken as being largely speculative.

Since the mid-60s there has been no absence of oratory and rhetoric about the plight of black people. Rhetoric extols the benefits of integration, internal separatism, complete independence, and the complete destruction of the American society by revolutionary means. Of the several alternatives, the last appears to be the least feasible because an attempt at armed revolution is most likely to meet with severe repressive measures. Many of the militant leaders of yesterday who called for an armed revolution have now begun to oppose it as a means, since the end results would be catastrophic for many blacks, urban guerila warfare not withstanding.[40]

There are numerous factors that militate against a successful armed revolution: (1) black people are generally highly concentrated in central

---

[39] For an excellent statement on the creation of a "new white consciousness" see Robert W. Terry, *For Whites Only* (Grand Rapids, Mich., W. B. Eerdmans Publishing Co., 1970).

[40] A recent example of this shift in philosophy is seen in a newspaper report of how Huey P. Newton turns away from Eldridge Cleaver's "pick-up-the-gun-now" philosophy and advocates working within the system to advance the social status of black people. *Kalamazoo Gazette* (Monday, Jan. 31, 1972).

city's ghettos, and this makes them vulnerable to the retaliatory actions of whites; (2) the preponderance of military strength rests in the hands of the white power structure; (3) virtually all the black organizations, especially the militant variety, have been infiltrated by informants and/or government agents; and (4) the proportion of blacks willing to stage total warfare against the white society is undoubtedly negligible. If an insurrection were to start in the cities it would not be a protracted affair. What is most likely to happen is that the black community would be encircled by military personnel and martial law would be declared to prevent freedom of movement of black people outside of their communities. Undoubtedly, in such an instance the black community again would be the victim, as in the riots of the 60s, with little damage exacted upon the institutions whose destruction was sought. As a matter of fact, if an insurrection is actually attempted the likelihood is that racist structures will be strengthened and the government will become more repressive toward black people. A factor that cannot be overlooked is that various levels of government have formulated plans to quell any attempt to overthrow the government. The riots of the 60s served as an impetus for the government to be ready in case the black people decided to change things through violent means.

The separatist route is also fraught with many dangers and uncertainties. Until recently, the Black Muslims envisioned that the white society would be destroyed by Allah rather than an armed struggle. Allah would take care of the white man in his own way, and therefore the black need not be concerned about the white man because his "day" was coming and then the black man would control his own destiny. Today, however, the experience of the Muslims has convinced them that such a vision was illusory and that it is virtually impossible to have a separate state within the confines of the United States. Thus, the Muslims are more concerned with the development of group solidarity and a strong economic base than with separation.[41]

What are the chances of a black group's gaining control of a state or several states where they can establish their own nation? The Republic of New Africa advocated taking over five Southern states. There is little chance that the government will turn over the several states, with the existing industries and business intact, to black people. This is too far-fetched to capture the imagination of any sizable number of blacks, regardless of their socioeconomic position. They feel strongly that, even in those states where there is a significant number of blacks, it would be impossible to take control of the state. This is suggested by the resistance to the acquisition of political and economic power by blacks in the South

---

[41]See Elijah Muhammad, "Message to the Black Man," in Arthur C. Littleton and Mary W. Burger (eds.), *Black Viewpoints* (New York, The New American Library, Inc., 1971), pp. 152–58. For a recent view of the Muslims see *Time*, March 14, 1977, p. 59.

through orderly and legal channels. The idea of a violent black secession is totally foreign and alien to the thinking of whites, therefore it seems axiomatic that pressures used to bring about an all-black state would meet effective resistance. Even the much milder program of the Black Muslims has stirred up local resistance to the expansion of their property holdings, and attempts at open secession would simply invite official repression.

Cultural nationalism, as an alternative, does not pose an immediate threat to the larger white society. Cultural nationalism is an attempt to bring about black consciousness. It might be said to be a mechanism to bring about a sense of peoplehood whereby black people recognize not only their shared common destiny, but also their cultural heritage. If blacks respond to this appeal, they would not be unlike other ethnic groups in this country who point with pride to their "home lands" and their cultural antecedents. Thus, like the Irish, Poles, Germans, Italians, and other groups, black Americans can benefit immensely from a cultural nationalism that will bring them to see themselves as psychological equals to others in the society. Perhaps from that position of strength they can chart out the direction in which they want to travel in the future. Cultural nationalism can be functional for black people to the extent that they and other Americans are able to see that black culture has made many contributions to the world in general and the United States in particular and will continue to do so. Within the black population resides the creative genius to move the country to a new level of awareness and existence. It has the potential power of bringing the dominant population to reevaluate and reassess many of the traditional myths about race and culture.

Partial evidence suggests that already black cultural nationalism is having some effect on white America. There is greater exposure of the black experience on television and in books and magazines, and the degree to which whites emulate the behavior and customs of blacks is in part a measure of the efficacy of cultural nationalism. Of course, another interpretation is that of exploitation, especially in the area of music, where whites have imitated the "soul sound" and have amassed a fortune while many black artists have remained obscure figures outside of the black community.

Cultural nationalism is not free of pitfalls and shortcomings, but the one that seems to stand out as the greatest impediment at the moment is that many young blacks appear too easily satisfied with the sheer superficialities of black cultural nationalism. More specifically, it appears that too frequently many black youth take black cultural nationalism to mean that they can ignore the forces and events of the larger white society. This can make them less effective in dealing with racism and at the same time more alienated and frustrated. To wear Afro garbs and Afro hairdos and to give the black power handshake and sign (clenched fist) is not enough.

These are outward signs of black pride and not ends in themselves. They should be seen as part of an essential strategy toward the eventual liberation of black people and only one aspect of a multifaceted orientation that blacks must adopt in order to change their status in the society. To withdraw into a shallow version of cultural nationalism will only impede the progress.

Black liberation philosophy holds great promise for moving blacks toward greater equality and freedom. It avoids many of the ideological shortcomings and pitfalls of the separatist tendency as well as those of the integrationist. Fundamentally, the real issue is the liberation of black people, not whether blacks are in the presence of whites. We would argue, however, that because of the magnitude and complexity of the race problems perhaps all the diverse groups are functional from a conflict model in the sense that a multifaceted approach may disrupt the equilibrium of a racist system sufficiently to bring about a new order—without exploitation, oppression, and racism—for all of the peoples regardless of race, creed, nationality, religion or color.

BLACK-WHITE INTERACTION PATTERNS IN THE UNITED STATES IN RELATION TO GENERALIZED PATTERNS

United States pattern. Until the mid-60s the overwhelming majority of black people were in favor of integration into the "main stream" of American culture. The freedom rides, the sit-in demonstrations, the March on Washington, and the rest, all were geared toward getting into the system. Congress passed many civil rights laws to ensure social equality, but there was a general recognition among blacks that there was little economic progress and that they were victimized by a racist society resistant to lowering the barriers for blacks. It appeared that the traditional methods of nonviolence were not achieving enough gains; thus more militant black groups came into existence in the hopes of waging a more successful battle against individual and institutional racism.

Generalized pattern. When the progress of a subordinated minority is constantly frustrated by opposition, militant groups will emerge and their goals and activities will be greater in comparison to previous groups.

United States pattern. In recent years there has been a greater sense of peoplehood among all blacks. Frazier's thesis that middle-class blacks did not identify with the black masses has been weakened by the trend for more and more blacks at all socioeconomic levels to realize their blackness and their common enemy—white racism. Yet there are cleavages among black people, especially when it comes to programs and methods to be used in overcoming racism.

Generalized pattern. Intragroup cleavages found among virtually any ethnic group will hamper that group in its struggle against the oppression of the dominant group.

United States pattern. In spite of the recent black cultural thrust there is a strong tendency in the United States for whites to view black culture as inferior to their own. It appears that, with the upsurge of ethnicity among many groups, more and more whites are resisting being "contaminated." It is not uncommon to hear whites say that blacks and other ethnic groups are going too far, and are forcing themselves on whites; that there is nothing wrong with white culture; that they are tired of white society being criticized by "those" ethnic groups; that if they do not like the country, they should leave it. As already mentioned, these attitudes have softened over the years, but they are prevalent and widespread enough to indicate that while "white ethnocentrism" may be on the wane it is far from dead.

Generalized pattern. The culture of a subordinated minority is usually denigrated and the dominant group tends to force its culture on minority group leaders.

United States pattern. Along with blacks, the Puerto Ricans, Indians, and Chicanos are keenly aware that, although some gains have been made in the past, relative gaps between themselves and whites are still substantial. The improvement which has come has stimulated the demand for further improvement.

Generalized pattern. Improvement among a subordinated minority tends to create a greater desire for the elimination of socioeconomic disparities.

United States pattern. Compared to the mid-60s the emphasis on black culture is very strong. When efforts to integrate into the white society were strongly resisted, blacks began to question the value of emulating white society, and to question why for many years they had rejected their blackness. Today, to deny one's blackness and culture is viewed as one of the most debilitating things that could happen to blacks. Most of the black man's African heritage was stripped away during slavery, but out of this experience and subsequent development has emerged a distinct black culture which has endured because attempts to integrate into white society were never successful. Had genuine integration occurred this distinct culture would never have arisen. Today blacks have turned inward for cultural expression and development.

Generalized pattern. When the subsystem of a subordinated minority is strong and the dominant group is strongly resistant to "genuine" integration, the tendency for retention of minority culture will be great.

United States pattern. Relative deprivation among blacks generated much of the frustration, anger and hostility that was manifested in the riots of the 60s. Negligible progress in employment, housing, politics, and so forth, leave black people with the feeling that the system is good at making promises, but most inept at making them a reality. Time and time again, high expectations have arisen that significant changes were going to take place only to be frustrated by a series of setbacks. Hence, many blacks, especially the youth, are unwilling to place their faith in the idea that meaningful changes will occur through the legal and orderly processes.

Generalized pattern. Substantial change without complete success often creates a sense of alienation and hopelessness that undermines the chance that change will occur through orderly procedures.

United States pattern. The black Muslims and the Republic of New Africa were two groups advocating a complete separation from the white society. The Muslims were harassed, threatened, and terrorized in their drive for independence. The chances for the success of the New Republic of Africa are not good at all within the political boundaries of the United States. Not too many whites take these groups seriously because the groups do not come into contact with them, but where the groups have had contact with whites they have encountered resistance. If they were to convince the white society that they stood a chance of being successful, the white power structure would devise a method to minimize or destroy their strength.

Generalized pattern. An attempt of a minority to achieve independence from the majority will not get the support of the majority but is most likely to be strongly resisted.

QUESTIONS

1. Why did the "indentured servant" classification fall into disuse and what important factors helped to accelerate the establishment of slavery as a definite system of forced labor?

2. How would you go about correcting the picture painted by some writers that during slavery an idyllic relationship existed between slaves and masters?

3. What important developments occurred near the end of the reconstruction period and what effect did they have on the subsequent progress of black people?

4. How would you characterize the status of black people in the South in post-Civil War years after the whites had regained control?

5. If you had to take a position on the progress black people have made in the United States would you take the majoritarian or the minoritarian viewpoint? Why? Defend fully.

6. Can you discern any historical factors that may help explain the malaise of black communities?

7. Why is there a need for greater community-police cooperation in the black communities? Do you think that "community control" of the police is a step toward the reduction of many of the problems plaguing black communities?

8. What factors are responsible for the strong black reaction against integration in recent years?

9. If you were asked to consider either the internal colonial model or the ethnic group model which would you defend as being a more accurate model to use in describing black America? Defend fully.

10. Do you see any inconsistencies in a position taken by a person who advocates integration and at the same time favors the concept of black power? Discuss fully.

11. In what sense did CORE and SNCC make a more drastic shift in their orientations than the NAACP or the National Urban League?

12. How do the black nationalist groups view white America and why are they opposed to the integrationist tendency?

13. Are there any salient differences between the four major expressions of black nationalism in the United States?

14. What does Lerone Bennett mean by the statement "the either/or proposition does not explicate the dialectics of development in which a negation is necessary for a synthesis?" Discuss fully.

15. Can you show, using a conflict model, how the various divergent black organizations may be functional to the progress of black people?

16. Are the chances for the integration of blacks in American society better or worse than the prospects of integration of the inhabitants of the French Antilles in the French Union? List the reasons for your viewpoint.

17. Do you think the black reaction along a more separatist line is a temporary or a long time trend? Will the majority of blacks eventually reject the integrationist organizations?

18. Is there an identity of interest between American blacks and the peoples of the third world?

19. Are the prospects for the elimination of racism better in the United States than in France or Britain? Why or why not?

20. Under ideal circumstances, what should be the direction of progress for American blacks; working toward a distinct and largely self-contained black community or toward complete assimilation and integration?

Chapter 12

The United States and Yugoslavia: Divergent approaches toward ethnicity

THE PARAMETERS OF COMPARISON

The United States and Yugoslavia follow contrasting patterns in both governmental organization and ethnic policies. These patterns, reflecting both past traditions and recent occurrences, can be discerned in the structure of governmental institutions, and point toward a preferred type of ethnic adjustment and institutional adaptation. The United States is a federation of individual states formed on the basis of territorial convenience rather than on the ethnic background of the inhabitants, while Yugoslavia developed into a federation based on the cultural differences of its peoples. Yugoslavia is a combination of several republics and provinces in which at least partially homogeneous populations have maintained a separate cultural identity for millennia. The memories of the glories of past kingdoms and the outrage at historic grievances combine to stimulate a jealous concern for the maintenance of cultural identity among its ethnically divergent populations.

In the United States ethnic groups can be classified according to their European or non-European heritage; the latter groups are sometimes referred to as different races and are composed of the indigenous American Indian population, the African and Asian populations, which were originally imported for labor, and those populations initially included in the United States by conquest, such as the Mexicans and Puerto Ricans.

In the United States the groups of non-European heritage have traditionally faced the greatest burdens of discrimination. They were economically and politically integrated into the larger community, which traced itself to a European background, but the occupations and political positions occupied by the groupings of non-European origin were generally low in status and in economic rewards.

The indigenous Indian populations of North and South America, the immigrant Asians, and the Africans could be easily identified by their physical appearance. Each of these groups has maintained an ethnic distinctiveness preserved in a pattern of separate communities. Nearly half of all American Indians live on reservations, the American Chinese commonly live in Chinatowns, the majority of urban American blacks reside in black ghettos, and the Spanish-speaking Mexican Americans and Puerto Ricans refer to their city quarters as *barrios*.

In the United States the major problem of intergroup relations is frequently seen as bringing the populations of non-European ancestry into the general pattern of assimilation, while, in Yugoslavia, the problem has been to guarantee an independent cultural identity to all groups in the face of major economic, educational, and social divergencies. Both Yugoslavia and the United States have a dominant ethnic group. In the United States it has been formed by the descendents of those Europeans who have most easily been assimilated to Anglo-Saxon culture and have established the pattern of living followed by the majority.[1] In Yugoslavia, the Serbs are the dominant nationality and represent nearly 40 percent of the population. Before World War II they contributed the ruling dynasty and held a majority of the important posts in government. In the United States, the dominance of the group sometimes characterized as white Anglo-Saxon Protestant has not been seriously questioned until recent years.

The civil rights movement, which reached its peak during the 1960s, marks an effort to destroy or, at least reduce, the barriers which have kept non-European groups, such as those of Mexican, Puerto Rican, American Indian, or black ancestry, from full participation in the American society and from full assimilation.

In Yugoslavia, similar changes took place in a much different manner as a result of World War II. The invasion of the country by the German armies forced the ruling dynasty into exile in 1941. Two guerrilla movements formed to resist the German occupiers: the Cetnik movement, led by General Draza Mihailovic, was composed entirely of Serbs and Montenegrins, while the Partisan movement led by Marshall Tito, appealed to

---

[1] Stewart G. Cole and Mildred Wiese Cole, *Minorities and the American Promise* (New York, Harper and Brothers, 1954), pp. 135–40.

all national groupings in Yugoslavia with a message of resistance and revolution. The forces of Tito were dominant over those of the Cetniks by the end of 1943, and the Partisans promised to found a new Yugoslavia which offered ethnic self-determination to all nationalities and minorities.

In the United States, the civil rights movement was supported by a democratic ideology, which proclaimed that all people had an equal right to participate in the society regardless of ethnic background. Socialism provided a somewhat similar egalitarian principle for Yugoslavia, since the formal aim of the government was cultural self-determination and the equalization of material conditions among all the peoples of Yugoslavia. The leadership of the Partisans stated that only the protection of minority rights could lead to full equality.[2]

It seemed for a time, in the United States, that the civil rights movement was eliminating the basis for racial conflict, while in Yugoslavia the government was establishing viable institutions based on cultural pluralism in that country. Both countries, however, have been disturbed by negative reactions to what promised to be a highly successful policy of intergroup adjustment. Both the United States and Yugoslavia have witnessed riots, assassinations, and other acts of lawlessness that resulted from ethnic alienation. Discontent in the United States is treated in Chapter 11. Before going into the details of ethnic conflict in Yugoslavia it is best to examine the intergroup relations in that country.

The following generalizations are stated at this point to help the reader more readily grasp the sociological relevance of the historical details as well as the subsequent ethnic relations: (1) a strong central government can either limit ethnic autonomy or promote economic equality among ethnic groups, and (2) the quest for justice in intergroup relations may move either from the individual to the group or vice versa.

POLITICAL ORGANIZATION AND ETHNICITY IN YUGOSLAVIA

The Socialist Federal Republic of Yugoslavia is a multinational state composed of five major nationalities, Serbs, Croats, Slovenes, Macedonians, and Montenegrins, and of more than nine other distinguishable ethnic minorities. The state is divided into six republics and two autonomous provinces. Five of the republics have a population primarily composed of one of the major nationalities. These five republics in order of size are

---

[2] The basic political principles had already been elaborated by the Communist Party of Yugoslavia in the prewar period, especially at its Fifth Conference in 1940. The principles are based on Lenin's premise that "the safeguarding of the rights of national minorities is indissolubly linked with the principle of full equality" from Lenin (Vladimir Ilyich Ulyanov), "Critical Notes on the National Question," quoted from Koča Jončič, *The Relations between Nationalities in Yugoslavia* (Beograd: Medunarodna Stampa, Interpress, 1967) p. 65.

Serbia, Croatia, Slovenia, Macedonia, and Montenegro. Montenegro is a republic, not because of a cultural distinctiveness, but rather because of the political traditions of this area; Montenegro was never really dominated by the Turks, and became the first independent state in the territories which comprise present-day Yugoslavia. The Montenegrins are culturally Serb. The sixth republic, Bosnia-Hercegovina, has a mixed population composed of Serbs, Croats, and Muslims, most of whom are culturally Slavic. Their ancestors were converted to Islam as a result of the special historical conditions under which the Ottoman Turks occupied the region in the 15th century.

The ethnic minorities which are not a majority in one of the republics were known, until 1971, as "national minorities." These "national minorities" constitute about one eighth of the population of Yugoslavia and will be referred to as "ethnic minorities" in this chapter. The nine largest minority populations in Yugoslavia include: the Albanians, Hungarians, Bulgarians, Rumanians, Slovaks, Czechs, Ruthenians, Italians, and Turks. Most of the ethnic minorities are culturally related to the populations of surrounding states.

The Socialist Republic of Serbia, which is the largest subdivision in Yugoslavia, contains 74.5 percent of the minority populations in Yugoslavia, and is further divided into the autonomous provinces of Vojvodina and Kossovo. The Vojvodina is the most ethnically mixed area in Yugoslavia; it contains mainly Hungarian, Slovak, Czech, Rumanian, Bulgarian, Serb, and Croat populations, all maintaining their national identities and living in close physical proximity. The Autonomous Province of Kossovo contains mainly Albanians and Serbs, with a small Turkish minority. Together, the Albanians and Turks comprise about 70 percent of the population in this province.[3]

Religion has played an important role in the divisions which have historically separated the peoples of Yugoslavia. The northern republics of Yugoslavia, Croatia, and Slovenia, were Hapsburg territories for many centuries. This historical inheritance meant that these two areas were Catholic in religion. The Austro-Hungarian Empire also carried with it a tradition of feudalism, the use of Latin as lingua franca, and the use of the Latin alphabet. The Hapsburg realms were a continuation of the Holy Roman Empire with its firm foundation of Roman and canon law, and this bestowed on these lands a political tradition which distinguished them sharply from the Orthodox Serbs.

---

[3] In 1971, Constitutional Amendment XX changed the term "national minorities" to "nationalities" with an English translation of "ethnic minorities." According to 1965 data, 40 of 84 communes in Serbia contain a majority of national minorities in the population. See Koča Jončič, *The Relations between Nationalities in Yugoslavia*, pp. 64, 68, 69, 70.

TABLE 12-1

Profile of Yugoslavia
(population according to nationalities
and national minorities [ethnic
groups])

	Total
Serbs	7,806,213
Croats	4,293,860
Slovenes	1,589,192
Macedonians	1,045,530
Montenegrins	513,833
Moslems (ethnic)	972,954
Yugoslavs	317,125
Albanians	914,760
Hungarians	504,368
Turks	182,964
Slovaks	86,433
Bulgarians	62,624
Rumanians	60,862
Russniaks°	38,619
Italians	25,615
Czechs	30,331
Gypsies, Vlachs† and others	142,627
Total	18,549,291

° Russniaks includes Russians and Ukranians; another term used is Ruthenians.
† Gypsies and Vlachs claim a distinct minority culture not related to a national state.
Source: *Statisticki godisnjak Jugoslavije 1964* (Belgrade: Savezni zavod za statistiku, 1964). Figures are from 1961 statistics.

The Serbs were heir to the Byzantine tradition. This meant that they were Orthodox in religion and used the Cyrillic alphabet in writing. While one can argue that there are separate Croat and Serb languages there are no educated Croats or Serbs who do not understand the spoken language of the other. The linguistic difference between the Serbs and Croats is not nearly as important as their separate historical development and separate political traditions. These divergences are reinforced in both areas by the differing religious establishments.

The Muslims constitute the third largest religious grouping in Yugoslavia. The Muslims are essentially members of three ethnic strains; the Muslims of Bosnia-Hercegovina are largely Slavs who converted to Islam, the Muslims of Kossovo are Albanians who converted to Islam, and the sprinkling of Turks in all areas of Yugoslavia once ruled by the Ottoman Empire remain Muslims. Traditionally, the greatest separation between the Muslim and the Christian populations existed in Serbia; Serbia was occupied for 500 years by the Turks, and the Muslim faith is considered to this day as the by-product of Ottoman occupation and collaboration. This set the tone for the historical antagonisms in both Kossovo and Bosnia-Hercegovina.

This historical heterogeneity among the Yugoslavs leads to conflicts which are exacerbated by economic jealousies, since industrial development in the various regions is far from uniform. This type of ethnic diversification has long contributed to political instability in Europe. Instability and conflict characterized the area both when it was a part of the Hapsburg Empire and when it formed the pre–World-War-II Kingdom of Yugoslavia.

One of the principal platforms of the Partisans during World War II was an appeal for the equal treatment of all the ethnic components of Yugoslavia as well as a federalism based on nationality. Yugoslavia was to be reconstituted into a multinational federation after World War II. At the same time the Partisan movement was influenced by the Soviet Union, which had developed strong central organs which dominated the local levels of government by a highly centralized political and economic bureaucracy. After the political leadership consolidated its power and reconstructed the country in the immediate aftermath of the war, it rejected the relevance of the Soviet model for Yugoslavia. In the 1950s the Yugoslav leadership introduced a system of workers' self-management which in time decentralized the decision-making powers of the government.

THE POLITICS OF ETHNIC CONFLICT IN YUGOSLAVIA

The evolution of the workers' self-management system led to a predictable liberalization of the political atmosphere in Yugoslavia which affected all spheres of national life. During the 1960s the government gradually transferred powers of taxation to the republics and to local units of government. This reform gave these bodies an independent basis for existence and a chance to chart their own policies of economic development. It was only natural for the more prosperous republics and regions to try to retain the locally earned revenues at the expense of the less developed areas, which were short of tax revenues for the maintenance of public services and investment funds to equalize the great disparities in economic welfare which exist in Yugoslavia. Nevertheless, the liberalization policy continued of its own momentum because it had brought rapid economic growth which had benefited all of Yugoslavia even though unequally.

This inequality led to political consequences which are at the root of the contemporary political conflict in Yugoslavia. During the year 1964–1965 Yugoslavia required new credits for modernizing the railways and stabilizing the currency. The Western lenders made it clear that Yugoslavia would not be able to expect new funds unless it put its fiscal house "in order" by devaluing its currency and imposing reforms which would end the costly practice of subsidizing enterprises, railroads, and other activities which could not stand on their own economically. This policy was urged by most Croat leaders, the Slovenes, and the intellectual elements in the Serbian community.

There was also substantial opposition to these efforts to introduce "market socialism" to Yugoslavia. The elements which opposed this policy were centered in the southern underdeveloped regions of Yugoslavia, but they also included influential institutions within the society such as the army and the police establishments. In both of these, the Serbs and Montenegrins predominated. This coalition of interest viewed the entire trend toward decentralization with suspicion because they felt that it would benefit the already prosperous areas of Yugoslavia disproportionately and also would erode the Serbian dominance of some institutions within the state and the leading role of the League of Communists itself.[4] The opposition to the reforms of 1965 found its spiritual leadership in the person of Alexander Rankovic, Vice President of Yugoslavia and former Minister of Interior. In Yugoslavia, the Ministry of Interior directs the activities of the secret police. Rankovic considered himself next in line as the successor to Tito and took imprudent steps to put himself into the best strategic position. The combination of these factors led to his removal from all offices and his early retirement in June 1966.

Rankovic was viewed as the real power behind the secret police, and that institution came under examination as he fell from influence. There were many exposés of the misdeeds of the secret police which ultimately had the result of discrediting the institution itself. This led to a major reduction in force, and the secret police became merely another agency within the country which was accountable to the League and to the Government. This downgrading of the secret police led to a greater feeling of security on the part of the Yugoslav public that expressed itself in an increased willingness to register open criticism. Other major consequences were that elective bodies and representative organs, both in government and in the self-managerial economic enterprises, expanded their authority and jurisdiction in the absence of any of the restraints previously exercised by the secret police. The liberal wing of the League of Communists came fully into its own, since those elements which were associated with Rankovic had temporarily lost their power and voice. The position of the liberals was bolstered by the unprecedented growth of prosperity, particularly in the most developed parts of Yugoslavia. This created the atmosphere which revived the Serb-Croat rivalry as a political issue and led to the student eruptions in Serbia in 1968.

---

[4] The Communist Party of Yugoslavia is known as the League of Communists; this title change took place at the Sixth Party Congress of 1952.

In the period when Rankovic was head of the secret police any open manifestation of Serb–Croat conflict was ruthlessly suppressed as a threat to civil order and Yugoslav unity. This policy of suppression was supported by many of the older people, who remembered the bitter feuds and the atrocities which resulted from ethnic conflict prior to the end of World War II. The younger generation, however, had no personal memories of World War II, and to them warnings about the danger of ethnic conflict sounded like the irrelevant prattle of old men. One of the features of a more "liberal" atmosphere was that ethnic concerns could be openly expressed. It was such a "liberal" atmosphere which allowed the "linguistic dispute" to become a major issue; in the Rankovic era such dissension was not allowed to surface.

Oddly enough, it was the effort to heal ethnic dissension which gave rise to one of the major points in the "linguistic conflict." This was the effort to lessen controversy over language usage by the development of a Serbo-Croatian language. This move was eventually denounced by several prominent Croatians, many of whom were members of the Communist Party and as such were assumed to be amenable to party discipline in behalf of Yugoslav unity. These Croatian leaders claimed that Serbian predominated in the mixed language and asked that Croatian be recognized as an official language.

This move produced an immediate Serb reaction expressed in the demand by 45 prominent Serbian writers, in the Belgrade daily Borba, that 600,000 Serbs living in Croatia use the Cyrillic alphabet for teaching and writing. Interest in the discussion increased and what started out as a somewhat academic debate escalated into a serious controversy. Finally the leaders of governmental and League organizations, including Tito, demanded that the debate cease.

Although forced to desist from public expression, the participants in the debate were not severely punished. Some were forced to resign their membership in the League of Communists, but in Yugoslavia this does not threaten status to the extent that would have been true in other Communist states. The relatively mild reaction in this case demonstrated to the public that draconian measures would not be employed against protest and paved the way for the next expression of dissent, the student strike in 1968.

The student strike included most of the students of Belgrade University, a majority of whom had grown up in the post–World-War-II era and thus had been socialized in the atmosphere of communist Yugoslavia. The strike was not directed so much at academic grievances as at conditions in Yugoslav society as a whole. In the years of prosperity and decentralization disparities in income between individual Yugoslav citizens had steadily increased. The students, who had been brought up on the rhetoric of socialism, deplored the distance between governmentally stated goals and

Yugoslav reality. Moreover, the student protest was bound to reverberate on the larger Yugoslav scene as discrepancies in income between nationalities were even greater than discrepancies between individual incomes.

The student strike was settled by the self-criticism of President Tito, who acknowledged the justice of the students' grievances and promised change. This solution was bound to act as a stimulant to other dissatisfied groups and to aggravate national conflicts. The decisive issue for the future survival and well-being of the Yugoslav state is the Serb-Croat relationship, which once again came to the forefront.

The League leadership believed that it was possible to maintain a fair degree of national cohesion with the widest dispersion of economic responsibility. All its political measures were based on this fundamental faith. During the same three years the powers of the League and the government were thoroughly decentralized by the constitutional amendments of 1968 and 1971 and the revised party statutes of 1969. The triumph of the students was also a victory for the liberalizing elements within the League. This federalization of power led to the logical consequence of merging economic demands with the politics of local nationalism. During the fall of 1971 the government of the Republic of Croatia was undergoing internal struggles within its own ranks between the liberals and conservatives, and with the central government. The liberal wing did not mind availing itself of nationalistic elements, both within and outside the League of Communists, principally through the medium of an old cultural organization known as *Matica Hrvatska*,[5] which propagated Croat nationalism through its own media. These evidences of nationalism were then transformed into concrete demands and into pressure both on the more ideologically conservative elements within the Croat government, symbolized by the former head of the Croatian League of Communists, Vladimir Bakaric, and on the federal government. The main demands concerned an increase of investment in Croatia, including the retention of Croatia's foreign exchange earnings within the Republic.

The government struck at the moment when it perceived that Matica Hrvatska was transforming itself into a political party with the connivance of the liberal wing of the Croatian Communist League. The central League organs summarily removed the Croat League leadership and then started purging the League members who were involved in Matica Hrvatska. After the liberal leaders in the League were relieved, the students of Zagreb University participated in major demonstrations and disturbances during which many students were arrested; most of them were subsequently released. These demonstrations protested the summary removal of the Croat leaders and demanded the restoration of autonomy to the

---

[5] Matica Hrvatska is an old Croatian cultural organization with nationalist overtones.

Croat League and the return of the dismissed League leaders. The episode points up the brittleness of Yugoslav institutional arrangements. The federal intervention was not planned and had the support of many Slovene leaders who saw their role as fending off any threat to the unity of Yugoslavia.

ETHNIC ADJUSTMENT IN THE
UNITED STATES AND YUGOSLAVIA

Historically, the United States and Yugoslavia evolved along different lines. Practically all the states which succeeded each other in the territories comprising present-day Yugoslavia accepted cultural divergence as a fact of life. This does not mean that the people of the Balkans escaped efforts by the Turks, Germans, Hungarians, Italians, and others to change the basic ethnic composition and national identification of the populations which inhabited these territories. Yet, from the very inception of Yugoslavia, progressive opinion, which would be described as liberal in the United States, identified with cultural self-determination for all ethnic groups represented in the country.

In the United States of America the trend might be justly labelled as the reverse; territorial autonomy and self-determination were discouraged and liberal opinion viewed integration, assimilation, and amalgamation as the *summum bonum* for American society. Integration was avidly pursued by most ethnic-racial groups.

The Anglo-Saxons and other English-speaking ethnic segments have been dominant in the United States since its inception. They established their ideas of legislation and judicial principles developed from an effort to harmonize the British stress on liberty with the French emphasis on equality. They addressed themselves to the establishment of a nonfeudal society in which commerce, the right to property, and individual civil liberties were highly protected, but ignored the rights of cultural groups, since American law acted essentially upon individuals, and not on groups. Some groups, such as the American blacks, the Chinese, and Indians, were excluded from legal definitions in theory and in practice by not being granted full status within the legal framework of the society.[6] The majority of Europeans who migrated and settled in the United States were gradually assimilated and denationalized. The thoroughness of the transi-

---

[6] In *People* vs. *Hall* (1854) Chief Justice of the California Supreme Court Hugh C. Murray declared the Chinese to be legally Indians, since both were presumed to have descended from the same Asiatic ancestor. In practice, the Chinese, the Indian, and also the Negro were prohibited from testifying in court for or against a white man. Although the ban was lifted against the Indian and Chinese in 1872, the practice itself continued. A more famous case, the Dred Scott decision, in 1857, ruled that Negroes did not have rights as citizens.

tion was more than the result of chance. With the establishment of public education, Americanization became one of the principal missions of the educational system. From that mission to the present day, public educa- tion still derives many of its traditions including the great emphasis on individual adjustment as opposed to concrete learning. Generations of im- migrants accepted the cultural extinction of their ethnic or national identi- ties for the benefits of their material betterment as individuals and also in the hopes of a better acceptance of their children. The social cost involved in this transformation was a frequent separation between generations in which children belittled their own parents and foreign backgrounds as a result of the competitive pulls between the home, on the one hand, and the school and the rest of the society, on the other. The entire weight of institutions was on the side of an Anglo-Saxon majority culture which pressed the immigrant into an American mold. The foreign-language schools seldom obtained public support, and even the Catholic parochial schools were primarily agencies of "Americanization" within a Catholic framework. As a result, the English-speaking school was the most available alternative, and it provided the assimilationist policy with substance. Foreign identification usually lasted through no more than three genera- tions, and in the third generation it was, to say the least, marginal. In ad- dition to an English-language school system, judicial proceedings also took place in English, without adequate protection to those who did not understand it.

The non-European minorities were also forced into an American mold. Spanish-speaking populations were assumed to use English as their pri- mary language, and children from such families were punished by the school authorities for using Spanish as their native tongue in the school room or on the school grounds.[7] Tests were administered in English and graded on the same basis as for English-speaking students. It is not sur- prising that large numbers of Mexican-American children found them- selves classified as mentally retarded when judged by such a testing sys- tem.[8] The American Indians found similar language problems in their schooling, compounded by efforts to acculturate them into the American way of life.[9]

---

[7] For a cogent study of every major bilingual school program in the Southwest United States, see Vera P. John and Vivian M. Horner, *Early Childhood Bilingual Education* (New York, Modern Language Association, 1971).

[8] The Department of Health, Education, and Welfare sent a memorandum to all school districts in the United States on May 25, 1970, to clarify the HEW policy relating to compliance with Title VI of the Civil Rights Act of 1964: "(2) School districts must not assign national origin minority group students to classes for the mentally re- tarded on criteria which measure English language, etc."

[9] The Navaho Indian leader, Robert Burnette, has recently commented on this policy: "Every Indian child knows, as I did when in school, that 'white was right,' and generations of Indian children underwent the brutal military training that aimed to

The contemporary Yugoslav federal system that took shape during World War II based its appeal on ideological premises by promising to build a postwar Yugoslavia in which all nationalities would be equal under a socialist government. No one was left in doubt by the Communist leadership that the future state would be based on an entirely new system. The prewar Yugoslav government had managed to antagonize wide segments of the public by its Serb nationalist policies and by an economic conservatism which favored the Serb establishment. The Serb Royal dynasty, maintained by a Serb civil service and a Serb military, did not permit those structural changes which would have been truly meaningful to the other nationalities to take place. The Partisan movement was able to build on the divisions resulting from Serb nationalism.

The federalism which was established in Yugoslavia was based on two major influences, each of which favored some degree of ethnic autonomy. The first flowed out of the very nature of Partisan warfare: as the Partisan movement spread the skein of resistance from the Austrian to the Greek borders, and as more nationalities were involved, the leadership had to delegate major decision-making powers to local commanders who knew their areas and could therefore adapt their appeals and tactics to suit local conditions. This was also necessitated by the generally poor communications between Partisan headquarters and the various regional branches of the movement. This led to a spontaneous growth of regional administrative units dominated by people from the locality, since the Partisans established an infrastructure of Partisan government in all territories under their control or influence. It was these local bodies, the national committees, which provided the Partisan leadership with the possibility for a smooth takeover after the termination of hostilities, and also provided continuity of personnel and administrative practice throughout the post–World-War-II era.

The second major influence on the Partisans was Soviet federalism and the attitudes of the Union of Soviet Socialist Republics toward nationality problems. The postwar Yugoslav Constitution of 1946 was closely patterned after the Soviet Constitution of 1936. It is generally agreed that these two documents were highly centralistic in administrative practice but they also provided the nationalities with substantial rights to preserve their separate cultural identities.[10] This meant that all groups could obtain

---

destroy the tiniest fragment of pride in one's identity as an Indian . . . the goal of the school system fostered by the Bureau of Indian Affairs is not education but acculturation." Quoted from Robert Burnette, *The Tortured Americans* (Englewood Cliffs, New Jersey: Prentice-Hall, 1971), p. 24.

[10] The Constitution of 1946, Article 13, stated that national minorities "shall enjoy the right to and protection of their cultural development and the free use of their language."

schooling in their respective languages and that free use of their language would extend to court proceedings and other official business. When proceedings could not be held in the language of the defendant, an interpreter would at least be provided. Even such small groups as the Slovaks and the Ruthenians were guaranteed their linguistic and legal rights as cultural entities.

In the immediate postwar period Soviet influence became paramount in Yugoslavia. The Yugoslav leadership, like that of other Soviet bloc states, tried to adapt Soviet practices and institutions to their own specific realities. This was frequently done by young administrators imbued with revolutionary spirit and with little administrative experience. The result of the Yugoslav effort to follow the Soviet example was the establishment of "administrative socialism" which allowed the ethnic groups cultural expression, but which vested all economic decisions in central bodies. The schools and other cultural organizations reflected the style and viewpoint of the ethnic groups involved, but economic decisions were made without much regard for ethnic autonomy. Decisions on prices, wages, and reinvestment policies were made by central government authorities, and the individual ethnic group was unable either to determine the economic policy within its own district or to influence it for the nation as a whole. Economic policy might involve either a shift in resources from a more developed to a less industrialized region or the increased investment in an already prosperous area which seemed likely to yield the greatest return in terms of increased production at relatively low cost. Whether the economic decision was to attempt a regional balance or to ignore balance in favor of maximizing the returns of investment, the specific nationality found itself at the mercy of the central authority, which assumed virtually complete power for the allocation of scarce resources.

This period was not conducive to an objective examination of the applicability of Soviet practices to the Yugoslav context. The Yugoslavs were not the pliant students the Soviet authorities in Yugoslavia expected. As a result, domestic criticisms accumulated, and the mounting grievances led the Soviet Union to support the expulsion of Yugoslavia from the Cominform, an organization of Soviet-sponsored Communist states. This ultimately caused the break between Yugoslavia and the Cominform bloc, in 1948. The grievances ranged from the behavior of Soviet representatives in Yugoslavia to such major issues as the Yugoslav right to sign separate treaties with the other Eastern bloc states. The Soviet suspicion that Yugoslavia wanted to become the leading state in a Balkan federation, and the open scorn in which Tito held Stalin, contributed to the break. The crux of the matter was that the Yugoslav leadership could not be considered a disciplined cog in the Soviet East European apparat.

This meant that the Yugoslav government could no longer count on Soviet power to underwrite its domestic or international policies, such as

Yugoslav claims to Trieste,[11] or such policies as agricultural collectiviza-tion. After the Cominform break, the Yugoslav leadership was forced to rely entirely on its national resources, since it was under a virtual eco-nomic and political blockade from the other East bloc states. This meant in practice that the Yugoslavs had to conciliate all those elements which had been antagonized by the centralism of the preceding three years. The centralistic phase of administrative socialism during 1945–1948 was now justified as having been necessary to mobilize the resources of the state for the massive reconstruction efforts necessitated by the destruction of World War II. The Yugoslav leadership claimed its right to govern on an ideological basis which was at variance with that of the Soviets. This marked the final break with the Soviet tradition of centralistic development.

WORKERS' SELF-MANAGEMENT AND ETHNICITY

In June 1950, when all hopes for reconciliation with the Cominform states had faded, Tito launched the workers' self-management movement which ultimately led to the decentralization of the entire system and the abolition of most central planning, with attendant shifts in personnel. The reforms were based on the premise that the Soviet state had developed into an overcentralized bureaucracy where the working class was more an object of manipulation than a dominant force. The Yugoslav system proposed to reverse this trend by making the workers in their enterprises the dominant force within society. Every enterprise and autonomous unit could be a decisive factor in decision-making through the worker-consti-tuted organs. The decision-making powers could be transferred from the planning agencies to the centers of production and to local units of gov-ernment. The Yugoslavs quickly discovered that, if they were serious about the implementation of these bold plans, they actually must curtail and abolish the central bureaucracies which had controlled all allocation of scarce resources during the period of administrative socialism. Without cur-tailment of the all-powerful central bureaucracy and the centrally directed organs of coercion, all efforts at dispersing the power of government would have failed.

The Fundamental Law of 1953 created a hierarchy of producers' coun-cils which attempted to synchronize the activities of the Yugoslav econ-omy at all levels, extending from the communes, which are the county-like basic units of Yugoslav local government, to the federal government. These were representative bodies delegated by the workers' councils that were elected in the individual enterprises throughout Yugoslavia, and they re-placed the central planning organs which had formerly given coherence

---

[11] See A. E. Moodie, "The Cast Iron Curtain," *World Affairs*, 4 (July 1950), p. 305.

to the Yugoslav economy. After 1953, the central planning agencies were largely confined to the task of statistical analysis.

Yugoslavia moved steadily toward the implementation of the principles of workers' self-management between 1953 and 1966. All its reorganizations and constitutional reforms increasingly yielded more power to local government and enterprises, so that by 1960 Yugoslav politics no longer moved according to the laws of the monistic model associated with Communist systems, but had become pluralized with many local centers of decision-making. Most of the reform measures were not aimed at providing a greater voice to national groupings, but were intended to provide the greatest possible economic decision-making authority to enterprises and to local units of government. This is not meant to imply, however, that these developments did not have profound ethnic implications.

The Yugoslav move away from central administration and toward principles of workers' self-management and control of individual enterprises was motivated primarily by economic and political considerations. The political considerations were based on a desire to be free from the oppressive power of a cumbersome centralized bureaucracy which tended to stifle initiative in the name of discipline and conformity. The economic considerations were simply a search for a method by which labor, capital, management, and new technological processes could be harnessed together for economic improvement. The workers' self-management reforms have succeeded in many of these aims. The power of the bureaucracy has been greatly restrained, workers' participation in decision-making has been increased and economic production has moved forward. However, in terms of ethnic implications, serious questions have begun to be raised about the workers' self-management policies.

These policies provided that the workers in each plant would decide the allocation of monies between wages and capital and that they would, in turn, determine how capital accumulation by the enterprise was to be reinvested. Although all of this was done in the name of socialism, it had the effect of making the rich ethnic groups richer and increasing the income gap between various sections of the country. As in the United States, income was much higher in the industrialized northern section than in the agricultural southern section. Since wages were partially set by the decision of workers, those in the more prosperous north would be paid wages several times that of the agricultural laborers in the south.[12] The workers'

---

[12] Slovenia moved from a per capita national income of 1,280 dinars in 1947 to 3,780 dinars in 1964, while the poorer Kosmet (Kossovo-Metohija area) moved from 380 dinars in 1947 to 710 dinars in 1964. This illustrates a widening gap. Source: *Jugoslavia statisticki pregled: 1945–1964* (Beograde Socijalisticka Federativna Republika Jugoslavija, Savezni zavod za statistiku, 1965), p. 89. According to Fredy Perlman's unpublished doctoral dissertation, *Conditions for the Development of a Backward Region* (University of Belgrade, 1966), p. 40, this represents a 3.7 percent per year increase for Kosmet, and an 8.4 percent per year for Slovenia. All figures are reported in new dinars.

council decision-making machinery was an effective way to maintain economic privilege for workers in the more advanced areas of the country. In reinvestment they sought the best returns, and these could be realized in areas of the country where the industrial infrastructure was already well developed. Hence, capital raised in the prosperous north was devoted to making it a still more prosperous area.

PROBLEMS OF DIFFERENTIAL GROUP DEVELOPMENT

One of the historical problems with which Yugoslavia must struggle is the great disparity in levels of development between those ethnic groupings which were under the dominion of Austria-Hungary in the late 19th and early 20th centuries and those which remained under Turkish rule until the Balkan Wars of 1912–1913. The areas which were under Austro-Hungarian or Serbian administration before World War I developed public services and public systems of education, while the former Turkish districts were backward in these respects; the degree of educational development in the regions of Southern Serbia, Kossovo, and Macedonia make it evident that two different levels of cultural development persist within the state of Yugoslavia.[13] The Yugoslav government strove to remove the burdens of this historical heritage by a major educational effort in the aftermath of World War II. They were confronted by a largely politically apathetic rural population and a dearth of public school teachers and other agents of acculturation who were qualified to teach their own nationalities. The Albanian minority is a case in point; before World War II, this group had been subjected to forcible assimilation, and there was no teaching in the Albanian language throughout that area. The Albanian minority did not feel a great loyalty to Yugoslavia during World War II. They regarded the Serbs as another group in the long line of occupiers who had swept over the area, while the Albanians continued to live in the isolated compactness of their villages. Albanian units joined the Partisans only late in the war, when it became apparent that the Partisans had assumed different attitudes than the previous governments. They accepted the principle of national self-determination, and made a serious effort to establish schools based on instruction in the Albanian language.[14] All these agriculturally–

---

[13] Neither the Albanians nor the Macedonians were recognized as ethnic minorities by the Royal Yugoslav government during the 1920s and 1930s; they were not protected by the Minorities Treaties under the League of Nations and were not guaranteed the use of their own language and schools as were the recognized minorities. These populations still showed over 73 percent illiteracy in 1948, according to Gabor Janoši, *Education and Culture of Nationalities in Yugoslavia* (Beograd: Medunarodna Politka, 1965), p. 20.

[14] According to Koča Jončič, Director of the Research Program on the Relations Between Nationalities in Yugoslavia at the Institute of Social Sciences in Belgrade, "The principle of the equality of the languages of the peoples and national minorities

based minorities organized to pool their resources in the best fashion they could in an effort to educate their own people. Operating under the Directives for the Opening and Operation of Schools for the National Minorities, which were adopted in August 1945, each group worked toward building adequately staffed schools for instruction in the language of that nationality.

By American standards the provision of schools in which various ethnic groups could have their children educated in their own language would be a major concession to cultural pluralism. Indeed in Yugoslavia itself the "majoritarian"[15] view was that the society had done everything possible to assure the integrity and survival of ethnic groups and to end all efforts at assimilation to a type of "Serbian conformity." The "minoritarian" view, that of some of the non-Serb ethnic groups, was a bit different. If they were prosperous, they feared that Serbian influence might divert some of their gains to other territories. If the nationalities in question were less prosperous, they were also discontented and inclined to feel that the central government was not really taking effective measures to aid in their development. Many of these fears were exacerbated by changes in economic policies in 1965.

Prior to these reforms the Yugoslav economy was one in which the influence of supply and demand factors was greatly restricted. Goods were bought and sold, but the prices bore no exact relation to costs or market demands. Many industries were subsidized by the state and the currency was not freely convertible. The reforms sought to make the Yugoslav currency convertible on the international money markets and to end the subsidies so that prices were set by supply and demand. Inefficient or unprofitable industries might go out of existence, while more prosperous industries might make large profits. Private capital played little role in the economy and most industry was socialized, but it was now a "market socialism."

These economic reforms raised a host of political issues which affected the nationalities as collective entities. The principal problem was the disproportionately rapid economic growth in the north in contrast with the agricultural south. In the early postwar years, Slovenia and Croatia were slated for major industrial investment because it was believed that these areas would return the investments much faster as a result of their already developed infrastructure. As in other Communist states, the agricultural sector bore a disproportionate share of the burdens of development be-

---

has been confirmed and incorporated in all the constitutions and other important documents since the last war. An official 'state' language does not exist in Yugoslavia. The languages of all the Yugoslav peoples are equal, and in each republic the official language is that of the native population." Quoted from: Koča Jončič, *The Relations between Nationalities in Yugoslavia*, p. 59.

[15] See discussion of majoritarian and minoritarian viewpoints in Chapter 10 pp. 316–18 and Chapter 11 pages 337–44.

cause of the artificially low agricultural prices due to government policy. The representatives from the agricultural areas resented that the north had achieved much higher living levels at their expense and only then had raised the issue of local economic autonomy. The policy of local autonomy permitted the northern areas to retain their profits after they had reached a much higher level of development than the south and many prime agricultural regions.

Market socialism was introduced at a juncture when many elements in the political situation were changing. As stated earlier, a new generation had grown up in Yugoslavia which did not share the reticence of their elders in discussing nationality issues. The more nationalistically oriented elements could now propagate views which would have been unmentionable during an earlier period. Such undeveloped areas, as the Autonomous Province of Kossovo, were beginning to develop an urban intelligentsia because of investment in the area. To an extent the revival of the nationality problem was a measure of the progress and prosperity of the country and the liberalization of the political atmosphere. It was these processes which led to the polarization of Yugoslav politics in which Alexander Rankovic was the loser and the liberalizing elements emerged victorious. The liberal leadership, in its efforts to defeat Rankovic and to downgrade the secret police, aired all of its past misdeeds. Some of the most serious revelations pertained to the suppression of the Albanian minority in Kossovo.

The secret police had viewed the large Albanian minority in southern Serbia as being potential subversives in the Federal Socialist Republic of Yugoslavia. The Albanians were associated with a neighboring country which had maintained its allegiance to Moscow or Peking and had frequently been violently critical of the Yugoslav government. Most Yugoslavs were Christian, while a majority of the Albanians were Muslim. Acts of terrorism by the secret police, such as the public beating of suspects on suspicion of hiding guns, were not uncommon. The Albanian feeling of injustice was aggravated by the lack of adequate representation on local governing bodies and in the court system.

The open discussion of the topic and the official admission of the misdeeds brought forth an Albanian reaction in terms of immediate demands for the rectification of past ills. The grievances embraced a wide range of issues all hinging on the charges of political, economic, and cultural discrimination against the Albanian minority. The Albanians represent the fastest-growing nationality in Yugoslavia because of a burgeoning birth rate. They constitute a compact, non-Slav population settled in an area which has great historical and sentimental value to the Serbs.[16]

---

[16] This region was the center of the medieval Serbian Kingdom which was toppled by the Turks in the battle of Kossovo in 1389. The Serbs view the Albanians as an

The rapid expansion of the Albanian population in Kossovo places strain on the resident Serbs by putting them in a minority position. The presence of the secret police, who were almost entirely Serb, had redressed the balance until 1966. The curbing of the secret police increased Albanian agitation for equal treatment, finally culminating in the Albanian disturbances of 1968. The main object of the demonstrations was to demand that Kossovo be granted republic status within Yugoslavia, but, above all, that the Albanians be given the same rights of national self-determination as other nationalities in Yugoslavia. While the Yugoslav government responded by meting out fairly stiff jail sentences to the rioters, it also established positive incentives which went a long way toward alleviating the Albanian complaints. The position of the Albanians in the Autonomous Province of Kossovo was upgraded significantly; more economic investment was promised, and the status of the faculties of Belgrade University in the provincial capitol of Priština was changed from a branch to that of the independent University of Priština. The normalization of relations in Kossovo had also the effect of improving relations between Yugoslavia and Albania.

Another dimension of the Albanian problem is that the Albanians migrated to the more developed parts of Yugoslavia, frequently to earn "bride price," and there occupied the most menial positions in the urban Yugoslav labor market. The alien nature of their culture and religion, coupled with their illiteracy and poverty, causes discrimination against the Albanian minority. The attitudes of prejudice expressed by the "common man" against them would not sound alien to American ears. Similar attitudes also apply to portions of the Gypsy population, particularly in the northern areas of the state; in Serbia there are permanently settled communities of Gypsies which enjoy good relations with their neighbors.

Like the Albanians, the Macedonians are affected by international politics. In the case of the Macedonians, the international complication is with Bulgaria, which also has a large Macedonian population. Both Albania and Bulgaria have attempted to stimulate discontent among their conationals in Yugoslavia. This discontent has been reduced by the fact that Yugoslavia is a more prosperous country than either Albania or Bulgaria. The Macedonians are recognized as a separate nationality within the Macedonian Republic of Yugoslavia. The Bulgars, on the other hand, regard them as Macedo-Bulgars without any ethnic identity apart from the Bulgarian one, and at various times they have laid claim to the Macedonian

---

essentially alien nationality which settled in the area only as the result of the Ottoman occupation which favored the Moslem Albanians. The area was a Serbian *irredenta* until the Balkan Wars, 1912–1913. The Albanians claim residence in the area which predates the Serbs; they also claim participation in the armies which fought the Turks in the battle of Kossovo.

parts of Yugoslavia. Bulgaria has been a staunch follower of Soviet policies, and, whenever there is a Soviet-Yugoslav issue, Bulgaria uses it as an excuse to revive the Macedonian question, although to date without any great degree of success.

There are numerous other complex minority patterns within Yugoslavia, but the major contention has been between the Serbs and the Croats, and it is to this issue that we now turn. The continuing discord in the Serb–Croat relationship stem from the unavoidable reality that the Serbs are the preponderant nationality within the state, constituting nearly 46 percent of the population, and that the federal capital is located in Belgrade, which is also the capital of the Serb Republic. The Serbs have continued to occupy a disproportionately large share of the positions in the armed forces and within the security services. This is due not only to discrimination, but because of essentially the same patterns which are noticeable in the United States; namely, that the people from less developed areas of a state find these occupations attractive careers, while the Croats and Slovenes tend to shun them in favor of occupations affording higher status. The more cosmopolitan Belgrade, which has grown up in the last 50 years, has overshadowed Zagreb, the capital of Croatia, as the first city of Yugoslavia despite the fact that economic conditions in the urban areas of Croatia were in no way inferior to those of Serbia. This loss of pre-eminence has stirred jealousy and resentment among the Croats. The Croats have also the largest proportion of workers employed abroad, partially because Croats are reluctant to migrate to other parts of Yugoslavia where there might be a market for their skills, and partially because the expansion of the Croat industries has not kept pace with the demand for new positions. This combination of factors causes fairly wide discontent among one of the best educated populations in the Yugoslav state. Current sources of discontent are coupled with long historical memories dating back to prewar Yugoslavia. Since the Croats represent the greatest potential threat to Yugoslav unity, overt expressions of Croat nationalism cause far more concern in Yugoslavia than similar expressions from any other nationality.

The Slovenes, the third major nationality of Yugoslavia, are essentially content within the Yugoslav state. Their self-perception as a small nationality of two million persons leads them to the belief that they have no chances for an existence in another type of state in which they might preserve their national identity. They also reside in the most prosperous part of Yugoslavia. This leads their politicians to take balancing positions within the framework of the Yugoslav state.

The basic question which confronts Yugoslavia is whether interethnic relations can be successfully arbitrated by the group processes on which Yugoslav governmental practice is based. Some Yugoslavs feel that the present one-party system represents the only alternative to the creation of a divisive multiparty system based on nationality divisions similar to those which placed prewar Yugoslavia in a continual crisis. Others fear that the present system of self-government and decentralization has actually created a multiparty system based on ethnicity, since it is becoming quite clear that adherence to a common ideology does not prevent League of Communist members from being good local patriots who will push their own national group interests as avidly as representatives in a multiparty system. In the past, only the practice of Communist party discipline prevented the worst manifestations of ethnic particularism. Should this restraint be removed Yugoslavia might well face difficult days. The question is whether these relationships can be arbitrated through the constitutional processes of the political system instead of by League intervention through the medium of party discipline.

CULTURAL PLURALISM VERSUS INTEGRATION IN THE UNITED STATES

In the United States, the drive for civil rights culminated with demands, not only for individual members of minorities, but also for redress to entire groups of the population which had been burdened legally, politically, and economically. Demands for recognition of a separate identity come primarily from non-European groups. The combined weight of such groups in the United States census of 1970 was about 17 percent of the total population. The black Americans are officially listed as composing 11.1 percent of the population, a percentage which amounts to about 22,500,000 people. To this figure can be added the Spanish-speaking and Spanish-named population of 5.5 percent, which totals about 11,000,000 people, and the American Indian population of around 800,000. Orientals contribute nearly 2,000,000 persons, including the Chinese, Japanese, Filipino, and "others." These populations are dispersed geographically and are far from homogeneous in economic status or political outlook.

The problem is complicated by the differential treatment minorities have been accorded historically in America. The discrimination was always the worst in the areas where a group could be found that was sufficiently large to maintain a coherent ethnic identity and thus constitute a possible threat to majority control, whether this was among the Puerto Ricans of New York, blacks in the South, or the Indians of the Southwest United States. The United States government is now facing demands for the recognition of a special identity which these ethnic groups wish to perpetuate within the larger American culture. Since they have not been successfully assimilated into American society, they are, in effect, asking for recognition as special cultural minorities and as special entities by the political, social, and legal system of the United States.

American Indians have found a united expression for demanding group rights through organizations such as the National Congress of the American Indian and the American Indian Movement.

Such demands are being heard from Spanish-speaking Americans, many of whom now are united within the Chicano movement,[17] which again has political, economic, and cultural overtones. Some militant portions of the black movement are also opting for a cultural separateness and are, in fact, demanding that amends be made to the blacks, as a group, in recognition of the past wrongdoings visited upon them by the society.[18] The people who are most vocal are minorities within the ethnic groups. For example, the Black Panther organization represents a minor percentage of the black populace, but there are no doubt many more who sympathize with its aims.

However, the majority of black and white opinion in the United States supports the premise that integration is desirable because there are few areas in the United States where black and white can be totally separated economically or in terms of patterns of residence. It is true that Newark, N.J., Washington, D.C., and some other major urban areas have a majority of blacks in the inner cities, but, because these inner cities are symbiotic with their white suburbs, true separation is no more feasible than in South Africa, where the government lends all its power to the principle of separation. This is not the case in the United States and, therefore, opinion which regards itself as progressive supports integration. This is true in both white and black communities.[19] Institutions have, however, become increasingly sensitive to the need for black representation if they are to retain their legitimacy in the eyes of both black and white populations.

---

[17] The etymology of *Chicano* is not fully clear. Young Mexican Americans, however, have given the term a positive meaning and prefer it, as a label, to "Mexican American." In fact, in their eyes, whether or not one is willing to call himself Chicano is a test of cultural loyalty. Although the U.S. Bureau of the Census, prior to 1970, has listed the Mexican American as part of the "white" population, it is estimated that nearly 5,000,000 Mexican Americans live in the United States. Spanish-speaking groups include: Latin Americans, Cubans, Puerto Ricans, and Spanish in addition to Mexican Americans.

[18] For example, the Black Economic Conference has demanded $5,000,000 in reparations for past wrongdoings from the white-supported churches; the Black Muslims support economic ownership by Muslims and separate living locations from the white population; the Republic of New Africa favors the establishment of a separate political state in the southern part of the United States, with black control and ownership. "Economic Programs of Militant Separatists" in William L. Henderson and Larry C. Ledebur, *Economic Disparity* (New York: The Free Press, 1971), pp. 75–104.

[19] Peter Goldman, *Report from Black America* (New York: Simon and Schuster, 1971), quotes from surveys among blacks showing that 74 percent indicated a preference for living in a "mixed" neighborhood and 78 percent said "yes" when asked if they preferred to see the children in their family go to school with white children. For exact figures see p. 179 and p. 267, respectively.

CONTRASTING ROLES OF FEDERAL GOVERNMENT IN THE UNITED STATES AND YUGOSLAVIA

The state structures of both Yugoslavia and the United States are federally based. Both countries possess strongly entrenched republican-state structures and strongly entrenched local authorities. Both have populations which greatly prize the existence of decision-making bodies on the local level because such institutions are deemed to be closer to the people and to meet their needs more adequately. Much of Yugoslav history is a record of social conflicts between the diverse nationalities and a powerful central government; as a matter of fact, the creation of post–World-War-II Yugoslavia rested on the platform of the recognition of equality of all nationalities and ethnic minorities. The Yugoslav system of law has gone to amazing lengths to ensure the right of the separate identity of each group, such as the right of the minorities to fly the state flag of the nation with which they are culturally identified. The entire trend of Yugoslav politics essentially supports the position which can be found in the Tenth Amendment of the United States Constitution, namely, that the powers not delegated to the federal government are reserved to the states or to the people.[20]

Yet, in the instance of the United States, the minorities and the ethnic groups suffered the worst at the hands of the local authorities. Discriminatory practices against black Americans and Spanish-speaking Americans were always defended on the basis of "states rights" and the rights of the local people to decide local issues. The most pernicious practices of segregation and judicial violence rested in the hands of state, city, and county authorities.

It was not until the Supreme Court applied the Constitution to the states in a forceful and resolute manner that the states lost the legal basis on which they had applied discriminatory policies against ethnic minorities. The executive, legislative, and judicial branches of the federal government became the best guarantor of equal rights. The Supreme Court initiated this record through a series of decisions which reversed longstanding judicial doctrines, and eventually resulted in the erasure of the "separate but equal" doctrine on the basis that separate was not equal.[21] The President of the United States practiced direct intervention, including

---

[20] The Tenth Amendment reads: "The Powers not delegated to the United States by the Constitution, nor prohibited by it to the States, are reserved to the States respectively, or to the people."

[21] One series of cases, starting with *Gitlow* vs. *New York*, 268 U.S. 652, in 1925, extended the "due process of law" clause in the Fourteenth Amendment back to the First Amendment, and gradually extended the rights guaranteed in the Bill of Rights to those citizens deprived of them by state laws. This shifted the grip of states rights. *Brown* vs. *Board of Education*, 347 U.S. 483 (1954), reversed the "separate but equal" doctrine as not consistent with the equal protection of the law clause in the Fourteenth Amendment.

the use of federal troops, in order to enforce these court decisions. The executive branch became a model employer; both the armed forces and the civil service of the United States became places where blacks and other minorities encountered relative freedom from discrimination, and the government followed policies of promoting minority group members into responsible positions.

From 1964 onward, the federal authorities started paying increased attention to the situation of de facto segregation in the North. Here, the major effort was the integration of housing and the integration of school systems, which in many instances are as rigidly segregated as those in the South. Segregation in the North rested on the compact patterns of residence which had developed around blacks and other racial-ethnic groups in the urban areas.[22] Some of it was voluntary, but much of it was involuntary. This problem has no ready analogy to any situation existing in Yugoslavia except to illustrate again the differential thrust in both societies in solving problems of ethnicity. The American thrust was entirely in the direction of integration. The effort was directed at integrating all groups, even those which resisted this effort and claimed the right to secure their national identity by voluntary isolation. Members of minorities, such as the black and Chinese groups, frequently saw the legal efforts of integration as a means to eradicate that which was distinctive in the black or Chinese culture. The law of the United States was again essentially blind to cultural collectivities and held that individual rights could best be safeguarded by equal treatment of individuals rather than by the recognition of the rights of groups as in Yugoslavia.

This basic formulation bedeviled judicial and administrative authorities from the beginning of the efforts to bring greater justice to minority and ethnic groups in the United States. The program began with the integration of the armed services by Executive Order 9981 in 1948. The remaining all-black units of the United States Army were dissolved, and their personnel were distributed among the existing white organizations. The assignment of personnel was no longer to be permitted along racial or ethnic lines but purely around the rank and Military Occupation Specialty (MOS), and the assigning authorities were ordered to be blind to such matters as the racial or ethnic origins of the soldiers involved. This transition to an integrated army was fairly smooth, where white and black units were involved, but the problems were infinitely greater in the case of the Spanish-speaking soldiers when the separate Puerto Rican units were dis-

---

[22] The Introduction to the Report of the National Advisory Commission on Civil Disorders says it better: "What white Americans have never fully understood—and what the Negro can never forget—is that white society is deeply implicated in the ghetto. White institutions created it, white institutions maintain it, and white society condones it." *Report of the National Advisory Commission on Civil Disorders* (New York: Bantam Books, 1968), p. vii.

solved. In the instance of the Puerto Ricans, the authorities attempted to enforce equality on a group which was culturally different from the majority. This resulted in frequent breakdowns in communication between officers and men, who simply did not understand each other's language, and in a major morale problem among both the Spanish-speaking soldiers and the army authorities who were attempting to make the army fairer by making no allowances for the de facto situation of the Spanish-speaking soldiers and officers.

The Yugoslav army has been used as an agency for ethnic acculturation. It has an explicit policy of sending Slovenes and Croats to underdeveloped parts of Yugoslavia, and Macedonians and Serbs to Slovenia and Croatia. Besides, it teaches urban living skills to soldiers who come from rural areas. In many instances, army service is the only link that citizens have with ethnic groupings other than their own.

In the United States, the laws and government are virtually blind to groups which have a strong drive to preserve their cultural integrity. The American constitution does not guarantee anything to such groups, whereas the Yugoslav Constitution of 1963, in Article 40, states, "Citizens are guaranteed the freedom to express their nationality and culture, and the freedom to use their own language." In the United States, the general policy of integration is supported by law which deals only with individuals, and may threaten entire groups with cultural extinction. This policy actually threatens all groups which try to preserve some modicum of special ethnic identity. An especially dramatic example of this policy, when carried to its final phase, is shown by the "termination" of Indian reservations in order to bring the Indians into the larger American society as integrated members. For instance the Menominee Indians of Wisconsin woke up one morning in 1961 to find that their reservation had been abolished, and that all of the special protections and provisions promised them by earlier treaties had disappeared.[23] It was further provided that no more Menominee Indians would be legally recognized after the present generation.

In Yugoslavia, the guarantee for use of the group culture and language extends into the schools, where instruction is available for any nationality in the mother tongue, wherever there are sufficient numbers of that group to warrant either a school or a class.[24] The guidelines for establishing the right to instruction in one's own language are federal, although each republic has instituted its own detailed plan. In Serbia, the Law of the Or-

---

[23] In 1954, five bills passed both houses of Congress which effectively terminated the tribal status of 8,000 North American Indians. This was known as the "termination policy." Gary Orfield, *A Study of the Termination Policy* (Denver, Colorado, National Congress of American Indians, 1965). President Nixon spoke against this policy in an official address on July 8, 1970.

[24] "General Law on the School System," *Official Gazette of the SFRY*, No. 4, Jan. 22, 1964.

ganization of Schools with Instruction in Languages of National Minorities in the Peoples' Republic of Serbia[25] guarantees lessons in the mother tongue wherever there are 15 students of the same nationality, while the Law on Bilingual Schools and Those in the Language of the National Minorities in Slovenia[26] provides for either bilingual schools for the nationalities, in which both Slovenian and another national language are used for instruction, or schools for nationalities in which only students are present who belong to a minority. The increase in the number of schools identified with a specific national minority is a strong indicator of the progress made toward establishing separate schools for different ethnic groups. The number of elementary and secondary schools in the languages of the nine minorities increased, between 1939 and 1964, from 271 to 1,506. Nearly half of these groups were not entitled to schools in their mother tongue before the war. Table 12–2 illustrates this point.

In the United States, minority groups usually have to resort to an en-

TABLE 12–2

Elementary and Secondary Schools in Languages of the
Nationalities (A comparative survey: 1938/1939 and 1963/1964)

| | | | Secondary | |
Nationality	Year	Elementary	Vocational	high school
Total	1938/39	266	1	4
	1963/64	1,419	56	31
Bulgarian	1938/39	——	—	—
	1963/64	87	—	1
Czechoslovakian	1938/39	42*	—	—
	1963/64	12	—	—
Italian	1938/39	——	—	—
	1963/64	133	1	5
Hungarian	1938/39	183	1	2
	1963/64	230	23	7
Rumanian	1938/39	33	—	1
	1963/64	34	1	1
Ruthenian	1938/39	3	—	—
	1963/64	4	—	—
Slovak	1938/39	42*	—	1
	1963/64	32	1	1
Albanian	1938/39	——	—	—
	1963/64	917	30	13
Turk	1938/39	——	—	—
	1963/64	60	—	3

* Czech and Slovak statistics for elementary school combined.
Sources: *Statistical Yearbook* (Beograd, 1964), p. 314; *Preliminary Data of the Federal Institute for Statistics,* 1965.

---

[25] *Official Gazette of the Peoples' Republic of Serbia* (Beograd No. 29, 1960).

[26] *People's Assembly of Slovenia, Executive Council* (Ljubljana, No. 61–2, April 9, 1962).

tirely privately financed system if they wish to maintain their distinct schools. Even such a system has to meet the high standards of the public schools if its students are to be certified for admission to colleges or universities or as transfer students. Needless to say, this is a very expensive method of educating cultural entities. Since 1967, experimental programs in bilingual instruction and community control in public city schools, located in ethnic locales, indicate some rethinking in this area.

ETHNICITY AND THE LAW

Since the American legal system deals with individual rights and not with the rights of groups, it is difficult to deal with libel and legal assault on the status and rights of entire groups. Any legislation dealing with the denial of rights of groups or libel against groups would run afoul of the First Amendment of the United States Constitution. There is no United States equivalent of the Yugoslav proscription against the dissemination of national hatred and overt discrimination as specified in the Constitution of the Socialist Federal Republic of Yugoslavia. Article 41 of that constitution states the official position most clearly in paragraph 3: "Spreading or practicing national inequality, and any incitement to national, racial or religious hatred or intolerance, is unconstitutional and punishable."

Any such provision in the Constitution of the United States of America would be against the entire tradition of Anglo-Saxon jurisprudence, which elevates the right of freedom of speech above the protection of groups from slander and libel. Such provisions may be difficult to enforce in any instance. The relative scarcity of prosecution under the provisions of the law in Yugoslavia attests to this. In both countries the amelioration of such problems is entrusted to the political process rather than to litigation. The United States Civil Rights Acts of 1957, 1960, and 1964[27] were a long step toward recognition that specified groups of the population might be injured by the discriminatory treatment of racial or minority groups. These laws were largely directed against state and local authorities which had traditionally taken a very cavalier attitude toward those rights which were already enunciated in the United States Constitution and in many Supreme Court decisions. As in Yugoslavia, the provisions of this law have been applied rarely and usually in the most flagrant cases.

---

[27] The Civil Rights Act of 1957 set up the Federal Civil Rights Commission. It is a temporary agency charged to investigate complaints alleging that citizens are being deprived of their right to vote by reason of their race, color, religion, or national origin or by reason of fraudulent practice, to study and collect information concerning legal developments constituting a denial of equal protection of the laws under the Constitution, to appraise Federal laws and policies with respect to equal protection of the laws, and to serve as a national clearinghouse for information in respect to denials of equal protection of the laws.

In Yugoslavia, all federal institutions have been organized on the principle of equal representation for the several nationalities as a constitutional right, since the Constitutional Amendments of December 1968. This principle is followed by both the government and the League of Communists. For example, the main legislative chamber is the Chamber of Nationalities, which is composed of 20 delegates from each republic and ten from each autonomous province. This organizing principle also prevails on the Federal Executive Council. The other five chambers, even though they are functional, reflect a somewhat proportional representation of the nationalities in Yugoslavia. The same reforms apply to the Presidential Council and to the major institutions of the League. These institutions have been under constant reorganization for the past 20 years. During the various changes, one tendency that remains constant is to give equal representation to the nationalities within the ruling councils of goverment and party. Before the reforms of 1968, the Serb and Montenegrin elements were heavily overrepresented in both party and government bodies.[28]

On the republic and provincial levels, the governments and party organizations are again composed in such a way as to give representation to the ethnic minorities within the republican, provincial, and communal territories. This applies to the institutions of both the government and the League. In highly mixed areas, such as the Province of Vojvodina, this constitutes a particularly difficult problem. According to official statistics for 1963, however, the communal councils within Yugoslavia showed a pattern of ethnic representation that was quite similar to the ethnic composition of the total population.[29]

Another important step in the same direction was the reorganization of the Yugoslav army in which a portion of the Yugoslav armed forces were placed under republican commands to organize the defense of their respective republican areas. This was done to reinforce the concept of territorial warfare which was always the dominant strategy of the Yugoslav military leadership, but also to circumscribe the powers of an officers' corps in which the Serbs and Montenegrins had a decisive majority.

Since the Yugoslav republics represent, to a large extent, different ethnic groups, the changes toward reducing the power of the central government and increasing the power of the republics also increase the autonomy of ethnic groups. The increased privileges of the Albanian minority indi-

---

[28] Paul Shoup, *Communism and the Yugoslav National Question* (New York: Columbia University Press, 1968), Appendix D, p. 274. Before the reforms of 1968 Serb and Montenegrin elements were heavily overrepresented in both party and governmental bodies.

[29] Statistics for the communal councils included 4.9 percent Albanians (against their 4.9 percent of the total Yugoslav population), 2.3 percent Hungarianrs (2.7 percent), 0.5 percent Slovaks (0.47 percent), 0.4 percent Bulgarians (0.34 percent), etc. Koča Jončič, *The Relations between Nationalities in Yugoslavia*, p. 70.

cate that Yugoslav leaders were indeed desirous of increasing ethnic self-determination. However, the removal of the Croatian League leadership indicates that the Yugoslav leaders are determined to maintain some degree of unity in the federation and will not willingly permit the development of secessionist trends. Since the break with the Soviet Union in 1948, Yugoslavia has moved steadily toward limiting the power of the federation and increasing the autonomy of the constituent units. Whether the removal of the Croat leaders represents an isolated reaction to an extreme challenge to the integrity of the state or is the beginning of a reversal of the policy which increased the authority of the republics and local government remains to be seen.

The minority groups within the United States are not territorially based, and the population is usually dispersed and unable to elect sufficient numbers of its group for adequate representation in a legislative body. This is especially true of the smaller minority groups in America. The black American, on the other hand, has developed an effective pattern of bloc voting among urban-based black populations and has elected black representatives to county, state, and federal offices. Indeed, in 1972 the number of black state legislators approached the black proportion of the population in Michigan, Alaska, Arizona, Colorado, Ohio, and Oklahoma, which is one effect of an increase in black-elected officials since 1967. In spite of this rise, studies show that in May 1972 the proportion of black elected officials has reached only 0.43 percent of the total number of elected officials in the country.[30] While minorities may be too dispersed to make bloc voting effective for national office, state and local office can be won by candidates operating from a small base of minority votes. Examples of this can be found in towns populated by a majority of Mexican-Americans, such as Crystal City, Texas, where the political party, La Raza Unida of Texas, was active and gained control of the school board and city council for the first time in 1970, or from among large concentrations of Indians, such as the Navaho of Arizona and New Mexico, who elected two of their numbers to the state legislature in 1964. After the 1966 elections, 15 Indians held seats in six legislatures of Western States by utilizing an untapped Indian vote for the first time. Coalitions between more than one minority group or between black and white groups have been successful in some cases, such as the election of the first black Newark mayor through a joint effort by blacks and Puerto Ricans in that city, or such as the election of the first black Cleveland mayor through a joint effort of committed black and white voters. In addition to these examples, minority individuals may be elected in districts not controlled by their group, as in the case of a Mexican-American, Joseph Montoya, United States Senator from New

---

[30] Research Bulletin, Joint Committee on Political Studies, (May 1972), p. 6.

Mexico, or a black American, Edward Brooke, United States Senator from Massachusetts. Government appointments also reflect a deliberate effort to recognize individuals from minority groups and to increase their numbers in office; this effort is closely associated with a recent pattern of setting up special government offices on minority affairs, such as the Office of Minority Business Enterprise in the Department of Commerce or the Office for Spanish-Speaking American Affairs in the Department of Health, Education and Welfare, and staffing them with members of the concerned group. An effort has also been made by both the public and private sector to recognize the achievement of individuals on their merits despite a minority ethnic status.

PROGRAMS TO SECURE FULL PARTICIPATION OF ETHNIC AND RACIAL GROUPS

Both Yugoslavia and the United States are saddled with a heritage which created great inequalities amongst segments of the population. In Yugoslavia these are largely regional and are the result of the differing historical experience of the nationalities which comprise today's Yugoslavia. The program of socialist development in Yugoslavia was partially aimed at the eradication of gross economic discrepancies between ethnic groupings. In the United States the problem is at least partially geographic as well. The Southern population included a large proportion of blacks in a section of the country which was disadvantaged by a low level of industrialization.[31] A handicapped black minority resided in an agricultural part of the United States which lagged behind national income averages. The same observation could be made of the Spanish-speaking population of the Southwestern states or of the American Indians. The government viewed the ethnic problem, at least partially, as an expression of the economic situation in which the minorities found themselves, whether interspersed among the general population of the poor or in compact regional settlements. In Yugoslavia, the analysis of retarded development rests on the foundations of Marxist philosophy. Yet the attack on the problem in the United States was quite consonant with Marxist thinking because it was aimed at altering the occupational structure of the minorities in the belief that altering the material basis of groups will also alter the social structure and abolish the condition of poverty.

The contrast in methods used to redress minority grievances points up the essential difference in the Yugoslav and the United States approach. In

---

31 The black population varied considerably in the South. For example, in the 1960 census, nearly one fourth of all counties in Mississippi had a black majority, but in no state did the black population exceed that of the white population. Louis Lomax, *The Negro Revolt* (New York: Signet Books, 1962), pp. 251, 266–67.

Yugoslavia, minorities were included on a group basis in representation by constitutional right. In the United States, individual rights are constitutionally guaranteed, and groups would be protected when the rights of individuals who made up the group were protected. In Yugoslavia, individuals would find access to social participation through the legal guarantees of their nationality group, while in the United States, treating an individual on the basis of ethnic group membership was considered discriminating behavior. Thus, the civil rights movement in the United States sought to remove ethnic classification as a basis for discrimination in the assignment of social rewards, while the Yugoslavs moved to give equal weight to both majority and minority ethnic categories. In short, this points up a fundamental difference in the ways in which the United States and Yugoslavia address themselves to individual and group grievances. The United States ignored ethnic groups and sought to protect the rights of individuals, while Yugoslavia sought to establish equality between ethnic groups as such. However, affirmative action programs and goals for ethnic representation in employment and education have brought the United States practices closer to the Yugoslav concept of group rights.

THE POLITICS OF INTEGRATION

There is little question that a powerful central government can implement many policies for the redistribution of income to poor areas. The central government can play this role only at the expense of local decision-making powers. This basic equation applies to any state, whether it be the United States or Yugoslavia. Political conflicts result from this basic fact of life in both societies. Yugoslavia, like the United States, has its agricultural underdeveloped areas in the south, and these areas are vitally interested in the redistribution of national wealth through the intermediacy of the federal government. In the United States, this demand has a somewhat paradoxical twist insofar as the greatest advocacy for states' rights also originates in the South.

In the United States, the white South has traditionally fought for the right to discriminate against nonwhite citizens by hoisting the banner of the right to local self-government. In the 1960s, when the civil rights movement began to agitate for black rights on the basis that such rights were guaranteed by the Constitution and other legal documents, the Southern resistance centered entirely on the issue of states' rights. Yet it can be amply demonstrated that states' rights to the South meant purely the privilege of racial discrimination. On the other issues which confronted the South, the elected representatives were among the most vocal backers of federal intervention because it meant essentially the redistribution of federal funds into such southern projects as education, highway construction, health services, and flood control. The voting record of the Southern

Congressmen and Senators was by and large fairly consistently on the side of the economic programs which enhanced federal power. The analogies to the Yugoslav case are more than superficially obvious. In Yugoslavia, the American equivalent of states' rights is a platform of those regions which are most prosperous, while those who seek increments in federal power tend to represent the poorer areas of the country for the same economic reasons as in the United States.

Nevertheless, Yugoslavia and the United States are moving from a platform of very different experience. In the United States, the forces which perceive themselves as being progressive by and large advocate an increase in federal power because they see local government as the seat of racial discrimination, corruption, and inefficiency. The higher standards of conduct in the civil service in the United States can be no doubt found in the federal government. The entire past history of the United States was a gradual buildup of these powers, which took a significant quantum jump in the 20th century and particularly under the administration of Franklin D. Roosevelt. Therefore the image of federal power tied to his stellar personality symbolized constructive change and progress. The Johnson administration finally federalized enforcement of voting rights and other civil rights which had been long denied by local powers.

The European experience in general, and the Yugoslav experience in particular, have been different from the American one. Europe evolved from feudal concepts of absolutism which made the individual subject to the exercise of governmental power, and much of the European struggle for civil rights or democracy has been against all-powerful central authorities which yielded their powers most reluctantly. This was certainly true of the absolutist traditions of the Hapsburg Monarchy or the Ottoman Empire. The entire interwar period in Yugoslavia was a record of struggle against the centralizing tendencies of the royal government and the Serb majority on which it rested. In the circumstances, it is not surprising that one can find many echoes of this historical development in present-day Yugoslavia.

SUMMARY

The ultimate solution to the problems outlined in this chapter, if there is an ultimate solution, can be found only in consonance with the political processes in the two countries under discussion. Historically, political processes have created many of the burdens with which the two states are saddled, whether these were 500 years of Turkish occupation in Yugoslavia or slavery in the United States. From a historical viewpoint, one cannot escape the conclusion that both states have taken vast strides in the last 30 years toward the alleviation of the inequities among their diverse populations.

The paths taken differed markedly. Yugoslavia restructured radically the entire constitutional framework of the state to satisfy the demands for equal rights among all the Yugoslav nationalities. The main thrust of the United States is still toward integration and freedom from individual discrimination. In the process of the political struggle which took place in the United States, largely during the past two decades, there is an increasing awareness that the goal of full integration may bring with it the denial of a separate identity which some groups strive toward.

In the very act of emancipating minority groups from discrimination there is an awareness that portions of the Indian and the Spanish-speaking populations would like to maintain their cultural identity, and this may in time be recognized at the programatic level. Congress has already recognized this need by setting up pilot projects, in 1967, under Title VII, the Bilingual Education Program, of the Elementary and Secondary Education Act of 1965.[32] The very fact that the Office of Education in the Department of Health, Education and Welfare has established entire bureaucratic structures to deal with problems of divergent ethnic and racial groups shows an increased awareness that these are group problems and not individual ones. The establishment of such organizations is increasingly found on the state and local levels. Institutions and businesses have become increasingly aware of the proportion of minority group members on their staff, and in some instances have set explicit quotas for minorities.

One could, perhaps, hypothesize about the emergence of a convergence pattern in which the United States is traveling more and more in the direction of the Yugoslav model for the treatment of minority problems with a distinct recognition that cultural divergencies may be a permanent factor in a complex multinational society. By the same token, Yugoslavia's experience of the last 20 years sets its course in the direction of greater individual rights as well as increased economic individualism. Both states firmly reject the notion that national and ethnic divergencies should be the source of discriminatory treatment for their respective citizens.

One of the paradoxes of United States and Yugoslav developments is that, while both governments framed major policies to insure the rights of their respective citizens, the approaches used were almost diametrically opposed. In the United States the federal government launched major efforts through the federal authorities as the only means of gaining redress for the minorities which suffered under the grip of vested local elites which controlled the economy and law enforcement. In Yugoslavia, the path

---

[32] Congress expressed concern over the inadequacy of language training in schools attended by non–English-speaking children by amending the Elementary and Secondary Education Act (1965) in the form of Title VII, the Bilingual Education Program, which provided for demonstration and pilot programs. These are primarily found in schools with Spanish-speaking children, and in a few Indian schools.

traveled was from central control to greater local control and therefore to more autonomy for ethnic groups. In the immediate postwar period, the Yugoslav government was not ethnically discriminatory, but implemented the revolution through rigid central control. It was only in the 1960s, with the rise of the workers' self-management movement, that substance was given to true self-government among the Yugoslav nationalities and national minorities. The question that remains is where the federal-local relationship will find its balance point. In the ultimate analysis, this basic question is the key to the success of the ethnic policies in both societies.

PATTERNS OF INTERGROUP BEHAVIOR

An inquiry into intergroup policies in Yugoslavia and the United States affords a comparison between a country with a group-centered polity and one with an individual-centered polity, between a country with a predominantly socialist economy and one with a predominantly capitalist economic system, and between a country with territorially based ethnic enclaves and one with relatively dispersed ethnic groups. Finally, practically all the Yugoslav population have an European–Near-Eastern background, while in the United States nearly a fifth of the population is of African, Latin American, Indian, or Oriental ancestry. These differences make even more significant any common factors which may appear in the delineation of intergroup relationships in the two countries.

Yugoslav-United States pattern.   Disparities in the socioeconomic status of ethnic and regional groups exist in both countries. In Yugoslavia and in the United States there is a north-south differential in income and also a differential between ethnic groups, with blacks receiving less than whites in the United States and Albanians with only a fraction of the per capita income of the Slovenes in Yugoslavia.

Generalized pattern.   Variations in natural resources of various regions and in the education and life styles of ethnic groups produce variations in the average income of group members which are difficult to equalize in either a socialist or a capitalist economic system.

Yugoslav-United States pattern.   In Yugoslavia, power was transferred from the central government to local units, partially in an effort to give greater autonomy to ethnic groups in local territories. In the United States power was centralized, partially to protect ethnic minorities from discrimination by local elites. The American centralized support of integration has been attacked as hostile to cultural pluralism, while Yugoslav decentralization has been attacked as a device to perpetuate economic inequalities between ethnically distinct regions.

Generalized pattern.   A powerful central government may limit ethnic autonomy, but only a strong central government can promote economic equality among ethnic groups.

Yugoslav-United States pattern. Both Yugoslavia and the United States have moved away from a situation in which majority ethnic status conferred special privilege. The Yugoslavs are working through group guarantees which attempt to insure cultural survival and proportionate representation of ethnic groups in governmental bodies. The United States has sought to achieve a situation in which ethnicity is unrelated to social, economic, or political participation and people are appraised on their individual merit.

Generalized pattern. The quest for justice in intergroup relations may move either from the group to the individual or vice versa. If the emphasis is on group parity, individual freedom is necessarily curtailed and many social classifications must be made on the basis of ethnicity rather than on individual qualities. If the emphasis is on individual rights, cultural groups may decay or disappear even though individuals associated historically with such groups advance in socioeconomic status.

QUESTIONS

1. Are there any fundamental differences in the manner in which the United States and Yugoslavia provide for the achievement of equality among their respective minority groups? Discuss fully.

2. How do you account for the fact that turmoil erupted in the United States and in Yugoslavia during the time when there was an increase in prosperity and liberalization? Defend your answer.

3. What evidence can you marshall to show that both the United States and Yugoslavia are moving into a period in which ethnic feelings are being revitalized and forcing changes in the two systems?

4. Historically, religion played an important role in keeping the peoples separated in Yugoslavia; what factor or factors played a similar role in the divisiveness of the American people?

5. What important developments are responsible for the emergence of the contemporary federal system in Yugoslavia and how does this new system favor ethnic autonomy?

6. How do you account for the fact that governmental reforms in Yugoslavia have not resulted in greater economic parity among the various minority groups? Discuss this fully.

7. What recommendations would you offer to bring about economic parity of the majority-minority groups in the United States? Could the same recommendations be applied toward the elimination of economic disparities in Yugoslavia? Defend your answer.

8. To what extent have the economic reforms and the decentralization of the government been detrimental to the bases of a socialist egalitarianism in Yugoslavia?

9. How could you account for the continued discord between the Serbs and the Croats and what steps could the government take to improve relations between these two groups?

10. Contrast the current legal approaches used by the United States and Yugoslavia in their attempt to solve interethnic group problems. In your opinion which legal approach seems most likely to succeed? Defend your answer.

11. What do you think would be some of the major consequences if the United States adapted a minority policy like that of Yugoslavia, where the various minority groups are guaranteed the freedom to express their own culture and nationality? Would such a policy call for a redistribution of the population in the United States?

12. Is there any evidence that the United States is moving in the direction of Yugoslavia in recognition and treatment of minority groups? If yes, how far do you think this trend will go and what are some of the major forces that would strongly oppose it?

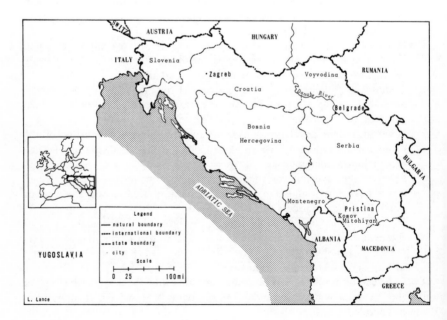

Chapter 13

The Peace Corps: A case of temporary minority adjustment

The Peace Corps and the people they served differed on many important social and cultural traits. The Peace Corps Volunteers were a fair cross section of educated American youth. This meant that the sexes were about equally represented, that most were white, and that, although some were Catholic, the majority came from Protestant or Jewish backgrounds. In Africa, this meant that a mostly white group was serving blacks. In the Philippines and Latin America, it meant that a mostly non-Catholic group was serving a predominantly Catholic population. In all cases, the Peace Corps enterprise involved Americans serving those of other nationalities, and citizens of a wealthy country serving those living in underdeveloped areas. Since many of these countries to which the Peace Corps was assigned had a strong tradition of male dominance, the Peace Corps situation often included women occupying roles usually reserved for men.

To be sure, the two-year period of Peace Corps service made the volunteers a highly transient minority, and transient minorities do have some privileges as contrasted with long-term residents. For one thing, since the period of residence is short, any threat of competition is only temporary. Nor are the Volunteers likely to be viewed as a political bloc, since both alien status and short tenure make normal political activity impossible. Pressures for assimilation are low, since it is assumed that sojourners will inevitably retain their alien culture. On the other hand, the success of the Peace Corps mission required a high degree of interaction between the Volunteers and citizens of the host country and the period during which this could take place was short.

The situation of temporary minority status is one that the Peace Corps shares with many other groups. Governmental technical experts, members of the armed forces, businessmen, missionaries, and diplomats have faced the problem of this kind of adjustment for many years. Their conditions of service, however, are sharply different from those of the Peace Corps Volunteers. With the exception of the military and the missionary, the financial remuneration of the ordinary United States citizen serving abroad is not only in excess of that received by natives of the country but usually in excess of that received by comparable fellow nationals in the United States. This differential is justified on the basis of the labor market, since most people are reluctant to leave their own country unless additional compensation is involved. Also, "hardship pay" is rationalized on the ground that tariffs and transportation costs may push the prices of Westernized types of products 25 percent to 100 percent above the level in the United States or a European country.

Neither the armed forces[1] nor the missionary societies use financial differentials as a recruitment device, and soldiers and missionaries usually receive less compensation than men in comparable occupations on the home base. In the case of the army, however, the element of compulsion comes into foreign duty, and in the case of missionaries, a service motive replaces the "hardship compensation." However, the compensation of both missionaries and soldiers is usually well above the income of the average native in the host country, even above that of the soldier or the clergyman with whom they might be most directly compared.

The Peace Corps Volunteer, on the other hand, sought to live in a manner typical of the people of the country and was employed at a compensation comparable to that of his native counterpart. The Peace Corps Volunteers were given adequate medical care and, if necessary, were furnished with transportation, but otherwise their intention was to live on an economic level which would not inhibit interaction with the populace. Rather than insulating the Volunteers from contact, the Peace Corps sought living conditions which would immerse them in the indigenous society.

Most transitory minority groups have made an adjustment through three types of escape mechanisms: enclave living, elite interaction, and task-oriented acculturation. Many examples of enclave living may be

---

[1] The military do receive a small overseas bonus, but are classed with missionaries on the grounds that, even with this bonus, military pay is usually less than that of comparable civilians in the home country.

found, such as the mission compound, the army base, the diplomatic quarters, the residences built by business concerns for their employees, and the special housing set up by the governments of developing countries for visiting Western experts. This type of enclave housing tends to minimize the interaction of the alien minority with the host nationals, since for their off-duty time they are located in a "gilded ghetto," in which the only nationals present are servants, or visitors who come by invitation. Usually the enclave is served by Western-type stores and amusements, worship facilities and schools, which provide a "little America," or whatever country is involved.

Enclave living cannot lead to complete isolation, or else the whole point of the individual's mission would be lost. The usual adjustment is to promote interaction with nationals of the host country who are intimately involved with the work in which the visiting minority is interested. Thus, there is exchange of hospitality between businessmen, government officials, military officers, missionaries and native clergy, etc. This close elite interaction is coupled with an isolation from the rest of the population except for the occasional servant, who frequently becomes not only a relief from the tedium of manual labor, but also an informant on the local culture and the channel through which the foreigner finds at least partial entry into the mysterious society in which he lives.

Like interaction, acculturation is also a task-oriented phenomenon which is restricted to those elements of the culture which impinge most directly on the individual's vocational role performance. He will probably pick up a few words of the native lagnuage, but most of his day-by-day contact will be with national counterparts or servants who are English-speaking. He will, perhaps, learn to eat a few of the better known items of food, but he will arrange for his own theaters, golf courses, clubs, swimming pools, and other types of social gatherings. Thus, he may live a reasonably comfortable life and be reasonably effective in his work performance, and yet come to know relatively little of either the values or the customs of the society in which he lives.

PEACE CORPS ADJUSTMENT TECHNIQUES

For the Peace Corps, task-oriented acculturation, elite interaction, and enclave ghetto living were contrary to two of its three directives, which were to help the people served to gain a better understanding of the American people and to promote a better understanding of other peoples on the part of the American people, as well as to meet "the needs for trained manpower."[2] Peace Corps Volunteers were engaged in specific functional

---

[2] Public Law 87–293, 87th Congress, Sept. 22, 1961, Section 2.

activities, but they were also in a real sense ambassadors of America, who were charged with a mission of becoming agents of understanding. As a result, their living arrangements were ideally those which placed them in a maximum of degree of contact with the native peoples, their interaction was on a broad scale, not restricted to a small elite, and their acculturation was of a type which would bring an insight into the general nature of the society.

Arriving at a suitable plane of living often represented a considerable problem for the Volunteer. There was no doubt that, compared to other Americans abroad, he was poor, but the idea that he should live as his local counterpart did not necessarily mean that no barriers of living standards existed to separate him from the bulk of the indigenous population. In the Philippines, most Volunteers lived in modest homes not too different from the bulk of the town population and scattered throughout the area. In most districts in Africa, however, teachers, like other government servants, had housing provided for them and lived in Western-style domiciles on the school campus, complete with all modern conveniences.

Such housing implied both a physical and a social separation from the African populace, even though the housing was shared by African teachers. Some Volunteers have forsaken the teacher's compound for life in a mud hut in the African quarters—an action which provokes a mixed type of reaction. Other teachers, either African or expatriate, were apt to feel that leaving the compound was an action which lowered standards and threatened the prerogatives of all teachers. Critics added that the only single women whom Africans are used to see living alone are prostitutes and that the female volunteer who leaves the teacher's enclave risked this kind of misinterpretation. Still other critics charged that the difficulty of housekeeping and the problems of sanitation reduced the individual's efficiency on the job. Perhaps the unkindest cut of all was the possibility that the individual who sought native quarters might face a suspicion of engaging in espionage.

On the other hand, Africans have remarked appreciatively that the Volunteers are almost the only foreigners who have voluntarily sought to live among the people with whom they work. Problems of convenience and sanitation have not been overwhelming, and Volunteers have been able to maintain a modest degree of comfort while living in traditional African housing. The experience certainly produced a cultural insight over and above that obtainable from study or observation. Occasionally, at least, it did produce a degree of sympathetic response from the neighbors. Thus one Nigerian government official, commenting on the Peace Corps, remarked that the Volunteers living in Zaria were the first white men for more than half a century who had lived in the old city and had really become friends and neighbors rather than aloof foreign experts.

Debate, however, continues on the proper course to follow with the bulk of the Volunteers accepting the housing provided by government for those engaged in their type of work. Housing, of course, is only one indication that the African secondary school teacher is part of a privileged sector of the population whose salary and fringe benefits enable him to drive a car, to eat imported food, and, in general, to live on a plane far above that of the majority. Many African schools are staffed largely by foreigners who view as an economic opportunity the position which the Volunteer has chosen on a service motivation. The African teacher himself is definitely one who has begun to "make good" and jealously guards the privileges which accompany his hard won social mobility. The Volunteer finds that smooth relations with his non–Peace-Corps counterparts are essential to his success and yet identifying with his vocational peers places him in an elitist position.

One instance in which the Volunteer gives in to the pattern established by other expatriates is in the matter of servants. To an American in the 1970s, a household servant seems like the epitome of privilege; a status distinction reserved for the very rich. When he finds that servants may be hired at a wage varying between three and eight dollars a week, this seems like the grossest sort of exploitation even though it may be an attractive wage to many of the inhabitants. The Volunteer may resolve that he would never be a "master" with a domestic subordinate, but this resolve quickly melts when he is confronted by the amount of work involved in shopping, washing clothes, and maintaining a minimal standard of sanitation. Further, the need for a trusted go-between to serve as a link between himself and a populace whose customs still baffle him and whose language he speaks very imperfectly leads to a reliance on servants.

To most foreigners serving in developing countries, the Volunteer appears either crazy or noble (according to the value judgment) in accepting a scale of material rewards far below that commanded by other resident aliens. To the indigenous populace the matter is not so clear. The Volunteer often shares some of the privileges provided for others in his vocational position, and even if his living quarters are those typical of the society, this is not regarded as hardship. Even the possession of a regular cash income, however modest, places one in a privileged position in most developing societies. On the other hand, the Volunteer is one who manifests an interest in local customs, tries to become acquainted with ordinary people, and foregoes at least some of the usual symbols of status. Barriers of economic privilege do remain, but at least they have been minimized to the point where social interaction on a partially egalitarian plane is not impossible.

The goal of the Peace Corps may be identified as "acceptance;" acceptance by the society of the Volunteer as one who is sympathetic and regards himself as being on the level of equality, and acceptance by the Volunteer of the worth and validity of the people and the culture in which he works. There is no clear criterion for measuring acceptance, but the Volunteer who is considered a friend and counselor by the people, who lives among the people and who spends much of his leisure time in recreational pursuits with the nationals of the area, would seem to have gone a long way.

The suggestion is made that perhaps intermarriage may be considered an index to the degree of acceptance and this would seem to have some validity. The rate of intermarriage is highest in places like the Philippines, where there are many common elements in the two cultures. However, it would certainly be a mistake to assume that the person who intermarries has accepted the culture, or that the person who does not find a mate among the nationals of the country is one who has failed to become *simpatico*.

Accepting the culture does not mean approving of all the goals and values of the country; neither does it mean that the Peace Corps Volunteer has been "de-tribalized" in the sense that he turns his back on American standards and ideals. Rather, it indicates that he has been able to accept the cultural matrix sufficiently, that he is at ease in his living situation, and that he can work constructively within the boundaries set by local customs and traditions.

WITHDRAWAL AND RETURN

The typical Peace Corps Volunteer has been heavily indoctrinated with the idea of cultural relativism during the training session, has usually begun to disdain the habits and way of life of the "enclave" Americans, and has made a solemn resolve that he himself is going to be an "acceptor." This, however, is a type of step which requires more than resolution, and it is common for many Volunteers to have a "withdrawal stage" in which they seek to find a type of retreat which, for a longer or shorter period, removes them from the necessity of contact with the national culture. Most reports of Peace Corps activities indicate that a weekend retreat in which Peace Corps Volunteers will visit each other, travel to the nearest city and engage primarily in interaction with fellow nationals is a common part of the Peace Corps experience and is described by many as being the only thing which makes it possible for them to stick out the trials of living during the week in surroundings where the familiar cultural cues fail to work. This weekly excursion routine represents a rhythmic pattern of withdrawal and return in which the Volunteer battles for five days with the task of cultural adjustment and then withdraws to more familiar haunts, only to resume the struggle the following week. It is hardly the optimum type of acceptance but it is a viable compromise which enables the Volunteer to function on the job and still obtain intermittent relief from cultural strain.

CULTURE FATIGUE AND CULTURE SHOCK

Even the minimum acceptance of the culture necessary for the performance of duties may be difficult for the Volunteer to achieve. Sometimes, the initial efforts of the Peace Corps Volunteer are rejected by the very people he desires to serve and the result is a kind of despondency illustrated in the following statement by a Volunteer in Colombia.

I began to develop a grudge against La Union and to make wild generalizations in my mind about the town and the people in it. I pretty much decided that I really didn't like the people and that it would be impossible to work with them. About the only adult I had met for whom I had any feelings of friendship at all was a young shoemaker who worked in a kiosk by the bus stop, an Indian from the Sierra who had dared to move down into the tropics. And God knows he wasn't really an adult at fifteen.

When I seriously thought about what I was going to do in this unrewarding spot for eighteen more months, it sent me spinning into a real depression. I locked myself in my room for three days and read Ian Fleming novels and drank about five gallons of coffee. In the afternoons when the little kids knocked at the door, I held my breath until they went away. I had thought that I could move into a completely different culture and, if not love, at least accept it enough that I could do the job I had been trained for. It came as an ego-shriveling shock to discover after the first month that I wasn't doing much of anything but reacting naively and emotionally to the poverty around me.[3]

The foregoing incident would be described as a case of cultural shock —a phenomenon which usually occurs in the early stages of contact. It is a situation much like homesickness, in which the absence of familiar customs and the inability to anticipate responses is so frustrating that the individual simply withdraws from interaction. Usually it is a malady from which the individual recovers in a few days; he is then able to face life in this strange new world which has become the scene of operation.

Cultural fatigue, by contrast, appears later in the individual's experience and may accompany a seemingly successful experience. One former Volunteer describes it as follows:

Cultural fatigue is the physical and emotional exhaustion that almost invariably results from the infinite series of minute adjustments required for long-term survival in an alien culture. Living and working overseas generally required that one must suspend his automatic evaluations and judgments; that he must apply new interpretations to seemingly familiar behavior; and that he must demand of himself constant alterations in the style and content of his activity. Whether the process is conscious or unconscious, successful or unsuc-

---

[3] Moritz Thomsen, *Living Poor* (Seattle, University of Washington Press, 1969), pp. 35–36.

cessful, it consumes an enormous amount of energy, leaving the individual decidedly fatigued.[4]

The Peace Corps policy of repudiating "enclave living" and encouraging maximum participation in the host society probably maximizes the prospect of both cultural shock and cultural fatigue. Occasionally individuals who appear to be outstandingly successful in bringing about constructive innovation fall victims to cultural fatigue and have to be shipped home, although the number of Volunteers who have been sent home for any reason is amazingly low. Eventually, intimate participation in an alien society brings a degree of understanding and familiarity which lessens emotional strain, but, in the short run, high expectations of social involvement may run the risk of a greater probability of culture shock and cultural fatigue.

Cultural differences are frequently regarded as matters of taste and custom, important to understanding but relatively superficial. Variations in clothes, diet, family practices, language usage, methods of greeting, and types of recreation are puzzling at first but with a bit of effort can be learned. Even concern for items high in American esteem such as sanitation can be minimized in behalf of intergroup amity. The really distressing intergroup differences are not variation in customary ways of life but different standards of value.

Even though intellectually they may be cautious in their claims, a belief in progress is implicit in the rapid change which all adult Americans have witnessed in their own lifetimes. Whatever their misgivings about the ultimate direction of history or even their ability to handle difficult day-by-day problems, Americans have a manipulative attitude toward their world. Fundamentally, the direct, vigorous, forthright approach is expected to yield the answer.

As one former Volunteer describes the American attitude:

There is an enormous cultural gap between industrialized countries and the preindustrial (ascending or developing) nations of the world. The host countries where the Peace Corps Volunteers are assigned have complex problems of population growth, nutrition, regional factionalism and leadership. The young American PCV enters the culture of the host country often without even having clearly defined the society of which he is a product. One might define the American culture briefly as: time-oriented, productive, qualitative, mechanical, organized, institution-oriented, wealthy, wasteful, violent, peace-seeking, educated and charitable. To this list a host national might add that Americans are insensitive, frank, exploitive, impersonal, generous, glamorous, ill-mannered and independent. Whether these behavioral characteristics do indeed describe

---

[4] David Szanton, "Cultural Configuration in the Philippines," in Robert B. Textor (ed.), *Cultural Frontiers of the Peace Corps*, (Cambridge, Mass., the M.I.T. Press, 1966), pp. 48–49.

Americans is not the point of importance. However, the existence of this stereotype in the minds of a great many of the peoples around the world is of enormous importance.[5]

Developing countries have seen change, but more frequently the change is seen as an erosion of ancient security and less frequently as a triumphant manipulation of nature for man's needs. Skepticism about the prospects of any quick change for the better leads to suspicion of the change advocate and a tendency to question his motives. Indirection is the way social disagreements are handled and elaborate subterfuges may be used to mask disagreement.

The following description of Philippine-American value differences would find an echo in most developing countries:

1.   The PCV who is "perfectly frank" with a Filipino, who expresses criticism openly, does so at considerable risk. In the Philippines such behavior can lead to painful embarrassment, loss of face, and shame—indeed to a sudden and severe denial of the social support needed to maintain the individual's psychological equilibrium. The forthrightly frank American is likely to evoke a reaction of hostility, or even possibly violence.

2.   A related fact is that the Filipinos place great stress on "Smooth Interpersonal Relations," or "SIR." They handle potential disagreements by ignoring them, by pretending that they do not exist, or by designating intermediaries to conduct negotiations between the parties involved. American directness and "sincerity" are hence quite out of place.

3.   Filipinos develop long-lasting mutual assistance alliances based on reciprocal obligations, which often override personal consequences, and often "get in the way" of accomplishing specific technological or managerial tasks. Americans, by contrast, tend toward more short-range, impersonal, contractual, functionally specific relationships.

4.   Open striving for power and prestige is socially acceptable (and expected) for individuals and families in the Philippines. Middle-class Americans tend to mask or deny their power drives.

5.   The Philippine kinship system gives greater prominence to relatives whom Americans consider distant. A Filipino's efforts and savings are hence likely to be "drained off" to the benefit of these "distant" relatives, rather than devoted to economic and technological investments.

6.   Deference to persons of higher status, including elderly people, is a much more pronounced feature of life in the Philippines than it is in egalitarian America.[6]

The work assignment of the Volunteer may act either to insulate him from the nationals of the area or to bring him into heightened interaction.

---

[5] Peter Limburg, Student Paper, used by permission.

[6] Szanton, "Cultural Configuration in the Philippines," pp. 43–44.

Occasionally, there is a Peace Corps job such as draftsman, which, by its very nature, tends to isolate the volunteer during working hours and also offers little stimulus to direct him toward off-duty contacts. A school assignment, and this is probably the most frequent type of duty, would seem to automatically involve a tremendous amount of interaction. Although there is, indeed, much interaction with students, it is highly structured and usually is confined to the classroom. To a lesser extent, the Volunteer interacts with non–Peace-Corps teachers. Sometimes this teacher interaction is intense in the school and carries over into community social life. In many situations the school interaction is formal and limited, with no shared activities outside of the school setting. The school assignment itself is a tremendously demanding and even exhausting type of experience and it is not uncommon for volunteers to find that the daily preparation of lessons and conduct of the classroom exhausts both their energies and their interests.

Community interaction may be either an extension of the Volunteer's official role or an escape from an unsatisfactory type of assignment. Most teaching Volunteers find their way into the community through their school contacts, but this is not the only route. In fact, an unsatisfactory school environment may actually push the Volunteer into seeking compensatory community contacts. In the Philippines, for instance, where an assignment as "teacher's aide" proved to be rather difficult to work out in practice, leaving many of the Volunteers suspended more or less in limbo, this was actually an inducement to community exploration. The Volunteer, finding his school duties light and not especially rewarding, rechanneled his efforts toward contact with the community and involvement with community enterprises.[7] Other assignments, such as community development work, are impossible to carry out without maximum interaction with the nationals of the area. To some extent work always offers a bridge, but it may also offer a refuge from less structured and more uncertain types of contacts.

The mutuality of interest between the Volunteers and the indigenous teachers is not always as great as might be expected. True, they are both engaged in the teaching process, but the indigenous teacher tends to develop bureaucratic security-oriented attitudes, while the Volunteer is anxious for quick results in the form of student improvement. The extent to which indigenous and Volunteer attitudes may diverge emerges quite sharply in the following letter of suggestions from a Volunteer to an Ethiopian educational official.

Provincial Education Officer
Ministry of Education
Asmara. Eritrea, Ethiopia

---

[7] Ibid., p. 41.

Dear ———

The following is an attempt to answer the question you put forth . . . : "How can we make education more meaningful for our students, and our schools more efficient?"

1.   A fact which I find abhorring is that teachers are impersonal to students and students are usually impersonal among themselves. An indication of this is the attendance record book which has only the student's number. The most important thing and sometimes the only thing they have is their name; as teachers, the least we can do is to learn it and use it. A reason for this impersonal attitude is probably the teaching method employed; i.e., the teacher enters the room and writes something on the blackboard; the student proceeds to copy it for later memorization. There is never any give and take between teacher and student. Never anything which requires listening and thought—memorization suffices. To break this vicious cycle and give man the dignity he deserves, I suggest a new method of teaching which takes into account the fact that students now possess text books.

2.   If Ethiopia at present needs an educated nucleus from which to build, tougher criteria for promotion must be adopted. It is my belief that every student deserves the opportunity to fail. According to a list of rules circulated by the Ministry of Education, "promotion should be automatic." A rule which works against the purpose of education must be invalidated. The prevailing culture is one which emphasizes "helping my brother," even to pass a test; put more simply, cheating! Not only among students, but teachers also "help" students. This "help" only serves to promote the incompetent; this developing country can ill afford any more incompetent officials. A basic change in cultural patterns is called for, but an immediate remedy to keep those who are not ready for promotion from being promoted is to have General Exams proctored by PCV's.

3.   Many teachers sincerely believe that they and their salaries are the "reasons for our schools." To say they are "misinformed" is a grave understatement. An idea to be drilled into all teachers is: Since education is the hope of our country's future, the welfare of all students is to be given priority. To be more specific: Teachers love to play soccer and basketball, but I believe it should be forbidden if it necessitates the teacher's absence from school so he can travel to the game site. Also, I believe it would be desirable in teaching the idea that our schools are for the learning of the students if it was made mandatory for a student team to accompany and play the other town on the same date as the faculty team.

4.   A top priority step in making our schools more efficient would be to make a "duties list" for each member of the staff (headmaster, classmaster, teacher, secretary, sportsmaster and custodians); e.g., our school has few windows, but have the custodians ever cleaned them? No, instead they have been known to walk into my room while class is in session and question my decision as a teacher. At least the non-teaching staff should be informed that their purpose is to support the teachers. Maybe the secretary could even relieve the classroom teacher of the tedious job of filling out report cards.

5.   The threat of student strikes is ridiculous and the students' power to do such must be broken. This could be done by giving headmasters instructions that

they are running their school and not the students, plus full authority to expel any and all rebellious students.

6.   To facilitate learning, it is believed that a short test each week in each subject would keep the students' efforts and thoughts directed more properly than one or two tests a semester.

7.   Exercises and questions should be used in all subjects which require the students thought process. A person who can't think has not been educated, and the biggest fool is one who memorizes facts obtainable in an *Almanac!* To decrease memorization, it might be advisable for less emphasis to be placed on the General Exam. Especially since math is the best subject for developing thought, its teachers should be advised never to give problems on a test which the students have previously worked and memorized.

8.   Students and teachers are lazy. I believe an outgrowth of this is the tendency that they all demonstrate as being hypochondriacs. In the hope that students do follow their teachers' example, teacher absenteeism must be stopped. Since medical permission for even an imagined headache is presently a good reason for many days' absence without any penalty, I recommend a rule of 5 days absence per year be established and every day thereafter be deducted from the offender's salary. Also, "permission" for the student must be made harder to obtain, along with the policy of expelling students who have an excessive number (possibly 10) of unjustified absences.

9.   Textbooks are of poor quality and circulated in a worse fashion. A student's mind is capable of grasping much more than these books disclose. Also, paperbound books are doing well if they last one year. Why not pay twice as much for books which are cloth bound and last 5 years?

Finally, it is simply amazing what can be accomplished by "trying"! It should become an official educational policy neither to accept nor offer excuses, but give an effort. If this idea is successfully ingrained in the minds of all of us connected with our schools, the amount of progress made will be unbelievable.

> Professionally,
> Edward A. Sullivan, P.C.V.[8]

The issues mentioned in Sullivan's letter are almost inevitable in the relationship between American Volunteers and the salaried officials of developing countries. The Volunteer is anxious to bring about change, the official either fears change or feels the situation is hopeless. The Volunteer is distrustful of any kind of bureaucratic process and presses for results; the official fears that an emphasis on results will bring his job into question. The Volunteer at home may have had the attitude that the important thing was to get through the system, i.e., finish school by the easiest possible route. Abroad, he sees the school in terms of what students learn and feels that an unearned diploma is of no value to the country and of no service to the individual. The official may endure shortages, since they are not his responsibility and he will not be blamed. The Volunteer is upset by any

---

[8] Excerpts from letter written by a P.C.V. in Ethiopia, the name Edward A. Sullivan is a pseudonym. Used by permission.

handicap to his mission and takes responsibility for seeing that these are remedied. The official is usually one with many interests besides his salaried position and feels that he has found a comfortable niche which does not require too much of his time and energy. The Volunteer has few other interests, feels the call of service, and must "prove" himself by some significant accomplishment. The resulting interaction may open new understanding to both the official and the Volunteer but is likely to be a bit traumatic for each.

RELATIONS WITH OTHER WESTERNERS

One of the complexities of the Peace Corps operation is that the Volunteer has to adjust not only to nationals of a developing country but, frequently, also to the individuals and the practices left by the colonial power, often Great Britain, which was previously the ruler of the area. Even with the best of good will, it is hard to avoid some sense of competition between the British, who were the representatives of Western civilization in the district for the previous hundred or more years, and the Americans who have just arrived with all of the confidence of people who are new to the scene and who have avoided the disillusionment which comes with experience.

Apart from actual competition there is frequently a difference between British and American folkways which is especially disturbing, since, on a superficial basis, the two cultures seem very similar. This difference in British and American practice shows up in a number of ways. In education, for instance, both British and Americans tend to be suspicious of the others' qualifications. The British tend to have a feeling that American education is superficial, while Americans are surprised to find that very few British secondary school teachers are graduates of institutions which would seem to approximate the American teachers' college, most of them having left school at the end of the sixth form, which Americans are apt to identify as the junior college level. The formality with which the British tend to cloak governmental concerns and the social distance which they tend to maintain from past or present subject peoples is another type of cultural difference which may be even harder for Americans to adjust to than the more obviously different customs of the indigenous population.

One example of the difficulties of British-American cooperation comes from the case of nurses in Malaya. The Peace Corps nurses were shocked by what they perceived as the attitude of the British that emergencies were situations which simply did not arise and that, therefore, plans for immediate adjustment to a crisis situation were unnecessary. Further, they were surprised by the strict social distance which marked off the hierarchies within the nursing profession and which separated nurses from other members of the medical services. On the other hand, the British were surprised that the American Peace Corps nurses were not trained in midwifery, since they tend to look upon this as an essential part of the nurse's equipment.[9]

On the whole, relations between British and Americans have been tolerable and difficulties are usually worked out over a period of time, but the process may involve more effort and more conscious adjustment than are anticipated. Even in matters of speech there are frequently differences in pronunciation and the use of words which give some strength to the old proverb that the "British and Americans are two people separated by a common language." Cowan's description of the Nigerian situation is a good summary of problems which arose between Volunteers and representatives of the ex–colonial power.

It should be added that not infrequently the problems of the Volunteers outside their specific job situation stemmed more from members of the expatriate community than from Nigerians. Both in ex-British and ex-French countries of West Africa, expatriates have frequently regarded the members of Peace Corps as the vanguard of American influence seeking to take over where the influence of former colonial power has begun to wane after independence. Perceiving a threat to their prestige and positions, these expatriates frequently voice criticism of the PVC's. This criticism, of course, must be expressed in terms that do not seem too transparently self-seeking. At its most convincing, it takes the form of pointing out how ill-prepared some of the PCV's are in a professional sense. Other criticism points to the Volunteers' youth and to their desire to help the African community apart from the purely formal instruction given in the classroom. The Volunteer, faced with this continuous criticism in the close contact of the day-to-day school situation and confronting resistance on the part of the African community toward his efforts at closer contact, found himself almost unconsciously absorbing the viewpoint of the colonial civil servant. By far the bulk of the Volunteers in Nigeria, however, were aware of this dilemma and made successful efforts to escape from it—sometimes at the cost of difficult personal relations with their European colleagues.[10]

While ideology may divide the Volunteers and the expatriates, their similarity in culture and color tends to draw them into a common classification. Color differences are, of course, immediately apparent and, while colonial powers in their later years tend to play down color discrimination, the memory of earlier days when the white face was frankly the badge of privilege is still present, along with continual tales of discrimination and racial strife coming from the United States. Usually the nationals of the country have had relatively little experience with American discrimination themselves, but they are quite aware of the stories that have circulated

---

[9] William H. Friedland, "Nurses in Tanganyika," in Textor, *Cultural Frontiers of the Peace Corps*, pp. 148–49.

[10] Gray L. Cowan, "The Nigerian Experience and Career Reorientation," in Textor, *Cultural Frontiers of the Peace Corps*, p. 163.

about the United States and as a result have a somewhat ambivalent attitude both toward American culture and toward the Volunteer, who, to some extent, is supposed to represent that culture. The words of a student from Ghana express quite well the twin attitudes of attraction and repulsion which occur.

In my opinion, the United States is one of the most developed countries in the world, but in spite of its civilization, there exists one of the most shameful acts in the world today, namely, racial discrimination . . .

Whites and blacks have separate schools, and they do not mix in cafes, restaurants and cinema places. If a black enters a "white" cafe by mistake, he is fought; a white will not go into a "black" cafe because it "degrades" him. In the combined parts of the cities, there are no fights but there is that old polite "they live their lives and we live ours" attitude between whites and blacks . . .

Racial discrimination spoils the good name of the United States. In spite of this, it must be a wonderful country to live in for it has many modern facilities. I'll prefer studying there to any other country. . . .[11]

If color represents somewhat of a hurdle of distrust and prejudice for the white Volunteers, its meaning for the black Volunteer is still more complex. It is hardly a carryover of the American position, for abroad he is at once a black man and an American. As an American, he is expected to be a representative of his country's viewpoints and the attitudes which are identified with Americans in general; as a black man he is expected to regard Africa, for instance, as his homeland. The more sophisticated Africans were often critical of the "Uncle Tom" type of mentality which they associated with the assimilated American Negroes; the black power approach, on the other hand, seemed to be something peculiarly American with very little relevance in Africa, where the black man was so obviously dominant that there seemed to be little point to elaborating the virtues of a reverse racism. The American black would find both a sense of continuity and also a sense of estrangement as he realized how drastic were the cultural differences which separated him from his African friends.

On the other hand, for at least a few of the black Volunteers this was an opportunity to establish identity, since this was a time when the black could return to his land of origin, could place his feet on the soil of his ancestors and yet at the same time was fully identified as an American. Hence, he had a twin identity, both black and American, and could face the future with a greater knowledge of his real roots than he had ever had before.

American racial concepts were not always applicable. Especially in countries outside of Africa, it was frequently true that gradations of color

---

[11] Arnold Zeitlin, *To the Peace Corps with Love* (Garden City, New York, Doubleday and Company, 1965), p. 98. Copyright 1965 by Arnold Zeitlin and Marion Zeitlin. Reprinted by permission of Doubleday & Company, Inc.

consciousness were so finely drawn that the simple black-white dichotomy expected in the American culture did not seem to apply. The experiences of a rather light-complexioned Negro in Colombia are a case in point.

The Negro volunteer's second assignment was in a site on the west coast of Colombia, where he did an amazing job. Someone who visited his site several months after he left found he was remembered with great respect and admiration. The community was largely Negro; the conclusion might be drawn that part of the reason the volunteer was so effective was that he, too, was Negro. However, inquiries among the people on this point elicited the response that, because of his light color, they did not regard this volunteer as Negro—an indication of how fine such distinctions may be in a country where minor gradations in skin color are directly related to social status.[12]

In almost every area, divisions within the society complicated the desire of the Peace Corps Volunteer to identify with the local inhabitants. In Southeast Asia, if he associated with the overseas Chinese he ran the risk that the dominant nationality groups might feel rejected. In Africa, friendship for one tribal group might increase suspicion from other tribes. In Latin America, the division between mestizos and Indians was often a complicating factor.

The mestizo-Indian divide was an especially difficult one for the Volunteer to bridge. In most cases he had, with difficulty, learned a smattering of Spanish, but he was totally unprepared for the task of tackling Indian dialects. The mestizo group were often officials with whom the Peace Corps had to work and their greater cultural similarity eased contacts. To associate with the mestizos was a move which came naturally, while the development of contact with the Indians required a special effort in which language ignorance was a serious handicap. On the other hand, Indians made up a large part of the population and any suspicion that the Peace Corps was in league with the mestizos produced an opposition from the Indians.

SEXUAL ROLES

In many countries, stereotypes about the proper role of the sexes presented almost as much of a problem as color. In the Philippines, women entered freely into most vocational fields, but a tradition of the social chaperonage of single women made it difficult for female Volunteers to move about freely without criticism. In other locations, such as Northern Nigeria, for instance, the pattern of female subordination was so strong that it was unusual for a woman to hold any type of salaried position. As aliens, the female Volunteers were partially exempted from local expecta-

---

[12] Morris L. Stein, *Volunteers for Peace* (New York, John Wiley and Sons, Copyright 1966), p. 9. Used by permission of John Wiley and Sons, Inc.

tions, but their deviation from the usual feminine roles still produced some consternation. The comments which Sullivan makes on the difficulties of the acceptance of feminine Peace Corps teachers in Ethiopia would apply in a great many places.

In a country where the role of the woman has traditionally been one of subservience, the acceptance of women as teachers has been mixed. Older staff members, particularly, have been slow to take to the idea of women instructors. One bright young girl, fresh from volunteer training, arrived in Addis Ababa to be told she had four distinct disadvantages; first, she was new; second, she was young; third, she was a woman; fourth, she was attractive. For many girl volunteer teachers, adaptability is a prime talent.[13]

COMMUNIST ATTACKS

It is perhaps a testimony to the effectiveness to which the Peace Corps won friends in the underdeveloped countries that it always became a marked target of Communist opposition. It was alleged that the Peace Corps representatives were associated with the CIA and that they were part of an imperialist plot to destroy the local culture as well as to carry back intelligence to the United States. As one former Peace Corps Volunteer in Liberia analyzes the situation:

Quite naturally the host country people will be suspicious of the "stranger" in their midst. They will often ask, "Why did you come here? Why did you leave your home? Can't you find work in your own country?" Accusations are sometimes made that the volunteer is a neocolonialist, imperialist, or C.I.A. agent.[14]

In Nigeria, during the days of the civil war, there were times when the suspicion of the Peace Corps as potential spies became so intense that it was difficult to even hold a meeting of Volunteers without facing accusations that some kind of espionage was being planned. In fact, the very effort of the Peace Corps to become friends with people in the locality and to penetrate the local culture in a manner which was not typical of expatriates in general, lent credence to the suspicion that here was a new and potentially effective type of spy. At times, even intermarriage has been described as a method of gaining entry into the local society for subversive purposes. If the Peace Corps Volunteer is withdrawn, he can be accused of being aloof and disdainful of the local society. If he participates actively, he is trying to capture control.

If the Volunteer is at all indiscreet in the remarks he makes about sanitation or the government administration, he is open to attack as one who is

---

[13] George Sullivan, *The Story of the Peace Corps* (New York, copyright by Fleet Press Corporation, 1964), p. 115.

[14] Joan Eileen Gay in a student paper.

insulting the country. The classic blunder of the Peace Corps girl in Nigeria who was indiscreet enough to write some critical comments about toilet customs on a postcard is a case in point. The postcard was intercepted by students on a Nigerian campus who immediately circulated it in a way which made these comments a cause celebre. The writer of the card had to be returned home, and for a while it seemed as though the entire Peace Corps effort in Nigeria had been placed in jeopardy. The changing winds of local politics have occasionally resulted in an entire Peace Corps contingent's being sent home, although usually a succeeding government will ask that the contract be renewed.

The Volunteer himself was frequently confused by this kind of warfare. He was reluctant to view himself as a participant in the cold war and considered himself engaged in a nonpolitical enterprise. He had been exposed to some lectures on the nature of Communism during the training program, lectures which he was inclined to disregard on the theory that this was some type of brainwashing attempt by the government. The mounting storm of criticism and disquiet over the United States role in Viet Nam did not exempt the Peace Corps, whose members shared the pattern of sentiments which were typical of many younger Americans. Thus, the Peace Corps Volunteer who was accused, however unjustly, of being an American spy may himself have suffered from guilt feelings, since he too may have been critical of American foreign policy.

Usually, the most effective answer to Communist propaganda has not been counterpropaganda but simply the evidence that the Peace Corps Volunteer was doing a job and that his efforts at friendliness and communication were sincere and rooted in a desire for helpfulness. In spite of a series of pamphlets, newspaper articles, and radio attacks inspired from Communist sources, the Peace Corps image has been surprisingly persistent. It is probably true that the example of rather attractive young men and women living seemingly selfless lives has been effective as "propaganda of the deed" for a favorable American image.

URBAN AND RURAL INTERACTION

One of the differences between the Peace Corps Volunteer and most of the people with whom he works is the extent of urban experience. Since farmers comprise only six percent of the American population, and since farm youth have been underrepresented among Peace Corps Volunteers, it is inevitable that most Volunteers come from an urban background. But the countries in which they work are primarily rural. Not only are the countries rural, but the rural areas are far more lacking in amenities than is usually the case in the United States, and the Volunteer in the rural area will find that he is a long way from the type of shopping center and recreational complex to which he has been accustomed.

It would seem that the isolation from Western-oriented facilities and people would place unbearable strain on the Peace Corps Volunteer and would lead to great difficulty in making adjustment. Quite the contrary seems to take place; various authorities have stated that there seems to be evidence that the adjustment of the Peace Corps Volunteer has been better in the rural areas,[15] and that the Peace Corps Volunteer is more nearly accepted and interacts to a greater extent in the countryside than he does in the urban center. This seemingly contradictory result may be explained by the comparative openness of rural society in an underdeveloped area. The Peace Corps Volunteer is necessarily known to people over a rather wide area and the custom of casual visiting is widespread, although patterns of formal hospitality may not be the ones expected by the Volunteer. The very fact that there is no European enclave to which he can resort and that commercial entertainment is nonexistent impels a Volunteer to seek to make friends and to immerse himself in community activities. Perhaps it is also true that the Peace Corps training has assisted in this kind of adjustment, since it has tended to romanticize life in the grass hut or the mud compound and has tried to prepare the Peace Corps volunteers to regard a rural assignment as an opportunity to demonstrate the extent of their dedication. On the other hand, the urban area offers many opportunities for escape from interaction and the generally impersonal type of environment means that contacts with the indigenous population are probably somewhat more difficult to establish and to maintain.

EQUALITY AND DIFFERENCES

The Volunteer tends to leave the Peace Corp training camp with a strong belief in the equality, and therefore the similarity, of people throughout the world. True, he has been exposed to many lectures on differences in culture, but these seem to be rather academic when placed beside the basic belief that all human beings must be essentially the same. This belief in the sameness of human beings breaks down in day-by-day contact with people who do not respond to the cultural cues with which he is familiar. When he finds that a clenched fist may be a sign of welcome, offers of hospitality may be ignored, that patterns of family relationship he has regarded as sacred may be completely disregarded, that values he assumed were self-evident are denied, the Volunteer becomes aware of the fact that people are different. The next question he faces is that if people really are different, if they have different standards, if they respond to different values, can he also hold to the feeling that people are equal?

---

[15] Gerald S. Maryanov, "The Representative Staff as Intercultural Mediators in Malaya," in Textor, *Cultural Frontiers of the Peace Corps*, p. 77, and Allen E. Guskin, "Tradition and Change in a Thai University," ibid., p. 99.

Perhaps the ultimate in acceptance comes when the Peace Corps Volunteer realizes that people are not similar in basic tastes and values and therefore equal, but different in tastes and values and still equal in their diverse representation of a common humanity.

CONCLUSIONS

Even though the Peace Corps did achieve both popularity with Congress and imitation by foreign countries, the long-term future of its programs is difficult to predict. Widespread distrust of the "establishment" among American youth tends to eliminate some idealistic young people who were anxious to flock to the banner during the Kennedy era. International opinion is subject to frequent shifts and the future may produce an atmosphere in which the Peace Corps may either be welcomed as representatives of a one-world philosophy or scorned as agents of American imperialism. Whatever the long run outlook, though, the experience of the Peace Corps offers some valuable insight into the nature of intergroup relations.

There are many types of personnel who share with the Peace Corps the aspect of temporary minority status, but there are few whose objectives and approach produce so sharp a variation from the usual practice. All such temporary minority migrants share in the experience of culture shock and culture fatigue and have worked out adjustments. The usual pattern is one of enclave living and elite interaction, with acculturation limited to the minimum required by the work role. This procedure offers the temporary minority a familiar cultural base with "their own kind of people" and just enough variation from the home country to provide a degree of the exotic. Some contact must take place with representatives of the indigenous culture but such interaction is usually limited in duration and confined to the most westernized part of the populace. Although diplomats, businessmen, and sometimes missionaries have operated fairly successfully on this basis for many years, the relationships do involve all the hazards we have reviewed in examining the experience of the Peace Corps.

Some people find even the minimal amount of intercultural cooperation necessary to their job too difficult to undertake and withdraw completely, others succumb to cultural shock and fatigue in spite of the relative insulation of their ethnic compound. Perhaps the most serious problem is that the degree of cross-cultural understanding generated in such a milieu is far less than might have been desired. The foreign minority and the indigenous population see each other only in segmented roles which reveal only a part of their outlook. Those who observe the "enclave American" abroad gain only a fragmented picture of American life, and Americans, in turn, learn only limited parts of the local culture. In this setting, cultural misunderstanding is easy and the so-called international experts of both countries have only a limited insight into other cultures.

In this chapter we will abandon the practice followed in the rest of the book of compiling a list of specific practices with the general notions that they seem to imply. Many of the experiences of the Peace Corps Volunteers reflect some of the patterns we have previously listed, but the main impact of the Peace Corps on intergroup relations is its method of relating people from an industrialized country to people whose countries are just beginning the process we rather arrogantly term "modernization." This relationship involves the transmission of ideas and methods, but the Peace Corps experience indicates that it may also involve the growth of mutual understanding.

The Peace Corps objectives were not limited to job performance but rather called both for exporting an understanding of America and for gaining an insight into other cultures. No one would maintain that these objectives have been completely met, but representatives of many countries have stated that the Peace Corps brought an image of America which had been only dimly perceived before their presence. At the same time, many Volunteers have found their cultural horizons expanded. Perhaps the most important lesson which emerges from this experience is that cultural acceptance can be substituted for cultural withdrawal as an antidote to cultural shock and fatigue. In the words of a returned Peace Corps Volunteer:

> The glaring implication which comes from this experience is that it is possible for the representatives of two cultures to meet without recourse to oppression, physical violence, or the maintenance of social distance; through understanding and accepting cultural differences both parties can grow and lead richer lives. Indeed the evidence tends to show that ethnocentrism with its concomitant racism and oppression which inhibit mutual acceptance, is merely a weak cultural factor which can be superseded with proper guidance, understanding and tolerance.[16]

Cultural acceptance implies a high degree of acculturation. Language learning is a must, the local foods will be explored, living quarters will be located in a setting which encourages interaction with a cross section of the indigenous population, and the standard of living will approximate that which is generally available in the locality.

The Peace Corps Volunteers survived a rigid "selecting out" process which was designed to weed out those whose personality framework would not allow them to make necessary adjustments; in addition a small number of Volunteers had to be sent back to the United States before their tour was completed. Further, most Volunteers are in their early 20s without family

---

[16] Student paper submitted by John L. Longman, former Peace Corps Volunteer in Ethiopia. Used by permission.

responsibilities and might be said to constitute a peculiarly adaptable group. In addition, some Volunteers chose to avail themselves of the support of enclave living, as a partial withdrawal from the host society, except for necessary work commitments; and most Volunteers perfected the ritual of weekend retreat to surroundings with less cultural strain.

With all these qualifications, there still remains a striking difference between the situation of many Volunteers and the typical temporary foreign minority. All of the difficulties of racial suspicion, ideological opposition, nationality conflict, and different interpretations of sex roles, which plague other groups are also problems for the Peace Corps. The difference is in the way in which such problems have been met. Rather than being given salaries that compete with United States pay scales, the Volunteers are placed on a stipend which approximates their native counterparts; rather than living in a protected milieu, they are encouraged to move into the community, and instead of retreating to an English-language enclave, they study local languages to the extent that many reach a substantial degree of fluency in their two-year assignment.

The most impressive aspect of the program is not that some Volunteers have failed and that others have evaded the program of cultural acceptance, but that so many have succeeded. Other agencies dealing with different types of personnel may not be able to follow the Peace Corps pattern completely, but many of them are giving a similar type of training to their recruits and stressing the rewards of cultural acceptance rather than the possibilities of cultural withdrawal. The idea that noncompetitive equal-status interaction holds at least the possibility of greater understanding is one of the findings of sociology which have been documented several times,[17] and the Peace Corps has demonstrated that the generalization applies in this particular type of intergroup relations.

The Peace Corps has been responsible for the instruction of thousands of students, the initiating and carrying on of community development programs, the mapping of uncharted districts, the provision of nursing services, and countless other activities. All these functions are important, but it is probable that the historians will conclude that its greatest contribution consisted in the pioneering application of a new brand of human

---

[17] Robin Williams, for instance, has made an analysis of the effect of intergroup contacts on prejudice in *Strangers Next Door: Ethnic Relations in American Communities* (New York, Prentice Hall, 1964), pp. 142–222. He finds that change is more likely to occur in the work context than in any other type of relationship. He also finds that change is especially likely when a person moves into a new community or group where the norms are different from those previously experienced. For the Peace Corps Volunteer both situations apply, i.e., he meets people from another group in the work context and he is confronting a community with different norms; hence one would prognosticate that a change in attitude is likely. For the people he meets change is less likely, but possible, since they are meeting Americans in a new context and hence must reformulate their role definitions.

relations in which sympathetic participation replaces detachment and cultural acceptance becomes the antidote for problems which other agencies have met by partial cultural withdrawal.

For a final word on the nature of the Peace Corps contribution we turn to an incisive statement by Lawrence Fuchs:

The Peace Corps is not the answer to what the rest of the world needs most. It is an answer to what Americans need most: to learn how to relate sensitively and empathetically with each other and with persons in other cultures and to learn how to ask assumption-challenging questions which break through the ethnocentrism in which nearly all of us are raised and bound.[18]

QUESTIONS

1. In terms of intergroup relations what is the difference between temporary and permanent migrants? Would the Peace Corps type of adjustment apply equally well to both classifications?
2. What is the basic principle underlying the techniques of enclave living, elite interaction, and vocationally oriented acculturation? How does the Peace Corps mode of adjustment differ?
3. Does an acceptance of a foreign culture imply the rejection of the culture of one's homeland?
4. Distinguish between culture fatigue and culture shock.
5. Is the weekend withdrawal pattern an aid to adjustment or a sabotage of the pattern of cultural participation?
6. To what extent is the Peace Corps adjustment pattern suitable for other types of temporary migrants?
7. Is there any way in which the Peace Corps could have avoided charges of espionage? Should Peace Corps Volunteers be allowed to demonstrate against United States foreign policy?
8. Would a group of Volunteers under the auspices of the United Nations be able to avoid the type of suspicions aroused by a United States Peace Corps? Why or why not?
9. How do you account for the fact that Volunteers from urban backgrounds seemed to adjust better to rural than to urban assignments?
10. What are the comparative merits of cultural acceptance versus enclave living as an antidote to cultural shock and fatigue? What are the implications of this issue for the assimilation of rural-urban migrants within a country?

---

[18] Lawrence H. Fuchs, "Inside Other Cultures," *Peace Corps Volunteer,* 6 (June 1968), p. 9.

Chapter 14

Persistent problems
and future prospects

In reading this brief description of ethnic interaction in many countries of the world, the student may well wonder from time to time what there is in common between areas so diverse in custom, geography, and ethnic composition. We have looked at a variety of religious, economic, and political entities covering all the continents of the earth except South America and Australia. We have looked at newly independent countries and those that have been self-governing for centuries, at countries slowly emerging into industrialism and at others where the problems of affluence seem as apparent as those of scarcity.

The common element in all of these case studies is that they are attempts to deal with ethnic diversity. These attempts may be classified into two broad categories. One is the effort to secure a homogeneous population and thereby limit the extent of the ethnic diversity with which the society must deal. The other category consists of societies which have accepted ethnic heterogeneity as an inevitable condition and have developed patterns by which people with different ethnic identities live together in a common framework.

METHODS OF LIMITING ETHNIC HETEROGENEITY

Attempts to secure an ethnically unified population run along three lines. The minority group may be eliminated by slaughter or expulsion, the territory may be divided in an effort to make national boundary lines coincide with ethnic distribution, or there may be a mixture of the populations so that the original lines of ethnic identity become blurred. In the last case a new composite society will emerge with a basic common identity for all. Slaughter or expulsion seemingly represents the triumph of ethnic hostility over any type of accommodation, since each method demonstrates a conviction that there is no way that different ethnic groups can live in the traditional territory. The next technique considered is that of partition, in which territories are divided and boundaries redrawn in an effort to attain ethnic homogeneity. Partition is a device adopted in the hope of avoiding ethnic conflict. Hostile ethnic groups may be allowed to remain in the same traditional geographic area, but the effort to retain a common government is abandoned and the new boundary lines attempt to eliminate most interethnic association. There are also other forms of separation and boundary changing, such as secession or annexation, which serve a similar function. The final method of attaining ethnic homogeneity is through amalgamation, in which a biological intermixture takes place, and assimilation, which is a blending of cultures. Amalgamation and assimilation are seldom the result of formal governmental policy and more frequently occur as a result of unplanned situations which promote interethnic contacts.

SLAUGHTER AND EXPULSION

We have not dealt with cases of slaughter, but the nearly successful attempt of Adolph Hitler to "solve the Jewish question" by the mass murder of European Jews is an event of recent history. There have been other massacres, and the 1972 and 1973 killing of the Hutus by the Watutsis in Burundi was apparently systematically conducted by the government authorities. However, the Hutu killings apparently were an effort to eliminate the educated elite rather than extermination of the entire tribe. In any event these and other massacres give somber evidence of the extremes to which ethnic conflict can be pushed.

Nor have we examined efforts to expel an entire people, although the policies toward Indians in Kenya may be a step in that direction—a step which Uganda has taken a bit further by the expulsion of all noncitizen Asians. For more thoroughgoing examples one could cite the expulsion of German nationals from surrounding countries after the end of World War II and the exchange of populations by Greece and Turkey after the end of their warfare in 1924. Similarly the flight of Jews from Arab countries and of Arabs from Israel has greatly changed population composition in these countries. Certainly mass expulsion has occurred in the past, is being approximated today, and could conceivably reappear in wholesale fashion if present trends continue.

PARTITION

We have cited two examples of partition; the creation of Northern Ireland and the Irish Free State and the separation of Belgium from the Netherlands. Our discussion also considered the decision of the British West Indies to separate themselves from Great Britain, and of Senegal to declare its independence from France as well as from other states in the area that might have become a French West African Federation.

Senegal and France were two nations which had never really merged; hence their separation might perhaps better be described as the breakup of a casual union rather than a divorce of married partners. Senegal had a veneer of French culture and there was a good deal of talk about assimilation. However, neither cultural diffusion nor political, educational, religious, and economic integration ever affected the majority of the Senegalese people. A small proportion of the elite attended French schools, became Catholic, participated in French political life, and were employed in France or in French-controlled enterprises. The majority of the Senegalese, however, continued to live in the pattern of their traditional societies, experiencing only indirect effects of the relationship with France. French economic policies might support the price of groundnuts, but French social security systems or labor unions were not extended to Senegal. Neither were the traditional tribal, religious, or communal customs greatly modified. In these circumstances, an initial inclination toward organic union with France quickly dissolved when a wave of independence spread through the rest of Africa. Senegal itself might be viewed as an artificial creation, since no nation by that name had ever existed before the French established it as an administrative unit. However, the precedent of the territorial lines established by the French gave rise to a number of vested interests and, in the absence of a strong push for consolidation, separate national independence seemed to be the easiest way out. Probably the basic conclusion to emerge from the Senegalese experience is that a long-term merger between two peoples requires a major degree of association and common enterprises involving the bulk of the population.

The British West Indies are somewhat different, since in these countries only vestiges of indigenous culture were left. The economic customs, the political forms and ideals, the language, the religion, and other basic patterns of social life were British. True, these were British patterns which had developed in an area separated by many miles from the British Isles and varying in many details; yet, certainly, the basic theme of the culture of these countries was far more British than African or Latin, as the case may be, if one chooses to refer to the ancestral land of origin or to countries in closest geographic proximity. In the historical development of government in the islands, one can observe a definite centrifugal tendency. As the islands developed and grew in population and commerce, the influence of the islanders was not expressed by participation in the British parliament, but in a greater separation from the British affairs and greater involvement in local government. This local government at first was restricted to the British settlers, but, once the pattern of local control was begun, the only question was who in the locality was going to exercise power. The pattern of relationship to Britain had been set. Unlike the French colonies that participated in the Chamber of Deputies, the British colonies turned more and more to their own concerns. As the non-European population gained greater power, they viewed independence as the logical end of the cycle—a step which probably would have been taken even if those in control had been of direct British ancestry.

The British West Indies nations are small countries greatly dependent on other powers for trade and protection. They might logically and economically benefit from incorporation in a greater union. In many ways, they were culturally similar to Britain, but·it appears that distant areas will separate from the mother country unless intensive policies involving two-way influence are followed. In the absence of such policies, the separation of the British West Indies islands was unavoidable.

The various types of partition are a different type of development from the attainment of independence. Partition involves peoples who have been intimately associated for many years, but who have maintained a separate identity and have found themselves in severe conflict. In both cases of partition, the same difficulty emerged. That is to say partition, while it seemed to solve one type of problem, developed new problems which seemed to be equally severe. These new problems arose because the new territories were still not ethnically homogeneous and because the ethnic divisions heavily overlapped with socioeconomic or "class" differences. The Belgians had separated from the Dutch, but the differences between Walloons and Flemish remained to perplex and divide the nation. The Protestants in Northern Ireland protected themselves from the dominance of the Catholic majority in the Irish Free State, but found themselves contending with a militant and discontented Catholic minority within their own zone.

Partition frequently seems to be the only solution in a country with violently antagonistic ethnic groups, but convincing evidence of its success is scarce. Apparently, in the modern world, it is next to impossible to carve out a territory which is both ethnically pure and economically viable. The search for a land which is peopled by only one ethnic group appears to be a futile quest which may limit the area of national territory without ending the rivalry between conflicting ethnic groups.

AMALGAMATION AND ASSIMILATION

Two countries in this category are Mexico and the United States. In Mexico, the creation of a common (socially categorized) mestizo physical type went hand in hand with assimilation to the Spanish culture. In the

United States, assimilation to a culture of Anglo-conformity blurred the sense of separate national identification of European immigrants, while the failure of racial amalgamation left various groups, of which the blacks are the largest, in a somewhat marginal position. The Indian in Mexico who leaves his ancestral village to take up employment in a factory finds that neither cultural distinctiveness nor physical type separates him from the bulk of the Mexican population. A part of moving to town is the acquisition of a variant of Spanish culture developed in the Mexican setting, while biological intermixture has made the mestizo classification one which can cover a wide range of color and physical types. Thus one does not find two sharply contrasting groups of Indian and Spanish ancestry, but rather finds that, for the most part, both of these, as well as the blacks who were brought into the country as slaves, have blended into the mestizo category. Two exceptions may be noted to this general picture of the homogenization of the population. One is that of the Indians, who still cling to a distinctive life style, and the other consists of aliens not recognized as either Spanish or Indian. About ten percent of the Mexicans are still identified as Indians and maintain traditional ways of life and ancient Indian languages. Mexico has not had the variety of immigration which the United States has seen, and those immigrants who are sharply different from either Spanish or Indians, such as the Chinese, have faced discrimination and prejudice.

To the degree to which Mexico has become the home of an ethnically unified people, the usual problems of intergroup hostility have been controlled if not completely eliminated. Such a development, however, was not the outcome of deliberate planning. The Spanish conquerors were as ethnocentric as any other invading group in any country of the world. Their eventual amalgamation with the Indian and black population seems to have been based, on the one hand, on a sex ratio in which Spanish females were in short supply, and, on the other, on a system of ethnic classification representing categories of ancestry which was so elaborate that it could not be carried out. Thus the processes of amalgamation and assimilation in Mexico, the merger of the Indian and the Spanish into one people, constitute a classic case of unplanned social development.

In the United States the various European immigrants found that the dominance of the English language in business, state, and school, together with the lack of permanent territorial enclaves, made assimilation on the basis of Anglo-conformity an expedient form of adjustment. Once the Europeans had become assimilated to Anglo culture, there was no longer a basis for a sharp differentiation, either in their own minds or in those of the older settlers, and the sharp divisions which had divided Europe into warring camps diminished almost to the point of disappearance. A similar process of assimilation took place for the Africans who were brought to the United States as slaves. In their case, the assimilation, however, was carried on primarily in the southern part of the country and in lower-class circumstances. The process of miscegenation during slavery and immediately thereafter gave many Americans a degree of racial intermixture and allowed some of the light-skinned mulattoes to "pass" into the white category. For the most part, however, blacks and whites were categorized as biologically separate, and, while the blacks' African culture had been destroyed almost totally, their Anglo-conformity was so conditioned by regional location and economic status that cultural distinctions remained.

When the barriers of open segregation and discrimination were lowered, blacks were appalled and indignant at the enormous handicaps which their historical development had placed on them in comparison with white Americans. Today, white Americans, with some recalcitrant exceptions, are trying to adjust to a situation in which blacks are no longer subordinate. Blacks themselves are uncertain of the type of relationship which they can or should attain in American society. The black separatists are driven by both racial pride and white rejection to develop, as far as possible, an enclave type of living which limits their interaction with white Americans even though they must remain a part of the same economic and social system. Other blacks feel that they must follow the pattern of European minorities into fairly complete integration in American life. Even while the conflict rages, still other voices urge the consideration of adjustments which will avoid a polarization between separatism and integration while every avenue toward liberation and development is sought. In the meantime, many whites are dismayed that changes made in the name of civil rights have led to rising expectations and increasing demands rather than gratitude and social peace. Hence, the United States is another example of the tendency of ethnic groups to resist complete incorporation in the national framework as long as they feel they are not wholeheartedly accepted.

The situation of blacks in the United States is, in many ways, unique. Blacks have kept their ethnic identity by virtue of a distinctive physical appearance, and yet the culture of black Americans is clearly a part of the composite American culture. Many of the distinctive characteristics of black culture have been affected by regional influences in the southern part of the United States and by low income and social status. Other distinctive qualities have been shaped by common experience as black people in a "white" society. One could argue that, on this basis, a separate culture is developing which sharply separates blacks from the pattern of Anglo-conformity which may be said to characterize white middle-class culture.

On the other hand, the movement of blacks from the South to the North, the growth of standardized mass communication such as television and radio, the increase in formal education of blacks, and the expansion of the black middle class are factors which might be expected to reduce cultural differences. Whites in the United States have been divided between a segregationist wing which wishes to stigmatize and isolate the black minority and an integrationist wing which seeks to remove color identification as a factor in social participation. In recent years, the integrationist wing has been gaining power among whites, but its program is meeting with some questioning from blacks. Blacks question both whether integration is possible, and, if possible, whether the sacrifice of black ethnicity which it involves is desirable. The nature of the controversy is indicated by the differences between the slogans, "Black is beautiful" and "Opportunity is color blind."

While strident voices are raised advocating extremes in either direction, such a choice is difficult for black Americans. On the one hand, they are brought into the general American culture by the fact that their period of residence in North America is longer than that of most Caucasian groups and hence their identification with American culture is close. Further, the greatest economic opportunities lie in a society which is not bounded by color restrictions. On the other hand, black suspicion, white rejection, the appeal of the Third World, and the possibility of gains from black pressure groups, all militate against an unquestioning acceptance of integration. The old segregated society is definitely on the way out, but the pattern of the new society is still not clearly discerned.

Neither Mexico nor the United States is a utopia with an absence of intergroup conflict. Both of them, though, demonstrate that ethnic divisions are not necessarily permanent and may yield to new and more inclusive types of identification. Future trends in relations between the American whites and blacks, as well as with Mexican Americans, Indians, and others, are uncertain. On the one hand, there is evidence of discontent, conflict, misunderstanding, and claims of grievances. On the other, there is a deliberate effort, unparalleled in most other countries of the world, to try to work out a modus vivendi between groups that find themselves part of a common society despite deep historical differences.

METHODS OF COPING WITH ETHNIC HETEROGENEITY

For many countries of the world, the social structure of various groups is so nearly complete and their relationships with other ethnic groups are so tangential that any type of merger through amalgamation or assimilation appears to be, at best, a matter of the remote future. Such societies must accept the fact of continuing diversity and develop some manner of meeting it. Various patterns have emerged in this process. The most prominent is cultural pluralism, which recognizes the legitimacy of the persistence of separate ethnic identity. Usually this has been the outcome of a relationship of peoples that has extended over many centuries. At other times, it may have occurred because of relatively recent movements of population in what had previously been comparatively homogeneous areas.

An example of this latter trend is the movement of non-European immigrants to France and Britain, bringing diverse languages, religions, and family customs into areas which previously had known only relatively minor regional variation. Another form of cultural pluralism develops when onetime colonies choose to unite with the former imperial country, rather than opting for independence, as in the case of Martinique and Guadeloupe. European imperialism is also responsible for other forms of ethnic diversity as, for instance, when nations were established in Africa made up of a number of tribes many of whom had a strong sense of distinct identity. Still another example of the influence of imperialism, seen both in Asia and Africa, is the bringing in, by an imperial power, of an alien working population which ultimately became the economic middle class of the country. This meant that the new element added to existing diversity was one whose marginal economic position made it a vulnerable and symbolically appropriate point of attack when the African or Asian nations reached the stage of independence and self-government. A final category is comprised of transient aliens who face the problem of temporary adjustment in a country of which they will never become a permanent part. In an interdependent modern world, there will be many people moving about for greater or longer periods, and the Peace Corps is cited as one pattern of such temporary accommodation.

CLASSIC CULTURAL PLURALISM

Four distinct examples of what might be called classic cultural pluralism have been considered. They include Swiss federalism, the Islamic millet system and the kinds of cultural pluralism recognized in the structure of the Union of Soviet Socialist Republics and Yugoslavia. The Swiss are unique because neither language differences nor religious cleavages have threatened a common loyalty to the Swiss nation. This unity is based upon a federal system in which comparative ethnic homogeneity in local districts gives an assurance of ethnic self-determinism, while a heterogeneous nation provides the advantage of cooperation with those of different ethnic background. The Islamic millet system was one in which community autonomy existed along with an acknowledgement of Islamic hegemony. It was a system which provided a degree of peace and security for many years, but has been threatened or superseded at present by the rise of states based on ethnic nationalism, using socialist enterprise to improve the economic fortune of the majority ethnic group while restricting the trading activities of minorities. The Soviet pattern is an attempt to avoid the ethnic rivalries which plagued the Czarist empire. Through the recognition of the languages and general culture of a variety of ethnic groups that make up about half of the population, the Union of Soviet Socialist Republics hopes to establish a federal system which is "nationalist in form and socialist in content." In addition to lingering suspicions between ethnic groups and the difficulty of dealing with "nationalities" like the Jews, which lack a territorial base, the basic question in the Soviet Union is whether a totalitarian, Communist system is compatible in the long run with cultural pluralism.

The Yugoslavian effort to carry out a scheme of cultural pluralism has seen a reaction against Soviet centralism. Rather than allowing some cultural freedom to ethnic groups while keeping all essential decisions in the hands of the federal government, the Yugoslavs decentralized decision making in the economic sphere to a considerable degree. Yugoslavia has great economic disparities between regions in which the peoples are separated by religious and language differences. The decentralization of decision making led to rapid economic progress in the more advanced areas, while the less developed regions felt neglected. Decentralization thus tended to increase the gap between the rich and poor regions and to intensify ethnic rivalries. At the same time regional power groups found their appetite for ethnic-regional nationalism growing with increased autonomy.

In the Yugoslavian pattern two problems emerged. First is the usual difficulty of reconciling regional-ethnic loyalty with allegiance to a superordinate federal government. Next is the task of maintaining enough federal control to move capital from the richer to the poorer regions without slowing down total economic development by less advantageous use of capital and burdening the economy with a cumbersome centralized decision-making apparatus. In the United States, a neglect of "group rights" has led to ethnic discontent, while in Yugoslavia an effort to give the greatest possible protection to ethnic regional groupings threatens the viability of the federal government.

Each of these three types of cultural pluralism has seen a period of comparative success and each faces difficulties in today's world. Swiss federalism may be foundering from the stress of migrations which are destroying the ethnic homogeneity of its local units. The Islamic millet system seems anachronistic in a world in which nationalistic states increasingly use political power in a totalitarian fashion that is hardly friendly to the existence of minority ethnic enclaves. Similarly, the hostility of Communism to religious institutions and voluntary associations which carry the culture of ethnic groups strikes at the very basis of the survival of the ethnic groups. Likewise, the insistence on industrialization under Communist auspices eliminates the economic functions unique to various ethnic groups and brings about a mixture of population in the industrialization process. Swiss federalism is based on a type of local ethnic territorialism which is rare in other countries and which may be passing in Switzerland. The Islamic and Communist patterns of cultural pluralism demonstrate that complete equality is probably impossible and that the existence of a pluralist society usually depends upon the acceptance of the domination of one ethnic group or, at least, of a particular social pattern. It is doubtful whether any pluralistic society can exist when the various ethnic groups do not recognize some type of control which transcends the ethnic groups themselves.

OTHER MULTI-ETHNIC COUNTRIES

The entry of non-European migrants into France and Britain is a new chapter in the history of developed and less developed countries. Previously, these contacts had been based on the compulsory type of relationship associated with the importation of slaves or the imposition of foreign rule by virtue of colonial conquest. The new non-European migrants are people leaving their homes in a preindustrial society and moving voluntarily into two of the world's most advanced industrialized societies. They are moving into societies which, at least in their homelands, do not have a tradition of segregation and discrimination or a permanent ascribed role for minorities.

Experience to date indicates that proclamations of formal equality or even attempts to enforce such equality through a civil rights commission are not an adequate answer to the problems of adjustment faced by this type of immigrant. Such policies do not assure satisfactory social mobility in the new country nor do they relieve the immigrant's anxiety, based on a fear of cultural denigration. In a free market, non-European immigrants will still probably be found heavily concentrated in the least rewarding occupations and crowded into the most unsatisfactory housing. When their children are welcomed in schools identical with those provided for native Britons or Frenchmen, the onetime colonial immigrants will probably find that their children fail to learn at the expected rate and will become bitter because the schools are not the avenues of opportunity which they expect. Natives living in school districts with immigrant children also become disillusioned. They find that, not infrequently, clashes develop between immigrant and native children and that, if the schools make a real effort to adjust to the immigrant children's needs, this results in a slowing down of instruction for the natives and a lowering of standards.

One viewpoint is that school assimilation is something which is seldom accomplished in one generation and that in two or three generations, when the bulk of the immigrants have ascended the economic scale at least to the level of the upper lower class, and have assimilated French or British culture, the problem will largely disappear. This certainly has been the case for other groups of immigrants and the logic may apply to those of non-European background as well. On the other hand, the differences of language, family life, and religion are far greater than they were for groups of immigrants of European background. This difference is accentuated by a Third World ideology which criticizes assimilation as a type of cultural imperialism. This Third World ideology is strengthened both by the extension of independence to non-European areas and by the difficulties which the immigrants face in adjustment to a European society.

In France, the fears of the natives that they are receiving a nonassimilable group of immigrants have been lessened because the largest single group, the Algerians, are mostly single men who leave their families in Algeria and whose residence in France is apparently one of a temporary nature. The United Kingdom seems to have attracted a more permanent type of immigrant, and the British have reacted against their fear of loss of cultural homogeneity by erecting rigid immigration restrictions which exclude even Commonwealth citizens. Both the extent of cultural differences and the British resistance to newcomers have made Anglo-conformity a difficult goal to achieve. Finding that assimilation was doubtful, the British have reacted by trying to limit the extent of the inevitable cultural enclaves which seem to be developing. No society in history has welcomed a deliberate shift from cultural homogeneity to cultural pluralism, and it is not surprising that the British, as they see it, are trying to limit the extent of the problem.

Still another situation is found in the French Antilles. Here, people with dark pigmentation speak the French language, practice the Roman Catholic religion, admire French culture, and journey freely back and forth between the Antilles and metropolitan France. In a time when the outlying possessions in general have been opting for independence, the French Antilles, like Hawaii and Puerto Rico, have chosen a continued identification with the onetime colonial power. This French identification runs squarely against the trend in other Third World countries and meets a degree of criticism from intellectuals within Martinque and Guadeloupe.

How long such a union between France and the French West Indies will persist is debatable, but, in the meantime, many of the French West Indians feel that they have the best of both worlds. Since they have a considerable degree of local autonomy, they can run their own show, and can avoid most of the stigmas of inferiority. On the other hand, they benefit from the French social security system, from the possibility of open immigration to France, and from their opportunity to play a role in the total French society. For the moment, at least, the French Antilles have been able to achieve considerable cultural homogeneity in spite of ethnic difference and to secure the loyalty of a people of distinct physical appearance through rather wholehearted inclusion in the total French nation. Like Mexico, the French Antilles is an area in which the effort to maintain an elaborate scheme of racial classification has led to a blurring of the distinction between white and colored and has placed a large part of the population in intermediate categories. This blurring of racial distinctions, in turn, dulls the edge of racial animosity and makes the association of European Frenchmen and French citizens of the West Indies an easier relationship.

One of the major questions of ethnic policy is whether the new African countries can achieve a sense of national unity in the face of ethnic or tribal diversity. The "tribe," which may vary from a few hundred to several million members, is not only the traditional form of social organization, but is a pattern which survives in modern democratic society. As traditional forms of organization have been modified or dissolved, the tribe often becomes a more diffuse collectivity, approaching the character of ethnic groupings in industrialized societies. Tribal or ethnic blocs form natural units for the support of political parties in a democratic state. Tribes usually have had an unequal exposure to European types of civilization and hence differ in their ability to compete in an industrial society. The resulting situation is one in which individual frustration may frequently kindle ethnic animosity and sharpen the tendency to define fellow Africans by tribe rather than by membership in the same nation.

The recent civil war in Nigeria is an understandable outcome of such a situation. One reason why the seceding Biafrans got little support from other African countries is that they too recognized the possibilities of disintegration from ethnic conflicts within their own borders. It is possible that the defeat of Biafra may have been as significant for the future of Africa as the American Civil War was for North America. Just as the defeat of the Confederacy indicated that the different regions of the United States were destined to continue in a common country, so the defeat of Biafra implies that secession will not be the answer to ethnic differences either in Nigeria or in other African countries.

One of the aspects of this situation is a search for a lingua franca which can be a means of cross-ethnic communication without raising the question of the priority of tribal languages. In East Africa, this lingua franca is now being sought in Swahili, and in North Africa, it is Arabic. In the rest of Africa, the independent nations have tended to retain either French or English as a national language.

If other ethnic questions are clouded, the future of the marginal trading class minorities in Africa and Asia seems to be distressingly clear. It seems obvious that, despite the cost in economic development and the embarrassment which may result from a denial of privileges which presumably were legally guaranteed, such groups are in for a difficult experience. National independence seems to increase discrimination. In the Philippines, the Chinese met severe discrimination against their business activities while securing citizenship was nearly impossible. Likewise the Indian population in Kenya has found that a solid type of guarantee is afforded neither by their claim to a British passport nor by Kenyan citizenship. The United Kingdom refused to honor their passports when confronted with what were viewed as a flood of colored immigrants, and' the Kenyan Africans have not hesitated to discriminate against Kenyan citizens of Indian background.

In the Philippines, a long history of assimilation and amalgamation of Chinese and Filipinos, together with the cessation of immigration, may make it possible for the Chinese minority to be absorbed into the mainstream of the Philippine population. Such a solution will not arrive easily or immediately, however, and, for a long time to come, one can picture a marginal group identified as ethnically Chinese which will have an increasingly difficult milieu in which to work. For the Indians in Kenya, the outlook is even more dismal. Sharp differences in physical appearance and in culture have limited assimilation and amalgamation. The restrictions against the Indians have been even more severe than those against the Chinese in the Philippines. Indians not only have been denied jobs and business opportunities, but have actually been deported from the country. Indications are that such repression will be more severe in the future than it has been in the past. New leaders will not share the charismatic prestige which Kenyatta received from his identification with independence. They will have to prove their nationalism, and the easiest way to do this is by stepping up discrimination against the Indian minority.

The situation of the citizens classified as alien by virtue of being in the marginal middle class contrasts with the position of those who came as citizens of the former imperial power. The British have found it possible to live and work in Kenya since independence, although not without rather severe adjustment. The Kenyan government has welcomed their capital and expertise and has even endeavoured to give some degree of security to the settler class of British farmers. The result is that, in recent years, the British migration into Kenya has actually exceeded the number of Britons leaving. In the Kenyan mind, the British appear as an asset to national development and the Indians as a threat.

The Chinese are still objects of suspicion and hostility by many people, but there are two very different groups which wish to end discrimination against the Chinese. One, the radicals who would rather use Americans as scapegoats than the Chinese. They regard the Chinese as fellow Asians who are allies in the battle to replace capitalism with socialism. They see Americans as offering undesirable images. American culture competes with indigenous Philippine culture, American business is an alternative to socialism and identification with America tends to place the Philippines outside the Afro-Asian bloc. Hence the radicals see the use of the Chinese as scapegoats for Philippine economic ills as a distraction from the issues they wish to emphasize.

The Marcos government also wishes to end discrimination against the Chinese, although its reasoning is almost the opposite of the Philippine radicals. The Marcos government has an all out committment to economic development. It sees the Chinese businessmen as a major source of enterprise and of capital and hence an ally in the developmental process. For these reasons, the Marcos government moved to end discrimination against the Chinese by making citizenship easily available. Neither the radical view nor the government view is popular with the majority of Filipinos and the Philippines could easily return to a policy of discrimination against resident Chinese.

The development of such marginal trading minorities as the Indians in Kenya and the Chinese in the Philippines was encouraged by colonialism and the future of these minorities now depends to a great extent on how Kenya and the Philippines define their relationships to the former imperial power. It is indeed a grim prospect when hatred for one group can only be relieved by finding an alternate target for national animosities.

Trends in the Republic of South Africa are directly opposite those in most of the rest of the world. It is a country with a permanent "settler" population in which the Europeans are unwilling either to leave the area or to submit to rule of the majority. The usual diagnosis of the situation has been that European domination would probably continue until African development made armed resistance possible. When this stage was reached, European domination would be ended in a blood bath which would wreck what had been the most highly economically developed countries in Africa.

In recent years, South Africa has been attempting to make some kind of compromise. The complete segregation of apartheid is being modified, black Africans are being upgraded in jobs and Bantustans are receiving their independence. Such concessions are gradually changing ethnic relations in South Africa but may not be enough to avoid a crisis. The countries bordering South Africa are now all ruled by black Africans and world pressure is mounting against the maintenance of white dominance.

So far, boycotts have been a mild nuisance and generally ineffective. With solid international support, a boycott might actually slow down the South African economy. In this case the white South Africans might (1) endure a shrinking economy in which the brunt of unemployment falls on the blacks, (2) yield to majority rule, (3) lose effective control and see chaos and violence wreck the country and the economy. It is extremely unlikely that the white settler population is going to give in to majority rule and the other alternatives seem like a doubtful improvement on the present situation. The issues are difficult but neither blacks nor whites can gain from all out conflict.

Some of the possible nuances of South African policy were indicated in the brief emergence of a policy of *verligtheid,* or "enlightenment," which offered a slightly more liberal image of the South African government. Apparently this policy produced both more ferment on the left, and more anti-government reaction on the right, than the regime was able to handle. The abandonment of the policy followed, but the fact that an apartheid government was able to move even briefly in a more permissive direction indicates that there may be more room for maneuver and compromise than many critics had assumed. The movement back to a more repressive regime may dampen any easy optimism, but the fact that *verligtheid* could emerge at all offers some hope that even the Nationalist Party may seek to avoid a seemingly inevitable polarization and the consequent all-out conflict. First attempts at reform often fail, but they do serve to render the concept less novel and therefore less suspect.

In the meantime, the economic basis of the existing policy is being questioned. Because South Africa is rapidly industrializing, the need is not so much for cheap unskilled labor as for skilled and technical workers, and many industrialists are now demanding freedom to upgrade African workers. This upgrading of African workers is resisted both by apartheid philosophy and by trade unions, which have designated practically all of the desirable economic slots as "white men's jobs." It is already true that, even though Africans live on a fraction of the white per capita income, their economic situation compares favorably with that of the people in the independent nations of Africa. It may well be that the logic of industrial advance will bring about further readjustment in the status of African workers with a consequent change in total social relationships.

These developments offer interesting possibilities which had hardly been foreseen at all by earlier observers. It is still difficult to conceive of a situation in which an African majority would allow the white population to keep their present privileges or in which the white population would trust African rule in any circumstances. One possible way out of the dilemma is the suggestion that, as futile as it has proved elsewhere, some type of partition may yet be a road to a peaceful solution of the South African question.

TEMPORARY ETHNIC MINORITIES

The ethnic situations which we have discussed previously are those dealing with relatively permanent aggregations of population. The world today witnesses two types of opposing trends. On the one hand, practically all countries are tightening up on immigration and restricting the possibilities of permanent change of residence. At the same time, increased ease of travel and communication and increased economic interdependence have brought about a substantial movement of people on a temporary basis. Businessmen, educators, diplomats, clergymen, and many types of skilled workers find themselves in foreign lands for limited periods.

The case of the Peace Corps has been included because it has developed a unique pattern of adjustment for such temporary foreign residence. Rather than seeking to isolate themselves from the natives and to preserve an ethnic enclave, the Peace Corps Volunteers have sought what might be called "short-time immersion." The have accepted a monetary compensation which places them on a standard of living similar to that of their native counterparts, they have learned the language of the people, and they have sought to understand its culture as completely as possible. Through the technique of almost total acceptance and understanding, they have sought to overcome the cultural shock and fatigue which tend to limit the effectiveness of the temporary worker. This pattern has had some degree of success in the Peace Corps, and it may offer some suggestions applicable to more permanent patterns of ethnic relations as well.

CRESCIVE INFLUENCES IN INTERGROUP RELATIONS

One of the most perplexing aspects of ethnic relations is the distortion or transformation of deliberately adopted ethnic policies by unplanned crescive developments. Sometimes ethnic policies have results quite the opposite of that which was intended, and, at other times, they are completely ineffective in the face of a general situation of a different tenor. An example of the first tendency is found in the fate of the elaborate Spanish socio-racial classification. This classification, which included from ten to 46 categories, according to the time and place involved, was the outcome of a desire to make exact lines of ancestry or descent the major aspect of social status.

Actually, the elaborate nature of the policy made this goal impossible to achieve. The gradations between categories were so slight that it was easy for individuals to shift from one category to the next. Since the details of the scheme were impossible to enforce, the whole plan became ineffective. Rather than being the major determinant of social status, racial category, or physical ancestry, became subordinate to cultural factors and the mixed (mestizo) classification became practically synonymous with "Mexican" as an ethnic category. Similar results have been observed in other areas of Spanish, French, or Portuguese influence, as contrasted with the two-category classification prevalent in Anglo-Saxon areas.

Conflict between specific ethnic policies and general trends in the society is a fairly common occurrence. One example of this is the effect of the invention of the cotton gin in the United States on the movement for the abolition or limitation of slavery. The cotton gin made the expansion of cotton production possible, thereby increasing the demand for labor and reinforcing the strength of the slavery pattern. Exactly the opposite kind of trend took place in the United States in the 1930s, when Southern support for segregation was rendered less effective by the impact of labor-saving devices such as the widespread use of tractors and cotton pickers, which reduced the need for labor and facilitated the exodus of millions of blacks from Southern plantations, where they had been subject to rigid white control. A similar example is found in the Republic of South Africa, in which an ideological commitment to apartheid and to African subordination conflicts with the need of an expanding industrialism for more skilled labor.

These observations do not indicate that deliberate planning in the ethnic sphere is ineffective. They do illustrate the point that ethnic relations cannot be viewed as something separate and apart but must be seen in the context of the total society. Where ethnic policies conflict with general social trends, some type of adjustment is bound to take place. Usually the ethnic policies are discovered to be a dependent, rather than an independent variable, and will conform to the prevailing trends in the total society.

Another instance of the limitations of deliberately designed ethnic policies is seen in the failure of written guarantees to protect the rights of ethnic minorities. The reactions of both Kenya and Great Britain toward the Indian population of Kenya illustrate this pattern. Indians who opted for Kenyan citizenship found that this did not protect them from a policy of "Africanization" which often made it difficult for them to earn a living. Likewise, Indians who had rejected Kenyan citizenship and kept their British passports found that the right of immigration was shut off at the time of greatest need. Still another example is found in the civil rights legislation passed during the reconstruction period of the United States after the Civil War. This legislation proved to be completely ineffective when Northern troops withdrew and political control passed to the white Southerners. In general, it may be said that written guarantees are effective only when the majority group of the society feels it is in their interest to carry them out. This conclusion is also supported by the failure of human rights guarantees to protect the Ibos in Nigeria against aggression from other Nigerian ethnic groups.

FREEDOM FOR THE INDIVIDUAL AND FOR THE GROUP

The ideal of perfection would seem to warrant both the right of the ethnic group to maintain its cultural distinctiveness and the right of the individual, regardless of ethnicity, to have complete freedom in determining his own life style. Unfortunately, these two rights often appear to be in conflict. If there is a rigid maintenance of the link between social participation and ethnic identity, then individual freedom is automatically diminished. On the other hand, if individual freedom leads a large number to deviate from loyalty to ethnically dictated standards, the group itself is in danger of disappearance.

Usually the society based on cultural pluralism gives a greater attention to the right of the ethnic group to preserve its identity, while the integrationist society is more concerned with the rights of the individuals. Thus, the American constitution and, to a considerable extent, American practice, give no protection at all to any inherent rights of ethnic groups, and, indeed, many such groups have disappeared as significant entities in American life. On the other hand, in Canada, both law and practice give substantial support to the maintenance of ethnic divisions.

The operation of ethnically related voluntary activities would seem to be a fairly clear-cut case, at least outside of the Communist orbit. In the Communist countries, voluntary activities of any type are under suspicion and the organizational support for ethnicity suffers accordingly. In countries where the state is less monolithic in its pretensions there would seem to be no reason for state interference with ethnic groups which wish to carry on cultural, welfare or recreational activities. This principle might also extend to the schools as long as they are privately supported and provide the student with the subject matter and the quality of instruction considered essential in the publicly supported curricula. There have been criticisms of the Chinese schools in the Philippines and of religious parochial schools in the United States as being possibly divisive. Actually, such schools tend to become mechanisms through which the minority can become assimilated to the majority culture in a more sympathetic milieu than in the general public institution. If the minority is sufficiently convinced of the value of its own school system to engage in financial support, there would seem to be no reason for the state to object.

The more difficult issue concerns the government support of ethnically focused activities. If this principle is accepted, ethnicity is guaranteed a longer life than it might have on the basis of strictly voluntary activities. Voluntary support will probably be forthcoming at a time when ethnic attachment is high and will dwindle as and if assimilation takes place. This provides for a recognition of ethnicity which is not based on some arbitrary assessment of its value, but on the actual sentiments of those who are involved. It further avoids the possibility that, with public support, individuals will be arbitrarily shunted to the institutions pertaining to their ethnic group as was the case in the southern part of the United States in the days of segregation, or that their personal freedom will be sacrificed to a rule for an entire district as is true of Flemish or Walloon districts in Belgium at the present time.[1] When people are free to support or abandon ethnic institutions, then the topic is removed from the sphere of political debate and ceases to be a politically divisive issue. Social peace would seem to require that society recognize the right of individuals to organize along ethnic lines and, at the same time, the right of individuals to engage in social participation independently of their ethnic classification.

---

[1] The principle of voluntary support for ethnically oriented schools is obviously difficult to apply in a country where, as in Belgium, groups are very nearly evenly divided. In such countries it may be wise for the state to provide different language schools in mixed areas and let individuals decide which school to attend.

SOCIAL UNITY AND ETHNIC DIVERSITY

Most of the discussion of ethnic relationships concerns the rights of ethnic minorities to self-determination. Relatively little attention is given to an equally important topic, namely, how enough unity can be secured to assure the support of a multinational state. Obviously, ethnic loyalty in itself does not necessarily lead to loyalty to the country and, in many cases, may work against it. Yet our examinaton of cases of partition indicates that it is practically impossible to secure a territory of significant size which is ethnically homogeneous. So the problem of maintaining national unity ranks at least equally with the problem of how to assure the freedom of individual ethnic groups.

What is needed is adherence to a formula which transcends loyalty to the particular ethnic structure. An example of the difficulties involved in this process is indicated by Philip Mason in his discussion of the adjustment of non-European minorities in France and Britain. In this discussion, he suggests that the problem is not only how to treat the minorities, but how to find a basis for the unity of the total British society. The previous basis was destroyed or at least greatly weakened with the destruction of the empire. Now that the empire is gone, this raises the question of the relationships not only of non-European ethnic peoples, but of all the peoples who might be included in the United Kingdom:

In both France and Britain people from former colonial territories are present in considerable numbers. The old imperial dilemma takes a new form; the problem had been how to reconcile the denial of democracy to colonial peoples. A nation-state with a strong sense of identity and some degree of internal democracy had ruled very diverse peoples autocratically. Now the question is how to transform what was once an essentially homogeneous nation-state into a society in which a variety of different groups can live side by side. The old nation had been united by a common culture, a language, a pride in past achievement, a sense of imperial power; also by the operation of a disciplined hierarchical system widely accepted, to which the opposite pole was a sturdy individualism, an admiration for individual initiative and individual craftsmanship. Regional and ethnic differences had been forgotten in the aura of the successful nation-state but today they revive; if the colonies are independent—ask the regions—why are not we? At the same time, authority is questioned, discipline decried, and individual initiative often resented.[2]

For Switzerland, the operating principle was a combination of diversity at the federal level and homogeneity at the communal and canton level; a very rare type of division which is both imperfect and apparently fading in Switzerland and which is not found elsewhere to anywhere near the

---

[2] Philip Mason, *Patterns of Dominance* (London, Institute of Race Relations, Oxford University Press, 1970), p. 330.

same degree. The Muslim millet was based on a recognition of the hegemony of Islam; French culture was the basic ingredient which bound the inhabitants of Martinique and Guadeloupe to France, just as Anglo-conformity is the assimilative process through which various European groups in the United States have minimized their ancient grievances. The dominance of Communism in the Soviet Union's version of cultural pluralism is quite obviously expressed in the slogan "National in form, socialist in content." This superordinate position of a particular culture, group, or ideology is often denounced as tyranny and, indeed, it may be carried to an oppressive extent. However, it is difficult to see how any type of plural society can exist without acknowledging the dominance of some unifying factor.

MAJORITARIAN AND MINORITARIAN PERSPECTIVES

One of the widely prevalent illusions in ethnic relations is the notion that a realization of the "facts" of the situation will bring interethnic peace and understanding. Not only are the facts often difficult to secure, but even when there is little argument as to their veracity, there may be a wide difference of interpretation of their meaning. This difference of interpretation usually runs along the line of majoritarian or minoritarian perspectives.[3]

Even when the facts are not in dispute, a change that is considered significant and important by observers from the majority group may be considered trivial and inconsequential by minority analysts. Since the majority spokesmen feel they have some responsibility for the society, they are likely to interpret any indication of minority progress as indicating the essential justice of the existing order. The minority spokesmen, on the other hand, secure their legitimacy by taking the role of leaders of an oppressed group. Any indication of progress under the existing system threatens both their individual status as spokesmen and the validity or need for having any minority spokesmen at all. Therefore, the minority spokesmen are impelled to belittle and minimize any gains which their group have made.

Apart from leaders, the ordinary members of majority and minority groups will also differ in their interpretation of a given rate of change. The majority group member, anxious to quiet both his own conscience and the protests of the minority, may be inclined to inflate the importance of a few exceptional people in the minority group who have achieved social mobility. The minority, on the other hand, are influenced by the principle of rising expectations. As their level of living increases, their standards and hopes also increase, so that however great real progress has been, the obvious moral is that still more change is needed.

---

[3] Michael Banton, *Race Relations* (New York, Basic Books, Inc., 1967), p. 388.

While this tendency toward a difference in interpretation according to majoritarian or minoritarian view is pervasive, it does not completely determine the issue. Societies will persist as long as the individuals who make up the different ethnic groups feel that there is a significant chance of reaching their individual goals within the society. The residents of the French Antilles, for instance, seem to be convinced that their best chance for personal and social improvement lies in keeping their status as citizens of the French union. Likewise, European immigrants to the United States have forsaken Old World customs in a belief that assimilation to an Anglo-conformity standard was a means of reaching their deepest aspirations. Interpretations of change are bound to vary with group perspective, but the maintenance of unity in a pluralist society depends on its ability to convince people in all groups that they have a chance for improvement within the common framework.

OUTLOOK FOR THE FUTURE

Much of our discussion has concerned either efforts of ethnic groups to break away from a larger national territory or friction between ethnic groups within a territory. This does not mean that national unity requires the complete abandonment of ethnic loyalty. Just as it is necessary for one to accept and to have a degree of pride in one's ancestors, so it is desirable to draw strength from association with an ethnic group whose traditions add richness to life. This does not mean that ethnic groups are immortal; they have changed and disappeared in the past and are in the process of changing and perhaps disappearing today. It does mean that they are persistent, that they cannot be ignored and must be dealt with constructively, if our world is to live in peace.

Axiomatically, racial and ethnic conflicts would be nonexistent in today's world had men who differed historically been satisfied to live apart from one another in self-sufficient communities. Obviously, man has not been content to live in a community of his own kind and, motivated and driven by many factors, has moved across the face of the globe, where he has come into contact with other peoples who differed in cultures or in physical appearance, or in both. These contacts, and the subsequent use of symbols to differentiate one group from another, formed the basis for much of the conflict that has occurred throughout the world. This is not meant to imply that contact inevitably leads to conflict, but that conflict is so pervasive that instances where it did not occur are indeed infrequent.

Robert Park, W. O. Brown, Clarence Glick, and other scholars concerned with race and ethnic cycles saw conflict as one of the phases that occur when two different groups come into contact with one another.[4] The

---

[4] Robert E. Park, *Race and Culture* (Glencoe, N. Y., The Free Press, 1949); W. O. Brown, "Culture Contact and Race Conflict, in E. B. Reuter (ed.), *Race and Culture*

nature of ethnic conflict will vary with the situation, and a policy that appears oppressive to one group may be desired by another. For instance, compare the relations of Jews and other nationalities in the Soviet Union with the relations of whites and blacks in South Africa. Jews are disturbed about the preservation of their cultural heritage in a society which appears determined to absorb them into a common culture. In South Africa, on the other hand, the dominant society is using a technique of segregation to encourage blacks to keep an indigenous culture and to limit their acquisition of European culture, as a means of assuring black subjugation. In the one case, assimilation was a cause of protest; in the other case, its enforced prohibition is considered an example of oppression.

It is also an axiom that virtually all groups are ethnocentric and want to preserve their own style of life when contact is made with "outsiders," but, at the same time, contact seems to make demands that are incompatible with this tendency. Certain concessions and compromises are essential in order for the two groups to sustain any long-term interaction, short of open warfare. Accordingly, contact often results in the breakdown of ethnocentrism to such an extent that ethnic differences may cease to be barriers to harmonious interethnic relations. Shibutani and Kwan write, " in all probability, then, human beings throughout the world will eventually acknowledge that they are fundamentally alike, descended from common ancestors in the remote past and that ethnic identity is a matter of little importance."[5]

Moreover:

> In spite of these seemingly insurmountable difficulties, the long-run prognosis for interethnic contacts is the termination of strife. The development of the media of mass communication is likely to break down the walls of ethnocentrism. The increasing availability of translated novels and of foreign motion pictures and television programs should facilitate the establishment of identification, for these channels enable audiences to participate vicariously in the lives of outsiders. As they become better able to understand the lives of people whose cultures are different, they will be able to appreciate that most of their preoccupations and motives are the same. If human nature is indeed universal, more efficient communication will eventually break down ethnic barriers.[6]

It should be emphasized that the realization of universality of a common human nature is not something which comes by ignoring human ethnic differences, but by exploring them. Our common humanity is almost

Contacts (New York, McGraw-Hill Book Company, 1934); Clarence Glick, "Social Roles and Types in Race Relations," in Andrew W. Lind, *Race Relation in World Perspective* (Honolulu, University of Hawaii Press, 1955), pp. 239–62.

[5] Tamotsu Shibutani and Kian M. Kwan, *Ethnic Stratification: A Comparative Approach* (New York, The Macmillan Company, 1965), p. 589. Copyright, The Macmillan Company, 1965. Reprinted by permission.

[6] Ibid., p. 588.

infinite in its capacity for variation, and we realize our essential similarity as we probe the nature of our differences. Human understanding is ill served either by the bigot who notices that people are in some ways different from himself and thereby condemns them, or by a bland, insensitive, determination to ignore differences on the grounds that all humans are essentially the same. Human ethnicity provides a rich variety of attitudes and traditions without which our world would be much the poorer.

We have explored some of the patterns upon which ethnic relations are constructed and examined the types of practices which determine the viability of the various systems. However, by their very definition, social systems are not impersonal mechanisms. They are carried on by human beings, and even the best designed will falter without adequate personal commitment. That personal commitment is best obtained, not by an ethnocentric blindness, but by an open determination to establish the basis for our common humanity through a more complete realization of the nature of the ethnic processes which have produced the various peoples of our world.

QUESTIONS

1. Other than those already discussed can you think of any case where the deliberate policy was one of assimilation and amalgamation? If so, how successful was it? Can you discern any crescive developments that either impeded or enhanced the chances of success?

2. Is there any reason to think that two groups that differed both racially and culturally would have a greater preference for partition as compared to two groups that differed only racially or culturally? Discuss the implications fully.

3. Why do you suppose some Indians in Mexico continue to resist being incorporated into the national framework of the society? Is it possible that they, not unlike black Americans, feel that they are not wholeheartedly accepted?

4. What factors seem to be a threat to the continued success of cultural pluralism in Switzerland, in Russia, and in the Islamic millet system?

5. Both France and England are resisting cultural pluralism. Since both countries are receiving non-European immigrants, why is England's task of limiting the extent of cultural pluralism more difficult than that of France?

6. Why does it appear that the existence of an ethnically pure and economically viable territory is virtually impossible in the modern world?

7. Are ethnic rivalries in the newly African countries a result of colonialism or was their emergence inevitable?

8. Are there any viable alternatives for the marginal trading-class minorities in Africa and Asia either in their present country of residence or in some new country? Discuss this fully.

9.   If you had the power to restructure the Republic of South Africa, what would you do to make it a just and equitable society for all of the peoples?

10. Does the Peace Corps provide any lessons of intergroup relations that may be used to bring about a viable solution to the problems of the marginal trading-class minorities in Africa and India?

11. Can you think of any illustrations or examples in the United States where deliberately adopted ethnic policies have been either distorted or transformed by unplanned crescive developments? What was the outcome?

12. In what sense may a black American experience conflict between his role as a member of the black group and his role as an individual trying to establish his own life style?

13. What real or potential problems are created by a society that gives greater attention to the right of the ethnic group as opposed to one that gives greater attention to the individual? Which emphasis is more likely to encourage and foster assimilation?

14. Can you think of a situation in which the members of various ethnic groups had to abandon their ethnic loyalty in order for the society to achieve national unity?

15. In what sense may "ethnocentric blindness" be both functional and dysfunctional for both the ethnic group and for the society?

16. Should the government support schools which maintain the culture of minority ethnic groups? Is this policy compatible with school integration?

17. How would acceptance of the majoritarian or the minoritarian perspective affect the evaluation of Flemish progress in Belgium? Of black progress in the United States?

18. Is the struggle in Northern Ireland a religious or an ethnic conflict? Can the two be separated?

19. Should government policy promote the mixing of population in a way which provides interpersonal contacts leading to intermarriage? Would such a policy be a greater threat to the survival of the majority or the minority?

20. As a long-term policy, should nations strive to cope with ethnic differences or to eliminate them? Defend your answer.

Bibliography:
Books and Articles

Abbott, Simon. "Profile of Kenyan Asians," *Institute of Race Relations Newsletter*, no. 1 (February 1958): 125–29.

Abrams, Mark. "Attitudes of Whites towards Blacks," *The Listener* (Nov. 6, 1969).

Adolff, Richard. *West Africa: The French Speaking Nations*. New York: Holt, Rinehart and Winston, 1964.

Adolff, Richard, and Thompson, Virginia. *French West Africa*, Stanford: Stanford University Press, 1957.

Allen, Robert L. *Black Awakening in Capitalist America*. New York: Doubleday, 1970.

Amber Paul. "Modernisation and Political Disintegration: Nigeria and the Ibos," *Journal of Modern African Studies* (September 1967): 163–79.

Awolowo, Obafemi. *Path to Nigerian Freedom*. London: Faber and Faber, 1947.

Baer, G. *Population and Society in the Arab East*. New York: Praeger, 1960.

Banfield, Edward C. *The Unheavenly City*. Boston: Little, Brown and Company, 1968.

Banton, Michael P. *The Coloured Quarter: Negro Immigrants in an English City*. London: Jonathan Cape, 1955.

———. *Race Relations*. New York: Basic Books, 1967.

———. *White and Coloured: The Behaviour of British toward Coloured Immigrants*. London: Jonathan Cape, 1959.

Baker, Pauline. "The Politics of Nigerian Military Rule," *Africa Reports,* 16 (February 1971): 18–21.

———. "The Emergence of Biafra: Balkanization or Nation-Building?" *Orbis,* 12 (Summer 1968): 518–33.

Beal, Ralph L. "Social Stratification in Latin America," *American Journal of Sociology,* 58 (January 1953): 327–39.

Bergson, Abram. *The Economics of Soviet Planning.* New Haven: Yale University Press, 1964.

Berger, Monroe. *The Arab World Today.* New York: Doubleday, 1962.

Bonjour, Edgar. *Swiss Neutrality: Its History and Meaning.* London: George Allen and Unwin Ltd., 1946.

Braithwaite, Lloyd. "Social Stratification in Trinidad," *Social and Economic Studies in the Caribbean,* 2 and 3 (October 1953): 90–98.

Bretton, Henry. *Power and Stability in Nigeria: The Politics of Decolonization.* New York: Praeger, 1962.

Bohannan, Paul and Curtin, Philip. *Africa and Africans.* New York: Doubleday, 1971.

Brooks, Robert C. *Civic Training in Switzerland.* Chicago: University of Chicago Press, 1930.

Brown, Leon Carl. "Color in Northern Africa," *Daedalus,* 96 (Winter-Spring 1967): 464–82.

Bryce, James. *Modern Democracies.* 2 vols., New York: The MacMillan Company, 1921.

Buchanan, K. M. and Pugh, J. C. *Land and People in Nigeria.* London: University of London Press, 1956.

Calley, Malcolm J. C. *God's People: West Indian Pentecostal Sects in England.* London: Oxford University Press, 1965.

Cantu, Caesar C. *Cortes and the Fall of the Aztec Empire.* Los Angeles: Modern World Publishing Company, 1966.

Churchill, Winston. *My African Journey.* London: Holland Press, 1964.

Cline, Howard F. *Mexico.* New York: Oxford University Press, 1963.

Coleman, James S. *Nigeria: Background to Nationalism.* Berkeley: University of California Press, 1965.

Coleman, James S., et al., *Equality of Educational Opportunity,* Office of Education, U.S. Dept. of Health, Education and Welfare, Washington, D.C., 1966.

Collins, Sydney. *Coloured Minorities in Britain.* London: Lutterworth, 1957.

Conant, James Bryan. *Slums and Suburbs.* New York: McGraw Hill Book Company, 1961

Conquest, Robert. *The Nation Killers: The Soviet Deportation of Nationalities.* New York: MacMillan, 1960.

Crowder, Michael. *Senegal: A Study of French Assimilation Policy.* London: Oxford University Press, 1967.

Crowder, Michael. *A Short History of Nigeria.* New York: Frederick A. Praeger, 1956.

Cumberland, Charles C. "The Sonora Chinese and the Mexican Revolution," *Hispanic American Historical Review,* 40 (May 1960): 191–211.

Daniel, W. W. *Racial Discrimination in England.* London: Penguin Books, 1968.

Davison, R. B. *Black British: Immigrants to England.* London: Oxford University Press, 1966.

Deakin, Nicholas. "Residential Segregation in Britain: A Comparative Note," *Race,* 11 (July 1964): 18–26.

DeKiewitt, Cornelius W. *A History of South Africa.* Oxford: Clarendon Press, 1941.

Dent, Martin. "Nigeria After the War," *World Today* 26 (March 1970): 103–9.

Desai, Rashmi. *Indian Immigrants in Britain.* London: Oxford University Press, 1963.

Duffy, James and Manners, Robert A. (eds.). *Africa Speaks.* Princeton: Van Nostrand, 1961.

Emerson, Rupert. *From Empire to Nation: The Rise to Self Government of Asians and African Peoples.* Cambridge, Mass.: Harvard University Press, 1960.

Epstein, Arnold L. *Politics in an Urban African Community.* Manchester, England: Manchester University Press, 1958.

Espiritu, Socorro C. and Hunt, Chester L. *Social Foundations of Community Development, Readings on the Philippines.* Manila: Garcia Publishing House, 1964.

Fanon, Frantz. *Toward the African Revolution.* Translated by Haakon Chevalier. New York: Grove Press, 1967.

Feuer, Lewis S. "Problems and Unproblems in Soviet Social Theory," *Slavic Review* 33 (March 1964): 117–28.

Folz, Richard. *From French West Africa to the Mali Federation.* New Haven: Yale University Press, 1965.

Fuchs, Lawrence H. "Inside Other Cultures," *Peace Corps Volunteer,* 6 (June 1968): 9–11.

Gann, L. N. *A History of Southern Rhodesia.* London: Chatto and Windus, 1965.

Gibson, Charles, *The Aztecs Under Spanish Rule.* Stanford: Stanford University Press, 1964.

Ginzberg, Eli, and Eichner, Alfred S. *The Troublesome Presence: American Democracy and the Negro.* New York: Mentor Book, New American Library, 1966.

Glazer, Nathan, et al. *Perspectives on Soviet Jewry.* New York: Ktav Publishing Company, 1971.

Goldhagen, Erich (ed.). *Ethnic Minorities in the Soviet Union.* New York: Frederick A. Praeger, 1968.

Gott, Richard. *Guerrilla Movements in Latin America.* New York: Doubleday, 1971.

Grant, Donald. "After Empires—What?" *Vista,* 5 (July–August 1969): 42–49.

Gruening, Ernest. *Mexico and Its Heritage.* New York: Greenwood Press, 1968.

Hargreaves, John D. "Assimilation in Eighteenth Century Senegal," *Journal of African History* 6 (1956): 529–36.

Harriman, Averell W. *America and Russia in a Changing World.* New York: Doubleday, 1971.

Harris, Marvin. "The Assimilation System in Portugese Mozambique," *African Special Report* 3 (November 1958): 7–12.

Hewsen, Robert H. "The Armenians in the Middle East," *Viewpoints* 6 (August–September 1966): 3–10.

Hill, Christopher R. *Bantustans: The Fragmentation of South Africa*. London: Oxford University Press, 1964.

Hodgkin, Thomas. "Uthman dan Fodio," *Nigeria Magazine* 9 (October 1960): 129–36.

Hoetink, H. *The Two Variants in Caribbean Race Relations*. New York: Oxford University Press, 1967.

Horowitz, Michael M. (ed.). *Peoples and Cultures of the Caribbean*. New York: Doubleday, 1971.

Hourani, A. H. *Minorities in the Arab World*. London: Oxford University Press, 1947.

Iwanska, Alicja. "The Mexican Indian: Image and Identity," *Journal of Inter-American Studies* 6 (October 1964): 529–36.

Johnson, William Weber. *Heroic Mexico: The Violent Emergence of a Modern Nation*. New York: Doubleday, 1968.

Jackson, John Archer. *The Irish in Britain*. London: Routledge and Kegan Paul, 1963.

Juviler, Peter H., and Morton, Henry W. (eds.). *Soviet Policy-Making*. New York: Praeger, 1967.

Kirk-Greene, A. H. M. *Crisis and Conflict in Nigeria: A Documentary Sourcebook*. 2 vols. London: Oxford University Press, 1971.

Kann, Robert A. *The Multi-National Empire*. 2 vols. New York: Columbia University Press, 1950.

Kochan, Lionel (ed.). *The Jews in Soviet Russia since 1917*. London: Oxford University Press, 1970.

Kuper, Leo, Watts, Hilstan, and Davies, Ronald. *Durban: A Study in Racial Ecology*. New York: Columbia University Press, 1958.

Kohn, Hans. *Nationalism and Liberty: The Swiss Example*. London: George Allen and Unwin Ltd., 1956.

Kolarz, Walter. *The Peoples of the Soviet Far East*. New York: Frederick A. Praeger, 1954.

Legum, Colin and Drysdale, John. *African Contemporary Record: Annual Survey and Documents—1968–69*. London: African Research Limited, 1969.

Lewis, Gordon K. "Protest Among the Immigrants: The Dilemma of Minority Culture," *Race* 20 (April 1970): 434–35.

Leys, Colin, *European Politics in Southern Rhodesia*. Oxford: Clarendon Press, 1959.

LeVine, Robert A. *Dreams and Deeds: Achievement and Motivation in Nigeria*. Chicago: University of Chicago Press, 1966.

Lind, Andrew W. *Race Relation in World Perspective*. Honolulu: University of Hawaii Press, 1955.

Little, Alan, Mabey, Christine, and Whitaker, Graham. "The Education of Immigrant Pupils in Inner London Primary Schools," *Race* 9 (April 1968): 439–52.

Little, Kenneth. "Some Aspects of Color, Class and Culture in Britain," *Daedalus* 96 (Winter-Spring 1967): 512–26.

Little, Malcolm. *The Autobiography of Malcolm X.* New York: Grove Press, 1965.

Littleton, Arthur C., and Burger, Mary W. (eds.), *Black Viewpoints.* New York: The New American Library, Inc., 1971.

Lorwin, Val R. "Segmented Pluralism: Ideological Cleavages and Political Cohesion in the Smaller European Democracies," *Comparative Politics* 3 (January 1971): 141–75.

Lowenthal, David. "Race and Color in West Indies," *Daedalus* 96 (Winter–Spring 1967): 580–626.

Luckham, Robin. *The Nigerian Military: A Sociological Analysis of Authority and Revolt, 1960–67.* London: Cambridge University Press, 1971.

Mead, Margaret. *Soviet Attitudes Toward Authority: An Interdisciplinary Approach to Problems of Soviet Character.* New York: Schocken, 1967.

Manuel, Arsenio E. *Chinese Words in the Tagalog Language.* Manila: Philippiniana Publications, 1948.

Mboya, Tom. *Freedom and After.* Boston, Mass: Little, Brown and Company, 1963.

McPhee, Marshall A. *Kenya,* New York: Frederick A. Praeger, 1968.

Marais, J. S. *The Cape Colored People, 1652 to 1937.* London: Longman, 1939.

Mason, Philip. *Patterns of Dominance.* London: (Institute of Race Relations) Oxford University Press, 1970.

Mayer, Kurt B. "Cultural Pluralism and Linguistic Equilibrium in Switzerland," *American Sociological Review* 16 (April 1951): 157–630.

———. "The Jura Problem: Ethnic Conflict in Switzerland," *Social Research,* 35 (1968): 727–41.

———. "Migration, Cultural Tensions and Foreign Relations: Switzerland," *Journal of Conflict Resolution* 11, (January 1967): 139–52.

[Medina], Belen Tan-Gatue. "The Social Background of Thirty Chinese-Filipino Marriages," *Philippine Sociological Review* 3 (July 1955): 3–13.

Melson, Robert and Wolpe, Howard (eds.). *Nigeria: Modernization and the Politics of Communalism.* East Lansing, Michigan State University Press, 1971.

Miller, Henry. "Race Relations and the Schools in Great Britain," *Phylon* 27 (Fall, 1966): 254–55.

Miner, Horace. *The Primitive City of Timbuctoo.* Princeton: Published for the American Philosophical Society by the Princeton Press, 1953.

Moritz, Thomsen. *Living Poor.* Seattle, Washington: University of Washington Press, 1969.

Morner, Magnus (ed.). *Race and Class in Latin America.* New York: Columbia University Press, 1970.

———. *Race Mixture in the History of Latin America.* Boston: Little, Brown and Company, 1967.

Moskos, Charles C. "Racial Integration in the Armed Forces," *The American Journal of Sociology* 72 (September 1966): 132–48.

Murch, Alvin W. "Political Integration as an Alternative to Independence in the French Antilles," *American Sociological Review* 33 (August 1968): 544–62.

Nalbandian, Louise. *The Armenian Revolutionary Movement*. Berkeley: University of California Press, 1963.

Neres, Phillip. *French Speaking West Africa*. London: Oxford University Press, 1962.

Nicholson, Irene. *The X in Mexico: Growth within Tradition*. New York: Doubleday, 1965.

Nodel, Emanuel. *Estonia: Nation on the Anvil*. London: Bookman Associates, 1963.

Nwankwo, Arthur Agwuncha, and Ifejika, Samuel Udochukwu. *The Making of a Nation: Biafra*. London: C. Hurst and Company, 1969.

Okpaku, Joseph (ed.). *Nigeria: Dilemma of Nationhood: An African Analysis of the Biafran Conflict*. New York: Third Press, 1972.

Olorunsola, Victor A. (ed.). *The Politics of Cultural Sub-Nationalism in Africa*. New York: Doubleday, 1971.

Osborn, Robert J. *Soviet Social Policies: Welfare, Equality, and Community*. Homewood, Illinois: The Dorsey Press, 1970.

Panter-Brick, S. K. (ed.). *Nigerian Political and Military Rule: Prelude to the Civil War*. London: Ahlone Press, 1970.

Park, Robert E. *Race and Culture*. New York: The Free Press, 1949.

Paton, Allan. *Hope for South Africa*. New York: Frederick A. Praeger, 1958.

Peck, Cornelius J. "Nationalism, 'Race' and Developments in the Philippine Law of Citizenship," *Journal of Asian and African Studies* 2 (January and April 1967): 128–43.

Pettigrew, T. F. *A Profile of the American Negro*. Princeton, New Jersey: Van Nostrand, 1964.

Quarles, Benjamin. *The Negro in the Making of America*. New York: MacMillan Company, 1969.

Record, Wilson. *The Negro and the Communist Party*. Chapel Hill: The University of North Carolina Press, 1951.

Reed, Alma M. *The Ancient Past of Mexico*. New York: Crown Publishers, 1966.

Reynolds, Hubert. "Overseas Chinese College Students in the Philippines: A Case Study," *Philippine Sociological Review* 5 (July–October 1968): 132–34.

Schubert, C. C. Liao. (ed.). *Chinese Participation in Philippine Culture and Economy*. Manila: Brookman Inc., 1964.

Shibutani, Tamotsu and Kwan, Kian M. *Ethnic Stratification: A Comparative Approach*. New York: The MacMillan Company, 1965.

Smal-Stocki, Roman. *The Captive Nations: Nationalism of the Non-Russian Nations in the Soviet Union*. New York: Bookman Associates, 1960.

Spores, Ronald. *Mixtec Kings and Their People*. Norman: University of Oklahoma Press, 1967.

Stalin, Joseph. *Marxism and the National and Colonial Question*. London: Lawrence and Wishart, 1936.

Steel, David. *No Entry: The Background and Implications of the Commonwealth Immigrants Act, 1968*. London: C. Hurst and Company, 1969.

Stein, Morris I. *Volunteers for Peace*. New York: John Wiley and Sons, 1966.

Strong, Anna Louise. *Peoples of the USSR*. New York: MacMillan Company, 1945.

Sullivan, George. *The Story of the Peace Corps.* New York: Fleet Press Corporation, 1964.

Tamune, Tekena. "Separatist Agitations in Nigeria Since 1914," *Journal of Modern African Studies* 8 (December 1970): 563–84.

Textor, Robert B. (ed.). *Cultural Frontiers of the Peace Corps.* Cambridge, Mass.: The M.I.T. Press, 1966.

Tiryakian, Edward A. "Sociological Realism: Partition for South Africa," *Social Forces* 46 (December 1967): 209–21.

Van Den Berghe, Pierre L. *Race and Ethnicity.* New York: Basic Books, 1970.

———. *South Africa: A Study in Conflict.* Berkeley: University of California Press, 1963.

Vardys, Stanley. "The Partisan Movement in Postwar Lithuania," *Slavic Review,* 22 (September 1963): 499–522.

Verschoyle, Vindes F. *Cecil Rhodes: Political Life and Speeches, 1881–1899.* London: Chapman and Hall, 1900.

Vucinich. Alexander, "Soviet Ethnographic Studies of Cultural Change," *American Anthropologist* 62 (October 1960): 867–77.

Wagely, Charles, and Harris, Marvin. *Minorities in the New World.* New York: Columbia University Press, 1958.

Wakin, Edward. "The Copts in Egypt," *Middle Eastern Affairs,* 12 (August–September 1961): 198–208.

———. *A Lonely Minority: The Modern Story of the Egyptian Copts.* New York: William Morrow, 1963.

Warren, Max. "Christian Minorities in Muslim Countries," *Race* 6 (July 1964): 41–51.

Wickberg, Edgar. *The Chinese in Philippines Life.* New Haven: Yale University Press 1965.

Wilhelm, Sidney M. *Who Needs the Negro.* New York: Doubleday, 1971.

Wilink, Henry, et. al. *Report of the Commission Appointed to Enquire into the Fears of Minorities and the Means of Allaying Them.* London: Her Majesty's Stationery Office, 1958.

Wilkie, James W. *Revolution in Mexico: Years of Upheaval, 1910–40.* New York: Doubleday, 1969.

Wolheim, O. D. "The Coloured People of South Africa," *Race* 5 (October 1963): 25–41.

Young, Jr., Whitney M. *Beyond Racism: Building An Open Society.* New York: McGraw-Hill, 1971.

Zeitlin, Arnold. *To the Peace Corps with Love.* New York: Doubleday, 1965.

Name index

Subject index

This book has been set in 10 and 9 point Cale-donia, leaded 2 points. Chapter numbers and titles are in 30 point Venus Bold Extended and 16 point Venus Medium Extended. The size of the type page is 27 x 45½ picas.